EMPLOYMENT LAW

NEW CHALLENGES IN
THE BUSINESS ENVIRONMENT

EMPLOYMENT LAW

NEW CHALLENGES IN
THE BUSINESS ENVIRONMENT

S E C O N D   E D I T I O N

JOHN JUDE MORAN, J.D., M.B.A.

PROFESSOR OF BUSINESS AND EMPLOYMENT LAW
WAGNER COLLEGE

Upper Saddle River, New Jersey 07458

Library of Congress Cataloging-in-Publication Data
Moran, John Jude.
    Employment law : new challenges in the business environment / John Jude Moran.—
2nd ed.
        p. cm.
    Includes indexes.
    ISBN 0-13-089607-1
    1. Labor laws and legislation—United States. I. Title.
KF3455 .M67 2002
344.7301—dc21

                                                                2001036279

VP/Editor-in-Chief: Jeff Shelstad
Acquisitions Editor: David Parker
Assistant Editor: Jennifer Surich
Editorial Assistant: Virginia Sheridan
Marketing Manager: Debbie Clare
Marketing Assistant: Brian Rappelfield
Managing Editor (Production): John Roberts
Production Editor: Maureen Wilson
Permissions Coordinator: Suzanne Grappi
Associate Director, Manufacturing: Vincent Scelta
Production Manager: Arnold Vila
Manufacturing Buyer: Diane Peirano
Cover Design: Kiwi Design
Cover Illustration/Photo: PhotoDisc
Full-Service Project Management and Composition: Carlisle Communications, Ltd.
Printer/Binder: Maple-Vail

Credits and acknowledgments borrowed from other sources and reproduced,
with permission, in this textbook appear on appropriate page within text.

10 9 8 7 6 5 4 3 2 1
ISBN 0-13-089607-1

*To my father and
grandmother*

CONTENTS

PREFACE

Employment law is an area that is constantly changing. Decisions are being rendered that redefine the parameters of selection, discrimination, privacy, and termination. Sexual harassment is the most litigated area of employment law. The number of cases involving disability discrimination is growing rapidly. Sexual orientation may soon be considered a suspect classification under gender discrimination. At-will employment may soon be displaced by the Model Termination in Employment Act's termination for cause contracts in lieu of an employee's right to sue. Arbitration will be the method for dispute resolution. The right of privacy advocates will continue to do battle with the proponents of drug and polygraph testing. As companies continue to find ways to improve the bottom line, diminishing employee theft of goods, services, and time will be a likely target. Surveillance will increase through the implementation of subtle methods. A trend has developed eliminating affirmative action in certain jurisdictions.

Employment issues used to be handled by personnel departments with a director as the head. Now, a human resources division is often in place with countless more workers and a vice president as its leader. At the other end of the spectrum, NAFTA and GATT will make inroads against unions, labor laws, OSHA, workers' compensation, unemployment insurance, pension and health benefits, minimum and hourly wage laws, child labor laws, and the number of high-paying skilled and office positions through the deployment of jobs to Mexico and overseas where these laws are not in effect. The global business environment will entice companies to seek out the most efficient labor force per dollar of wages and the least expensive manufacturing plants and office space. American workers will have to work longer, harder, and more efficiently while continuously learning skills to keep them competitive.

Employment issues are now high profile. The study of employment law is important because of the impact it will have on businesses, management, and employees. The focus of *Employment Law: New Challenges in the Business Environment* is on discrimination and employment regulation. As with my first book, *Practical Business Law,* I have written this book presenting principles of law in a step-building approach and illustrating those principles with stimulating employment perspectives (there are more than 100 employment perspectives).

Ninety percent of cases are 1995 to date with 80 percent of the 120 cases new to this edition. A chapter checklist appears at the beginning of each chapter with a hypothetical scenario illustrating employment law problems confronted by a small business. Employer and employee lessons and a chapter summary close out each chapter.

Employment Law: New Challenges in the Business Environment is a simple approach to employment law, with a foundation of legal principles explained in the layperson's language. The principles, once learned, can be applied to understand the judges' opinions in the cases presented.

The ultimate task in learning is to apply the principles of law to factual situations. This can be accomplished through the use of cases and chapter review questions to stimulate class discussions. Cases are included in each chapter that focus on the important principles of law to be learned. These cases are extracted from actual cases to enhance class discussions while providing the student with a pragmatic view of the reasoning behind court decisions. This makes the book timely. This provides the student with a text he or she can truly understand and appreciate. At the same time, the text affords the professor the opportunity to discuss the principles more fully by introducing his or her own examples and instances of practical experience.

A hypothetical scenario involving a small business, its owners, and their attorney continues through the text. In each chapter, the owners are confronted with a legal challenge involving their employees. With the legal guidance of their attorney, they attempt to resolve the conflict.

Chapter checklists are incorporated into each chapter to highlight the important principles students should glean from the text.

Employer and employee lessons located toward the culmination of each chapter speak to the issues that employers and employees should concern themselves with to minimize potential litigation.

One hundred percent of the cases, which are incorporated into the end of the chapter review questions, are from no earlier than 1990.

Part I sets forth the parameters of the relationship between employer and employee and independent contractor. The distinction between an employer and independent contractor is identified. The rights and duties of the parties are spelled out in the employment contract along with the resulting liability should a breach occur.

The procedure for selecting and testing employees is also discussed. A considerable problem for employers is employee theft. Balancing the privacy interests of employees with the employer's desire to utilize testing, investigations, inspections, and surveillance is discussed. Finally, the issues of at-will employment, termination for cause, and wrongful discharge are explained.

Part II presents the Civil Rights Act, affirmative action, and the various forms of discrimination found in employment. Hot issues include sexual harassment, racial discrimination, disability discrimination, and sexual orientation.

Part III addresses government regulation of the workplace with regard to unions, collective bargaining, minimum and maximum wage hours, safety, health, compensation for injuries, and pension and health benefits.

Web site addresses will be cited at the end of each chapter for student reference. The Web Sites are current as of September 2001.

Finally, excerpts from the relevant statutes for each of the above topics are included in a companion web site. This will promote greater use by the student through ease of access.

This book was written because of the timeliness and importance of employment law and its interaction with the business curriculum. It is important that students understand the impact employment law has on both management and employees.

I wish to express gratitude to my parents, Rita and John, for their love and support.

I am indebted to Anthony Ginetto, for his thought-provoking and inciteful commentary in the foreword. Mr. Ginetto is a highly regarded legal scholar in the field of employment law. He received his J.D. degree from St. John's University Law School and his L.L.M. degree from New York University Law School.

I appreciate the tireless efforts of the following individuals from Prentice Hall: Virginia Sheridan, Editorial Assistant, John Roberts, Managing Editor of Production, Maureen Wilson, Production Editor, Debbie Clare, Marketing Manager, and Jeff Shelstad, Editor-in-Chief. Ann Imhof at Carlisle Publishers Services did an exemplary job regarding the layout and composition, for which I am grateful.

I wish to thank the following people for their review of the manuscript: Dr. Sandra Powell, Weber State University; William McDevitt, Saint Joseph's University; and Michele Longeau, University of Phoenix.

J. J. Moran, J. D.

FOREWORD

When I was asked to write the foreword for Professor Moran's textbook *Employment Law: New Challenges in the Business Environment,* second Edition, my first thought was what can I possibly say about this comprehensive and informative text that has not already been said? Well, as a practitioner who has specialized in the area of employment law for twenty-five years, in both federal service and private industry, I have found that this text has not only been an informative tool for my use as an Adjunct Professor, but has also served as an invaluable resource to me in researching legal issues in this very complex area.

Employment law has been subject to numerous substantial changes in the last 10 years: notably the erosion of the "at-will employment" concept, development of new affirmative defenses in sexual harassment cases, the extension of the hostile work environment doctrine from sexual harassment to race and age discrimination cases; and Supreme Court recognition that sexual orientation discrimination may be prohibited under Title VII. In addition to changes in traditional labor law, the text also covers succinctly new areas of employment law previously not encountered: privacy, drug and polygraph testing, and new OSHA ergonomic rules, first issued and then withdrawn by joint Congressional Resolution.

Today in corporate America, companies are paying particular attention to diversity issues in the workplace. In this regard, employment lawyers and human resource professionals must keep current with new laws and decisions in order to insure compliance with them and achieve a diverse workforce. With so many demands one may be overwhelmed by the accumulation of so much to learn and know. Professor Moran's text deals with all of these areas in a manner which has helped me keep abreast of new developments while keeping significant past developments fresh.

I highly recommend Professor Moran's text for attorneys, Human Resource professionals, and those who, while not specialists in the area, wish to become more informed about an area of law which has an impact on us all. I am certain that students will find this text to be informative and written in a style that will easily facilitate their understanding of a very complex area of law. Many may even be encouraged to further pursue their studies in this increasingly dynamic and important facet of the business world.

Anthony C. Ginetto, J. D., L.L.M.
Associate General Counsel
Employment Law Division
MetLife Insurance Co.

ABOUT THE AUTHOR

John Jude Moran was born in Bay Ridge, Brooklyn, New York. After graduating from Xaverian High School at the age of sixteen, John received his Bachelor's Degree in Business Administration from St. John's University's Notre Dame College in two years at the age of eighteen. John then attended New York Law School from which he received his Doctor of Law Degree at the age of twenty-one. John's first teaching experience was at the City University of New York, which he began while still in law school. John also taught part-time at St. John's University MBA program. After becoming a member of the New York Bar, John worked for a law firm and then a corporation in Manhattan.

In 1982, John moved to Cameron Lake in Staten Island. At this time, John began writing his first book, *Practical Business Law*. This book was published in 1985. It is now in its third edition and has been used in almost 100 colleges in the United States and six foreign countries. John returned to St. John's University to pursue an MBA in Finance, which he received at the age of thirty.

After teaching at St. Peter's College for one year, John became a member of Wagner College's faculty in 1985. He has served as Chairman of the Department of Business Administration and is currently a Professor of Business and Employment Law. John still resides in Grasmere, Staten Island, with his dogs, Cupcake, Cuddles, and Honey Bunch.

EMPLOYMENT RELATIONSHIP

INTRODUCTION

The employment relationship is a contractual one between an employer and a worker. The worker may be either an employee or an independent contractor. Distinguishing between the two is very important. It has an effect on compensation, benefits, harassment, family leave, workers' compensation, unemployment insurance, and discrimination.

In an employment relationship, authority is conveyed by an employer to an employee. Deciding what kinds of authority and how much authority to grant are important issues for employers to resolve. Inherent in every employment relationship is the employee's duties of loyalty and good faith and the employer's duties to compensate and maintain a safe working environment. Violations of these duties give rise to contractual and tort liability. A contract is a legally enforceable agreement. A tort is a private civil wrong. Tort liability encompasses assault and battery, defamation, invasion of privacy, and negligence. The key to an employer's responsibility is whether or not the tort was committed within the scope of employment. In other words, "On the Job." Finally, employers may attempt to employ restrictive covenants also known as "covenants not to compete." These covenants are used to protect the employer's business against theft of trade secrets, stealing clients, and competing against the former employer. Courts generally do not like to restrict people from working, but the courts will enforce these covenants where they are voluntarily signed and designed to protect the business from unfair competition.

CHAPTER CHECKLIST

❖ Define employment relationship.

❖ Distinguish between an employee and an independent contractor.

❖ Understand the duties of the employer and the worker.

❖ Appreciate the types of authority given to the worker.

❖ Know the parameters of a "covenant not to compete" and when it is enforceable.

❖ Discern when an employee's actions occurred within the scope of employment.

❖ Identify situations that could lead to potential liability involving contract disputes and the torts of assault, battery, defamation, and invasion of privacy.

EMPLOYMENT SCENARIO

Tom Long and Mark Short form a business entitled, "The Long and the Short of It" and abbreviated, "L&S."

L&S is a men's clothing store dedicated to large, tall, and short men. These are sizes not generally catered to by department stores and other men's clothing stores. Tom and Mark met while working at a well-known men's clothing store. Their idea for L&S stemmed from their experience of being unable to fulfill requests for clothing from customers who were very large, tall, or short. Niche marketing had intrigued both of them. They wanted to open their own clothing store and thought it was far better to specialize rather than attempt to be all things to all people.

For the first eight months of the business Tom and Mark handled the ordering, selling, measuring, and tailoring. Through an effective advertising campaign emphasizing the name of the company and its owners, many customers are attracted to the store. Sales are brisk. Tom and Mark begin to feel overwhelmed by the amount of work. Currently, store hours are Monday through Friday 10:00 A.M. to 6 P.M. and Saturday 12:00 noon to 6 P.M. The tailoring and paperwork are done after hours.

Tom and Mark make an appointment with Susan North, an employment law specialist. They retain her services and ask her to advise them as employment issues arise with the growth of the business.

The word *employment* may be defined as the rendering of personal service by one person on behalf of another in return for compensation. The person requesting the service is the *employer*. The person performing the service may be either the *employee* or an *independent contractor*. Employment law has its roots in the law of agency.

Agency is a contractual relationship, involving an agent and a principal, in which the agent is given the authority to represent the principal in dealings with third parties. The most common example is an employer-employee relationship wherein an *agent* (employee) is given the power by a *principal* (employer) to act on his or her behalf. An agent may be an employee or an independent contractor. A principal is a person who employs an agent to act on his or her behalf. A principal (employer) has full control over his or her employee. The employee must complete the work assigned by following the instructions of the employer.

The issue in this case is whether the term *employees* includes former employees.

ROBINSON v. SHELL OIL COMPANY

519 U.S. 337 (1997)

JUSTICE THOMAS delivered the opinion of the Court.

Section 704(a) of Title VII of the Civil Rights Act of 1964 makes it unlawful "for an employer to discriminate against any of his employees or applicants for employment" who have either availed themselves of Title VII's protections or assisted others in so doing. We are asked to decide in this case whether the term "employees," as used in sect; 704(a), includes former employees, such that petitioner may bring suit against his former employer for post employment actions allegedly taken in retaliation for petitioner's having filed a charge with the Equal Employment Opportunity Commission (EEOC). The United States Court of Appeals for the Fourth Circuit, sitting en banc, held that the term "employees" in sect; 704(a) referred only to current employees and therefore petitioner's claim was not cognizable under Title VII. We granted certiorari and now reverse.

Respondent Shell Oil Co. fired petitioner Charles T. Robinson, Sr., in 1991. Shortly thereafter, petitioner filed a charge with the EEOC, alleging that respondent had discharged him because of his race. While that charge was pending, petitioner applied for a job with another company. That company contacted respondent, as petitioner's former employer, for an employment reference. Petitioner claims that respondent gave him a negative reference in retaliation for his having filed the EEOC charge.

Petitioner subsequently sued under sect; 704(a), alleging retaliatory discrimination. On respondent's motion, the District Court dismissed the action, adhering to previous Fourth Circuit precedent holding that sect; 704(a) does not apply to former employees. Petitioner appealed, and a divided panel of the Fourth Circuit reversed the District Court. The Fourth Circuit granted rehearing en banc, vacated the panel decision, and thereafter affirmed the District Court's determination that former employees may not bring suit under sect; 704(a) for retaliation occurring after termination of their employment.

We granted certiorari in order to resolve a conflict among the Circuits on this issue.

Our first step in interpreting a statute is to determine whether the language at issue has a plain and unambiguous meaning with regard to the particular dispute in the case. Our inquiry must cease if the statutory language is unambiguous and "the statutory scheme is coherent and consistent."

The plainness or ambiguity of statutory language is determined by reference to the language itself, the specific context in which that language is used, and the broader context of the statute as a whole. In this case, consideration of those factors leads us to conclude that the term "employees," as used in sect; 704(a), is ambiguous as to whether it excludes former employees.

At first blush, the term "employees" in sect; 704(a) would seem to refer to those having an existing employment relationship with the employer in question. This initial impression, however, does not withstand scrutiny in the context of sect; 704(a). First, there is no temporal qualifier in the statute such as would make plain that sect; 704(a) protects only persons still employed at the time of the retaliation. That the statute could have expressly included the phrase "former employees" does not aid our inquiry. Congress also could have used the phrase "current employees." But nowhere in Title VII is either phrase used—even where the specific context otherwise makes clear an intent to cover current or former employees.

Similarly, that other statutes have been more specific in their coverage of "employees" and

3

"former employees" proves only that Congress *can* use the unqualified term "employees" to refer only to current employees, not that it did so in this particular statute.

Second, Title VII's definition of "employee" likewise lacks any temporal qualifier and is consistent with either current or past employment. Section 701(f) defines "employee" for purposes of Title VII as "an individual employed by an employer." The argument that the term "employed," as used in sect; 701(f), is commonly used to mean "performing work under an employer-employee relationship," begs the question by implicitly reading the word "employed" to mean "*is* employed." But the word "employed" is not so limited in its possible meanings, and could just as easily be read to mean, "*was* employed."

Third, a number of other provisions in Title VII use the term "employees" to mean something more inclusive or different than "current employees." For example, sect; 706(g)(1) and 717(b) both authorize affirmative remedial action (by a court or EEOC, respectively) "which may include . . . reinstatement or hiring of employees." As petitioner notes, because one does not "reinstate" current employees, that language necessarily refers to former employees. Likewise, one may hire individuals *to be* employees, but one does not typically hire persons who already *are* employees.

Of course, there are sections of Title VII where, in context, use of the term "employee" refers unambiguously to a current employee, for example those sections addressing salary or promotions. But those examples at most demonstrate that the term "employees" may have a plain meaning in the context of a particular section— not that the term has the same meaning in all other sections and in all other contexts. Once it is established that the term "employees" includes former employees in some sections, but not in others, the term standing alone is necessarily ambiguous and each section must be analyzed to determine whether the context gives the term a further meaning that would resolve the issue in dispute.

Finding that the term "employees" in sect; 704(a) is ambiguous, we are left to resolve that ambiguity. The broader context provided by other sections of the statute provides considerable assistance in this regard. As noted above, several sections of the statute plainly contemplate that former employees will make use of the remedial mechanisms of Title VII. Indeed, sect; 703(a) expressly includes discriminatory "discharge" as one of the unlawful employment practices against which Title VII is directed. Insofar as sect; 704(a) expressly protects employees from retaliation for filing a "charge" under Title VII, and a charge under sect; 703(a) alleging unlawful discharge would necessarily be brought by a former employee, it is far more consistent to include former employees within the scope of "employees" protected by sect; 704(a).

In further support of this view, petitioner argues that the word "employees" includes former employees because to hold otherwise would effectively vitiate much of the protection afforded by sect; 704(a). This is also the position taken by EEOC. According to EEOC, exclusion of former employees from the protection of sect; 704(a) would undermine the effectiveness of Title VII by allowing the threat of post-employment retaliation to deter victims of discrimination from complaining to EEOC, and would provide a perverse incentive for employers to fire employees who might bring Title VII claims.

We hold that the term "employees," as used in sect; 704(a) of Title VII, is ambiguous as to whether it includes former employees. It being more consistent with the broader context of Title VII and the primary purpose of sect; 704(a), we hold that former employees are included within sect; 704(a)'s coverage. Accordingly, the decision of the Fourth Circuit is reversed.

Judgment for Robinson.

Case Commentary

When a term is ambiguous, it is within the court's discretion to clarify its meaning. In this case, the Supreme Court of the United States ruled that the term "employee" includes former employees. Thus, Charles Robinson can proceed with his case for retaliatory discrimination against Shell Oil in the District Court.

Case Questions

1. Do you agree with the court's decision?
2. Why do you think the Fourth Circuit decided otherwise?

3. What protection would be afforded to former employees under the Fourth Circuit's reasoning?

An independent contractor is an individual hired by an employer to perform a specific task. The employer has no control over the methods used by the independent contractor. The following are among those who act independently of an employer: electricians, carpenters, plumbers, television repairpersons, and automobile mechanics. Independent contractors also include professional agents such as lawyers, physicians, accountants, securities brokers, insurance brokers, real estate brokers, and investment advisors. Independent contractors may also employ others in their field who will be bound to them as employees.

At times there is conflict over whether or not a worker is an employee or an independent contractor. This arises with workers who are sales people, delivery and car service drivers, home workers, and others who work for tips or commissions. Employers prefer the independent contractor status because there is no paid vacation, sick time, or personal leave as well as any life, health, and unemployment insurance involved. In addition, pension benefits do not have to be paid; there are no workers' compensation suits; taxes do not have to be withheld; there are no minimum wages, maximum hours, or overtime, and there is minimal or no tort liability for the actions of the independent contractor. Employers initially designate a worker as an employee or an independent contractor. The Internal Revenue Service weighs in on this as well concerning tax matters. How then is the distinction made? Courts often employ an Economic Realities' test, which encompasses an employer's control over the worker's behavior. First, factors indicating behavioral control include instructing, training, setting work hours, designating dress codes as well as where, when, and how the work is to be done, and restricting the worker from being employed by others. Second, financial control is determined by the following: the worker does not have a significant investment in the business, the worker cannot perform services for the public, the worker has no unrealized personal profit or loss, the worker does not pay business expenses or provide tools, the worker is compensated for a job on an hourly basis, and the worker files reports as required by the employer. Third, the type of relationship is indicative of employment status. Factors include: the relationship is continuous; the worker plays an essential part in the business; the worker has no power to employ others without the employer's authorization; the worker is liable if the job is done poorly or is not completed; and the worker may be terminated at will, not solely for breach of contract.

Affirmative responses to the above criteria would indicate that the worker is an employee. Negative responses signify that the worker is an independent contractor. Often, indicators are split between employee and independent contractors. Some courts have used a balanced approach, in which the criteria supporting employee status will be counted or weighed against the criteria supporting independent contractor status, to determine the employment relationship.

EMPLOYMENT SCENARIO

Long and Short inform Susan that they are considering expanding store hours and advertising. They wish to concentrate their efforts on management and growth. There are several workers they wish to hire, but they are uncertain whether or not these workers would be designated as employees or independent contractors. Susan asks Long and Short to describe the nature of each position, the hours worked, and the control they exercise over each worker. Jack Walker, Grant Worthington, and Phil Costello are first-rate sales people who have extensive experience in selling men's clothing. They would each work forty hours and be paid a base salary plus commission. The salesmen would be prohibited from working elsewhere. They would be required to wear a suit, and their work schedule would be set by L&S. Paid vacation and sick leave would be given as well. Jack, Grant, and Phil would have no discretion in deciding on whether to attend to a customer's needs or not, and they would have no authority to hire assistants.

Nancy Cooke is being employed as an administrative assistant. Her duties will include bookkeeping, ordering, and typing, as well as telephone reception. She will work from 10 A.M. to 6 P.M. Monday to Friday. Susan advises L&S that by employing an Economic Realities test these workers would qualify as employees. The employment relationship has permanency and L&S has control over the sales people's behavior and compensation.

Designation of hours to be worked, dress code, compensation, permanency of the relationship, inability to select customers and hire assistants, plus termination of employment at will are all indicative of employee status.

Martha Winslow, a seamstress by trade, is being hired to perform the necessary alterations on the clothing. She would be available for appointments on Tuesdays and Thursdays from 6 P.M. to 8 P.M. and on Saturday afternoons from 2 P.M. to 4 P.M. Martha would set her own hours in addition to these, depending on the workload. Martha has set a fee schedule covering the various types of alterations performed on a per item basis.

Stephanie Russo is a web page design specialist with a degree in Graphic Arts. She is being trained to create a web page for "The Long and the Short of It." After that she will act as a consultant for purposes of web advertising. Lastly, Lucy Johnson is being hired to clean the store after hours. She will set her own schedule, and estimates working one to two hours per night. Stephanie is being paid on a one-time fee basis for the web design work and then will be retained on an hourly basis as a consultant. Lucy is being paid a flat fee per night regardless of the length of time it takes for her to clean the store. Susan ponders the information given and suggests that Martha, Stephanie, and Lucy would all appear to be independent contractors. They set their own hours, control how the work is to be performed, and will be held liable if the work is not done properly. Martha, Stephanie, and Lucy have a significant investment in their own materials, to wit: sewing machine, computer, and cleaning apparatus, respectively. They can employ others to assist them in conducting their business. Although their work is important, the store will not fail without them. An argument can be presented that each worker exhibits some traits of being an employee, because the employer designates where the work is to be performed, as with Martha and Lucy, and control over the compensation for Stephanie's consulting services. However, these traits pale in comparison, both in number and significance, to those traits of an independent contractor, which they exhibit. Long and Short graciously thank Susan for elucidating the difference between an employee and independent contractor. L&S promises Susan that it will implement her advice.

The issue in this case is whether the delivery drivers are to be considered employees or independent contractors.

CASE

ALEXIS M. HERMAN, SECRETARY OF LABOR v. EXPRESS SIXTY-MINUTES DELIVERY SERVICE

161 F.3d 299 (5th Cir. 1998)

PARKER, Circuit Judge.

Appellant, the Secretary of Labor, brought this FLSA action seeking to enjoin appellee Express 60-Minutes Delivery Service, Inc. from violating the minimum wage, overtime compensation, and record keeping provisions of the Act. After a six-day bench trial, the district court concluded that no violation of the FLSA occurred because the courier delivery drivers were independent contractors.

FACTUAL BACKGROUND

Drivers

Express operates a courier delivery service in Dallas and Tarrant Counties, Texas. Express contracts with various businesses, including law firms, hospitals, and laboratories, to deliver packages on a 24-hour basis in and around the Dallas-Fort Worth metropolitan area. Over 50% of the packages delivered by Express contain medical

blood or tissue samples. Express averages around 525 deliveries each day. To make these deliveries, Express relies on about fifty drivers on its payroll at any given time. The drivers are recruited by Express through newspaper advertisements and word of mouth.

Customers of Express choose among various delivery options under which Express agrees to complete its deliveries within either one, two, or four hours of when an order is placed. Express uses a computer-dispatch system wherein orders are taken by customer service personnel over the telephone, entered into the computer, and transferred to dispatchers who assign the deliveries. The dispatchers communicate with the drivers by pager, two-way closed-channel radio, and telephone. While different factors guide their decisions, the dispatchers generally offer a delivery to the last on-duty driver to have received an offer who is closest to the pick-up point.

Express bills its customers based upon several factors including the size of the package, the priority of its delivery, and the distance between the pick-up and delivery points.

Potential drivers are required to attend an orientation session at which they must sign an Independent Contractor Agreement providing that they will make deliveries for Express using their own vehicles in exchange for receiving a commission for each delivery equal to a percentage of the customer's cost. Under the agreement, drivers also pay the costs of their gasoline, vehicle maintenance, and insurance. Most drive a vehicle that they also use personally.

The Independent Contractor Agreement also provides that drivers will furnish their own uniforms, radios and pagers, as well as the biohazard bags and dry ice required for transporting medical samples. These items are supplied to the drivers by Express, which leases some of the items to the drivers and deducts the cost from their first few paychecks. Drivers supply their own dollies and MAPSCOs, and, if needed, their own tarps and cords for covering and securing items.

The drivers can and do negotiate for increased commissions, but most drivers do not negotiate their commissions. The drivers have no input into how Express's business is conducted, the amount charged its customers, or the allocation or frequency of deliveries.

The drivers may use only those radios supplied by the company, because the radios operate on a private channel that Express licenses from the Federal Communication Commission. Most drivers wear a uniform consisting of a blue shirt and khaki pants. One shoulder of the shirt has a patch with an Express logo and the other shoulder sports an Independent Contractor patch. Uniforms are not required, but preferred.

Pursuant to their contracts, drivers agree to make themselves available to work on-call for Express's 24-hour delivery service. A majority of the drivers who testified stated either that they were required to work on-call or that they had no input into when their on-call time was scheduled. Express posts the on-call schedules at its offices and informs drivers that if unable to work, they are responsible for finding a replacement.

Drivers work for Express for varying lengths of time, with the majority working for relatively short periods. Several drivers testified that they had worked for other courier companies in the Dallas-Fort Worth area either prior to or after working for Express. Only one driver testified that he worked for another courier company while working for Express. The Independent Contractor Agreement does not contain a covenant-not-to-compete.

No prior experience is necessary to become a courier driver, but couriers need to be able to drive, read maps, and be courteous to customers. By using their judgment as to the best routes available and their knowledge about area traffic patterns, drivers may earn more money because they can make their deliveries faster and be available to make more deliveries.

Under the terms of the contract, the drivers have the right to accept or reject individual offers of delivery jobs, and have no obligation to accept any specified number of jobs during any given period. Drivers confirmed that they could decline offers without being subjected to retaliation.

In addition to the drivers that Express considers independent contractors, the company employs four drivers it considers employees. The employee-drivers run errands for Express and make routine deliveries when the office is busy. They attend the same initial orientation session as the other drivers. Unlike the contract drivers, the employee-drivers (1) report for work at a specified time; (2) are paid by the hour; (3) work a set number of hours that are determined by Express; (4) are required to wear a uniform; (5) are provided with a company vehicle and all of the necessary tools of the trade; (6) are reimbursed for expenses; (7) are not allowed to turn down deliveries; and (8) are under the control and supervision of Express.

ANALYSIS

Drivers

To determine employee status under the FLSA, we focus on whether the alleged employee, as a matter of economic reality, is economically dependent upon the business to which he or she renders his or her services.

In other words, our task is to determine whether the individual is, as a matter of economic reality, in business for himself or herself.

To aid us in this task, we consider five factors: the degree of control exercised by the alleged employer; the extent of the relative investments of the worker and alleged employer; the degree to which the worker's opportunity for profit and loss is determined by the alleged employer; the skill and initiative required in performing the job; and the permanency of the relationship.

No single factor is determinative.

We review the district court's findings as to these five factors for clear error, but we review the district court's ultimate determination of employee status de novo.

1. Degree of control exercised by the alleged employer

The district court found that Express had minimal control over its drivers. We agree. The drivers set their own hours and days of work and can reject deliveries without retaliation. It is preferred that drivers wear a uniform and become notaries, but it is not required of all contract drivers. The drivers can work for other courier delivery systems, and the Independent Contractor Agreement does not contain a covenant-not-to-compete. Although the drivers are required to attend an orientation session and required to be on-call, these facts do not outweigh the other facts indicating a lack of control and independent contractor status. This result is even clearer when one contrasts Express's employee-drivers who, unlike contract drivers, report for work at a specified time; are paid by the hour; work a set number of hours that are determined by Express; are required to wear a uniform; are not allowed to turn down deliveries; and are under the control and supervision of Express.

The degree-of-control factor points toward independent contractor status. Such a finding by the district court is not clearly erroneous.

2. Relative investment of worker and alleged employer

The district court found that the investment on the part of the drivers was significant. The district court first pointed out that Express does not provide drivers with any equipment—drivers were required to purchase or lease all the necessary tools of the trade including a vehicle, automobile insurance, dolly, MAPSCO, tarp, two-way radio, pager, and a medical delivery bag. The drivers also were responsible for all fuel, maintenance, and depreciation of their vehicles.

The Secretary counters that most drivers use their automobiles for personal and recreational purposes as well as for business, so that the capital risk on the part of the drivers is not substantial. Further, the Secretary argues that the relative investment of Express far exceeds that of the drivers, explaining that Express operates offices in two locations, uses a sophisticated computer system, purchases the equipment that it leases to its drivers, pays to license a closed-channel radio frequency from the Federal Communications Commission, and pays the salaries of twenty-five office employees. While the Secretary did not discuss in her brief the dollar amount of investment of Express, an independent review of the record reveals the following:

a. monthly lease on Fort Worth office = $1500–$1900
b. Monthly lease on Dallas office = several hundred dollars
c. 60–65 radios at $600 a piece
d. Air time for radio = $17 per month for each radio
e. Biweekly payroll = approximately $19,000
f. four vehicles = approximately $14,000 each
g. fax machine = $250
h. computer system = $25,000

The relative investment by Express is indeed significant. Although the driver's investment of a vehicle is no small matter, that investment is somewhat diluted when one considers that most drivers also use the vehicle for personal purposes.

The district court also concluded that, although no direct testimony was presented on this point, the aggregate investment of all the contract drivers is substantially more than that of Express. However, we find no support for the application of an aggregation principle with respect to the relative investment factor.

The relative investment factor weighs in favor of the Secretary and toward employee status.

3. Degree to which employee's opportunity for profit and loss is determined by the alleged employer

The district court found that the drivers are compensated on a commission basis. According to the district court a driver's profit or loss is determined largely on his or her skill, initiative, ability to cut costs, and understanding of the courier business. The district court observed that the drivers who made the most money appeared to be the most experienced and most concerned with efficiency, while the less successful drivers tended to be inexperienced and less concerned with efficiency.

Although the Secretary maintains that Express controls customer volume and the amount charged to customers, we cannot say that the district court clearly erred in finding that the drivers' opportunity for profit and loss was determined by the drivers to a greater degree than Express. This is especially true because the drivers had the ability to choose how much they wanted to work and the experienced drivers knew which jobs were most profitable.

This factor points toward independent contractor status. The district court did not clearly err.

4. Skill and initiative required

The district court found that once a job is offered to the driver, the driver is not told which route to take—the driver must rely on his own judgment, knowledge of traffic patterns and road conditions in the Dallas-Fort Worth metroplex, ability to read a MAPSCO, and ability to anticipate the need for an alternate route. According to the district court, experienced drivers possess specialized skills beyond that of merely driving an automobile and more experienced drivers tended to make more money than less experienced drivers.

The Secretary argues that the contract drivers are more like wage earners than independent entrepreneurs seeking a return on their risky capital investment. The Secretary is correct. The district court did not discuss initiative during its evaluation of this factor. We agree with the Secretary that the skill and initiative factor

points toward employee status. The district court clearly erred in finding to the contrary.

5. Permanency of the relationship

The Secretary conceded at oral argument that the district court correctly determined the permanency issue. We agree. The majority of drivers work for Express for a short period of time. Drivers are able to work for other courier delivery companies, and the Independent Contractor Agreement does not contain a covenant-not-to-compete. The permanency factor points toward independent contractor status.

6. Other factors

Both sides encourage the court to look to other factors in addition to the preceding five factors. The Secretary emphasizes that the work performed by the drivers is an integral and indispensable part of Express' business. Express argues that the contract provided that the drivers were independent contractors and the drivers' uniforms indicate same.

The determination of employee status is very fact intensive, and as with most employee-status cases, there are facts pointing in both directions.

In this case, three of the five traditional factors point toward independent contractor status. We conclude that the district court did not err in finding that the drivers were independent contractors.

We are confident in this result not only because the various factors weigh in favor of independent contractor status, but also because of Supreme Court precedent with respect to this issue.

The conclusion of the district court that the drivers were independent contractors is affirmed.

Judgment for Express.

Case Commentary

This case illustrates that a worker can exhibit traits of both an employee and an independent contractor. Here, the Fourth Circuit employed a five-prong test. The conclusion reached was that three criteria pointed to independent contractor status, while two criteria pointed to employee status. Thus, the workers for Express were independent contractors. It is not necessary that all factors point one way or the other.

Case Questions

1. Do you agree with the court's assessment of the criteria?

2. Is a simple 3 to 2 majority sufficient to make a decision here?

3. Why do some businesses prefer the independent contractor designation for their employees?

Employment is a contractual relationship wherein the employee or independent contractor is given authority to act on behalf of the employer. All the requirements of contract law are applicable to the creation of employment.

ELEMENTS OF AN EMPLOYMENT CONTRACT

An *employment contract* is a legally enforceable agreement. For an agreement to be legally enforceable, the following elements must be present: a mutual agreement, executed in proper form, voluntarily made by two or more capable parties wherein each party promises to perform or not to perform a specific legal act for valuable consideration. Each element in this definition must be satisfied by each party for the contract to be valid. The validity of the contract is what gives it legal effect. The elements of an employment contract are:

- Lawful purpose
- Agreement
- Legal capacity
- Promise to perform
- Consideration
- Executed in proper form

Employment contracts are personal service contracts. Personal service contracts are contracts in which one person promises to perform a service for an employer in return for the employer's promise to provide compensation for the services rendered. Personal service contracts include employment contracts, in which an individual is employed on a salary basis, as well as contracts with professionals or independent contractors, in which performance is on an hourly or per case basis.

Assignments of employment contracts are permissible under certain circumstances.

PROPER APPLICATION OF STATE LAWS

Each state has its own law of contracts. State laws are enacted to interpret and enforce contracts. The state must have sufficient interest to interpret the contract and legally enforce the rights and duties of the parties involved. To determine the proper application of state laws, the following rule applies: When a contract is made between two parties of a state and the contract is to be performed in that state, the law of that state will govern. Employment contracts are generally governed by the state in which substantial performance is to be rendered; however, as stated before, the parties may stipulate otherwise.

EMPLOYMENT PERSPECTIVE

The Daily Times in Sun Valley, Idaho, buys the *Morning Star* newspaper, which is based in Jupiter, Florida. Mike Marra signs a contract with the Planet to be editor-in-chief of the *Morning Star.* After six months, the Times is suing Mike Marra for nonperformance of his duties. Which state law governs? Florida's because it is the state where performance is to be rendered. Could this have been altered by contract? Yes, the parties could designate Idaho law if they wish. ▪

An employment contract may be created expressly, through a writing or a verbal conversation, or impliedly, through the actions of the parties. Generally employment contracts are not required to be in writing because they are indefinite in nature.

EMPLOYMENT PERSPECTIVE

AT&T hires Francine Pell and Rita Morse to perfect their telephone and telegraph systems by an oral agreement made on January 1. Pell is to begin work on April 1 and to complete the work on January 31, ten months later. Morse, who is eighty-seven years of age, has a lifetime contract. Neither agreement is in writing. Are the contracts enforceable? Pell's contract is not enforceable. To be enforceable, it must be in writing because its duration is thirteen months, commencing at the time the contract is made—January 1. This situation is true even though Pell does not begin to work until April 1. Morse's contract is enforceable. A lifetime contract does not have to be in writing because it is possible that the person may die within one year of making the contract. ■

However, if the employee's or independent contractor's duties involve entering into a contract on behalf of the employer, which is required to be in writing under the statute of frauds, then the employment contract must also be in writing. The statute of frauds is a list of those contracts required to be in writing. Employment contracts with a duration in excess of one year must be in writing.

TYPES OF AUTHORITY

ACTUAL AUTHORITY

The scope of an employee's authority is usually determined by the employer. Actual authority is the express authority conveyed by the employer to the employee, which also includes the implied authority to do whatever is reasonably necessary to complete the task. This implied authority also gives the employee power to act in an emergency. Implied authority is authority which the employee actually has. It comes with the job.

EMPLOYMENT PERSPECTIVE

Charlie Moore is a garage mechanic at the Seagate Service Station. His actual authority is limited to servicing automobiles. He has no authority to enter into contracts with customers for his services and has no authority to decide on which cars he will work. One day while the gas attendant is out to lunch, a customer pulls up to the gas pump. Does Charlie Moore have the authority to service the customer? Yes! Inherent in the authority delegated to Charlie is the implied authority to perform those routine tasks necessary for the continuation of the business when the other mechanics or gas attendants are out to lunch or otherwise occupied. Is Charlie an employee or an independent contractor? If Charlie works exclusively for Seagate, he would be an employee. For example, if a boy threw a brick through the office window and it had to be repaired before closing, Charlie would have the authority to board up the window or have a glazier replace the glass—assuming that the service station manager could not be notified—because Charlie would be acting in an emergency. ■

APPARENT AUTHORITY

Apparent authority is the authority the employee professes to have which induces a reasonable person to believe in the employee. The reliance on apparent authority must be justifiable. With apparent authority, the employee appears to have the authority to act, but he or she actually does not.

EMPLOYMENT PERSPECTIVE

In the previous example, suppose Charlie is alone at the service station, finishing a tune-up on a Monte Carlo, when Arthur Moriarity drives up in his Rolls-Royce. Charlie had previously been assigned by his manager to perform a brake job on this Rolls six months ago. Moriarity recognizes Charlie and informs him that there is a rumbling sound in the engine. Charlie inspects the engine and informs Arthur Moriarity that the valves are worn and need to be reseated. Moriarity agrees to leave the car overnight. The next morning Charlie has completed the valve job, but the engine's rumbling has become worse. When Moriarity calls for the Rolls-Royce, he threatens to sue the service station for negligence in its attempted repair of his car. Can the service station raise the defense that Charlie Moore acted without authority. No! Although Charlie did not possess the actual authority to bind the Seagate Service Station to a contract, he appeared to have the authority in entering into the contract of repair. Arthur Moriarity was justified because a reasonable person would believe a garage mechanic would possess the authority to decide whether a car could be repaired at the service station for which he or she worked. ■

How could Seagate prevent Charlie from agreeing to service cars on Seagate's behalf? Seagate could post conspicuous notices instructing customers to speak only with the manager and it could warn Charlie that if he takes it upon himself to accept a car for service, he would be severely reprimanded or terminated.

DUTIES OF EMPLOYEES AND INDEPENDENT CONTRACTORS

DUTY OF LOYALTY

The relationship between employers and employees or independent contractors is a fiduciary one, based on trust and confidence. Inherent in this relationship is the employee's or independent contractor's duty of loyalty. An employee has a duty to inform, to obey instructions, and to protect confidential information. An employee or independent contractor has a duty to disclose all pertinent information he or she learns of that will affect the employer, the employer's business, or the task at hand. An employee or independent contractor must not take advantage of the employer's prospective business opportunities or enter into contracts on behalf of the employer for personal aggrandizement without the employer's knowledge. An employee, and in some cases an independent contractor (lawyer, investment banker, sports-team scout), may not work for two employers who have competing interests.

EMPLOYMENT PERSPECTIVE

Peter Stapelton works as a sales clerk and mechanic in South Shore Auto Parts and Repair Shop. One day Stapelton is approached by Malcolm Ripkin, owner of Ripkin's Limousine Service, who informs him that he would like South Shore to maintain his fleet of seventeen limousines. Stapelton takes Ripkin's card, but instead of passing it along to the owners of South Shore, he decides to negotiate with Ripkin on his own behalf. Stapelton reasons that if he can get the contract for the maintenance of the seventeen limousines, it would enable him to establish his own auto repair station. Stapelton enters into a personal service contract with Ripkin and then contracts with South Shore to purchase all the supplies he needs at wholesale prices. Six months later, South Shore learns of Stapelton's disloyalty. What recourse does the company have? South Shore may sue Stapelton for breach of contract because he violated his duty of loyalty in failing to disclose Ripkin's offer and in taking advantage of South Shore's business opportunity. Stapelton also contracted on behalf of South Shore for his own benefit without informing the company of what he was doing. Stapelton will be liable to South Shore for consequential damages—that is, the loss of profits South Shore sustained because of Stapelton's unauthorized contracts made on behalf of South Shore with himself at wholesale prices. South Shore will be able to recover the difference between the wholesale price and the retail price, and may also fire Stapelton for his disloyal actions. ∎

DUTY TO ACT IN GOOD FAITH

An employee or independent contractor has an obligation to perform all duties in good faith. He or she must carry out the task assigned by using reasonable skill and care. The employee or independent contractor has a further duty to follow the employer's instructions and not to exceed the authority delegated to him or her.

EMPLOYMENT PERSPECTIVE

Steve Torrino worked in a Burgerville Restaurant for three years. During his employment, he felt that the manager was continually mistreating him by using abusive language, assigning him hours which purposely conflicted with his class studies, and making him perform janitorial services that were not included in his job description. When an opening arose at a nearby House of Burgers on a late shift, Torrino accepted the position, but he retained his regular job with Burgerville. During the manager's absence one busy Saturday afternoon, Torrino neglected his routine duties and took charge of the cash register. He proceeded to give away three jumbo burgers free with every purchase of a small soda. He informed the customers that it was an anniversary celebration. Torrino's intent was to repay the Burgerville manager for his unkindness by causing him to lose profits. What recourse does the Burgerville manager have against Torrino? Torrino violated his duty of loyalty to Burgerville by working for a competing employer, House of Burgers, and by purposely causing Burgerville to lose profits. Torrino refused to obey instructions to perform his delegated duties. He exceeded his authority through the authorization of a free offer. If Torrino was displeased with his job, he should have left to find another position rather than allowing his resentment to build up for three years. In all respects, Torrino violated his duty to act in good faith. ∎

DUTY TO ACCOUNT

An employee or independent contractor has a duty to account for all compensations received, including kickbacks. Upon the employer's request, an employee or independent contractor must make a full disclosure, known as an accounting, of all receipts and expenditures. The employee or independent contractor must not commingle funds but rather must keep the employer's funds in an account separate from his or her own. Furthermore, an employee or independent contractor must not use the employer's funds for his or her own purposes.

EMPLOYMENT PERSPECTIVE

Ted Murphy is a securities broker at a branch office of Pearlman & Associates, located in Silver City, New Mexico. All of Murphy's clients signed an agreement appointing him as their agent to buy and sell securities. Murphy would often borrow from individual accounts in order to further his own investment opportunities. He did this without informing either the client or the company; later he would repay the amount borrowed. Since Silver City is not a large city, many clients make deposits in cash. Murphy would stamp the deposit slip but then deposit the cash in his own account, expecting to repay the money at a later date. Finally, Murphy has a streak of bad luck and is unable to repay the money before the monthly statements are sent out. The clients sue Pearlman & Associates and Ted Murphy, for conversion of the funds in their accounts. What recourse does Pearlman & Associates have against Murphy? The company may sue Murphy for breach of contract and for reimbursement of any of the clients' losses. Murphy breached his duty of loyalty, his duty to act in good faith, and his duty to disclose fully all deposits he received. He commingled clients' funds with his own for the purpose of furthering his own investment schemes. ■

EMPLOYER'S DUTIES

DUTY TO COMPENSATE

An employer has the duty to compensate the employee or independent contractor for the work performed. An employee or independent contractor will be entitled to the amount agreed upon in the contract; otherwise he or she will be entitled to the reasonable value of the services rendered. Sales representatives are usually paid according to a commission-based pay structure, which incorporates a minimum level of compensation against which the sales representatives are entitled to draw. An employer must also reimburse an employee for the expenses incurred by the employee during the course of conducting the employer's business. For tax purposes, an employer has a duty to keep a record of the compensation earned by an employee and the reimbursements made for expenditures. Employers are required to withhold payroll taxes from employees' paychecks. This is not so with fees paid to independent contractors.

DUTY TO MAINTAIN SAFE WORKING CONDITIONS

The maintenance of safe working conditions is another obligation placed on the employer. Any tools or equipment furnished to the employee must be in proper working order; otherwise, the employer may be liable for the harm resulting to an employee under the Occupational Safety and Health Act.

If an employee is injured during the scope of employment, then the employee will be covered under workers' compensation. The scope of employment means the worker is on the job.

EMPLOYMENT PERSPECTIVE

Dolores Wright, an agent of the Green Bay Housing Authority, is in charge of tenant complaints regarding lack of heat and hot water. She is a part-time employee who works only during the winter months. Wright's office is in a three-story building located in the downtown section and owned by the city. In February, the building's oil burner malfunctioned. Dolores Wright made numerous calls to her superiors, but no action was taken. When Dolores called the oil company people, they said the burner needed to be replaced. It was not replaced. Of her own volition, she bought and paid for a heater, insulated her office, and continued to work through the month of February. At that time, she became ill with pneumonia and was hospitalized. Since she was a part-time employee, the city did not pay for her medical plan. She thereupon sued the city for her medical bills, loss of compensation while she was hospitalized, and the expenses she incurred in attempting to make the office habitable during the month of February. Is she entitled to be reimbursed? Yes! The city is liable for her medical expenses because it failed to provide her with a safe and healthy working environment. She is entitled to compensation for the time she lost from work because the lost time was directly caused by the city's negligence. Also she is entitled to reimbursement for the expenses she incurred in attempting to create a healthy environment in the office. If Dolores never reported the burner's malfunction, would the city have been liable? No! Dolores must put the city on notice to cure the defect before it results in harm to an employee. What if Dolores in a fit of rage or frustration threw a chair through a window and became ill eventually from the cold air blowing in. Would the city be responsible for her illness? No! Dolores caused the problem by her own purposeful act. ■

RESTRICTIVE COVENANTS

Contracts not to compete are generally found to be not in the best interests of the public. However, contracts containing a covenant not to compete may be lawful where the contract involves employment. A noncompete clause in an employment contract may prevent an employee from working in the same field for a certain length of time. The courts do not look with favor upon such clauses because enforcing these clauses prevents a worker from earning a livelihood in his area of expertise. Courts will enforce noncompete clauses only when the employee has knowledge of trade secrets or where the employer will suffer loss of customers and/or profits. Restrictive covenants usually contain time and geographic restrictions. Reasonable time limitations are usually for a three- to five-year period. Geographic restrictions are limited to where the employer does business. If the employer conducts business only within a city, then the employee cannot compete within the city.

The limitations set forth in the contract must be reasonable. The courts will not enforce restrictions upon employees that are unduly harsh and permit employers to derive more protection than that necessary to guard their secrets or to protect their business interests.

EMPLOYMENT PERSPECTIVE

David Williams bought a liquor store on the South Side of Chicago. He hired Brian Jackson to manage the store for him. A provision in the contract prohibited Brian from opening a liquor store within the city limits for the rest of his natural life. After learning the trade, Brian quit and opened his own place in the downtown section of Chicago known as the Loop. Can David enforce the provision? No! The provision is too broad in its geographical area and much too unreasonable in its time restraints. ■

EMPLOYMENT SCENARIO

L&S approaches Susan with a concern over whether it can restrict its salespeople from leaving to work for a competitor. Susan explains that a covenant "not to compete" would have to be drafted designating the duration and geographical restriction. The latter is usually limited to the area from where L&S draw its customers. Each salesperson would have to sign the "noncompete" agreement. The enforceability of this covenant hinges upon whether or not L&S could show harm to its business. Susan adds that courts do not look with favor upon these covenants absent the showing of actual loss of profits to the business, because the employee would be precluded from working in his or her profession. Enforcement of such a clause mandates relocation or a career change. L&S states that it is the salespeople who develop a rapport with the customers. L&S worries that the salespeople, upon leaving, could influence customers to follow them to another store. Susan cautions that the result might be to depress the morale of the sales staff because the covenant evidences a lack of trust in them. The restriction may also force them to refuse the job. The salespeople may consider that if they are unhappy working for L&S, their freedom to work elsewhere will be restricted. L&S counters with a compromise that restricts the salespeople from establishing their own large, tall, or short men's clothing store or working for another clothing establishment that specializes in this line of work. Susan agrees to draft a "noncompete" agreement, which integrates these stipulations.

PROMISSORY ESTOPPEL

When a person changes his or her position in reliance on a promise, and that change in position is foreseeable, the person making the promise will be stopped from asserting that there is no consideration to enforce the contract. This is the doctrine of *promissory estoppel*. It is equitable in that enforcement of a promise may be upheld for reasons of fairness and justice even though the recipient of the promise gave no consideration in return. To invoke the doctrine of promissory estoppel, the person making the promise must reasonably expect it to motivate the other person to change his or her position by taking some substantial and justifiable action in reliance on the promise. The person taking the action must be going to suffer a detriment for his or her reliance on that promise if it is not carried out. This is the reason for enforcing the promise— to prevent the person relying on the promise from suffering a loss.

EMPLOYMENT PERSPECTIVE

It was the middle of a scorching hot summer. Timothy Woodwirth, who worked on the night shift for the Brooklyn D.A.'s office, was out pounding the pavement during the day in his three-piece suit looking for a higher paying position. He entered the reception area of the law firm of Collins, Egbert, and Phillips. He informed the receptionist of his request for an interview and she notified Mr. Phillips. Mr. Phillips spoke to Timothy and then introduced him to Mr. Egbert. After the interviews, Timothy was offered a position with a salary of $25,000. He was to begin work in two weeks. In the interim, Mr. Collins returned from an extended vacation. He strenuously objected to the hiring of Timothy because of his lack of experience in civil litigation. As senior partner in the firm, he won out. Meanwhile, Timothy had resigned from the D.A.'s office and was ready to begin work when he was advised of Mr. Collins's decision. Has Timothy any recourse? Yes! Although Timothy gave no consideration in return for the promise made by Mr. Egbert and Mr. Phillips to hire him, he relied on their promise by resigning from the D.A.'s office to work for their firm and thus suffered a real detriment, loss of a job. Under the doctrine of promissory estoppel, the law firm must compensate Timothy for lost wages until he finds another suitable legal position. ■

BREACH OF CONTRACT

Most employment contracts are completed without significant problems. Parties generally fulfill their promises under the contract. Breach of contract occurs when a party does not fulfill his or her promise to perform. The breach, which is a failure to perform a material contractual obligation, may take the form of renunciation of the contract, restraining the other party's performance, as well as failure to perform.

INJUNCTION

An *injunction* is an equitable remedy that prevents a party breaching a contract from rendering the same performance elsewhere. An injunction is personal in nature and negative in effect in that it precludes a person from performing certain acts. However, since the breaching party cannot be compelled to perform a certain act, an injunction can prohibit the party from performing the same act elsewhere. An injunction acts as a restraint against the party breaching an employment contract. An injunction is the appropriate remedy to enforce a restrictive covenant (non-compete clause).

EMPLOYMENT PERSPECTIVE

Wild Bill Cary is under a five-year contract with the Texas Tornadoes to play quarterback for them for $100,000 per year. After leading his team to successive central division titles, he is offered a four-year contract from the Hawaii Hurricanes for $500,000 per year. There are still three years remaining on Wild Bill's contract with Texas, but he decides to accept Hawaii's offer. Can Texas prevent Wild Bill from quarterbacking for Hawaii? Yes! An injunction can be granted, but Texas cannot legally force Wild Bill to quarterback for them through specific performance. Wild Bill is bound to Texas for the three years remaining on his contract unless they renegotiate his contract or trade him.

The terms of Wild Bill's original contract were designed to protect him from being cut from the team while insuring him a substantial yearly salary. After the contract expires, Wild Bill will have free agent status. ▪

CONTRACTUAL CONDITIONS

A condition occurs when the parties' contractual duties are contingent upon the occurrence of a future event. Parties must expressly agree when making the contract if they are conditioning their obligations on the occurrence of a particular event.

Sales quotas in car dealerships, insurance, brokerage, and so forth, are conditions that must be continuously satisfied for the worker to retain his or her job.

LIABILITY OF EMPLOYEES AND INDEPENDENT CONTRACTORS

Employees and independent contractors will be liable for breach of contract if they fail to uphold their duties, including duty of loyalty, duty to act in good faith, and duty to account for all receipts and expenses. An employee will be liable for all unauthorized acts or misrepresentations made to third parties in the principal's name.

An employee's and independent contractor's liability extends to situations in which they contract in their own name or on behalf of their employer without authority. To protect themselves against personal liability, they should always sign the employer's name and then their own name as agent.

EMPLOYMENT PERSPECTIVE

Robert McMillen lists farmland that he owns north of Cheyenne, Wyoming, with Tumbleweed Real Estate and gives it an exclusive agency. After four months of attempting to locate a buyer, Tumbleweed learns that an interstate highway will proceed north from Denver and Cheyenne through McMillen's farmland, thus enhancing the purchase price. Tumbleweed contracts with McMillen to purchase the farmland for Dexter Brady, supposedly an out-of-state principal who has given Tumbleweed power of attorney to act on his behalf. Tumbleweed is actually purchasing the land for itself. Brady is a fictitious principal who does not exist. McMillen is happy with the purchase price until he learns about the interstate highway plan. He sues Tumbleweed Real Estate and Dexter Brady, only to discover Brady is nonexistent. What recourse does McMillen have against Tumbleweed? Tumbleweed can be compelled to return the farmland to McMillen even though there were no other ready, willing, and able buyers. Tumbleweed attempted to defraud McMillen by purportedly acting for a principal who did not exist, while they were actually buying the land for themselves.

Assume that there was no interstate highway plan and that Dexter Brady really existed and gave Tumbleweed authority to act for him. Suppose that Tumbleweed contracted with McMillen in its own name and that Brady later reneged on the purchase;

would Tumbleweed be liable on the contract for the sale of McMillen's farmland? Yes! An independent contractor who signs in his or her own name is personally liable to a third party unless the employer admits he or she is liable by approving the agent's acts. Although Tumbleweed may be liable to McMillen, it may sue Brady for breach of his agency contract with the company. ■

LIABILITY OF EMPLOYERS

CONTRACTUAL LIABILITY

An employer is bound by his or her employee's or independent contractor's contract with a third party where the employee or independent contractor acted with actual authority, either express or implied, or with apparent authority. An employer is not liable for the unauthorized acts of the employee or independent contractor unless the employer ratifies the unauthorized acts.

EMPLOYMENT PERSPECTIVE

Clifford Branch and James Alworth were both attending an auction at Porter's Auction House. Branch was representing the Ford Foundation as he had done on numerous occasions in the past. Alworth was representing a man named Vanderbilt, an undisclosed employer. During the auction, Branch was declared the highest bidder on paintings by Paul Cézanne and Henri Matisse for $850,000 and $700,000, respectively. Alworth was successful with his $1,450,000 bid for a Van Gogh. Both Branch and Alworth signed a contract agreeing to deliver the purchase price within two weeks, at which time the painting would be transferred. Branch signed "Ford Foundation by Clifford Branch, Agent." Alworth signed his own name. If the Ford Foundation claimed that Branch exceeded his authority by paying a sum greater than the agreed-upon $500,000 for each painting, would this be a good defense to a suit by Porter's? No! Branch had actual authority to pay up to $500,000 and apparent authority beyond that, since he had acted for the Ford Foundation on prior occasions. The Ford Foundation must pay for the painting. Its sole recourse lies against Branch for exceeding his actual authority. If Vanderbilt refuses to pay for the Van Gogh, will Alworth be liable? Yes! Porter's may sue Alworth because he signed the contract in his own name. The prudent move for Alworth would have been to disclose Vanderbilt's identity and produce the employment contract with Vanderbilt. Porter's may then proceed against either Alworth or Vanderbilt but most likely will choose the deepest pocket to be sure of collecting payment. If Alworth paid for the painting, would he have any recourse against Vanderbilt? Yes! Alworth would be entitled to sue Vanderbilt for indemnification of the loss Alworth suffered because of Vanderbilt's breach of duty. ■

An employer is not liable for the unauthorized acts of an employee or independent contractor in cases where the third party has a duty to inquire about the agent's actual authority when that authority is not apparent. A third party who takes it for granted that the employee or independent contractor possesses the authority to contract and is not justified in so relying will have no recourse against the employer, but will be restricted to recovering from the employee or independent contractor alone.

TORT LIABILITY

An employer is liable for any *tort* committed by his or her employee if the tort is committed within the scope of employment—that is, if it is related to the business at hand. A tort is a private civil wrong as opposed to a crime which is a wrong committed against the public. Money damages are awarded to compensate a party who has been injured by a tort. Employers may contract for liability insurance to minimize their risk and to avoid paying for the damages out of the profits of the business. However, an employer is not liable for the torts of an independent contractor even if the torts are committed during the scope of employment because the employer has no control over the work of an independent contractor.

EMPLOYMENT PERSPECTIVE

Luis Manulto is a construction worker who was hired by Valenti Construction Company. Currently, Luis is working on the forty-fourth floor of an office building in downtown Houston. Manulto has his toolbox at his feet, but when someone calls him abruptly, he accidentally knocks it off the beam. The toolbox falls onto a pedestrian walkway that was covered by a heavy plastic grating. Linda Anderson, who was walking through the passageway at the time, is severely injured. Is Manulto an employee or an independent contractor? Manulto is an employee because he works exclusively for Valenti and is under Valenti's direct control. Who is liable for Linda's injuries? Linda may sue both Luis Manulto (employee) and Valenti Construction Company (employer). Manulto acted negligently in knocking over the toolbox. Valenti Construction Company is liable for Manulto's negligence because it occurred during his scope of employment; the accident was related directly to the business at hand.

Suppose that at lunchtime, Manulto stops at a bar across the street to drown his sorrows and that a patron comments, "I saw the whole episode, and it was a real stupid thing you did." Manulto, angered by the patron's comments, punches him in the face, causing the patron to suffer a fractured nose and a concussion. Is the principal liable for Manulto's acts? No! Valenti Construction Company is not liable for Manulto's tort of assault and battery because it did not occur within the scope of employment—the tort was not related to the business at hand. Manulto will be solely liable. ■

EMPLOYMENT SCENARIO

One evening at the L&S store, Martha is measuring the inseam on a customer, Fred Nichols. Fred comments, "I like when you touch me there. It makes me feel real good." Martha is very embarrassed. Salesperson Grant Worthington is privy to Fred's comments. Grant confronts Fred by saying, "How could you talk to a woman like that?" Fred replies, "She was purposely touching me there, so butt out, geek!" Grant clocks Fred with a left uppercut that would make Mike Tyson proud. Fred sustains a broken jaw and sues L&S for the torts of assault and battery. L&S retains Susan North for its defense. Susan states that liability is determined by whether the tort was committed within the scope of employment, or in other words, "on the job." Susan tells L&S that Grant should have requested the customer to leave the store and to escort him out in the process. L&S will be liable to Fred for the injuries he received.

The case presented below is concerned with whether a store is liable for the negligent acts of its security guard and whether a federal court determination has any bearing on a subsequent state court trial.

CASE

GUIDRY v. HARP'S FOOD STORES, INC.

987 S.W.2d 755 (Ark. 1999)

MEADS, Judge.

This appeal is brought from the trial court's entry of summary judgment in favor of appellee, Harp's Food Stores, Inc. The court found that certain issues decided in a federal civil rights suit brought by appellant precluded appellant from relitigating those issues in a tort suit prosecuted in state court. We reverse and remand.

David Jones, a Rogers city policeman, worked for appellee during his off-duty hours as a loss-prevention officer. On March 25, 1996, he supposedly observed appellant stealing a pack of cigarettes. Appellant was apprehended and arrested and charged with shoplifting. It was later determined that the cigarettes did not come from appellee's store, and the shoplifting charge was **nolle prossed.** As a result of the incident, appellant filed suit in federal court against David Jones, the City of Rogers, and the city's police chief. In the same action, he sued appellee for battery, assault, false imprisonment, defamation, malicious prosecution, and negligence. The federal court granted summary judgment, ruling that Jones's arrest and detention of appellant was reasonable, even if mistaken, thus entitling Jones to qualified immunity under federal law. Further, the court found that appellant failed to prove that Jones used excessive force in making the arrest, having offered no evidence that he suffered anything beyond minor injury or discomfort. At the conclusion of these findings, the court exercised its prerogative to decline jurisdiction over the state tort claims.

Following the federal court ruling, appellant filed suit in state court against appellee.

According to the complaint, David Jones, in the presence of store employees and customers, wrongly accused appellant of shoplifting, then detained him by use of force. The complaint further alleged that appellee commenced a criminal proceeding against appellant without probable cause. Based upon these allegations, appellant asserted that appellee, acting through its agent, Jones, committed the torts of battery, assault, false imprisonment, malicious prosecution, defamation, and outrage. Appellant also asserted a cause of action for conversion based upon appellee's retention of the cigarettes he was suspected of stealing, and a cause of action for negligence based upon appellee's failure to train its security guards or investigate their backgrounds. After discovery was undertaken in the case, appellee filed a motion for summary judgment. The motion contended that, at the time of the incident, Jones was acting as a city police officer, not as appellee's employee. However, the gravamen of appellee's argument was that the federal court ruling conclusively established the reasonableness of Jones's actions, thereby leaving no basis for appellant's tort claims. A copy of the federal court ruling was attached to the motion, along with various affidavits, depositions, and answers to interrogatories. Through these exhibits, appellee presented the following evidence: Jones believed he saw appellant put a pack of cigarettes in his pocket without paying for them. Jones then approached appellant, identified himself as a police officer, and asked appellant to accompany him to the manager's office. Appellant refused and called Jones a "racist pig." When appellant tried to leave the store, Jones held him, and a scuffle ensued. Jones warned appellant that he would have to physically restrain him if he kept fighting. Appellant ignored the warnings, and Jones put him on the floor, holding him there until on-duty officers arrived. The cigarettes that appellant was holding were confiscated and were held at appellee's store until they were picked up by the police a week later. The charges against appellant were dropped when the city attorney's office learned that the tax identification number on the cigarettes showed that they did not come from appellee's store. Appellant responded to the motion by arguing that the findings made by the federal court were based upon Jones's conduct as a police officer as viewed in light of constitutional requirements, not as a private actor viewed in light of state tort law. He attached depositions that were primarily directed to appellee's assertion that Jones was not acting as its employee. The depositions indicated, however, that up to twenty-five people may have observed the incident and that Jones had received no training or guidance from appellee regarding the apprehension of suspected shoplifters.

After a hearing, the trial judge found that the federal court ruling "knocked out the underpinning" of appellee's state tort claims, thus barring them under the doctrine of collateral estoppel. With regard to the negligence claim, the judge found that there was no causation between appellee's alleged negligence in training Jones and appellant's damages. It is from this ruling that appellant brings his appeal.

Appellant's federal action was brought pursuant to 42 U.S.C. § 1983, which provides a cause of action against persons who, under color of law, subject a citizen to deprivation of rights, privileges, and immunities secured by the Constitution. The purpose of section 1983 is to deter state actors from using the badge of their authority to deprive individuals of their federally guaranteed rights.

As to appellant's defamation claim, an officer may make a defamatory statement about a suspect, even though his arrest and detention of the suspect were not plainly incompetent or knowingly illegal for section 1983 purposes.

These examples illustrate that the issue sought to be precluded, *i.e.,* whether Jones's conduct was tortious, is not the same as the issue litigated in federal court, *i.e.,* whether Jones was entitled to qualified immunity.

In addition to his ruling on the collateral-estoppel question, the trial judge ruled that appellant could not show that his damages were proximately caused by appellee's failure to properly train Jones or investigate his background. A careful reading of the court's comments reveals that this ruling was also based upon the federal court's finding that Jones's actions were reasonable. In light of our holding, this part of the summary judgment must also be reversed.

Judgment for Guidry.

Case Commentary

Guidry was accused of shoplifting by Jones, an off-duty policeman hired as a security guard by Harp's Food Store. Guidry was detained by force. In the federal court suit, Jones's actions were determined to be reasonable. In state court, the Arkansas judge ruled that the federal court ruling left no triable issue to decide.

The Arkansas Court of Appeals held that the federal court ruled Jones was entitled to qualified immunity because he was a police officer. This is different from the State court issue of whether Jones's actions were tortious. This case was sent back to the Arkansas trial court to resolve the issue.

Case Questions

1. Why did the Arkansas trial court judge rule that the federal court ruling would be binding on the state tort claim filed by Guidry?
2. Do you think Guidry will win when the tort claim is tried?
3. Do you believe Jones acted reasonably in detaining Guidry?

4. Should police officers be entitled to qualified immunity?
5. Would the outcome be different if Jones was a security guard who was not a police officer?

The issue in this case is whether the WMATA is immune from assault, battery, and negligent hiring lawsuits by virtue of its status as a governmental agency.

CASE

BURKHART v. WASHINGTON METROPOLITAN AREA TRANSIT AUTHORITY

112 F.3d 1207 (DC Cir. 1997)

SENTELLE, Circuit Judge.

Washington Metropolitan Area Transit Authority appeals from a judgment following a jury verdict finding WMATA (1) directly liable for negligent hiring, training, and supervision of its bus operators; (2) directly liable for violations of the Americans with Disabilities Act and the Rehabilitation Act of 1973 and (3) vicariously liable for assault, battery, and infliction of emotional distress.

WMATA raises a myriad of issues on appeal, many of which have been waived and others of which are frivolous. We need only consider certain of the issues, finding them sufficient to reverse the judgment of the trial court as to the ADA and Rehabilitation Act claims and the negligent hiring, training, and supervision claims. However, we affirm the trial court's judgment as to the assault, battery, and infliction of emotional distress claims.

I. BACKGROUND

This case arises from a physical altercation that took place in northern Virginia between Eduardo Burkhart, plaintiff-appellee, and Archie Smith, a WMATA bus operator. On May 5, 1994, Burkhart and a friend, Basram Salman, both of whom are deaf, boarded a Metrobus in Arlington, Virginia. Burkhart and Salman each placed a thirty-cent token in the fare box. The correct fare for those with disabilities is fifty-cents. As the bus pulled away from the curb, Smith called both Burkhart and Salman back to pay the correct fare.

However, because they are deaf, neither Salman nor Burkhart understood Smith's request. The events that followed this exchange are in substantial dispute. It is sufficient for our purposes to say that a series of blows was exchanged between Smith and Burkhart.

When the bus reached its destination at the Pentagon Metrorail Station, Burkhart exited the bus and began looking for a transit officer. At this point, the evidence is in dispute as to whether Burkhart was pointing to Smith or was sticking his finger in Smith's chest. In any event, Smith then grabbed Burkhart's finger. Burkhart responded by kicking Smith in the groin, causing him to release his hold of Burkhart's finger. Smith then picked up a stick, at which point he was restrained.

Ultimately, Transit Police Officer Jonathan Gray arrived on the scene. Officer Gray and Burkhart communicated by writing notes on a notepad. Both Smith and Burkhart were charged with assault and battery. However, these charges were ultimately dropped.

Burkhart subsequently filed suit against WMATA and Smith for injuries sustained as a result of the altercation with Smith. Burkhart asserted claims against Smith, and against WMATA vicariously, for assault, battery, gross negligence, and infliction of emotional distress. In addition, Burkhart alleged that WMATA negligently hired, trained, and supervised its bus operators and, as a result, caused the assault and battery at issue. Still further, Burkhart alleged that he was subject to discrimination, by reason of his disability, in violation of both the ADA and Rehabilitation Act in that WMATA failed to take appropriate steps to ensure that communications with him were as effective as communications with others. The case was tried to a jury with a magistrate judge presiding. At trial,

WMATA admitted that Smith was acting within the scope of his employment with WMATA when the events at issue occurred. As a result, the district court granted Smith's unopposed motion that the claims against him be dismissed.

At the conclusion of trial, the jury returned a verdict for Burkhart. The jury concluded that WMATA was vicariously liable for assault and battery, and awarded Burkhart $373.65 in damages for medical expenses incurred. In addition, the jury found WMATA vicariously liable for infliction of emotional distress, and awarded Burkhart $510.00 for medical expenses. Further, the jury found WMATA directly liable for negligent hiring, training, and supervision, and awarded Burkhart $50,000 for injuries caused by the defendants' acts. Finally, the jury found WMATA directly liable for violations of the ADA and Rehabilitation Act, and awarded Burkhart another $50,000 in damages for injury, embarrassment, humiliation, frustration, inconvenience, indignity and/or the stigma of discrimination. As a result, the trial court entered a judgment for Burkhart in the amount of $100,883.65 and awarded him attorneys' fees and costs of $62,071.46 on the ADA claim. WMATA appeals raising thirteen separate issues of which three warrant discussion.

II. ANALYSIS

Negligent Hiring, Training, and Supervision Claims.

WMATA also urges that we reverse the judgment of the district court as to the negligent hiring, training, and supervision claims.

WMATA was created as the result of a compact signed by Maryland, Virginia, and the District of Columbia and consented to by Congress. The WMATA Compact provides that the Authority shall be liable . . . for its torts and those of its Directors, officers, employees and agents committed in the course of any proprietary function . . . but shall not be liable for any torts occurring in the performance of a governmental policy judgment and involving an exercise of political, social, or economic judgment.

Applying this test, we hold that decisions concerning the hiring, training, and supervising of WMATA employees are discretionary in

nature, and thus immune from judicial review. The parties have pointed to no law or policy specifically prescribing guidelines for the hiring, training, or supervision of WMATA employees. The WMATA compact confers upon WMATA broad power to create and abolish . . . employments and provide for the qualification, appointment, and removal . . . of its . . . employees without regard to the laws of any of the signatories, establish, in its discretion, a personnel system based on merit and fitness, and control and regulate . . . the service to be rendered.

These provisions hardly constrain WMATA's determination of whom it will employ or how it will train and supervise such employees. Thus, WMATA has choices to make.

The hiring, training, and supervision choices that WMATA faces are choices susceptible to policy judgment. The hiring decisions of a public entity require consideration of numerous factors, including budgetary constraints, public perception, economic conditions, individual backgrounds, office diversity, experience and employer intuition.

Similarly, supervision decisions involve a complex balancing of budgetary considerations, employee privacy rights, and the need to ensure public safety. The extent of training with which to provide employees requires consideration of fiscal constraints, public safety, the complexity of the task involved, the degree of harm a wayward employee might cause, and the extent to which employees have deviated from accepted norms in the past. Such decisions are surely among those involving the exercise of political, social, or economic judgment.

As a result, we conclude that the hiring, training, and supervision of WMATA personnel are governmental functions. WMATA is therefore immune from suit for negligence in the performance of such functions. The district court erred in refusing to dismiss Burkhart's negligent hiring, training, and supervision claims against WMATA.

III. CONCLUSION

For the foregoing reasons, we affirm the judgment of the district court as to the assault, battery, and infliction of emotional distress claims. We reverse the judgment of the district court as to the negligent hiring, training, and supervision claims, as well as the ADA and Rehabilitation Act claims. Because WMATA is immune from suit for negligent hiring, training, and supervision, we remand the case for retrial only of the ADA and Rehabilitation Act claims.

Case Commentary

The District of Columbia Circuit Court of Appeals held the WMATA liable for the intentional torts of its employee Archie Smith because they were committed on the job during the scope of employment. The WMATA was not held liable for negligent hiring, training, and supervision because this was a governmental function immune from lawsuit.

Case Questions

1. Should the WMATA be immune from lawsuit for negligent hiring because it is a governmental agency?

2. Do you think the ADA award of $50,000 was excessive?

3. Were the combined intentional tort awards of $883.65 adequate?

An employer is also liable for the fraud or misrepresentations committed by an employee where the principal has placed the employee in a position that leads people to believe that the agent has the apparent authority to make certain actual representations.

EMPLOYMENT PERSPECTIVE

Keith Stewart, a representative of Super Duper Vacuum Company, calls on Thelma Williams at her house. Although at first Thelma is reluctant to make a purchase, Stewart convinces her when he makes the false representation that this household vacuum cleaner will also clean basements and garages, with the separate purchase of certain attachments. He does this intentionally to get the sale. Thelma purchases the vacuum cleaner as well as the attachments. When her husband comes home, she gives him a demonstration in the living room, where the vacuum cleaner works perfectly. Then using the attachments, Thelma's husband attempts to clean the garage floor. The machine breaks down. Thelma and her husband sue Super Duper Vacuum Company and Keith Stewart for fraud. Super Duper never instructed Stewart to make false statements of fact and never advertised its vacuum cleaner for anything more than household use. Who will be responsible for the fraud? If Keith is an employee working exclusively for Super Duper, then both Super Duper and Keith Stewart will be liable. Super Duper is liable for its employee's fraudulent representations because it placed Stewart in a position where people would reasonably believe that he had the authority to make such a statement. Super Duper may seek indemnification from Stewart because of his breach of duty of loyalty. Stewart breached the duty by exceeding his authority through the making of statements which were false and unauthorized. ■

EMPLOYMENT PERSPECTIVE

One day while strolling through Richmond Hill Mall, Bill Cominsky decides to browse around Peter's Jewelry Store. He spots what appears to be a gold necklace on sale for $49. He figures this would be perfect for his fiancee's upcoming birthday. Bill goes in and asks the clerk, Marjorie Travers, whether the necklace is made of gold. She excuses herself and goes into a back room where she questions Bernard Peters, the store owner. He replies that the necklace is 14K gold, knowing this to be false. Marjorie conveys the message to Bill, ignorant of its falsehood. Bill, relying on the statement, makes the purchase. On his fiancee's birthday, they discover that the necklace is not 14K gold. What recourse is available to Bill Cominsky? Bill may sue Marjorie Travers, the employee, for misrepresentation and Bernard Peters, the employer, for fraud. Marjorie Travers made a material misrepresentation of fact that Bill justifiably relied on to his detriment. She made this statement innocently, without an intent to defraud. Bernard Peters is guilty of fraud because his misrepresentation was intentional. ∎

NEGLIGENCE

Negligence is the failure to perceive a risk which results in an injury that was foreseeable. Negligence is caused by conduct that falls below the standard established by law for the protection of others against risk of harm. The negligent party must have had a duty to perceive the risk of harm that he or she fails to meet. The key to negligence is that the defendant failed to act as a reasonable person would in light of the risk. The plaintiff has the burden of proving this. The elements that give rise to negligence are the following:

- Negligent act
- Duty owed
- Proximate cause
- Forseeable injury
- Resulting loss

Negligence is an act performed in a careless manner, or an omission to act, that proximately causes injury to another. Liability for the negligence does not arise until it is established that the person who was careless owed a duty toward the person bringing the suit. A duty to exercise reasonable care arises whenever there is a danger of one person's causing injury to another. The injury to the plaintiff must have been proximately caused by the negligent act of the defendant.

Proximate cause means the negligent act must have been reasonably connected to the plaintiff's injury. The injury to the plaintiff must be foreseeable. A foreseeable injury is that which would be reasonably anticipated as a consequence of the defendant's negligence. In most states, the defendant is responsible for damages resulting from only foreseeable injuries. The plaintiff must sustain a definable loss or damage and prove that this loss or damage resulted from the injury caused by the defendant's negligence. The plaintiff's loss is recompensed with money damages.

The doctrine of foreseeability may also be applied to situations where one party's negligence has injured a person and caused others to attempt to rescue. Under the doctrine of "danger invites rescue," the negligent party is responsible for injury to the rescuers, where they act reasonably and where it is foreseeable that people might go to the rescue of the injured person.

EMPLOYMENT PERSPECTIVE

Lauren, a French-family owned corporation, is building a trestle bridge across Niagara Falls. The company employs Jack Hill as their chief carpenter and general contractor. One day Jack, who is rushing to finish work in order to leave for his home, omits three of the four nails securing one of the tracks. Two months later, the bridge opens and the first Loco, Inc. train rolls across. John Phillips and his cousin Fred Goodman are among the last to board the train. The two men are forced to stand between the cars because the train is overcrowded. Because the train's engineer misjudges the correct speed needed to make a smooth transition around a curve, Phillips is sent flying out the door. The train stops 100 feet down the tracks. Fred Goodman bolts off the train to look for his cousin. When he steps onto the track that is not properly secured, it gives way, and he joins his cousin in Niagara Falls. Their estates sue the Lauren Corp. and Loco, Inc. for wrongful death. What is the result? Loco, Inc. is responsible for Phillips's death due to the negligence of its engineer. Lauren Corp. is liable for Goodman's death because of the negligence of its carpenter, Jack Hill. Fred Goodman's estate may also recover from Loco Corp. under the doctrine that danger invites rescue, because it was foreseeable that Fred Goodman might go to the rescue of his cousin. ■

RATIFICATION OF AN EMPLOYEE'S UNAUTHORIZED ACTS

Ratification is the approval or sanction given by the employer to the unauthorized acts of an employee. The employer may ratify the unauthorized contracts made by the employee as well as the torts committed by the employee. The following requirements are necessary for ratification:

- Employee acts in excess of or without authority.
- Employer is made aware of all important facts.
- Employer ratifies entire act, not part of it.
- Ratification must be made in the same manner as the authority given to the employee.

Ratification may be implied when an employer fails to condemn an employee's acts within a reasonable time after the employer acquires knowledge of all the important facts. Once the employer ratifies the employee's contractual acts and the third party is notified, a contract exists between the employer and the third party which the employer is now legally obligated to perform. When notice is conveyed to a third party that the employer assumes all responsibilities for an employee's torts, the employer will be liable for the injuries sustained by that third party.

EMPLOYMENT PERSPECTIVE

Christopher Evans is a salesclerk in Montclair's Electronics Store. Evans is greeted one morning by an enthusiastic salesman offering to sell the store two hundred videotapes on consignment. Evans believes the sale of video movies will greatly enhance the store's business, especially the sale of its video players and recorders. Evans signs the contract on behalf of Montclair even though he has no authority to do so. When apprised of Evans's action, Montclair believes it to be a smart move and notifies the salesman of his approval. If Montclair changes his mind and claims Evans's acts were not authorized, who will be responsible, Evans or Montclair? Evans was originally liable for breaching his duty of loyalty by exceeding the authority given to him. However, once Montclair ratified Evans's actions, Evans is no longer liable. Montclair will be solely liable to the third party—the videotape distributor. Would it be the same if Evans advised Montclair of his unauthorized act and Montclair said nothing? Yes! Ratification may be implied by silence, if the employer fails to disaffirm responsibility for the employee's acts after learning all the facts. Would Montclair be liable to the videotape distributor if he immediately notified the distributor that he would not assume liability for Evans's unauthorized acts? It would depend on whether it was the usual practice in the trade for a salesclerk to order new merchandise. If so, Montclair would be liable because Evans acted with apparent authority. If it was not the usual practice, then the salesclerk should have known that a salesclerk does not possess the authority to contract with a new concern and the owner should have been consulted. ▪

❖ EMPLOYER LESSONS

- Develop an understanding of the implementation of the Economic Realities test as it relates to the distinction between employees and independent contractors.
- Discern what kind of authority employees should have and how much authority should be given to them.
- Reprimand employees if they exceed the authority given to them.
- Indoctrinate employees concerning the loyalty owed to the employer and their need to always act in the best interests of the company.
- Implore employees to act in good faith, give their best effort, and carry out their jobs in a responsible manner.
- Compensate employees fairly and be concerned about their workplace safety to enhance employee morale.
- Understand when employees' actions occur within the scope of employment.
- Appreciate the torts of defamation, invasion of privacy, and interference with business relations when speaking to others about employees.
- Remember that contracts are binding and lawsuits are filed for breaches of contracts.
- Minimize tort liability by emphasizing to employees that they should never assault, defame, harass, inflict emotional distress, or interfere in the business relations of others.

❖ EMPLOYEE LESSONS

- Know whether or not your employment status is that of an employee or independent contractor.
- Understand the rights and responsibilities of both.
- Learn what authority you have been given.
- Acknowledge the limits of your authority by not exceeding them.
- Recognize that you are to be loyal to your employer and act in the best interests of your employer.
- Undertake your tasks in good faith by giving your best efforts.
- Appreciate the concept of "scope of employment" and make certain to act within it.
- Refrain from assaulting, defaming, invading the privacy of others, interfering with the business relations of others, harassing or inflicting emotional distress on customers, management, or co-workers.
- Remember that contracts are binding and lawsuits result from breaches of contracts.
- Discern the effects of limiting one's employment opportunities by signing a covenant "not to compete."

❖ SUMMARY

The key to a successful business is the existence of a positive relationship between employers and employees. Employers are confronted with issues concerning employees' authority, duties, compensation, and liability. Employers must be concerned with elucidating in a clear and concise manner the employees' authority and duties. Employers must fairly compensate their workers. Employers should limit their liability by adequately educating and training their employees with regard to specific torts and breaches of contracts. Adapting the concept of "scope of employment" (which means whether the action or complaint occurred on the job) to the business will clearly define an employer's liability for torts and breaches of contracts.

A good understanding of the appropriate time to employ a covenant "not to compete" in an employment contract is essential. Finally, the distinction between employees and independent contractors has been defined. Courts employ an "economic realities test" to determine the extent of control the employer has over the behavior and compensation of workers and whether the relationship is permanent.

❖ REVIEW QUESTIONS

1. Define *agency, principal, agent, employment, employer, employee,* and *independent contractor.*
2. What is the difference between express and implied actual authority? Give an example of each.
3. What is apparent authority? Give an example.
4. Define the employee's duty of loyalty, duty to act in good faith, and duty to account, and give an example of a breach of each duty.
5. Explain the employer's duty to compensate and the employer's duty to maintain safe working conditions.
6. What is the main difference between an employee and an independent contractor?
7. Why does employment create a fiduciary relationship?
8. When will a restrictive covenant be enforced?
9. When is an employer contractually liable?
10. Explain the types of torts for which an employer may be liable.
11. Debi Eyerman worked her way up through the ranks of Mary Kay Cosmetics until she was appointed a national sales director. At that time, she signed a National Sales Director Agreement, which provided that Eyerman would be an independent contractor, not an employee, and that she would earn a commission based on the performance of her sales group. Eyerman was required to maintain an office, provide advice to salespersons, and attend meetings when necessary. She was given no power to enter into a contract on behalf of Mary Kay Cosmetics, and the company would exercise no control over her as well. Either party could cancel the agreement upon sixty days' notice. Is Eyerman an employee or an independent contractor? *Eyerman v. Mary Kay Cosmetics, Inc.,* 967 F.2d 213 (6th Cir. 1992)
12. Lorentz was hired by Coblentz, who had an appliance-repair business. Lorentz had to provide his own truck and stock his own parts. At 8:00 every morning, Lorentz had to call in to receive his assignments for the day. He was paid a 50 percent commission. Coblentz withheld federal payroll taxes. Is Lorentz an employee or an independent contractor? What was the result? *Lorentz v. Coblentz,* 600 S.2d 1376 (La. App. 1 Cir. 1992)
13. Mrs. Amoroso was injured by a defective crossbar on a sailboat, which she and her husband had rented at the Diplomat Hotel. The sailboats were owned and operated by Sunrise Water Sports. The rental stand was on the hotel's grounds, the rental fee was billed to the hotel room, and the rental service was advertised in the hotel room. Mrs. Amoroso sued the Diplomat on the theory of apparent authority. What was the result? *Amoroso v. Samuel Friedland Family* Ent., 604, So.2d 827 (Fla. App. 4 Dist. 1992)

14. Raymond Berta was a partner in the Decker, Berta and Co. Accounting firm. When the business was sold, he remained as an employee and signed the following document:

    "RESTRICTIVE COVENANT. For a period of three (3) years from the date of the termination of his employment, the Employee will not, within a thirty-five (35) mile radius of any present places of business of Employer, directly or indirectly own, manage, operate, or control, or be connected in any manner with any business of the type and character of business engaged in by the Employer at the time of such termination."

    When the contract expired, Berta joined another accounting firm. He brought his father-in-law's account with him. Berta also phoned several other former clients, asking them to switch firms. Decker, Berta and Co. sought a preliminary injunction alleging Berta violated the restrictive covenant.

    Is this restrictive covenant enforceable? *Decker v. Berta,* 587 N.E.2d 72 (Ill. App. 4 Dist. 1992)

15. Dennis Harris was police chief of Plano, Illinois, when Bud Johnson was elected mayor. Harris asked Johnson if Johnson wanted Harris to remain as police chief; otherwise, he would take advantage of other opportunities offering similar pay. Johnson told Harris he would appoint him if he stayed on but later terminated Harris' employment. Harris was forced to take another position with a substantial reduction in pay. Therefore, Harris sued Johnson for breach of promise, asked for the difference in pay as the measure of damages, and cited the promissory estoppel doctrine. What was the result? *Harris v. Johnson,* 578 N.E.2d 1326 (Ill. App. 2 Dist. 1991)

16. David Duwell left Bobcat Enterprises for Portman Equipment Co., a competitor. This action was in violation of the restrictive covenant Duwell signed while employed with Bobcat. Bobcat sought an injunction. Duwell's current position involves renting industrial forklifts, a business Bobcat does not engage in. What was the result? *Bobcat Enterprises, Inc. v. Duwell,* 587 N.E.2d 905 (Ohio App. 12 Dist. 1990)

17. Gregory Harthcock was hired as a chemist by Zep Manufacturing. He signed a nondisclosure covenant that restricted work in the same field for two years and that did not specify geographic location. Subsequently, he left Zep's employ for a job with its competitor, Panther Industries. Zep sought to enforce the restrictive covenant; Harthcock claimed it was indefinite in its terms. What was the result? *Zep Mfg. Co. v. Harthcock,* 824 S.W.2d 654 (Tex. App.-Dallas 1992)

18. P.M. Palumbo, Jr., M.A., Inc., is a professional corporation providing medical services. Dean Bennett was hired as an independent contractor according to the employment contract. The contract contained a restrictive covenant prohibiting Bennett from competing. Subsequently, Bennett terminated the employment and violated the restrictive covenant. When sued, Bennett argued that the contract is void because the law does not permit a professional corporation to provide services through an independent contractor. The court agreed. Palumbo argued that this technicality should not prevent the court from enforcing the restrictive covenant. What was the result? *P.M. Palumbo, Jr., Inc. v. Bennett,* 409 S.E.2d 152 (Va. 1991)

19. D&B Computing Services sold Nomad, a software product, to Must Software. The contract for sale assigned to Must the right to enforce any violation of the employment agreement related to the sale of Nomad. Larry Parcler, a former D&B employee, started Diversified Business Systems to provide consulting services to users of Nomad. Two former D&B employees, who had been at Must, left to join Diversified. The issue is whether the restrictive covenant in an employment contract that is assigned when the business is sold still has validity. What was the result? *U3S Corp. of America v. Parker,* 414 S.E.2d 513 (Ga. App. 1991)

20. Petitioners Sandra Sheffield and Mary Kay Schroeder, nurses who worked for the hospital, were charged with two specifications of unprofessional conduct in the practice of nursing by practicing nursing beyond its scope in that they measured, weighed,

compounded, and mixed ingredients in preparation of intravenous solutions and prescriptions. They contend that the nursing practice in question has been going on at the hospital for more than 25 years and that since 1988 the Health Department regulations explicitly permit not only nurses but licensed practical nurses under the supervision of a nurse to prepare intravenous solutions, including those ultimately administered to patients by other nurses. What was the result? *Sheffield v. State of New York, Education Dept.,* N.Y. Sup. Ct. App. Div. (3rd Dept. 1991)

21. Amoco leased a service station to Tommy Baker. The lease provided that Amoco would be responsible for major repairs including the replacement of the furnace. Baker had full discretion over hiring. He hired Anna Jessee to work as cashier. Subsequently, the heating system did not function. Baker advised Amoco, which then hired Standard Heating to replace the system. After installation, Jessee became ill and was rushed to the hospital to be treated for carbon monoxide poisoning. She suffered brain damage. Because the fresh-air-return duct was not reconnected to the new furnace, the cashier's booth became filled with carbon monoxide. Standard Heating was hired to install the furnace but not to reconnect the ducts.

    The issue is whether Amoco is liable for the work of Standard Heating, an independent contractor. *Jesse v. Amoco Oil Co.* 594 N.E.2d 1210 (Ill. App. 1 Dist. 1992)

22. Hennessy's claims arise as a result of receiving internal contamination by radiation while he was working in ComEd's Dresden nuclear power station.

    Hennessy claims no physical injury as a result either of his internal or his external contamination and exposures. Hennessy has stated that no one has ever told him that he presently has, or in the future may have, any physical ill effects as a result of his internal exposures. No doctor has ever told Hennessy that he has an increased risk of cancer.

    Hennessy's emotional distress derives from a fear of cancer or other illness allegedly associated with the radiation exposure he received. What was the result? *Hennessy v. Commonwealth Edison Co.,* 764 F.Supp. 495 (N.D. Ill. 1991)

23. Kenny Collum sold a mobile home to the Dawsons. He arranged with Stanley Wilson to have a septic tank installed. During installation, Wilson knocked over fifteen fruit trees on the adjacent property owned by the Argos. The Argos brought suit against Collum alleging that Wilson was in Collum's employ when Wilson committed the trespass. The issues are whether Collum is Wilson's employer and whether an employer is liable for the torts of his or her employee. *Collum v. Argo,* 599 So.2d 1210 (Ala. Civ. App. 1992)

24. Hampton and his co-workers were cleaning the area around the MDI unit, when a phosgene leak occurred, through the fault of Rubicon. Phosgene, commonly known as "mustard gas," is a highly toxic gas, which is used in the production of plastics. Hampton and several of his co-workers were exposed to phosgene for about ten minutes. Because of this exposure, Hampton and his co-workers were taken to the first aid station within the plant. No doctor was available, and they were given minimal, if any, medical treatment. They were then sent home with instruction to contact the plant doctor if they felt any effects from the gas. After arriving home, Hampton became seriously ill, and his wife rushed him to the emergency room at Our Lady of the Lake Hospital in Baton Rouge. Despite all of the hospital's efforts, Hampton's condition rapidly worsened, and he died during the early morning hours of the following day, after suffering extreme pain for several hours. What was the result? *Hampton v. Rubicon Chemicals, Inc.,* 579 So.2d 485 (La. App. 1 Civ. 1991)

25. Equitable Life Assurance instructed Dr. Arora to administer a stress test to Sidney Rosenberg, a fifty-one-year-old man with a history of heart problems. Rosenberg died a month after taking the stress test, and it was determined to be the proximate cause of his death. His estate sued Equitable for wrongful death. What was the result? *Rosenberg v. Equitable Life Assurance Society,* 584 N.Y.S.2d 765 (Ct. App. 1992)

26. Sparks sued the Northeast Alabama Regional Medical Center, her employer, claiming to be sexually harassed by Dr. Garland. Sparks alleged that Dr. Garland joked about her breast size and sex life and cursed at her for being late in front of her coworkers. The hospital claimed that this was outside the scope of Dr. Garland's employment. What was the result? *Sparks v. Regional Medical Center Bd.,* 792 F.Supp. 735 (N.D. Ala. 1992)

27. Kimberly Bunce entered the Parkside Lodge for rehabilitation from a cocaine addiction. Bryan Brown, a senior counselor, comforted Bunce on a few occasions. This situation led to a sexual relationship. After several encounters, Bunce revealed her relationship with Brown to Parkside, then left the facility. Brown resigned. Bunce sued Parkside for sexual assault, malpractice, and intentional infliction of emotional distress.

Parkside claimed that it was not responsible for the intentional torts of its employee. What was the result? *Bunce v. Parkside Lodge of Columbus,* 596 N.E.2d 1106 (Ohio App. 10 Dist. 1991)

28. Cory Grote, a 16-year-old, was a high school rodeo champion. After receiving permission from Bruce Bushnell, foreman, he was allowed to visit his brother Brad at Joy Ranch, a division of Meyers. During his visit, Cory helped Brad release twelve colts into a corral. One of the colts, known to the ranchers to be uncontrollable, kicked Cory, causing him to have a skull fracture. Cory sued the ranch, claiming that the ranch was negligent in not informing him of the colt's dangerous propensities. Is the ranch liable for its employees' failure to warn Cory? *Grote v. Meyers Land and Cattle Co.,* 485 N.W.2d 748 (Neb. 1992)

❖ WEB SITES

www.gov.on.ca/lab/es/ese.htm
www.lycos.com/business/cch/guidebook.html?lpv=1&docnumber=PO5
www.asksam.com/cgi-bin/as_web.exe?bar+b+state%20%2d%20employment%20cases
www.findlaw.com
www.employment-law.freeadvice.com
http://businessweek.lycos.com/smallbiz/content/sep2000/sb20000928_014.htm
www.employmentlegaladvisor
www.lycos.com/business/cch/guidebook.html?lpv=1&docnumber=P05_8105
www.lycos.com/business/cch/guidebook.html?lpv=1&docnumber=P05_0100
http://lawsmart.lawinfo.com

2

SELECTION

INTRODUCTION

The purpose of this chapter is to give instruction on the proper methods for selecting employees for employment, training, and promotion. Recruiting a broad range of candidates is key. Nepotism and promoting from within are acceptable so long as they do not compromise this end. Accurate record-keeping is essential for evidence in EEOC investigations and lawsuits. Screening candidates for job-related criminal convictions to preclude negligent hiring is an important task.

CHAPTER CHECKLIST

❖ Understand that the selection process must be nondiscriminatory.

❖ Identify when an employer's recruitment process may be discriminatory.

❖ Distinguish between job-related questions and questions that are discriminatory.

❖ Understand the importance of undertaking a job analysis that will define the qualifications necessary for the job.

❖ Appreciate why record-keeping is important.

❖ Discern when the EEOC may investigate for discrimination.

❖ Know why job-related criteria should be established before employees are evaluated for a promotion.

❖ Understand why only criminal convictions related to a particular job should be checked.

❖ Appreciate the employer's liability for a negligent hire.

DISCRIMINATION IN SELECTION

The purpose of recruitment and selection is to obtain the best possible workers for a business. Discrimination is permissible with respect to selecting candidates based on interpersonal relations, communication skills, training, and education. It is not permissible with respect to suspect classifications such as race, religion, gender, age, disability, and national origin. Because employees are valuable assets to a business, employers must be able to choose those employees who will perform the best work for the business. Education, training, communication skills, and interpersonal relations are key qualities that employees must possess to help a business be more successful.

The easiest way to discriminate against individuals is to do so in the recruitment and selection process. Employers may use a myriad of methods to evaluate an individual and his or her particular traits. Testing, interviews, writing samples, demonstrations, and role playing are a few examples. If these methods are job-related, then the employer has every right to use them. What an employer may not do is discourage potential candidates who belong to a particular suspect classification as defined by Title VII of the Civil Rights Act, the Age Discrimination in Employment Act, and the Americans with Disabilities Act.

EMPLOYMENT PERSPECTIVE

Speedy Delivery Service (SDS) delivers packages to residential and business customers. All the delivery personnel are men, and SDS would like to keep it that way. Sandra Musial applied for a position. SDS discouraged her by showing her extremely bulky and heavy parcels. Sandra was told she would have to carry these packages up two, sometimes three, flights of stairs. Sandra withdrew her application. Later, she learned that other female applicants were told the same story but males were not. Sandra filed a claim with the EEOC. Will she win? Yes! The selection process is tainted. Males are encouraged, females are not. They must be treated the same. Suppose SDS advertised the position only in a men's fitness magazine, would this be discriminatory? Yes! It would be designed to attract only male applicants. If the job entailed only minor lifting, but in its advertisements, SDS stated that heavy lifting was required in order to discourage female applicants, would this be discriminatory? Yes! SDS would be misrepresenting the requirements for the position. ■

Employers may also not seek prospective applicants from pools that do not contain certain groups, such as recruiting from predominantly white male schools.

EMPLOYMENT PERSPECTIVE

SDS is at it again. This time the company is recruiting candidates exclusively from Prestige College, a predominantly white male school. Is this practice discriminatory? Yes! SDS's purpose is to exclude women and minorities from its hiring process. ■

SELECTION PROCESS

The selection process must be free of discrimination. Great care must be taken to ensure that statements, overtures, and advertisements are not suspect. References to age must not be made because age is not a qualitative criterion to be used in the selection process. In an advertisement of a job description, the use of terms such as high school student, college student, recent college graduate, boy, girl, and only those under forty need apply are all examples of possible violations of the Age Discrimination in Employment Act.

ADVERTISING AND RECRUITING

Employers are barred from indicating in any advertisement for employment that they prefer an applicant of a particular race, religion, gender, or national origin. An exception to this condition exists if it can be shown that a bona fide occupational qualification requires a person of a particular religion, gender, or national origin. There is no exception for race and color.

EMPLOYMENT PERSPECTIVE

Lilly's Lingerie Shop places an advertisement in a local paper for a position admitting women to its dressing room area. The ad stated that only females need apply. Is this advertisement in violation of Title VII? Most likely! Lilly's must establish that it is a business necessity that only a woman should work in this position where the attendant is in such close proximity to an area where female customers are undressing. However, if the attendant is visibly outside the dressing room area where other employees and customers are, then no invasion of privacy exists to warrant a same sex attendant. ■

Recruiting at colleges, graduate schools, and professional schools has long been a practice followed by many companies. This is a process in which a large pool of people seeking professional and office work are located and, for the most part, are unemployed. This practice may not in and of itself be discriminatory unless done exclusively. A company or professional firm that recruits only students at graduation is discriminating against people already in the labor force and possibly those without the mandated degree. Recruiting candidates solely from colleges for a position where a degree is not a justifiable necessity is discriminatory.

EMPLOYMENT PERSPECTIVE

Rhodes, Lucas and Reed is a prestigious accounting firm that recruits its entry level candidates solely from college. The firm advertises, "entry level positions available for this year's graduates only." Amanda Stewart graduated from college two years ago and has been working with a local accountant. She applies for the entry level position with Rhodes, Lucas and Reed because it would provide a sizeable salary increase and great experience. Amanda is rejected because of her experience. She claims discrimination. The firm argues that students right out of college can be trained and indoctrinated more easily. Amanda argues that her experience would not hamper that process in the least. Who wins? Amanda has a good chance of winning because of the exclusivity of the firm's policy with regard to hiring only college students. ■

EMPLOYMENT PERSPECTIVE

Safe T Alarm Systems advertises a position available for alarm-system planning and installation. Scott Feeney, age 50, applies for the position but is rejected because he does not possess a college diploma. Scott argues an alarm system installer does not need a college education. Safe T recounts that college graduates have better interpersonal skills for dealing with people and possess sound reasoning skills for planning the layout of the alarm system. Who will be victorious? Scott! Although Safe T may incorporate reasoning ability and interpersonal skills in its job qualifications, its argument will most likely fail because a college diploma is not a justifiable business necessity for this type of position. This requirement discriminates against older workers who do not possess a college degree. Many individuals can and do perform this job adequately without possessing the college degree. While college graduates may be more qualified on average, it does not mean there are no qualified candidates among the remainder. To exclude this entire group because they do not possess a characteristic not crucial to the job is arbitrary and capricious. ▪

EMPLOYMENT PERSPECTIVE

Simon, Matthews and Stevens, a Park Avenue law firm, consistently recruit new associates from three predominantly white male schools exclusively. Their firm is comprised of seventeen attorneys all of whom are protestant white males. They will not visit any other law schools. Simon, Matthews and Stevens conduct on-site interviews and, if interested, invite the select few for a visit to their office. Is the procedure discriminatory? Definitely! The firm is dismissing other qualified applicants without a justifiable reason. Simon, Matthews and Stevens may be looking to perpetuate the old-boy network by persisting in the maintenance of their policy of exclusivity. ▪

QUESTIONING

Questioning an applicant about his or her religion, national origin, race, and age is discriminatory. Inquiries regarding marital status, the number of children, or the prospects of having children are also suspect. An employer may not require an applicant to state whether he or she has a disability or to submit information concerning the disability. This would be an unfair employment practice. However, the employer may require the applicant to undergo a physical or mental examination to determine whether the person has the ability to perform the job. The examination must relate only to the essential job-related functions and must not be a fishing expedition. It must be required of all applicants, not just those with a perceived disability.

EMPLOYMENT SCENARIO

During an office visit with Susan North, Esq., Tom Long and Mark Short ask Susan her opinion regarding some problems they have encountered during the interview process. Susan listens as Tom and Mark recall their experiences. Tom mentioned that he asked Martha if she had small children. He thought that was a legitimate concern given the evening hours needed for coverage. Mark wondered about what country Lucy Jimenez was from and asked her about it. Tom remembered that both he and Mark refused to hire Bruce Wood because of his effeminate mannerisms. They thought that he was gay. Mark added that Mildred Peterson was refused employment as a sales representative because she was a woman. They told her that this was a men's clothing store. Tom and Mark were seeking affirmation for their business conduct. Susan replied, "I am sorry to disappoint you, but you are disillusioned in believing your actions are vindicated. First, asking a woman about having small children presupposes that she has not arranged for their care and will not be committed to her job. Believing that the mother will leave work every time her children are sick, lonely, or in trouble is an outdated stereotype. Day care centers house most children of working mothers. The centers are well equipped to handle children and the problems that confront them." Susan cautions that "questioning Martha in this manner amounts to sex discrimination in accordance with the Civil Rights Act if she was not hired and if there were fifteen or more employees in their business." Second, Susan states, "Asking Lucy about what country she is from is tantamount to national origin discrimination. Acting in a discriminatory manner is not an intelligent way to enhance the reputation of your business." The question is not job related; therefore it serves no purpose other than to satisfy Mark's curiosity. Although many people have trouble distinguishing among various ethnic backgrounds, making inquiries regarding such matters is not appropriate in a job interview.

Third, even though the Civil Rights Act has not been extended to protect homosexuals from employment discrimination, they may be covered under individual state or local statutes. Furthermore, the gay and lesbian lobby is a powerful foe once antagonized. This presupposes Bruce is gay. If he is not, their statement to that effect may be defamatory.

Fourth, denying a woman a sales position in a men's clothing store is not justified as a bona fide occupational qualification. Women are potentially as knowledgeable about men's fashion as men. This is another example of sex discrimination. However, the fifteen-employee requirement of the Civil Rights Act will preclude Mildred from pursuing her legal cause of action in federal court. In the future, Tom and Mark should guard themselves against repeating these mistakes and should judge candidates based on their job qualifications. For some employers, deleting all personal questions renders the job interview sterile. Susan pontificates, although that may be true, "It is better to err on the side of caution."

The Americans with Disabilities Act (ADA), along with most state civil rights acts, prohibits discriminating against an individual in the selection process because of a disability. A disability is defined as a physical or mental condition that results in a substantial handicap. The employer may be required to reasonably accommodate disabled individuals to enable them to perform the jobs that but for their handicap they would be qualified to do.

EMPLOYMENT PERSPECTIVE

Mary Thomas applied for a position as a computer programmer with Computer Wizard. She was given a computer language exam. Her references and educational background were checked, and she was required to undergo a physical examination. Mary's qualifications were superb except for the physical examination, which disclosed that she had had a breast removed four years ago because of cancer. Mary was not hired. She filed a claim with the EEOC, alleging disability discrimination. Computer Wizard claimed it did not want to hire someone with a history of cancer. Such a person might incur huge medical expenses in the future, and the company's medical insurance premiums might skyrocket. Is this a valid reason for not hiring her? No! Her breast removal is not related to an essential job-related function. Had she been missing fingers or an arm that related to her typing skills, that disability might be a consideration. However, even then a reasonable accommodation may be made or possibly the person may type as fast with one arm as someone with two arms. In that case, the disability would have no effect. ▪

UNIFORM GUIDELINES ON EMPLOYEE SELECTION PROCEDURES

Uniform Guidelines on Employee Selection Procedures was enacted in 1978 to provide counsel in the proper methodology used in the selection process to avoid infringement of Title VII, Equal Employment Opportunity Act (Affirmative Action) and the Equal Pay Act. While not applying directly to the Age Discrimination in Employment Act and the Americans with Disabilities Act, other guidelines are available for consultation in these areas.

The main thrust of the Uniform Guidelines is to recognize and encourage the discontinuance of selection procedures that have a disparate impact on minorities and women. *Disparate impact* may be defined as having an adverse or detrimental effect on a particular group. Men are also covered in situations where gender is a determining factor in the selection process. Minority groups include Blacks, Hispanics, Asians, and American Indians.

To eliminate a disparate impact, records must be kept of the number of each minority group and gender that apply and the number of each group selected. If the percentage of minorities selected is at least 80 percent of the percentage of whites selected, there is no adverse effect. If the 80 percent rule is not met, then a detriment in employment selection exists against the particular group of minority or women applicants.

EMPLOYMENT PERSPECTIVE

ABC Mutual Fund places an advertisement for customer service representatives. One hundred positions are available. Three hundred applicants are received: 100 women and 200 men, including 150 whites, 50 Blacks, 50 Asians, and 50 Hispanics. The selections made were 20 women and 80 men, including 75 whites, 5 Blacks, 20 Asians, and 0 Hispanics. Does the selection procedure have an adverse effect on the minorities and women? Yes. A disparate impact exists against Blacks, Hispanics, and women. The percentage of whites chosen out of those whites who applied was 50 percent. That means all minority group selection rates must be within 80 percent of the 50 percent white rate. Minority groups selection rates must be at least 40 percent. The selection rate of Asians met the test, 50 applicants of which 20 were chosen—that is 40 percent. The Black selection rate was 10 percent, and the Hispanic selection rate was 0 percent. Both of these fall far short of the required rate and are evidence of discrimination, according to the Uniform Guidelines of Employee Selection Procedures. The selection rate of women was 20 percent: 20 out of 100. The selection rate of men was 40 percent: 80 out of 200. The women's percentage was only one-half, or 50 percent, of the men's percentage. This result does not meet the 80 percent rule and is evidence of discrimination. ▪

SELECTION PROCEDURE

The term *selection procedure* encompasses the use of aptitude testing, physical evalua-tions, educational credentials, employment experience, training programs, probationary terms, resumes, interviews, and application forms to evaluate prospective candidates. These guidelines apply to employers, employment agencies, testing organizations, and labor unions.

EMPLOYMENT PERSPECTIVE

E. J. Roberts receives about fifty unsolicited resumes each month for positions with his marketing research firm. He dumps most of these in the garbage. Every once in a while he leafs through a few while he is having a cup of herbal tea. If something catches his eye, he notifies his secretary to contact the person for an interview. Is E. J.'s procedure in contradiction with the Uniform Guidelines on Employee Selection Procedures? Yes! There is no objective standard of judgment employed in E. J.'s procedure. It is arbitrary and capricious. ■

The employer's right to investigate the employee's background including past criminal records is based on the employer's showing of a justifiable business necessity.

EMPLOYMENT SCENARIO

Roger Thorpe, an African-American candidate, was refused employment after revealing during an interview with L&S that he had a prior conviction for the sale of cocaine fourteen years ago. Tom and Mark discussed this situ-ation with Susan after the fact. Susan asked Tom and Mark how they came to know of the prior drug conviction. They responded that during the inter-view they required every candidate to reveal all prior criminal convictions. Susan pleaded with Tom and Mark to seek her counsel before making such rash judgments and explained that prior convictions related to the job at hand are the only ones that need be required. In this case, one's prior convic-tions for arson, burglary, larceny, robbery, and receipt of stolen goods would be appropriate questions to pose.

Susan continued to say that refusal of employment to a person of a class protected under Title VII of the Civil Rights Act based on an unrelated con-viction could be considered discriminatory. In this case, it could constitute race discrimination.

The issue in the following case deals with whether an applicant for a teaching position should be denied a teaching license because of a prior drug sale conviction.

THE MATTER OF ARROCHA v. BOARD OF EDUCATION OF THE CITY OF NEW YORK

93 N.Y.2d 361 (1999)

LEVINE, Judge

In 1996, petitioner applied for a Pedagogical Certificate from the Board of Education of the City of New York licensing him to teach high school Spanish in the New York City public school system. In his application, petitioner disclosed that he had been convicted in 1987, at age 36, of criminal sale of a controlled substance (a B felony) for selling a $10 bag of cocaine to an undercover officer, and subsequently served the minimum of a two-to-six year prison term. As evidence of rehabilitation, petitioner submitted to the Board a certificate of relief from disabilities, designed to remove any automatic bar to employment or licensure . He also provided five current letters of recommendation, attesting to his teaching ability and professional skills, as well as evidence of his educational achievements during and since incarceration.

The Board nevertheless denied petitioner's application, stating that his conviction "is serious in nature" and that the granting of employment "would pose a risk to the safety and welfare of the student population and Board of Education employees." Petitioner thereafter challenged the Board's determination in this article 78 proceeding, arguing that the Board's reliance on the nine-year-old conviction was arbitrary and capricious and in violation of article 23-A of the New York Correction Law which prohibits discrimination against ex-offenders. Supreme Court agreed and ordered the Board to grant petitioner the teaching license. The Appellate Division affirmed over a two-Justice dissent. The Board appealed to this Court as of right, and we now reverse. The Board's decision denying petitioner the privilege of a teaching license is the type of administrative action that, at common law, was subject to challenge through a writ of mandamus to review and thus cannot be disturbed unless it is arbitrary and capricious. In such situations, " 'the courts cannot interfere unless there is no rational basis for the exercise of discretion' " by the administrative agency. " 'It is well settled that a court may not substitute its judgment for that of the board or body it reviews unless the decision under review is arbitrary and unreasonable and constitutes an abuse of discretion'."

Mindful of these restraints on the judicial power of review here, we turn to petitioner's claims that the Board acted unlawfully, and thus arbitrarily, when it denied him a high school teaching license on the basis of his previous conviction. Article 23-A of the Correction Law provides that "no application for any license or employment shall be denied by reason of the applicant's having been previously convicted of one or more criminal offenses." The statute, however, recognizes exceptions either where there is "a direct relationship between the previous criminal offense and the specific license or employment sought," or where granting the license or employment would "involve an unreasonable risk to property or to the safety or welfare of specific individuals or the general public."

Here, the Board denied petitioner's license under the second exception, stating in its letter to petitioner denying the license that, in light of his prior conviction, his employment in the City's high schools would "pose a risk to the safety and welfare of the student population and Board of Education employees." Such a finding of unreasonable risk "depends upon a subjective analysis of a variety of considerations relating to the nature of the license or employment sought and the prior misconduct." Thus, Correction Law § 753 sets forth a series of eight factors to be considered by the Board in determining whether it would pose an unreasonable risk to issue a license. Specifically, the Board must consider:

a. "The public policy of this state, as expressed in this act, to encourage the licensure and employment of persons previously convicted of one or more criminal offenses.

b. The specific duties and responsibilities necessarily related to the license or employment sought.

c. The bearing, if any, the criminal offense or offenses for which the person was previously convicted will have on his fitness or ability to perform one or more such duties or responsibilities.

d. The time which has elapsed since the occurrence of the criminal offense or offenses.

e. The age of the person at the time of occurrence of the criminal offense or offenses.

f. The seriousness of the offense or offenses.

g. Any information produced by the person, or produced on his behalf, in regard to his rehabilitation and good conduct.

h. The legitimate interest of the public agency or private employer in protecting property, and the safety and welfare of specific individuals or the general public."

The statute also creates a presumption of rehabilitation where, as here, the applicant has obtained a certificate of relief from disabilities. Nonetheless, the certificate does not establish a prima facie entitlement to the license or employment, but only establishes, if not rebutted, that the applicant has been rehabilitated—just one of the eight factors that the Board must consider in determining whether an exception applies.

On the record before Supreme Court, there is evidence that the Board considered all eight of the factors set forth in section 753 in reaching its conclusion. Significantly, the Board considered those positive factors on which petitioner heavily relies, namely that the conviction was nine years old[d] , the positive references submitted on petitioner's behalf [g][evidence of rehabilitation]), his educational achievements and the presumption that he is rehabilitated.

The Board, however, balanced these considerations against the other five factors delineated by the statute. In particular, the Board averred that it considered the fact that high school teachers must serve as role models to students at an impressionable age and are held to a high ethical standard and that petitioner's conviction might impact his ability to serve as such a role model [c][bearing of prior conviction on applicant's fitness to perform responsibilities]). The affidavit submitted by the Board noted that petitioner was a mature adult when he committed the crime [e]), and that the offense was a serious felony conviction[f]. Finally, the Board considered the fact that criminal sale of a controlled substance is one of the six specifically enumerated crimes that the Board has deemed to be of special concern with respect to carrying out its duty to protect the welfare of New York City school children[h] [interest of public agency in protecting welfare of specific individuals]).

Nevertheless, the courts below annulled the Board's determination because the Board failed to submit any evidence to rebut the presumption of rehabilitation and because the Board unduly relied on the prior drug sale conviction in the face of the evidence of petitioner's more recent academic and professional accomplishments. As previously discussed, the presumption of rehabilitation does not preclude the Board from considering any of the other seven factors, unrelated to rehabilitation, including prior convictions in the context of the license or employment being sought. We stated in Bonacorsa v Van Lindt that, even where an applicant has the benefit of a presumption of rehabilitation:

> "in some cases, consideration of other factors such as severity of the criminal offenses, the age of the offender at the time of the offenses, the passage of time between the offenses and the application, and the nature of the license or employment sought can warrant denial of the license notwithstanding the absence of new evidence specifically addressed at overcoming the presumption of rehabilitation."

Thus, the Board was not obligated to rebut the presumption of rehabilitation and was entirely justified in considering the nature and seriousness of this particular crime, a B felony cocaine sale committed by petitioner at the mature age of 36, of overriding significance when issuing a high school teaching license.

Moreover, all that the record establishes here is that, in denying petitioner a high school teaching license, the Board gave greater weight to the statutory factors adversely affected by the fact and circumstances of his conviction than to the statutory factors favorably affected by his subsequent accomplishments and the presumption of rehabilitation. This did not afford a basis for the lower courts to conclude that factors favorable to petitioner were not considered, and there is nothing additional in the record that would support that conclusion. Thus, there is no justification for overturning the Board's determination without engaging in essentially a re-weighing of the factors, which is beyond the power of judicial review.

Accordingly, the order of the Appellate Division should be reversed, without costs, and the petition dismissed. Judgment for the Board of Education

Case Commentary

The Board of Education applied an eight-prong test to determine whether the prior drug sale conviction posed a threat to the safety of the students and employees of the school system. In doing so, the Board gave greater weight to a drug sale conviction than to the applicant's subsequent rehabilitation and accomplishments. The New York Court of Appeals stated there is no justification for overturning the Board of Education's decision.

Case Questions

1. Do you believe Arrocha was entitled to the license?

2. Should the Board of Education be entitled to assign different weights to the licensing criteria?

3. Should the court have the right to review the weight assigned to each criterion?

INVESTIGATION AND RECORD-KEEPING

To properly conduct an investigation, the EEOC has the right to evidence which has a bearing on the alleged unlawful employment practice. This would include the right of access to documentation, as well as to the coworkers, superiors, and subordinates of the employee alleging a Title VII violation for the purpose of questioning them.

Employers are obligated to keep records relating to their methods of selection, compensation, promotion, training, and termination of employees. Test scores and the chronological order of applications for hiring, training, and promotion must be part of the record-keeping.

These records must be made available to the EEOC to enable them to determine whether unlawful employment practices have been committed. An employer may seek an exemption from the EEOC if it can prove the burden of record-keeping presents undue hardship. A notification of excerpts of Title VII is required to be posted by each employer in a conspicuous setting to apprise current employees as well as applicants of the existence of Title VII.

Record-keeping can be burdensome, especially for small firms that do not have a human resources department. In addition to keeping records denoting the number of persons who applied and the number of persons who were selected in each job category for each suspect classification, similar record-keeping must be kept for promotions and terminations as well.

SAMPLES

Where the number of applicants and those selected are so numerous that maintaining records on every individual would be too burdensome, the Uniform Guidelines on Employee Selection Procedures permit the company to select samples and maintain records on them. The sample must be adequate in size and representative of the various groups. If it is not, then the sample may be challenged and an inference of discrimination may be drawn. If the sample is viable but results in a disparate impact, the company is bound by it. The company may not dispute the authenticity of its own sample.

THE BOTTOM LINE

The Uniform Guidelines on Employee Selection Procedures adopts the bottom line approach where a myriad of selection procedures are utilized. If one criterion is tainted, the selection process will not be found to be discriminatory where other criteria have offset it and the final results do not violate the 80 percent rule.

EMPLOYMENT PERSPECTIVE

Thompson Meat Packing Plant employs three criteria in its employee selection process: a weight-lifting test, a dexterity test, and an application form. Hispanics, Asians, and women who apply have difficulty with the weight-lifting test because of their small stature. Their overall selection rate satisfies the 80 percent rule. Regardless, these groups claim that a greater number of them would have been selected but for this test and that weight-lifting is not a job necessity. Will they win? No! Since a significant number of women, Asians, and Hispanics are being selected, the bottom line is not discriminatory. The weight-lifting component does not have to be justified as a business necessity. ∎

DISCRIMINATION IN PROMOTIONS

The reason that certain groups are promoted less frequently is due in part to discrimination and in part to social factors. Promotions often entail more responsibility, longer hours, travel requirements, attendance at social affairs, decision-making requirements, and greater stress. Young people, a greater number of whom are single, may welcome the traveling and may not mind the longer hours. Older individuals with families, especially women who are mothers, may find the benefits of the promotion outweighed by their presumption that their quality of life will decline. The requirements need not change so long as they are job related. If any individual cannot travel or work longer hours, that person will not get the position. The point is to refrain from stereotyping. Many women with small children may be willing to travel and some men may not be willing to travel. The Equal Employment Opportunity Act presumes an equal percentage of all groups seek promotions. Overcoming this premise is a difficult task for the employer.

PROMOTION CRITERIA

When a possibility exists within a firm for a promotion or transfer, the employer must post the job along with its description in a conspicuous manner, and a formal evaluation procedure must be followed. The procedure must utilize criteria which are job-related, and the imposition of these criteria must be uniformly applied to every applicant. The managers who are in charge of recommending candidates for promotion must be judged on the basis of their recommendations to determine whether they are acting in conformity with equal employment opportunity guidelines. Finally, the racial, ethnic, and gender composition of the manager will be looked into where a breach of equal opportunity employment occurs.

NEPOTISM AND PROMOTING FROM WITHIN

Nepotism is the hiring of family members. Some companies forbid this action; others allow it if the employed family member does not take part in the decision process. Still others encourage it wholeheartedly. This approach, as well as the concept of promoting from within, is incestuous because it may discourage diversity. If that is so, discrimination exists. Employers argue that promoting from within allows the company to reward an individual who is known and respected. While there is substance in that argument, if the result is the creation of a disparate impact against a suspect class, the tradition will be held to be discriminatory and will need to be abandoned.

EMPLOYMENT SCENARIO

The Long and Short of It (L&S) approach Susan with a plan to hire relatives, friends, and individuals referred by those employed at L&S. Tom and Mark's explanation is that they are comfortable with the composition of their present staff and they would prefer hiring similar people. Susan sanctions their plan as a sound idea for a small company, but she cautions that, as L&S grows, this plan may have a disparate impact against certain classes of people. At that time, L&S should consider advertising to create a pool of candidates from diverse backgrounds. Tom retorts that that is exactly what he wants to guard against. Susan rebukes Tom, stating that L&S can forestall the inevitable for a while, but eventually L&S may be confronted with litigation. She advises Tom to get "with it" by adopting an open-minded attitude.

This case presents two issues: whether nepotism includes in-laws, and whether the nepotism policy was consistently enforced.

CASE

BLACKBURN v. UNITED PARCEL SERVICE

179 F.3d 81 (3rd Cir. 1999)

BECKER, Chief Judge.

In this diversity case, we are asked to review the District Court's grant of summary judgment for defendant United Parcel Service, which was grounded on the view that the conduct of plaintiff Benjamin Blackburn did not constitute protected activity under the New Jersey whistleblower statute, the Conscientious Employee Protection Act (CEPA). Being doubtful of the correctness of this conclusion of the District Court, we will assume that Blackburn has met his burden of establishing a prima facie case of retaliation under CEPA. We will instead affirm the District Court's judgment on the alternative ground that Blackburn has failed to offer sufficient admissible evidence to rebut UPS's proffered legitimate justification for his discharge—his putative violation of UPS's anti-nepotism, favoritism, integrity, and accountability policies. In order to reach the pretext issue, and so as to determine which evidence of Blackburn's might be admissible at trial, we must consider the contours of a number of exceptions to the rule against admitting hearsay evidence. In particular, we must interpret the seldom-invoked exception for reputation evidence concerning family relationships, which bears on Blackburn's defense to the nepotism charges. Ultimately, we conclude that an insufficient quantum of evidence would be admissible at trial to rebut UPS's proffered legitimate justification for discharging Blackburn; hence, we affirm.

I. FACTS PROCEDURAL HISTORY

Blackburn worked for UPS for approximately eight years. He began work as a driver in June 1986, and was promoted several times, first becoming a manager in 1990. In early 1992, Blackburn was transferred to a division of the company that priced UPS products and services. His duties included development of a flexible pricing project, the Incentive Administration System. In September 1993, he was promoted to Marketing User Representative for the Marketing Information Group in Mahwah, New Jersey. In this position, his responsibilities included addressing, through the IAS or otherwise, UPS's loss of accounts and significant amounts of business to a competitor, Roadway Package Service. His principal supervisor at that time was Gary Hopwood, who was based in Atlanta. Hopwood's supervisor was Nicholas Bain, who was also Atlanta-based.

UPS contends that Blackburn was fired for violations of UPS's anti-nepotism, favoritism, integrity, and accountability policies.

UPS has had an anti-nepotism policy in its Policy Book for management employees since 1965.

The 1992 version, in effect during the period in question, states:

We Strictly Limit the Employment of Relatives. . . .

We prohibit hiring—for either full-time or part-time employment—relatives of active employees. . . .

For the same reasons, we discourage continuation of the full-time or part-time employment of any employee who marries another employee while either person holds a management position in the same district, the same region office or Corporate Headquarters.

The Policy Book does not define relatives. The favoritism policy states, We Treat Our People Fairly and Without Favoritism. . . . We have the responsibility to avoid any relationship that may result in actual or perceived favoritism. The integrity policy states:

We Insist Upon Integrity in Our People. . . .

We insist on integrity in the preparation and approval of all reports.

We expect our people to be honest with respect to intangible things as well—in the time, effort, and full performance of their jobs; in fair play in dealing with others; and in the acknowledgment of mistakes or other shortcomings.

When we do discover a dishonest person in our organization, we deal with that individual quickly and firmly.

Finally, the accountability policy states:

We Are All Accountable for Compliance With Our Policies. As individuals, we do not have the authority to change or disregard any of our company's policies. We are expected to follow existing policies, even if not always in complete agreement with them. We must be careful not to misinterpret or violate a policy's spirit and intent. If in doubt, we should check with others for guidance.

Our managers and supervisors set the example for carrying out our policies. . . . They, therefore, are expected to lead the way for other UPS people—by word and action—in living up to our policies.

As a management employee, Blackburn received a copy of the Policy Book and was aware of these policies.

Blackburn married Loren Morrissey in April of 1990. On September 29, 1993, Linda Shepard, Morrissey's sister, applied for a job at UPS's Mahwah facility. Shepard stated on her employment application that she did not have any relatives employed by UPS. In December of 1993, Shepard was hired as a Methods Analyst at Mahwah, and began work in the same building as Blackburn. Blackburn was aware that Shepard had applied for and gotten the job, and at times commuted to work with Shepard and had contact with her during the workday by, for example, meeting her for lunch. At no time before September 1994 did Blackburn disclose his relationship with Shepard to UPS.

At various times after Shepard's hiring, and before September 1994, Blackburn recommended Shepard for other UPS positions without informing those to whom he made the recommendations that Shepard was his sister-in-law.

On September 14, 1994, UPS's Loss Prevention Department received an anonymous complaint, forwarded to Patricia Knowles of UPS's Human Resources Department at Mahwah, that Blackburn was Shepard's brother-in-law. The complaint also expressed concern that Shepard might be promoted because of Blackburn's influence. That same day, Knowles and UPS manager Nigel Watson met with Shepard and questioned her regarding her relationship with Blackburn. After initially denying that Blackburn was her brother-in-law, Shepard eventually admitted that he was married to her sister. However, she gave an incorrect date for Blackburn's marriage to her sister, claiming that they were married in April 1994, after Shepard had been hired by UPS.

After verifying the actual date of Blackburn's marriage (through UPS's Human Resources Department in Atlanta), Knowles confronted Blackburn on September 15, 1994. Blackburn denied that he was related to Shepard but admitted that he was married to her sister. He also expressed disbelief that the relationship was of concern to UPS. On September 16, Knowles met again with Shepard, who claimed that Blackburn was aware that Shepard was interviewing with UPS when she originally sought a job there. On September 29, 1994, UPS offered Shepard a chance to resign, on the grounds that she had lied on her application (by indicating that she was not

related to anyone at UPS) and had lied to Knowles when confronted with this information. Shepard resigned on September 30, 1994.

Also in September, Blackburn's supervisor, Hopwood, was informed of the events surrounding Shepard's hiring and her relationship to Blackburn. Hopwood spoke with Blackburn and, upon learning the identity of Blackburn's sister-in-law, realized that she was the person Blackburn had recommended to him and another manager for openings in the department without informing them that she was his sister-in-law. Blackburn allegedly refused to acknowledge that his conduct was inappropriate, and told Hopkins that UPS would regret it if it pursued the matter.

On September 29, 1994, Hopwood's supervisor Bain and Human Resources manager James Daniels met with Blackburn, who stated that he was not related to Shepard but that he was her brother-in-law. He denied any misconduct in permitting her to be hired, recommending her for positions without revealing the nature of their relationship, and claiming not to be related to her. Bain advised Blackburn that he had violated the anti-nepotism policy and the policies on favoritism, integrity, and accountability. That day, after consultation with Daniels and two Human Resources coordinators, Bain fired Blackburn.

The Ensuing Litigation

In August 1995, Blackburn filed suit in New Jersey state court, claiming that UPS had fired him in violation of CEPA, and seeking compensatory and punitive damages, attorneys' fees, costs, and such other relief as the court might provide. UPS removed the case to the District Court for the District of New Jersey on the basis of diversity jurisdiction.

Following discovery, UPS moved for summary judgment.

The District Court found that Blackburn's conduct was not covered by CEPA, and it therefore granted summary judgment for UPS.

UPS's Stated Reason for the Discharge

UPS's stated reason for firing Blackburn was his violation of the company's anti-nepotism, favoritism, integrity, and accountability policies, which it placed in the record. UPS adduced evidence that Blackburn failed to divulge that

Shepard was his relative, and that he recommended her for positions within UPS without disclosing to the relevant decisionmakers that she was his sister-in-law. UPS also offered evidence that it has consistently enforced its anti-nepotism policy, which supports its proffer that Blackburn's violation of this policy was the actual reason he was discharged. Indeed, Blackburn himself conceded at his deposition that UPS has regularly enforced the anti-nepotism policy (although he offers purported examples of the policy's nonenforcement). Therefore, UPS has met its burden of production at the second step of the burden-shifting analysis.

While Blackburn has suggested that the anti-nepotism policy does not apply to his situation because Shepard is not a blood relation, he does not press this point, relying instead on UPS's purported nonenforcement of the policy. However, UPS alleges that Blackburn's conduct also violated its favoritism, integrity, and accountability policies, and he has offered little evidence in response to this proffer.

Blackburn's Evidence

In order to meet his burden, Blackburn must point to admissible evidence in the record showing that there is a genuine issue for trial. In attempting to show that UPS's stated reason for firing him was pretextual, Blackburn claims that he never hid his relationship with Shepard. Rather, he testified that he regularly commuted to and from work with her, entered the building with her each day, often met her for lunch and breaks, displayed a wedding picture prominently on his desk with Shepard in the wedding party, and was otherwise open about the relationship, including the fact that they shared an address. Similarly, Shepard testified that she told colleagues about the relationship and even inquired about it at her initial interview, and nothing was done. Blackburn also testified that he assumed that the prohibition on the hiring of relatives included only blood relatives.

We find the foregoing less than persuasive evidence to support Blackburn's burden, even at summary judgment, of proving that UPS's stated reason was pretextual. The only portion of this evidence that is probative of pretext—i.e., that UPS knew of Blackburn's relationship to Shepard but did nothing about it, and later fired

him for his whistleblowing activity under the pretext of its anti-nepotism policy—is Shepard's allegation that, when she applied for a job at UPS, she informed the initial interviewer that her brother-in-law worked for UPS. There is no indication that the decisionmakers who fired Blackburn for his violations of the anti-nepotism and related policies were informed of Shepard's comments at her interview. In fact, although UPS's policy was less than clear in defining the prohibited relationships, the clarity of the policy or the reasonableness of Blackburn's alleged misreading of the policy are not necessarily relevant to the pretext issue. If the policy actually covered relationships such as Blackburn and Shepard's, and if this (along with the concomitant violations of the other policies) was the real reason that Blackburn was discharged, Blackburn's CEPA case must fail. The record evidence overwhelmingly supports the conclusion that the relevant UPS managers were unaware of Blackburn's relationship with Shepard until the anonymous tip was received in September 1994, at which time immediate action was taken against both Shepard and Blackburn.

Blackburn's stronger argument for pretext—and one that would be sufficient to preclude summary judgment, if supported by adequate admissible evidence—is that UPS did not consistently enforce its anti-nepotism policy, which, according to UPS, was the primary basis for his discharge. If Blackburn has presented admissible evidence that would raise a fact question whether UPS enforced its anti-nepotism policy, it would be for a jury to decide whether UPS's proffered reason for firing him was pretextual. Given our assumption that Blackburn has presented sufficient evidence to meet his prima facie burden under CEPA, we would have to reverse summary judgment in UPS's favor if a fact issue regarding pretext existed.

In support of his pretext argument, Blackburn provides numerous examples of UPS employees who were related to other employees yet allegedly were not disciplined or terminated for this apparent violation of the anti-nepotism policy. His examples include brothers-in-law, siblings, spouses, uncles and nephews, fathers and sons, and intimate relationships between employees who were dating or living together. UPS responds with evidence that, within the last five years, twenty-nine people at Mahwah left UPS in accordance with the anti-nepotism policy, and that no exceptions currently exist there.

Blackburn's testimony regarding UPS employees he believes to be related includes the following: Jackie and Sal Biancardi, a married couple who work at the UPS facility in Morristown; an uncle and nephew working together at a UPS facility; Mark Hopkins and his wife, Beth; Bill, and Art Weyrauch, brothers. Blackburn has no personal knowledge of any of the alleged relationships listed above. Rather, he testified in his deposition that he was told of these relationships by other persons. The alleged relationships are offered for their own truth. Therefore, Blackburn's information is based on hearsay.

We conclude that Blackburn's evidence that UPS decisionmakers were aware of his relationship to Shepard, and later fired him for his whistleblowing activity under the pretext of its anti-nepotism policy, is, without more, insufficient to overcome summary judgment. As we have detailed, we find that virtually none of his evidence regarding other UPS employees who were allegedly related would likely be admissible at trial as relevant evidence that falls within a hearsay exception. We must therefore determine whether Blackburn has offered sufficient evidence to create a genuine issue of material fact regarding UPS's stated reason for firing him.

In sum, on this record, we are satisfied that, even assuming that Blackburn has met his prima facie burden under CEPA, he has failed to adequately rebut UPS's proffered reason for his discharge by pointing to sufficient inconsistencies or anomalies that could support an inference that the employer did not act for its stated reasons.

The judgment of the District Court will therefore be affirmed.

Case Commentary

The Third Circuit Court suggested Blackburn could have argued that a sister-in-law does not qualify as a relative. UPS does not clearly define this term. Instead, Blackburn focused on whether UPS was consistent in enforcement of its anti-nepotism policy. Blackburn uncovered numerous violations of this policy, but did not have the documentation to prove the violations. Blackburn's argument was based totally on inadmissible hearsay.

Case Questions

1. Do you believe an in-law qualifies as a relative?
2. Was UPS consistent in enforcement of its anti-nepotism policy?

3. Should Blackburn's evidence of UPS's policy violations have been admissible?

The case that follows addresses the question of whether an employer who promotes from within can set promotion quotas for minorities and females. Nonminority males allege that they are being skipped over when promotions arise.

DALLAS FIRE FIGHTERS
v. CITY OF DALLAS

885 F.Supp. 915 (N.D. Tex. 1995)

KENDALL, District Judge.

This lawsuit challenges the promotion practices of the Dallas Fire Department ("DFD") as discriminatory based upon race and gender-conscious promotions made under the City of Dallas' ("The City") Affirmative Action Plan ("AAP"). More specifically, the Plaintiffs challenge certain "skip promotions" which were made by the DFD in accordance with goals established by the City in its voluntary Affirmative Action Plan.

The Dallas Fire Fighters Association of Dallas filed suit on behalf of individual white and Native American firefighters who sought, but did not receive, promotions between 1991 and 1993. In response to other challenges to its promotion program, the City has changed various features of the process, including eliminating the rank of Second Driver, reducing time-in-grade promotion eligibility requirements, and ending the practice of adjusting test scores upward for seniority. These actions were taken in addition to making the skip promotions at issue here.

The Dallas Fire Department's promotional process is not unlike many others across the nation. DFD does not make lateral hires from other fire departments, but fills positions above the entry level by promoting from within the department. Beginning with the entry level, current firefighter ranks are: fire and rescue officer, driver-engineer, lieutenant, captain, battalion chief, deputy chief, assistant chief and the fire chief. Among the various requirements for promotion for the ranks up to and including battalion chief is a promotional exam. Firefighters eligible for promotion are placed on a promotion list in descending order according to their scores on the exam. Unless a specific reason exists to pass over a particular candidate due to unsatisfactory job performance, disciplinary reasons, non-paramedic status or other reasons, members are promoted as vacancies occur by going down the eligibility list according to an individual's score on the exam.

Plaintiffs' complaints in these consolidated cases allege that all plaintiffs are now and were at the time the skip promotions were made, employed as firefighters by the Defendant City of Dallas. The Plaintiffs further allege that from 1991 to 1993, the City promoted various members of the Fire Department in the ranks of Driver, Lieutenant, Captain and Deputy Chief. Each of the Plaintiffs, all of whom are white males, with the exception of Plaintiff Wallace J. Graves who is a Native American, applied for promotions by taking and passing the promotional exam. The Plaintiffs were passed over for promotion in favor of lower ranked individuals. Plaintiffs' complaint asserts that they were passed over solely because of race or gender in an attempt by the City and DFD to promote minorities in accordance with the City's Affirmative Action Plan. Plaintiffs allege that these promotions violate the Equal Protection Clause of the United States Constitution. The Plaintiffs also assert claims under the Civil Rights Act of 1871. Plaintiffs further allege violation of the Equal Rights Clause of the Texas Constitution.

In Defendants' answer, the City denies that the skip promotions were made on the sole basis of sex or race. Further, the City denied that it acted in violation of either the United States Constitution, the Texas Constitution or any statutory prohibitions. The City asserts several affirmative defenses against the Plaintiffs. The City first asserts that the Plaintiffs have not been injured by a constitutionally defective policy or custom of the City. Second, the City asserts that some of Plaintiffs' claims are barred by the statute of limitations. Finally, the City asserts that a number of the Plaintiffs lack standing because they would not have been promoted even if the skip promotions had not been made.

This factor concerns the goals set by the AAP with relation to the labor pool of qualified applicants. As stated above, the Dallas Fire Department does not hire laterally from other fire departments. Therefore, each rank is composed of those individuals qualified for promotion from the rank below. The promotional goals should be statistically related to the number of qualified applicants in each rank below. The affirmative action goals of the City's 1992 adopted AAP state that annual promotion goals are based on a ratio of African-American and Hispanics in the population of Dallas, Texas at a level not to exceed 40%. The goals also show that representation goals for upper-ranks and executives are based on calculations of availability plus a five point acceleration factor when applicable. However, the promotion goals for all ranks within the fire department above Fire & Rescue Officer are the same. The City in the 1992 AAP, set promotion goals across the board in all ranks above Fire & Rescue Officer at 23.4% for African-Americans, 16.6% for Hispanics and 10% for Females. The percentage of qualified individuals in each rank below necessarily fluctuates; the Court does not find how a single broad percentage goal for each rank can be adequately related to the number of qualified applicants in the appropriate feeder pool.

The City argues that because no unqualified candidates were considered for promotion and the Plaintiffs were only denied an employment opportunity, not deprived of their existing jobs ("denial of a future employment opportunity is not as intrusive as loss of existing job") that the impact on the Plaintiffs is not significant. Certainly, "a DFFA member denied a promotion is not in as bad a position as the victim of a layoff." However, the City's interest in race-conscious promotion policies is not as strong as the rights and expectations surrounding seniority. DFD has validated its promotional exams, it no longer adjusts the scores for seniority and it has established policies and customs which are aimed at racial parity. The Plaintiffs have had their promotional opportunities affected and many are not eligible to take upcoming promotional exams. They would have been eligible for these exams had the City promoted according to its own promotional ranking. The policy of ranking scores on validated tests creates an expectation in *all* firefighters that promotion can be earned by studying for the test. The City should not undermine this expectation with skip promotions that are not narrowly tailored.

For the above reasons, the Court finds that the City's policy of skip promotions in the fire department is not narrowly tailored and the Plaintiff's motion for summary judgment, as to the Equal Protection violation, is granted.

The case before this Court is factually distinguishable from the *Johnson* case. While the legal standards set out in *Johnson* are applicable to this case, the promotional methodology at issue here is starkly different. The Dallas Fire Department utilizes two criteria in making its promotional decisions, a passing score on an exam and a ranked order of all passing scores. In the positions at the time, with the exception of a subjective interview, there is no evidence of an individual evaluation of the applicants to be promoted, there is no evidence of an evaluation of the applicants based upon their past job performance, experience or personal attributes. All of these factors are present in *Johnson*. In this case, there is evidence that race has become a trump card in the hands of a municipal government in its quest for a diverse workforce in the shortest amount of time. To paraphrase George Orwell, the City's argument seems to be that all factors are equal, but some factors are more equal.

The leading case in determining whether or not a race or gender-conscious remedy comports with Title VII is *Johnson v. Transportation Agency of Santa Clara*. In *Johnson,* the Santa Clara County Transit District Board promoted, in accordance with an affirmative action plan, a female employee with a lower qualifying score over a male employee who had scored two points higher on the interview scale. During the selection process, both applicants cleared the initial hurdle of being deemed qualified. Both applicants were included in a group of applicants interviewed by a two-person panel. Those applicants who scored above 70 on this interview were certified as eligible for selection by the appointing authority. The next step of the process was an interview by three Agency supervisors who made a final recommendation. Despite the panel's recommendation of the male applicant, the

Affirmative Action Plan Coordinator recommended to the Director of the Agency that the female applicant be promoted. The Director of the Agency heeded that recommendation and promoted the female applicant. Subsequently, the male applicant filed a lawsuit.

The Supreme Court held that the Plan used by the Transit Board was permissible because the sex of the applicant was but one of numerous factors taken into account in arriving at the decision. "The Agency earmarks no positions for anyone; sex is but *one of several factors* that may be taken into account in evaluating qualified applicants for a position." The Supreme Court also stated that the decision to consider sex as one factor among many was made pursuant to an affirmative action plan that represented a moderate, flexible, case-by-case approach.

The Court acknowledges that "there is no precise formula for determining whether or not an affirmative action plan trammels the rights of [nonminorities]." When reviewing affirmative action plans involving race or gender-based entry-level hiring goals, the Supreme Court has noted that the impact on nonminorities is diffused, spread across all those in society who might deserve the entry-level position. Entry-level hiring goals, while burdening some innocent persons, do not impose the same type of injury on nonminorities as that imposed by the use of race or gender to determine layoffs. Because layoffs impose the entire burden on

particular individuals, often causing serious disruption to their lives, the Supreme Court has determined that this burden is too intrusive. These two situations present the extremes of employment decisions based on race or gender. The instant situation, however, does not neatly fall at one end of the spectrum or the other.

This case involves neither hiring or layoffs, but instead concerns skip promotions made under the City's affirmative action plan. The Eleventh Circuit has held that a promotion situation lies between entry-level hiring and layoffs in terms of the burden permitted on nonminorities. This Court agrees with that holding. The burden of the City of Dallas' skip promotion policy is not diffused throughout society, nor even diffused throughout the entire fire department. Instead, this policy resembles the layoff situation because only specific individuals are burdened.

The Court does not find that in order to unnecessarily trammel on nonminorities rights, there must be a firing or a layoff decision based upon race or gender. As stated above in the discussion of the Equal Protection claim, this Court finds that the promotional goals adopted by the City in its AAP are not reasonably related to the applicable pools of qualified employees for each job classification in the Fire Department ranks. A single percentage for the promotional goal in each rank seem to be arbitrarily selected.

Judgment for Dallas Fire Fighters.

Case Commentary

The Northern District Court of Texas determined that an affirmative action plan designed to enable minorities to become promoted by skipping over higher-ranked white candidates

was in violation of the Equal Protection Clause of the Fourteenth Amendment, in that it had an adverse impact on higher qualified white candidates.

Case Questions

1. What is a skip promotion?
2. Do you agree with the court's decision?

3. If minorities are not skipped, how will the disparate impact in the higher ranks be remedied?

NEGLIGENT HIRING

Many job applications and résumés contain false representations made by prospective applicants specifically with regard to their employment history and educational background. Many candidates resort to this falsification to improve their prospects of being hired. Employers must be diligent in confirming the authenticity of the offered information. If the individual is hired and causes damage or injury to a third party, the employer will be liable.

EMPLOYMENT PERSPECTIVE

Dennis Michaelson applied for a position as a resident gynecologist at Fairview Hospital in Brooklyn. According to Dennis's résumé, he graduated from one of the top medical schools and had an extensive private practice on the Kohala Coast on the big island of Hawaii. Dennis explained that after his wife's recent death, he wanted to return to his roots. Dennis's appearance, demeanor, and expertise convinced the hospital board to retain his services. The hospital was so impressed that it did not check with the medical school or on the references he had submitted. Dennis was at the hospital for fourteen months before he was questioned intensively about his diagnosing two cases of ovarian cancer as being benign growths. Dennis suddenly heard the call of the islands and disappeared. Fairview was sued by the two cancer victims as well as countless others who were treated by the fraud. When Fairview investigated, it learned that Dennis was not a licensed physician; he was just a con artist in disguise. Is the hospital liable? Yes! Fairview is liable for negligent hiring. ■

EMPLOYMENT SCENARIO

In questioning potential salespeople, Long & Short asked each applicant if he or she had any criminal convictions. Dan Wilson responded that he had been convicted of larceny. L&S hired Dan in spite of his conviction because it believed his other attributes were outstanding. Six months after being hired, Dan appropriated $120 in cash and a Rolex watch from a customer. Scott Thornton, the customer, after disrobing, left his pants, which contained his wallet and Rolex, inside the dressing room. Scott was with Martha, the seamstress, who was making adjustments to a suit Scott had purchased. Scott discovered the loss of his Rolex and the cash after he arrived home. By that time the store was closed. Dan left the employ of L&S that evening for parts unknown. Scott sued L&S for the cash and the value of the Rolex. Susan defended L&S. On its behalf, she claimed that Dan's theft occurred outside the scope of employment. She admonished Tom and Mark that this defense was weak due to the negligent hire of Dan, who they knew had a propensity to steal based on his prior conviction of larceny. After losing the case and paying damages, Tom and Mark resolved to consult Susan when a potential candidate has a prior conviction.

The issue presented in the following case is whether a business owes a duty to a member of the general public when one of its employees commits a tortious act against an individual.

POE v. DOMINO'S PIZZA, INC.

139 F.3d 617 (8th Cir. 1998)

ARNOLD, Chief Judge.

Gina Poe brought this lawsuit against Domino's Pizza after she was abducted and raped by James Sturtz, a Domino's employee. She alleges, negligent hiring and supervision. The District Court granted Domino's motion for summary judgment. We affirm.

Because the case comes to us on appeal from the grant of a summary judgment, we state the facts in the light most favorable to the party opposing that motion, here the plaintiff, Ms. Poe. Domino's hired Mr. Sturtz in early 1994. On March 7th of that year, he was distributing pizza coupons door-to-door near the college Ms. Poe attended in Cedar Rapids, Iowa. Ms. Poe was waiting at a bus stop, and Mr. Sturtz approached her, told her she had missed the bus, and offered her a ride. Ms. Poe declined and told him she would wait for the next bus. Mr. Sturtz asked Ms. Poe where she was going, and, when she told him, said he was going that way. Mr. Sturtz told Ms. Poe he worked for Domino's and that it would be okay for her to ride with him, and he showed her the coupons he was passing out. Ms. Poe got into the car, and Mr. Sturtz drove to a remote area of Cedar Rapids where, at knife-point, he raped Ms. Poe.

Mr. Sturtz had previous convictions for sexual assault and abuse, and when he applied for a job with Domino's, he lied on the form, saying he had never been convicted of a felony. Ms. Poe alleges that it was negligent of Domino's to fail to check Mr. Sturtz's criminal background thoroughly, to ensure that he had a two-year uninterrupted driving record, and to follow up with the references Mr. Sturtz provided. She also alleges that Domino's violated its own policy by not supervising Mr. Sturtz while he was distributing the coupons. Under Iowa law, however, the case turns on whether a special relationship existed between Domino's and Ms. Poe that gave rise to a legal duty owed by Domino's to Ms. Poe. We conclude that the District Court did not err when it held that Ms. Poe failed to establish the existence of such a duty.

The plaintiff concedes that Mr. Sturtz was not acting within the scope of his employment when he committed the acts complained of. The theory of respondeat superior is therefore not available as a basis of liability in this case. Plaintiff proceeds on a theory of negligent hiring. The Iowa courts hold that a special relationship must exist in order for the plaintiff to prevail in a negligent-hiring case. Whether a duty exists is a matter for the court to determine.

The District Court reviewed three factors to determine whether a special relationship existed: whether the plaintiff and the employee were in places where each had a right to be when the wrongful act occurred; whether the plaintiff met the employee as a direct consequence of the employment; and whether the employer would receive some benefit, even if only a potential or indirect benefit, from the meeting of the employee and the plaintiff had the wrongful act not occurred. The Court held that Domino's did not cause the meeting between Ms. Poe and Mr. Sturtz, that the meeting did not arise out of Mr. Sturtz's employment, and that Domino's received no benefit from the meeting. Ms. Poe was not a customer of Domino's, nor was she an owner or resident of a house where Mr. Sturtz was going to leave an advertisement for Domino's.

Ms. Poe claims there was a special relationship because Domino's considers all members of the public to be potential customers and encourages its drivers to have frequent contact with targeted customers such as college students. She also argues that Mr. Sturtz lured her into his car by telling her he worked for Domino's and by showing her the coupons he was distributing. The District Court found this unpersuasive, and, under Iowa law, so do we. Ms. Poe was not a customer, and she was not one to whom Domino's owed a duty because of its coupon distribution.

She got into Mr. Sturtz's car for the purpose of getting a ride to her destination. We believe the District Court correctly held there was no special relationship. Ms. Poe had no more connection with Domino's than any other member of the general public that Mr. Sturtz might have victimized.

Affirmed.

Case Commentary

In this case, the Eighth Circuit Court of Appeals determined that since negligent hiring is based on the tort of negligence, a duty must be owed to the victimized person. Domino's owes a duty of care to its customers and possibly to those individuals it is attempting to solicit. Here, since Gina Poe was neither a customer nor a solicitee, Domino's was not responsible for James Sturtz's actions. Furthermore, Gina Poe voluntarily accepted a ride from Sturtz. There is no conceivable way Domino's could have prevented this.

Case Questions

1. Was Gina Poe entitled to believe she would be safe with a Domino's employee?
2. Does it matter whether the vehicle had a Domino's sign on it?
3. Should Domino's be liable to the public for injuries sustained when it sends an employee out of its store?
4. Should Domino's have done a more extensive background check on James Sturtz, knowing he would be venturing out among the public on behalf of Domino's?

❖ EMPLOYER LESSONS

- Address the concerns of those candidates who have been refused employment expeditiously and with great care.
- Establish criteria for promotions that are necessary for those positions.
- Draft policies for nepotism and promoting from within that will not hamper the attainment of a diverse workforce.
- Evaluate which criminal convictions are related to an available job before you ask candidates about their criminal records.
- Guard against negligent hiring by screening candidates thoroughly.
- Attempt to achieve a work environment that is free from discrimination.
- Query candidates about the qualifications that are related to the job.
- Train interviewers to refrain from asking those questions that may be discriminatory.
- Recruit from as wide a variety of sources as possible to assure a diverse pool of candidates.
- Maintain accurate records.

❖ EMPLOYEE LESSONS

- Recognize inappropriate questions asked during an interview.
- Decide prior to an interview how you intend to respond if an inappropriate question is asked.
- Understand if you take issue with the interviewer that you may not get the job for that reason.
- Do not expect the interviewer to apologize because he or she may be wrong.

- Be prepared for a time-consuming and possibly expensive lawsuit to resolve the conflict.
- Ask what the job qualifications are for the position for which you are applying.
- Inquire as to the criteria employed and the decision-making process utilized in determining promotions.
- Learn the employer's policy on nepotism and promoting from within.
- Appreciate the fact that employers should only inquire into prior criminal convictions that are related to the job.
- Respond to questions honestly or refuse if inappropriate, but never lie; otherwise you may be discharged for being dishonest.

❖ SUMMARY

The selection process has become a complicated procedure for employers. They must carefully choose questions based on job qualifications. They risk litigation if they ask inappropriate questions which can be inferred as discriminatory. Employers must recruit from a diverse pool of candidates. Employers must keep accurate records of these candidates, such as who applied and who was hired. Employers must establish job-related criteria necessary for promotions. Employers must perform background checks on employees to guard themselves against negligent hiring, but these checks are limited to activities or criminal convictions that are job related. Policies with regard to nepotism and promoting from within should also be drafted by the employer. The selection process is a daunting but necessary undertaking for the employer. As most of us know, it is an equally stressful experience for workers.

❖ REVIEW QUESTIONS

1. Is discrimination possible in the selection process?
2. What is the Uniform Guidelines On Employee Selection Procedures?
3. Can an employer be guilty of negligent hiring?
4. Is nepotism permissible?
5. Are promotions from within the company discriminatory?
6. Are firms who recruit at colleges practicing discrimination?
7. What records is an employer required to keep with regard to its employees?
8. Can an employer specify "recent college graduates only" in an employment ad?
9. What is the procedure a company should follow when a job becomes available that would entail promoting someone within the company?
10. Does an employer have to be careful where it advertises for potential job applicants to avoid acting in a discriminatory manner?

11. Sitgraves' request to be transferred was denied. Sitgraves filed suit claiming discrimination. Allied Signal argued that a new and distinct relationship would not have been forthcoming had the request been granted. Therefore, Sitgraves has no grounds for bringing the suit. What was the result? *Sitgraves v. Allied Signal, Inc.* 953 F.2d 570 (9th Cir. 1992)
12. Carter applied for a transfer to a division through which eligibility for a promotion would occur. The transfer was denied. Carter brought suit claiming discrimination in the denial of a promotion. What was the result? *Carter v. South Central Bell,* 912 F.2d 832 (5th Cir. 1990)
13. Michelle LeGault applied to become a firefighter in Johnston, Rhode Island. Although she ranked among the highest on the written examinations, she was passed over because she did not complete the required run and hose pull within the allotted time period. She

contended that these tests were never validated according to the National Fire Protection Association standards, which have no run or hose pull requirement. Mayor Arruso argued that he instituted a stringent test to find the best qualified people for this dangerous job. What was the result? *LeGault v. Arrusso*, 842 F.Supp. 1979 (D.N.M. 1994)

14. Ms. Stukey had several experiences in teaching. Ms. Stukey directed educational seminars at Central State University and Antioch College from 1978 until 1981. In addition, Ms. Stukey had conducted seminars on a variety of legal topics, including labor law and housing law. Ms. Stukey had also been managing attorney for the Greene County Legal Aid Office from 1978 until 1981.

    In contrast, one successful male candidate had only taught freshman chemistry at the University of Maryland in 1966–67. Nevertheless, the selection committee gave the male candidate substantially more teaching points than Ms. Stukey in the selection committee's evaluation.

    Prior to the start of the March 25, 1985, interview, selection committee member Earnest Spitzer spoke with Ms. Stukey. In this conversation, Mr. Spitzer questioned Ms. Stukey about her divorce and her child care arrangements. Ms. Stukey claimed she was rattled by these questions, which as a labor lawyer, she knew were improper. What was the result? *Stukey v. U.S. Air Force*, 809 F.Supp. 536 (S.D. Ohio 1992)

15. According to Ulrich, he has not progressed at Exxon to the level merited by his qualifications, abilities, and performance. He complains that Exxon utilizes a highly subjective and arbitrary system for job performance evaluation, which includes a ranking system where employees who are determined to be within the same peer group are ranked from best to worst. Additionally, Exxon supervisors are required to prepare a "career potential assessment" of employees, which is critical to an employee's ability to advance within the company. Ulrich alleges that "in order to attempt to escape closer scrutiny by state and federal agencies enforcing statutory provisions for equal employment opportunity, Exxon has direct-

ed that individuals representing racial minorities be hired and promoted and placed in positions designed to provide maximum visibility to the incumbents." He contends that these efforts have been utilized to manipulate personnel decisions in disregard of individual ability and performance. He asserts, for example, that managers may artificially inflate the rating and ranking of selected minority employees to fill positions in preference to white employees of established merit and experience. As a result of these alleged practices, Ulrich asserts that he has been arbitrarily and capriciously ranked and assessed well below the level merited by his knowledge, training, experience, and performance, leading to a loss of pay and promotional opportunities. Defendants assert that Ulrich has not presented even a *prima facie* case of race discrimination. What was the result? *Ulrich v. Exxon Co. U.S.A. A Div. of Exxon Corp.*, 824 F.Supp. 677 (S.D. Tex 1993)

16. At a meeting on November 21, 1989, the weed board and county board became aware that the only two applicants for the superintendent's position were plaintiff and Gary Craig. Kenneth Luce, a member of the weed board, testified that after discussing the applicants, three members of the weed board stood up and announced they wished to hire Gary Craig as the new superintendent. When Kenneth Luce reminded the three that interviews had not yet been held, they sat down and the meeting continued.

    Plaintiff was then interviewed. Unlike Gary Craig, she was not provided with a written job description and list of questions prior to or at any point during her interview.

    At the meeting the weed board voted 3–2 to hire Gary Craig.

    As a result of defendants' actions in rejecting her for the position of weed superintendent, plaintiff testified that she suffered both emotionally and physically. She became depressed, was unable to sleep, became emotional and cried when she saw people on the street, and felt as though her reputation in the community had been destroyed. What was the result? *Bruhn v. Foley*, 824 F.Supp. 1345 (D.Neb. 1993)

❖ WEB SITES

www.usnews.com/usnews/wash/affhigh.htm
www.findlaw.com
www.lawinfo.com
www.usccr.gov/index.html
www.hodes.com/research.html
http://sacramento.bcentral.com/sacramento/stories/1997/08/04/smallb6.html

CHAPTER 3

TESTING

INTRODUCTION

Employers are seeking to employ qualified workers who will do the best job. Aside from interviewing candidates, evaluating their experience, and checking their references, testing provides the most useful source of information for employers. The tests most often used are aptitude, residency, psychological, honesty, polygraph, and drug tests. Concerns over privacy and discrimination lead to litigation regarding the use of tests. With regard to privacy, the employer's desire to know must be balanced with the employee's right to safeguard his or her personal information. With respect to discrimination, the tests must be designed to determine the ability of the worker to perform the task. The tests themselves must be a business necessity, and the questions must be related to the job. The tests cannot be used for the purpose of refusing employment to women and minorities. With that in mind, an analysis should be undertaken for each position. Job qualifications should be determined. A job description should be written based on the analysis and should include appropriate qualifications. An evaluation should be made to determine if testing is necessary and, if so, what type of testing is required. Then, a test should be drafted utilizing questions specific to determining whether the worker has the qualifications for the particular job.

CHAPTER CHECKLIST

❖ Distinguish between the different tests available to employers.

❖ Determine when it is appropriate to use a specific test.

❖ Decide whether the test questions are related to the job.

❖ Balance the employer's need to know against the worker's desire for privacy.

❖ Establish whether the test is being used to deny employment to women and minorities.

❖ Understand the ramifications of the Employee Polygraph Protection Act.

❖ Identify the exceptions to that act.

❖ Appreciate the employer's concern for restricting employment to workers who do not engage in the use of alcohol and drugs.

❖ Be familiar with the Drug-Free Workplace Act.

❖ Appreciate the impact the Fourth Amendment has had on drug testing.

EMPLOYMENT SCENARIO

In two years, the Long and Short of It has grown to three stores with each having at least 1,500 square feet of floor space. L&S employs 48 workers, 42 of whom are employees. Recently, L&S has experienced customer complaints regarding employee knowledgeability about some of L&S's clothing lines. In addition, on three occasions, salespeople have lost their cool with indecisive customers, alleging the customers were wasting the salespeoples' time. To remedy this, L&S planned to require those applicants selected for employment as salespeople to take written aptitude and psychological tests. Tom and Mark ask Susan North, Esq. for her perspective. Susan advises that, in order for a test to defeat a challenge for being discriminatory or an invasion of privacy, the test must be based on a business necessity, and the questions must be job related. Susan believes general aptitude and psychological tests will not be permissible for this type of employment. Susan counsels L&S to create a test where the questions are job related and narrowly tailored to evidence knowledge of the specific tasks required for the job. She adds that role-playing or short essay questions can be asked to determine how the candidate would handle a customer who becomes indecisive or annoying. Tom and Mark appreciate Susan's guidance.

APTITUDE TESTS

Employers must justify the use of employing an aptitude test by showing that the tests are job related and, if so, are used for the sole purpose of identifying qualified applicants. If the tests are used as a pretext to disqualify members of a suspect classification, then the employer's action is discriminatory.

Opponents of general tests argue that they are biased against women and minorities. Proponents insist that scholarly individuals at impartial testing facilities established these tests. Their use is widespread, and their reliability is reinforced by a long tradition.

The following case addresses the issue of whether the state may test the competency of its teachers through the administration of aptitude exams. The teachers felt that this was a violation of the Civil Rights Act and the Age Discrimination in Employment Act.

FRAZIER v. GARRISON

980 F.2d (5th Cir. 1993)

BROWN, Circuit Judge.

Texas Examination for Current Administrators and Teachers (TECAT). The teachers alleged that the TECAT, a state administered examination for teachers that tested basic reading and writing skills, violated Title VI and Title VII of the 1964 Civil Rights Act, the Age Discrimination in Employment Act (ADEA), the Equal Educational Opportunities Act of 1974, and the Due Process and Equal Protection Clauses of the Constitution. The Teachers also moved the trial court to certify them as a class for purposes of maintaining a class action. The trial court refused to certify the class, denied the Teachers' motion to consolidate, and granted summary judgment in favor of the School Districts on the Title VI claim, the Title VII claim, the ADEA claim, and the Due Process and Equal Protection claims. This is an appeal from the district court's final judgment. We affirm.

TECAT

On July 23, 1984, the Texas legislature passed into law House Bill 72 which contained numerous provisions for education reform including school funding, school finance reform, teacher raises, establishment of a teacher career ladder, provisions for school discipline management, restructuring of the State Board of Education and teacher competency testing. Section 13.047 of the act, which provides for teacher competency testing, is the section at issue on this appeal.

(a) The board shall require satisfactory performance on an examination prescribed by the board as a condition to continued certification for each teacher and administrator who has not taken a certification examination.

(b) The board shall prescribe an examination designed to test knowledge appropriate to teach primary grades and an examination designed to test knowledge appropriate to teach secondary grades. The secondary teacher examinations must test the knowledge of each examinee in the subject areas listed in Section 21.101 of this code in which the examinee is certified to teach and is teaching. If a teacher is not tested in an area of certification, the teacher must take the examination for that area within three years after beginning to teach that subject. The administrator examinations must test administrative skills, knowledge in subject areas, and other matters that the board considers appropriate. The examinations must also test the ability of the examinee to read and write with sufficient skill to perform satisfactorily as a professional teacher or administrator.

(c) In developing the examinations, the board shall solicit and consider the advice of classroom teachers and administrators.

(d) Each teacher must perform satisfactorily on the applicable examination on or before June 30, 1986, to teach the subject at a particular level unless a school district establishes to the satisfaction of the commissioner of education that there is an emergency need. A teacher may not teach under a determination of an emergency need for more than one school year.

(e) The board, in conjunction with school districts, shall provide teachers and administrators with an opportunity for board-developed preparation for the examination.

The teachers had not presented any direct evidence of intent to discriminate. Since the School Districts' knowledge of the allegedly adverse impact of the TECAT on minority teachers and the raising of the cutoff rate are the Teachers' only possible proof of intent to discriminate, we conclude that the district court's grant of summary judgment was appropriate on the disparate treatment claim. There is no evidence that the School Districts acted with discriminatory intent.

The teachers contend that the trial court erred in refusing to certify the Teacher's class for purposes of maintaining a suit under the Age Discrimination in Employment Act. This court held that the four elements that a plaintiff must initially prove under *McDonnell Douglas Corp. v. Green* to maintain a Title VII case are also required to support a claim under the ADEA. Specifically, the court held that a rejected job applicant must show the following in order to bring a discrimination suit: that he belongs to a racial minority, that he applied and was qualified for a job for which the employer was seeking applicants, that despite his qualifications, he was rejected, and that after his rejection, the position remained open and the employer continued to seek applicants from persons of complainant's qualifications. The district court concluded, that the Teachers had not applied for positions for which they were qualified (non-certified teaching positions) and therefore, could not bring suit under either Title VII or the ADEA.

Judgment for Garrison and the School Board.

Case Commentary

Minority teachers in the Texas school system claimed the requirement of an examination designed to test the competency of its teachers is discriminatory. Their argument failed because they offered no evidence to prove intent to discriminate on the part of the Texas legislature.

Case Questions

1. Is the requirement of a teacher competency test a business necessity?
2. Why are the teachers reluctant to take the test if they are qualified?
3. Do you agree with the decision of the court?

RESIDENCY TESTS

Cities, towns, countries, and municipalities may require that applicants for civil service positions be residents. In other localities, preference may be given to applicants. This mandate of preference must be clearly stated in a local ordinance.

Residency requirements may not be instituted by state or local governments in public contracts given to private contractors unless they are implemented to alleviate the loss of economic benefits to the state or to alleviate the state's high unemployment.

The following case presents the test for determining whether residency is a permissible requirement for employment.

A. L. BLADES & SONS v. YERUSALIM

121 F.3d 865 (3rd Cir. 1997)

SCIRICA, Circuit Judge.

The issue on appeal is whether Pennsylvania Act 1935-414 § 154 violates the Privileges and Immunities Clause of the United States Constitution by requiring contractors to employ only Pennsylvania residents as laborers and mechanics on Commonwealth-funded public works projects. Because the statute's discrimination is not substantially justified; we hold it is unconstitutional.

I.

On May 12, 1994, the Pennsylvania Department of Transportation accepted bids for the Potter County highway improvement construction project. A.L. Blades & Sons, a New York based highway construction contractor, was the apparent low bidder. After awarding the contract, PennDOT notified Blades that the #154 residency requirement would be strictly enforced.

Section 154 of Pennsylvania Act 1935-414 provides:

154. Resident laborers and mechanics

The specifications upon which contracts are entered into by the Commonwealth, county, municipality, or other subdivisions of the Commonwealth, for the construction, alteration, or repair of any public works shall contain the provision that laborers and mechanics employed on such public works shall have been residents of the Commonwealth for at least ninety days prior to their employment; and failure to keep and comply with such provision shall be sufficient legal reason to refuse payment of the contract price to the contractor.

This statute was enacted during the Great Depression to ensure that Pennsylvania residents, and particularly those unemployed, would be the sole beneficiaries of state funds spent on public works.

To comply with the Act, PennDOT includes in each construction contract a provision which reads:

Residence requirements.

Laborers and mechanics to be employed for work under the contract are required by Act 1935-414 to have been residents of the State for at least 90 days prior to their starting work on the contract. Failure to comply with these provisions will be sufficient reason to refuse paying the contract price.

Nevertheless, Blades employed Jeffrey Elliot and Simon Barnes who were New York residents. In November and December 1994, PennDOT notified Blades that continued employment of nonresident workers could result in withholding contract payments and could affect its pre-qualification status to do future work in Pennsylvania. Following this notification, Blades fired Elliot and Barnes.

In December 1994, Blades, Elliot, and Barnes brought this action against the Pennsylvania Secretary of Transportation and other officials. The complaint alleged that Pennsylvania Act was invalid because it violated (1) the Privileges and Immunities Clause of the United States Constitution, the Equal Protection Clause of the United States Constitution, and the Pennsylvania State Constitution. In January 1995, the district court granted Blades preliminary injunctive relief prohibiting enforcement of the residency requirement on the Potter County project during the pendency of the action. Thereafter Blades completed the project.

Both Blades and the Commonwealth filed motions for partial summary judgment on the Privileges and Immunities claim. The Privileges and Immunities challenge may be brought on behalf of the individual plaintiffs but not A.L. Blades & Sons since it is a corporation.

The Privileges and Immunities Clause of Article IV of the United States Constitution provides: "The citizens of each state shall be entitled to all privileges and immunities of citizens in several states." The Clause is designed to prevent the discriminatory treatment of citizens from other states. As the Supreme Court held: "it was undoubtedly the object of the Privileges and Immunities Clause . . . to place the citizens of each State upon the same footing with citizens of other States, so far as the advantages resulting from citizenship in those States are concerned."

But this protection is not absolute. There is a three prong test.

The Clause only precludes discrimination against nonresidents when the governmental action burdens one of the privileges and immunities protected under the clause, and the government does not have a substantial reason for the difference in treatment or the discrimination practiced against the nonresidents does not bear a substantial relationship to the government's objectives. In the first instance, we must determine whether the Act burdens one of those privileges and immunities protected by the clause.

Typically the right to employment is considered fundamental under the Privileges and Immunities Clause.

We hold that direct public employment is not a privilege or fundamental right protected by the Privileges and Immunities Clause of Article Four.

Nonetheless there is a fundamental right to employment where the employee is hired by a private employer who receives a government contract to work on a public project. Blades has satisfied the first prong of the test.

The second prong of the test is whether there is a substantial reason for the statute's discriminatory approach beyond the mere fact that the targeted group is comprised of citizens of other states such as alleviating high unemployment in the Commonwealth's construction industry and avoiding the loss of economic benefits resulting from the expenditure of Commonwealth funds on nonresident workers. The district court rejected the unemployment justification, but held the loss of economic benefits attributed to nonresident workers removing their earnings to their states of residency justified the statute's discriminatory approach. Because we find the Commonwealth's reasons insufficient to substantially justify # 154's discriminatory approach, we will not reach the third prong that requires the State to demonstrate the discrimination practiced against nonresidents bears a substantial relationship to the State's objective.

For the foregoing reasons we will reverse the district court's grant of summary judgment for the Commonwealth. We will remand this matter to the district court with instruction to enter judgment for plaintiffs.

Judgment for Blades & Sons.

Case Commentary

The Third Circuit ruled that residency requirements are not applicable to private employers who work on public projects unless they are used to relieve high unemployment or to stymie a loss of economic benefits to the state.

Case Questions

1. Do you agree with the decision in this case?
2. Should Pennsylvania be able to determine who works on public projects?

3. Should the decision in Question #2 rest on whether the employer is public or private?

HONESTY TESTS

Honesty tests are those which measure physiological changes in the person tested. They are usually referred to as lie-detector tests. Polygraphs, voice stress analyzers, and psychological stress evaluators are the most prevalent types. Some employers also attempt to determine veracity through the use of psychological questionnaires of personal judgments based on demeanor or physical behavior.

PSYCHOLOGICAL TESTING

Psychological tests may be administered only where the employer can show a compelling need. Employees are considered to be patients of the physicians conducting the examinations. In that respect, the patients are entitled to examine their medical reports.

EMPLOYMENT PERSPECTIVE

Excelsior Bank, a specialist in investment banking, established along with a team of psychologists a psychological profile of people who work best under pressure. Every new applicant is required to take the test. The result is a prime determinant as to whether the applicant is given the job. Susan Morgan, who was otherwise qualified, is refused employment as a result of her low score on the psychological profile. Excelsior Bank's employees are overwhelmingly white males. Susan claims the test is not job related and is used as a pretext to discriminate. Is she correct? Yes! Excelsior has not shown a compelling need for the administration of the psychological test. Its use by Excelsior is to eliminate women and minorities from the selection process. ■

The issue in the next case is whether employees qualify within the definition of patients in their quest to obtain copies of their psychological test results.

CASE

CLEGHORN v. HESS
853 P.2d 1260 (Nev. 1993)

ROSE, Chief Justice.
Respondent Wackenhut Services, Inc. (Wackenhut) is under contract with the United States Department of Energy (DOE) to provide security services at the Nevada Test Site and related nuclear weapons facilities in Nevada. Appellant Michael Cleghorn (Cleghorn) is a security inspector for Wackenhut and has been a Wackenhut employee since May 24, 1982. Under a contract with Wackenhut, respondent Dr. Hess, a licensed psychologist, examines, tests, and evaluates Wackenhut employees and applicants for employment to determine their psychological suitability for employment. The psychological testing is conducted in accordance with the terms of a collective bargaining agreement between Wackenhut and appellant Independent Guard Association of Nevada, Local 1 (IGAN), and as part of a medical and psychological suitability testing program for the Doe Human Reliability Personnel Assurance Program (PAP). As a con-

dition of employment for a security personnel, the DOE requires Wackenhut to employ only those persons who meet PAP medical standards.

Wackenhut referred Cleghorn to Dr. Hess for psychological testing on May 9, 1982 (pre-employment), and again on July 6, 1990. Cleghorn requested copies of his psychological records and test results. Dr. Hess and Wackenhut refused Cleghorn's repeated requests for copies of his psychological test results. Thereafter, Cleghorn brought an action for declaratory and injunctive relief, seeking to obtain the test results of his psychological testing.

The sole issue on review is whether the district erred in concluding that NRS 629.061 does not entitle Cleghorn and IGAN to obtain copies of their psychological test results. NRS 629.061 provides, in pertinent part: "1. Each provider of health care shall make the health care records of a patient available for physical inspection by: (a) the patient or a representative with written authorization from the patient...." Cleghorn and IGAN argue that NRS 629.061 entitles them to receive copies of the test results of the psychological testing done by Hess for the following reasons: (1) Hess is a provider of health care as defined in NRS 629.031; (2) Cleghorn and the IGAN members are patients because they are persons seeking medical services for examination or treatment; and (3) the records requested are medical records as defined in NRS 629.021.

Dr. Hess and Wackenhut asserted that Hess is not a provider of health care under the statute. They further assert that Cleghorn and the IGAN members were not patients of Hess pursuant to NRS 629.061 because Hess did not provide health care to them, they did not expect any treatment from Hess, and the examinations were for the sole benefit of Wackenhut.

As a licensed psychologist, Dr. Hess is clearly a "provider of health care" under NRS 629.031. The information sought by Cleghorn and IGAN are written reports and records produced by Dr. Hess containing information relating to Dr. Hess' examination of Wackenhut employees, including Cleghorn, and thus are "health care records" as defined in NRS 629.021. Although there is no definition of patient provided in Chapter 629, a "patient" is defined in our evidence statute as "a person who consults or is examined or interviewed by a doctor for purposes of diagnosis or treatment." NRS 49.215(3). The word patient has similarly been defined as "a person seeking medical services for examination or treatment." The Wackenhut employees were undeniably interviewed and examined by Hess in order to determine their psychological suitability for employment.

Furthermore, to say in the instant case that the employees were not patients because they did not receive treatment is to split hairs. The employees were tested, examined, and evaluated by a psychologist. The definition of "patient" utilized by other jurisdictions when considering tort liability is not necessarily appropriate in the instant case, and a more liberal definition of "patient" would be in harmony with the legislative intent behind the enactment of NRS 629.061. The intent of the legislature is the controlling factor in statutory interpretation. When the language of a statute is clear on its face, its intention must be deduced from such language. The statute is clearly intended to provide, rather than prevent, access to medical records by specific persons, while at the same time protecting the patient's privacy rights: only the patient or patient's representative, the attorney general or grand jury or an authorized representative or investigator of the state licensing board may access the medical records. The Nevada Legislature set forth detailed requirements and procedures for the retention, copying, and inspection of a patient's medical records to facilitate the obtaining of that information. A narrow interpretation of who is a patient would defeat the purpose of the statute. We therefore conclude that Cleghorn and the IGAN members are patients for the purpose of NRS 629.061.

Judgment for Cleghorn.

Case Commentary

The Supreme Court of Nevada decided that an employee who is required to undergo psychological testing pursuant to a collective bargaining agreement that mandates testing of all security personnel is entitled to copies of his psychological records and the test results.

Case Questions

1. Why should the physician have to divulge his records to the plaintiff if the plaintiff was not a patient?
2. Why does the employer have to relinquish psychological test results that were paid for by the employer?
3. Do you agree with the decision in this case?
4. Has the employee's privacy been invaded by mandating that he go for a psychological exam?

POLYGRAPH TEST

Polygraphs are a form of lie-detector test. Their use is prohibited in all but a select set of instances because the reliability is questionable and their use amounts to an invasion of privacy.

EMPLOYEE POLYGRAPH PROTECTION ACT OF 1988

Under the Employee Polygraph Protection Act, employers cannot directly or indirectly suggest or require an employee to take a lie-detector test, nor can an employer use an employee's results from a lie-detector test. The term "lie detector" encompasses a polygraph, voice stress analyzer, psychological stress evaluator, or any similar device used to determine the honesty of a person. A fine up to $10,000 is imposed on any employer found to be in breach of this act. If employee selection or termination is determined by the polygraph, the Secretary of Labor may order employment, promotion, reinstatement, and reimbursement for lost wages and benefits. The employee may also seek these remedies in a private civil action. The Employee Polygraph Protection Act applies to all employers engaged in commerce. It does not apply to the federal government or to any state and local governments. There are other exemptions. Polygraphs may be used by an armored car company, a security alarm system firm, or a security personnel provider, with regard to their screening of employee applicants who are being hired to protect any facility impacting on the national health or safety of the United States, and any facility supplying electric, nuclear, or public water, shipments of radioactive or other toxic wastes, public transportation, currency, securities, precious commodities, or drug manufacture.

EMPLOYMENT SCENARIO

The Long and Short of It experienced a wave of property thefts over a two-week period. The Company estimates that more than $18,000 in clothing was stolen from two of its stores. L&S decides to require all 48 workers to submit to a polygraph. L&S contacts Susan, but she is away on vacation. Tom and Mark forge ahead rather than wait for her to return. In addition to questions about the $18,000 theft, they propose asking the following: Have you ever stolen anything? Do you ever think of stealing? Have you ever taken drugs and, if so, which drugs? Are you currently taking drugs? How much alcohol do you consume daily? Sarah Michels, a bookkeeper for L&S, refuses to take the polygraph. L&S immediately terminates her and threatens to notify the authorities that it has reason to believe she is a prime suspect if she does not divulge information about the theft and make restitution. Sarah files a complaint with the EEOC. The EEOC fines L&S for violation of the Employee Polygraph Protection Act and orders reinstatement and reimbursement for lost wages and benefits. When Susan returns she scolds Tom and Mark for their impatience and impulsiveness. Instead of resolving the crime, they have added to their misery.

The issue in the following case is whether a tape recorded conversation used with a voice exemplar qualifies as a form of a lie-detector test whose use is in violation of the Employee Polygraph Protection Act.

CASE

DARRYL VEAZEY v. COMMUNICATIONS & CABLE OF CHICAGO, INC.

194 F.3d 850 (7th Cir. 1999)

COFFEY, Circuit Judge.

Darryl Veazey contends that his former employer, LaSalle Telecommunications, Inc., incorrectly sued as Communications & Cable Co. of Chicago, violated the Employee Polygraph Protection Act ("EPPA"), when it discharged him because he refused to provide the specific tape-recorded voice exemplar his superiors had requested. The district court dismissed his suit under Federal Rule of Civil Procedure for failure to state a claim. Because it is possible to hypothesize a set of facts consistent with Veazey's complaint that would entitle him to relief, we reverse the district court's ruling and remand for further proceedings.

I. BACKGROUND

In the fall of 1996, Darryl Veazey's employer, LaSalle Telecommunications, Inc., suspected that Veazey, who was employed as an outage coordinator/dispatcher, had left a hostile and threatening anonymous message on the voicemail of another employee at LaSalle. Accordingly, LaSalle set up an interview with Veazey concerning the incident. Mike Mason, LaSalle's Customer Fulfillment Manager, and Jack Burke, a "cable troubleshooter," questioned Veazey about the message during a four hour interview. Veazey maintained his innocence at all times.

Despite Veazey's denials, Mason and Burke requested that Veazey read a verbatim transcript of the threatening message into a tape recorder, which would in turn enable LaSalle to create a voice exemplar. Veazey refused to read the ver-

batim transcript of the message for he was concerned about how the tape might be used and because he thought the message was offensive. In a counteroffer, Veazey agreed to provide a tape-recorded voice exemplar of his reading of a different message. Because of his refusal to provide the specific voice exemplar requested, Mason suspended Veazey without pay. Three days later, Mason and Burke again summoned Veazey to a meeting, and once again Veazey refused to provide LaSalle with a voice exemplar of him reading a transcript of the threatening message. Based on Veazey's continued refusal to provide the requested voice exemplar, Mason discharged him for insubordination.

Thereafter, Veazey filed suit against LaSalle alleging that LaSalle's decision to terminate him after he refused to provide the specific tape recorded message violated the EPPA's prohibition against employers, like LaSalle, from administering lie detector tests. LaSalle responded to Veazey's complaint with a motion to dismiss for failure to state a claim under Federal Rule of Civil Procedure. The district court granted the motion to dismiss, agreeing with LaSalle that the tape recording requested by Mason and Burke did not qualify as a lie detector test as that term is used in the EPPA. Veazey appeals. We reverse and remand this case for further proceedings.

II. ISSUES

The issue in this case is whether LaSalle's specific request that Veazey produce a voice exemplar of him reading a transcript of the threatening voicemail message amounts to a "lie detector test" under the EPPA.

III. ANALYSIS

A. Standard of Review

We review a dismissal taking a plaintiff's factual allegations as true and drawing all reasonable inferences in the plaintiff's favor.

B. The History of the Lie Detector

The polygraph is composed of a combination of devices which measure certain, specified physical data. In 1895, an Italian psychiatrist and criminologist named Cesare Lombroso made the unprecedented claim that he could "detect lies" by monitoring a person's blood pressure and "reading" the changes in it. Lombroso asserted that by understanding the typical criminal responses and physical characteristics he could distinguish "criminal types" from the rest of society. Over a hundred years later, his claims continue to shape society's perceptions of polygraphs and account for their popularity. In order to understand the importance of the EPPA, and why LaSalle may have violated it, we believe it is helpful for one to understand the evolution of the lie detector and its impact on employers and employees.

Before the EPPA, federal law regulated the use of polygraph machines mainly in law enforcement contexts, but made no attempt to control or monitor their use in the private workplace. It was not a surprise when private employers took it upon themselves to administer more polygraph examinations than either the federal government or state criminal investigators. In fact, a 1978 survey of four hundred major U.S. corporations found that more than fifty percent of the commercial banks and retailers that had responded to the survey used polygraphs. The survey also noted that these companies were more likely to test all job applicants and employees than to conduct random sampling.

As polygraph machines gained popularity in the American business world, many researchers and defense lawyers began to question the accuracy of the machine that was dictating numerous people's employment fate. Several studies concerning polygraph validity were published in the late 1970's and early 1980's, and contributed greatly to the understanding of the lie detector's limitations, motivating the United States Congress to pass the EPPA.

FIELD STUDIES

In 1982, Kleinmuntz and Szucko obtained the charts of one hundred polygraph examinations which were performed by the then well-known Reid Polygraph Agency in Chicago, Illinois. The study consisted of fifty charts that had been verified as deceptive by the subsequent confessions of the examinees and fifty charts that had been verified as truthful by the subsequent confessions of other people. Polygraphers from the well recognized Reid agency then independently rescored all one hundred charts, incorrectly classifying 39% of the verified innocent examinees as guilty.

Barland & Raskin, An Evaluation of Field Techniques in Detection of Deception. In this study, the guilt or innocence of the suspects was determined by an expert panel of one judge, two defense lawyers, and two prosecutors who examined each suspect. Barland then administered polygraph examinations to ninety-two criminal suspects, and Raskin independently scored those charts.

Based on the decisions of the expert panel, Raskin incorrectly classified 55% of the innocent suspects as deceptive when they denied their guilt. Once again, the survey suggests that employees (or employers for that matter) might fare just as well if their fate was determined by a simple flip of a coin.

Barland Study (1981)

In 1981, Barland conducted one of the few validity studies ever done on the use of polygraphs in pre-employment screening by testing military personnel who worked in the intelligence field. For the study, Barland told half of the participants to lie when responding to one of the questions—offering twenty dollars if they could produce a truthful reading during the polygraph examination. Again, without going into the specifics of the study, the O.T.A. stated in its 1983 report that "the results of the Barland study raise serious questions about the usefulness of directed lie control questions in screening procedures as well as, in general, the validity of polygraph testing for pre-employment and counterintelligence purposes, especially if used alone."

As we shall see, LaSalle may have been trying to skirt the EPPA's prohibition on lie detector tests when it requested Veazey to provide a tape recording, and discharged him for refusing to do so.

The Employee Polygraph Protection Act

As stated above, Congress enacted the Employee Polygraph Protection Act in 1988 in response to justified concerns that employers were many times misusing lie detectors or their derivatives (as the case may have been here) and were too frequently relying on inaccurate, inconclusive, or unfounded lie detector results to make employment decisions. Accordingly, the EPPA makes it illegal, with limited exceptions, for employers to use lie detector tests. In particular, the provisions applicable to this case provide, in relevant part:

It shall be unlawful for any employer engaged in or affecting commerce or in the production of goods for commerce—

(1) directly or indirectly, to require, request, suggest, or cause any employee or prospective employee to take or submit to any lie detector test;

(3) to discharge, discipline, discriminate against in any manner, or deny employment or promotion to, or threaten to take any such action against—

(A) any employee or prospective employee who refuses, declines, or fails to take or submit to any lie detector test.

The statute defines the term "lie detector" to include "a polygraph, deceptograph, voice stress analyzer, psychological stress evaluator, or any other similar device (whether mechanical or electrical) that is used, or the results of which are used, for the purpose of rendering a diagnostic opinion regarding the honesty or dishonesty of an individual." We point out the illuminating language in this statute (which is obviously broad enough to preclude the resolution of this case on a motion to dismiss) and query whether today's technology permits a tape recording, if used in conjunction with other devices enumerated in the statute, to achieve the results of a "lie detector." The case is about the tape recording LaSalle requested being used in conjunction with other devices that would have allowed LaSalle to directly gauge whether Veazey was telling the truth

when he denied leaving the threatening message on another employee's answering machine.

Initially, LaSalle contends that a tape recorder, the device it wanted to use to make the requested voice exemplar, is not a "lie detector" as defined by the EPPA because it, by itself, does not directly gauge a person's truthfulness; it merely records sounds. LaSalle's characterization of the statutory definition of "lie detector" is, in our opinion, too narrow because it overlooks the significance of the phrase "the results of which are used . . . for the purpose of rendering a diagnostic opinion regarding the honesty or dishonesty of an individual." LaSalle concedes that a voice exemplar, evaluated by a voice stress analyzer or similar device, might be and often is used in the rendering of a "diagnostic opinion regarding the honesty or dishonesty of an individual." We are of the opinion that the application of basic logic necessitates that a tape recorder might very well be considered as an adjunct to a "lie detector" determination under the EPPA because the results of a tape recording (a voice exemplar) can be used to render a diagnostic opinion regarding the honesty or dishonesty of an individual when evaluated by a voice stress analyzer or similar device. Accordingly, a tape recorder, when used in conjunction with one of the devices enumerated in the statute or a similar device, may fit within the definition of a "lie detector" under the EPPA.

Furthermore, the narrow interpretation advanced by LaSalle removes many of the protections afforded by the EPPA. For instance, if an employer could tape record an interview with an employee, then turn around and analyze the tape recording with a voice stress analyzer, the EPPA's prohibition on the use of voice stress analyzers would be eviscerated. As the Supreme Court has stated, it is extremely unlikely that an interpretation that allows a statute to be so easily evaded would be the correct one.

Accordingly, we conclude that the EPPA's definition of "lie detector" does not, as a matter of law, exclude the use of the specific voice exemplar LaSalle requested Veazey to produce.

Our holding in this case does not mean that a tape recorder invariably must be considered a "lie detector" under the EPPA. A tape recorder would not fall within the statutory definition if it was not used in conjunction with another device that assists in the gauging of a person's truthfulness.

There is nothing in the EPPA or Veazey's complaint that excludes the possibility that the specific tape recording LaSalle requested qualifies as a lie detector test under the EPPA. Accordingly, we hold that it was improper for this case to have been dismissed for failure to state a claim under Rule 12(b)(6). We REVERSE the judgment of the district court and direct that this case be REMANDED for further proceedings consistent with this opinion.

Despite the fact that LaSalle Telecommunications, Inc. does not appear as a named party in the caption, the parties represent that LaSalle is properly identified as the defendant-appellee. Accordingly, we will refer to the defendant-appellee as LaSalle Telecommunications, Inc.

A voice exemplar is simply a recording of a person's utterances used to capture the physical properties of that person's voice.

Judgment for Veazey.

Case Commentary

The Seventh Circuit concluded that the use of a tape recorded conversation together with mandating that an employee provide a voice exemplar with which to compare it would fall within the umbrella of a lie-detector test, whose use is prohibited by the Employee Polygraph Protection Act.

Case Questions

1. Did the court make the correct judgment in this case?
2. Is a tape recorded conversation coupled with a voice exemplar really a form of a lie-detector test?
3. Should the Employee Polygraph Protection Act extend to Veazey in this case?

A polygraph test may also be administered to an employee against whom the employer has a reasonable suspicion for believing the employee is involved in a theft of property or information. The lie-detector test may be administered as part of an investigation. The employer must submit a signed statement setting forth the specific property misappropriated or the damage which may be caused by the transfer of the secret information, the access the employee had to the property or information, and why the employer believes the employee was involved in a theft.

When a polygraph test is administered, the questions must relate to the job and to general matters for the purpose of determining the subject's veracity. Questions about private personal matters unrelated to the business are not permitted.

EMPLOYMENT PERSPECTIVE

Linda Merrit applies for a job with Bull and Bear Securities Firm. The firm requires Linda to take a polygraph test. She consents. The questions include Linda's religious affiliation, political affiliation, beliefs on race relations, sex life, and labor unions. Linda feels very uncomfortable about divulging her answers to these private matters. Has Bull and Bear conducted the polygraph examination in accord with the Employee Polygraph Protection Act? No! Questions relating to these matters are prohibited by the Act. ■

POLYGRAPH LICENSING

The polygraph examiner must be licensed by the state if so required and must post a substantial bond of professional liability coverage. The examiner's conclusion must be derived solely from the polygraph charts and cannot be based on a subjective evaluation. The examiner can give no opinion on whether the employer should hire the person examined. Disclosure of the results of a polygraph may be given only to the employee, employer who commissioned the test, and a court, should the matter arise in the course of litigation. The pertinent provisions of the Employee Polygraph Protection Act must be conspicuously posted in the workplace.

DRUG TESTING

Businesses lose many billions of dollars each year because of employee drug use. Employees using drugs are less productive; the quality of their work is suspect because of impairment to their reasoning capabilities. Drug users may be negligent in the assembly of a product; the driving of a motor vehicle, train, or airplane; the security of documents, currency, office, or other real or personal property, and the preparation of food and beverages. The list goes on and on. Employee drug users may also steal from their company to support their drug habit. Employers wish to safeguard against abuses by drug users that could jeopardize the safety of the company, its employees, and its customers. To do so, many companies beef up security, increase supervision, create drug-rehabilitation programs, propagate the antidrug message, advocate a drug-free work environment through a written policy conspicuously posted in the workplace, and test for drugs.

FOURTH AMENDMENT

The use of drug testing is a volatile issue because of concern about privacy. The argument put forth against drug testing because it infringes on a person's privacy is based on the Fourth Amendment. The Fourth Amendment affords individuals the right to be secure in their person, property, and effects; individuals do not have to submit to unreasonable searches and seizures. Opponents of drug testing claim that mandating a person to turn over a sample of his or her urine is an infringement on the right of that person to be secure in his or her person, because the urine is then seized for the purpose of subjecting it to a search for illegal drug contaminants. Proponents of drug testing argue that the search and seizure is not unreasonable in light of the pervasiveness of employee theft.

SUSPICIONLESS DRUG TESTING

Suspicionless drug testing is permissible in those situations where the employee is working in a safety sensitive area. There may be no evidence of a drug problem, but the safety of those concerned would be jeopardized if the employer waited until a significant drug problem arose before implementing the drug test. The need to be drug free must clearly outweigh the employees' reasonable expectation of privacy.

The following is the first major drug testing case dealing with the right to a suspicionless search of employees' blood and urine samples.

SKINNER v. RAILWAY LABOR EXECUTIVES' ASSN.

489 U.S. 602 (1989)

JUSTICE KENNEDY delivered the opinion of the Court.

The Federal Railroad Safety Act of 1970 authorizes the Secretary of Transportation to "prescribe, as necessary, appropriate rules, regulations, orders, and standards for all areas of railroad safety." Finding that alcohol and drug abuse by railroad employees poses a serious threat to safety, the Federal Railroad Administration (FRA) has promulgated regulations that mandate blood and urine tests of employees who are involved in certain train accidents. The FRA also has adopted regulations that do not require, but do authorize, railroads to administer breath and urine tests to employees who violate certain safety rules. The question presented by this case is whether these regulations violate the Fourth Amendment.

I

A

The problem of alcohol use on American railroads is as old as the industry itself, and efforts to deter it by carrier rules began at least a century ago. For many years, railroads have prohibited operating employees from possessing alcohol or being intoxicated while on duty and from consuming alcoholic beverages while subject to being called for duty. More recently, these proscriptions have been expanded to forbid possession or use of certain drugs. These restrictions are embodied in "Rule G," an industry-wide operating rule promulgated by the Association of American Railroads, and enforced, in various formulations, by virtually every railroad in the country. The customary sanction for Rule G violations is dismissal.

Comments submitted in response to this request indicated that railroads were able to detect a relatively small number of Rule G viola-tions, owing, primarily, to their practice of relying on observation by supervisors and co-workers to enforce the rule. At the same time, "industry participants . . . confirmed that alcohol and drug use did occur on the railroads with unacceptable frequency," and available information from all sources "suggested that the problem included 'pockets' of drinking and drug use involving multiple crew members (before and during work), sporadic cases of individuals reporting to work impaired, and repeated drinking and drug use by individual employees who are chemically or psychologically dependent on those substances." "Even without the benefit of regular post-accident testing," the FRA "identified 34 fatalities, 66 injuries and over $28 million in property damage (in 1983 dollars) that resulted from the errors of alcohol and drug-impaired employees in 45 train accidents and train incidents during the period 1975 through 1983." Some of these accidents resulted in the release of hazardous materials and, in one case, the ensuing pollution required the evacuation of an entire Louisiana community. In view of the obvious safety hazards of drug and alcohol use by railroad employees, the FRA announced in June 1984 its intention to promulgate federal regulations on the subject.

B

After reviewing further comments from representatives of the railroad industry, labor groups, and the general public, the FRA, in 1985, promulgated regulations addressing the problem of alcohol and drugs on the railroads. The regulations prohibit covered employees from using or possessing alcohol or any controlled substance. The regulations further prohibit those employees from reporting for covered service while under the influence of, or impaired by, alcohol, while having a blood alcohol concentration of 0.04 or more, or while under the influence of, or impaired by, any controlled substance. The regulations do not restrict, however, a railroad's authority to impose an absolute prohibition on the presence of alcohol or any drug in the body fluids of persons in its employ, and, accordingly, they do not "replace Rule G or render it unenforceable."

To the extent pertinent here, two subparts of the regulations relate to testing. Subpart C, which is entitled "Post-Accident Toxicological Testing," is mandatory. It provides that railroads "shall take all practicable steps to assure that all covered employees of the railroad directly involved . . . provide blood and urine samples for toxicological testing by FRA," upon the occurrence of certain specified events. Toxicological testing is required following a "major train accident," which is defined as any train accident that involves (i) a fatality, (ii) the release of hazardous material accompanied by an evacuation or a reportable injury, or (iii) damage to railroad property of $500,000 or more. The railroad has the further duty of collecting blood and urine samples for testing after an "impact accident," which is defined as a collision that results in a reportable injury, or in damage to railroad property of $50,000 or more. Finally, the railroad is also obligated to test after "any train incident that involves a fatality to any on-duty railroad employee." After occurrence of an event which activates its duty to test, the railroad must transport all crew members and other covered employees directly involved in the accident or incident to an independent medical facility, where both blood and urine samples must be obtained from each employee. After the samples have been collected, the railroad is required to ship them by prepaid air freight to the FRA laboratory for analysis. There, the samples are analyzed using "state-of-the-art equipment and techniques" to detect and measure alcohol and drugs. The FRA proposes to place primary reliance on analysis of blood samples, as blood is "the only available body fluid . . . that can provide a clear indication not only of the presence of alcohol and drugs but also their current impairment effects." Urine samples are also necessary, however, because drug traces remain in the urine longer than in blood, and in some cases it will not be possible to transport employees to a medical facility before the time it takes for certain drugs to be eliminated from the blood-

stream. In those instances, a "positive urine test, taken with specific information on the pattern of elimination for the particular drug and other information on the behavior of the employee and the circumstances of the accident, may be crucial to the determination of" the cause of an accident. The regulations require that the FRA notify employees of the results of the tests and afford them an opportunity to respond in writing before preparation of any final investigative report. Employees who refuse to provide required blood or urine samples may not perform covered service for nine months, but they are entitled to a hearing concerning their refusal to take the test.

Respondents, the Railway Labor Executives' Association and various of its member labor organizations, brought the instant suit in the United States District Court for the Northern District of California, seeking to enjoin the FRA's regulations on various statutory and constitutional grounds. In a ruling from the bench, the District Court granted summary judgment in petitioners' favor. The court concluded that railroad employees "have a valid interest in the integrity of their own bodies" that deserved protection under the Fourth Amendment. The court held, however, that this interest was outweighed by the competing "public and governmental interest in the . . . promotion of . . . railway safety, safety for employees, and safety for the general public that is involved with the transportation." The District Court found respondents' other constitutional and statutory arguments meritless.

A divided panel of the Court of Appeals for the Ninth Circuit reversed.

We granted the federal parties' petition for a writ of certiorari, to consider whether the regulations invalidated by the Court of Appeals violate the Fourth Amendment. We now reverse.

II

The Fourth Amendment provides that "the right of the people to be secure in their persons, houses, papers, and effects, against unreasonable searches and seizures, shall not be violated . . . ." The Amendment guarantees the privacy, dignity, and security of persons against certain arbitrary and invasive acts by officers of the Government or those acting at their direction. Before we consider whether the tests in question are reasonable under the Fourth Amendment, we must inquire whether the tests are attributable to the Government or its agents, and whether they amount to searches or seizures. We turn to those matters.

A

We have long recognized that a "compelled intrusion into the body for blood to be analyzed for alcohol content" must be deemed a Fourth Amendment search.

The Government's interest in regulating the conduct of railroad employees to ensure safety, like its supervision of probationers or regulated industries, or its operation of a government office, school, or prison, "likewise presents 'special needs' beyond normal law enforcement that may justify departures from the usual warrant and probable-cause requirements." The hours of service employees covered by the FRA regulations include persons engaged in handling orders concerning train movements, operating crews, and those engaged in the maintenance and repair of signal systems. It is undisputed that these and other covered employees are engaged in safety-sensitive tasks.

Our cases indicate that even a search that may be performed without a warrant must be based, as a general matter, on probable cause to believe that the person to be searched has violated the law. When the balance of interests precludes insistence on a showing of probable cause, we have usually required "some quantum of individualized suspicion" before concluding that a search is reasonable. We make it clear, however, that a showing of individualized suspicion is not a constitutional floor, below which a search must be presumed unreasonable. In limited circumstances, where the privacy interests implicated by the search are minimal, and where an important governmental interest furthered by the intrusion would be placed in jeopardy by a requirement of individualized suspicion, a search may be reasonable despite the absence of such suspicion.

We believe this is true of the intrusions in question here.

More importantly, the expectations of privacy of covered employees are diminished by reason of their participation in an industry that is regulated pervasively to ensure safety, a goal dependent, in substantial part, on the health and fitness of covered employees. We conclude,

therefore, that the testing procedures contemplated by Subparts C and D pose only limited threats to the justifiable expectations of privacy of covered employees.

By contrast, the Government interest in testing without a showing of individualized suspicion is compelling. Employees subject to the tests discharge duties fraught with such risks of injury to others that even a momentary lapse of attention can have disastrous consequences.

While no procedure can identify all impaired employees with ease and perfect accuracy, the FRA regulations supply an effective means of deterring employees engaged in safety-sensitive tasks from using controlled substances or alcohol in the first place. The railroad industry's experience with Rule G persuasively shows, and common sense confirms, that the customary dismissal sanction that threatens employees who use drugs or alcohol while on duty cannot serve as an effective deterrent unless violators know that they are likely to be discovered. By ensuring that employees in safety-sensitive positions know they will be tested upon the occurrence of a triggering event, the timing of which no employee can predict with certainty, the regulations significantly increase the deterrent effect of the administrative penalties associated with the prohibited conduct, thereby increasing the likelihood that employees will forgo using drugs or alcohol while subject to being called for duty.

We conclude that the compelling Government interests served by the FRA's regulations would be significantly hindered if railroads were required to point to specific facts giving rise to a reasonable suspicion of impairment before testing a given employee. In view of our conclusion that, on the present record, the toxicological testing contemplated by the regulations is not an undue infringement on the justifiable expectations of privacy of covered employees, the Government's compelling interests outweigh privacy concerns.

In light of the limited discretion exercised by the railroad employers under the regulations, the surpassing safety interests served by toxicological tests in this context, and the diminished expectation of privacy that attaches to information pertaining to the fitness of covered employees, we believe that it is reasonable to conduct such tests in the absence of a warrant or reasonable suspicion that any particular employee may be impaired. We hold that the alcohol and drug tests contemplated by the FRA's regulations are reasonable within the meaning of the Fourth Amendment. The judgment of the Court of Appeals is accordingly reversed.

Judgment for Railway Labor Executives Assn.

JUSTICE MARSHALL, with whom JUSTICE BRENNAN joins, dissenting.

The issue in this case is not whether declaring a war on illegal drugs is good public policy. The importance of ridding our society of such drugs is, by now, apparent to all. Rather, the issue here is whether the Government's deployment in that war of a particularly Draconian weapon—the compulsory collection and chemical testing of railroad workers' blood and urine—comports with the Fourth Amendment. Precisely because the need for action against the drug scourge is manifest, the need for vigilance against unconstitutional excess is great. History teaches that grave threats to liberty often come in times of urgency, when constitutional rights seem too extravagant to endure.

In permitting the Government to force entire railroad crews to submit to invasive blood and urine tests, even when it lacks any evidence of drug or alcohol use or other wrongdoing, the majority today joins those shortsighted courts which have allowed basic constitutional rights to fall prey to momentary emergencies. The majority holds that the need of the Federal Railroad Administration (FRA) to deter and diagnose train accidents outweighs any "minimal" intru-sions on personal dignity and privacy posed by mass toxicological testing of persons who have given no indication whatsoever of impairment. In reaching this result, the majority ignores the text and doctrinal history of the Fourth Amendment, which require that highly intrusive searches of this type be based on probable cause, not on the evanescent cost-benefit calculations of agencies or judges.

The majority purports to limit its decision to postaccident testing of workers in "safety-sensitive" jobs, much as it limits its holding in the companion case to the testing of transferees to jobs involving drug interdiction or the use of firearms. But the damage done to the Fourth Amendment is not so easily cabined. The majority's acceptance of dragnet blood and urine testing ensures that the first, and worst, casualty of the war on drugs will be the precious liberties of our citizens. I therefore dissent.

For the reasons stated above, I find nothing minimal about the intrusion on individual liberty that occurs whenever the Government forcibly draws and analyzes a person's blood and urine. Several aspects of the FRA's testing program exacerbate the intrusiveness of these procedures. Most strikingly, the agency's regulations not only do not forbid, but, in fact, appear to invite criminal prosecutors to obtain the blood and urine samples drawn by the FRA and use them as the basis of criminal investigations and trials. This is an unprecedented invitation, leaving open the possibility of criminal prosecutions based on suspicionless searches of the human body.

Case Commentary

Justices Marshall and Brennan believe suspicionless searches contravene the Fourth Amendment prohibition against unreasonable searches and seizures. They believe a search must be based on probable cause. The majority agrees probable cause is necessary in criminal cases, but not in civil cases where public safety is at issue.

Case Questions

1. Are Justices Marshall and Brennan correct in this case?
2. Do you need probable cause in all cases?

3. Why are the dissenting justices opposed to suspicionless drug testing?
4. What are they afraid will happen?

In the following case, the issue is whether suspicionless drug testing of candidates for governor is permissible.

CHANDLER v. MILLER

520 U.S. 305 (1997)

JUSTICE GINSBURG delivered the opinion of the Court.

The Fourth Amendment requires government to respect "the right of the people to be secure in their persons . . . against unreasonable searches and seizures." This restraint on government conduct generally bars officials from undertaking a search or seizure absent individualized suspicion. Searches conducted without grounds for suspicion of particular individuals have been upheld, however, in "certain limited circumstances." These circumstances include brief stops for questioning or observation at a fixed Border Patrol checkpoint, or at a sobriety checkpoint, and administrative inspections in "closely regulated" businesses.

Georgia requires candidates for designated state offices to certify that they have taken a drug test and that the test result was negative. We confront in this case the question whether that requirement ranks among the limited circumstances in which suspicionless searches are warranted. Relying on this Court's precedents sustaining drug testing programs for student athletes, customs employees, and railway employees, the United States Court of Appeals for the Eleventh Circuit judged Georgia's law constitutional. We reverse that judgment. Georgia's requirement that candidates for state office pass a drug test, we hold, does not fit within the closely guarded category of constitutionally permissible suspicionless searches.

The prescription at issue, approved by the Georgia Legislature in 1990, orders that "each candidate seeking to qualify for nomination or election to a state office shall as a condition of such qualification be required to certify that such candidate has tested negative for illegal drugs." Georgia was the first, and apparently remains the only, State to condition candidacy for state office on a drug test.

Under the Georgia statute, to qualify for a place on the ballot, a candidate must present a certificate from a state approved laboratory, in a form approved by the Secretary of State, reporting that the candidate submitted to a urinalysis drug test within 30 days prior to qualifying for nomination or election and that the results were negative. The statute lists as "illegal drugs": marijuana, cocaine, opiates, amphetamines, and phencyclidines. The designated state offices are: "the Governor, Lieutenant Governor, Secretary of State, Attorney General, State School Superintendent, Commissioner of Insurance, Commissioner of Agriculture, Commissioner of Labor, Justices of the Supreme Court, Judges of the Court of Appeals, judges of the superior courts, district attorneys, members of the General Assembly, and members of the Public Service Commission."

Candidate drug tests are to be administered in a manner consistent with the United States Department of Health and Human Services Guidelines, or other professionally valid procedures approved by Georgia's Commissioner of Human Resources. A candidate may provide the test specimen at a laboratory approved by the State, or at the office of the candidate's personal physician. Once a urine sample is obtained, an approved laboratory determines whether any of the five specified illegal drugs are present, and prepares a certificate reporting the test results to the candidate.

Petitioners were Libertarian Party nominees in 1994 for state offices. The Party nominated Walker L. Chandler for the office of Lieutenant Governor, Sharon T. Harris for the office of Commissioner of Agriculture, and James D. Walker for the office of member of the General Assembly. In May 1994, about one month before the deadline for submission of the certificates required by sect;21-2-140, petitioners Chandler, Harris, and Walker filed this action in the United States District Court for the Northern District of Georgia. They asserted that the drug tests required by sect;21-2-140 violated their rights under the First, Fourth, and Fourteenth Amendments to the United States Constitution. Naming as defendants Governor Zell D. Miller and two other state officials involved in the administration of sect;21-2-140, petitioners requested declaratory and injunctive relief barring enforcement of the statute.

In June 1994, the District Court denied petitioners' motion for a preliminary injunction. Stressing the importance of the state offices sought and the relative unintrusiveness of the testing procedure, the court found it unlikely that petitioners would prevail on the merits of their claims. Petitioners apparently submitted to the drug tests, obtained the certificates required by sect;21-2-140, and appeared on the ballot. After the 1994 election, the parties jointly moved for the entry of final judgment on stipulated facts. In January 1995, the District Court entered final judgment for respondents.

A divided Eleventh Circuit panel affirmed. It is settled law, the court accepted, that the drug tests required by the statute rank as searches. We granted the petition for certiorari and now reverse.

To be reasonable under the Fourth Amendment, a search ordinarily must be based on individualized suspicion of wrongdoing. But particularized exceptions to the main rule are sometimes warranted based on "special needs, beyond the normal need for law enforcement." When such "special needs"—concerns other than crime detection—are alleged in justification of a Fourth Amendment intrusion, courts must undertake a context specific inquiry, examining closely the competing private and public interests advanced by the parties. "In limited circumstances, where the privacy interests implicated by the search are minimal, and where an important governmental interest furthered by the intrusion would be placed in jeopardy by a requirement of individualized suspicion, a search may be reasonable despite the absence of such suspicion." In evaluating Georgia's ballot access, drug testing statute—a measure plainly not tied to individualized suspicion—the Eleventh Circuit sought to " 'balance the individual's privacy expectations against the State's interests,' " in line with our precedents most immediately in point: *Skinner,* *Von Raab,* and *Vernonia.* We review those decisions before inspecting Georgia's law.

In *Von Raab,* the Court sustained a United States Customs Service program that made drug tests a condition of promotion or transfer to positions directly involving drug interdiction or requiring the employee to carry a firearm. While the Service's regime was not prompted by a demonstrated drug abuse problem, it was developed for an agency with an "almost unique mission," as the "first line of defense" against the smuggling of illicit drugs into the United States. Work directly involving drug interdiction and posts that require the employee to carry a firearm pose grave safety threats to employees who hold those positions, and also expose them to large amounts of illegal narcotics and to persons engaged in crime; illicit drug users in such high risk positions might be unsympathetic to the Service's mission, tempted by bribes, or even threatened with blackmail. The Court held that the government had a "compelling" interest in assuring that employees placed in these positions would not include drug users. Individualized suspicion would not work in this setting, the Court determined, because it was "not feasible to subject these employees and their work product to the kind of day to day scrutiny that is the norm in more traditional office environments."

Finally, in *Vernonia,* the Court sustained a random drug testing program for high school students engaged in interscholastic athletic competitions. The program's context was critical, for local governments bear large "responsibilities, under a public school system, as guardian and tutor of children entrusted to its care." An "immediate crisis," caused by "a sharp increase in drug use" in the school district, sparked installation of the program. District Court findings established that student athletes were not only "among the drug users," they were "leaders of the drug culture." Our decision noted that " 'students within the school environment have a lesser expectation of privacy than members of the population generally.' " We emphasized the importance of deterring drug use by schoolchildren and the risk of injury a drug using student athlete cast on himself and those engaged with him on the playing field.

Turning to those guides, we note, first, that the testing method the Georgia statute describes is relatively noninvasive; therefore, if the "special need" showing had been made, the State could not be faulted for excessive intrusion. Georgia's

statute invokes the drug testing guidelines applicable to the federal programs upheld in *Skinner* and *Von Raab*. The State permits a candidate to provide the urine specimen in the office of his or her private physician; and the results of the test are given first to the candidate, who controls further dissemination of the report. Because the State has effectively limited the invasiveness of the testing procedure, we concentrate on the core issue: Is the certification requirement warranted by a special need?

Our precedents establish that the proffered special need for drug testing must be substantial—important enough to override the individual's acknowledged privacy interest, sufficiently vital to suppress the Fourth Amendment's normal requirement of individualized suspicion. Georgia has failed to show a special need of that kind.

The statute was not enacted in response to any fear or suspicion of drug use by state officials:

"QUESTION: Is there any indication anywhere in this record that Georgia has a particular problem here with State officeholders being drug abusers?

"COUNSEL FOR RESPONDENTS: No, there is no such evidence. . . . and to be frank, there is no such problem as we sit here today."

A demonstrated problem of drug abuse, while not in all cases necessary to the validity of a testing regime would shore up an assertion of special need for a suspicionless general search program. Proof of unlawful drug use may help to clarify—and to substantiate—the precise hazards posed by such use. Thus, the evidence of drug and alcohol use by railway employees engaged in safety sensitive tasks in *Skinner,* and the immediate crisis prompted by a sharp rise in students' use of unlawful drugs in *Vernonia,* bolstered the government's and school officials' arguments that drug testing programs were warranted and appropriate.

In contrast to the effective testing regimes upheld in *Skinner, Von Raab,* and *Vernonia,* Georgia's certification requirement is not well designed to identify candidates who violate antidrug laws. Nor is the scheme a credible means to deter illicit drug users from seeking election to state office. The test date—to be scheduled by the candidate anytime within 30 days prior to qualifying for a place on the ballot—is no secret. As counsel for respondents acknowledged at oral argument, users of illegal drugs, save for those prohibitively addicted, could abstain for a pretest period sufficient to avoid detection. Moreover, respondents have offered no reason why ordinary law enforcement methods would not suffice to apprehend such addicted individuals, should they appear in the limelight of a public stage. Section 21-2-140, in short, is not needed and cannot work to ferret out lawbreakers, and respondents barely attempt to support the statute on that ground.

What is left, after close review of Georgia's scheme, is the image the State seeks to project. By requiring candidates for public office to submit to drug testing, Georgia displays its commitment to the struggle against drug abuse. The suspicionless tests, according to respondents, signify that candidates, if elected, will be fit to serve their constituents free from the influence of illegal drugs. But Georgia asserts no evidence of a drug problem among the State's elected officials, those officials typically do not perform high risk, safety sensitive tasks, and the required certification immediately aids no interdiction effort. The need revealed, in short, is symbolic, not "special," as that term draws meaning from our case law.

However well meant, the candidate drug test Georgia has devised diminishes personal privacy for a symbol's sake. The Fourth Amendment shields society against that state action.

We reiterate, too, that where the risk to public safety is substantial and real, blanket suspicionless searches calibrated to the risk may rank as "reasonable"—for example, searches now routine at airports and at entrances to courts and other official buildings. But where, as in this case, public safety is not genuinely in jeopardy, the Fourth Amendment precludes the suspicionless search, no matter how conveniently arranged.

For the reasons stated,
the judgment of the Court of Appeals
for the Eleventh Circuit is *Reversed.*

Case Commentary

This case appears to be at odds with the Sixth Circuit decision in the Knox County Association case. In that case, a suspicionless search of school teachers and administrators was justified because of their influence and supervision of children. Here, the Supreme Court appears to

believe the public safety is not in jeopardy. But, the governor has authority over the state police and national guard within the state. Applying the Supreme Court's reasoning to the Knox case would probably lead to a different result.

Case Questions

1. Is the Supreme Court correct that the public safety would not be endangered if the governor was a drug user?
2. What is the appropriate criteria in deciding whether to implement suspicionless drug testing?
3. In what occupations do you believe suspicionless drug testing is warranted?
4. Why did the Sixth Circuit in Knox render a decision that appears to be in conflict with this Supreme Court decision?
5. Can the Knox case be distinguished from this case?

REASONABLE SUSPICION DRUG TESTING

When applying the Fourth Amendment, there must be probable cause to believe that the person committed a crime before a warrant will be issued to conduct a search. The standard for reasonable suspicion drug testing is less strict. It may be justified when an employer can document its reasonable suspicion. Suspicion-based drug testing requires that an employer must have a reasonable suspicion that the employee is using drugs before a drug test can be required. A reasonable suspicion exists where a rational inference can be drawn from the facts and circumstances in the employment. Suspicion-based drug testing may be undertaken at any time during the worker's employment upon the satisfaction of the following criteria: reasonable suspicion that the employee is selling or using drugs; is in possession of drugs or alcohol at the workplace; is working under the influence of drugs or alcohol; is exhibiting significant behavioral changes that may be related to the use of drugs or alcohol; is engaging in criminal activity with a connection to the sale or use of drugs or alcohol; or is involved in an accident while operating in an impaired state. The employer must document in writing the circumstances that formed the basis for the reasonable suspicion that led to the requirement of the drug testing. The sources of information must be credible. The legitimate interests of the employer are balanced against the intrusion on an individual's physical solitude. In those cases where random drug testing has been found permissible, the need must overwhelmingly outweigh the unwanted invasion of privacy.

EMPLOYMENT PERSPECTIVE

Victory College's administrators are arch conservatives who abhor the use of drugs and alcohol. The college institutes a policy that all faculty and staff submit to drug testing at the beginning of each semester. The faculty and staff claim the drug testing is an invasion of their privacy and that the invasion of privacy is not outweighed by the college's need to know. Who will win? Most likely the faculty and staff. While the use of drugs always impairs an employee's ability to function, the implementation of a drug testing program will be allowed where the safety of the public or the security of the workplace is at issue. The college has not shown this to be the case. ■

One day, while visiting the store's restroom, Mark smelled a sweet, pungent odor. He surmised it must be marijuana. As a result, he and Tom decided to implement random drug testing of all workers. However, before acting impulsively this time, they sought Susan's counsel. Susan stated that L&S would have to show a compelling need to drug test. Employee morale and trust might be compromised. There is no widespread drug use among L&S's employees. It is even possible that a customer smoked pot in the restroom. L&S might be making a big deal over an insignificant problem. Susan advises that it would be preferable to evaluate each employee on his or her merits. If drug use is affecting a worker's job performance, then L&S can require the employee to participate in a drug rehabilitation program or terminate the worker. In addition, L&S can admonish all employees against using drugs or alcohol while at work.

The issue in the following case is whether schoolteachers should be subject to a suspicionless search of their urine for drugs upon being offered a teaching position and a suspicion-based search of their urine at any time during their employment if they are using or selling drugs, because their position of looking after the well-being of children is safety sensitive.

CASE

KNOX COUNTY EDUCATION ASSOCIATION v. KNOX COUNTY BOARD OF EDUCATION

158 F.3d 361 (6th Cir. 1998)

ROSEN, District Judge.

BACKGROUND

Plaintiff Knox County Education Association ("KCEA"), which represents professional employees in the Knox County School System, initiated this action to challenge drug and alcohol testing procedures adopted by Defendant Knox County Board of Education ("Board"), which is the body responsible for the administration, management, and control of the Knox County School System. In the District Court, KCEA made a facial attack on the Board's "Drug-Free Workplace Substance Abuse Policy," seeking declaratory and injunctive relief. The policy establishes two different levels of testing: (1) suspicionless drug testing for all individuals who apply for, transfer to, or are promoted to, "safety sensitive" positions within the Knox County School system, including teaching positions; and (2) "reasonable suspicion" drug and/or alcohol testing of all school employees. KCEA challenged both testing programs as violative of the Fourth Amendment's prohibition against unreasonable searches and seizures.

The matter was tried on November 12, 1996. In an Opinion and Order dated March 4, 1997, the District Court found that the Board's drug testing policy violated the Fourth Amendment to the extent that (1) it permitted any suspicionless drug testing; and (2) in the manner by which it permitted alcohol testing upon reasonable suspicion. The District Court enjoined the Board from further implementation and enforcement of those sections of the Policy, and found the remainder of the policy facially valid.

This matter is now before the Court on the cross-appeals of the parties.

III. Facts

Thirty-two hundred teachers are employed in the Knox County Schools.

1994 Drug Testing Policy

On June 1, 1994, in response to Judge Jordan's decision, the Board of Education met in regular session and voted to adopt the "Drug-Free Workplace Substance Abuse Policy" for implementation in the Knox County School system. As adopted, the Policy establishes a comprehensive drug and alcohol testing program for the Board of Education's employees. The Policy notes that the Federal Anti-Drug Act, 41 U.S.C. § 702, requires federal grant recipients, such as the Board, to establish a drug-free workplace. The Policy describes its goals and objectives as follows:

1. To establish, promote, and maintain a safe, healthy, working and learning environment for employees and students.
2. To aid the affected employee in locating a rehabilitation program for employees with self-admitted or detected substance abuse problem.
3. To promote the reputation of the Knox County School System and its employees as responsible citizens of public trust and employment.
4. To eliminate substance abuse problems in the workplace.
5. To aid in the reduction of absenteeism, tardiness, and apathetic job performance.
6. To provide a clear standard of job performance for Knox County Schools employees.

7. To provide a consistent model of substance-free behavior for students.

The Policy divides the tested employees into two distinct groups: (1) those who may be the subject of suspicionless testing (those who may be tested pre-employment for "safety sensitive" positions, pre-transfer for "safety sensitive" positions, and upon return to duty after undergoing rehabilitation); and (2) those who may be tested for reasonable suspicion of drug or alcohol impairment while at work (all employees). The substance abuse policy prohibits any Board of Education employee from being under the influence of an illegal drug or alcohol while on duty, on Knox County Board of Education property, or in attendance at a System-approved or school-related function.

1. Suspicionless Testing The Policy allows suspicionless testing for people applying for positions that are "safety sensitive." The Policy defines "safety sensitive" positions as those positions "where a single mistake by such employee can create an immediate threat of serious harm to students and fellow employees." According to the Policy, and consistent with the ruling in KCEA I, this category includes principals, assistant principals, teachers, traveling teachers, teacher aides, substitute teachers, school secretaries and school bus drivers.

Applicants for these positions are tested after they are offered a job but before their employment has commenced (i.e., post-offer, pre-employment). They are to be given a copy of the Policy in advance of the physical and are to sign an acknowledgment prior to substance screening, permitting the summary result to be transmitted to the Medical Review Officer ("MRO") and Director of Personnel. An applicant refusing to complete any part of the drug testing procedure will not be considered a valid candidate for employment with the school system, and such refusal will be considered as a withdrawal of the individual's application for employment. If substance screening shows a confirmed positive result for which there is no current physician's prescription, a second confirming test may be requested by the MRO. If the first or any requested second confirming test is positive, any job offer will be revoked.

Current employees attempting to transfer into safety sensitive positions—including those who already hold such positions—are also tested. Employees who test positive for illegal drugs on a promotion/transfer test will no longer be considered an applicant for that position. Employees seeking a transfer or promotion who refuse any portion of the drug testing procedure forfeit the opportunity to transfer to, or advance into, a safety sensitive position and are subject to discipline for insubordination (including termination).

2. Reasonable Suspicion Testing   Section .05 of the Policy provides for drug and/or alcohol screening based upon reasonable suspicion as follows:

Whenever the Knox County Board of Education, through its Director of Personnel or the person authorized to act as the Director in the Director's absence, and/or the Medical Review Officer, reasonably suspects that an employee's work performance or on-the-job behavior may have been affected in any way by illegal drugs or alcohol, or that an employee has otherwise violated the Knox County Board of Education Drug-Free Workplace Substance Abuse Policy, the employee may be required to submit a breath and/or urine sample for drug and alcohol testing. When a supervisor observes or is notified of behavior or events that lead the supervisor to believe that the employee is in violation of the Drug-Free Workplace Substance Abuse Policy, the Supervisor should notify the Director of Personnel.

An employee who is required to submit to drug/alcohol testing based upon such reasonable suspicion and refuses will be charged with insubordination and subject to the disciplinary sanctions, including possible termination.

Further, an employee testing positive on a reasonable suspicion test will be found to be in violation of the Policy, and such a violation will constitute grounds for termination. The Policy notes that the School System Director of Personnel, or the person authorized to act in that person's absence, or the MRO are the only individuals in the Knox County School System authorized to make a determination that reasonable suspicion, or cause, exists to order a drug screen, and are the only individuals in the School System who may order an employee to submit to a drug screen.

The Policy describes two types of cases for which the reasonable suspicion procedures may be invoked:

(1) Chronic case

Deteriorating job performance or changes in personal traits characteristics where the use of alcohol or drugs may be reasonably suspected as the cause. These cases may develop over a fairly long period of time.

(2) Acute case

Appearing in a specific incident or observation to then be under the present influence of alcohol and/or drugs is reasonably suspected to be a contributing cause. Regardless of previous history, immediate action is necessary.

The Policy further enumerates the circumstances under which substance screening may be considered, which include, but are not limited to, the following:

1. Observed use, possession, or sale of illegal drugs and/or use, possession, sale, or abuse of alcohol and/or the illegal use or sale of prescription drugs.
2. Apparent physical state of impairment of motor functions.
3. Marked changes in personal behavior not attributable to other factors.
4. Employee involvement in or contribution to an accident where the use of alcohol or drugs is reasonably suspected or employee involvement in a pattern of repetitive accidents, whether or not they involve actual or potential injury.
5. Violations of criminal drug law statutes involving the use of illegal drugs, alcohol, or prescription drugs and/or violations of drug statutes.

The above circumstances under which substance screening may be considered "are strictly limited in time and place to employee conduct on duty or during work hours, or on or in Knox County Board of Education property, or at school system-approved or school related functions."

3. Testing Procedures   Section .11 of the Policy describes the drug and alcohol abuse testing procedures. The Board has designated a physician as the MRO. The MRO is responsible for reviewing the results of drug tests before they are reported to the Board's Director of Personnel; reviewing and interpreting each confirmed positive test to determine if there is an alternative medical explanation for the positive result; conducting an interview with the individual testing positive;

reviewing the individual's medical history and medical records to determine if the positive result was caused by legally prescribed medication; requiring re-test of the original specimen if the MRO deems it necessary; and verifying that the laboratory report and the specimen are correct. The MRO is expected to follow the Medical Review Officer's Manual published by the U.S. Department of Health and Human Services. However, if the MRO determines that there is a legitimate medical explanation for the positive test other than the use of a prohibited drug, the MRO will conclude that the test is negative and take no further action. If the MRO concludes that a particular test is scientifically insufficient, the MRO will conclude that the test is negative for that individual. If the MRO determines that there is no legitimate explanation for the positive test other than the use of a prohibited drug, the MRO will communicate the test results as positive to the Director of Personnel.

In the case of drug testing, urine specimens are to be collected in accordance with Department of Transportation Workplace Testing Programs with some exceptions. Procedures for collecting urine specimens shall allow privacy unless there is reason to believe that a particular individual may alter or substitute the specimen. The initial test performed on the urine at the laboratory will be an Enzyme-Multiplied Immunoassay Technique (EMIT) screen which will be used to eliminate negative urine specimens from further consideration. All specimens identified as positive on the initial test will then be confirmed using gas chromatography/mass spectrometry (GC/MS) techniques.

With respect to the alcohol testing procedures, the Policy provides only that the Knox County Sheriff's Department will be requested to perform, and will be responsible for administering, a breath analysis test. If the breath analysis test is positive, a second breath analysis may be taken. The breath analysis test level to be considered positive will be .02. The alcohol urinalysis will be an EMIT screen followed by confirmatory gas chromatography tests on positive screens. Either test will be considered positive if the results are .04 or more. In contrast to the D.O.T. procedures—which contain detailed regulations concerning training for individuals who administer breathalyzers, standards for breathalyzer machines, and standards for administering

the initial test—the Policy provides few guidelines regarding the administration of a breathalyzer test.

Procedurally, the Policy describes the reasonable suspicion testing as follows:

Once the determination has been made that an employee is to be tested based upon reasonable suspicion, the Director of Personnel should then transport the employee to the collection site, or make other appropriate arrangements for transportation. The collection site personnel should be notified that the reason for testing is reasonable suspicion.

Upon arriving at the collection site, the employee will be asked to sign a release for testing and to assist in completing the necessary forms for testing. After the employee has signed the necessary releases for testing, then the standard procedures for drug and alcohol testing should be followed by the collection site personnel.

Once the procedure has been completed, the employee should be transported back to the Director of Personnel's office where the employee will be placed on administrative leave with pay until the results of the tests are available and given instruction to call the Director of Personnel each work day, before the normal reporting time for that employee, for further instructions.

If the employee refuses to sign the release or refuses to be tested by NPL, the employee should be advised that refusal under the Board Policy is insubordination. If the employee continues to refuse, the employee should be transported back to the Director of Personnel's office. The Director of Personnel will place the employee on administrative leave with pay with instructions to call his/her office before the normal reporting time for that employee on the following work day.

If Director of Personnel feels that the employee is in no condition to operate a vehicle, then the employee should be transported home. In the event of positive test results, the MRO will contact the Director of Personnel who will then review other records of the employee and contact the Knox County Law Director to work out proper disciplinary procedures. The Policy recognizes that information regarding an individual's drug testing results is confidential and "will be released by the MRO and the Director of Personnel only upon the written consent of the individual, except the results may be released and relied upon by the Knox County Board of Education in any administrative or court action by the employee involving the drug test, or any discipline resulting from a violation of this policy, including employment and court proceedings." The Policy further provides that the substance screens will be maintained by the MRO in a secure fashion and disclosed to the Director of Personnel only to the extent necessary to address any work-related safety risks occasioned by either the drug or alcohol use. All personnel records and information regarding referral, evaluation, substance screen results, and treatment are to be maintained in a confidential manner and no entries concerning such will be placed in the employee's personnel file. In effect, two separate files will be maintained: one with the MRO indicating the results of the substance abuse tests and another maintained as part of the employee's personnel record.

Since the Board instituted its initial drug testing in December of 1989, four individuals have tested positive for drug/alcohol use: two teachers, one teacher applicant, and one employee in a non-safety-sensitive position. Three of those individuals were subject to drug testing on the basis of reasonable suspicion, and the other was subject to suspicionless pre-employment drug testing.

Balancing the intrusion on privacy that resulted from suspicionless testing against the state's interest in such testing, the District Court concluded that the balance tilted heavily in favor of individual privacy interests. Thus, the District Court held that the suspicionless testing program violated the Fourth Amendment.

Reasonable Suspicion Testing

The District Court ruled that the reasonable suspicion drug testing program was constitutional but that the reasonable suspicion alcohol testing program was constitutionally flawed.

ANALYSIS

The Fourth Amendment safeguards the privacy of individuals against arbitrary and unwarranted governmental intrusions by providing that "the right of the people to be secure in their persons, houses, papers, and effects against unreasonable searches and seizures, shall not be violated." However, "the Fourth Amendment does not proscribe all search-

es and seizures, but only those that are unreasonable." It is now well-settled that drug testing which utilizes urinalysis is a "search" that falls within the ambit of the Fourth Amendment

A. Suspicionless Testing As a general rule, in order to be reasonable, a search must be undertaken pursuant to a warrant issued upon a showing of probable cause. ("Except in certain well-defined circumstances, a search or seizure in such a case is not reasonable unless it is accomplished pursuant to a judicial warrant issued upon probable cause."). That is, a valid search must ordinarily be based on an "individualized suspicion of wrongdoing." But particularized exceptions to the main rule are sometimes warranted based on "special needs, beyond the normal need for law enforcement." When such "special needs"—concerns other than crime detection—are alleged in justification of a Fourth Amendment intrusion, courts must undertake a context-specific inquiry, examining closely the competing private and public interests advanced by the parties. Thus, where a Fourth Amendment intrusion serves special needs, "it is necessary to balance the individual's privacy expectations against the Government's interests to determine whether it is impractical to require a warrant or some level of individualized suspicion in the particular context." Quite simply, then, in evaluating the constitutionality of the Board's drug testing Policy here, we must balance the government's (or public's) interest in testing against the individual's privacy interest.

1. Public Interest in Testing With regard to the government's interest in testing, the Supreme Court has traditionally focused its analysis on two central factors: (1) whether the group of people targeted for testing exhibits a pronounced drug problem; and, if not, whether the group occupies a unique position such that the existence of a pronounced drug problem is unnecessary to justify suspicionless testing; and (2) the magnitude of the harm that could result from the use of illicit drugs on the job.

Thus, as would be expected when using a balancing test, in cases in which a pronounced drug problem exists within the target group, a drug testing regime has a higher likelihood of being deemed constitutional because the more pernicious the drug problem is, the greater the public's interest is in abridging it.

In this case, there is little, if any, evidence of a pronounced drug or alcohol abuse problem among Knox County's teachers or other professional employees. Specifically, there is no empirical or historical evidence of an ongoing abuse problem or evidence of a newly blossoming epidemic of abuse. In fact, since the Policy was implemented in 1989, only one prospective hire has failed the suspicionless drug test. In short, although the record evidence does not reflect that the Knox County District school teachers and other such officials have a track record of a pronounced drug problem, the suspicionless testing regime is justified by the unique role they play in the lives of school children and the *in loco parentis* obligations imposed upon them.

The second factor we must consider in the balancing test analysis focuses on the magnitude of harm that could result from the use of illicit drugs in any given set of circumstances. The validity of this argument hinges in large part upon whether or not teachers, principals, and the other school officials covered by the testing actually occupy "safety-sensitive" positions.

Although the position of school teacher may not fit neatly into the prototypical "safety-sensitive" position, we do not read the definition of "safety-sensitive" so narrowly as to preclude application to a group of professionals to whom we entrust young children for a prolonged period of time on a daily basis. Simple common sense and experience with life tells us "that even a momentary lapse of attention can have disastrous consequences," particularly if that inattention or lapse were to come at an inopportune moment. For example, young children could cause harm to themselves or others while playing at recess, eating lunch in the cafeteria (if for example, they began choking), or simply while horsing around with each other. Children, especially younger children, are active, unpredictable, and in need of constant attention and supervision. Even momentary inattention or delay in dealing with a potentially dangerous or emergency situation could have grievous consequences.

This is equally true of teaching at the high school level. Not only must teachers observe and report drug use, but they are also charged, by law, with reporting assaults as well: "every teacher observing or otherwise having knowledge of an assault and battery or vandalism endangering life, health or safety committed by a student on school property shall report such action immediately to the principal of the school." Fifty such incidents occurred in Knox County schools in the 1995–96 school year, and 77 in the 1994–95 school year.

The Court believes that a local school district has a strong and abiding interest in requiring that teachers and other school officials be drug-free so that they can satisfy their statutory obligation to insure the safety and welfare of the children. The fact that the Board has not been able to cite any one specific example in which a teacher or other employee responsible for children has allowed any harm to the children by being in an impaired condition while on the job is certainly not dispositive of the question of whether teachers and administrators hold "safety-sensitive" positions. We do not believe that the Board must wait passively for a disaster to occur before taking preemptive action to minimize the risks of such an occurrence. Indeed, we have no doubt that if a tragedy were to befall one or more of the school children of Knox County that in some manner implicated a teacher or administrator being under the influence of an illegal substance, the members of that community would rightly question why the Board had not taken all efforts possible in advance to prevent such an occurrence.

2. Privacy Interest of Employees   Having ruled that the public interest in suspicionless testing is very strong, an analysis of the employee's privacy rights is necessary to determine which of the competing values should prevail in this case. As will become evident in the course of this analysis, because teachers' legitimate expectation of privacy is diminished by their participation in a heavily regulated industry and by the nature of their job, the public interest in suspicionless testing outweighs that private interest.

The tests screen for the following drugs: marijuana, cocaine, phencyclidine, amphetamines, methamphetamine, phenobarbital, secobarbital, amobarbital, butalbital, pentobarbital, propoxyphene, methadone, morphine, codeine, monacetilmorphine, and benzodiazepines. In this respect, the Policy departs from D.O.T. procedures, which allow testing for five (but effectively seven) of these eighteen drugs. The five drugs tested for under the D.O.T. guidelines are classified as Schedule I, II, or III drugs under the Controlled Substances Act, whereas the remaining drugs for which Defendant screens include Schedule IV and V drugs, i.e., drugs that have an accepted medical use and a lower potential for abuse. The additional drugs for which Defendant screens can be found in medications such as Robitusson A-C and Robitusson DAC (used to treat chest colds); Axocet, Egsic-Plus, Fiorinal, Fioricet, and Sedapap (used to treat tension headaches); Arco-Lase Plus and Donnatal (used to relieve gastrointestinal disorders); Bellergal (used to treat menopausal disorders); Quadrinal (used to treat asthma and chronic bronchitis); and Valium and Dizac (used to treat stress).

Under the relevant Supreme Court precedents discussed above, the expectation of privacy associated with not submitting to a drug test may be diminished if the employee participates in a heavily regulated industry.

For all of the reasons stated here, we believe that the privacy interest for the employees not to be tested is significantly diminished by the level of regulation of their jobs and by the nature of the work itself. The ultimate inquiry before the Court is whether the search at issue here—the one-time, suspicionless testing of people hired to serve in teaching and administrative positions—is reasonable. On balance, the public interest in attempting to ensure that school teachers perform their jobs unimpaired is evident, considering their unique *in loco parentis* obligations and their immense influence over students. These public interests clearly outweigh the privacy interests of the teacher not to be tested because the drug-testing regime adopted by Knox County is circumscribed, narrowly-tailored, and not overly intrusive, either in its monitoring procedures or in its disclosure requirements. This is particularly so because it is a one-time test, with advance notice and with no random testing component, and because the school system in which the employees work is heavily regulated, particularly as to drug usage.

Therefore, we REVERSE the District Court's finding this portion of the statute unconstitutional.

B. Suspicion-Based Testing   The Court now turns to the suspicion-based testing, and finds that this portion of the Policy is also constitutional under the Fourth Amendment.

1. Drug Testing   The Policy provides for testing of an employee if the Director of Personnel "reasonably suspects" that an employee's work performance or on-the-job behavior may have been affected by illegal drugs or alcohol. The Policy further enumerates the circumstances under which substance screening may be considered.

These requirements of "reasonable cause" sufficiently limit the discretion of the officials administering the rule and, because the testing is clearly based upon a finding of individualized suspicion, this portion of the Policy comports with the reasonableness requirement of the Fourth Amendment. Thus, for these reasons and those identified by the District Court, we **AFFIRM** the District Court's ruling on this aspect of the suspicion-based testing program.

2. Alcohol Testing   As the District Court noted, the record does not contain any evidence regarding whether the broad range of the alcohol testing and particularly the low threshold is reasonably related to the purpose of the testing, nor does it indicate the amount and timing of consumption that would result in that low level reading. Therefore, it is unclear from the record why the Board believes impairment at the relatively low .02 level is significant, and how that level is related to the purpose of the testing. It may be that there is no such nexus and, if this is so, this portion of the Policy is indeed unconstitutional. However, we cannot conclude that from this record (just as we cannot conclude that there is some relationship between the nature of the test and levels established and the identified need for testing). Therefore, the issue of whether this portion of the test is constitutional is REVERSED AND REMANDED to the District Court to determine whether the .02 level is reasonably related to the purpose of the testing.

VII. CONCLUSION

Therefore, for the reasons stated, The District Court's ruling as to the suspicionless testing portion of the Policy is REVERSED. The District Court's ruling as to the suspicion-based portion of the Policy is AFFIRMED, except regarding the issue of whether the alcohol testing is constitutional, which is REVERSED AND RE-MANDED for proceedings not inconsistent with this opinion.

Case Commentary

The Sixth Circuit decided that suspicionless testing is reasonable when individuals are hired for teaching or administrative positions. The Court came to this conclusion even though drug use was not a widespread problem among teachers and staff. The decision is based on the influence teachers have and the supervisory role they play in the lives of their students. Other courts may differ as to the result.

Case Questions

1. Does the teacher's position alone justify drug testing?
2. Should widespread drug use among teachers be required before drug testing is permitted?
3. Does the level set for alcohol consumption bear any relationship to impairment?
4. Why did the Sixth Circuit in *Knox* render a decision that appears to be in conflict with the Supreme Court decision in *Chandler?*
5. Can this case be distinguished from the *Chandler* case?

The question presented in the following case is whether the disclosure of the results of a drug test taken while the employee was in a hospital giving birth is an invasion of privacy. The employee lost her job as a result.

CASE

KRUSE v. STATE OF HAWAII

68 F.3d 331 (9th Cir. 1995)

PREGERSON, Circuit Judge.
Plaintiffs-Appellants, Sue Kruse and Lance Caspary, filed a 42 U.S.C. Section 1983 action in state court against the State of Hawaii and employees of Hawaii's Department of Human Services ("DHS") for allegedly violating their various rights under the U.S. Constitution and state law. The State removed the case to federal court. The district court granted the State's motion for judgment on the pleadings on claims barred by the Eleventh Amendment and on the supervisory liability claims. The court also granted the State's motion for summary judgment on the qualified immunity issue. The court then remanded the state law claims to state court.

Kruse filed the instant appeal. She claims that the district court did not have jurisdiction because the action was improperly removed. Kruse also claims that the district court erred as a matter of law in: (1) finding that Kruse's claims for injunctive relief against DHS officials in their official capacity were retroactive and therefore barred by the Eleventh Amendment; (2) ruling that the officials were entitled to qualified immunity; and (3) admitting certain pieces of evidence. We affirm.

I. BACKGROUND

On July 7, 1991, Kruse gave birth to her son Kanoa. The next day, the hospital staff found that Kanoa was jittery and easily arousable, and that Kruse's breath smelled of marijuana. A urine test revealed the presence of marijuana in Kanoa's system. A hospital social worker reported the results to Child Protective Services ("CPS"), a division of Hawaii's Department of Human Services ("DHS"). That afternoon, Kruse allegedly admitted to a CPS caseworker that she occasionally used marijuana and smoked it once a week during her pregnancy.

On July 10, 1991, Luana Ogi, a CPS social worker, visited Kruse's home. During the visit, Kruse allegedly told Ogi that she smoked marijuana when she was on her way to the hospital to give birth to Kanoa. Kruse then agreed to participate in a family support services program, Mothers and Infants Support Team ("MIST").

During this time, Kruse was employed as a child care worker at the Mauna Lani School, a child care facility under the jurisdiction of DHS. Under Hawaii Administrative Rules ("HAR"), a child care facility can terminate an employee if the employee's employment history indicates that the employee may pose a danger to children because of prior acts of violence, drug, or alcohol abuse, or if the employee "has been identified as, and substantiated to be the perpetrator of child abuse or neglect."

Some time before July 19, 1991, Kruse allegedly told Angela Thomas, her employer, that she had used marijuana and was under CPS investigation. On July 19, 1991, Ogi related the facts of Kruse's investigation to Deborah Arnett, a DHS official responsible for overseeing the Mauna Lani School. Arnett asked that Kruse submit to a drug test as a condition of her continued employment. On July 25, 1991, Kruse agreed to submit to a drug test but requested a delay of thirty days before taking the test so that she would be certain to test negative.

On August 7, 1991, officials of MIST (the family support services program) found that Kruse was in a high risk situation because (1) she was potentially addicted to marijuana and cigarettes, (2) she and Caspary were not married, (3) her job was potentially at risk because of her drug use, and (4) Kanoa was her first child. MIST officials recommended that Kruse enter a drug rehabilitation program, that

CPS monitor Kanoa's condition, that Kruse and Caspary enter counseling, and that Kruse be tested for drugs.

Kruse refused to take a drug test. On August 29, Thomas fired Kruse. The termination letter stated that Kruse was being fired because the in utero transmission of marijuana to a fetus constitutes "abuse and neglect of the child," which disqualifies Kruse from working at a child care facility. Thomas told CPS that she would not rehire Kruse because Kruse's marijuana use had become known in the community, and that this situation could harm the preschool's reputation.

On July 2, 1993, Kruse and Caspary, on behalf of themselves and Kanoa ("Kruse"), filed the instant suit in state court against the State of Hawaii and various DHS and CPS employees in their official and individual capacities (collectively "the State"). Kruse argued that under Hawaii law, there was no legal basis for CPS to intervene in traditional family relationships based on prenatal exposure to parental drug-use, and claimed negligence, negligent hiring, emotional distress, and interference with contractual relations. Kruse also claimed that the State's failure adequately to hire, supervise, train, instruct, and control CPS employees violated Kruse's federal constitutional right to privacy and due process. Kruse sought declaratory, injunctive, and monetary relief.

The district court denied Kruse's motion for abstention and granted the State's motion for judgment on the pleadings on the supervisory liability claims and on the claims barred by the Eleventh Amendment. The district court also granted the State's motion for summary judgment in favor of the DHS employees on the ground that they were entitled to qualified immunity. The district court then remanded the state law claims to state court. Kruse now appeals.

CONCLUSION

For the foregoing reasons, the district court's judgment is AFFIRMED.

Case Commentary

After testing positive for marijuana as a result of a urine test taken after giving birth, Sue Kruse lost her job as a child care worker. A case worker reported the test results to her employer. Kruse claimed that the disclosure of the drug test results was an invasion of privacy.

Case Questions

1. Should positive drug test results be kept confidential?
2. Did Kruse's employer have the right to test Kruse for drugs?
3. If the DHS caseworker did not have a qualified immunity, would Kruse have won?

DRUG-FREE WORKPLACE ACT

A strong argument for random drug testing in cases involving public safety or national security can be made under the Drug-Free Workplace Act of 1988. This Act applies to contractors that provide more than $25,000 worth of property or services to the federal government and to those employers receiving federal grant monies. Under the Drug-Free Workplace Act, the employer must publish a conspicuous notice in the workplace that drug use is prohibited. This notice must also be sent to all employees. The employer must educate its employees about the dangers of drug use, the availability of counseling and drug treatment programs, and the consequences the employee will suffer if he or she does not seek assistance. Notification must be given to the appropriate federal agency by the employer within 10 days of learning that an employee has been convicted for drug use. Employees must notify their employer if they have been convicted within five days of said conviction. The employer must in all respects make a good faith effort to ensure a drug-free workplace.

JOB RELATEDNESS

The Fourth Amendment applies to the federal government. Through the due process clause of the Fourteenth Amendment, the Fourth Amendment, along with the rest of the Bill of Rights, was applied to state and local governments. The application to others, including private employers, is essentially based on public policy decisions in court cases and the Privacy Act of 1974. The test applied, which is one of reasonableness, requires that the reason for the drug testing must be significantly job related. Adequate safeguards must be taken, and the intrusion on a person's physical solitude must be minimal. Job relatedness means that the purpose of the test must affect the public safety, the national security, or the safety and security of the workplace. Adequate safeguards must be instituted to assure that the testing is done by a qualified, independent laboratory.

LAB TESTING

Laboratory drug testing has become a lucrative business. It is important that both the laboratory and the test it performs are reliable. Laboratories conducting drug testing for federal agencies are required to be certified. The initial tests, immunoassay, or thin-layer chromatography are usually expeditious and inexpensive to perform. If a positive result is found, a gas chromatography/mass spectrometry test may be used to confirm the finding. This test is more expensive and more reliable than the others.

The examination of hair follicles is an alternative method, which is said to provide more detailed information. The collection of the sample is less intrusive, but the results are more intrusive as they provide the quantity and duration of the drug use.

TESTING PROCEDURE

It is important that the results be absolutely confirmed before aggressive action is taken. The procedure for gathering the urine specimen should be conducted by an independent source. The process from urination to labeling the vial to transportation to the laboratory to the performance of the actual test itself must be properly controlled. To allow the employer to do it would create a conflict of interest. Employees would find it intrusive and would allege tampering upon the determination of a positive finding. The collection of the urine sample must be observed to verify that the employee has not substituted another person's sample for his or her own. The observer may stand behind the man and outside the stall while listening for the sound of urination by the female. These methods are not unreasonably intrusive. The consequences of confirming drug use may be a warning, required counseling, admission to a drug-treatment program, or termination.

EMPLOYEE ACCEPTANCE

The best approach is for employers to attempt to elicit an acceptance of the program by the employees. This can be accomplished by emphasizing safety, security, and a more productive work environment. The latter translates into greater profits, less theft, and possibly a sharing of this new-found wealth with the employees through better raises or bonuses. Advocating an employer/employee partnership in the fight against drugs will go a long way in easing the implementation of a drug-testing program into the workplace.

❖ EMPLOYER LESSONS

- Conduct an analysis for each position.
- Identify the qualifications necessary for each job.
- Draft a job description based on those qualifications.
- Evaluate the necessity of commissioning a test to determine those job qualifications.
- Design specific questions to establish those job qualifications.
- Gauge employee morale when testing is introduced.
- Educate the employees as to why testing is necessary.
- Balance the gain in knowledge from testing with the potential loss of employee trust.
- Assure confidentiality with regard to test results.
- Refrain from using test results to discriminate.

❖ EMPLOYEE LESSONS

- Inquire into the employer's purpose for administering the test: What does the employer hope to achieve?
- Ask if the test result will be kept confidential.
- Identify legitimate objections to testing.
- Distinguish between the different tests available and know when each is appropriate.
- Query the employer on whether the test questions are job related.
- Familiarize yourself with the protections afforded by the Employee Polygraph Protection Act.
- Respect the significance of the Drug-Free Workplace Act.

- Understand the impact of the Fourth Amendment on drug testing.
- Appreciate the amount of information gleaned from the hair follicle drug test.
- Protect your privacy to the best of your ability.

❖ SUMMARY

With respect to information concerning the employee, the employer and the employee are often adversaries. The employer's need to know is at odds with the employee's privacy concerns. That is why courts will often require an employer to establish a compelling interest in the need for information to overrule invasion of privacy concerns. Although they may not eliminate the controversy, employers may reduce the hostility and build trust by sharing with employees the concerns that have driven the employers to want to implement testing. It's not always what you say or do, but how you say or do it.

❖ REVIEW QUESTIONS

1. What is a polygraph?
2. Is the use of polygraphs generally acceptable?
3. When can polygraphs be used?
4. What is the importance of the Fourth Amendment as it relates to testing?
5. Why are employers interested in testing their employees?
6. Are laboratory tests reliable?
7. What is the most informative method of testing for drug use?
8. When is random drug testing permissible?
9. What other types of testing devices can be utilized to determine an employee's honesty?
10. Explain the significance of the Drug-Free Workplace Act of 1988.
11. An employee was required as a condition of employment to submit to a medical examination. The employee asked to see the test results. The physician refused, arguing that the employee was not a patient and need only be notified if a dangerous condition was discovered. What was the result? *Green v. Walker,* 910 F.2d 291 (5th cir. 1990)
12. Sibi Soroka applied for a position as a security officer with Target Stores. He was required to pass a psychological screening, the purpose of which is to judge the emotional stability of the applicants. Numerous questions related to the applicant's sex life, sexual orientation, and sexual thoughts. Soroka questioned the job-relatedness of this test. A security guard's primary function is to prevent shoplifting. What was the result? *Soroka v. Dayton Hudson Corporation,* 1 Cal. Rptr. 2d 77 (1991)
13. Howard Saari was employed by Smith Barney, Harris Upham & Co., Inc. as an account executive beginning in July 1988, and alleges that at all times his work was satisfactory. According to Saari's complaint, on or about December 14, 1988, a "sum of money, supposedly belonging to a client of Smith Barney, was supposedly stolen from the desk of a Smith Barney employee." Saari alleged he was questioned about the theft and was later asked to take a polygraph test concerning the incident, which he refused. Saari claims he was then terminated for his refusal to take the polygraph examination.

   Saari became a registered representative of the New York Stock Exchange and thereby subject to its Rule 347 which provides that:

   > Any controversy between a registered representative and any member or member organization arising out of the employment or termination of employment of such registered representative by and with such member or member organization shall be settled by arbitration.

   Saari contends that the enforcement provisions of EPPA show no such flexibility. Is the arbitration requirement in violation of the Employee Polygraph Protection Act? *Saari v. Smith Barney,* 968 F.2d 877 (9th Cir. 1992)

❖ WEB SITES

www.waldentesting.com
www.brgarrison.com
www.employeeselect.com
www.caliperonline.com
www.polygraph.org/apa5.htm
www.criminology.fsu.edu/journal/volume1.html
www.passyourdrugtest.com

PRIVACY, THEFT, AND WHISTLE-BLOWING

INTRODUCTION

Freedom and privacy are sacred to Americans. The Bill of Rights safeguards these principals. But the right to privacy is not absolute. In employment law, a balancing test is used. When an employer can show that its need to know outweighs the employee's right to privacy, then an invasion of that employee's privacy will be warranted. Conversely, when an employee's right to privacy is paramount, then it will be protected. Certain situations may be clear-cut, while others are controversial. Surveillance, security guards, tape recorded conversations, credit checks, and E-mail monitoring may be used by employers. But an employer's rights are not absolute. The employer's need to know must be business related. Listening to personal phone conversations, reading the contents of private E-mails, and installing cameras in employee bathrooms and lounges are not permissible. In any event, an employer must evaluate the benefits to the business from invading employee privacy versus depressing employee morale, creating a lack of trust, and causing employees to leave the business for a competitor who will not infringe upon employee privacy. Employees should be cognizant of privacy intrusions and decide whether to be docile, resign in protest, or object and litigate. The financial and emotional makeup of each employee will dictate the approach taken.

CHAPTER CHECKLIST

❖ Understand the employer's motives for invading the privacy of employees.

❖ Appreciate the employee's rationale for objecting to invasion of privacy.

❖ Familiarize yourself with the safeguards afforded by the Privacy Act, Omnibus Crime Control and Safe Streets Act, Electronic Communications Act, and Fair Credit Reporting Act.

❖ Learn whether an employer's actions fall within one of the defined categories of invasion of privacy.

❖ Distinguish between an opinion and a defamatory statement.

❖ Know when someone is intentionally interfering with a business relationship.

❖ Appreciate the negative impact employee theft has on business.

❖ Discern when an employer has the right to conduct an office search and whether the parameters of the search are justified.

❖ Be able to define whistle-blowing and the protections afforded by the Whistleblower Protection Act.

❖ Understand the dilemma confronting a potential whistle-blower: the desire to reveal wrongdoing versus possible retaliation.

PRIVACY ACT OF 1974

The Privacy Act of 1974 was enacted to safeguard private information of Federal Employees from being disclosed by the Federal Government. Under the act, no information pertaining to an employee may be released before obtaining prior written consent of the employee. There are many exceptions to this procedure. Other employees of the agency may access the records of a particular worker on a need-to-know basis, if their position so requires. A court, civil or criminal law enforcement agency, Congress, the Census Bureau, or the National Archives may have access to an employee's records for a justifiable reason. Unless exempted under the Privacy Act, the information should be kept in a secure facility that guards against easy access by unauthorized people. Civil and criminal penalties can be imposed for breaches of trust.

FREEDOM OF INFORMATION ACT OF 1966

Under the Freedom of Information Act of 1966, records relating to employment may be disclosed unless disclosure would constitute an invasion of privacy. A balance test is used between the need for disclosure and the intrusion. The employee's information may be disclosed upon the showing of a compelling reason relating to health or safety. A mailing to the employee's address is required for notification. A firm that is conducting a statistical analysis may have access to employee records for purely statistical reasons when the employee's identification has been deleted. At all times, employees have the right to view their files. The employer must be able to justify why the files are kept and why the particular information contained in the files is needed. The employee must be afforded the opportunity to correct any information which is not accurate.

OMNIBUS CRIME CONTROL AND SAFE STREETS ACT

Title III of the Omnibus Crime Control and Safe Streets Act of 1968 prohibits employers from listening to the private telephone conversations of their employees or from publicly disclosing the contents of these conversations. Employers who eavesdrop intentionally when employees are justified in expecting their conversations to be private are in violation of the act. Employers may ban personal calls and then monitor conversations for violations, but they may not listen to the entire conversation for the purpose of discerning its content. Violators may incur fines up to $10,000.

EMPLOYMENT PERSPECTIVE

Sheena Whitmore placed a call to her physician concerning the results of a blood test she had taken to determine whether she had contracted a sexually transmitted disease. This call was intercepted by her employer, who then stayed on the line to hear the test results. Is this an invasion of privacy? Yes! The employer's actions are in violation of Title III of the Omnibus Crime Control and Safe Streets Act. Sheena was expecting privacy. Her employer invaded that privacy by listening to her test results. ∎

ELECTRONIC COMMUNICATIONS ACT

The Electronic Communications Act of 1986 extended people's privacy protection to E-mail. Unauthorized access or interceptions are subject to stiff civil and criminal penalties. Federal law also prohibits tampering with E-mail. However, there is an exception for employers who access employees' E-mail during the course of business. Employers may monitor E-mail for quality control, sexual, racial, and abusive language. Employers should not divulge the contents of the E-mail communications. Employees should be on guard when transmitting E-mail because of the limited protection afforded to them.

FAIR CREDIT REPORTING ACT

The Fair Credit Reporting Act of 1970 allows consumer-reporting agencies to furnish credit reports for employment purposes. These reports contain basic information about the individual and his or her credit worthiness. The employers who seek this information need not notify the employee or prospective applicant of their intention to do so. If the employer wishes to have a more detailed background check done by the consumer-reporting agency with regard to interviews of the employee or of the applicant's friends, neighbors, and coworkers, then notice must be given to the individual. In all respects, the employer's reason for doing so must be job related. If the report goes beyond what is considered to be a business necessity, an invasion of privacy suit may ensue. If the individual falls into a suspect classification (race, gender, religion, national origin, age, or disability), then grounds for a discrimination suit may exist.

DEFAMATION

Defamation is a false statement communicated to at least one other person, orally or in a permanent form such as a writing, that causes harm to a third person's reputation. *Libel* is written defamation, while *slander* is oral defamation. Libel is actionable without proof of special damages because a writing remains in existence and could be distributed widely, whereas oral defamation is usually temporary and limited to the range of a person's voice, except when the oral statement is recorded and continuously broadcast on television, radio, or sound tracks.

LIBEL

The requirement for libel is a false statement that is published and read by someone other than the one about whom it is written. The true intention of the writer is that which is apparent from the natural and ordinary interpretation of the written words and, when applied to individuals, the interpretation placed upon those words by people acquainted with the plaintiff and the circumstances. General damages are automatically awarded for harm to reputation in the community or in business, and for personal embarrassment and mental anguish. Special damages may be awarded if the victim can prove he or she suffered an actual pecuniary loss from the harm to his or her reputation.

EMPLOYMENT PERSPECTIVE

The *Star Gazette* published an article that accused Lawrence Binghamton, president of the town's savings bank, of pilfering depositors' money through the authorization of several large personal loans to himself. These statements are proven untrue. Nonetheless, Binghamton's bank loses numerous depositors. Has Binghamton any recourse? Yes! He may sue for libel by claiming that the statement was false and proving that it led to a decline in his business. ■

SLANDER

Slander requires a defamatory statement that is heard by someone other than the person against whom it is directed. Special damages must be proved except in four situations where general damages are recoverable without proof. These situations include: derogating some characteristic important to a person in that person's trade or business, such as honesty or integrity; accusing a person of committing a crime of moral turpitude; denouncing someone by stating that he or she has contracted a loathsome disease; or imputing that a woman is unchaste.

EMPLOYMENT PERSPECTIVE

Peter J. Roberts is a local attorney who has a well regarded real estate law practice. Matthew Brady is also an attorney. Out of jealousy, he informs several real estate brokers who refer clients to Peter J. Roberts that Roberts has cheated his clients in several real estate deals. Even though Brady's statements are false, Roberts's business suffers a severe decline as a result. Does Peter J. Roberts have any recourse? Yes! Roberts may recover general damages for the harm suffered to his business reputation. ■

TRUTH AND MALICE

Truth is an absolute defense when the statement made is fully true. However, the truth must be proved. There is a special rule pertaining to defamatory statements made by the media concerning public figures. Even if the statement cannot be proved to be true, the media will not be liable unless malicious intent can be substantiated. *Malice* is the making of a false statement with the intent to injure another.

EMPLOYMENT PERSPECTIVE

In the previous situation, assume that Matthew Brady's allegations concerning Peter J. Roberts were the truest words ever spoken but that Brady has no way of proving them to be true. What would be the result? The result would be the same:

▌ Roberts will recover general damages. Although truth is an absolute defense, if Roberts meets his initial burden of proof, the burden then shifts to the person who made the statement. ■

The issue in the case below is whether Dr. Moran was defamed by statements made by administrators of the Kansas Medical Center.

CASE

MORAN v. STATE OF KANSAS

985 P.2d 127 (Kan. 1999)

ALLEGRUCCI, Judge.

Jon F. Moran, M.D., former head of the Department of Cardiothoracic Surgery at the University of Kansas Medical Center (KUMC), brought this action against defendants, alleging that they made false and defamatory statements about him and his stewardship of KUMC's heart transplant program. Individual defendants are KUMC administrators. The district court granted summary judgment in favor of defendants on the ground that Moran had produced no evidence that he suffered damage to his reputation as a result of defendants' statements. Moran appealed from the entry of summary judgment. Defendants cross-appealed on their claim of immunity under the Kansas Tort Claims Act (KTCA), and on their contention that a defamation plaintiff must show a quantifiable pecuniary or economic loss or detriment.

Moran claims the district court erred in (1) finding he did not establish that his reputation was damaged by defendants' statements, and (2) requiring that he must show injury to his reputation when defendants have acted with actual malice. In their cross-appeal, defendants claim they are immune from liability under the discretionary function exception of the KTCA, and Moran is required to prove special damages or a quantifiable pecuniary or economic loss or detriment in order to make out a prima facie case for defamation.

Moran was chairman of the Department of Cardiothoracic Surgery at KUMC from June 1985 to April 1994. He remained on staff at KUMC until he resigned on March 3, 1995.

At issue are statements made by KUMC administrators in May 1995.

1. The impact of the *Star's* May 7 article lay in its pairing of the fact that no heart transplants had been performed at KUMC from early May 1994 to late March 1995 with the paradox that patients continued to be admitted and added to the heart transplant waiting list. In investigating the circumstances, the reporter talked to Moran and Dr. Clay Beggerly, the program's two former surgeons. The account that Moran gave the reporter was that he had complained for many months of a lack of surgeons and qualified nurses. When the complaints produced no changes, Moran asked twice in early June 1994 that the program be suspended. His request was not granted. In early November, he told administrators that he would do no more heart transplants.

Jon Jackson, an associate administrator of KUMC, was quoted in the *Star's* article:

" 'There was not any indication given to us that he was not operating a program,' said Jon Jackson, an associate administrator. 'Had Dr. Moran told us that we're not going to do transplants prior to his letter of Nov. 4, we would have made other arrangements for those procedures to take place.' "

Kim Russel, chief operating officer, was quoted as denying Moran's allegations of shortages of qualified nurses.

2. The May 10 open letter from A. L. Chapman, Acting Executive Vice Chancellor, began by quoting the entire response prepared by Daniel Hollander, Executive Dean, and Glenn Potter, Vice Chancellor for Hospital Administration, to the May 7 *Star* article. Chapman added several paragraphs, including the following one:

"It is important to point out that after Dr. Moran announced he would do no more transplants, Dr. Hannah and KU cardiologist Dr. Steven Gollub jointly accepted responsibility to accept or reject donor hearts. A review shows that none were turned down for other than medical reasons after November, 1994. To be acceptable, donor hearts must closely match tissue type and body size of the recipient as well as meet other clinical criteria."

3. The Viewpoint commentary by Hollander and Potter placed responsibility for collapse of the heart transplant program squarely on Moran:

"For about 10 years, heart transplantation surgery was headed by Dr. Jon Moran. As the physician in charge, it was Dr. Moran who made medical decisions about his patients.

"It was Dr. Moran who decided which patients were put on a waiting list for a heart transplant, and which hearts to accept or reject. These medical decisions were made by Dr. Moran, not by hospital or medical center administrators."

As shown by the date in the May 7 article, Dr. Moran on his own began to curtail the volume of heart transplant surgery in 1993. He did fewer transplants in 1993 and 1994 than he had in previous years. Although he continued to assign new patients to his waiting list, he began to refuse almost all hearts that were offered to him for transplantation, but did not notify administration of this fact until November 1994. The hearts that were offered to Dr. Moran—but refused by him—were then offered to other national programs and were either accepted or declined by them. Finally, in November 1994, Dr. Moran formally announced that he would no longer do heart transplants.

For the purpose of their motion for summary judgment, defendants did not dispute that they made the statements Moran complains of, that the statements were false and defamatory, and that Moran had proven actual malice. For his part, Moran conceded that he is required to show actual malice.

In granting defendants' motion for summary judgment, the district court gave only one reason for its decision: "Based upon the record established by the parties and presented to the court in this motion the court can find no evidence that plaintiff suffered any damage to his reputation as a result of any statements made by any defendant."

In his answers to defendants' interrogatories, plaintiff set forth a number of ways in which defendants' defamatory statements had harmed his reputation:

'While I am still able to practice as a cardiothoracic surgeon, my academic advancement has been markedly impaired by defendants' actions. Specifically, the frequency with which I have been approached about considering positions as division or department chief of an existing CTS program, or to start a new CTS (or heart transplant) program, or as a transplant surgeon in an existing transplant program, have decreased dramatically since the defendants' libelous communications. Similarly, the frequency with which I have been asked to write scholarly articles or to review articles submitted for publication in major journals has decreased. My reputation within the academic surgical community, as well as the community at large, has been damaged. This damage is significant and, I believe, is likely to be permanent.'

"All of plaintiff's testimony is couched in terms of what *he* believes he has suffered. Yet he can bring forward no one else who says that he has been approached less frequently about new employment positions, new transplant programs or authorizing or reviewing scholarly publications. Nor is there any evidence other than his own conjecture that he has been sued in medical malpractice cases or will be unable to obtain insurance in the future. Even if the court gives plaintiff the benefit of these facts based solely on plaintiff's opinion and finds that all of these things have occurred, there is still no evidence that any of defendants' statements caused these results. The record here contains other publications not attributable to defendants that contain information which one could construe as possibly damaging to plaintiff and, for that matter, to several other people involved with Kansas University Medical Center. The jury would have nothing but speculation before it on the question of whether it was defendants' statements rather than those of others that caused any of plaintiff's alleged damages.

"It's undisputed that plaintiff has the same job now that he had just prior to publication of the statements in question. He is a professor of surgery at East Carolina University School of Medicine. He also is chief of the pedia tric cardiothoracic surgical program, director of the surgical assistants, and in charge of recruitment for the division of cardiothoracic surgery."

The evidence presented by Moran is unquestionably thin. However, when the evidence is viewed in a light most favorable to Moran and he is given the benefit of all inferences that reasonably may be drawn from it, a reasonable person might reach conclusions other than the one reached by the trial court.

Defendants contend that under this discretionary function exception of the KTCA they are immune from liability on Moran's allegations. The trial judge expressed disbelief that a state employee who made false and defamatory statements would be statutorily shielded from liability.

The district court's order of summary judgment is reversed, and the case is remanded for further proceedings consistent with this opinion.

Judgment for Moran.

Case Commentary

The Supreme Court of Kansas reversed the summary judgment decision of the Kansas District Court, thereby giving Jon Moran an opportunity to present his evidence in a trial before the Kansas District Court. A court generally grants summary judgment when it believes there is no triable issue to decide. The court will view the case in a light most favorable to the party against whom the summary judgment is requested before it is granted. In this case, the Supreme Court of Kansas believed that although Moran's case was weak, he could possibly persuade a jury that he was defamed. Therefore he is entitled to a trial.

Case Questions

1. How would you argue the case for Moran when it goes to trial?
2. Do you agree with the decision of the Supreme Court of Kansas?
3. Can a person's opinion of another be defamatory?

INVASION OF PRIVACY

Personal privacy is protected against invasions causing economic loss or mental suffering. There are four distinct invasions: intrusion on a person's physical solitude; publication of private matters violating ordinary decencies; putting a person in a false position in the public eye by connecting him or her with views he or she does not hold; appropriating some element of a person's personality for commercial use, such as photographs.

EMPLOYMENT PERSPECTIVE

Statler Beer is introducing a new beer called Sparkling Lite. To market the product, Statler is featuring an unauthorized poster of the Reverend Luther Winthrop advocating the purchase of Sparkling Lite. The Reverend Winthrop is a well-known fundamentalist minister who openly decries the consumption of alcohol. Has Reverend Winthrop any recourse? Yes! He may sue Statler Beer, asserting that the poster was not consented to and that it puts him in a false position in the public eye by connecting him with a view that he does not hold and a product that he does not deem appropriate. ■

EMPLOYMENT PERSPECTIVE

Rob Peters is a pension benefits specialist for Americana Insurance Company. One of his assistants, Brad Matthews, informs Rob that he must leave work two hours early this Tuesday for medical reasons. Rob asks Brad for specifics, citing company policy. Brad declines at first, but when pressed, Brad admits that he has the HIV virus and is being tested for AIDS. After Brad departs early on Tuesday, Jim Waters, a coworker, asks Rob why Brad left early. Rob responds, "You wouldn't believe it, Jim!" Jim retorts, "Try me." Rob blurts out, "Brad's got AIDS!" Jim responds in astonishment, "No!" Then Jim sends an E-mail message to the other coworkers. Brad's AIDS test comes back negative. Who does Brad have recourse against? Since it was company policy for the manager to inquire about the specific medical condition of the employee, Brad may sue Americana for invasion of privacy. Brad may also sue Rob for slander, because Rob made a false statement about Brad's having AIDS. Brad may sue Jim for invasion of privacy and libel, because the false statement was in written form. Rob and Jim may have been motivated by curiosity and gossip, not intent to harm, but the damage to Brad's reputation still occurred. ■

EMPLOYMENT SCENARIO

Long and Short phone Susan to inquire as to whether or not they can ask employees questions about their medical conditions when the employees ask for time off for illness. L&S also wish to know if it can share that information when queried by coworkers. Susan vehemently responds, "No!" to both queries. Both questions are invasions of privacy. If L&S wants to verify its employees' veracity, the company should ask for medical confirmation. A physician need only state that the request for medical leave is valid. Under no circumstances should any medical information of an employee be shared with coworkers.

On a separate note, L&S think it would be great to include in advertising how good Shaquille O'Neal, Kareem Abdul-Jabbar, and Patrick Ewing would look after shopping at "The Long and the Short of It." Susan again cautions against using specific basketball players' names, because the advertisement would place them in a false position in the public eye, connecting them with an image they may not wish to express. The ad could be interpreted as though they do not already dress with style. Long and Short ask Susan whether or not a life-size, cardboard cutout photo of Michael Jordan holding Dr. Evil's Mini Me (from the Austin Powers movie) with the store's name on it, "The Long and the Short of It," could be placed at its entrance directly above the photo. Susan applauds L&S's imagination and creativity but rebukes them for appropriating an element of Michael Jordan and Mini Me's personalities through photographs for commercial purposes without compensation. Susan informs L&S that the above proposals are forms of invasion of privacy that could subject the company to litigation. Susan suggests that L&S use their imagination and creativity to develop an advertisement that is unique.

The issue in this case is whether the searches were motivated by race discrimination.

CASE

WAL-MART, INC. v. STEWART

990 P.2d 626 (Alaska 1999)

COMPTON, Justice.

I. INTRODUCTION

Elvis R. Stewart sued Wal-Mart for violating Alaska's civil rights statute, for invading his common-law right to privacy, and for negligent and intentional infliction of emotional distress. He sought both compensatory and punitive damages. At the close of Stewart's case, Wal-Mart moved for a directed verdict. The court denied the motion. The jury returned a verdict in favor of Wal-Mart on Stewart's civil rights claim, but found for Stewart on his claims of invasion of privacy and intentional infliction of emotional distress. The jury awarded Stewart both compensatory and punitive damages. Wal-Mart moved for, and was denied, a judgment notwithstanding the verdict (JNOV) on the issue of punitive damages. Wal-Mart appeals the court's denial of its motions for a directed verdict and a JNOV. Wal-Mart also appeals numerous evidentiary rulings and the court's failure to remove an allegedly conflicted juror. We affirm.

II. FACTS AND PROCEEDINGS

A. Facts

In July 1994 Elvis R. Stewart, an African-American, began working for the McDonald's restaurant located inside the Wal-Mart store on Benson Boulevard in Anchorage. Stewart was hired to work the grill area; eventually he was moved to the area of the restaurant where people eat. Stewart's shift was from 7:30 P.M. until closing, the time of which varied. Stewart also worked at Taco Bell. Stewart's shift at Taco Bell

was from 11:30 A.M. until 7:00 P.M. In order to work both shifts, Stewart carried a change of clothes and personal items in a duffel-type bag. He would change out of his Taco Bell uniform, and into his McDonald's uniform, in the Wal-Mart bathroom. He also took the time between shifts to freshen up, i.e., wash himself with soap and a washcloth that he carried in his bag, and brush his teeth. He used the Wal-Mart bathroom, instead of the Taco Bell bathroom, because it was larger and less crowded with customers.

Wal-Mart had a nation-wide policy of stationing a member of its management team at its exits to check for receipts of purchases made by Wal-Mart and McDonald's employees, and to check for stolen items that might be concealed in their personal bags. Management conducted the checks before employees left the store at the end of their shifts. Randy Hardy, a Wal-Mart assistant manager, testified that management did not check women's purses, because women sometimes carry in their purses personal items that may be embarrassing to them.

The first few weeks Stewart worked at McDonald's, he exited the Wal-Mart store at the close of his shift without incident. According to Stewart, sometime during his third week of employment, Hardy stopped Stewart as he was exiting McDonald's at the end of his shift. Hardy asked to search Stewart's bag, and then proceeded to dump the contents of Stewart's bag onto the counter and look through it. According to Stewart, this type of bag search continued until mid-February 1995. Stewart testified that he routinely objected to the searches. On February 15 Stewart was again searched by Hardy. Hardy questioned Stewart about some candy bars in his bag, for which Stewart produced a receipt. After Hardy completed the bag search he allowed Stewart to leave. The next day Stewart came to McDonald's to speak with Sheila Hay, the wife of the franchise owner of the McDonald's where Stewart worked. It was Stewart's day off. He told Hay that he felt that Hardy was singling him out for bag searches. Hay took Stewart to speak with Mark Divis, the Wal-Mart store manager. Stewart repeated to Divis that he felt that Hardy was singling him out for bag searches. Divis called Hardy into the office. Hardy denied singling out Stewart for searches. Stewart testified that during the meeting Hay asked Hardy who else he searched. Stewart asked Hardy whether he searched certain people because they were black; Hardy answered yes. Divis promptly ended the meeting and conferred with Hay outside the presence of Hardy and Stewart.

On February 23 Stewart wrote a letter to Divis commending him on his "efforts with enforcing Wal-Mart [p]olicy, as it is in regards to the checking of All bags. . . ." But after he had written the letter, Stewart testified that things "drifted back to the same old way that—people started being singled out."

B. Proceedings

In August 1995 Stewart sued Wal-Mart, Divis, and Hardy (hereinafter Wal-Mart, unless specifically referring to Hardy's searches), alleging that: (1) the bag searches, conducted solely on the basis of his race, violated rights protected by AS 18.80.220(a); [Fn. 1] (2) the searches of his bag and person negligently [Fn. 2] and intentionally inflicted emotional distress upon him; and (3) the searches violated his common-law right to privacy guaranteed by article I, section 23 of the Alaska Constitution. Stewart sought compensatory and punitive damages. The jury returned a verdict in favor of Wal-Mart on Stewart's civil rights claim. However, it did conclude that Stewart had proved by a preponderance of the evidence that Wal-Mart intentionally inflicted emotional distress on him, and that it had invaded his privacy. Lastly, the jury concluded that Stewart had proved by clear and convincing evidence that Wal-Mart's conduct warranted punitive damages because it had been "the result of malicious or hostile feelings toward plaintiff Stewart, or was undertaken with reckless indifference to his interests or

rights and was outrageous." The jury awarded Stewart $7,800 in compensatory damages and $50,000 in punitive damages. After the special verdict form was read in open court, the jury was polled and discharged. After the jury had been discharged, Wal-Mart moved for a JNOV with regard to punitive damages. The court denied Wal-Mart's motion.

Wal-Mart appeals the trial court's denial of its motions for a directed verdict.

The Trial Court's Decision that Wal-Mart Was Not Entitled to a Directed Verdict on Any Count Was Correct.

1. Invasion of privacy

We have recognized that all persons are entitled to the common-law "right to be free from harassment and constant intrusion into one's daily affairs." The trial court instructed the jury that

[i]n order to recover, plaintiff must prove by a preponderance of the evidence that:

1. One or more defendants intentionally intruded upon the solitude, seclusion or private affairs or concerns of plaintiff Stewart; and
2. A reasonable person would find this a highly offensive intrusion.

Our review of the record discloses sufficient evidence that would allow reasonable minds to conclude that Wal-Mart searched Stewart's bag in an unreasonable manner or for an unlawful reason.

a. Unreasonable manner   Stewart presented witnesses who testified to the manner in which Hardy searched Stewart's bag. The following are examples of this evidence:

1. Stewart testified that Hardy told him to "empty out his pockets, all—everything, all that was in his pockets."
2. Stewart testified that Hardy "snatched" his bag off of his shoulder.
3. Stewart testified that Hardy aggressively dumped everything out of his bag onto the counter.
4. Mary Ann Dias testified that she saw Hardy take "everything out of Stewart's bag and lay it on the counter. Opened it up and took everything out, and then put everything back."

Based on this type of evidence, reasonable jurors could find that Hardy intentionally intruded upon the solitude or private affairs or concerns of Stewart and that a reasonable person would find this a highly offensive intrusion, concluding that the searches were done in an unreasonable manner.

b. Unlawful reason   Ample evidence was presented that also would permit reasonable jurors to find that Hardy searched Stewart's bag for an unlawful reason, i.e., because he is an African-American. The following are examples of this evidence:

1. Stewart testified that he "interjected, sprung open a question to Hardy, so you search us because we're black. And he recalled Mr. Hardy saying yes."
2. Mary Ann Dias testified that, prior to Stewart's complaint, she never saw any Caucasian McDonald's employees get their backpacks searched.
3. Travis Witcher testified that "So the next day I guess they searched everybody or a majority of the blacks, just—they just searched—searched them. There were no—no white associates that day got searched." He also testified that Hardy asked him to open his jacket and patted him down, while Hardy did not search the bag of a white associate who was walking out with Witcher.

While Hardy testified that his search of Stewart was not motivated by the fact that Stewart was an African-American, a reasonable juror could have found Hardy's testimony not credible. Based on this type of evidence, reasonable jurors could find that Hardy searched Stewart for an unlawful reason, i.e., solely on the basis of his race.

c. Consent   Wal-Mart argues that consent is a defense to an invasion of privacy claim, and that a reasonable juror could not have concluded that the searches of Stewart's bag were anything but consensual. Wal-Mart also asserts that "the evidence showed that Stewart consented to the searches by continuing to carry his bag, because the jury found that Stewart's bag was not searched for the illegal motive of racial basis." Wal-Mart's final point is that "where a legal bag search procedure is in effect, consent is implied."

Reasonable jurors could find that Stewart did not consent to the searches. Not only was there evidence presented that could lead reasonable jurors to conclude that Stewart was mistaken or under duress when he "consented" to the searches, but, as the superior court noted, there was also evidence presented that Stewart never in fact consented. The superior court stated: "On the issue of consent, again there is evidence on both sides that Mr. Stewart essentially voiced his dissent numerous times when he was being searched." Specifically, Stewart did not consent to Hardy's vigorous and overly-thorough searches.

The following are examples of this evidence:

1. Stewart testified that the first time he was searched he "was thinking that the reason he was stopped was race, and he was also thinking perhaps there was a mistake somewhere, perhaps someone had described somebody that looked like him, maybe they thought he was someone that was stealing from the store."
2. Stewart testified that "as he was protesting the searches, Mr. Hardy said to him shut up, I'm not going to argue with you; as long as I'm working, I'm going to search you every night."

Whether consent is implied when a store has a legal bag search policy is irrelevant. Even were we to conclude that a consent is implied when a legal bag search procedure is in effect, Stewart's suit was premised on the notion that he was not searched pursuant to Wal-Mart's legal bag search policy. Rather, Stewart successfully argued at trial that the searches of his bag invaded his privacy because they were done for an unlawful purpose or in an unreasonable manner.

2. Intentional infliction of emotional distress

The elements necessary for establishing a prima facie case of IIED are: "(1) the conduct is extreme and outrageous, (2) the conduct is intentional or reckless, (3) the conduct causes emotional distress, and (4) the distress is severe."

We conclude that it was not an abuse of discretion for the superior court to make the threshold determination, based on the evidence presented, that Hardy's conduct was sufficiently outrageous, and Stewart's emotional distress was sufficiently severe, to submit the IIED claim to the jury. The following are examples of this evidence:

1. Stewart testified that Hardy admitted that the reason he searched the people that he did was because they were African-Americans.
2. Stewart testified that he was told to empty his pockets, and that Hardy grabbed his duffel bag off of his shoulder.
3. Numerous witnesses testified that Stewart and other people of color were searched very often, while Caucasians were either allowed to exit the store without being searched or were searched much less frequently.

C. The Trial Court's Decision that Wal-Mart Was Not Entitled to a Directed Verdict or a JNOV on the Punitive Damages Claim Was Correct.

IV. CONCLUSION

We conclude that the superior court properly denied Wal-Mart's motions for a directed verdict and a JNOV. It did not abuse its discretion in any of its evidentiary rulings. Wal-Mart waived its right to appeal numerous evidentiary rulings and the court's decision to leave Hostman on the jury. The jury instructions were not plain error. We AFFIRM the judgment of the superior court.

Case Commentary

The lessons to be learned from this case are to treat all employees alike and to treat them in a humane manner. Do not distinguish between employees on the basis of personal prejudices.

Case Questions

1. Could Hardy's searches of only black employees ever be justified?
2. Do you agree with the Alaska Supreme Court's decision?
3. If all employees were searched, would it be an invasion of privacy?

Publication of private matters that are newsworthy is privileged as long as it does not violate ordinary decencies. A false report by the media of a matter of public interest is protected by the First Amendment right of free press, in the absence of proof that it was published with malice.

INTERFERENCE WITH BUSINESS RELATIONS

A person who intentionally interferes in a business relationship through the use of fraudulent inducement or other unethical means that result either in an unfavorable contract or in the loss or breach of a favorable contract is liable for damages. The victim must prove damages, such as the specific loss of a customer, except where the nature of the falsehood is likely to bring about a general decline in business.

EMPLOYMENT PERSPECTIVE

Phil Murray owns a service station in Mobile, Alabama. The On-The-Spot Car Service Company approaches Phil about maintaining their twelve-car fleet. This opportunity would greatly enhance Phil's business. While they are still negotiating, Michael Dean, owner of a rival service station, circulates a false rumor that Phil Murray is incompetent and unreliable when it comes to servicing cars. As a result, Phil loses the contract with On-The-Spot Car Service. Thereafter, he discovers that Michael Dean originated the false rumor and sues him for damages. Will Phil be successful? Yes! Michael Dean's intentional interference with the contractual negotiations between Phil Murray and On-The-Spot Car Service caused Phil to lose the contract. Phil is entitled to the profits that he lost because of Michael Dean's interference. ■

EMPLOYMENT SCENARIO

Due to a personality conflict with Tom Long, Ray Costello decides to leave L&S. Ray finds a job at Giant Department Store in the men's clothing section. On his employment application form, Ray lists L&S as his prior employer with Mark Short as his supervisor. Sam Hong, the men's clothing manager at Giant Department Store, phones Mark for a reference. Tom answers and explains to Sam that although Ray is a competent salesperson, Ray possesses a bad attitude in his relations with management. Ray's hostility is apparent to other employees and fills the working environment with tension. Tom says, "Sam, Ray will make your life very difficult." Based on Tom's candor, Sam does not hire Ray. Ray believes something is awry. He questions Sam, who denies any bad-mouthing by L&S. Ray sues L&S for interference with Ray's business relations and subpoenas Sam to testify to any conversations Sam had with Tom or Mark. Under oath, Sam testifies as to his conversation with Tom. There is a likelihood that Ray may recover damages for interference with business relations because Tom laid the framework for Ray's being a problem employee and then conjectured that Ray would be a future problem for Sam. Tom's motive was to influence Sam not to hire Ray. Susan counsels Tom that in the future he should set aside any personal hostility toward any former employee and limit the information given to position held and dates of employment.

EMPLOYEE THEFT

Theft by employees accounts for billions of dollars in losses for businesses each year. Employee theft can be narrowly or broadly defined. The narrow definition is the appropriating of personal property belonging to the business for an employee's own personal use. This appropriation can be temporary, but most often it is permanent.

EMPLOYMENT PERSPECTIVE

Harry Tubbs and Pete Jackson work as a team for Moving On Van Lines. They often make long-distance moves. After being assigned a job, they often complete it in less time by working late hours. Then they use the company van for making short moves from which they derive a profit. Harry and Pete believe that as long as they perform their assigned work within the allotted time, they are doing their job, and the company should not be concerned. Are they guilty of employee theft? Yes! Their theft is temporary, but the consequences are still severe. A van's useful life and maintenance costs will directly correspond to its mileage. Harry's and Pete's ventures are lowering the van's useful life to the company and increasing its maintenance costs. There is no difference between doing this and keeping the equivalent amount of money from a customer's cash payment. Both acts are theft. In addition, if they are in an accident while performing their personal work, the accident could subject Moving On to liability for damages and injuries. If Harry and Pete are injured, most likely Moving On will incur medical expenses, and workers' compensation benefits will be paid out. Harry and Pete are not entitled to any of this because this occurrence happened outside the scope of their employment, but Moving On may have to pay for it if the theft is not known. Some companies will want their employees prosecuted, but most will not because of the bad publicity it would bring. Dismissal with or without restitution is the most likely consequence. ◾

EMPLOYMENT PERSPECTIVE

When Marge Adams resigned from Pentangel Publishing, everything in her office was intact. That evening, Phil Thomas took the computer, printer, lamp, office supplies, and fax machine from Marge's office and brought them home. Phil believed his actions were justified because most likely Marge was not going to be replaced. Is Phil's reasoning sound? No! Phil has stolen company property for his own personal aggrandizement. ◾

EMPLOYMENT SCENARIO

Fred Samuels has knowledge that Ruth Gurdon, head buyer for L&S, has been procuring imitation brand name jeans through the black market, while charging L&S at the rate charged by the brand name merchants. Ruth is pocketing the rest. Fred is afraid to whistle-blow because he knows Ruth is dating Mark Short. Fred does not want to lose his job because of this, but he still wants to do the right thing. Fred asks Tom Long to recommend a competent attorney. Tom suggests Susan North, L&S's attorney. Fred relates the story to Susan. Susan acknowledges the dilemma, but advises Fred that he has a duty of loyalty to L&S to act in its best interests. Susan suggests Fred draft the details in writing. She will present the evidence to Tom and Mark in her office without divulging Fred's identity. Susan reveals Ruth's fraudulent scheme to Tom and Mark. She warns them of the potential harm to L&S's reputation as a result of this scheme, and of the possibility of litigation from the name brand merchants. Although initially taking a defensive posture, Mark recognizes Ruth may have been taking advantage of him. Mark confronts Ruth with the evidence. She denies it, quits the job on the spot, and tells Mark the relationship is over. Mark is stunned. Tom reassures Mark that although Mark may feel personally hurt, their business reputation has been saved.

CONVERSION

Conversion is the unlawful taking of personal property from the possession of another. It is the converting of another's property for one's own use. Conversion may be made by mistake, but if it is done intentionally, it amounts to criminal theft, which is considered under the headings of larceny, embezzlement, and robbery.

> **EMPLOYMENT PERSPECTIVE**
>
> Mary Rodgers works as a cashier in Macy's Department store. She takes a break one afternoon to go to the powder room. She mistakenly leaves her pocketbook at the register. When she returns, her pocketbook is there but her wallet has been removed. The store detective apprehends Debbie Wilson, a stock clerk, with Mary's wallet in her hand. Has Mary Rodgers any civil recourse for Debbie Wilson's theft? Yes! Mary may sue Debbie in tort for conversion. Debbie may also be criminally prosecuted for the crime of larceny or theft. ■

Employee theft occurs when a worker, usually a cashier or someone in billing, charges a customer, who is generally a friend, less than the amount owed. Although the employee may not be benefiting directly, the employee is instrumental in making the theft happen. There would be no difference between the preceding example and that of an employee stealing the merchandise and giving it to a friend. Both acts are thefts.

> **EMPLOYMENT PERSPECTIVE**
>
> Missy Atkins is a waitress at the Busy Body Diner. Missy, who is shy and unassuming, wants to become more popular with the in-crowd at school. Whenever they come in for burgers, fries, and sundaes, Missy charges them only for the sundaes. Missy's popularity is increasing fast, but is she gaining it at Busy Body's expense? Yes! Missy is guilty of employee theft. ■

EMBEZZLEMENT

Embezzlement is the fraudulent taking of property during the course of employment.

The following case addresses the issue of whether an employee who has stolen funds should be liable to make restitution for the funds converted as well as for the expenses the employer incurred to straighten out its accounting records.

CASE

BENTON v. STATE OF DELAWARE

711 A.2d 792 (Del. 1998)

HOLLAND, Justice.

Following a jury trial in the Superior Court, the defendant-appellant, Melissa Benton ("Benton"), was convicted of Felony Theft and Falsifying Business Records. She was found to have embezzled funds in the course of her employment as an accounts receivable clerk. In this appeal, Benton does not contest the merits of her convictions. She only challenges the Superior Court's judgments with regard to the total amount of $21,450.65 in restitution that she was ordered to pay.

Benton contends that the Superior Court erred, as a matter of law, by ordering her to pay restitution in an amount that exceeded the State's evidence at trial. She argues, alternatively, that there was insufficient evidence to support the Superior Court's order of restitution. In a related claim, Benton submits that the Superior Court erred by ordering her to make restitution to her employer because her employer had signed a general release of all claims pursuant to its receipt of payment under an insurance surety bond. Benton also argues that the Superior Court's order of restitution constituted an excessive fine in violation of the Eighth Amendment to the United States Constitution. Finally, Benton argues that the Superior Court failed to consider her inability to repay the restitution it ordered.

We have carefully considered each of Benton's arguments. We have concluded that the record reflects no error. Accordingly, the judgment of the Superior Court is affirmed.

FACTS

In January 1995, Benton went to work as a bookkeeper for the Angola By The Bay Property Owners Association ("the Association"). The Association controls a housing development and resort in Sussex County. Its members are lot owners in the resort. The Association is responsible for the maintenance and upkeep of the common facilities at Angola By The Bay.

The Association receives a yearly assessment of $250 per lot from each property owner. It also receives revenue from boat slip rentals, boat ramp usage fees, boat rack rentals, pool passes and soft drink sales. During the time Benton was the bookkeeper, she was responsible for receiving payments for these fees and services, entering the amount received in the financial records of the Association, preparing deposit slips, and depositing the cash and checks in the Association's bank account.

Benton voluntarily left her employment at the Association in June 1995. Shortly after she resigned, it was discovered that Benton had embezzled money from the Association. Benton's embezzlement scheme was explained by the evidence presented during the State's case at trial. The record reflects that, when Benton received cash on behalf of the Association, she would frequently keep the money for herself. Benton was able to hide her embezzlement by a scheme known as "lapping." Pursuant to this scheme, Benton would note in the financial records of the Association that she had received

a cash payment from a property owner or customer. In fact, however, Benton would convert the cash to her own use. The amount of cash embezzled would be replaced in the daily bank deposit with one or more payments by check from other property owners. The "lapping" scheme delayed the discovery of Benton's thefts until property owners, who had made payments by check, realized that their accounts had not been given proper credit.

For example, if Benton received a $250 assessment payment in cash from property owner A, and a $250 property assessment payment by check from property owner B, she might credit property owner A with cash payment in the Association's books and on a deposit slip, but keep the cash for herself and actually deposit the $250 check from property owner B. Under a classic lapping scheme, once the funds are diverted for the embezzler's own use, successive accounting book entries are made to hide the defalcations by crediting those customers' accounts as paid, using subsequent payments in the same amounts but received from other customers.

The State's evidence at trial showed that Benton had stolen at least $2,300 from her employer. Benton was convicted of Felony Theft and Falsification of Business Records. On October 25, 1996, Benton was sentenced to probation. She was also ordered to make restitution. Benton's original appeal from that sentence to this Court was voluntarily dismissed.

A restitution hearing was held on May 13 and July 10, 1997. The Superior Court determined that $2,300 had been misappropriated from the payments for lot assessments by Benton in her "lapping" scheme. The Superior Court concluded that a $100 traveler's check and a $155.45 Association check had been diverted to Benton's personal use. The Superior Court also concluded that Benton had embezzled an additional amount of $1,589.20 from soda sales, $325 from pool passes, $225 from boat racks, $825 from marina stickers, and $425 from ramp stickers. The Superior Court aggregated the total theft from the Association by Benton at $5,994.65 The Superior Court also determined that Benton should pay restitution for the following amounts, which reflect a portion of the fees the Association had paid its accountants: $6,660 to ascertain the amount stolen by Benton through the "lapping" scheme;

$1,336 in expenses for trial preparation; and $7,460 for restoring the Association's financial records because of the damage done by Benton's falsifications.

In an amended sentencing order dated August 15, 1997, the Superior Court directed Benton to pay restitution in the total amount of $21,450.65. Prior to the Superior Court's order quantifying Benton's restitution, the Association had received the proceeds of a $10,000 bond under a policy of theft insurance, as a result of Benton's theft. Therefore, the Superior Court divided the restitution. The first $11,450.65 was ordered to be paid to the Association and the remaining $10,000 to the insurer.

RESTITUTION AMOUNT PROPERLY EXCEEDED TRIAL EVIDENCE

Benton submits that the maximum amount of restitution she could be ordered to pay is limited to the evidence presented during her criminal trial. Therefore, Benton contends that the Superior Court erred by ordering her to pay an amount of restitution in excess of $2,300. Benton bases this claim on the trial testimony by an accountant for the Association. According to that accountant, prior to trial he had only been able to determine that Benton had embezzled at least $2,300 and had attempted to conceal that theft by her "lapping" scheme.

Benton's contention disregards the legal distinction between evidence that is either relevant or necessary to establish the elements of an offense at a criminal trial and evidence that is admissible at a hearing to determine the appropriate amount of restitution. There is no constitutional or statutory mandate that the complete economic consequences of a defendant's illegal conduct be established at the criminal trial. In fact, the complete economic consequences of a crime would frequently be irrelevant and inadmissible during the criminal trial, e.g., out-of-pocket losses and other expenses. There are separately enumerated statutory factors, however, which either permit or require the complete economic ramifications of the convicted defendant's illegal conduct to be taken into account by the sentencing judge for purposes of ordering restitution.

Benton was charged with Falsification of Business Records and Felony Theft. The State

met its burden by proving the elements of those offenses at the criminal trial. The State presented evidence that Benton had embezzled more than $500 from the Association and had falsified records in order to conceal her theft. The jury was convinced, beyond a reasonable doubt, that Benton was guilty of both crimes.

The Delaware Criminal Code imposes separate statutory responsibilities upon the Superior Court for the purposes of sentencing. Section 841(d) provides that, "upon conviction, the sentencing judge shall require full restitution to the victim for any monetary losses suffered. . . ." Accordingly, Section 4106(b) directs the sentencing judge to "determine the nature and amount of restitution, if any, to be made to each victim of the crime of each convicted offender."

The statutory criteria for making that determination are set forth in Section 4106(a):

any person convicted . . . shall be liable to each victim of the offense for the value of the property or property rights lost to the victim and for the value of any property which has diminished in worth as a result of the actions of such convicted offender and shall be ordered by the court to make restitution. If the court does not require that restitution be paid to a victim, the court shall state its reason on the record. The convicted offender shall also be liable for direct out-of-pocket losses, loss of earnings and other expenses and inconveniences incurred by victim as a direct result of the crime. . . .

Thus, the statutory scheme for restitution expressly provides for the victim to recover for the value of the property rights lost or diminished by the defendant's criminal conduct, as well as "direct out-of-pocket losses, loss of earnings and other expenses and inconveniences."

In determining the amount of restitution to order for the total actual theft by Benton, the Superior Court relied upon the testimony of the Association's accountant, who had also testified at the criminal trial, and the testimony of the Association's president. The accountant had testified, based on his pre-trial review of the Association's financial records, that Benton had embezzled at least $2,300. At the restitution hearing, the president of the Association described the post-trial calculations which reflected Benton's embezzlement of more than $3,600 in additional money from the Association. The

Superior Court properly admitted evidence regarding the full amount of Benton's actual theft at the restitution hearing.

In addition to restitution for the total amount stolen, Section 4106(a) contemplates that a restitution award will include compensation to the victim for out-of-pocket losses and other expenses directly resulting from the defendant's criminal acts. The Superior Court's restitution order included the $7,460 accountant's fee charged for the reconstruction of the Association's financial records that had been falsified by Benton as part of her embezzlement scheme. The Superior Court also ordered for restitution of 90% of the accountant's fee required to determine the extent of the money missing as part of the lapping scheme ($6,660) and one-half of the amount charged by the Association's accountants to prepare for trial ($1,336). The total accountant's fee included in the Superior Court's order of restitution was $15,456.

The Superior Court correctly concluded that Section 4106(a) authorized it to order restitution for the accounting fees incurred by the Association. The record reflects that those out-of-pocket expenses were incurred as a result of Benton's theft from the Association and her falsification of the Association's business records. In cases of embezzlement, accounting fees for restoration of financial records and preparation of the case against the defendant are properly awarded to the victim as part of the amount of restitution for out-of-pocket expenses.

CONCLUSION

The judgment entered by the Superior Court, pursuant to its amended sentencing order, is affirmed.

Case Commentary

The moral of this case is that an employee who is caught stealing will have to make restitution to the employer for the amount he or she converted to his or her own use as well as all expenses incurred by the employer as a consequence of the employee's conversion.

Case Questions

1. As punishment for a total theft of $5,994.65, do you believe it is fair to make Melissa Benton pay an additional $15,456 for accounting fees to straighten out the employer's records?

2. Do you think this type of judgment will discourage future acts of theft?
3. What is the difference between the evidence presented in Melissa Brown's criminal trial and the civil trial above?

PADDED PAYROLL

A padded payroll is one to which a dishonest employee has added names that are unauthorized and frequently fictitious. Checks are issued to these fictitious payees and endorsed by the dishonest employee. The person or bank receiving the endorsed instrument is not liable if they acted in good faith and exercised ordinary care.

EMPLOYMENT PERSPECTIVE

Jonathan Rhodes worked as the treasurer for the Whitney and Myers Department Store. There were 92 employees of the store. Rhodes issued 95 checks each week. The three additional checks were issued to Kelly, Paige, and Evan—fictitious employees of the department store who supposedly worked with mannequins. Rhodes endorsed the names of the payees and negotiated the checks to the Williamsburg Savings Bank in return for cash. When the department store discovered Rhodes's scheme, he had left for a permanent vacation in the Bahamas. Has the department store any recourse against the bank? No! The endorsement of Rhodes, the impostor, is effective against the company as long as the bank acted in good faith. ∎

In the following case, a worker was passing embezzled funds through his best friend's checking account. The friend had no knowledge of any wrongdoing, but was implicated. After the friend extricated himself, he sought damages from the worker's employer for infliction of emotional distress. The issue is whether he is entitled to relief.

CASE

ITT CONSUMER FINANCIAL CORP. v. TOVAR

932 S.W.2d 147 (Tex. 1996)

BARAJAS, Justice.

This is an appeal from a judgment on a jury verdict awarding Appellee actual and punitive damages for negligence, gross negligence and intentional infliction of emotional distress. We reverse and render.

I. Summary of the Evidence

Appellee holds a degree in criminal justice and works as a paralegal specialist for the United States Customs Service. In late 1987, Appellee bought a home and invited his best friend from high school, Frank Chavira, who was working at Appellant's consumer loan office as an assistant manager, to share the house. Chavira paid for a room of his own and a half share of the utilities.

Appellee, however, had problems getting Chavira to pay his rent and bills in a timely fashion. Therefore, beginning in 1988, Appellee allowed Chavira to deposit checks into his personal bank account. When Chavira needed money, Appellee would either write him a check, withdraw money from an ATM, or give Chavira his ATM card to withdraw a specific amount.

Appellant is engaged in the business of consumer lending nationwide and had several branches in El Paso. Appellant employed approximately a dozen auditors who conducted periodic branch audits pursuant to a program encompassing 250 areas of office operation. The El Paso Number One Branch ("the Branch"),

where Chavira worked, was audited (the "250-point audit") in December 1987, and it received an above average "C+" rating, meaning that the Branch was running generally within company guidelines. It is undisputed that this auditing program was not designed to detect fraud.

The Branch was not audited again until 1992. According to Appellant's former audit supervisor, a branch receiving a "C" grade would generally be audited again within approximately two years after the previous audit.

In addition to the 250-point audits, Appellant employed regional managers, each responsible for eight to twelve branches, who were required to audit the branches in their region every 120 days by taking a statistical sampling of loans made since the previous 120 day audit. The sample loans were reviewed pursuant to a twenty point check system to determine whether they complied with company policy.

On December 29, 1989, Rose Santana, a Branch employee, discovered irregularities in six accounts. Neither the aforementioned 250-point audit nor the 120 day audit had uncovered these irregularities. This finding launched a lengthy investigation by Regional Manager Ray Chavez and Director of Security and Special Investigations Jim Klein. On January 4, 1990, Chavira confessed to embezzling through eighteen fraudulent accounts. Appellant immediately suspended him without pay and turned him over to the El Paso Police.

It was eventually revealed that Chavira, between May 1987 and January 1990, embezzled $59,178 from Appellant by creating twenty-nine fictitious loans. Chavira created files to make the fictitious loans appear legitimate, then later destroyed the files for twenty-seven of the twenty-nine accounts. Chavira would prepare a loan application and then instruct other branch employees to do the required pre-loan verifications, explaining that the customer would come to the office after hours to close the loans with him. Chavira also made entries into the computer system indicating that a check was received. Thus, employees, believing that a post-dated check had been received, would not follow up with the customer. Beginning in October 1989, Chavira kept control of all post-dated checks received by the Branch, making it more difficult for employees to know what checks had been received. Eventually, he used one month deferments to make the delinquent accounts appear current. Although Appellant allowed customers two deferments a year, some accounts had as many as nineteen deferments.

For the first twelve months of the fraud, Chavira passed the fraudulent checks through his own MBank checking account. Thereafter, Chavira closed his account and began using Appellee's El Paso Teacher's Credit Union checking account to clear the checks and obtain the cash proceeds. Chavira eventually deposited seventeen embezzled checks totaling $34,523.66 into Appellee's account. Although Appellee had two accounts with Appellant, neither account was affected by Chavira's embezzling and money laundering schemes. Regarding the money deposited into Appellee's account and the fact that he was unaware of the deposits, Appellee testified as follows:

Q. Did they (Chavez and Klein) ask you if you were balancing—or how you balanced your checking account?

A. Yes, sir, they did.

Q. And what did you tell them about that?

A. I told them that I do receive statements and that I do look at them. However, my main method of balancing my checkbook was to call the bank and they give you the information, if you want the last five checks, or the last three checks, the last deposits, and I would—I personally preferred doing it that way.

On March 27, 1990, Jim Klein and Appellee had a telephone conversation regarding the seventeen embezzled checks deposited into his account Klein explained that each of the checks bore a first endorsement in the customer's name and a second endorsement in the name of Appellee. Appellee declared that he had no knowledge of the checks.

The following day, Appellee went to Appellant's offices to examine the checks. Klein asked Appellee if he knew Chavira, but at no time informed him about the underlying fraudulent loans. Appellee examined twelve of the embezzled checks and confirmed his account number which appeared on each of the checks below the endorsement in Appellee's name. Appellee again denied knowledge of the checks and stated that the endorsements in his name were forgeries. Appellee stated that he did not have any roommates who might have access to his account without his knowledge.

Chavira was arrested on December 29, 1991. Appellee bailed him out of jail the next day and took him to see an attorney. At this point, Appellee was informed about the fraud and the money being laundered through his account.

On May 15, 1990, Chavez and Klein gave the El Paso Police Department their investigative report entitled "Statement Regarding Embezzlement." This report provided, in pertinent part to Appellee:

PURPOSE OF THIS STATEMENT

This statement provides information relating to the admitted embezzlement of over $20,000 by an ITT Financial Services employee, Frank Chavira.

ITT Financial Services requests the information presented herein be reviewed and further investigated by law enforcement officials for the purpose of filing criminal charges, on Frank Chavira and other co-conspirators, as appropriate.

DISPOSITION OF DIVERTED CHECKS

Seventeen (17) checks, totaling $34,523.66, appear to have been deposited to account # 38179 at the El Paso Teachers Credit Union. All the checks have a (fraudulent) first endorsement in the alleged customer's name followed by a second endorsement in the name of Daniel Tovar and account # 38179.

J. M. Klein and I interviewed Daniel Tovar on March 28, 1990, at the El Paso # 1 branch office (Exhibit 6). Tovar confirmed that account # 38179 was his account, however he denied having any knowledge of the ITT checks being deposited to the account. Tovar examined the purported endorsements in his name and stated that they were forgeries. Tovar said that no one else had authority to sign on his account.

Tovar acted as if someone must be using his account without his knowledge. Tovar said he probably did not detect the activity in the account because he never looked at his monthly account statement. Tovar refused to provide a written affidavit concerning the forgeries. Delacruz (whose name Chavira used on a fraudulent account) said that he also knows Daniel Tovar and that Chavira and Tovar are also friends.

Several ITT Financial Services branch employees stated that Chavira received many calls from a "Danny." Chavira told employees that Danny was his brother. (This has not been confirmed.) ITTFS employee Francis Trejo recalls that in January or February, 1990, Daniel Tovar came into the branch and made a payment on his account. While he was in the office, Tovar asked about what happened to Chavira. Tovar said that Chavira told him that he left ITTFS because he was being forced to transfer.

CONCLUSION

The evidence presented above supports that Frank Chavira knowingly and willfully engaged in fraudulent deceptive acts designed to embezzle monies from his employer, ITT Financial Services. Chavira's actions, supported by his admissions, indicate that he acted intentionally, fully understanding the outcome of his acts and knowing that he had no legal basis for engaging in these fraudulent activities. His deceptive actions were accomplished without the effective knowledge or consent of ITT Financial Services.

The case was assigned to Dempsey Gunaca, Chief Investigator of the District Attorney's White Collar Crime Unit. Gunaca subpoenaed bank records in an effort to determine the disposition of the embezzled funds. He also hired a handwriting expert to determine whether the endorsements in Tovar's name were forgeries.

Regarding the prosecution of Appellee, Gunaca testified as follows:

Q. Who made the decision to indict Daniel Tovar?

A. I made that—to indict him? The grand jury did. To present it to the grand jury, I did.

On August 4, 1992, Appellee filed this action against Appellant alleging malicious prosecution, defamation, intentional infliction of emotional distress, negligence and gross negligence. At the close of Appellee's case-in-chief the trial court directed a verdict in favor of Appellant on Appellee's malicious prosecution and defamation claims. The trial judge, who also heard Appellee's criminal case, ruled as follows on Appellant's motion for directed verdict:

With regards to the motion for directed verdict on the malicious prosecution claim, the Court finds that the Defendant ITT did not initiate the case against Mr. Tovar, but rather, that was left to the discretion of the district attorney's office, and rather, it was the district attorney's office who initiated and procured the prosecution against Mr. Tovar.

And let me further add that I find the district attorney's supervision of its assistants negligent and grossly negligent in that had there been some thought applied and some knowledge of the law applied to the review of that case, and had there been some temperance on the part of the district attorney—assistant district attorney handling the case when it was ready to go to trial, that prosecution would have been dismissed. And that the Court actually instructed the assistant district attorney handling that case to review the case because the Court felt that they would not be able to make the charges or present the evidence sufficient to establish a case against Mr. Tovar. And perhaps the district attorney's office should have been a defendant in this case.

The Court finds that there was probable cause for the acts that ITT took in its presentation of the case to the district attorney's office and that they were not actually initiating or procuring a complaint against Mr. Tovar, but simply presented the facts as they knew them. And I further find that there was no malice in the actions of the Defendant ITT in presenting the case to the district attorney's office. So the motion for directed verdict as to that cause of action is granted to the Defendant.

The negligence, gross negligence, and intentional infliction of emotional distress claims were submitted to the jury. The jury returned a verdict awarding Appellee $1,204,750 in actual damages and $1,500,000 in punitive damages,[5] which precipitated this appeal.

The actual damages questions were answered as follows:

Question

What sum of money, if paid now in cash, would fairly and reasonably compensate Daniel Tovar for his damages, if any, that were proximately caused by the negligence you have found?

***

Answer:

  a. Medical expenses of Daniel Tovar; $7000.00
  b. Lost income of Daniel Tovar; $14,000.00
  c. Legal fees related to the defense of the $6220.00 criminal charges brought against Daniel Tovar;
  d. Cost of the bail bond; $2530.00
  e. Damage to the reputation of Daniel Tovar; $250,000.00
  f. Daniel Tovar's mental anguish; and $400,000.00
  g. Daniel Tovar's physical pain and suffering. $25,000.00

Question

What sum of money, if paid now in cash, would fairly and reasonably compensate Daniel Tovar for his damages, if any, that were proximately caused by the intentional infliction of emotional distress you have found?

  a. Daniel Tovar's emotional distress.

Answer: $500,000.00

The jury could have reasonably concluded that Tovar was his, and ITT's, best hope for recovering some money.

Klein left ADA Meraz with the impression he did not believe Tovar's story. Klein also told ADA McDonald, after Tovar was indicted, that Klein thought Tovar was an accomplice. His actions, when examined in the context in which they occurred, are factually sufficient evidence that Klein went beyond "all possible bounds of decency" and ensured that Tovar would be tried. We find nothing extreme or outrageous in the conduct of Klein or Chavez. Indeed, seventeen fraudulent checks totaling almost $35,000 going through an account would make anyone, even Appellee, suspicious:

Accordingly, finding that Chavira was not acting in the scope of his employment and that the conduct of Chavez and Klein was not so outrageous and extreme in degree as to "go beyond all bounds of decency," we find that the evidence is legally insufficient to support a finding of severe emotional distress.

Judgment for ITT Consumer Financial Corporation.

Case Commentary

The Texas Appellate Court concluded that infliction of severe emotional distress requires unreasonable and unauthorized action on the part of the employer. Here, ITT's actions were reasonable in light of Tover's permitting Chavira to deposit and clear checks through Tovar's account. If not for Tovar's lack of supervision of his own checking account, he would never have been implicated in a criminal proceeding.

Case Questions

  1. Do you agree with the Texas Appellate Court's decision?
  2. What do you think of the Court's comment that the District Attorney's office should have been a codefendant?
  3. Should Tovar be permitted to commence a lawsuit where he is contributorily negligent?

THEFT OF TIME

The broad definition of employee theft would also include theft of time. This would encompass longer lunch breaks, arriving late, leaving early, conducting personal business on company time, and just goofing off. The old expression "time is money" is true. An employee who commits this theft of time is not giving the employer adequate work in return for the wage bargained for. The employee is wrongfully inflating his or her wage at the employer's expense, which is a form of theft. Theft of time will not result in prosecution but may result in dismissal or demotion.

EMPLOYMENT PERSPECTIVE

Pamela Hall is a research assistant at Bull and Bear Stockbrokerage. She often spends time in the firm's library researching information on companies that her father, an avid market player, is interested in investing in. Is this act employee theft? Yes! Pamela is guilty of theft of time. What if Pamela had no work assigned? Then she should ask her supervisor for an assignment or educate herself on some aspect of the company's business. ■

EMPLOYMENT PERSPECTIVE

Justin Sheldon is a data entry clerk for Miracle Drug Pharmaceutical Company. Justin often spends an hour or two a day making personal calls and running errands. He then works overtime at time-and-a-half to accomplish what he could not do in the eight-hour day. Obviously, Justin is not closely supervised. In any event, is he guilty of employee theft? Yes! Justin is not only stealing time but also charging the company at the overtime rate for the time he spent on personal business. ■

FOURTH AMENDMENT

Employee theft is a very serious problem. It undermines business profitability as well as giving the unethical employees an unfair advantage over their honest counterparts. Some solutions are closer supervision through time sheets, electronic surveillance, desk and office searches, security guards, and tape-recorded phone lines. Many employees feel that such steps are an invasion of privacy, but what degree of privacy should an employee have at the workplace? The Fourth Amendment to the United States Constitution guarantees the right of the People to be secure in their person, property, and effects from unreasonable searches and seizures. In the workplace, absent an overcoat or a briefcase, what personal effects or property belong to the employee? Aren't the office and the desk company property? That would seem to be the case.

Americans have safeguarded their privacy rights since the inception of this nation. Today privacy is a major concern in the workplace. Employees have argued the Fourth Amendment prohibition against unreasonable searches and seizures should be extended to office searches, E-mail monitoring, tape recording telephone conversations, and drug testing. With the advent of suspicionless searches, employees seem to be slowly losing ground. At the same time, employers feel that employees' reasonable expectation of privacy should give way due to the increase in employee theft and drug use.

SURVEILLANCE

Many companies use time sheets and electronic surveillance. Time sheets require an employee to justify his or her time spent during the workday, but they can be doctored. However, supervisors should be able to distinguish fabrications by comparisons with other similarly engaged employees and from experience with the work habits of the employee in question. Electronic surveillance is often installed by retail companies under the guise of identifying shoplifters, but equally important to the company is the electronic supervision of the work habits of its employees and the recognition of those who steal. Tape-recorded conversations are often used in the securities industry to record conversations between broker and customer for the purpose of verification should a miscommunication occur. Tape-recorded conversations can also discourage an employee from receiving personal calls. The use of polygraphs, otherwise known as lie-dectector tests, is severely restricted to cases in which the employer has a reasonable suspicion that an employee has committed a theft.

EMPLOYMENT SCENARIO

The Long and Short of It feels it can improve its profits by discouraging employee theft and shoplifting through the conspicuous use of surveillance cameras. L&S is also contemplating tape recording phone conversations to monitor personal phone use, which it believes has become a problem. Finally, L&S wants to prohibit use of its E-mail system for private messages after receiving a complaint from a customer who received a sexual joke from L&S's E-mail. The joke was mistakenly sent to the customer by Rodney Fraizer, an employee, instead of to his friend. But the damage was done. L&S consults with Susan North for a critique of the above security measures. Susan asks L&S if the workers know of the problems L&S wants to address. L&S answers in the negative. Susan counsels L&S that before it adopts a dictatorial approach, it might want to bring the workers onboard to solve the dilemma. Encouraging the workers to take ownership of the company's problems makes it easier to find a solution that satisfies almost everyone. L&S says that it will heed Susan's advice.

SECURITY

The mere presence of security guards is a deterrence to many employees who would otherwise want to steal. Security guards, though, cannot be everywhere and see everything. They are also expensive when compared with the other alternatives. An additional method would be the use of inventory control. This requires limiting access to inventory to certain employees and instituting accounting controls and physical checks for verification. Inconsistencies can be investigated, and thefts are more easily traceable. When companies are lax in determining the existence of theft, it encourages employees so inclined to steal because there is little chance of detection. When controls are instituted, employees are more wary.

OFFICE SEARCHES

Desk and office searches are often used primarily to locate drug use but also to identify the conducting of work unrelated to the company by the employee while on the job. Many employees find this to be particularly intrusive and an invasion of privacy. Most courts come down on the side of the employer if it has a justifiable business reason. However, employees who have been with an employer for a lengthy period of time develop a reasonable expectation of privacy in at least their desk and file cabinets.

The following case addresses the question of whether the contents of a physician's office can be searched by the hospital that employs him. The resolution revolves around the issue of whether the Fourth Amendment protects the physician's privacy.

CASE

O'CONNOR v. ORTEGA

480 U.S. 709 (1986)

O'CONNOR, JUSTICE.

This suit under 42 U.S.C. 1983 presents two issues concerning the Fourth Amendment rights of public employees. First, we must determine whether the respondent, a public employee, had a reasonable expectation of privacy in his office, desk, and file cabinets at his place of work. Second, we must address the appropriate Fourth Amendment standard for a search conducted by a public employer in areas in which a public employee is found to have a reasonable expectation of privacy.

Dr. Magno Ortega, a physician and psychiatrist, held the position of Chief of Professional Education at Napa State Hospital for 17 years, until his dismissal from that position in 1981. As Chief of Professional Education, Dr. Ortega had primary responsibility for training young physicians in psychiatric residency programs.

In July 1981, Hospital officials, including Dr. Dennis O'Connor, the Executive Director of the Hospital, became concerned about possible improprieties in Dr. Ortega's management of the residency program. In particular, the Hospital officials were concerned with Dr. Ortega's acquisition of an Apple II computer for use in the residency program. The officials thought that Dr. Ortega may have misled Dr. O'Connor into believing that the computer had been donated, when in fact the computer had been financed by the possibly coerced contributions of residents. Additionally, the Hospital officials were concerned with charges that Dr. Ortega had sexually harassed two female Hospital employees, and had taken inappropriate disciplinary action against a resident.

Dr. O'Connor selected several Hospital personnel to conduct the investigation, including an accountant, a physician, and a Hospital security officer. Richard Friday, the Hospital Administrator, led this "investigative team." At some point during the investigation, Mr. Friday made the decision to enter Dr. Ortega's office. The petitioners claim that the search was conducted to secure state property. Initially, petitioners contended that such a search was pursuant to a Hospital policy of conducting a routine inventory of state property in the office of a terminated employee. At the time of the search, however, the Hospital had not yet terminated Dr. Ortega's employment; Dr. Ortega was still on administrative leave. Apparently, there was no policy of inventorying the offices of those on administrative leave. Before the search had been initiated, however, petitioners had become aware that Dr. Ortega had taken the computer to his home. Dr. Ortega contends that the purpose of the search was to secure evidence for use against him in administrative disciplinary proceedings.

The resulting search of Dr. Ortega's office was quite thorough. The investigators entered the office a number of times and seized several items from Dr. Ortega's desk and file cabinets, including a Valentine's Day card, a photograph, and a book of poetry, all sent to Dr. Ortega by a former resident physician. These items were later used in a proceeding before a hearing officer of the California State Personnel Board to impeach the credibility of the former resident, who testified on Dr. Ortega's behalf. The investigators also seized billing documentation of one of Dr. Ortega's private patients under the California Medicaid program. The investigators did not otherwise separate Dr. Ortega's property from state property because, as one investigator testified, "trying to sort State from non-State, it was too much to do, so I gave it up and boxed it up." Thus, no formal inventory of the property in the office was ever made. Instead, all the papers in Dr. Ortega's office were merely placed in boxes, and put in storage for Dr. Ortega to retrieve.

Dr. Ortega commenced this action against petitioners in Federal District Court under 42 U.S.C.1983, alleging that the search of his office violated the Fourth Amendment.

The Fourth Amendment protects the "right of the people to be secure in their persons, houses, papers, and effects, against unreasonable searches and seizures. . . ." Our cases establish that Dr. Ortega's Fourth Amendment rights are implicated only if the conduct of the Hospital officials at issue in this case infringed "an expectation of privacy that society is prepared to consider reasonable."

Because the reasonableness of an expectation of privacy, as well as the appropriate standard for a search, is understood to differ according to context, it is essential first to delineate the boundaries of the workplace context. The work-

place includes those areas and items that are related to work and are generally within the employer's control. At a hospital, for example, the hallways, cafeteria, offices, desks, and file cabinets, among other areas, are all part of the workplace. These areas remain part of the workplace context even if the employee has placed personal items in them, such as a photograph placed in a desk or a letter posted on an employee bulletin board.

Not everything that passes through the confines of the business address can be considered part of the workplace context, however. An employee may bring closed luggage to the office prior to leaving on a trip, or a handbag or briefcase each workday. While whatever expectation of privacy the employee has in the existence and the outward appearance of the luggage is affected by its presence in the workplace, the employee's expectation of privacy in the contents of the luggage is not affected in the same way. The appropriate standard for a workplace search does not necessarily apply to a piece of closed personal luggage, a handbag, or a briefcase that happens to be within the employer's business address.

Within the workplace context, this Court has recognized that employees may have a reasonable expectation of privacy against intrusions by police. As with the expectation of privacy in one's home, such as expectations that have deep roots in the history of the Amendment.

Given the societal expectations of privacy in one's place of work, we reject the contention made by the Solicitor General and petitioners that public employees can never have a reasonable expectation of privacy in their place of work. Individuals do not lose Fourth Amendment rights merely because they work for the government instead of a private employer. The operational realities of the workplace, however, may make some employees' expectations of privacy unreasonable when an intrusion is by a supervisor rather than a law enforcement official. Public employees' expectations of privacy in their offices, desks, and file cabinets, like similar expectations of employees in the private sector, may be reduced by virtue of actual office practices and procedures, or by legitimate regulation.

The Court of Appeals concluded that Dr. Ortega had a reasonable expectation of privacy in his office, and five Members of this Court agree with that determination. Because the record does not reveal the extent to which Hospital officials may have had work-related reasons to enter Dr. Ortega's office, we think the Court of Appeals should have remanded the matter to the District Court for its further determination. But regardless of any legitimate right of access the Hospital staff may have had to the office as such, we recognize that the undisputed evidence suggests that Dr. Ortega had a reasonable expectation of privacy in his desk and file cabinets. The undisputed evidence discloses that Dr. Ortega did not share his desk or file cabinets with any other employees. Dr. Ortega had occupied the office for 17 years and he kept materials in his office, which included personal correspondence, medical files, correspondence from private patients unconnected to the Hospital, personal financial records, teaching aids and notes, and personal gifts and mementos.

On the basis of this undisputed evidence, we accept the conclusion of the Court of Appeals that Dr. Ortega had a reasonable expectation of privacy at least in his desk and file cabinets.

Judgment for Ortega.

Case Commentary

The United States Supreme Court decided that after occupying the same office for seventeen years, the employee is entitled to a reasonable expectation of privacy in his desk and file cabinets. Since their decision is specific to this employee, it does not provide guidance for employees who occupy an office for a much shorter period of time or an employee who works in a cubicle or at a desk in an open floor plan with many others.

Case Questions

1. Do you agree with the court's decision?
2. Why did the court bother hearing this case if they were not going to make a decision that would provide guidance for employers who want to conduct office searches and for employees who want to know the extent of their privacy?
3. Does the fact that the desk, file cabinets, computer, and office belong to employers give them the right to search their contents?
4. Must notice be given to employees if an employer wants to conduct a search?

COMPANY POLICY

Establishing a policy against employee theft is an important consideration for a company. The policy should include a definition encompassing all the property that the company feels if taken or allowed to be taken would constitute theft. The policy should spell out what the consequences for thefts will be and whether the company intends to have the employee prosecuted. A statement should be included stipulating that the policy applies to all employees from executives on down. The company must disseminate this policy to all its employees along with conspicuous posting. Finally the company should follow through rigorously, identifying and then enforcing breaches of this policy in a consistent manner.

WHISTLE-BLOWING

Whistle-blowing is the notification by an employee to management about a coworker's unlawful activities or to the appropriate federal and state agencies about the company's illegal activities.

Whistle-blowing is a noble and ethical act that sometimes requires a courageous effort on the part of an employee. Whistle-blowers may be heroes in the movies, but are often labeled troublemakers and treated with disdain by management and coworkers for the disruption they cause. On the other hand, some workers whistle-blow as an act of spite or revenge. They may fabricate the event or blow it out of proportion. These workers are not acting in an ethical manner.

The following case addresses the issue as to whether trivial disclosures are protected under the Whistle-blower Protection Act.

CASE

HERMAN v. DEPARTMENT OF JUSTICE

193 F.3d 1375 (Fed. Cir. 1999)

MICHEL, Circuit Judge.

The Petitioner, Dr. Richard Herman, filed an Individual Right of Action ("IRA") appeal to the Merit Systems Protection Board ("Board" or "MSPB"), alleging that he was reassigned in retaliation for whistleblowing activities. On the government's motion, the Board dismissed the appeal for lack of jurisdiction, ruling that none of the disclosures upon which Dr. Herman based his complaint was a protected disclosure under the Whistleblower Protection Act ("WPA"). Because both the specific language in the Act and our case law interpreting the Act support the Board's conclusion, we affirm.

BACKGROUND

In September 1997, Dr. Herman was laterally reassigned from the position of Chief Clinical Psychologist, GM-13, at the Federal Prison Camp, Eglin Air Force Base, Florida, to that of Staff Clinical Psychologist, GM-13, at the Federal Correctional Complex, Coleman, Florida. Dr. Herman filed a complaint about his reassignment with the United States Office of Special Counsel ("OSC"). The OSC terminated its investigation without taking corrective action. Dr. Herman timely appealed to the MSPB.

Before the MSPB, Dr. Herman alleged that his reassignment to a new facility was a "prohibited personnel action" which was taken in retalia-

tion for two separate whistleblowing disclosures. Dr. Herman contended that the first disclosure was a memorandum given in July 1997 to the associate warden at the prison camp urging the warden to either formalize an agreement with the Base hospital for use of its facilities in the event there is a suicidal inmate or create a suicide watch room at the prison camp. Before the Board, Dr. Herman asserted that the memorandum indicated that failure to have a formal written agreement with the hospital, or have a suicide watch room at the camp itself, potentially posed a substantial and specific danger to the public health and safety within the meaning of the WPA and violated the U.S. Department of Justice/Federal Bureau of Prisons Suicide Prevention Program ("SPP").

Dr. Herman contended that the second disclosure was a statement he made in June 1997, by telephone to the national Employee Assistance Program ("EAP") Coordinator in Washington, DC, and in writing to the associate warden that EAP Directives requiring confidentiality of counseling information may have been violated when his department's telephone log was copied during an investigation of his conduct by prison officials. The EAP provision, Directive P.S. 3792, states that the "confidential nature of EAP counseling information of all employees referred for assistance shall be preserved with the same enhanced level of confidentiality as counseling records of employees with alcohol and drug abuse problems." Dr.

Herman contended that the copying of the telephone log during an investigation of Dr. Herman's alleged unauthorized use of the telephone could have been a violation of Directive P.S. 3792 and of other federal laws and regulations.

The Administrative Judge ("AJ") conducted a pre-hearing conference in which she questioned whether the disclosures qualified as protected disclosures under the WPA and ordered Dr. Herman to submit evidence and argument that his disclosures met any of the criteria set forth in 5 U.S.C. § 2302(b)(8). Following receipt of the parties' written responses, the AJ concluded that Dr. Herman did not establish that a reasonable person in Dr. Herman's position would believe that the disclosures were protected disclosures under the WPA and dismissed Dr. Herman's IRA appeal without an evidentiary hearing for lack of jurisdiction.

Dr. Herman's First Disclosure

The legislative history of the initial whistleblower provisions indicates that the Act was not intended to apply to disclosure of trivial or de minimis matters.

The legislative history explains that:

the Committee intends that only disclosures of public health or safety dangers which are both substantial and specific are to be protected. Thus, for example, general criticisms by an employee of the Environmental Protection Agency that the agency is not doing enough to protect the environment would not be protected under this subsection. However, an allegation by a nuclear regulatory commission engineer that the cooling system of a nuclear reactor is inadequate would fall within the whistle blower protections.

We agree with the Board that Dr. Herman's memorandum, discussing the absence of a formal agreement between the hospital and the prison camp, did not disclose a "substantial and specific danger to public safety" that, according to legislative intent, warrants protection under the WPA.

Further, at the time Dr. Herman made his statement about the suicide watch room, the prison camp had not placed an inmate on suicide watch in at least three years. Dr. Herman has failed to identify any prison inmates, or any other members of the public, needing access to a suicide watch room, or even that there is a specific and substantial likelihood that there will be individuals in the future needing access to the suicide watch room.

Dr. Herman's Second Disclosure

The AJ based her decision on the fact that Dr. Herman had not provided any evidence whatsoever that any confidential "counseling information" was copied. Thus, there simply was no violation. The AJ therefore correctly held that Dr. Herman's memorandum expressing his concern about the possible effect that copying the telephone logs may have on the integrity and the confidentiality of the program is not a protected disclosure.

If supervisors have to fear that every trivial lapse in their own behavior will be the subject of a whistleblowing complaint when they critically appraise their employees, as they are obligated to do, they will be deterred from carrying out honest appraisals. Poor performers will be protected by any minor lapse in a supervisor's conduct. This was not the purpose of the WPA, which merely was intended to root out real wrongdoing.

Dr. Herman must allege facts that, if proven, would establish that he was subject to an adverse personnel action because he made a protected disclosure, that is, information which he reasonably believed evidenced a violation of law, rule, or regulation, or gross mismanagement, a gross waste of funds, an abuse of authority, or a substantial and specific danger to public health and safety. As stated above, even accepting as true all that Dr. Herman alleges, none of Dr. Herman's disclosures were protected disclosures under the WPA.

Accordingly, the decision of the Board is
AFFIRMED.

Case Commentary

The purpose of the Whistleblower Protection Act is to encourage employees who have knowledge of danger to public health and safety, an illegal activity, gross mismanagement, or an abuse of funds to come forward with the assurance that they will be protected from retaliation. In this case, the actions taken by Dr. Herman's employer are not retaliatory because Dr. Herman's disclosures do not qualify as whistleblowing activities.

Case Questions

1. Do you believe Dr. Herman's actions qualify as whistle-blowing activities?
2. What is the purpose of the Whistleblower Protection Act?
3. Would evaluations undertaken by supervisors be undermined if employees could claim any adverse action of the supervisor was motivated by retaliation?

While the authorities encourage whistle-blowing, more could be done to protect people who do risk their jobs for the truth to be known.

The Whistleblower Protection Act of 1989 was enacted to safeguard workers who report major violations of the law from being discharged or otherwise retaliated against by their employers.

EMPLOYMENT PERSPECTIVE

Stellar Industries, a manufacturer of tires for commercial aircraft, is located in Oklahoma City. Times have been tough for Stellar.

The last recession had caused Stellar to trim its workforce by 40 percent. Recently Stellar was awarded a contract by Heavenly Airlines for designing a more durable tire. This contract will triple Stellar's revenues over a five-year period. Also, the contract enabled Stellar to rehire half the people it had laid off as well as some new people.

One of the people rehired was Megan Thomas. Her assignment is to run the testing of the tire tread wear. She will work directly under Russ Heflin, who is the chief engineer and the person directly responsible for the design of the durable tires. The purpose of the testing is to assure Heavenly that the plane will land 50 times before the tires have to be replaced. After the first round of tests, a tire blows out after the thirty-sixth landing. Megan Thomas informs Russ of the result. He instructs her to test again. This time the tires last through the thirty-fourth landing. Both Megan and Russ realize that a mistake has been made. Megan asks Russ if he will inform Heavenly that Stellar can guarantee only 30 landings and that the tires will have to be replaced more frequently. Russ explains that Heavenly Airlines intends to replace the tires after thirty landings. The 50 landing guarantee provides them with a cushion. Therefore, Russ states that although no damage will occur, the failure to guarantee 50 landings is a breach of contract. Heavenly will go elsewhere to have the tires manufactured and will sue for the difference between the contract price and the market price, the price paid elsewhere. Stellar not only will have to pay damages but also will lose the revenue guaranteed over the next five years. Stellar's reputation for quality will also be harmed, and its financial stability will be undermined.

Russ orders Megan to do whatever is necessary to see to it that the tires will last fifty times, such as allowing the plane to coast after landing rather than applying full pressure to the brake pads. Russ's behavior is clearly unethical. What should Megan do?

A likely response is to speak to Russ's boss. Fred Worthingham, vice president for manufacturing, is Russ's superior. Fred is also the one who negotiated the contract with Heavenly and who signed his name thereto. He is the person ultimately responsible for the deal. Upon learning this, should Megan still seek out Fred?

Megan decides to talk the situation over with Fred. Fred informs Megan that her duty is to follow the orders given by her direct superior. He says that the responsibility for those decisions lies with the company. Megan tells Fred that she cannot live with this decision and would rather resign.

Fred tells Megan that he will assign her to a different job. Does that relieve Megan from ethical responsibility, or must she whistle-blow by informing Heavenly Airlines, the FAA, and/or the attorney general's office? Whistle-blowing would be the most ethical decision, but the consequences can often be severe: loss of job; blacklisted from the industry, threats of physical harm, or even murder, as was intimated by the movie about Karen Silkwood.

The possibility of loss of life from the tires is a major consideration for whistle-blowing as compared with defective tray tables or food carts on an airplane. Although ethical responses should be unconditional, is it realistic to expect a person to whistle-blow or lose a job over defective tray tables or food carts? Ethically, no one should produce defective equipment regardless of the consequences of the defect, because to do so would be to breach the duty to act in good faith.

When the rehirings took place, Russ Heflin specifically asked for Megan because she is a diligent worker. Megan was thrilled because her husband, Phil, was recently placed on disability from his job because of a back injury. She is now the primary supporter of her husband and four children. Knowing her gratefulness for being rehired and her personal financial dilemma, Russ emphasizes that his favor to her must be repaid; otherwise, the consequences of losing her job would leave Megan and her family in dire financial straits. Now Megan must balance her desire to do the right thing against her family's livelihood. Megan decides to discuss the matter with her husband. Phil tells her that as long as the vice president accepts full responsibility and relieves her from any accountability, then she should do as he says. Now lacking support from her husband, Megan gives in. She is practical, but is she unethical? Must she sacrifice everything to do the right thing? What if a plane crashes because she followed orders by doctoring the tests or failed to prevent that from happening by remaining silent and accepting the transfer? What if she whistle-blows, loses her job, ruins her family life, and no one believes her accusations, and furthermore, no plane ever crashes? ■

❖ EMPLOYER LESSONS

- Consider the effect surveillance and security measures have on employee morale.
- Balance that against money lost through theft and slacking off.
- Refrain from listening to the contents of employees' personal telephone calls.
- Never utter statements about employees which are false or damaging to their reputation.
- Protect the privacy of employees by refusing to divulge confidential information.
- Refrain from reading the contents of personal letters or E-mail directed to or sent by an employee.
- Investigate thoroughly and compile evidence before accusing an employee of theft.
- Never accuse an employee of committing any crime in front of others. In case you are wrong, it's defamation.
- Share the problem that is forcing you to implement security measures with your employees.
- Encourage whistle-blowers to come forward with information which, if not disclosed, would result in harm to the business.

❖ EMPLOYEE LESSONS

- Familiarize yourself with the protections afforded by law to safeguard your privacy.
- Question employers who have or are implementing security measures, in order to determine their motives.
- Decide if you want to work in an environment where your privacy is restricted.
- Refrain from stealing property from the business.
- Avoid conducting an inordinate amount of personal business on company time.
- Do not use company property, such as vehicles or equipment, for personal tasks without consent.
- Refrain from abusing phone, fax, and copying privileges.
- Know when you have been subjected to the torts of defamation, invasion of privacy, and interference with business relations.
- Never justify your immoral or illegal action against the business out of revenge for its ill-treatment toward you.
- Acquaint yourself with the Whistleblower Protection Act.
- Comprehend the ramifications that could befall you for whistle-blowing and evaluate whether your decision to do so is justified.

❖ SUMMARY

Employers and workers have strong opinions on privacy, theft, and whistle-blowing, and most often their interests are adverse. Absent litigation, these conflicts can only be resolved through a thorough understanding of the other party's concerns. Fostering communication is key here. Open or secret retaliation can result in a war zone where sides are drawn. This can only hurt the business. Power struggles and authoritative behavior are ultimately no match for compromise and balance.

❖ REVIEW QUESTIONS

1. Explain the significance of the Privacy Act of 1974.
2. What implications does the Omnibus Crime Control and Safe Streets Act of 1968 have on privacy?
3. How has the right to privacy been affected by the Electronic Communications Act of 1986?
4. In what respect has the Fair Credit Reporting Act of 1970 improved the right to privacy?
5. What types of property are encompassed under the heading of employee theft?
6. What types of action have been taken by employers to combat employee theft?
7. Do any of these security actions infringe on an employee's right to privacy?
8. How can both interests be effectively balanced?
9. Is an employer entitled to conduct office searches?
10. Lenzer was employed as a physician assistant by ARC under the supervision of Drs. Baucom and Harman. She was in the process of satisfying the requirement for state certification. However, Drs. Baucom and Harman withdrew supervision from Lenzer, causing her to lose the certification she needed to maintain her position with ARC. The physicians' reason was that Lenzer counseled patients about child abuse. This action was outside the scope of a physician assistant's duties. There was no dispute over Lenzer's competence, and actually her counseling had been tolerated for a long time. Lenzer claims that her counseling is protected by the First Amendment's Free Speech. Lenzer is suing for Drs. Baucom's and Harman's interference with her contract with ARC. What was the result? *Lenzer v. Flaherty*, 418 S.E. 2d 276 (N.C.App. 1992)

11. Jimmy Piersall, a former major league all-star, was hired by Jerry Reinsdorf, owner of the Chicago White Sox, to be a commentator for "Sports Vision," a cable TV program. Piersall was also a radio announcer for WMAQ. During the early 1980s Piersall made the following statements:

    a. Wives of baseball players are "horny broads who say yes very easily."
    b. The writers for *The Sun Times* were "a bunch of alcoholics."
    c. "There is no one in the White Sox organization smart enough to hold a gun to anyone's head," in response to a recent player trade.

    After the first game of the 1983 season, Piersall was discharged. Reinsdorf made the following statements about Piersall and former White Sox announcer Harry Cary:

    "I don't mind criticism, but they both told a lot of lies. They wanted us to lose. They thought they were bigger than the club and did not want the attraction shifting to the field." (*Chicago Sun Times*, September 19, 1983)

    and

    "The public could not know the truth about them; they are both liars. They both said things on the air they knew were not true." (*Chicago Tribune*, September 19, 1983)

    Piersall sued Reinsdorf for libel. The issue is whether Reinsdorf's statements were made with actual malice. *Piersall v. Sportsvision of Chicago*, 595 N.E.2d 103 (Ill. App. 1 Dist. 1992)

❖ WEB SITES

www.epic.org/privacy/consumer/states.html
www.netatty.com/privacy/privacy.html
www.employeetheft.com
www.privacy.gov.au/issues/p7_4.html
www.woodsrogers.com/articles/2art-5g.htm
www.publaw.com/privacy.html
www.encyclopedia.com/articles/13815.html
www.discriminationattorney.com/whistle.html

5

TERMINATION

INTRODUCTION

The majority of employment relationships are oral contracts for an indefinite period of time. As such, these relationships can be ended at the will of either of the parties without a reason. That is how the term "at-will" employment originated. It is a source of major controversy in the field of employment law. Public policy exceptions have been carved into the at-will employment doctrine. Every state has its own list of exceptions, but the major ones are the following: discrimination, retaliation for whistle-blowing, instituting a workers' compensation claim, and filing or testifying in a harassment or discrimination lawsuit against the employer.

CHAPTER CHECKLIST

❖ Understand the significance of at-will employment.

❖ Appreciate the controversy surrounding this topic.

❖ Be aware of the public policy exceptions to at-will employment.

❖ Consider how an employer can vitiate at-will employment through an employee handbook.

❖ Learn how an employee proceeds with an objection to the termination.

❖ Understand the compromise of the Model Employment Termination Act.

❖ Comprehend the impact this act has on both employer and employee.

❖ Imagine why an employer may retaliate against an employee by discharging him or her.

❖ Identify when an uncomfortable employment environment transforms itself into constructive discharge.

❖ Be familiar with the other reasons for concluding an employment relationship.

Fred Williams was hired by the Long and the Short of It three months ago. His position is market analyst. Fred's function is to anticipate fashion trends and to make purchase recommendations as to the type of clothing, the brand name, and the quantity. Fred has been way off-the-mark on all of his recommendations. Tom Long and Mark Short inform Fred that his work is unsatisfactory, and therefore he is being discharged. Fred states he should not be judged based on one mistake. He implores Tom and Mark to reconsider; otherwise, he will be forced to sue. Tom and Mark consult with Susan North, Esq. concerning their discharge of Fred. Susan explains that L&S is located in a state that advocates employment at will. Tom and Mark are free to discharge employees without cause so long as they are not acting in a discriminatory or retaliatory manner.

TERMINATION OF EMPLOYMENT

Termination is the discharge of an employee by an employer with or without cause. An employment relationship may terminate in the following ways:

- Employment at will
- Agreement
- Fulfillment of purpose
- Unfulfilled condition
- Operation of law

EMPLOYMENT AT WILL

Employment at will is the employer's right to revoke the worker's authority and to terminate him or her at will.

An employer may dismiss an employee without cause where the employment relationship is considered to be at will. *At will* means either the employer or the employee can terminate the relationship upon giving proper notice. Proper notice is considered to be the duration of the pay period, i.e., one week, two weeks, or one month. (That is where the phrase "two-week notice" is derived from.) Employers feel that if employees are free to leave at will, then employers should be free to discharge employees at will, too. However, some employers provide in their employee handbooks that employees will not be dismissed except for cause or in case of layoffs. In this context, the employer has given up its ability to terminate at will.

In the case that follows, the issue is whether an at-will employee is entitled to protection from reprisals and intimidation when he is asked to appear as a witness against superiors.

HADDLE v. GARRISON

525 U.S. 121 (1998)

CHIEF JUSTICE REHNQUIST delivered the opinion of the Court.

Petitioner Michael A. Haddle, an at-will employee, alleges that respondents conspired to have him fired from his job in retaliation for obeying a federal grand jury subpoena and to deter him from testifying at a federal criminal trial. We hold that such interference with at-will employment may give rise to a claim for damages under the Civil Rights Act.

According to petitioner's complaint, a federal grand jury indictment in March 1995 charged petitioner's employer, Healthmaster, Inc., and respondents Jeanette Garrison and Dennis Kelly, officers of Healthmaster, with Medicare fraud. Petitioner cooperated with the federal agents in the investigation that preceded the indictment. He also appeared to testify before the grand jury pursuant to a subpoena, but did not testify due to the press of time. Petitioner was also expected to appear as a witness in the criminal trial resulting from the indictment.

Although Garrison and Kelly were barred by the Bankruptcy Court from participating in the affairs of Healthmaster, they conspired with G. Peter Molloy, Jr., one of the remaining officers of Healthmaster, to bring about petitioner's termination. They did this both to intimidate petitioner and to retaliate against him for his attendance at the federal-court proceedings.

Petitioner sued for damages in the United States District Court for the Southern District of Georgia, asserting a federal claim and various state-law claims. Petitioner stated two grounds for relief: one for conspiracy to deter him from testifying in the upcoming criminal trial and one for conspiracy to retaliate against him for attending the grand jury proceedings.

Respondents moved to dismiss for failure to state a claim upon which relief can be granted. Because petitioner conceded that he was an at-will employee, the District Court granted the motion on the authority of Morast v. Lance. In Morast, the Eleventh Circuit held that an at-will employee who is dismissed pursuant to a conspiracy has no cause of action. The Morast court explained that "to make out a cause of action the plaintiff must have suffered an actual injury. Because Morast was an at will employee, . . . he had no constitutionally protected interest in continued employment. Therefore, Morast's discharge did not constitute an actual injury under this statute." Relying on its decision in Morast, the Court of Appeals affirmed.

The Eleventh Circuit's rule in Morast conflicts with the holdings of the First and Ninth Circuits. We therefore granted certiorari. At issue is whether petitioner was "injured in his property or person" when respondents induced his employer to terminate petitioner's at-will employment as part of a conspiracy prohibited by §1985(2).

Section 1985(2), in relevant part, proscribes conspiracies to "deter, by force, intimidation, or threat, any party or witness in any court of the United States from attending such court, or from testifying to any matter pending therein, freely, fully, and truthfully, or to injure such party or witness in his person or property on account of his having so attended or testified." The statute provides that if one or more persons engaged in such a conspiracy "do, or cause to be done, any act in furtherance of the object of such conspiracy, whereby another is injured in his person or property, . . . the party so injured . . . may have an action for the recovery of damages occasioned by such injury . . . against any one or more of the conspirators." Our review in this case is accordingly confined to one question: Can petitioner state a claim for damages by alleging that a conspiracy proscribed by §1985(2) induced his employer to terminate his at-will employment?

We disagree with the Eleventh Circuit's conclusion that petitioner must suffer an injury to a "constitutionally protected property interest" to state a claim for damages under §1985(2). Nothing in the language or purpose of the proscriptions in the first clause of §1985(2), nor in its attendant remedial provisions, establishes such a requirement. The gist of the wrong at which §1985(2) is directed is not deprivation of property, but intimidation or retaliation against witnesses in federal-court proceedings. The terms "injured in his person or property" define the harm that the victim may suffer as a result of the conspiracy to intimidate or retaliate. Thus, the fact that employment at will is not "property" for purposes of the Due Process Clause does not mean that loss of at-will employment may not "injure petitioner in his person or property" for purposes of §1985(2). The kind of interference with at-will employment relations alleged here is merely a species of the traditional torts of intentional interference with contractual relations and intentional interference with prospective contractual relations. This protection against third-party interference with at-will employment relations is still afforded by state law today. Even though a person's employment contract is at will, he has a valuable contract right which may not be unlawfully interfered with by a third person.

The judgment of the Court of Appeals is reversed, and the case is remanded for further proceedings consistent with this opinion.

Judgment per Haddle.

Case Commentary

Most employment positions are at will. If at-will employees were not protected from intimidation, then practically all employees could be exposed to this harm without recourse.

Case Questions

1. What do you think of the Eleventh Circuit's decision in Morast referenced above?
2. Do at-will employees deserve any protection?
3. To what measure of damages is Haddle entitled?

EMPLOYMENT HANDBOOKS

An employment handbook is usually construed by courts to be a contract and, as such, employers will be bound by its terms, including termination for cause. Therefore, in an at-will employment state, employers have to be careful not to compromise their ability to discharge at will by specifying in the handbook that employees will be terminated only for cause.

EMPLOYMENT SCENARIO

Tom Long and Mark Short approach Susan with a query about whether L&S should compose an employment handbook. Susan states that an advantage of a handbook is that it can spell out for employees all the rules and regulations concerning employment behavior. Policies regarding dress codes, facial jewelry, nepotism, promoting from within, sexual harassment, family leave, privacy, etc., can be discussed. However, with regard to termination, the less said the better. Susan mentions that the handbook can stipulate the fact that employment is at will, meaning an employee can be terminated without cause. Susan reiterates that it is important that an employer do nothing to jeopardize its right to terminate employees at will.

BREACH OF CONTRACT

A breach of contract occurs when the employee's reasonable expectations under the contract have not been fulfilled. Breach of contract suits arise in the following situations:

1. When a contract is made for a definite period of time, and the employee is terminated before the expiration of that time period without cause, the employer will be liable for the duration of the contract.
2. When an employer specifies in an interview the reasons why an employee may be terminated, then discharge will be limited to those reasons.
3. When an employment handbook recites a litany of causes for an employee's discharge, then the employer will be bound to what it has stipulated.

In the following case the issue presented is whether a change in the Personnel Rules compromised the employer's right to discharge regular employees at will. The employee filed a breach of contract claim as a result of the discharge.

CASE

ALASKA HOUSING FINANCE CORP. v. SALVUCCI

950 P.2d 1116, (Alaska 1997)

MATTHEWS, Justice.

I. INTRODUCTION

This is an appeal by the Alaska Housing Finance Corporation (AHFC) from certain rulings of the superior court in favor of former AHFC employee Pat Salvucci. The superior court directed a verdict for Salvucci on his breach of contract claim. Salvucci also was granted prejudgment interest on lost past and future wages and benefits as well as on punitive damages. We remand the award of prejudgment interest on lost past and future wages and benefits, reverse the award of punitive damages, and affirm in all other respects.

II. FACTS AND PROCEEDINGS

In 1989 Salvucci was hired by AHFC as its Internal Auditor. At the time of his hire, Salvucci signed a letter stating that his "employment at AHFC is at all times subject to AHFC Personnel Rules and any future amendments to those rules." The Personnel Rules divided employees into two groups, the "Regular" and "Executive" Service. Personnel Rule, Section 2.01.0. While the former could be terminated only for cause and only following a disciplinary procedure, the latter could be terminated at will by the Executive Director. All Regular Service employees received contractual employment protection, set forth in Rules 4, 11 and 13; only Executive Service employees did not receive the protection afforded by these rules.

The Executive Service became a part of AHFC Personnel Rules in August 1989 when AHFC's Board of Directors adopted Personnel Rule 2, Section 2.03.03. One of the positions designated Executive Service by Section 2.03.03 was the Internal Auditor position. Regular Service was defined as "positions within the Corporation that are not in the executive service."

The AHFC's Audit Charter, authored by Salvucci and adopted in June 1990, defined the duties and role of the Internal Auditor. The Charter set forth the reporting procedure, specifically that the Internal Auditor reported administratively to the chief executive officer and functionally to the Audit Committee of the Board of Directors. Further, it mandated that the Internal Auditor's removal required the concurrence of the Audit Committee.

In 1992 AHFC Personnel Rule 2.03.03 was amended. The amended rule shortened the list of Executive Service positions and omitted the Internal Auditor position from the list of positions in the Executive Service. The definition of Regular Service was not changed.

In July 1993 Will Gay became AHFC's Executive Director. In November Gay placed Salvucci on administrative leave, subject to an approval vote by the Audit Committee. In December the Audit Committee concurred in Gay's decision and Salvucci's employment was terminated. Salvucci was not given any reason for his termination and was not afforded a prior disciplinary process, as required for the termination of Regular Service employees.

Salvucci filed a grievance, pursuant to Personnel Rule 13. AHFC refused to consider his grievance and also declined to consider his appeal of the grievance refusal, both instances on the ground that the Personnel Rules were inapplicable to the position of Internal Auditor. After the denial of his internal remedies, Salvucci filed a complaint in superior court alleging breach of contract, breach of the implied covenant of good faith and fair dealing, due process violations, and violation of the Whistleblower Act.

The superior court denied AHFC's motions for summary judgment on Salvucci's claim for punitive damages. The court granted a directed verdict for Salvucci on his breach of contract claim, finding that the 1992 amendment removed the Internal Auditor position from the Executive Service, placing the Internal Auditor within the Regular Service, with its accompanying contractual protections.

The jury awarded Salvucci $43,200 in lost past wages and benefits, $144,234 in lost future wages and benefits, and $500,000 in punitive damages. The superior court awarded Salvucci prejudgment interest on his wage and benefit award and on his punitive damage award, for a total of $62,493.30 in prejudgment interest. The court did not specify what amount of prejudgment interest was awarded for wages and benefits, and what amount of prejudgment interest was awarded for punitive damages.

The Breach of Contract Claim

AHFC contends that the superior court improperly granted a directed verdict for Salvucci on the breach of contract claim. AHFC argues that evidence presented at trial allowed a reasonable jury to conclude either that the Internal Auditor position was never removed from the Executive Service or that the Internal Auditor position enjoyed a unique classification falling outside either the Regular or Executive Service. AHFC argues that the Internal Auditor was a "corporation director" within the meaning of amended Rule 2, Section 2.03.03.

At the time the Audit Charter was passed, the Internal Auditor was an Executive Service position. The Charter did not refer to or alter the Service categorization of the Internal Auditor; rather it created a distinct process of reporting and removal for the Internal Auditor. Pursuant to the Charter, the Executive Director did not have sole discretion to appoint or remove the auditor; any such action required the concurrence of the Board of Director's Audit Committee.

In 1991 Barry Hulin, then Executive Director, proposed amending the Personnel Rules to narrow the categories of positions in the Executive Service. The proposal removed the Internal Auditor from the Executive Service. In presenting the proposal to the Board of Directors, Hulin specifically stated that the amendment took the Internal Auditor out of the Executive Service. Hulin also specifically informed the Board that those persons not in the Executive Service are subject to termination only for a "performance-related cause" and cannot be terminated before receiving "progressive discipline" in accordance with contractual employment protections. In 1992 the amendment was adopted.

All parties agree that the terms of Salvucci's employment contract are governed by his employment letter, the Audit Charter and the Personnel Rules. The text of Section 2.03.03 before and after the amendment makes evident that the Internal Auditor position was included in the Executive Service before the amendment and excluded once the section was amended. Hulin's testimony confirms that one intention of the amendment was to remove the Internal Auditor from the Executive Service, and further confirms that the Board was informed of this intent before it approved the amendment. The record shows that AHFC's Deputy Executive Director and AHFC's Personnel Director were also aware that one purpose of the amendment was to remove the Internal Auditor from the Executive Service.

We have held that when the provisions of a personnel manual create reasonable expectations that employees have been granted certain rights, the employer is bound by the representations contained in those provisions. Similar reasoning applies in this case. AHFC created a reasonable expectation that Salvucci was granted the rights of Regular Service employees after the 1992 amendment.

The employment letter required Salvucci to sign a statement that the Personnel Rules and any subsequent amendments to those rules governed the terms and conditions of his employment. When the Personnel Rules were amended in 1992 to delete the Internal Auditor from the list of Executive Service, Salvucci was bound to accept the amendment and the accompanying obligations or rights imposed by the Personnel Rules. Hulin informed Salvucci that the rules had been changed to remove him from the Executive Service. Salvucci read the transcript of the Board meeting at which the Board was told it was being asked to remove the Internal Auditor from the Executive Service.

As Salvucci reasonably believed that he was a Regular Service employee after the amendment, and as the superior court's analysis of the contract turns largely on his reasonable expectation, Based on the binding nature of the employment letter, the clear text of Section 2.03.03 before and after amendment, the absence of any language in the Audit Charter creating a category other than Executive or Regular Service for the Internal Auditor, Hulin's statements of intent to remove the Internal Auditor from the Executive Service to the Board before its passage of the amendment, and Salvucci's reasonable expectations, we hold that in 1993, at the time Salvucci was terminated, the Internal Auditor position was in the Regular Service.

It is undisputed that in November 1993 Gay informed Salvucci that Salvucci would be placed on administrative leave and, subject to approval by the Audit Committee, would be terminated. It is further undisputed that Salvucci was not given any reason by Gay or the Audit Committee for his termination, and that he was not afforded the protection of progressive disciplinary procedures. Given AHFC's failure to afford Salvucci the contractual protections due Regular Service employees, we hold that the superior court correctly directed a verdict in favor of Salvucci on his breach of contract claim.

Judgment for Salvucci.

Case Commentary

The Alaska Supreme Court held that Salvucci was entitled to recover for breach of contract. Salvucci's position was changed from Executive to Regular. AHFC failed to adhere to its procedure for terminating Regular employees only for performance-related reasons and only after they have been disciplined. Here, Salvucci was terminated without reason.

Case Questions

1. Is the court's decision regarding the breach of contract claim valid?
2. Was AHFC's amendment to the Personnel Rules the determining factor in Salvucci's victory?
3. Did AHFC's Personnel Rules compromise its right to terminate Salvucci at will?

An employee's or an independent contractor's authority may be revoked if the duration of the contract is indefinite or if no time limit has been specified. The employer may also revoke an employee's or an independent contractor's authority for cause where the employee or independent contractor has breached one of the duties owed. The employee or independent contractor must be notified that his or her authority is revoked. If the employment contract was in writing, then the revocation must also be in writing. Under other circumstances, it may be oral. This notice is effective when the employee or independent contractor receives it.

Notice of termination by revocation or mutual agreement must also be communicated to third persons who have dealt with the employer through the employee or independent contractor. Otherwise, the employer will be liable to third persons who contract with the employee or independent contractor. The employer's liability is based on apparent authority to act based on prior dealings that the third party is justified in believing. Third parties who have dealt with the employee or independent contractor on prior occasions must be sent actual notice of termination. This becomes effective when the third party receives it. For all other third parties, the employer's duty to notify may be satisfied by publishing a statement regarding termination of authority in a newspaper.

EMPLOYMENT PERSPECTIVE

Bob Kaufman was the managing agent for the Barons, a singing group that performed at clubs and weddings. When it came time to renew his contract, Kaufman demanded that his commission be increased from 10 percent to 15 percent of the band's gross earnings. Although the Barons informed him that they would consider his request, they subsequently informed him that they would not accede to his request and terminated his employment. Infuriated by their reply, Kaufman, who was in the process of negotiating with several clubs for bookings, informed each of the clubs that the Barons would perform on the dates requested for $250 less than their usual price. Kaufman said, "They're glad to get the work." The Barons were familiar with these particular clubs but never informed them of the termination of Kaufman's employment. Are they bound to perform at the club for the lower fee? Yes! The Barons, as employer, have a duty to inform the clubs of Kaufman's termination. Otherwise, as in the case here, the clubs are justified in relying on Kaufman's apparent authority because they have dealt with the Barons through him on past occasions. ■

AGREEMENT

An employment contract can be terminated, like any other contract, by the mutual agreement of the parties. This termination is valid even if the contract had called for a longer term of employment.

FULFILLMENT OF PURPOSE

The authority of an employee or an independent contractor hired for a specific term of employment, as in an employee–employer relationship, will terminate upon the expiration of that term. An agency relationship created for the fulfillment of a specific purpose will terminate when that purpose is completed.

EMPLOYMENT PERSPECTIVE

Jonathan Murrow, a lawyer, was engaged by Marvelous Mini-Bikes, Inc., to represent it in several product liability suits. Murrow hired Timothy Hines, a paralegal, to assist him by researching the numerous cases in point and writing a legal memorandum of the principles of law applicable to the issues presented. Hines was hired for two years, by which time Murrow figured the suits would be settled. What is the status of the employment relationships created, and when will they terminate? Jonathan Murrow is an independent contractor hired by Marvelous Mini-Bikes and is free to use his own methods to handle the case. This employment will terminate when all of the product liability suits against Marvelous Mini-Bikes have been settled. Timothy Hines is an employee of Jonathan Murrow. Hines must follow Murrow's instructions with regard to the work he undertakes. This employment relationship will expire at the end of the two-year term of employment. ■

UNFULFILLED CONDITION

The creation of an employment relationship may be conditioned on the happening of an event. If the condition precedent fails, the employment will not be created. Employment may also be created with its continued existence dependent on the fulfillment of a condition subsequent. If this condition should fail, the employment will be terminated.

EMPLOYMENT PERSPECTIVE

George Larsen applied to Chevrolet for a franchise in order to open a dealership. Confident that his request would be approved, Larsen called Kenneth Washburn and asked him to be a sales agent for the new dealership if the franchise was approved. If the franchise is approved, the condition precedent has been met, and an employment relationship has been created between Larsen and Washburn. If not, there will be no employment relationship. Suppose that the franchise is approved and Larsen hires Washburn on the condition that Washburn sells seventy cars each year. During the first two years of his employment, Washburn meets his quota, but in the third year he sells only fifty-seven cars and is dismissed. Has he any recourse? No! Washburn's employment is terminated because he failed to continue to meet the required condition. ■

PROHIBITED BY OPERATION OF LAW

Employment may terminate by operation of law in the following ways:

- Bankruptcy of the employer or the employee terminating the employee's authority in financial transactions.
- Insanity or death of the employee or employer if he or she is a sole proprietor.
- Destruction or loss of the subject matter, if the employment was created for a purpose related to that subject matter.

If the termination is not legally justifiable, then it is considered wrongful. This discussion does not apply to instances in which an employee voluntarily resigns or in which an employment contract for a designated period has reached its end. An employer may dismiss an employee for cause when the employee is in breach of contract or has committed a tort or a crime or has not otherwise complied with the rules and regulations set forth by the employer. These regulations would include those laws imposed upon the employer such as the Occupational Safety and Health Act, Title VII of the Civil Rights Act, or the Americans with Disabilities Act. Termination with cause protects employees from being arbitrarily dismissed.

EMPLOYMENT PERSPECTIVE

Molly Player, Caitlin Dempsey, and Jason Simington are employees of the Texas Gentlemen, a fine men's-apparel store. One of Molly's responsibilities was to fold sweaters after customers had unfolded them to get a better idea as to whether they liked the sweaters. Molly continuously neglected her duty despite her recognition of the Texas Gentlemen's image of being meticulous in appearance.

Caitlin's function was to replenish the retail inventory from storage in the back of the store. On occasion, she would remove an article of clothing from the premises as a present for her boyfriend. Finally, she was apprehended by the security guard.

Jason was in charge of safety maintenance. One day a fire broke out in the storage area. The sprinklers malfunctioned, and the fire extinguishers, which were placed in the rear of the store, could not be reached, so that substantial damage resulted. Molly, Caitlin, and Jason were all terminated for cause. They claim that Texas Gentlemen's actions amount to wrongful discharges. Are they correct? No! Molly was insubordinate and therefore was in breach of contract. Caitlin was guilty of the tort of conversion and the crime of larceny. Jason violated OSHA laws by failing to adhere to federal safety standards. ■

MODEL EMPLOYMENT TERMINATION ACT

The Model Employment Termination Act was designed to permit employers to discharge employees only for cause. In turn, employees would have to relinquish their right to sue in favor of arbitration. The advantage to the employer is to forgo the time and expense of litigation. The advantage to the employee is that he or she could no longer be terminated at will.

An employer may terminate for good cause when the employee has been derelict in his or her duties of loyalty, duty to act in good faith and duty to account; acting in excess of or without authority; performing work outside the scope of employment; harassing coworkers or subordinates; and engaging in employee theft. The employer may also discharge for good cause when the employer downsizes its workforce because of a consolidation, reorganization, or divestiture.

Under the Act, termination refers to dismissal for cause, layoff pursuant to downsizing, and resigning by an employee due to the employer's intolerable actions.

Within 180 days of termination, the employee may file a complaint. The matter will then be arbitrated. After the arbitration hearing, a decision will be rendered within thirty days. If the arbitrator finds for the employee, an award may be made for reinstatement, back pay, reimbursement for benefits lost, or a lump sum if reinstatement is not permissible.

CONTESTING THE TERMINATION

Claims for wrongful termination are filed with the department of labor in the state of employment. The department of labor will forward a claim of discrimination to the employer. The employer will be afforded the opportunity to settle the claim pursuant to a no-fault agreement. If a settlement cannot be reached, the department will proceed with its fact finding investigation. A fact finding conference may be held with mandatory attendance required of the employer and the employee. A decision regarding the employer's fault will then be made. If the employer is at fault, the Department will attempt to reach a conciliation agreement with the employer regarding damages and/or reinstatement of the employee. If an agreement cannot be reached, a complaint will be filed by the Department of Labor with the Equal Employment Review Board. The parties may submit written briefs prior to the hearing. After the hearing, the Board will make its decision and pronounce a remedy. The Board's decision can be appealed to the State's General Trial Court. The court's function is to determine whether the Board's decision was substantiated by sufficient evidence.

Because downsizing has become a widespread phenomenon among companies, hundreds of thousands of employees have been laid off as a result. When a company downsizes for economic reasons, the employee has no recourse. Economic reasons may encompass a broad spectrum from saving a company from filing for bankruptcy to improving the price of the stock by increasing earnings.

WRONGFUL DISCHARGE

An employer is guilty of wrongful discharge where its motivation for termination is discriminatory. This situation gives the employee the right to sue under Title VII of the Civil Rights Act, the Americans with Disabilities Act, the Age Discrimination in Employment Act, or The Equal Pay Act, to name a few. Furthermore, employees may not be discharged for exercising their constitutional rights such as freedom of speech or freedom of religion.

The case that follows addresses the question of whether an employer can dismiss an employee for his or her political affiliation.

CASE

PIERCE v. MONTGOMERY COUNTY OPPORTUNITY BD., INC.

884 F.Supp. 965 (E.D.Pa. 1995)

JOYNER, District Judge.

This litigation arises out of the termination of Plaintiff Frances Pierce from her position as Executive Director of the Montgomery County Opportunity Board, Inc. (MCOB). Pierce is and has been a Republican Committeewoman at all material times and votes for Republican political candidates. In August, 1990, Pierce was made the Acting Executive Director of MCOB. At some point after August 1990, State Defendants, presumably Democrats, resolved to have Pierce removed from the head of MCOB, allegedly for political reasons. In June 1991, Pierce was appointed MCOB's Executive Director for a 5-year term at a certain salary and with certain benefits.

In November 1991, State Defendants arranged to terminate MCOB's federal funding, allegedly because Pierce's active Republicanism created a prohibited conflict of interest under Federal regulations. In May 1992, MCOB Defendant Harvey Portner was appointed to the MCOB Board and at some point became its

President. He apparently asked Pierce to resign as Executive Director, and when she refused, embarked upon a campaign to impugn Pierce's reputation. In August 1992, the MCOB's Defendants (including at least one Republican) joined in a conspiracy with Portner and the State Defendants to remove Pierce from MCOB on account of her Republicanism.

In December 1992, Portner resigned as President of the Board so as to "create an aura of non-involvement," but nonetheless, "maintained effective control over the Opportunity Board." He was replaced by MCOB Defendant Aaron Schell, a Republican.

On December 16, 1992, Schell informed Pierce that the MCOB Board was to meet with the Department of Community Affairs, told Pierce that he did not know the purpose of the meeting, and then did not attend the meeting himself. At this meeting, State Defendants informed the board that they were there to close down MCOB. According to the Amended Complaint, the "purpose of the attendance of defendants Darling and Weisberg was to give a basis for the actions which were planned sub rosa to remove Frances Pierce as Executive Director." One month later the MCOB Board voted to remove Pierce as Executive Director.

In Pennsylvania, an at-will employee can be discharged for any reason or for no reason at all. The exception to this rule is the public policy exception. This provides that when there is no plausible and legitimate reason for a termination, and a clear mandate of public policy is violated by the termination, even an at-will employee has a claim for wrongful discharge. Pennsylvania does not, however, permit a wrongful discharge claim if statutory relief is available to the plaintiff.

Here, Pierce alleges that "The Opportunity Board of Montgomery County, Inc. could not discharge an employee for utilizing the right to freedom of speech in the employee's off hours, such discharge as here complained of, being in violation of the public policy of the Commonwealth of Pennsylvania." Elsewhere in the Amended Complaint, Pierce alleges that she was terminated solely on account of her participation in Republican party politics. As the Third Circuit has held, "an important public policy is in fact implicated wherever the power to hire and fire is utilized to dictate the term of employee political activities." Pierce alleges that she was terminated for engaging in protected First Amendment activities. We find that this states a claim for wrongful discharge, for which, if the allegations are proved, relief can be granted.

Judgment for Pierce.

Case Commentary

The Eastern District Court of Pennsylvania held that a public policy exception to the at-will termination doctrine exists where the employee is engaging in protected First Amendment activities. Here Frances Pierce was discharged for her political affiliation.

Case Questions

1. Should a person's political affiliation be entitled to protection?
2. Do you believe this was the real reason why she was discharged?
3. What public policy exceptions do you believe should exist to the at-will employment doctrine?

RETALIATORY DISCHARGE

If an employee has made a claim of discrimination or is to appear as a witness in a discrimination investigation, the employer may not take retaliatory action against the employee.

EMPLOYMENT PERSPECTIVE

EMPLOYMENT PERSPECTIVE
Cindy Thomas has filed a gender-based discrimination claim against Star Enterprises for not receiving a promotion. Nicole Robinson will be appearing as a witness on Cindy's behalf. In the interim, Cindy has been discharged, and Nicole has been demoted. Do they have a recourse? Yes! Cindy may amend her claim to include the charge of retaliation. Nicole may commence an action for violation of Title VII against Star Enterprises based on its retaliatory behavior. ■

In addition, it is wrongful when a worker is discharged for filing a workers' compensation claim, or blowing the whistle on a company's illegal activity. The employee may bring an action for retaliatory discharge against the employer.

EMPLOYMENT PERSPECTIVE
Carly Fisher worked the night shift at Top Cat Chemical Corporation. One evening while on a break, she observed several workers emptying barrels into the Pristine River adjacent to the plant. Carly notified the Environmental Protection Agency. Because their investigation revealed that toxic waste had been dumped, the company was fined heavily. One month later, Carly was discharged after a poor performance rating. For six years, Carly had received satisfactory ratings. Is this a case of retaliatory discharge? Yes! Top Cat's actions in dismissing Carly were motivated by its desire for revenge against her for whistle-blowing. ■

The issue in the case that follows is whether the employee was discharged for performing poorly or in retaliation for filing a workers' compensation claim.

CASE

BLACKWELL v. SHELTER MUTUAL INSURANCE CO.

109 F.3d 1550 (10th Cir. 1997)

BRORBY, Circuit Judge.
In August 1994, Shelter Mutual Insurance Company ("Shelter Mutual") terminated Kathleen Blackwell from employment after twenty years of service with the company. Thereafter, Ms. Blackwell filed suit against Shelter Mutual in the United States District Court for the Western District of Oklahoma, alleging her termination was in retaliation for exercising her rights under Oklahoma's Workers' Compensation Act. The district court determined Ms. Blackwell failed to establish a prima facie case of retaliatory discharge and granted summary

judgment in favor of Shelter Mutual. Ms. Blackwell appeals the district court's entry of summary judgment. We exercise jurisdiction over Ms. Blackwell's appeal and affirm.

I. FACTUAL AND PROCEDURAL BACKGROUND

Ms. Blackwell was employed by Shelter Mutual for approximately twenty years, beginning in 1974. In January 1993, Ms. Blackwell injured her back while lifting a ladder on the job. Ms. Blackwell sought medical treatment for her injury, but continued working until March 1993. On March 1, 1993, Ms. Blackwell's supervisor, Steve Duke, advised Ms. Blackwell to see a neurologist regarding her back injury. Following her visit to the neurologist, Ms. Blackwell missed approximately four months of work because of her injury. Ms. Blackwell continued to receive full salary during her leave of absence. While out of work, Mr. Duke called Ms. Blackwell and inquired as to when she would be able to return to work. Although Mr. Duke informed her the workload was heavy and she was needed back at the office, Mr. Duke did not state her job was in jeopardy if she did not return to work. However, Ms. Blackwell claims she "got the feeling" from Mr. Duke's "mannerism" that he did not want Ms. Blackwell on workers' compensation. Furthermore, Ms. Blackwell thinks other adjusters implied to her that her job would be in jeopardy if she did not return to work. In addition, a Shelter Mutual employee in the Tulsa office told Ms. Blackwell that he did not believe he was treated fairly by Shelter Mutual after he filed a workers' compensation claim. Ms. Blackwell returned to work at Shelter Mutual on July 6, 1993. In May 1994, Shelter Mutual branch manager Don Ridlon recommended a merit increase in salary for Ms. Blackwell. However, Mr. Ridlon advised Shelter Mutual to place a "hold" on the merit increase after he received some "strong allegations" against Ms. Blackwell regarding her involvement in the improper handling of salvage vehicles. Apparently Mr. Ridlon learned that several vehicles Ms. Blackwell determined to be total losses were later owned by Ms. Blackwell's son or processed through the business of Ms. Blackwell's husband. Mr. Ridlon also became aware of allegations concerning an insurance claim Ms. Blackwell improperly paid after another agent had previously denied this same claim. Mr. Ridlon learned that Ms. Blackwell may have removed or destroyed pictures in the file related to this claim. This incident has been referred to as the "Schwartz incident" throughout this litigation. On May 24, 1994, Mr. Duke sent Ms. Blackwell a five-page written reprimand outlining a number of problems with her job performance. Mr. Duke's reprimand stated, in pertinent parts, as follows: Your work product has been faltering and, as you have

mostly failed to respond to my verbal suggestions, you have left me no other option but to outline the problems that have been created by your work over the last few months. . . . The agents in your territory, not one, but a majority, are calling in, expressing concern that they are having to cover for you way too much. They feel your work over the last few months is causing damage to the service reputation of their agencies, and Mr. Ridlon and I feel their complaints to be valid. . . . Service is not being provided as required by your employer. Your investigations are often haphazard; many times, either delayed or incomplete. . . . We are seeing more and more people calling, including agents, stating that you are not returning their calls. . . . Some of your files make me very nervous, as to their ability to comply with requirements in the Fair Claims Practice Act. As a result, I feel that some of your investigations are not of an acceptable standard. I need to see a speed and quality improvement immediately in this very serious area of concern. Mr. Duke's letter went on to list a number of procedures Shelter Mutual expected Ms. Blackwell to "adhere to religiously" in order to improve her work performance. In conclusion, Mr. Duke warned there would be "difficult decisions for both of us to make" if Ms. Blackwell did not substantially improve her performance. On several occasions in May and June of 1994, Ms. Blackwell and Mr. Ridlon discussed the Schwartz incident, as well as Ms. Blackwell's alleged involvement in the misappropriation of salvage. Ms. Blackwell told Mr. Ridlon she could not remember much about the circumstances surrounding the loss or the adjustment of the Schwartz file. Ms. Blackwell also advised Mr. Ridlon she had never profited from any of her salvage dealings. On July 14, 1994, Mr. Ridlon sent a twenty-two-page memorandum concerning Ms. Blackwell to Ray Warner, regional claims director of Shelter Mutual. The memorandum detailed Mr. Ridlon's investigation into the Schwartz incident and the alleged misappropriation of salvage by Ms. Blackwell. In the report, Mr. Ridlon stated he did not believe Ms. Blackwell provided him with "straight answers" to many of his questions surrounding the incidents. Mr. Duke evaluated Ms. Blackwell's job performance in July and August of 1994. In each of these evaluations,

Mr. Duke noted Ms. Blackwell's performance had improved in a number of areas. Also, in the July 14, 1994 memo to Mr. Warner, Mr. Ridlon stated Ms. Blackwell had begun addressing the problems detailed in Mr. Duke's letter of May 24, 1994. On July 7, 1994, Ms. Blackwell informed Mr. Duke her back was still causing her trouble. Mr. Duke advised Ms. Blackwell to schedule a follow-up visit with her doctor. According to a company memorandum, Shelter Mutual's Legal and Human Resources department recommended terminating Ms. Blackwell on August 22, 1994, "due to numerous problems." The author of the company memorandum noted he or she believed Ms. Blackwell would have a workers' compensation claim. On August 25, 1994, Don Ridlon terminated Ms. Blackwell's employment with Shelter Mutual. Mr. Ridlon explained she was being terminated due to "unresolved performance problems," problems with salvage, and the Schwartz file. Approximately one month after her discharge, Ms. Blackwell filed a workers' compensation claim against Shelter Mutual. In May 1995, Ms. Blackwell initiated this retaliatory discharge lawsuit against Shelter Mutual. However, in April 1996, the district court entered summary judgment in favor of Shelter Mutual, concluding Ms. Blackwell failed to establish her termination was in retaliation for pursuing workers' compensation relief.

II. ISSUES

Ms. Blackwell raises two issues on appeal: (1) whether she presented sufficient evidence to establish the exercise of her rights under Oklahoma's Workers' Compensation Act was a significant factor motivating Shelter Mutual's decision to terminate her and, if so, (2) whether Ms. Blackwell presented sufficient evidence to prove Shelter Mutual's proffered explanation for her discharge was pretextual.

To establish a prima facie case of retaliatory discharge, a discharged employee must prove the following four elements: (1) employment; (2) on-the-job injury; (3) medical treatment which put the employer on notice that treatment had been rendered for a work-related injury; and (4) consequent termination. If the discharged employee establishes a prima facie case, the burden shifts to the employer to rebut the inference of a retaliatory motive by articulating a legitimate, non-retaliatory reason for the termination. The employer's burden is simply one of production, not persuasion. If the employer satisfies this burden, the presumption of retaliatory motive is successfully rebutted. At that point, the discharged employee can only prevail by proving his termination was significantly motivated by retaliation for his exercise of statutory rights, or by proving the employer's proffered reason for the discharge was pretextual. Here, there is no dispute Ms. Blackwell can establish the first three elements of a prima facie case.(1) The focus of this appeal is on the fourth and final element—whether a consequent termination occurred. The district court concluded Ms. Blackwell could not establish the occurrence of a consequent termination and granted summary judgment in favor of Shelter Mutual.

Here, the temporal relationship between the protected activity and Ms. Blackwell's discharge is even more attenuated. Shelter Mutual fired Ms. Blackwell thirteen months after her leave of absence from work. Although Ms. Blackwell informed Shelter Mutual her back was still causing her problems in July 1994, there is no evidence this information influenced her termination. Since no inference of retaliation was raised, we conclude the timing of the discharge in the present case does not raise an inference of retaliation. Looking to the entire evidence in the light most favorable to Ms. Blackwell, we do not believe a reasonable jury could conclude her discharge was significantly motivated by retaliation for exercising her rights under the Workers' Compensation Act.

CONCLUSION

For the foregoing reasons, we AFFIRM the district court's order granting summary judgment in favor of Shelter Mutual Insurance Company.

Case Commentary

Here an employee who had been performing poorly attempted to mask this behavior by filing a claim for retaliation over a prior unrelated workers' compensation claim.

Case Questions

1. Do you believe Shelter Mutual Insurance Company's allegation of Kathleen Blackwell's poor performance was pretextual?

2. Was Blackwell's termination appropriate?

3. Should Shelter Mutual Insurance have done something more before discharging Blackwell?

The following case illustrates the issue of whether the Fair Labor Standards Act's protection against retaliation is extended to a personnel director who notifies upper management of noncompliance with that act.

CASE

McKENZIE v. RENBERG'S INC.

94 F.3d 1478 (10th Cir. 1996)

EBEL, Circuit Judge.

Plaintiff-Appellant Lori G. McKenzie brought this action against her former employer, Renberg's Inc., and its president, Robert Renberg (collectively "defendants"), asserting claims for retaliatory discharge in violation of the Fair Labor Standards Act ("FLSA") and wrongful discharge in violation of Oklahoma public policy. The district court dismissed McKenzie's state law wrongful discharge claim prior to trial. McKenzie received a favorable jury verdict on her retaliation claim, but the district court thereafter entered judgment as a matter of law for defendants. McKenzie now appeals these two rulings. We have jurisdiction and we affirm. We hold that McKenzie did not engage in protected activity when, in her capacity as personnel director, she undertook to advise Renberg's that its wage and hour policies were in violation of the FLSA.

BACKGROUND

Renberg's, Inc. ("the company") hired McKenzie as a receptionist in July 1984. She was promoted to Assistant Personnel Director in October 1984, and in May 1985, she became the company's Personnel Director. As Personnel Director, McKenzie was responsible for monitoring compliance with state and federal equal employment opportunity laws, wage and hour laws, and other laws regulating the workplace.

In August 1991, a co-worker of McKenzie, Marsha McElroy, attended a seminar on wage and hour laws and returned with various informational materials. McElroy gave these materials to McKenzie, who, after reviewing them, became concerned that certain employees of the company were not receiving proper compensation for working overtime. McKenzie discussed the matter with McElroy, and then decided to disclose her concerns to the company attorney, Steve Andrew. McKenzie and McElroy met with Andrew on September 4, 1991, and later that same day, McKenzie also discussed the wage and hour problem with Robert Renberg ("Renberg"), the company president. Sixteen days later, on September 20, 1991, McKenzie was terminated by Renberg.

Believing she had been retaliated against for reporting the company's possible wage and hour violations, McKenzie filed suit in the United States District Court. In her complaint, McKenzie asserted an FLSA retaliatory discharge claim. This statutory provision makes it unlawful for an employer to discharge or in any other manner discriminate against any employee because such employee has filed any complaint or instituted or caused to be instituted any proceeding under or related to this chapter, or has testified or is about to testify in any such proceeding, or has served or is about to serve on an industry committee.

McKenzie also asserted a state law claim for wrongful discharge in violation of Oklahoma public policy. The district court dismissed the public policy claim. The FLSA retaliation claim was tried to the jury.

Renberg denied that McKenzie's discharge was in retaliation for her protected FLSA activity. Renberg testified that he fired McKenzie for two legitimate reasons: (1) for disclosing confidential information in her role as personnel director; and (2) for notarizing a "contract" between two company employees for sexual favors. The "contract," which was entered into by Brenda Jagels, an on-call sales clerk, and David Childers, a company vice-president, provided in relevant part as follows:

AREA OF CONTENTION: Renberg's Christmas Bonus

TERMS OF THE AGREEMENT: Should Christmas bonuses not be paid in their usual manner to the employees of Renberg's Inc., a company operating in Tulsa, Oklahoma, then David Childers will provide Brenda Jagels with the following:

(1) Fendi Parfum 1.4 oz.
(1) Fendi EDT
(1) Fendi Body Lotion or Creme
(1) Erno Laszlo Eye Creme

However, should Christmas bonuses be paid then Brenda Jagels will provide David Childers with a very special and provocatively intimate evening; time, place and duration to be negotiated.

PAYMENT: Made on or before December 25, 1989.

Brenda, this letter is intended to be a binding contract. Please signify your agreement with the foregoing provisions by signing below and returning one copy for my file.

At trial, McKenzie admitted that she had notarized the sex contract, but stated that she had neither read it nor was aware of its content when she notarized it. McKenzie also admitted that she had made a mistake by notarizing the contract.

The district court granted the Motion for Judgment as a Matter of Law, and ruled that the Motion for New Trial was moot. McKenzie now appeals.

Under the district court's approach, the dispositive question is whether the defendants would have been justified in terminating McKenzie for notarizing the sex contract. This approach, however, disregards both the jury's express findings of fact and the "but for" test of causation. Under the "but for" standard, only those employees "who would have suffered exactly the same adverse action even if they had not engaged in FLSA activities will be unprotected. . . ." Thus, the mere existence of a non-retaliatory motive that would justify an employee's discharge does not absolve an employer of liability for a retaliatory employment decision; rather, the employer must actually rely on that non-retaliatory reason as the sufficient, motivating reason for the employment decision. As the Supreme Court recently stated, "proving that the same decision would have been justified . . . is not the same as proving that the same decision would have been made."

Here, the defendants were given the opportunity at trial to persuade the jury that McKenzie was terminated not for reporting her wage and hour concerns, but for notarizing the sex contract. The jury, however, was not convinced. The jury instead found that the "but for" cause of McKenzie's discharge was her FLSA activity, and that the defendant's asserted "sex contract" rationale was a pretext. Given these findings of fact, it is immaterial whether the defendants would have been justified in discharging McKenzie for notarizing the sex contract, as the jury concluded she was not actually discharged for this reason.

According to defendants, McKenzie was not asserting any rights under the FLSA but rather was merely performing her everyday duties as personnel director for the company.

Here, McKenzie never crossed the line from being an employee merely performing her job as personnel director to an employee lodging a personal complaint about the wage and hour practices of her employer and asserting a right adverse to the company. McKenzie did not initiate a FLSA claim against the company on her own behalf or on behalf of anyone else. Rather, in her capacity as personnel manager, she informed the company that it was at risk of claims that might be instituted by others as a result of its alleged FLSA violations. In order to engage in protected activity, the employee must step outside his or her role of representing the company and either file (or threaten to file) an action adverse to the employer, actively assist other employees in asserting FLSA rights, or otherwise engage in activities that reasonably could be perceived as directed towards the assertion of rights protected by the FLSA. Here, McKenzie did none of these things. McKenzie therefore lacks an essential ingredient of a retaliation claim; that is, she did not take a position adverse to her employer or assert any rights under the FLSA. Accordingly, McKenzie did not engage in activity protected, and we affirm the judgment as a matter of law in favor of the defendants on this alternative ground.

Judgment for Renberg's Inc.

Case Commentary

This case emphasizes the point that an individual who seems to have everything going for her to win the case may lose on a technicality. Here, McKenzie sought to help her employer correct a wrongdoing and in so doing lost her job because of the employer's retaliatory act. McKenzie was not protected because the issues she raised occurred while she was acting in furtherance of her position as personnel director. Only actions taken adverse to the employer are protected.

Case Questions

1. Do you believe this case was fairly decided?
2. Is the law applicable to this case unjust?
3. What could she have done differently to protect herself?
4. What modifications to the law would you recommend?

The following case presents the issue of whether the employee was terminated for poor performance or in retaliation for her making an allegation of sexual harassment against her superior.

CASE

BEALL v. ABBOTT LABORATORIES

130 F.3d 614 (4th Cir. 1997)

MAGILL, Senior Circuit Judge.

Judith Beall appeals the district court's grant of summary judgment to defendants Abbott Laboratories (Abbott), Michael Budlong, and Michael Maiocco on Beall's claims of retaliation and sexual harassment under Title VII of the Civil Rights Act of 1964, and the grant of summary judgment to defendants Budlong and Maiocco on her claim of malicious interference with business relations. We affirm.

I.

In 1985, Judith Beall began working as a territory manager (TM) for Ross Laboratories (Ross), a division of Abbott that manufactures and markets Similac infant formula and other pediatric nutritional products. TMs sell Ross's products in hospitals and doctors' offices. Beall worked in northern Virginia and was supervised by Michael Budlong, the manager of the Virginia district. District managers are responsible for helping

TMs increase Ross's market share, which is calculated by the "Mothers' Survey," a monthly questionnaire mailed to 63,000 new parents to determine the dietary habits of infants during the first six months of life. Approximately once per month, the district manager accompanies each TM on a field visit and coaches the TM on sales techniques. An evaluation of the TM's performance follows each visit.

According to Budlong, Beall was difficult to manage at times, particularly because she did not respond well to criticism. However, Budlong and Beall worked together without incident until shortly after Beall returned from maternity leave to deliver her second child in early 1993. During an April 1993 field visit to a local hospital, Beall excused herself to go to the lactation room and use her breast pump. Budlong then allegedly remarked that "he would come into the room with Beall and do some paperwork while Beall pumped."

While driving together the next day, Beall told Budlong that she wanted to stop at the Fairfax Hospital lactation room to use the breast pump. According to Beall, Budlong replied, " 'I don't want to stop now, pull your car off the road, get in the back seat of your car and get out your breast pump.' " Although she recognizes that "the nature of her business is to discuss breast feeding," Beall was upset by these comments. One year later, in April 1994, Budlong required Beall and another female TMs to assemble their own promotional materials. All other male and female TMs in the Virginia district either received assembled materials or were permitted to arrange for their assembly. When Beall complained, Budlong told her that " 'the girls could put their own promotional boxes together.' " Beall "didn't like to be referred to as 'the girls.' "

In a July 1994 field visit to a doctor's office, Beall took offense to a comment Budlong made about Beall's weight loss. Beall claims that Budlong said, " 'Get over here and get on this scale, I want to see how much you weigh.' " According to Budlong, however, Beall had lost a significant amount of weight and often discussed her weight loss and related medical problems with Budlong.

In November 1994, Budlong allegedly yelled at Beall to move her car after Beall suffered a diabetes-related dizzy spell. Beall also alleges that Budlong "frequently spoke to me in a demeaning and condescending tone and yelled at me during our monthly supervisory work visits."

Beall's performance declined during this time. Although generally giving Beall "outstanding" or "commendable" performance ratings throughout 1994, Budlong's evaluations made several references to flaws in Beall's sales presentation and to Beall's inability to establish effective Similac Welcome Addition Club (SWAC) programs. SWAC programs provided expecting parents with educational literature and coupons for Ross products. On August 25, 1994, Ross conducted a detailed analysis of the Virginia district's sales data. This meeting was attended by Budlong, regional manager Michael Maiocco, and two other Ross executives. The analysis revealed that Beall's Mothers' Survey trends had declined over the past four quarters and that Beall's market share ranked last among the forty-three TMs in the region. Beall also had poor SWAC enrollment numbers. During the August 30, 1994 field visit, Budlong informed Beall of the problems in Beall's performance. According to Beall, this was the most upsetting work visit she ever had.

On September 12, 1994, Beall wrote a letter to Maiocco alleging that Budlong had "created a hostile and intimidating work environment" and "inaccurately and unfairly attacked my performance."

Three days later, Beall met with Maiocco and discussed both the alleged sexual harassment and her poor performance analysis. Maiocco investigated the harassment allegation by interviewing Budlong and five TMs in Budlong's district. On September 26, Maiocco again met with Beall and informed her that his investigation did not substantiate her harassment claim.

At the September 26 meeting, Maiocco gave Beall a letter formally placing her on Unsatisfactory Performance status (USP) for sixty days. Ross's official objective in placing employees on USP is "to restore employees to a satisfactory level of performance." The USP letter stated that Beall was being placed on USP because she had the lowest market share in the district for the second quarter of 1994, the lowest SWAC enrollment numbers in the district, and a flaw in her sales presentation. The letter also set forth goals which Beall needed to meet before returning to satisfactory performance. Beall was to (1) maintain a specific market share of infants discharged from Fairfax Hospital and add 300 newborns at other hospitals; (2) establish new promotional programs at eight pediatricians' offices and eight obstetricians' offices; (3) increase prenatal SWAC enrollment to meet the district average and add sixteen new SWAC programs in obstetricians' offices; (4) utilize Ross's five-step sales presentation; and (5) be present in her territory every day from 8:30 A.M. to 5:00 P.M.

The defendants contend that, although Beall's district ranking improved to twenty-eighth out of forty-three TMs, Beall did not meet the goals of the September 26 letter. Specifically, the defendants determined that (1) Beall did not add 300 newborns; (2) she established new promotional programs at only one pediatrician's office and only seven obstetricians' offices; (3) she fell short of the SWAC enrollment goals by over 100 prenatal enrollees; and (4) she established only ten of the required sixteen new SWAC programs. On December 16, 1994, Beall was placed on final probation, which gave Beall another sixty days to meet the same USP goals.

In January 1995, Beall took short-term disability leave because of complications from her third pregnancy. She stayed on disability leave throughout the remainder of her employment at Ross. Her territory had been covered by other TMs during her absence. In June 1995, Abbott decided to reduce its Ross sales force by eliminating twelve TM positions. According to Ross's policy, the territory of any TM who is on leave for more than six months is considered vacant and a new individual is hired to fill the opening. Beall's six-month period ended July 10, 1995. Rather than hiring a new TM, Ross eliminated or "collapsed" Beall's territory pursuant to its reduction in force on September 27, 1995. Beall's clients were assigned to other TMs.

Beall filed a complaint with the Equal Employment Opportunity Commission (EEOC) on March 17, 1995. The EEOC declined to act on Beall's complaint, and in October 1995 Beall obtained a right-to-sue letter from the EEOC.

Beall sued Abbott, Budlong, and Maiocco for retaliation, claiming that the decisions to place her on USP and final probation and to eliminate her position were made in retaliation for her complaints to Maiocco and the EEOC regarding Budlong's alleged harassment.

The district court granted summary judgment for the defendants on all claims.

While the district court held that Beall had established a prima facie case of retaliation, the district court concluded that the defendants rebutted the prima facie case by showing legitimate nondiscriminatory justifications for each action. Because Beall did not produce sufficient evidence to show that the defendants' nonretaliatory justifications were pretextual, the district court granted summary judgment against her. Beall now appeals.

Beall argues that her employer's decisions to place her on USP and final probation and to collapse her territory were made in retaliation for her complaining about the alleged harassment. On appeal, Beall argues that there are genuine issues of material fact concerning whether the defendants' nonretaliatory reasons were merely pretextual. We disagree.

To state a prima facie case of retaliation, a plaintiff must show that (1) the plaintiff engaged in a protected activity, such as filing a complaint with the EEOC; (2) the employer acted adversely against the plaintiff; and (3) the protected activity was causally connected to the employer's adverse action. Once this is shown, the burden is on the employer to rebut the presumption of retaliation by articulating a legitimate nonretaliatory reason for its actions. The plaintiff must then demonstrate that the employer's reason was mere pretext for retaliation by proving " 'both that the reason was false, and that discrimination was the real reason' for the challenged conduct." The plaintiff always has the ultimate burden of persuading the trier of fact that the defendant engaged in retaliatory conduct.

We assume, arguendo, that Beall stated a prima facie case of retaliation. However, we agree with the district court that the defendants rebutted Beall's prima facie case with legitimate nonretaliatory reasons for each of their adverse actions. The defendants first contend that they placed Beall on USP because of Beall's decline in performance, as measured by the Mothers' Survey results and the SWAC enrollment numbers. The defendants further contend that they placed Beall on final probation because of Beall's failure to meet the USP objectives. Finally, the defendants contend that they eliminated Beall's position because of Ross's need to eliminate jobs and its policy of collapsing vacant territories. Because the defendants have articulated legitimate nonretaliatory reasons for their actions, any presumption raised by the plaintiff's prima facie case "drops from the case."

Beall also has not shown that the defendants' reason for placing Beall on final probation was mere pretext. The letter of September 26, 1994, clearly set forth the requirements that Beall needed to meet in order to return to satisfactory performance. The defendants contend that she did not meet these goals. In response, Beall asserts that the defendants mistakenly assessed her performance during the USP period. She asserts that her delivery of promotional boxes to doctors' offices should count as establishing a promotional program at each office. She relies on the number of promotional boxes she delivered as evidence of the total number of new infants using Ross products. However, absent evidence of retaliatory motive, we leave to the employer's discretion the method of evaluating

an employee's job performance. Accordingly, Beall has not demonstrated a genuine issue of material fact concerning the defendants' reason for placing her on final probation.

Finally, Beall cannot show that the decision to collapse her territory was retaliatory. Beall's position was eliminated pursuant to a reduction in force at Ross and according to Ross's vacant territory rules. Beall has not presented evidence to show that the need for a reduction in force was pretextual or that Ross applied its policy with a retaliatory motive. Beall has thus failed to show how any of the justifications for her employer's actions were mere pretext for retaliation against Beall. Accordingly, the defendants are entitled to summary judgment on Beall's retaliation claim.

For the reasons stated above, we affirm the district court's grant of summary judgment in favor of the defendants.

Judgment for Abbott Labs.

Case Commentary

In this case, an employee who had performed poorly attempted to characterize her employer's decision to terminate her as retaliation. The employer responded with evidence of employee Beall's poor performance. The Civil Rights Act

was enacted to remedy injustices of termination for discriminatory motives. The Civil Rights Act was never intended to strip away an employer's right to make critical judgments with regard to the performance of its employees.

Case Questions

1. Do you agree with the decision in this case?
2. Was Beall treated fairly?
3. Should an employer's right to judge the performance of its workers be safeguarded?
4. If not, under what conditions could an employee be terminated, and who would make the judgment?

CONSTRUCTIVE DISCHARGE

As opposed to outright termination, an employer may make the work environment so intolerable that the employee may be forced to resign. This process amounts to constructive discharge. These actions may be motivated by discrimination, general dislike, or retaliation. The employer may act directly or through the targeted employee's coworkers. The coworkers themselves may act on their own initiative.

The issue in this case is whether the employer made the work environment so intolerable for the employee in retaliation for whistle-blowing to amount to a constructive discharge.

MINTZMYER v. DEPARTMENT OF THE INTERIOR

84 F.3d 419 (Fed. Cir. 1996)

MAYER, Circuit Judge.

Lauretta L. Mintzmyer petitions for review of a final decision of the Merit Systems Protection Board dismissing her individual right of action appeal. We affirm.

BACKGROUND

In 1980, Mintzmyer became the Regional Director of the Rocky Mountain Region of the National Park Service, a bureau within the United States Department of the Interior (agency). As such, she was in the Senior Executive Service working in Denver, Colorado. In October 1991, Mintzmyer and two other directors of different regions were part of a three-way rotation, in which Mintzmyer was reassigned as Regional Director of the Mid-Atlantic Region in Philadelphia, Pennsylvania.

Displeased with her transfer, Mintzmyer filed an Equal Employment Opportunity complaint with the agency, claiming that her reassignment was due to gender and age discrimination and was in retaliation for whistle-blowing. In April 1992, Mintzmyer retired. She then amended her EEO complaint to allege that she had been coerced into retiring for the same reasons.

In October 1992, Mintzmyer filed a complaint against the agency in the United States District Court for the District of Colorado, alleging, *inter alia,* violations of Title VII of the Civil Rights Act of 1964, and the Age Discrimination in Employment Act of 1967. The case was transferred to the United States District Court for the District of Columbia.

On January 12, 1995, the district court entered judgment in favor of the agency on seven of Mintzmyer's eight claims, but awarded her $5,025 for a year-end bonus it found she was wrongfully denied in reprisal for filing a discrimination complaint against the agency. The court

expressly rejected Mintzmyer's claim that she had been constructively discharged for filing a discrimination complaint against the agency.

The WPA prohibits government personnel actions taken against an employee in reprisal for whistleblowing. Except when there exists an independent right to appeal an adverse personnel action directly to the board, an employee or former employee aggrieved by the action must first seek corrective action from the Office of Special Counsel. Only after the Office of Special Counsel has notified the employee or former employee that it has terminated its investigation or has failed to commit to pursuing corrective action within 120 days may that person file an IRA appeal to the board.

At the Office of Special Counsel, Mintzmyer argued that the agency had taken the following personnel actions against her in reprisal for whistleblowing: (1) reassigned her; (2) denied her a salary step increase; (3) denied her a bonus; and (4) constructively discharged her through a course of "harassing and retaliatory behavior." Before the board, Mintzmyer alleged that the agency also had taken the following "retaliatory actions": (1) threatened to reprimand her; (2) continuously threatened her with "prosecution"; (3) made several false and slanderous statements "with regard to actions taken against and by" her; and (4) declared that she was a threat to President George Bush just prior to a visit he made to the Mid-Atlantic Region.

Mintzmyer was required "to articulate with reasonable clarity and precision the basis for her request for corrective action under the WPA" to the Office of Special Counsel. Her failure to do so deprived the board of jurisdiction over these four claims; thus, its dismissal was proper.

The legal standard for establishing a constructive discharge is the same regardless of whether the discharge was allegedly in retaliation for whistleblowing or for filing a discrimination claim. The district court required Mintzmyer to establish that the agency intentionally made working conditions intolerable, thereby forcing her to involuntarily retire. The test the court applied was whether the agency created or tolerated "retaliatory working conditions that would drive a reasonable person to resign." The board has adopted the same test in examining whether an appellant has been constructively discharged in reprisal for whistleblowing. Mintzmyer does not argue that this test is inappropriate in whistleblower cases, and we endorse the board's use of it.

In addition to the identity of the legal issue raised by both claims, the facts raised by Mintzmyer in support of each claim are identical. The board explicitly found that "the underlying facts relied upon by Mintzmyer to support her claims of constructive discharge before the Board and the District Court are the same." She has not established that this finding is unsupported by substantial evidence. Before the district court, Mintzmyer alleged that the agency had constructively discharged her by undermining her ability to manage her staff in the Mid-Atlantic Region. She argued that a number of different agency actions, viewed cumulatively and in context, rendered her position there untenable, forcing her to retire. In rejecting this claim, the court addressed three controversial situations she faced upon assuming her post as Mid-Atlantic Regional Director and insulting treatment she received from security officials who viewed her as a security risk to President Bush.

In her IRA appeal, Mintzmyer claimed that she was "subjected to continuing harassment with regard to . . . employees under her supervision." As part of her prehearing submission to the board, she explained further that the agency had subjected her to a continuous stream of harassment in Philadelphia that undermined her relationship with her subordinates and decreased her effectiveness, resulting in a constructive discharge. Although she argues on appeal that the factual basis for her whistleblower claim differs from that of her discrimination claim and notes that the district court "refused to hear or decide any of the facts going to constructive discharge caused by whistleblower retaliation," she has alleged no acts of harassment to which she was subjected in Philadelphia that differ from those she relied upon in litigating her discrimination claim.

Judgment for the Department of the Interior.

Case Commentary

This case is an example of where an employee, perturbed over a reassignment, attempts to feign an action for constructive discharge and for whistle-blowing. The Whistleblower Protection Act was not enacted to be used by disgruntled employees whose cases have no merit.

Case Questions

1. Was the court's decision appropriate?
2. Did the agency's actions toward Mintzmyer constitute constructive discharge?

3. Do you believe Mintzmyer's complaint had any merit?

EMPLOYMENT PERSPECTIVE

Sean Stockton works for Premier Motors Manufacturing in their quality control division. He uncovers a scheme to shortcut the process by continuing assembly before the adhesives dry. Sean notifies his superiors, but he is told to ignore the problem. Sean approaches senior management, who appreciate his forthrightness. Sean's superiors and coworkers are severely disciplined. Later, though, he begins to receive threatening notes, his car windshield has been smashed, his tires have been flattened, and he has been demoted. Sean complains to senior management, but they tell him to deal with the problems in his own way. After being assaulted, Sean leaves the company, claiming constructive discharge. Is he correct? Yes! His coworkers and superiors have made the work environment so intolerable that it is no longer conducive to Sean's mental and physical well-being to continue on the job. If the individuals responsible had been discharged because of Sean's whistle-blowing, then Premier's duty to protect Sean and safeguard his property extends only while Sean is on the premises. Once he departs, he is on his own. This is a major risk that a whistle-blower must bear on his or her own. It may not be foreseeable to the whistle-blower that retaliatory acts will be directed against him or her. However, it would be wise for the employee to consider all of the possible ramifications for whistle-blowing and the recourses available for protection. ■

❖ Employer Lessons

- Comprehend the law relating to at-will employment.
- Be careful to identify reasons for termination, as they may compromise at-will employment.
- Use a consistent set of criteria for evaluating employees for discharge.
- Establish a grievance procedure within the company that culminates in arbitration.
- Avoid bad publicity and litigation.
- Refrain from discrimination when terminating employees.
- Do not retaliate against employees when they whistle-blow, file a workers' compensation claim, or initiate or testify in a lawsuit based on discrimination or harassment.
- Avoid acting maliciously toward an employee by making the work environment so intolerable for him or her that it constitutes constructive discharge.

❖ Employee Lessons

- Familiarize yourself with the at-will employment doctrine of the state in which you are employed.
- Read the company's employment handbook if one exists.
- Focus on any language surrounding the discharge of employees.
- Determine whether or not the employer has ever given a litany of reasons for discharge.
- Ask the new employer for a written employment contract guaranteeing you employment for a certain period of time if you are in a strong bargaining position when relocating or giving up a good job.
- Know your rights upon termination if you have been the subject of discrimination, retaliation, or constructive discharge.
- Identify whether or not the company has a grievance procedure that culminates in arbitration.
- Learn the time constraints in this procedure and abide by them.
- Identify whether or not you have been discharged in a manner that is not consistent with the treatment of other employees.

❖ Summary

Generally, employers do not take termination as personally as do employees. However, it can be a difficult process for both sides, especially if the employee believes that the discharge is wrongful.

At-will termination protects the rights of employers to terminate employees. Therefore, employees must evaluate the evidence to discern whether or not it meets one of the public policy exceptions to the at-will doctrine.

Employers must guard against compromising their protection under the at-will employment doctrine by stipulating that employees will be discharged only for cause or by listing explicit reasons for discharge in an employment handbook or in conversation with an applicant or an employee.

❖ REVIEW QUESTIONS

1. What constitutes a wrongful discharge?
2. Is downsizing a form of discriminatory conduct?
3. What does at-will employment mean?
4. Explain retaliatory discharge.
5. Is retaliatory discharge ever justifiable?
6. How can an employee be constructively discharged?
7. What does it mean to be dismissed for cause?
8. Define termination.
9. Can an employee be dismissed without cause?
10. Explain the significance of the Model Employment Termination Act.
11. How can a termination be contested?
12. Hercules, motivated by bad faith and malice, wrongfully discharged the Plaintiff in violation of the public policy against employment discrimination based on age, as codified in the ADEA and the Delaware Fair Employment Practicers Act (FEPA).

    First, it could be a claim for discharge of an at-will employee in violation of public policy. Second, it could be read as alleging a common law tort claim of malicious discharge.

    The Delaware Supreme Court has never recognized a public policy exception to an employer's ability to dismiss an at-will employee. However, in *Merrill v. Crothall American, Inc.,* the Delaware Supreme Court recognized that an implied covenant of good faith and fair dealing may be breached in some circumstances by termination of an at-will employee.

    In this case, should the Delaware Court create a public policy exception to the doctrine of employment at will? *Finch v. Hercules, Inc.,* 809 F.Supp. 309 (D. Del. 1992)
13. On January 26, 1988, while Patricia Williams Howard was on the air, Keith Holcombe drove to the station and informed her that

she was fired. When he fired her, Holcombe told her that she was being fired because Karen Wolff, whose husband owned Wolff Broadcasting Corporation ("Wolff"), did not want any females on the air. On that same night, Howard typed a letter stating that she was fired because Karen Wolff did not want any females on the air. Howard says this letter was signed by Keith Holcombe.

On October 2, 1989, Howard filed a complaint against Wolff, alleging fraud and breach of contract, and against Karen Wolff, alleging intentional interference with business relations.

The determinative question on that issue is whether Howard's employment contract was terminable at will. What was the result? *Howard v. Wolff Broadcasting Corp.* 611 SO.2d 307 (Ala. 1992)
14. In November 1990, J. Walter Company Ltd. ("Walter Ltd.") formed J. Walter Inc. ("Walter Inc.") as an independent corporation responsible for the sale of Walter products in the United States. Walter Inc. is a Delaware corporation with its principal place of business in Hartford, Connecticut. On November 1, 1990, Manfred Thiede was hired as the president of Walter Inc. and Patrick Mochelle was hired as a salesman for Walter Inc. and continued to sell Walter products in the United States.

On January 14, 1992, Thiede fired Mochelle from Walter Inc. for failing to perform his job duties and for failing to communicate with his supervisor, Thiede, despite repeated warnings.

Plaintiff claims that he was fired from his employment at "Walter" because of his political aspirations and his desire to run for political office. Walter Ltd. contends that it cannot be liable because it was not the employer of Mochelle during the period of the alleged political interference. Walter Inc. admits that it was the employer of Mochelle at the time of the alleged political interference, but contends that it cannot be liable because it does not have the requisite twenty employees mandated by the statute. What was the result? *Mochelle v. J. Walter, Inc.* 823 F.Supp. 1302 (M.D.L.A. 1993)

15. Governor James Thompson of Illinois, on November 12, 1980, issued an executive order proclaiming a hiring freeze for every agency, bureau, board, or commission subject to his control. The order proclaims that "no exceptions" are permitted without the Governor's "express permission after submission of appropriate requests to his office." Requests for the Governor's "express permission" have allegedly become routine.

Cynthia B. Rutan has been working for the State since 1974 as a rehabilitation counselor. She claims that since 1981 she has been repeatedly denied promotions to supervisory positions for which she was qualified because she had not worked for or supported the Republican Party. What was the result? *Rutan et al. v. Republican Party of Illinois*, 497 U.S. 62 (1990)

16. In this case, Clowes's ADEA claim and the judgment she won were predicated on the assertion that she has been constructively discharged. Clowes was never threatened with discharge; nor did her employer ever urge or suggest that she resign or retire. Similarly, Clowes's employer did not demote her or reduce her pay or benefits. Clowes was not involuntarily transferred to a less desirable position, and her job responsibilities were not altered in any way. She was not even given unsatisfactory job evaluations but merely received ratings of "fair."

It is also highly significant that Clowes, prior to leaving her position with the hospital, never requested to be transferred to another position, never advised the hospital that she would feel compelled to leave if changes regarding the manner in which she was being supervised were not made, and did not even attempt to file a grievance until long after she had stopped working at the hospital.

Moreover, it is significant, in our view, that Clowes's complaint focused exclusively on Malloy's allegedly overzealous supervision of her work. Clowes has not brought to our attention a single case in which a constructive discharge has been found based solely upon such supervision. *Clowes v. Allegheny Valley Hosp.*, 911 F.2d 1159 (3rd Cir. 1993)

❖ **WEB SITES**

www.Majlaw.com/terminate.html
www.findlaw.com
http://sacramento.bcentral.com/sacramento/stories/1996/11/18/smallb3.html
www.gov.on.ca/lab/es/terminae.htm
www.ucop.edu/humres/policies/spp64.html
www.ilrg.com/forms/terminat.html
www.counsel.net/chatboards/emp-law/topic227/8.27.00.18.19.29.html

CHAPTER

6

CIVIL RIGHTS ACT

INTRODUCTION

Shortly after the conclusion of the Civil War in 1865, the Thirteenth, Fourteenth, and Fifteenth Amendments to the U.S. Constitution were adopted. The Thirteenth Amendment abolished slavery. The Fifteenth Amendment gave black men the right to vote. But, it was the Equal Protection Clause of the Fourteenth Amendment that laid the basis for equal rights in employment. The Equal Protection Clause basically states that all people are entitled to equal protection under the law. A few years after its enactment, the Supreme Court of the United States, in *Plessy v. Ferguson*, interpreted this to mean that separate but equal facilities would satisfy the Fourteenth Amendment requirement. Segregation persisted into the 1970s, but inroads began to be made in the mid-1950s with the *Brown v. Board of Education* decision, which mandated integration in public schools. This decision had a reverberating effect throughout society. In 1964, Congress passed the Civil Rights Act to legislate integration in schools, housing, restaurants, transportation, shopping, employment, etc. Title VII of the Civil Rights Act speaks to employment. It prohibits discrimination because of religion, race, color, sex, and national origin.

There are two main types of discrimination: disparate impact, which is discrimination against a class of people, and disparate treatment, which is discrimination against an individual. The two major cases defining these forms of discrimination are *Griggs v. Duke Power Co.*, which deals with disparate impact, and *McDonnell Douglas Corp. v. Green*, which deals with disparate treatment. Both of these cases are set forth in this chapter.

CHAPTER CHECKLIST

❖ Appreciate the history of events leading up to passage of the Civil Rights Act.

❖ Understand the purpose of Title VII of the Civil Rights Act.

❖ Comprehend the decisions in *Griggs v. Duke Power Co.* and *McDonnell Douglas Corp. v. Green*.

❖ Distinguish between disparate impact and disparate treatment.

❖ Learn what constitutes business necessity and job relatedness.

❖ Understand the issue of whether an employer's decision was a pretext.

❖ Appreciate the function of the Equal Employment Opportunity Commission.

❖ Be able to explain the 80 percent rule.

❖ List the significant features of the Civil Rights Act of 1991.

❖ Identify the exemptions to Title VII of the Civil Rights Act.

Employment Scenario

One day during lunch with Susan, Tom Long and Mark Short ask her whether Title VII of the Civil Rights Act applies to The Long and The Short of It. As she digests her grilled salmon and baked sweet potato, Susan replies in the affirmative. L&S has four stores with a total of 62 employees. Growth has been phenomenal. Susan explains L&S has been subject to Title VII since it hired its fifteenth employee. At that time, Susan reminded Tom and Mark that she sent them a memo detailing the requirement that they keep records regarding their selection process of potential candidates. These records must be made available to the EEOC upon request. Susan advised Tom and Mark to notify her if anyone filed a claim against L&S for discrimination. She also cautioned them to be consistent in their treatment of employees. She reminded them not to favor or discourage any class of workers. Susan warned them not to favor the employment of one sex over the other by stereotyping certain jobs. Treating everyone equally is the key to an employer's peaceful coexistence with its employees.

The question presented in the case that follows is whether separate but equal facilities are discriminatory.

CASE

BROWN v. BOARD OF EDUCATION OF TOPEKA

347 U.S. 483 (1954)

CHIEF JUSTICE WARREN

The decision in this lawsuit was rendered in response to a number of cases having the same constitutional question concerning the segregation of white and colored children in public schools.

In each case, colored children have made applications to schools attended by white children and in most cases they have been denied admission based on the separate but equal doctrine formulated in 1896. That doctrine provided that equal treatment of races is satisfied when the races are provided separate, but equal facilities. The parties bringing these lawsuits contended that segregated public schools are not "equal."

The issue is whether segregation in public schools is unconstitutional in violation of the Equal Protection clause of the Fourteenth Amendment.

In 1954, the United States Supreme Court held that segregation in public schools was unconstitutional. They cited as their reasoning a finding made by the court in the Kansas case which, although holding segregation to be constitutional, declared "Segregation of white and colored children in public schools has a detrimental effect upon the colored children. The impact is greater when it has the sanction of the law; for the policy of separating the races is usually interpreted as denoting the inferiority of the Negro group. A sense of inferiority affects the motivation of a child to learn." The Supreme Court added "In these days, it is doubtful that any child may reasonably be expected to succeed in life if he or she is denied the opportunity of an education. Such an opportunity, where the state has undertaken to provide it, is a right which must be made available to all on equal terms."

Judgment for Brown.

Case Commentary

The United States Supreme Court concluded that separate but equal facilities are discriminatory because separating a class of people is tantamount to claiming they are inferior. This was the landmark case for the Civil Rights movement.

Case Questions

1. Why did it take almost ninety years for the Supreme Court to abolish the separate but equal doctrine?
2. What solution did the Court provide to effectuate integration?
3. Did the Court state that all public schools must be integrated, or only those in racially diverse neighborhoods?
4. Was busing the appropriate response to the Court's decision?

Ten years later, the Civil Rights Act was introduced to codify existing statutes and case law. Enforcement of the Civil Rights Act continued to wane until the *Griggs v. Duke Power* case of 1971 set forth the criteria for bringing a discrimination suit based on the disparate impact of an employer's selection and promotion procedure.

One year later, the Supreme Court laid out the process for an individual to bring a discrimination action based on disparate treatment in *McDonnell Douglas v. Green.*

Title VII of the Civil Rights Act of 1964 is the main authority governing employment discrimination. Because it is a federal law, it is binding on all employers throughout the United States. An employer is a person or business employing at least 15 individuals for 20 weeks of the year. The employer's business must have some connection with interstate commerce for Title VII to be applicable. Basically, a business is engaged in interstate commerce if it ships goods to a state other than the one in which it is located, performs services in another state, or performs services intrastate for individuals traveling interstate. Interstate commerce has been construed so broadly that it would be difficult for a business to seek exemption from Title VII under the auspices of not participating in interstate commerce.

The main thrust of Title VII is that it is an unlawful practice to discriminate in failing or refusing to hire, train, discharge, promote, compensate, or in any other aspect of the employment relationship because of an individual's religion, race, color, sex, or national origin. Employers may not segregate employees or classify them in such a way as to deprive any of them of employment opportunities or to adversely affect their status as employees.

EMPLOYMENT PERSPECTIVE
Redeye truck stop is located on interstate 80 in Pennsylvania. It refuses to serve women and minority truckers. Redeye argues that it is not subject to the Civil Rights Act because all of its business is transacted in Pennsylvania. Is this argument valid? No! Although Redeye's business is conducted intrastate, it services truckers who are traveling interstate. Therefore, its business affects interstate commerce. ■

The term *employer* includes individuals, partnerships, corporations, associations, unincorporated organizations, and governments. Employment agencies and labor unions are also subject to Title VII. For purposes here, *employer* will also refer to employment agencies and labor unions where appropriate. It does not include the United States, an American Indian tribe, or a tax exempt, bona fide private membership club. Religious societies and religious educational institutions are also exempt insofar as they have the right to employ only individuals of their religion.

EMPLOYMENT PERSPECTIVE
George Feinstein, who is Jewish, has just received a college degree in education. Neither the public schools nor the Jewish schools have openings for teachers. George applied to the Catholic Diocese, where positions are readily available. He was turned down because he is not a practicing Catholic. Is this discrimination? No! Catholic schools, as well as any other religious-affiliated institutions, may restrict employment to members of their own particular faith. ■

The issue in the next case concerns whether employees who work part-time or who are hired midweek count for the purposes of fulfilling the 15-employee threshold of the Civil Rights Act.

CASE

WALTERS v. METROPOLITAN EDUCATIONAL ENTERPRISES, INC.

519 U.S. 202 (1997)

JUSTICE SCALIA delivered the opinion of the Court.

Title VII of the Civil Rights Act of 1964 applies to any employer who "has fifteen or more employees for each working day in each of twenty or more calendar weeks in the current or preceding calendar year." These cases present the question whether an employer "has" an employee on any working day on which the employer maintains an employment relationship with the employee, or only on working days on which the employee is actually receiving compensation from the employer.

I.

Petitioner Darlene Walters was employed by respondent Metropolitan Educational Enterprises, Inc., a retail distributor of encyclopedias, dictionaries, and other educational materials. In 1990, she filed a charge with the Equal Employment

Opportunity Commission (EEOC), claiming that Metropolitan had discriminated against her on account of her sex in failing to promote her to the position of credit manager. Soon after that, Metropolitan fired her.

On April 7, 1993, petitioner EEOC filed suit against Metropolitan and its owner, respondent Leonard Bieber (hereinafter collectively Metropolitan), alleging that the firing constituted unlawful retaliation. Walters intervened in the suit. Metropolitan filed a motion to dismiss for lack of subject-matter jurisdiction, claiming that the company did not pass the 15-employee threshold for coverage under Title VII.

The District Court granted Metropolitan's motion to dismiss. On appeal from the District Court's judgment, the Court of Appeals reaffirmed Zimmerman. We granted certiorari.

II.

Petitioners' suit rests on Title VII's antiretaliation provision, which makes it unlawful for an employer to discriminate against any of its employees for filing complaints of discrimination. Metropolitan was subject to Title VII, however, only if, at the time of the alleged retaliation, it met the statutory definition of "employer," to wit: "a person engaged in an industry affecting commerce who has fifteen or more employees for each working day in each of twenty or more calendar weeks in the current or preceding calendar year."

Metropolitan's "working days" are Monday through Friday, and the "current" and "preceding" calendar years for purposes of the retaliatory-discharge claim are 1990 and 1989. The parties have stipulated that Metropolitan failed to satisfy the 15-employee threshold in 1989. During most of 1990, Metropolitan had between 15 and 17 employees on its payroll on each working day; but in only nine weeks of the year was it actually compensating 15 or more employees on each working day (including paid leave as compensation). The difference resulted from the fact that Metropolitan had two part-time hourly employees who ordinarily skipped one working day each week.

A.

The parties agree that, on any particular day, all of the individuals with whom an employer has an employment relationship are "employees" of that employer. Thus, individuals who are not receiving compensation from their employer on the day in question nonetheless qualify as "employees" on that day for purposes of Section(s) 2000e(b)'s definition of "employer." Respondents contend, however, and the Seventh Circuit held here, that an employer "has" an employee for a particular working day within the meaning of Section(s) 2000e(b) only when he is actually compensating the individual on that day. This position has also been adopted by the Eighth Circuit.

Petitioners contend that the test for when an employer "has" an employee is no different from the test for when an individual is an employee: whether the employer has an employment relationship with the individual on the day in question. This test is generally called the "payroll method," since the employment relationship is most readily demonstrated by the individual's appearance on the employer's payroll. The payroll method was approved in dictum by the Fifth Circuit and was adopted by the First. The payroll method has also been adopted by the EEOC under the Age Discrimination in Employment Act of 1967, which defines "employer" in precisely the way Title VII does. The Department of Labor has likewise adopted the payroll method under the Family and Medical Leave Act of 1993, which defines "employer" as a person who "employs 50 or more employees for each working day during each of 20 or more calendar workweeks in the current or preceding calendar year." In its administration of Title VII, the EEOC has expressed a preference for the payroll method, but it lacks rulemaking authority over the issue.

We think that the payroll method represents the fair reading of the statutory language, which sets as the criterion the number of employees that the employer "has" for each working day. In the absence of an indication to the contrary, words in a statute are assumed to bear their "ordinary, contemporary, common meaning occur with sufficient frequency to merit inclusion in a federal anti-discrimination statute." But it is not a matter of carving out special treatment for this (supposedly minuscule) class-as would be the case if, without the phrase "for each working day," part-week employees would unquestionably be counted toward the statutory minimum. Without the phrase one would not be sure whether to count them or not, and in at least some cases the matter would have to be litigated. (Does a company have 15 employees "in" a week where, on all except the last workday, it has only 14? "In" a week where it hires a new employee on Saturday, a nonworkday, to begin on the next Monday? "In" a week where, in mid-week, one of 14 employees quits and is replaced by a different 14th employee?) We are decidedly of the view that the "mere" elimination of evident ambiguity is ample-indeed, admirable-justification for the inclusion of a statutory phrase; and that purpose alone is enough to "merit" enactment of the phrase at issue here. Moreover, the phenomenon of mid-week commencement and termination of employment seems to us not as rare as the Court of Appeals believed. For many businesses pay-day, and hence hiring and firing-day, is the end of the month rather than the end of the week. Metropolitan itself experienced 10 mid-week arrivals or departures from its roughly 15-employee work force during 1990.

As we have described, in determining the existence of an employment relationship, petitioners look first and primarily to whether the individual in question appears on the employer's payroll. Metropolitan did not challenge this aspect of petitioners' approach; its objection was the more basic one that existence of an employment relationship was not the criterion. For their part, petitioners emphasize that what is ultimately critical under their method is the existence of an employment relationship, not appearance on the payroll; an individual who appears on the payroll but is not an "employee" under traditional principles of agency law would not count toward the 15-employee minimum. We agree with petitioners that the ultimate touchstone under Section(s) 2000e(b) is whether an employer has employment relationships with 15 or more individuals for each working day in 20 or more weeks during the year in question.

The parties' stipulation concerning the number of weeks in 1990 during which Metropolitan satisfied the 15-employee threshold using the payroll approach does not correspond precisely to the counting method petitioners have advocated here. The stipulation was arrived at by counting the number of employees on the payroll in each week of 1990, without regard to whether these employees were employed on each working day of the week. However, subtracting the nine weeks in which Metropolitan experienced mid-week employment changes in 1990 from the 47 weeks of that year in which, according to the parties' stipulation, Metropolitan had employment relationships with 15 or more employees, leaves 38 weeks in which Metropolitan satisfied the 15-employee threshold under the interpretation we adopt. Therefore, Metropolitan was an "employer" within the meaning of Section(s) 2000e(b) for purposes of petitioners' retaliatory-discharge claim.

The judgment of the Court of Appeals is reversed, and the cases are remanded for further proceedings consistent with this opinion.

Judgment for Walters.

Case Commentary

The U.S. Supreme Court concluded Metropolitan had the requisite number of employees required under the Civil Rights Act.

Case Questions

1. Do you agree with the court's decision?
2. What is the rationale for the 15-person requirement?
3. Is the 15-employee threshold necessary or should it be lower?

DISPARATE TREATMENT

Disparate treatment exists where an employer treats an individual differently because that individual is a member of a particular race, religion, gender, or ethnic group. The complaining party must show that he or she is a member of a particular Title VII class;

that the employer in question was seeking applicants for a position; that he or she was rejected; and that the employer continued to seek applicants with similar qualifications.

EMPLOYMENT PERSPECTIVE

Thomas Johnson, who is black, responded to an advertisement offering a position with the law firm of Mayer, Morgan and Marconi. The law firm was seeking a person who graduated in the top half of his or her class from an Ivy League law school. Johnson met those qualifications. However, he was told that the position had already been filled. The same advertisement continued to run in the newspaper, though. Johnson claimed disparate treatment. Is he correct? Yes! The law firm lied to Johnson about the position's being filled, because it did not want to hire a black person. ■

The following case, which set the standard for qualifying for disparate treatment, is a landmark case. To qualify for Title VII protection, a person must show that (1) he or she is a member of a protected class; (2) he or she applied for a position for which he or she was qualified and for which the employer had openings; (3) he or she was rejected; (4) the position remained open. At this point, the burden of proof has been met by the employee or the applicant and then shifts to the employer to establish a justifiable reason for its action. Finally, the employee must prove that the employer's reason was just a pretext for its refusal to hire.

CASE

McDONNELL DOUGLAS CORP. v. GREEN

411 U.S. 792 (1972)

JUSTICE POWELl delivered the opinion of the Court.

The case before us raises significant questions as to the proper order and nature of proof in actions under Title VII of the Civil Rights Act of 1964, 42 U.S.C. 2000e.

Petitioner McDonnell Douglas Corp., is an aerospace and aircraft manufacturer headquartered in St. Louis, Missouri, where it employs over 30,000 people. Respondent, a black citizen of St. Louis, worked for petitioner as a mechanic and laboratory technician from 1956 until August 28, 1964 when he was laid off in the course of a general reduction in petitioner's work force. Respondent, a long-time activist in the civil rights movement, protested vigorously that his discharge and the general hiring practices of petitioner were racially motivated. As part of this protest, respondent and other members of the Congress on Racial Equality illegally stalled their cars on the main roads leading to petitioner's plant for the purpose of blocking access to it at the time of the morning shift change. The District Judge described the plan for, and respondent's participation in, the "stall-in."

Some three weeks following the "lock-in" on July 25, 1965, petitioner publicly advertised for qualified mechanics, respondent's trade, and respondent promptly applied for re-employment. Petitioner turned down respondent, basing its rejection on respondent's participation in the "stall-in" and "lock-in." Shortly thereafter, respondent filled a formal complaint with the Equal Employment Opportunity Commission, claiming that petitioner has refused to rehire him because of his race and persistent involvement in the civil rights movement, in violation of 703 (a)(1) and 704 (a) of the Civil Rights Act of 1964. The former section generally prohibits racial discrimination in any employment decision while the latter forbids discrimination against applicants or employees for attempting to protest or correct allegedly discriminatory conditions of employment.

The language of Title VII makes plain the purpose of Congress to assure equality of employment opportunities and to eliminate those discriminatory practices and devices which have fostered racially stratified job environments to the disadvantage of minority citizens.

The complainant in a Title VII trial must carry the initial burden under the statute of establishing a prima facie case of racial discrimination. This may be done by showing (i) that he belongs to a racial minority; (ii) that he applied and was qualified for a job for which the employer was seeking applicants; (iii) that, despite his qualifications, he was rejected; and (iv) that, after his rejection, the position remained open and the employer continued to seek applicants from persons of complainant's qualifications. In the instant case, we agree with the Court of Appeals that respondent proved a prima facie case. Petitioner sought mechanics, respondent's trade, and continued to do so after respondent's rejection. Petitioner, moreover, does not dispute respondent's qualifications and acknowledges that his past work performance in petitioner's employ was "satisfactory."

The burden then must shift to the employer to articulate some legitimate, nondiscriminatory reason for the employer's rejection. We need not attempt in the instant case to detail every matter which fairly could be recognized as a reasonable basis for a refusal to hire. Here petitioner has assigned respondent's participation in unlawful conduct against it as the cause for his rejection. We think that this suffices to discharge petitioner's burden of proof at this stage and to meet respondent's prima facie case of discrimination.

Respondent admittedly had taken part in a carefully planned "stall-in," designed to tie up access to and egress from petitioner's plant at a peak traffic hour. Nothing in Title VII compels an employer to absolve and rehire one who has engaged in such deliberate, unlawful activity against it.

"We are unable to conclude that Congress intended to compel employers to retain persons in their employ regardless of their unlawful conduct, to invest those who go on strike with an immunity from discharge for acts of trespass or violence against the employer's property."

Petitioner's reason for rejection thus suffices to meet the prima facie case, but the inquiry must not end here. While Title VII does not, without more, compel rehiring of respondent, neither does it permit petitioner to use respondent's conduct as a pretext for the sort of discrimination prohibited by 703(a)(1). On remand, respondent must, as the Court of Appeals recognized, be afforded a fair opportunity to show that petitioner's stated reason for respondent's rejection was in fact pretext. Especially relevant to such a showing would be evidence that white employees involved in acts against petitioner of comparable seriousness to the "stall-in" were nevertheless retained or rehired. Petitioner may justifiably refuse to rehire one who was engaged in unlawful, disruptive acts against it, but only if this criterion is applied alike to members of all races.

In sum, respondent should have been allowed to pursue his claim under 703(a)(1). If the evidence on retrial is substantially in accord with that before us in this case, we think that respondent carried his burden of establishing a prima facie case of racial discrimination and that petitioner successfully rebutted that case. But this does not end the matter. On retrial, respondent must be afforded a fair opportunity to demonstrate that petitioner's assigned reason for refusing to re-employ was a pretext or discriminatory in its application. If the District Judge so finds, he must order a prompt and appropriate remedy. In the absence of such a finding, petitioner's refusal to rehire must stand.

The judgment is vacated and the cause is hereby remanded to the District Court for further proceedings consistent with this opinion.

Judgment for Green.

EQUAL EMPLOYMENT OPPORTUNITY COMMISSION

The Equal Employment Opportunity Commission was established in 1972 when the Equal Employment Opportunity Act amended Title VII of the Civil Rights Act of 1964. It is composed of five members, no more than three of which may be Republican or Democrat. The President of the United States shall appoint these members with the advice and consent of the U.S. Senate for a period of five years. Although the Civil Rights Act of 1964 is the cornerstone of the movement against employment discrimination, it is important to understand that legislative policy on employment discrimination has developed over time through the enactment of several different laws.

The Commission's responsibility is to enforce the provisions of Title VII against unlawful employment practices. A person claiming a violation of Title VII has 180 days to file the complaint with the EEOC. There is no cost to file.

Violations of Title VII are brought before the Equal Employment Opportunity Commission (EEOC). Within 10 days of receipt of a complaint, the EEOC notifies the employer and conducts an investigation that entails questioning employees and/or obtaining physical evidence. A determination must be made by the EEOC. If there is a reasonable cause to believe the charges are true, the EEOC will attempt to persuade the offender to change its practices. None of these proceedings are made public. The offender has 30 days to comply. If the violation is charged against a government or one of its agencies, the EEOC shall refer the matter to the Attorney General of the United States, who may then proceed in Federal District Court. There are 98 Federal District Courts located throughout the United States. These are the general trial courts in the Federal Court System. Appeals from them go to one of the 11 Circuit Courts of Appeals and then to the United States Supreme Court.

If a state or local law exists prohibiting the unlawful employment practice, the complainant must first proceed within the state or locality before filing with the EEOC. After 60 days of instituting the suit with the state, the time limit for filing with the EEOC shall be extended to the earlier of 300 days or 30 days after the state or local action has been resolved.

If at the time of filing, the EEOC or Attorney General's office believes that irreparable harm will result if the employer's unlawful employment practices are not immediately halted, they can apply for a temporary restraining order or a preliminary injunction against the employer.

After the initial investigation, the EEOC will determine whether there is a reasonable basis to believe that the allegation is true. If the EEOC believes that there is no basis, the complaining party is informed and is given a right to sue letter. He or she is free to proceed with a civil suit in a Federal District Court within 90 days of notification.

The District Court may enter a permanent injunction against the employer to refrain from engaging in the unlawful employment practice cited in the complaint. Furthermore, the Court may authorize the employer to hire the individual or individuals issuing the charge, reinstate them if they have been discharged, reimburse them with back pay, promote them, or give them any other type of equitable relief that the Court deems necessary. The Court may also allow the prevailing party reasonable fees for attorney representation, as well as for expert testimony. The charge for discrimination under Title VII is limited to race, color, religion, national origin, or sex. Discrimination for age and disability are covered under separate acts discussed later.

The question in the following case is whether the plaintiffs' lawsuit was filed within the time constraints provided by the Civil Rights Act.

CASE

ARMSTRONG, ET AL. v. MARTIN MARIETTA CORP.

138 F.3d 1374 (11th Cir. 1998)

TJOFLAT, Circuit Judge.

This case arises under the Age Discrimination in Employment Act, 29 U.S.C. § 621 *et seq.* (1994) (the "ADEA"). The thirty-one appellants in the instant case are former Martin Marietta employees who lost their jobs between 1992 and 1993. Following their terminations, twenty-nine appellants filed timely charges of age discrimination with the Equal Employment Opportunity Commission (the "EEOC"), as is required by statute.

At various times, the EEOC notified each appellant that his or her charge of age discrimination was dismissed. Receipt of such notice triggers the statute of limitations for bringing a civil action in court, and the plaintiff must then file suit within ninety days. This ninety-day limitations period is tolled, however, while the plaintiff is a putative member of a class action. Twenty-eight of the thirty-one appellants opted into *Carmichael v. Martin Marietta Corp.*, an age discrimination class action that was already proceeding in the Middle District of Florida, on June 4, 1993. The remaining three appellants—Davis, Havlish, and Hinduja—were named plaintiffs in the *Carmichael* action.

On April 7, 1994, the district court in *Carmichael* determined that the appellants were not "similarly situated" to the other *Carmichael* plaintiffs. The *Carmichael* court therefore certified a plaintiff class that did not include as members the appellants in the instant case. The court then dismissed the claims of appellants Davis, Havlish, and Hinduja without prejudice, and

denied the remaining appellants' requests to opt into the *Carmichael* class. None of the appellants requested leave to file an interlocutory appeal from that order under 28 U.S.C. § 1292(b).

On October 11, 1994, more than ninety days after the *Carmichael* court's partial denial of class certification, the thirty-one appellants and fourteen additional plaintiffs filed the complaint that commenced the instant action in the district court.

On January 17, 1995, Martin Marietta filed a motion for partial summary judgment against the thirty-one appellants, on the ground that they had failed to file their individual lawsuits within ninety days after their dismissal from the *Carmichael* class action. Martin Marietta also sought summary judgment against appellants Clarke-Iley, Johnson, and Shaw on the alternative ground that each had failed to file a charge of age discrimination with the EEOC within 300 days of the alleged discrimination.

On March 22, 1995, a magistrate judge issued a report recommending that the district court grant Martin Marietta's motion for partial summary judgment. The magistrate judge recommenced the *Carmichael* court dismissed their claims. Therefore, because the appellants' instant claims were filed more than ninety days after the dismissal in *Carmichael*, those claims were barred by the statute of limitations.

On May 10, 1995, the district court adopted the magistrate judge's report and recommendation, and granted partial summary judgment against the thirty-one appellants. On September

14, 1995, the district court amended its order and replaced the partial summary judgement with a final judgment pursuant. This appeal followed.

The primary issue on appeal is whether the district court was correct in holding that the statute of limitations, which was tolled while the appellants were putative members of the class action, resumed running when the *Carmichael* court dismissed the appellants' claims in that case. We hold that the limitations period for filing an individual suit (and for intervening in an extant action) did so resume.

The ADEA's statute of limitations requires the plaintiff to file suit within ninety days after receiving notice that the EEOC has dismissed the plaintiff's age discrimination charge. Membership in a pending class action, however, tolls the ninety-day period for filing an individual lawsuit. The purpose of such tolling is to encourage class members reasonably to rely on the class action to protect their rights. Without tolling, class members would have to take action prior to the running of the statute of limitations in order to protect themselves in case class certification is later denied, even when they may reasonably expect to receive relief through the already-filed class action. Once the district court enters the order denying class certification, however, reliance on the named plaintiffs' prosecution of the matter ceases to be reasonable, and, we hold, the excluded putative class members are put on notice that they must act independently to protect their rights.

The appellants, however, argue that the statute of limitations should continue to be tolled, even after the district court's denial of class certification, because the denial of certification in an interlocutory order may be reversed by the district court at any time before final judgment, or by the court of appeals after final judgment or, in rare cases, on interlocutory review. We disagree. No reasonable person would rely on the hope that either the district court or this court might someday determine that the suit should have proceeded as a class action.

Judgment for Martin Marietta.

Case Commentary

The Eleventh Circuit Court of Appeals decided that the plaintiff's action was time barred by the ADEA's statute of limitation.

Case Questions

1. Do you agree with the decision of this case?
2. Did the plaintiffs have a legitimate reason for filing late?

3. Should exceptions be made for late filing if there is a valid reason?
4. If a law applicable to this case is unfair, what can be done?

EQUAL OPPORTUNITY PLAN

In addition to the application of the preceding stated requirements of Title VII, the EEOC shall be responsible for approving an equal employment opportunity plan for each department and agency, and also reviewing progress reports at least twice a year from each department and agency, and evaluating on an annual basis the operation of the equal opportunity plan for each department and agency.

CIVIL RIGHTS ACT OF 1991

The Civil Rights Act of 1991 amended in part the Civil Rights Act of 1964. Jury trials are permitted. Juries are primarily comprised of workers who may be more sympathetic to the plight of employees with whom they can identify. Compensatory and punitive damages are now recoverable. Individuals who are covered by the Americans with Disabilities Act of 1990 and the Rehabilitation Act of 1973 are now covered by the Civil Rights Act of 1964 for the purpose of recovering compensatory and punitive damages. Punitive damages are recoverable when the employer has acted with malice or in reckless disregard of an individual's civil rights.

COMPENSATORY AND PUNITIVE DAMAGES

Compensatory damages include emotional pain and suffering, mental anguish, loss of enjoyment of life, inconvenience, as well as other nonpecuniary losses. Punitive damages are awarded to punish the party who has committed the wrong. Compensatory and punitive damages are awarded where there has been intentional discrimination on the part of the employer. These damages are granted in addition to back pay, which is still recoverable under the Civil Rights Act of 1964. The total of compensatory and punitive damages may not exceed $50,000 for employers with 15 to 100 employees; $100,000 for employers with 101 to 200 employees; $200,000 for employers with 201 to 500 employees; and $300,000 for employers with more than 500 employees. The employee claiming the violation may request a jury trial. The term *complaining party* now encompasses a disabled person as well as a member of a minority race, religion, sex, and national origin. Attorney fees may also be granted in the courts discretion.

BUSINESS NECESSITY

The Civil Rights Act of 1991 adopted the concepts of "business necessity" and "job related" as enunciated by the Supreme Court in *Griggs vs. Duke Power Company* (1971). The test for business necessity is not met where the employment practice that excludes a particular class is not job related. In such a case, the practice is prohibited.

It shall be an unlawful practice to adjust scores, establish different cutoff scores, or alter scores on employment-related tests for a particular race, religion, gender, or national origin.

GLASS CEILING COMMISSION

Congress has found that there still exists barriers to the advancement of women and minorities in the workplace. They remain underrepresented in management decision-making positions. Under the Civil Rights Act of 1991, Congress established the Glass Ceiling Commission to rectify this problem. The Commission must consider how prepared women and minorities are for advancement, what opportunities are available, and what policies businesses follow in making such promotions, as well as making comparisons with businesses that have actively promoted women and minorities and their reasons for success.

The issue in the case that follows is whether the EEOC has the power to award compensatory damages.

WEST, SECRETARY OF VETERANS AFFAIRS v. GIBSON

527 U.S. 212 (1999)

JUSTICE BREYER delivered the opinion of the Court.

The question in this case is whether the Equal Employment Opportunity Commission (EEOC) possesses the legal authority to require federal agencies to pay compensatory damages when they discriminate in employment in violation of Title VII of the Civil Rights Act of 1964. We conclude that the EEOC does have that authority.

I

A

Title VII of the Civil Rights Act of 1964 forbids employment discrimination. In 1972 Congress extended Title VII so that it applies not only to employment in the private sector, but to employment in the Federal Government as well. This 1972 Title VII extension, found in sect;717 of Title VII, has three relevant subsections.

The first subsection, sect;717(a), sets forth the basic Federal Government employment anti-discrimination standard. It says that

"all personnel actions affecting employees or applicants for employment of specified Government agencies and departments ... shall be made free from any discrimination based on race, color, religion, sex, or national origin."

The second subsection, sect;717(b), provides the EEOC with the power to enforce the standard. It says (among other things) that

"the Equal Employment Opportunity Commission *shall have authority to enforce the provisions of subsection (a) . . . through appropriate remedies,* including reinstatement or hiring of employees with or without back pay, as will effectuate the policies of this section. . . ."

The third subsection, sect;717(c), concerns a court's authority to enforce the standard. It says that, after an agency or the EEOC takes final action on a complaint (or fails to take action within a certain time),

"an employee or applicant ... who is still aggrieved ... may file a civil action as provided in section 706, dealing with discrimination by private employers ..., in which civil action the head of the department, agency, or unit, as appropriate, shall be the defendant."

In 1991 Congress again amended Title VII. The amendment relevant here permits victims of intentional employment discrimination (whether within the private sector or the Federal Government) to recover compensatory damages. The relevant portion of that amendment, which we shall call the Compensatory Damages Amendment (CDA), says:

"In an action brought by a complaining party under section 706 dealing with discrimination by private employers or 717 dealing with discrimination by the Federal Government against a respondent who engaged in unlawful intentional discrimination . . . , the complaining party may recover compensatory . . . damages. . . ."

The CDA also sets forth certain conditions and exceptions. It imposes, for example, a cap on compensatory damages (of up to $300,000 for large employers). And it adds: "If a complaining party seeks compensatory . . . damages under this section . . . any party may demand a trial by jury. . . ." Once the CDA became law, the EEOC began to grant compensatory damages awards in Federal Government employment discrimination cases.

B

Respondent, Michael Gibson, filed a complaint with the Department of Veterans Affairs charging that the Department had discriminated against him by denying him a promotion on the basis of his gender. The Department found against Gibson. The EEOC, however, subsequently found in Gibson's favor and awarded the promotion plus backpay. Three months later Gibson filed a complaint in Federal District Court, asking the court to order the Department to comply immediately with the EEOC's order and also to pay compensatory damages. The Department then voluntarily complied with the EEOC's order, but it continued to oppose Gibson's claim for compensatory damages.

Eventually, the District Court dismissed Gibson's compensatory damages claim. On appeal, the Department supported the District Court's dismissal with the argument that Gibson had failed to exhaust his administrative remedies in respect to his compensatory damages claim; hence, he could not bring that claim in court. The Seventh Circuit, however, reversed the District Court's dismissal. It rejected the Department's argument because, in its view, the EEOC lacked the legal power to award compensatory dam-

ages; consequently there was no administrative remedy to exhaust.

Because the circuits have disagreed about whether the EEOC has the power to award compensatory damages we granted certiorari in order to decide that question.

II

The language, purposes, and history of the 1972 Title VII extension and the 1991 CDA convince us that Congress has authorized the EEOC to award compensatory damages in Federal Government employment discrimination cases. Read literally, the language of the statutes is consistent with a grant of that authority. The relevant portion of the Title VII extension, namely, sect;717(b), says that the EEOC "shall have authority" to enforce sect;717(a) "through appropriate remedies, including reinstatement or hiring of employees with or without back pay." After enactment of the 1991 CDA, an award of compensatory damages is a "remedy" that is "appropriate."

The decision of the Court of Appeals is vacated, and the case is remanded for further proceedings consistent with this opinion.

Judgment for West, Secretary
of Veterans Affairs.

Case Commentary

The United States Supreme Court decided that it is within the purview of the EEOC to award compensatory damages.

Case Questions

1. Do you agree with the decision in this case?
2. Are compensatory damages appropriate in a discrimination case?
3. Should the awarding of compensatory damages be reserved to the court?

The issue in the following case revolves around the requirements for granting punitive damages.

KOLSTAD v. AMERICAN DENTAL ASSOCIATION

527 U.S. 526 (1999)

JUSTICE O'CONNOR delivered the opinion of the Court.

Under the terms of the Civil Rights Act of 1991(1991 Act), punitive damages are available in claims under Title VII of the Civil Rights Act of 1964 (Title VII), and the Americans with Disabilities Act of 1990 (ADA), Damages are limited, however, to cases in which the employer has engaged in intentional discrimination and has done so "with malice or with reckless indifference to the federally protected rights of an aggrieved individual." Here we consider the circumstances under which punitive damages may be awarded in an action under Title VII.

I

A

In September 1992, Jack O'Donnell announced that he would be retiring as the Director of Legislation and Legislative Policy and Director of the Council on Government Affairs and Federal Dental Services for respondent, American Dental Association (respondent or Association). Petitioner, Carole Kolstad, was employed with O'Donnell in respondent's Washington, D.C., office, where she was serving as respondent's Director of Federal Agency Relations. When she learned of O'Donnell's retirement, she expressed an interest in filling his position. Also interested in replacing O'Donnell was Tom Spangler, another employee in respondent's Washington office. At this time, Spangler was serving as the Association's Legislative Counsel, a position that involved him in respondent's legislative lobbying efforts. Both petitioner and Spangler had worked directly with O'Donnell, and both had received "distinguished" performance ratings by the acting head of the Washington office, Leonard Wheat.

Both petitioner and Spangler formally applied for O'Donnell's position, and Wheat requested that Dr. William Allen, then serving as respondent's Executive Director in the Association's Chicago office, make the ultimate promotion decision. After interviewing both petitioner and Spangler, Wheat recommended that Allen select Spangler for O'Donnell's post. Allen notified petitioner in December 1992 that he had, in fact, selected Spangler to serve as O'Donnell's replacement. Petitioner's challenge to this employment decision forms the basis of the instant action.

B

After first exhausting her avenues for relief before the Equal Employment Opportunity Commission, petitioner filed suit against the Association in Federal District Court, alleging that respondent's decision to promote Spangler was an act of employment discrimination proscribed under Title VII. In petitioner's view, the entire selection process was a sham. Counsel for petitioner urged the jury to conclude that Allen's stated reasons for selecting Spangler were pretext for gender discrimination, and that Spangler had been chosen for the position before the formal selection process began. Among the evidence offered in support of this view, there was testimony to the effect that Allen modified the description of O'Donnell's post to track aspects of the job description used to hire Spangler. In petitioner's view, this "preselection" procedure suggested an intent by the Association to discriminate on the basis of sex. Petitioner also introduced testimony at trial that Wheat told sexually offensive jokes and that he had referred to certain prominent professional women in derogatory terms. Moreover, Wheat allegedly refused to meet with petitioner for several weeks regarding her interest in O'Donnell's position.

Petitioner testified, in fact, that she had historically experienced difficulty gaining access to meet with Wheat. Allen, for his part, testified that he conducted informal meetings regarding O'Donnell's position with both petitioner and Spangler, although petitioner stated that Allen did not discuss the position with her.

The District Court denied petitioner's request for a jury instruction on punitive damages. The jury concluded that respondent had discriminated against petitioner on the basis of sex and awarded her backpay totaling $52,718. Although the District Court subsequently denied respondent's motion for judgment as a matter of law on the issue of liability, the court made clear that it had not been persuaded that respondent had selected Spangler over petitioner on the basis of sex, and the court denied petitioner's requests for reinstatement and for attorney's fees.

Petitioner appealed from the District Court's decisions denying her requested jury instruction on punitive damages and her request for reinstatement and attorney's fees. Respondent cross-appealed from the denial of its motion for judgment as a matter of law. In a split decision, a panel of the Court of Appeals for the District of Columbia Circuit reversed the District Court's decision denying petitioner's request for an instruction on punitive damages. In so doing, the court rejected respondent's claim that punitive damages are available under Title VII only in " 'extraordinarily egregious cases.' " The panel reasoned that, "because 'the state of mind necessary to trigger liability for the wrong is at least as culpable as that required to make punitive damages applicable,' " the fact that the jury could reasonably have found intentional discrimination meant that the jury should have been permitted to consider punitive damages. The court noted, however, that not all cases involving intentional discrimination would support a punitive damages award. Such an award might be improper, the panel reasoned, in instances where the employer justifiably believes that intentional discrimination is permitted or where an employee engages in discrimination outside the scope of that employee's authority. Here, the court concluded, respondent "neither attempted to justify the use of sex in its promotion decision nor disavowed the actions of its agents."

We granted certiorari, to resolve a conflict among the Federal Courts of Appeals concerning the circumstances under which a jury may consider a request for punitive damages.

II

A

Prior to 1991, only equitable relief, primarily backpay, was available to prevailing Title VII plaintiffs; the statute provided no authority for an award of punitive or compensatory damages. With the passage of the 1991 Act, Congress provided for additional remedies, including punitive damages, for certain classes of Title VII and ADA violations.

The 1991 Act limits compensatory and punitive damages awards, however, to cases of "intentional discrimination"–that is, cases that do not rely on the "disparate impact" theory of discrimination. Section 1981a(b)(1) further qualifies the availability of punitive awards:

> "A complaining party may recover punitive damages under this section against a respondent (other than a government, government agency or political subdivision) if the complaining party demonstrates that the respondent engaged in a discriminatory practice or discriminatory practices *with malice or with reckless indifference to the federally protected rights of an aggrieved individual.*"

The very structure of § 1981a suggests a congressional intent to authorize punitive awards in only a subset of cases involving intentional discrimination. Section 1981a(a)(1) limits compensatory and punitive awards to instances of intentional discrimination, while § 1981a(b)(1) requires plaintiffs to make an additional "demonstration" of their eligibility for punitive damages. Congress plainly sought to impose two standards of liability—one for establishing a right to compensatory damages and another, higher standard that a plaintiff must satisfy to qualify for a punitive award.

Moreover, § 1981a's focus on the employer's state of mind gives some effect to Congress' apparent intent to narrow the class of cases for which punitive awards are available to a subset of those involving intentional discrimination. The employer must act with "malice or with reckless indifference *to the plaintiff's federally protected rights.*" The terms "malice" or "reckless indifference" pertain to the employer's knowledge that it may be acting in violation of federal law, not its awareness that it is engaging in discrimination.

There will be circumstances where intentional discrimination does not give rise to punitive damages liability under this standard. In some instances, the employer may simply be unaware of the relevant federal prohibition. There will be cases, moreover, in which the employer discriminates with the distinct belief that its discrimination is lawful. The underlying theory of discrimination may be novel or otherwise poorly recognized, or an employer may reasonably believe that its discrimination satisfies a bona fide occupational qualification defense or other statutory exception to liability.

B

The inquiry does not end with a showing of the requisite "malice or . . . reckless indifference" on the part of certain individuals, however. The plaintiff must impute liability for punitive damages to respondent.

The Restatement of Agency places strict limits on the extent to which an agent's misconduct may be imputed to the principal for purposes of awarding punitive damages:

"Punitive damages can properly be awarded against a master or other principal because of an act by an agent if, but only if:

"(a) the principal authorized the doing and the manner of the act, or

"(b) the agent was unfit and the principal was reckless in employing him, or

"(c) the agent was employed in a managerial capacity and was acting in the scope of employment, or

"(d) the principal or a managerial agent of the principal ratified or approved the act."

The Restatement, for example, provides that the principal may be liable for punitive damages if it authorizes or ratifies the agent's tortious act, or if it acts recklessly in employing the malfeasing agent. The Restatement also contemplates liability for punitive awards where an employee serving in a "managerial capacity" committed the wrong while "acting in the scope of employment."

We have concluded that an employer's conduct need not be independently "egregious" to satisfy § 1981a's requirements for a punitive damages award, although evidence of egregious misconduct may be used to meet the plaintiff's burden of proof. We leave for remand the question whether petitioner can identify facts sufficient to support an inference that the requisite mental state can be imputed to respondent. The parties have not yet had an opportunity to marshal the record evidence in support of their views on the application of agency principles in the instant case, and the en banc majority had no reason to resolve the issue because it concluded that petitioner had failed to demonstrate the requisite "egregious" misconduct. Although trial testimony established that Allen made the ultimate decision to promote Spangler while serving as petitioner's interim executive director, respondent's highest position, it remains to be seen whether petitioner can make a sufficient showing that Allen acted with malice or reckless indifference to petitioner's Title VII rights. Even if it could be established that Wheat effectively selected O'Donnell's replacement, moreover, several questions would remain, *e.g.*, whether Wheat was serving in a "managerial capacity" and whether he behaved with malice or reckless indifference to petitioner's rights. It may also be necessary to determine whether the Association had been making good faith efforts to enforce an antidiscrimination policy. We leave these issues for resolution on remand.

For the foregoing reasons, the decision of the Court of Appeals is vacated, and the case is remanded for proceedings consistent with this opinion.

Judgment for the American Dental Association.

Case Commentary

The United States Supreme Court decided that the granting of punitive damages is contingent upon proving the employer's conduct was so egregious as to warrant punishment to dissuade the employer from acting in the same vein in the future.

Case Questions

1. Do you agree with the decision in this case?
2. Is egregious conduct the appropriate standard for awarding punitive damages?
3. Did Carole Kolstad meet this criterion?

EXEMPTIONS

There are a number of classifications which are exempt from the Civil Rights Act. In these situations, discrimination would be permissible.

BONA FIDE OCCUPATIONAL QUALIFICATION

Employers may discriminate because of religion, gender, and national origin if they can establish that there is a bona fide occupational qualification. This condition does *not* generally apply to race and color, except for the casting of certain actors in the movies and theatre.

EMPLOYMENT PERSPECTIVE

Mary Jacobs applied for a position as a rest-room attendant at the Nautilus Health and Fitness Club. A total of seven women, but no men, applied for the position. After another woman was selected for the position of attendant to the female locker-room, Mary asserted that she should be considered for attendant to the male locker-room. Nautilus refused on the ground that Mary is a woman. Is this discrimination? No! Gender is bona fide occupational qualification in the selection of a locker-room attendant. ■

COMMUNISTS

Title VII does not apply to individuals who are members of the Communist party of the United States.

EMPLOYMENT PERSPECTIVE

Igor Musnovec, a Communist party member, applied for a job as a checkout clerk at a local Foodway supermarket. His application was not considered because he is a Communist. Is this discrimination? No! It is lawful to discriminate against a Communist. ■

DRUG ADDICTS

It is lawful for an employer to refuse to hire individuals who are using illegal drugs as long as this practice was not adopted intentionally to discriminate against a particular class.

EMPLOYMENT PERSPECTIVE

Julio Gonzalez, who is currently participating in drug rehabilitation, has applied for a job as a clerk in Save Mart Department Store. Save Mart refuses to hire Julio because of his drug addiction. Does Julio have any recourse? No! Julio's only recourse would be if he could prove that Save Mart had instituted the stipulation with the intention of enforcing it only against Hispanics. ■

MERIT PAY

Employers may compensate individuals differently on the basis of merit, seniority, quality, or quantity of work performed, or location of employment. It is understood that employers cannot discriminate under the guise of the protected categories of the Civil Rights Act. If it turns out that discrimination is the employer's intention, then the employer will be in violation of Title VII. Professionally developed ability tests may be designed and administered to determine hiring and promoting as long as the test is job related, not intended to discriminate.

❖ EMPLOYER LESSONS

- Educate officials, managers, and workers about the Civil Rights Act.
- Persuade officials, managers, and workers to conduct themselves in such a manner as to avoid discrimination.
- Guard against retaliation.
- Keep in mind the 80 percent rule when hiring.
- Maintain records on employee hiring and retention.
- Be familiar with the authority of the Equal Employment Opportunity Commission.
- Understand the different avenues available to an employee in maintaining an action for discrimination.
- Be apprised that compensatory and punitive damages are now available.
- Appreciate the requirements of business necessity and job relatedness when formulating qualifications for a job.
- Be cognizant of the exemptions to the Civil Rights Act.

❖ EMPLOYEE LESSONS

- Familiarize yourself with the protections afforded to you under the Civil Rights Act.
- Be apprised of the types of damages recoverable and the monetary caps.
- Be aware of the exemptions to the Civil Rights Act.
- Know what rights are available to you under state law.
- Understand the functions of the Equal Employment Opportunity Commission.
- Discern whether the employer has retaliated against you.
- Know what the deadlines are for filing discrimination claims.

❖ SUMMARY

In hindsight, the Civil Rights Act of 1964, along with subsequent amendments, has had the most profound impact on employment since the proliferation of unions. The Civil Rights Act opened the door to employment opportunities and promotions for minorities and women. These two groups comprise more than half the workforce. Neglecting them for so long was an egregious mistake. Forgetting them in the future would be economically disastrous.

Securing a well-paying job is the main step for an individual to increase his or her standard of living and to secure better housing. Without employment opportunities, women and minorities are relegated to welfare, unemployment, or ministerial positions with low pay. In turn, minorities and women providing sole support for a family have the lowest economic status. Making ends meet is a day-to-day goal. The Civil Rights Act, while not being a panacea, provided an area of opportunity for those on the lowest levels of society. Women and minorities are now significantly represented in professional and graduate school programs. They are also present in middle-level management positions. Attaining upper-level positions is much harder to realize because it is easier for decision-makers to integrate those departments that are beneath them than it is to integrate their own. Also, while it takes time for qualified candidates to work their way up through the ranks, that moment is at hand because enough time has passed for these candidates to emerge. It is now that access to the executive level and the boardroom should begin to increase. It will likely remain a slow process, though, for these positions involve sizeable amounts of pay and, more importantly, power.

Societies should not be judged on the basis of their most wealthy citizens. If they were, Mexico and certain Arabian countries would score very high. The average standard of living is not the most satisfactory basis either, because great wealth can give the average an upward bias. Instead, societies should be judged on how well their poor are doing. The greater the number of people in this classification, the more likely the society has failed to serve the needs of all its people. When a society can boast that even the least of its members has a job that provides the means for a satisfactory subsistence, then a society has achieved its greatest goal.

The Civil Rights Act has provided an impetus for achieving this goal. Raising the bottom up is its underlying purpose. However, improvements in education, life at home, and the community have not kept pace with the advancement made in employment opportunities. Employment opportunities are the goal for a young person who has honed his or her intellect and been brought up in a stable community, with a family oriented toward principles and values. When education and environment leave a lot to be desired, employment opportunities are difficult to take advantage of. In order for the Civil Rights Act to fulfill its main purpose of lifting the lower echelon of society to a more suitable level, similar strides must take place in education and the community and family environment.

❖ REVIEW QUESTIONS

1. Explain the significance of the Civil Rights Act of 1964.
2. Who is covered under the Civil Rights Act?
3. What changes were made by the 1991 Civil Rights Act?
4. What is a bona fide occupational qualification?
5. Are Communists covered by the Civil Rights Act?
6. Is the use of merit pay permissable?
7. Elucidate the difference between disparate treatment and disparate impact.
8. Give an example of the 80 percent rule.
9. Does the employee have recourse if the employer retaliates?
10. May drug addicts be discriminated against?
11. What is the function of the EEOC?
12. What is the purpose of the Glass Ceiling Commission?
13. When are punitive damages awarded?
14. What is the test for business necessity?
15. Does the EEOC have the right to access employment records regarding the makeup of a company's employees?
16. Is the 80 percent rule ethical?
17. If a plaintiff has established a prima facie case and further shows that the employer's articulated reasons are pretextual, is the plaintiff entitled to recovery for illegal discrimination? *Blare v. Husky Injection Molding Systems Boston, Inc.,* 646 N.E.2d 111 (1995)
18. J. Walter, Inc. and J. Walter, Ltd. are two separate companies. In November 1990,

Mochelle was hired by J. Walter, Inc., as a salesman. In August 1991, Mochelle informed his supervisor of his intention to run for political office. In October 1991, he lost the election. In January 1992, Mochelle was fired for failing to perform his duties. Mochelle claimed he was fired because he ran for political office and brought suit against J. Walter, Ltd., contending that the two companies were interrelated. The reason for this was that Walter, Inc., does not have enough employees to qualify for a Title VII action. Walter, Ltd., contended that it has separate offices, employees, records, phone numbers, and tax returns. What was the result? *Mochelle v. J. Walter, Inc.,* 823 F. Supp. 1302 (M.D. LA. 1993)

19. When does a joint employer relationship exist? *Texas World Service Co., Inc. v. NLRB,* 928 F.2d 1426 (5th Cir. 1991)

20. Betty Lattanzio initiated this employment discrimination action against Security National Bank (the Bank) pursuant to Title VII of the Civil Rights Act of 1964 (Title VII) and the Pennsylvania Human Relations Act (PHRA). Lattanzio alleges that the Bank discriminated against her on the basis of her age and sex in discharging her from employment on December 19, 1990. The Bank contends that because it employed fewer than 15 individuals during 1989 and 1990, the Plaintiff's complaint fails to state a cause of action and this Court lacks subject matter jurisdiction under Title VII. What was the result? *Lattanzio v. Security Nat. Bank,* 825 F. Supp. 86 (E.D.Pa.1993)

❖ WEB SITES

www.eeoc.gov
www.findlaw.com
www.westbuslaw.com
www.usccr.gov/index.html
www.eeoc.gov/laws/cra91.html
www.watson.org/~lisa/blackhistory/early-civilrights/
www.usbr.gov/laws/civil.html

AFFIRMATIVE ACTION

INTRODUCTION

Affirmative action attempts to achieve equal employment opportunity by actively selecting minorities and women where they have been underrepresented in the workforce. Although affirmative action programs are considered temporary, many remain in force for a long time until equilibrium is achieved. To determine whether an affirmative action program is needed, a number of factors must be considered: the minority population of the area and their percentage of the total population in the area; the number of minorities employed and unemployed, together with their respective percentages; the skills of the minority; the labor pool; the amount of training the employer can reasonably undertake; and the availability of other minorities or women in the organization who can be promoted or transferred. The same criteria are considered in determining the need for an affirmative action program for women. After procedures are in place, the goals must be achieved following reasonable timetables. The rate of success must be measured.

CHAPTER CHECKLIST

❖ Understand the origin of the concept of affirmative action.

❖ Appreciate the role of affirmative action in accomplishing the goals of the Civil Rights Act of 1964.

❖ Distinguish between voluntary and court ordered affirmative action programs.

❖ Discern the difference between an affirmative action plan and a quota.

❖ Reconcile the decisions of the United States Supreme Court in *United Steelworkers of America v. Weber* and *University of California Regents v. Bakke*.

❖ Be able to explain the significance of reverse discrimination.

❖ Understand the significance of the Equal Employment Opportunity Act.

❖ Consider whether affirmative action is still needed.

❖ Comprehend the impact of California's Proposition 209.

❖ Understand the ramifications of the settlement reached in *Taxman v. School Board of Piscataway.*

EMPLOYMENT SCENARIO

Tom and Mark consult with Susan about the handling of Debbie Brown's disparate impact claim. Tom and Mark resent the allegation that their actions may be viewed as prejudicial. Susan retorts that they must put aside their personal feelings and view the claim objectively. She suggests that L&S voluntarily adopt an affirmative action program to recruit and hire minorities. Tom and Mark are perturbed. Susan counsels them that L&S is located in a state that still supports affirmative action. Susan suggests that the EEOC would most likely require L&S to formulate a plan to hire minority employees until minority hires reach 40 percent, the same proportion as is reflected in the community. Rather than risk extensive litigation and possible bad publicity, Tom and Mark voluntarily adopt an affirmative action program. Tom and Mark reluctantly see the light and propose that Susan collaborate with them to accomplish this goal.

HISTORY OF AFFIRMATIVE ACTION

Equal employment opportunity had its roots in a series of executives orders and acts. In 1940, President Roosevelt issued Executive Order 8587, which prohibited the denial of public employment based on race. Several orders and acts followed that were designed to prohibit other forms of discrimination in public employment, such as on the basis of religion and color. The emphasis was on what the administrative agencies could *not* do. There was no mandate as to what they *should* do.

1955 marked the beginning of a transformation from passive to active programs. In Executive Order 10050, President Eisenhower stipulated, ". . . it is the policy of the United States Government that equal opportunity be afforded all qualified persons, consistent with law, for employment in the Federal Government." Equal employment opportunity was formally recognized and confirmed by President Kennedy in 1961; Executive Order 10925 called for ". . .. positive measures for the elimination of any discrimination, direct or indirect, which now exist."

The concept of affirmative action first arose out of an Executive Order promulgated by President Lyndon Johnson in 1964. It provided that contractors who were supplying goods or services to the federal government were required to take an affirmative action, that employees are to be hired without regard to race, color, religion, sex, or national origin, and that once selected, promotion, compensation, training, and termination are made without discrimination. Subcontractors hired by federal contractors were held to the same standards.

Those federal contractors whose employees were underrepresented with regard to women and minorities were forced to correct that injustice by developing an affirmative action plan designed to hire and/or promote more women and minorities.

EMPLOYMENT PERSPECTIVE

Blackwell Enterprises is a federal contractor located in the city of Atlanta, which employs 100 workers, 10 of whom are minorities. The minority population of the city of Atlanta is approximately 50 percent. Will Blackwell jeopardize its federal contracts because of the underrepresentation of minorities in its workforce? Yes, unless it establishes an affirmative action plan designed to increase the number of minorities hired! How should this plan be designed? Blackwell may create a plan that for every three new positions that become open, two must be filled by qualified minorities. Thus, when the first position becomes available, if there is a qualified minority applicant, he or she will receive the job. With the second position, if there are no qualified minority applicants, a white person may be hired; but then preference will be given to the minority applicant for the third position. ■

In 1965, President Johnson, through Executive Order 11246, placed the responsibility for equal employment opportunity with the Civil Service Commission. Johnson followed that in 1967 with Executive Order 11375 that added sex discrimination. However, it was not until 1969 that affirmative action was used to address the problem of those seeking employment as well as those stuck in low-level positions.

President Nixon's Executive Order 11478 issued in 1969 provided that equal employment opportunity "...applies to and must be made an integral part of every aspect of personnel policy and practice in the employment, development, advancement and treatment of civilian employees of the Federal Government." It also set forth the procedure for affirmative action, as well as the requirement for training programs to enable low-level employees to gain the experience necessary to be eligible for upper-level positions.

The Executive Order resulted in the Equal Employment Opportunity Act of 1972.

What if an employer is having difficulty finding qualified minority candidates? The employer must make every effort to locate potential candidates through advertisements in newspapers that are likely to be read by minorities. The employer must also contact employment agencies who service minority job-seekers. The burden is on the employer to put the word out in the minority community.

EMPLOYMENT PERSPECTIVE

The CPA firm of Glick, Worthington and Sutherland has 50 accountants and 150 staff members. The latter includes administrative assistants, typists, and file clerks. During tax season, the firm's accountants and staff put in 80 plus hour workweeks. For this reason, the firm refuses to hire women during their child bearing years. Young women who are refused employment claim this provision creates a disparate impact. Is this correct? Yes! The Court will impose an order on the CPA firm to establish an affirmative action plan to hire females including those who are in their child bearing years. If females make up 40 percent of accountants, then a plan to hire two out of three will suffice. Does the firm have to discharge men and replace them with women? No! The entire injustice does not have to be remedied immediately, as long as the process begins in a timely manner. As long as an affirmative action plan is implemented as the accounting firm expands or as existing accountants leave, justice is served. ■

TITLE VII VIOLATORS

Those employers who have intentionally discriminated or who have been guilty of creating an employee environment where a disparate impact exists against a class of people of race, color, religion, sex, or national origin, may receive a court order to establish an affirmative action plan to remedy the discrimination.

EMPLOYMENT PERSPECTIVE

Fredericks Meat Packing in Kansas City has 150 managers and 500 workers. Minority employees consist of 400 workers and no managers, although the population of Kansas City is approximately one-third minority. A claim is registered with the EEOC against Fredericks for discrimination. The EEOC files suit in Federal District Court and secures a judgment. How will the court remedy this injustice? The District Court will issue a court order mandating Fredericks to establish an affirmative action plan to increase the number of minority managers to reflect more adequately the percentage of minorities in the Kansas City population. This plan may be achieved either through recruitment or promotion. ■

VOLUNTARY ACTION

Rather than wait for potential lawsuits to force the correction of Title VII violations many employers have created their own voluntary plans. In many instances quotas were instituted to increase the number of women and minorities; the quotas require a set number of women and minorities to be hired. In effect, if qualified applicants cannot be found, unqualified ones must be hired. Quotas are not mandated by law and are thought to be necessary only where the racial imbalance is severe and has been intentionally disregarded. Although the word *quota* sparks controversy, it seems that every plan designed must have a goal of some fraction or percentage allocating two out of three or 60 percent of new hirings or promotions. This would appear to be equivalent to a quota, but strictly speaking it is not.

Affirmative action plans require that only qualified women and minorities have to be hired, unlike quotas where the hiring is done without regard to qualification. If there are no qualified women or minorities, white males may be hired in their place. But as mentioned earlier, the employer must make every effort to attempt to locate qualified women and minority applicants.

Affirmative action plans are designed to address manifest imbalances in the racial makeup of the work force. Once the imbalance is eradicated, the affirmative action plan will be discontinued. Affirmative action plans are not designed to remain indefinitely to maintain equilibrium. If a discrepancy occurs in the future, then the affirmative action plan can be put into effect again.

Affirmative action plans do not place existing employees in jeopardy regarding termination or disciplinary action; which must be applied equally to all employees. However, it is lawful for an employer to hire qualified women and minorities over white men who are more qualified. The key is that the women and minorities must be qualified.

> **EMPLOYMENT PERSPECTIVE**
>
> Express Airlines requires that applicants who wish to be considered for the job of pilot must have completed 750 hours of air flight-training. Currently, Express employs 100 pilots, none of whom are women or minorities. Express then implements an affirmative action program. The next five openings are filled by two women, two minorities, and one white male. There were 15 qualified applicants. The women and minorities chosen were among them. Although the women and minorities selected were not among the top five persons most qualified, they were chosen to fulfill the affirmative action plan. Is this lawful? Yes, because they were qualified! If they had not been qualified, Express would have been justified in hiring all white male employees, as long as its requirement met the strict standard of being a business necessity. In this situation, Express Airlines might be persuaded to initiate a training program for women and minorities to enable them to become pilots. ∎

The following case addresses the question of whether a private employer and a union can in a collective bargaining agreement provide for an affirmative action plan. The plan reserved 50 percent of the openings for black applicants until the racial makeup of the workplace was indicative of the local community.

CASE

UNITED STEELWORKERS OF AMERICA v. WEBER

443 U.S. 193 (1978)

JUSTICE BRENNAN delivered the opinion of the Court.

Challenged here is the legality of an affirmative action plan—collectively bargained by an employer and a union—that reserves for black employees 50 percent of the openings in an in-plant craft-training until the percentage of black craftworkers in the plant is commensurate with the percentage of blacks in the local labor force. The question for decision is whether Congress in Title VII of the Civil Rights Act of 1964, left employers and unions in the private sector free to take such race-conscious steps to eliminate manifest racial imbalances in traditionally segregated job categories. We hold that Title VII does not prohibit such race-conscious affirmative action plans.

In 1974, petitioner United Steelworkers of America (USWA) and petitioner Kaiser Aluminum & Chemical Corp. (Kaiser) entered into a master collective-bargaining agreement covering terms and conditions of employment at 15 Kaiser plants. The agreement contained an affirmative action plan designed to eliminate conspicuous racial imbalances in Kaiser's then almost exclusively white craftwork forces. Black crafthiring goals were set for each Kaiser plant equal to the percentage of blacks in the respective local labor forces. To enable plants to meet these goals, on-the-job training programs were established to teach unskilled production workers—black and white—the skills necessary to become craftworkers. The plan reserved for black employees 50 percent of the openings in these newly created in-plant training programs.

This case arose from the operation of the plan at Kaiser's plant in Gramercy, La. Until 1974, Kaiser hired as craft-workers for that plant only persons who had had prior craft experience. Because blacks had long been excluded from craft unions, few were able to present such credentials. As a consequence, prior to 1974 only 1.83 percent (5 out of 273) of the skilled craftworkers at the Gramercy plant were black, even though the work force in the Gramercy area was approximately 39 percent black.

Pursuant to the national agreement Kaiser altered its craft-hiring practice in the Gramercy plant. Rather than hiring already trained outsiders, Kaiser established a training program to train its production workers to fill craft openings. Selection of craft trainees was made on the basis of seniority, with the proviso that at least 50 percent of the new trainers were to be black until the percentage of black skilled craftworkers in the Gramercy plant approximated the percentage of blacks in the local labor force.

During 1974, the first year of the operation of the Kaiser-USWA affirmative action plan, 13 craft trainees were selected from Gramercy's production work force. Of these, seven were black and six white. The most senior black selected into the program had less seniority than several white production workers whose bids for admission were rejected. Thereafter one of those white production workers, respondent Brian Weber (hereafter respondent), instituted this class action in the United States District Court for the Eastern District of Louisiana.

The complaint alleged that the filling of craft trainee positions at the Gramercy plant pursuant to the affirmative action program had resulted in junior black employees' receiving training in preference to senior white employees, thus discriminating against respondent and other similarly situated white employees in violation of Section 703 (a) and (d) of Title VII. The District Court entered a judgment in favor of the plaintiff class, and granted a permanent injunction prohibiting Kaiser and the USWA "from denying plaintiffs, Brian F. Weber and all other members of the class, access to on-the-job training programs on the basis of race." A divided panel of the Court of Appeals for the Fifth Circuit affirmed, holding that all employment preferences based upon race, including those preferences incidental to bona fide affirmative action plans, violated Title VII's prohibition against racial discrimination in employment. We granted certiorari. We reverse.

We emphasize at the outset the narrowness of our inquiry. Since the Kaiser-USWA plan does not involve state action, this case does not present an alleged violation of the Equal Protection Clause of the Fourteenth Amendment. Further, since the Kaiser-USWA plan was adopted voluntarily, we are not concerned with what Title VII requires or with what a court might order to remedy a past proved violation of the Act. The only question before us is the narrow statutory issue of whether Title VII forbids private employers and unions from voluntarily agreeing upon bona fide affirmative action plans that accord racial preferences in the manner and for the purpose provided in the Kaiser-USWA plan.

Congress' primary concern in enacting the prohibition against racial discrimination in Title VII of the Civil Rights Act of 1964 was with "the plight of the Negro in our economy." Before 1964, blacks were largely relegated to "unskilled and semi-skilled jobs." Because of automation the number of such jobs was rapidly decreasing. As a consequence, "the relative position of the Negro worker was steadily worsening. In 1947 the nonwhite unemployment rate was 64 percent higher than the white rate; in 1962 it was 124 percent higher." as Senator Humphrey explained to the Senate:

"What good does it do a Negro to be able to eat in a fine restaurant if he cannot afford to pay the bill? What good does it do him to be accepted in a hotel that is too expensive for his modest income? How can a Negro child be motivated to take full advantage of intergrated educational facilities if he has no hope of getting a job where he can use that education?

"Without a job, one cannot afford public convenience and accommodations. Income from employment may be necessary to further a man's education, or that of his children. If his children have no hope of getting a good job, what will motivate them to take advantage of educational opportunities?"

These remarks echoed President Kennedy's original message to Congress upon the introduction of the Civil Rights Act in 1963:

"There is little value in a Negro's obtaining the right to be admitted to hotels and restaurants if he has no cash in his pocket and no job."

Accordingly, it was clear to Congress that the crux of the problem was to open employment opportunities for Negroes in occupations which have been traditionally closed to them and it was to this problem that Title VII's prohibition against racial discrimination in employment was primarily addressed.

Clearly, a prohibition against all voluntary, race conscious, affirmative action efforts would disserve these ends. We therefore hold that Title VII's prohibition in section 703(a) and (d) against racial discrimination does not condemn all private, voluntary, race-conscious affirmative action plans.

We need not today define in detail the line of demarcation between permissible and impermissible affirmative action plans. It suffices to hold that the challenged Kaiser-USWA affirmative action plan falls on the permissible side of the line. The purposes of the plan mirror those of the statute. Both were designed to break down old patterns of racial segregation and hierarchy. Both were structured to "open employment opportunities for Negroes in occupations which have been traditionally closed to them."

At the same time, the plan does not unnecessarily trammel the interest of the white employees. The plan does not require the discharge of white workers and their replacement. Nor does the plan create an absolute bar to the advancement of white employees; half of those trained in the program will be white. Moreover, the plan is a temporary measure; it is not intended to maintain racial balance, but simply to eliminate a manifest racial imbalance.

Judgment for United Steelworkers of America.

Case Commentary

The United States Supreme Court set forth a four-prong test to determine whether an affirmative action plan is in violation of Title VII's prohibition against race discrimination: The plan must be remedial in purpose; it must have a limited duration; the minority workers hired under the plan must be qualified; and current white employees must not be discharged to provide positions for minorities. Here, Weber, who is white, was not hired even though he was more qualified than several black candidates who were selected. The Court upheld the affirmative action plan because it met all of the requirements.

Case Questions

1. Do you agree with the Supreme Court's decision?
2. Is the four-prong test set forth in *Weber* the most accurate method for justifying an affirmative action program?

3. Should the most qualified individual be entitled to the job?

EQUAL EMPLOYMENT OPPORTUNITY ACT OF 1972

This was the first major amendment to Title VII of the 1964 Civil Rights Act. The Act provided the Civil Service Commission with the power to address all federal employment issues and to remedy injustices with reinstatement and back pay. Each agency director was required to apply the law. The Equal Employment Opportunity Act of 1972 states that all employment decisions ". . . shall be made free from any discrimination based on race, creed, color, religion, sex, or national origin."

To insure compliance, evaluation will be made and record-keeping will be required on the employment of women and minorities. ". . . nothing contained in the act shall relieve any Government agency or official of its or his primary responsibility to assure non-discrimination in employment as required by the Constitution and statutes or its or his responsibility under Executive Order 11478 relating to equal employment opportunity in the Federal Government."

Each administrative agency, as well as each department within the agency, was required to set forth an affirmative action plan. This was even required to be done on a regional basis to help the Civil Service Commission identify areas in need of particular attention. Agencies were required to develop education and training programs geared to aiding its employees achieve their greatest potential. To implement these programs, agencies were required to secure qualified personnel to administer these programs. Program content and personnel size and competency were both subject to scrutiny by the Civil Service Commission. On-site inspections were conducted routinely. After annual review, the Civil Service Commission would publish reports on each agency's progress. Employees were encouraged to file complaints if they have not been afforded an equal employment opportunity. The Commission would reach a resolution after investigation. If dissatisfied with the resolution, access to the courts was now available to an aggrieved employee. Court decisions over time have developed a body of case law, which now provide legal precedent in certain areas of employment discrimination (*i.e.,* the U.S. Supreme Court decisions of *Griggs v. Duke Power Co.* and *McDonnell Douglas Corp. v. Green*).

Agencies were required to administer Skill Utilization Surveys to identify the skill that each employee had and to determine whether those skills were being utilized. Nonutilization of a skill may be grounds for an adaptation of the current job or a transfer or a promotion of that employee to a job in which the skill will be more fully utilized. An illustrative questionnaire was given to all employees for purposes of eliciting meaningful responses regarding their skills. Then the supervisors were asked to evaluate each response to determine whether the skills were being utilized in the current job and whether they could be utilized there or at another position within the agency.

Many deficiencies were noted by the Civil Service Commission in reviewing the affirmative action plans of the administrative agencies. These included lack of specificity in the development of employment opportunities, failure to file timely reports, refusal to set timetables for achievement of plan goals, designating inadequate and inexperienced personnel to the plan, and relegating employment and supervision to human resource departments rather than integrating them throughout the agency.

The Civil Service Commission redefined its mandate to correct these deficiencies. In developing the plan, the commission called for agencies to file an assessment report to single out departments where access had been denied or rarely given to women and minorities. Consultation with women and minority groups was strongly suggested for the valuable input they could give. Next, specific remedies were required to address the problems identified in the assessment report. Each department was to tailor the plan to meet its respective needs. Timetables were then required to be attached to each plan of action to monitor progress and ultimately resolution. Although the plans permitted flexibility, movement toward the goal was necessary. These plans would then be reviewed by the Commission annually, and agency directors would be called to explain noncompliance.

A breakdown of the composition of women and minorities for each department and each grade level in the administrative agency should be an integral part of the assessment. The percentage of women and minorities in maintenance, clerical, managerial, technical, and professional areas should also be included. Once jobs become available, each agency should endeavor to discover those women and minorities in their workforce who have the capability for advancement. In addition, agencies should seek out potential recruiting venues for women and minority employment candidates.

Discriminatory complaints must be grouped according to job category and grade level. Solutions should be proposed for reoccurring complaints, while unique dilemmas must be handled on an ad hoc basis. The goal of an affirmative action plan is not an instantaneous resolution, but one of constant movement toward the accomplishment of equal opportunity in employment for all.

With the assessment report in hand, specific actions can be taken. Expeditious resolution of discriminatory complaints is the key toward ensuring that women and minorities continue to have faith in the system. Advertising job opportunities in promotional mediums, which are earmarked specifically toward recruiting women and minorities, is imperative to secure greater applicants from that cohort. Instituting programs in the community to enhance the potential pool of prospective employees is a proactive step. These might include helping an employee find adequate housing, aiding the community in establishing day-care centers or providing on-site day-care centers instead, and fostering relations with women and minority groups. The designing of proficient training programs will enable women and minority employees to become the most qualified they can be. Self-evaluation of the affirmative action program's proficiency is an important tool when future reassessment is made.

AFFIRMATIVE ACTION PLAN GUIDELINES FOR THE PRIVATE SECTOR

The key to establishing an affirmative action plan is to garner the commitment of management. Once committed, management can emphasize its importance and lead by example. An assessment must be made of the number of women and minorities and their current status within the organization. This data will prove invaluable as a benchmark against which the program's progress can be measured. Once the problem areas are identified, then recruitment and promotion issues must be addressed. A critical look at the current methods utilized must be taken, and a plan must be instituted to remedy its deficiencies. To bolster recruitment, notification should be sent to the placement offices of schools with significant or exclusive women or minority populations. Women and minority organizations can also be advised of the need for prospective candidates. Advertisements in newspapers, magazines, radio, and television designed for women and minorities will enable a company to tap into that particular circle. Company tours for students and community groups are also beneficial. Relying solely on referrals and traditional recruitment techniques will only reinforce discrimination.

Career counseling to direct women and minorities toward career paths and training programs to help them realize these accomplishments must be created or embellished. The fact that counseling and training programs exist is not sufficient. They must be made available or specifically developed with women and minorities in mind.

Job descriptions must also be perused for possible barriers against women and minorities. If found, the descriptive narration must be rethought. All requirements must be job-related. Any which are not should be eliminated, especially unnecessary education or experience; otherwise, discrimination will continue. Testing should also be restricted to when it is absolutely necessary and its reality and job-relatedness can be proved. The assignment of grade levels to jobs must also be reviewed for bias in favor of men. If discovered, such bias must be readjusted. Interviewers must be indoctrinated to no longer believe that women and minorities can perform only certain jobs—those involving routine ministerial tasks. They must avoid asking women and minorities personal questions about marital status, other sources of income, number of children, criminal record, and other issues that are not job-related and are not routinely asked of white men.

Job categories, job descriptions, promotional materials, and in-house rules and regulations must be redrafted to be gender-neutral, both in written communications and pictorials.

EMPLOYMENT PERSPECTIVE

In an advertisement brochure, Sunshine Chemicals states that the men in its employ are the most qualified in the industry. Several pages of pictorials of white men follow. Is this material discriminatory toward the women and minorities who are employed there? Yes! The language is not gender-neutral, and the pictorials are neither gender- nor racially-neutral. ▥

The affirmative action plan should be in written form and distributed throughout the company. A director should be appointed to administer the plan. A letter from the director as well as the CEO should confirm that it is the company's intention to refrain from discrimination both maliciously as well as accidentally and that the company expects all of its employees to act accordingly or face disciplinary measures. Lip service will not be tolerated.

The director should be developing companywide goals for recruitment, training, promotion, and termination; companywide applies to top management equally. There can be no exceptions, or else a good example will not be set, and the plan will fail because of selective application. Each of the goals should be tailored appropriately to work within individual departments. Discussions should be held at all levels to explain the reasoning behind the plan. Getting as much support as possible from top to bottom will thwart divisiveness, prejudice, and subversion. Unions should be encouraged to embrace and promote the plan. Whenever a positive attribute of the plan is realized, it should be publicized throughout the company as well as externally. It is wise to clear up any misunderstanding or resentment about the purpose of the plan by counseling those feeling so inclined. Educating employees goes a long way to resolving prejudice and conflict. The director should have an open-door policy for all employees and should communicate periodically with the CEO.

REVERSE DISCRIMINATION

Reverse discrimination exists when the affirmative action plan is unfair to white males in that it selects unqualified women and minorities over them, establishes mandatory quotas, or bars the selection of white males completely. Often reverse discrimination is claimed when qualified women and minorities are given preference over higher-qualified white males. Although there have been conflicting cases, it is generally agreed that this is an acceptable practice when a racial imbalance exists.

EMPLOYMENT PERSPECTIVE

Oakville is going to employ twenty new police officers. Oakville has very few women and minority police officers. A score of 70 on the police exam is required to be qualified. Oakville plans to hire ten minorities and five women, if they are qualified. The ten minorities selected scored 74 to 90. The five women selected scored 78 to 87. Jim Newman, a white male, scored 94 but was not selected because five other white males scored higher. He sues Oakville, claiming reverse discrimination. Will he win? Most likely not. The issue is not who is more qualified, but whether the individuals selected are qualified. As long as they are qualified, as is the case here, the affirmative action plan will be upheld. If they were not qualified, then Jim's claim of reverse discrimination would be granted, and he would be given a position. ■

Without affirmative action plans, it is unlikely that women and minorities would have the opportunity of obtaining certain jobs, especially those involving managerial positions.

The following case addresses the issue of whether a school can set aside a definitive number of seats for minority applicants. A white applicant argued that race should not be the determining factor in making an admissions decision.

CASE

UNIVERSITY OF CALIFORNIA REGENTS v. BAKKE

438 U.S. 265 (1977)

JUSTICE POWELL announced the judgment of the Court.

This case presents a challenge to the special admissions program of the petitioner, the Medical School of the University of California at Davis, which is designed to assure the admission of a specified number of students from certain minority groups. The Superior Court of California sustained respondent's challenge, holding that petitioner's program violated the California Constitution, Title VII of the Civil Rights Act of 1964, and the Equal Protection Clause of the Fourteenth Amendment. The court enjoined petitioner from considering respondent's race or the race of any other applicant in making admissions decisions.

Following the interviews, each candidate was rated on a scale of 1 to 100 by his interviewers and four other members of the admissions committee. The rating embraced the interview-

ers' summaries, the candidate's overall grade point average, grade point average in science courses, scores on the Medical College Admissions Test (MCAT), letters of recommendation, extracurricular activities, and other biographical data. The ratings were added together to arrive at each candidate's "benchmark" score. Since five committee members rated each candidate in 1973, a perfect score was 500; in 1974, six members rated each candidate, so that perfect score was 600. The full committee then reviewed the file and scores of each applicant and made offers of admission on a "rolling" basis. The chairman was responsible for placing names on the waiting list. They were not placed in strict numerical order; instead, the chairman had discretion to include persons with "special skills."

The special admissions program operated with a separate committee, a majority of whom were members of minority groups. On the 1973

Class Entering in 1974

			MCAT [Percentiles]			
	SGPA	*OGPA*	*Verbal*	*Quantitative*	*Science*	*Gen. Info.*
Bakke	3.44	3.46	96	94	97	72
Average of regular admittees	3.36	3.29	69	67	82	72
Average of special admittees	2.42	2.62	34	30	37	18

application form, candidates were asked to indicate whether they wished to be considered as "economically and/or educationally disadvantaged" applicants; on the 1974 form the question was whether they wished to be considered as members of a "minority group," which the Medical School apparently viewed as "Blacks," "Chicanos," "Asians," and "American Indians." If these questions were answered affirmatively, the application was forwarded to the special admissions committee. No formal definition of "disadvantaged" was ever produced, but the chairman of the special committee screened each application to see whether it reflected economic or educational deprivation. Having passed this initial hurdle, the applications then were rated by the special committee in a fashion similar to that used by the general admissions committee, except that special candidates did not have to meet the 2.5 grade point average cutoff applied to regular applicants. About one-fifth of the total number of special applicants were invited for interviews in 1973 and 1974. Following each interview, the special committee assigned each special applicant a benchmark score. The special committee then presented its top choices to the general admissions committee. The latter did not rate or compare the special candidates against the general applicants, but could reject recommended special candidates for failure to meet course requirements or other specific deficiencies. The special committee continued to recommend special applicants until a number prescribed by faculty vote were admitted. While the overall class size was still 50, the prescribed number was 8; in 1973 and 1974, when the class size had doubled to 100, the prescribed number of special admissions also doubled, to 16.

Allan Bakke is a white male who applied to the Davis Medical School in both 1973 and 1974. In both years Bakke's application was considered under the general admissions program, and he received an interview. His 1973 interview was with Dr. Theodore C. West, who considered Bakke "a very desirable applicant to the medical school." Despite a strong benchmark score of 468 out of 500, Bakke was rejected. His application had come late in the year, and no applicants in the general admissions process with scores below 470 were accepted after Bakke's application was completed. There were four special admissions slots unfilled at that time, however, for which Bakke was not considered. After his 1973 rejection, Bakke wrote to Dr. George H. Lowrey, Associate Dean and Chairman of the Admissions Committee, protesting that the special admissions program operated as a racial and ethnic quota.

Bakke's 1974 application was completed early in the year. His student interviewer gave him an overall rating of 94, finding him "friendly, well tempered, conscientious and delightful to speak with." His faculty interviewer was, by coincidence, the same Dr. Lowrey to whom he had written in protest of the special admissions program. Dr. Lowrey found Bakke "rather limited in his approach" to the problems of the medical profession and found disturbing Bakke's "very definite opinions which were based more on his personal viewpoints than upon a study of the total problem." Dr. Lowrey gave Bakke the lowest of his six ratings, at 86; his total was 549 out of 600. Again, Bakke's, application was rejected. In neither year did the chairman of the admissions committee, Dr. Lowrey, exercise his discretion to place Bakke on the waiting list. In both years, applicants were admitted under the special program with grade point averages, MCAT scores, and benchmark scores significantly lower than Bakke's.

After the second rejection, Bakke filed the instant suit in the Superior Court of California. He sought mandatory, injunctive, and declaratory relief compelling his admission to the Medical School. He alleged that the Medical School's special admissions program operated to exclude him from the school on the basis of his race, in violation of his rights under the Equal Protection Clause of the Fourteenth Amendment. The University cross-complained for a declaration that its special admissions program was lawful.

Applicants admitted under the special program also had benchmark scores significantly lower than many students, including Bakke. Bakke was rejected under the general admissions program, even though the special rating system apparently gave credit for overcoming "disadvantage."

The special admissions program is undeniably a classification based on race and ethnic background. To the extent that there existed a pool of at least minimally qualified minority applicants to fill the 16 special admissions seats, white applicants could compete only for 84 seats in the entering class, rather than the 100 open to minority applicants. Whether this limitation is described as a quota or a goal, it is a line drawn on the basis of race and ethnic status.

The guarantees of the Fourteenth Amendment extend to all persons. Its language is explicit: "No State shall . . . deny to any person within its jurisdiction the equal protection of the laws." The guarantee of equal protection cannot mean one thing when applied to one individual and something else when applied to a person of another color. If both are not accorded the same protection, then it is not equal.

If petitioner's purpose is to assure within its student body some specified percentage of a particular group merely because of its race or ethnic origin, such a preferential pupose must be rejected not as insubstantial but as facially invalid. Preferring members of any one group for no reason other than race or ethnic origin is discrimination for its own sake. This the Constitution forbids.

In such an admissions program, race or ethnic background may be deemed a "plus" in a particular applicant's file, yet it does not insulate the individual from comparison with all other candidates for the available seats. The file of the particular black applicant may be examined or his potential contribution to diversity without the factor of race being decisive when compared, for example, with that of an applicant identified as an Italian-American if the latter is thought to exhibit qualities more likely to promote beneficial educational pluralism. Such qualities could include exceptional personal talents, unique

work or service experience, leadership potential, maturity, demonstrated compassion, a history of overcoming disadvantage, ability to communicate with the poor, or other qualifications deemed important. In short, an admissions program operated in this way is flexible enough to consider all pertinent elements of diversity in light of the particular qualifications of each applicant, and to place them on the same footing for consideration, although not necessarily according them the same weight. Indeed, the weight attributed to a particular quality may vary from year to year depending upon the "mix" both of the student body and the applicants for the incoming class.

This kind of program treats each applicant as an individual in the admissions process. The applicant who loses out on the last available seat to another candidate receiving a "plus" on the basis of ethnic background will not have been foreclosed from all consideration for that seat simply because he was not the right color or had the wrong surname. It would mean only that his combined qualifications, which may have included similar nonobjective factors, did not outweigh those of the other applicant. His qualifications would have been weighed fairly and competitively, and he would have no basis to complain of unequal treatment under the Fourteenth Amendment.

It had been suggested that an admissions program which considers race only as one factor is simply a subtle and more sophisticated—but no less effective—means of according racial preference than the Davis program. A facial intent to discriminate, however, is evident in petitioner's preference program and not denied in this case. No such facial infirmity exists in an admissions program where race or ethnic background is simply one element—to be weighed fairly against other elements—in the selection process.

In summary, it is evident that the Davis special admissions program involves the use of an explicit racial classification never before countenanced by this Court. It tells applicants who are not Negro, Asian, or Chicano that they are totally excluded from a specific percentage of the seats in an entering class. No matter how strong their qualifications, quantitative and extracurricular, including their own potential for contribution to educational diversity, they are never afforded the chance to compete with applicants from the preferred groups for the special admissions seats. At the same time, the preferred applicants have the opportunity to compete for every seat in the class.

The fatal flaw in petitioner's preferential program is its disregard of individual rights as guaranteed by the Fourteenth Amendment. Such rights are not absolute. But when a State's distribution of benefits or imposition of burdens hinges on ancestry or the color of a person's skin, that individual is entitled to a demonstration that the challenged classification is necessary to promote a substantial state interest. Petitioner has failed to carry this burden. For this reason, that portion of the California court's judgment holding petitioner's special admissions program invalid under the Fourteenth Amendment must be affirmed.

In enjoining petitioner from ever considering the race of any applicant, however, the courts below failed to recognize that the State has a substantial interest that legitimately may be served by a properly devised admissions program involving the competitive consideration of race and ethnic origin. For this reason, so much of the California court's judgment as enjoins petitioner from any consideration of the race of any applicant must be reversed.

With respect to respondent's entitlement to an injunction directing his admission to the Medical School, petitioner has conceded that it could not carry its burden of proving that, but for the existence of its unlawful special admissions program, respondent still would not have been admitted. Hence, respondent is entitled to the injunction, and that portion of the judgment must be affirmed.

Judgment for Bakke.

Case Commentary

The Supreme Court of the United States decided the medical school's admission policy was discriminatory toward white applicants because it was based on a quota. A certain number of seats were reserved exclusively for minorities. This amounted to reverse discrimination in violation of the Civil Rights Act of 1964's prohibition against race discrimination.

Case Questions

1. Do you agree with the decision in this case?
2. What is the difference between a quota and an affirmative action program?
3. Should a school have a lower set of criteria for minorities?

The most qualified standard applies only to candidates of the same race; where candidates are of different races, being qualified is sufficient. Thus, the fact that the black workers were not the most qualified is immaterial because they were qualified. Both Bakke and Weber were denied admission because they were not the most qualified candidates within their racial classification (white). When selecting among candidates of different races, being qualified is all that matters. But, when deciding among people of the same race, being the most qualified is the deciding factor.

REQUIREMENTS OF AN AFFIRMATIVE ACTION PLAN

An affirmative action plan will be upheld if it is remedial in nature. A remedial purpose can be determined by the following criteria:

1. the plan creates a balance in the workforce that would not have existed absent discrimination;
2. the plan's duration is limited to the achievement of its objective;
3. only qualified applicants will be hired;
4. white candidates are not barred from being hired.

The following case brought by a white male concerns the validity of an affirmative action plan. The question presented is whether sufficient statistical facts have been introduced to show the plan has a reverse discrimination effect on white males.

CASE

HANNON v. CHATER

887 F. Supp. 1303 (N.D. Cal. 1995)

INFANTE, Judge.

In the instant case, the OHA's (Office of Housing Administration) Affirmative Action Plan is designed to increase over a five-year period, and by varying specific percentages, the numbers of women and minorities who are ALJs (Administrative Law Judges) through "reaching out to inform potential applicants about ALJ employment opportunities at OHA."

The Government's "latest statistics" indicate that five of every six ALJs nationwide are white males. Hannon has not shown, nor even suggested, that the entire United States is an inappropriate labor market for the purpose of evaluating an affirmative action plan for hiring ALJs for Los Angeles. Nor has he supplied evidence whatsoever suggesting that the Government's statistics are mistaken or that such statistics are disproportionate to the qualified labor force. Finally, Hannon has not established that women and minorities are not "underutilized" as ALJ's—i.e., that there does not exist a "manifest imbalance" between the percentage of women and minorities who are ALJs and the percentage of women and minorities qualified to be ALJs. Without the comparative statistics, Hannon cannot carry his burden of showing, on the basis of the undisputed facts, that OHA's Affirmative Action Plan is invalid.

Hannon has also failed to make any showing establishing that the OHA's Affirmative Action Plan unnecessarily trammels the rights of white male ALJ applicants or creates a bar to their advancement. The OHA's plan is, by its terms, "limited to reaching out to inform potential applicants about ALJ employment opportunities at OHA." Insofar as affirmative action policies are necessary evils, the OHA's plan could hardly be more benign. It does not establish quotas nor set aside positions for women or minorities. Moreover, Hannon did not have an "absolute entitlement" to or "legitimate firmly rooted expectation" of obtaining a position as an ALJ.

Finally, Hannon has not offered an iota of proof that the OHA's Affirmative Action Plan is a permanent feature of the OHA's landscape which seeks to establish in perpetuity a work force whose sexual composition mirrors that of the relevant labor force. Indeed, to the contrary, Hannon argues that the Affirmative Action Plan lapsed, and was no longer in force, prior to 1993.

In sum, Hannon has not made a showing sufficient to establish the existence of any elements essential to his disparate impact claim, on which he would bear the burden of proof at trial, and as such the Government is entitled to summary adjudication of Hannon's disparate impact claim.

Judgment for Chater.

Case Commentary

The northern District Court of California concluded that the OHA's AAP met the Weber test.

Case Questions

1. Do you believe Hannon was a victim or reverse discrimination?

2. What determination would achieve a result that would be fair to all parties?

The issue in the case that follows is whether race can be taken into account when a school is formulating its admissions procedure.

CASE

HOPWOOD v. STATE OF TEXAS

21 F.3d 603 (5th Cir. 1996)

SMITH, Circuit Judge.

With the best of intentions, in order to increase the enrollment of certain favored classes of minority students, the University of Texas School of Law ("the law school") discriminates in favor of those applicants by giving substantial racial preferences in its admissions program. The beneficiaries of this system are blacks and Mexican Americans, to the detriment of whites and non-preferred minorities. The question we decide today is whether the Fourteenth Amendment permits the school to discriminate in this way.

We hold that it does not. The law school has presented no compelling justification, under the Fourteenth Amendment or Supreme Court precedent, that allows it to continue to elevate some races over others, even for the wholesome purpose of correcting perceived racial imbalance in the student body. "Racial preferences appear to 'even the score' . . . only if one embraces the proposition that our society is appropriately viewed as divided into races, making it right that an injustice rendered in the past to a black man should be compensated for by discriminating against a white."

As a result of its diligent efforts in this case, the district court concluded that the law school may continue to impose racial preferences. We reverse and remand, concluding that the law school may not use race as a factor in law school admissions. Further, we instruct the court to reconsider the issue of damages in accordance with the legal standards we now explain.

I.

A.

The University of Texas School of Law is one of the nation's leading law schools, consistently ranking in the top twenty. Accordingly, admission to the law school is fiercely competitive, with over 4,000 applicants a year competing to be among the approximately 900 offered admission to achieve an entering class of about 500 students. Many of these applicants have some of the highest grades and test scores in the country. Numbers are therefore paramount for admission. In the early 1990's, the law school largely based its initial admissions decisions upon an applicant's so-called Texas Index ("TI") number, a composite of undergraduate grade point average ("GPA") and Law School Aptitude Test ("LSAT") score. The law school used this number as a matter of administrative convenience in order to rank candidates and to predict, roughly, one's probability of success in law school. Moreover, the law school relied heavily upon such numbers to estimate the number of offers of admission it needed to make in order to fill its first-year class.

Of course, the law school did not rely upon numbers alone. The admissions office necessarily exercised judgment in interpreting the individual scores of applicants, taking into consideration factors such as the strength of a student's undergraduate education, the difficulty of his major, and significant trends in his own grades and the undergraduate grades at his respective college (such as grade inflation). Admissions personnel also considered what qualities each applicant might bring to his law school class. Thus, the law school could consider an applicant's background, life experiences, and outlook. Not surprisingly, these hard-to-quantify factors were especially significant for marginal candidates.

Because of the large number of applicants and potential admissions factors, the TI's administrative usefulness was its ability to sort candidates. For the class entering in 1992—the admissions group at issue in this case—the law school placed the typical applicant in one of three categories according to his TI scores: "presumptive admit," "presumptive deny," or a middle "discretionary zone." An applicant's TI category determined how extensive a review his application would receive.

Blacks and Mexican Americans were treated differently from other candidates, however. First, compared to whites and non-preferred minorities, the TI ranges that were used to place them into the three admissions categories were lowered to allow the law school to consider and admit more of them. In March 1992, for example, the presumptive TI admission score for resident whites and non-preferred minorities was 199. Mexican Americans and blacks needed a TI of only 189 to be presumptively admitted. The difference in the presumptive-deny ranges is even more striking. The presumptive denial score for "nonminorities" was 192; the same score for blacks and Mexican Americans was 179.

While these cold numbers may speak little to those unfamiliar with the pool of applicants, the results demonstrate that the difference in the two ranges was dramatic. According to the law school, 1992 resident white applicants had a mean GPA of 3.53 and an LSAT of 164. Mexican Americans scored 3.27 and 158; blacks scored 3.25 and 157. The category of "other minority" achieved a 3.56 and 160.

These disparate standards greatly affected a candidate's chance of admission. For example, by March 1992, because the presumptive denial score for whites was a TI of 192 or lower, and the presumptive admit TI for minorities was 189 or higher, a minority candidate with a TI of 189 or above almost certainly would be admitted, even though his score was considerably below the level at which a white candidate almost certainly would be rejected. Out of the pool of resident applicants who fell within this range (189-192 inclusive), 100% of blacks and 90% of Mexican Americans, but only 6% of whites, were offered admission.

The stated purpose of this lowering of standards was to meet an "aspiration" of admitting a class consisting of 10% Mexican Americans and 5% blacks, proportions roughly comparable to the percentages of those races graduating from Texas colleges. The law school found meeting these "goals" difficult, however, because of uncertain acceptance rates and the variable quality of the applicant pool. In 1992, for example, the entering class contained 41 blacks and 55 Mexican Americans, respectively 8% and 10.7% of the class.

In addition to maintaining separate presumptive TI levels for minorities and whites, the law school ran a segregated application evaluation process. Upon receiving an application form, the school color-coded it according to race. If a candidate failed to designate his race, he was presumed to be in a nonpreferential category. Thus, race was always an overt part of the review of any applicant's file.

The law school reviewed minority candidates within the applicable discretionary range differently from whites. Instead of being evaluated and compared by one of the various discretionary zone subcommittees, black and Mexican American applicants' files were reviewed by a minority subcommittee of three, which would meet and discuss every minority candidate. Thus, each of these candidates' files could get extensive review and discussion. And while the minority subcommittee reported summaries of files to the admissions committee as a whole, the minority subcommittee's decisions were "virtually final."

Finally, the law school maintained segregated waiting lists, dividing applicants by race and residence. Thus, even many of those minority applicants who were not admitted could be set aside in "minority-only" waiting lists. Such separate lists apparently helped the law school maintain a pool of potentially acceptable, but marginal, minority candidates.

B.

Cheryl Hopwood, Douglas Carvell, Kenneth Elliott, and David Rogers (the "plaintiffs") applied for admission to the 1992 entering law school class. All four were white residents of Texas and were rejected.

The plaintiffs were considered as discretionary zone candidates. Hopwood, with a GPA of 3.8 and an LSAT of 39 (equivalent to a three-digit LSAT of 160), had a TI of 199, a score barely within the presumptive-admit category for resident whites, which was 199 and up. She was dropped into the discretionary zone for resident whites (193 to 198), however, because Johanson decided her educational background overstated the strength of her GPA. Carvell, Elliott, and Rogers had TI's of 197, at the top end of that discretionary zone. Their applications were reviewed by admissions subcommittees, and each received one or no vote.

II.

The plaintiffs sued primarily under the Equal Protection Clause of the Fourteenth Amendment; they also claimed derivative statutory violations of 42 U.S.C. 1981 and 1983 and of title VI of the Civil Rights Act of 1964, 42 U.S.C. 2000d ("title VI"). The plaintiffs' central claim is that they were subjected to unconstitutional racial discrimination by the law school's evaluation of their admissions applications. They sought injunctive and declaratory relief and compensatory and punitive damages.

After a bench trial, the district court held that the school had violated the plaintiffs' equal protection rights. The plaintiffs' victory was pyrrhic at best, however, as the court refused to enjoin the law school from using race in admissions decisions or to grant damages beyond a one-dollar nominal award to each plaintiff. The district court, however, did grant declaratory relief and ordered that the plaintiffs be allowed to apply again without paying the requisite fee.

Significantly, on the second justification, the court rejected the plaintiffs' argument that the analysis of past discrimination should be limited to that of the law school; instead, the court held that the State of Texas's "institutions of higher education are inextricably linked to the primary and secondary schools in the system."

Accordingly, the court found that Texas's long history of racially discriminatory practices in its primary and secondary schools in its not-too-distant past had the following present effects at UT law: "the law school's lingering reputation in the minority community, particularly with prospective students, as a 'white' school; an underrepresentation of minorities in the student body; and some perception that the law school is a hostile environment for minorities." The court also noted that "were the Court to limit its review to the University of Texas, the Court would still find a 'strong evidentiary basis for concluding that remedial action is necessary.' "

III.

The central purpose of the Equal Protection Clause "is to prevent the States from purposefully discriminating between individuals on the basis of race. It seeks ultimately to render the issue of race irrelevant in governmental decisionmaking."

Accordingly, discrimination based upon race is highly suspect. "Distinctions between citizens solely because of their ancestry are by their very nature odious to a free people whose institutions are founded upon the doctrine of equality," and "racial discriminations are in most circumstances irrelevant and therefore prohibited. . . ." Hence, "preferring members of any one group for no reason other than race or ethnic origin is discrimination for its own sake. This the Constitution forbids." These equal protection maxims apply to all races.

In order to preserve these principles, the Supreme Court recently has required that any governmental action that expressly distinguishes between persons on the basis of race be held to the most exacting scrutiny.

Indeed, the purpose of strict scrutiny is to "smoke out" illegitimate uses of race by assuring that the legislative body is pursuing a goal important enough to warrant use of a highly suspect tool. The test also ensures that the means chosen "fit" this compelling goal so closely that there is little or no possibility that the motive for the classification was illegitimate racial prejudice or stereotype.

Under the strict scrutiny analysis, we ask two questions: (1) Does the racial classification serve a compelling government interest, and (2) is it narrowly tailored to the achievement of that goal?

Finally, when evaluating the proffered governmental interest for the specific racial classification, to decide whether the program in question narrowly achieves that interest, we must recognize that "the rights created by . . . the Fourteenth Amendment are, by its terms, guaranteed to the individual. The rights established are personal rights." Thus, the Court consistently has rejected arguments conferring benefits on a person based solely upon his membership in a specific class of persons.

With these general principles of equal protection in mind, we turn to the specific issue of whether the law school's consideration of race as a factor in admissions violates the Equal Protection Clause.

We agree with the plaintiffs that any consideration of race or ethnicity by the law school for the purpose of achieving a diverse student body is not a compelling interest under the Fourteenth Amendment. Finally, the classification of persons on the basis of race for the purpose of diversity frustrates, rather than facilitates, the goals of equal protection. Within the general principles of the Fourteenth Amendment, the use of race in admissions for diversity in higher education contradicts, rather than furthers, the aims of equal protection. Diversity fosters, rather than minimizes, the use of race. It treats minorities as a group, rather than as individuals. It may further remedial purposes but, just as likely, may promote improper racial stereotypes, thus fueling racial hostility.

The use of race, in and of itself, to choose students simply achieves a student body that looks different. Such a criterion is no more rational on its own terms than would be choices based upon the physical size or blood type of applicants. Thus, the Supreme Court has long held that governmental actors cannot justify their decisions solely because of race.

While the use of race per se is proscribed, state-supported schools may reasonably consider a host of factors some of which may have some correlation with race in making admissions decisions. The federal courts have no warrant to intrude on those executive and legislative judgments unless the distinctions intrude on specific provisions of federal law or the Constitution. A university may properly favor one applicant over another because of his ability to play the cello, make a downfield tackle, or understand chaos theory. An admissions process may also consider an applicant's home state or relationship to school alumni. Law schools specifically may look at things such as unusual or substantial extracurricular activities in college, which may be atypical factors affecting undergraduate grades. Schools may even consider factors such as whether an applicant's parents attended college or the applicant's economic and social background.

For this reason, race often is said to be justified in the diversity context, not on its own terms, but as a proxy for other characteristics that institutions of higher education value but that do not raise similar constitutional concerns. Unfortunately, this approach simply replicates the very harm that the Fourteenth Amendment was designed to eliminate.

The assumption is that a certain individual possesses characteristics by virtue of being a member of a certain racial group. This assumption, however, does not withstand scrutiny. "The use of a racial characteristic to establish a pre-sumption that the individual also possesses other, and socially relevant, characteristics, exemplifies, encourages, and legitimizes the mode of thought and behavior that underlies most prejudice and bigotry in modern America."

Plaintiff Hopwood is a fair example of an applicant with a unique background. She is the now-thirty-two-year-old wife of a member of the Armed Forces stationed in San Antonio and, more significantly, is raising a severely handicapped child. Her circumstance would bring a different perspective to the law school. The school might consider this an advantage to her in the application process, or it could decide that her family situation would be too much of a burden on her academic performance.

We do not opine on which way the law school should weigh Hopwood's qualifications; we only observe that "diversity" can take many forms. To foster such diversity, state universities and law schools and other governmental entities must scrutinize applicants individually, rather than resorting to the dangerous proxy of race.

In sum, the use of race to achieve a diverse student body, whether as a proxy for permissible characteristics, simply cannot be a state interest compelling enough to meet the steep standard of strict scrutiny. These latter factors may, in fact, turn out to be substantially correlated with race, but the key is that race itself not be taken into account. Thus, that portion of the district court's opinion upholding the diversity rationale is reversibly flawed.

In sum, for purposes of determining whether the law school's admissions system properly can act as a remedy for the present effects of past discrimination, we must identify the law school as the relevant alleged past discriminator. The fact that the law school ultimately may be subject to the directives of others, such as the board of regents, the university president, or the legislature, does not change the fact that the relevant putative discriminator in this case is still the law school. In order for any of these entities to direct a racial preference program at the law school, it must be because of past wrongs at that school.

Next, the relevant governmental discriminator must prove that there are present effects of past discrimination of the type that justify the racial classifications at issue: To have a present effect of past discrimination sufficient to justify the program, the party seeking to implement the program must, at a minimum, prove that the effect it proffers is caused by the past discrimination and that the effect is of sufficient magnitude to justify the program.

Moreover, as part of showing that the alleged present effects of past discrimination in fact justify the racial preference program at issue, the law school must show that it adopted the program specifically to remedy the identified present effects of the past discrimination.

In sum, the law school has failed to show a compelling state interest in remedying the present effects of past discrimination sufficient to maintain the use of race in its admissions system. Accordingly, it is unnecessary for us to examine the district court's determination that the law school's admissions program was not narrowly tailored to meet the compelling interests that the district court erroneously perceived.

IV.

While the district court declared the admissions program unconstitutional, it granted the plaintiffs only limited relief. They had requested injunctive relief ordering that they be admitted to law school, compensatory and punitive damages, and prospective injunctive relief preventing the school from using race as a factor in admissions.

In this case, there is no question that a constitutional violation has occurred and that the plaintiffs were harmed thereby.

Obviously, if the school proves that a plaintiff would not have gained admittance to the law school under a race-blind system, that plaintiff would not be entitled to an injunction admitting him to the school. On the other hand, the law school's inability to establish a plaintiff's non-admission—if that occurs on remand—opens a panoply of potential relief, depending in part upon what course that plaintiff's career has taken since trial in mid-1994. It then would be up to the district court, in its able discretion, to decide whether money damages can substitute for an order of immediate admission—relief that would ring hollow for a plaintiff for whom an education at the law school now is of little or no benefit.

We note, however, that if the law school continues to operate a disguised or overt racial classification system in the future, its actors could be subject to actual and punitive damages.

In summary, we hold that the University of Texas School of Law may not use race as a factor in deciding which applicants to admit in order to achieve a diverse student body, to combat the perceived effects of a hostile environment at the law school, to alleviate the law school's poor reputation in the minority community, or to eliminate any present effects of past discrimination by actors other than the law school. Because the law school has proffered these justifications for its use of race in admissions, the plaintiffs have satisfied their burden of showing that they were scrutinized under an unconstitutional admissions system. The plaintiffs are entitled to reapply under an admissions system that invokes none of these serious constitutional infirmities. We also direct the district court to reconsider the question of damages, and we conclude that the proposed intervenors properly were denied intervention.

The judgment is REVERSED and REMANDED for further proceedings in accordance with this opinion.

Judgment for Hopwood.

Case Commentary

The Fifth Circuit held that race should not be a factor in the admissions process where there has been no past evidence of discrimination on the part of the school that is seeking to implement the affirmative action plan.

Case Questions

1. Do you agree with the Court's decision?
2. Where there is inadequate representation of minorities, should entrance requirements be lowered to increase minority enrollment?
3. How would the United States Supreme Court have decided this case?

In the following case, the questions presented are whether the affirmative action program was remedial in nature and whether it had a deleterious effect on white employees.

CASE

TAXMAN v. BOARD OF EDUCATION OF THE TOWNSHIP OF PISCATAWAY

91 F.3d 1547 (3rd Cir. 1996)

MANSMANN, Circuit Judge.

In this Title VII matter, we must determine whether the Board of Education of the Township of Piscataway violated that statute when it made race a factor in selecting which of two equally qualified employees to lay off. Specifically, we must decide whether Title VII permits an employer with a racially balanced work force to grant a non-remedial racial preference in order to promote "racial diversity."

It is clear that the language of Title VII is violated when an employer makes an employment decision based upon an employee's race. The Supreme Court determined in United Steelworkers v. Weber, however, that Title VII's prohibition against racial discrimination is not violated by affirmative action plans which first, "have purposes that mirror those of the statute" and second, do not "unnecessarily trammel the interests of the non-minority employees."

We hold that Piscataway's affirmative action policy is unlawful because it fails to satisfy either prong of Weber. Given the clear antidiscrimination mandate of Title VII, a non-remedial affirmative action plan, even one with a laudable purpose, cannot pass muster. We will affirm the district court's grant of summary judgment to Sharon Taxman.

I.

In 1975, the Board of Education of the Township of Piscataway, New Jersey, developed an affirmative action policy applicable to employment decisions. The Board's Affirmative Action Program, a 52-page document, was originally adopted in response to a regulation promulgated by the New Jersey State Board of Education. That regulation directed local school boards to adopt "affirmative action programs," to address employment as well as school and classroom practices and to ensure equal opportunity to all persons regardless of race, color, creed, religion, sex or national origin.

The 1975 document states that the purpose of the Program is "to provide equal educational opportunity for students and equal employment opportunity for employees and prospective employees," and "to make a concentrated effort to attract . . . minority personnel for all positions so that their qualifications can be evaluated along with other candidates." The 1983 document states that its purpose is to "ensure equal employment opportunity . . . and prohibit discrimination in employment because of race. . . ."

The operative language regarding the means by which affirmative-action goals are to be furthered is identical in the two documents. "In all cases, the most qualified candidate will be recommended for appointment. However, when candidates appear to be of equal qualification, candidates meeting the criteria of the affirmative action program will be recommended." The phrase "candidates meeting the criteria of the affirmative action program" refers to members of racial, national origin or gender groups identified as minorities for statistical reporting purposes by the New Jersey State Department of

Education, including Blacks. The 1983 document also clarifies that the affirmative action program applies to "every aspect of employment including . . . layoffs. . . ."

The Board's affirmative action policy did not have "any remedial purpose"; it was not adopted "with the intention of remedying the results of any prior discrimination or identified underrepresentation of minorities within the Piscataway Public School System." At all relevant times, Black teachers were neither "underrepresented" nor "underutilized" in the Piscataway School District work force. Indeed, statistics in 1976 and 1985 showed that the percentage of Black employees in the job category which included teachers exceeded the percentage of Blacks in the available work force.

A.

In May, 1989, the Board accepted a recommendation from the Superintendent of Schools to reduce the teaching staff in the Business Department at Piscataway High School by one. At that time, two of the teachers in the department were of equal seniority, both having begun their employment with the Board on the same day nine years earlier. One of those teachers was intervenor plaintiff Sharon Taxman, who is White, and the other was Debra Williams, who is Black. Williams was the only minority teacher among the faculty of the Business Department.

Decisions regarding layoffs by New Jersey school boards are highly circumscribed by state law; nontenured faculty must be laid off first, and layoffs among tenured teachers in the affected subject area or grade level must proceed in reverse order of seniority. Seniority for this purpose is calculated according to specific guidelines set by state law. Thus, local boards lack discretion to choose between employees for layoff, except in the rare instance of a tie in seniority between the two or more employees eligible to fill the last remaining position.

The Board determined that it was facing just such a rare circumstance in deciding between Taxman and Williams. In prior decisions involving the layoff of employees with equal seniority, the Board had broken the tie through "a random process which included drawing numbers out of a container, drawing lots or having a lottery." In none of those instances, however, had the employees involved been of different races.

In light of the unique posture of the layoff decision, Superintendent of Schools Burton Edelchick recommended to the Board that the affirmative action plan be invoked in order to determine which teacher to retain. Superintendent Edelchick made this recommendation "because he believed Ms. Williams and Ms. Taxman were tied in seniority, were equally qualified, and because Ms. Williams was the only Black teacher in the Business Education Department."

While the Board recognized that it was not bound to apply the affirmative action policy, it made a discretionary decision to invoke the policy to break the tie between Williams and Taxman. As a result, the Board "voted to terminate the employment of Sharon Taxman, effective June 30, 1988. . . ."

At her deposition, Paula Van Riper, the Board's Vice President at the time of the layoff, described the Board's decision-making process. According to Van Riper, after the Board recognized that Taxman and Williams were of equal seniority, it assessed their classroom performance, evaluations, volunteerism and certifications and determined that they were "two teachers of equal ability" and "equal qualifications."

B.

Following the Board's decision, Taxman filed a charge of employment discrimination with the Equal Employment Opportunity Commission. Attempts at conciliation were unsuccessful, and the United States filed suit under Title VII against the Board in the United States District Court for the District of New Jersey. Taxman intervened, asserting claims under both Title VII and the New Jersey Law Against Discrimination (NJLAD).

A trial proceeded on the issue of damages. By this time, Taxman had been rehired by the Board and thus her reinstatement was not an issue. The court awarded Taxman damages in the amount of $134,014.62 for backpay, fringe benefits and prejudgment interest under Title VII. A jury awarded an additional $10,000 for emotional suffering under the NJLAD.

The Board appealed, contending that the district court erred in granting Taxman summary judgment as to liability.

As in other areas of employment, statistics for educational institutions indicate that minorities and women are precluded from the more prestigious and higher-paying positions, and are relegated to the more menial and lower-paying jobs. While in elementary and secondary school systems Negroes accounted for approximately 10% of the total number of positions in the higher-paying and more prestigious positions in institutions of higher learning, blacks constituted only 2.2% of all positions, most of these being found in all-black or predominantly black institutions. Women are similarly subject to discriminatory patterns. Not only are they generally under-represented in institutions of higher learning, but those few that do obtain positions are generally paid less and advanced more slowly than their male counterparts. Similarly, while women constitute 67% of elementary and secondary school teachers, out of 778,000 elementary and secondary school principals, 78% of elementary school principals are men and 94% of secondary school principals are men.

The Board admits that it did not act to remedy the effects of past employment discrimination. The parties have stipulated that neither the Board's adoption of its affirmative action policy nor its subsequent decision to apply it in choosing between Taxman and Williams was intended to remedy the results of any prior discrimination or identified underrepresentation of Blacks within the Piscataway School District's teacher workforce as a whole. Nor does the Board contend that its action here was directed at remedying any de jure or de facto segregation. Even though the Board's race-conscious action was taken to avoid what could have been an all-White faculty within the Business Department, the Board concedes that Blacks are not underrepresented in its teaching workforce as a whole or even in the Piscataway High School.

Rather, the Board's sole purpose in applying its affirmative action policy in this case was to obtain an educational benefit which it believed would result from a racially diverse faculty. While the benefits flowing from diversity in the educational context are significant indeed, we are constrained to hold, as did the district court, that inasmuch as "the Board does not even attempt to show that its affirmative action plan was adopted to remedy past discrimination or as the result of a manifest imbalance in the employment of minorities," the Board has failed to satisfy the first prong of the Weber test.

We turn next to the second prong of the Weber analysis. This second prong requires that we determine whether the Board's policy "unnecessarily trammels . . . nonminority interests. . . ." Under this requirement, too, the Board's policy is deficient.

We begin by noting the policy's utter lack of definition and structure. While it is not for us to decide how much diversity in a high school faculty is "enough," the Board cannot abdicate its responsibility to define "racial diversity" and to determine what degree of racial diversity in the Piscataway School is sufficient.

The affirmative action plans that have met with the Supreme Court's approval under Title VII had objectives, as well as benchmarks which served to evaluate progress, guide the employment decisions at issue and assure the grant of only those minority preferences necessary to further the plans' purpose. By contrast, the Board's policy, devoid of goals and standards, is governed entirely by the Board's whim, leaving the Board free, if it so chooses, to grant racial preferences that do not promote even the policy's claimed purpose. Indeed, under the terms of this policy, the Board, in pursuit of a "racially diverse" work force, could use affirmative action to discriminate against those whom Title VII was enacted to protect. Such a policy unnecessarily trammels the interests of nonminority employees.

Moreover, valid affirmative action plans are "temporary" measures that seek to " 'attain,' " not "maintain" a "permanent racial . . . balance." The Board's policy, adopted in 1975, is an established fixture of unlimited duration, to be resurrected from time to time whenever the Board believes that the ratio between Blacks and Whites in any Piscataway School is skewed. On this basis alone, the policy contravenes Weber's teaching.

Finally, we are convinced that the harm imposed upon a nonminority employee by the loss of his or her job is so substantial and the cost so severe that the Board's goal of racial diversity, even if legitimate under Title VII, may not be pursued in this particular fashion. This is especially true where, as here, the nonminority employee is tenured. In Weber, when considering whether nonminorities were unduly encumbered by affirmative action, the Court found it significant that they retained their employment.

Accordingly, we conclude that under the second prong of the Weber test, the Board's affirmative action policy violates Title VII. In addition to containing an impermissible purpose, the policy "unnecessarily trammels the interests of the nonminority employees."

While we have rejected the argument that the Board's non-remedial application of the affirmative action policy is consistent with the language and intent of Title VII, we do not reject in principle the diversity goal articulated by the Board. Indeed, we recognize that the differences among us underlie the richness and strength of our Nation. Our disposition of this matter, however, rests squarely on the foundation of Title VII. Although we applaud the goal of racial diversity, we cannot agree that Title VII permits an employer to advance that goal through non-remedial discriminatory measures.

Having found that the district court properly concluded that the affirmative action plan applied by the Board to lay off Taxman is invalid under Title VII, and that the district court did not err in calculating Taxman's damages or in dismissing her claim for punitive damages, we will affirm the judgment of the district court.

Judgment for Taxman.

Case Commentary

The tests for determining whether an affirmative action program is enforceable are whether the enactment of the plan was in response to a disparate impact against minorities, and whether the implementation of the plan will have an adverse effect on white employees. The Piscataway Board of Education's plan failed in both respects. There were a suffcient number of minorities employed; therefore remediation was unnecessary, and a white employee, Sharon Taxman, suffered the loss of her job because of the implementation of the plan.

Case Questions

1. Do you agree with the decision in this case?
2. Does this mark the end of affirmative action?

3. How would the United States Supreme Court have decided this case?

The question presented in the case that follows is whether a state referendum approved by the voters disbanding affirmative action programs is in violation of the Fourteenth Amendment's Equal Protection Clause.

CASE

THE COALITION v. PETE WILSON

122 F.3d 692 (9th Cir. 1997)

O'SCANNLAIN, Judge.
We must decide whether a provision of the California Constitution prohibiting public race and gender preferences violates the Equal Protection Clause of the United States Constitution.

On November 5, 1996, the people of the State of California adopted the California Civil Rights Initiative as an amendment to their Constitution. The initiative, which appeared on the ballot as Proposition 209, provides in relevant part that the state shall not discriminate against, or grant preferential treatment to, any individual or group on the basis of race, sex, color, ethnicity, or national origin in the operation of public employment, public education, or public contracting.

The California Legislative Analyst's Office portrayed Proposition 209 to the voters as a measure that would eliminate public race-based and gender-based affirmative action programs. The California Ballot Pamphlet explained to voters that: A YES vote on Proposition 209 means: The elimination of those affirmative action programs for women and minorities run by the state or local governments in the areas of public employment, contracting, and education that give "preferential treatment" on the basis of sex, race, color, ethnicity, or national origin.

A NO vote on this measure means State and local government affirmative action programs would remain in effect to the extent they are permitted under the United States Constitution.

The Ballot Pamphlet also included arguments by proponents and opponents of Proposition 209. Proponents urged a "yes" vote, arguing that: A generation ago, we did it right. We passed civil rights laws to prohibit discrimination. But special interests hijacked the civil rights movement. Instead of equality, governments imposed quotas, preferences, and set-asides. And two wrongs don't make a right! Today, students are being rejected from public universities because of their RACE. Job applicants are turned away because their RACE does not meet some "goal" or "timetable." Contracts are awarded to high bidders because they are of the preferred RACE.

That's just plain wrong and unjust. Government should not discriminate. It must not give a job, a university admission, or a contract based on race or sex. Government must judge all people equally, without discrimination!

And, remember, Proposition 209 keeps in place all federal and state protections against discrimination!

Opponents of Proposition 209 urged a "no" vote, responding that: California law currently allows tutoring, mentoring, outreach, recruitment, and counseling to help ensure equal opportunity for women and minorities. Proposition 209 will eliminate affirmative action programs like these that help achieve equal op-

portunity for women and minorities in public employment, education and contracting. Instead of reforming affirmative action to make it fair for everyone, Proposition 209 makes the current problem worse. . . .

The initiative's language is so broad and misleading that it eliminates equal opportunity programs including: tutoring and mentoring for minority and women students; affirmative action that encourages the hiring and promotion of qualified women and minorities; outreach and recruitment programs to encourage applicants for government jobs and contracts; and programs designed to encourage girls to study and pursue careers in math and science.

Proposition 209 passed by a margin of 54 to 46 percent; of nearly 9 million Californians casting ballots, 4,736,180 voted in favor of the initiative and 3,986,196 voted against it.

On the day after the election, November 6, 1996, several individuals and groups ("plaintiffs") claiming to represent the interests of racial minorities and women filed a complaint in the Northern District of California against several officials and political subdivisions of the State of California ("the State").

The complaint, brought under 42 U.S.C. S 1983, alleges that Proposition 209, first, denies racial minorities and women the equal protection of the laws guaranteed by the Fourteenth Amendment, and, second, is void under the Supremacy Clause because it conflicts with Titles VI and VII of the Civil Rights Act of 1964, and Title IX of the Educational Amendments of 1972. As relief, plaintiffs seek a declaration that Proposition 209 is unconstitutional and a permanent injunction enjoining the State from implementing and enforcing it.

With their complaint, plaintiffs filed an application for a temporary restraining order ("TRO") and a preliminary injunction. The district court entered a TRO on November 27, 1996, and granted a preliminary injunction on December 23, 1996. The preliminary injunction enjoins the State, pending trial or final judgment, "from implementing or enforcing Proposition 209 insofar as said amendment to the Constitution of the State of California purports to prohibit or affect affirmative action programs in public employment, public education or public contracting."

The district court provided extensive findings of fact and conclusions of law in support of the injunction. This lawsuit, the court explained, challenges Proposition 209's prohibition against race and gender preferences, not its prohibition against discrimination. Plaintiffs' constitutional challenge is "only to that slice of the initiative that now prohibits governmental entities at every level from taking voluntary action to remediate past and present discrimination through the use of constitutionally permissible race- and gender-conscious affirmative action programs."

The elimination of such programs, the district court found, would reduce opportunities in public contracting and employment for women and minorities. It further would cause enrollment of African-American, Latino, and American Indian students in public colleges to fall, though enrollment of Asian-American students would increase. Finally, the court found that minorities and women, to reinstate race-based or gender-based preferential treatment, would have to re-amend the California Constitution by initiative.

From these findings of fact the district court concluded, first, that plaintiffs have demonstrated a likelihood of success on their equal protection claim. Proposition 209, the court reasoned, has a racial and gender focus which imposes a substantial political burden on the interests of women and minorities.

The district court concluded, second, that plaintiffs have also demonstrated a likelihood of success on their preemption claims. Title VII, the court reasoned, preserves the discretion of public employers voluntarily to use race and gender preferences. To the extent that Proposition 209 bans such preferences statewide, the court held that Title VII preempts it under the Supremacy Clause.

As a general rule, federal courts "ought not to consider the Constitutionality of a state statute in the absence of a controlling interpretation of its meaning and effect by the state courts."

From the district court's findings, however, we are satisfied, to answer the Supreme Court's question, that "yes—this conflict really is necessary." We may now address the merits.

In granting the preliminary injunction, the district court first concluded that plaintiffs have demonstrated a likelihood of success on their claim that Proposition 209 violates the Equal Protection Clause of the Fourteenth Amendment. We must examine whether the district court's conclusion is based on an erroneous legal premise as a matter of "conventional" equal protection analysis, which looks to the substance of the law at issue, or as a matter of "political structure" equal protection analysis, which looks to the level of government at which the law was enacted. We shall apply each mode of analysis to Proposition 209 in turn.

As a matter of "conventional" equal protection analysis, there is simply no doubt that Proposition 209 is constitutional. The Equal Protection Clause provides that "no State shall . . . deny to any person within its jurisdiction the equal protection of the laws." The central purpose of the Equal Protection Clause "is the prevention of official conduct discriminating on the basis of race." The Fourteenth Amendment forbids such conduct on the principle that "distinctions between citizens solely because of their ancestry are by their very nature odious to a free people whose institutions are founded upon the doctrine of equality."

Racial distinctions "threaten to stigmatize individuals by reason of their membership in a racial group and to incite racial hostility."

The ultimate goal of the Equal Protection Clause is "to do away with all governmentally imposed discrimination based on race." Therefore, "whenever the government treats any person unequally because of his or her race, that person has suffered an injury that falls squarely within the language and spirit of the Constitution's guarantee of equal protection." The Equal Protection Clause also protects against classifications based on gender. "Without equating gender classifications, for all purposes, to classifications based on race or national origin, the Court . . . has carefully inspected official action that closes a door or denies opportunity to women or to men." The standard of review under the Equal Protection Clause does not depend on the race or gender of those burdened or benefited by a particular classification.

When the government prefers individuals on account of their race or gender, it correspondingly disadvantages individuals who fortuitously belong to another race or to the other gender.

"Consistency does recognize that any individual suffers an injury when he or she is disadvantaged by the government because of his or her race." Proposition 209 amends the California

Constitution simply to prohibit state discrimination against or preferential treatment to any person on account of race or gender. Plaintiffs charge that this ban on unequal treatment denies members of certain races and one gender equal protection of the laws. If merely stating this alleged equal protection violation does not suffice to refute it, the central tenet of the Equal Protection Clause teeters on the brink of incoherence.

A legislative classification will deny equal protection only if it is not "rationally related to a legitimate state interest." Id. (citations omitted).

The general rule does not apply, however, when a law classifies individuals by race or gender. Any governmental action that classifies persons by race is presumptively unconstitutional and subject to the most exacting judicial scrutiny. To be constitutional, a racial classification, regardless of its purported motivation, must be narrowly tailored to serve a compelling governmental interest, an extraordinary justification. When the government classifies by gender, it must demonstrate that the classification is substantially related to an important governmental interest, requiring an "exceedingly persuasive" justification.

The first step in determining whether a law violates the Equal Protection Clause is to identify the classification that it draws. Proposition 209 provides that the State of California shall not discriminate against, or grant preferential treatment to, any individual or group on the basis of race or gender. Rather than classifying individuals by race or gender, Proposition 209 prohibits the State from classifying individuals by race or gender. A law that prohibits the State from classifying individuals by race or gender a fortiori does not classify individuals by race or gender. Proposition 209's ban on race and gender preferences, as a matter of law and logic, does not violate the Equal Protection Clause in any conventional sense. Can a statewide ballot initiative deny equal protection to members of a group that constitutes a majority of the electorate that enacted it? Plaintiffs allege that Proposition 209 places procedural burdens in the path of women and minorities, who together constitute a majority of the California electorate. Is it possible for a majority of voters impermissibly to stack the political deck against itself? The Supreme Court leaves us, quite frankly, a little perplexed as to the answer. The difficulty, however, lies in recon-

ciling what seems to be that eminently sensible conclusion with the principle that the Fourteenth Amendment guarantees equal protection to individuals and not to groups. That the Fourteenth Amendment affords individuals, not groups, the right to demand equal protection is a fundamental first principle of "conventional" equal protection jurisprudence. The Equal Protection Clause, after all, prohibits a state from denying "to any person within its jurisdiction the equal protection of the laws." U.S. Const. amend. Where a state denies someone a job, an education, or a seat on the bus because of her race or gender, the injury to that individual is clear. The person who wants to work, study, or ride but cannot because she is black or a woman is denied equal protection. Where, as here, a state prohibits race or gender preferences at any level of government, the injury to any specific individual is utterly inscrutable. No one contends that individuals have a constitutional right to preferential treatment solely on the basis of their race or gender. Quite the contrary. What, then, is the personal injury that members of a group suffer when they cannot seek preferential treatment on the basis of their race or gender from local government? This question admits of no easy answer. The legal question for us to decide is whether a burden on achieving race-based or gender-based preferential treatment can deny individuals equal protection of the laws.

The Supreme Court has recognized an explicit distinction "between state action that discriminates on the basis of race and state action that addresses, in neutral fashion, race related matters." The former denies persons against whom the law discriminates equal protection of the laws; the latter does not. Into which category Proposition 209 falls we must now determine.

When, in contrast, a state prohibits all its instruments from discriminating against or granting preferential treatment to anyone on the basis of race or gender, it has promulgated a law that addresses in neutral-fashion race-related and gender-related matters. It does not isolate race or gender antidiscrimination laws from any specific area over which the state has delegated authority to a local entity. Nor does it treat race and gender antidiscrimination laws in one area differently from race and gender antidiscrimination laws in another. Rather, it prohibits all race and gender preferences by state entities.

Plaintiffs challenge Proposition 209 not as an impediment to protection against unequal treatment but as an impediment to receiving preferential treatment. The controlling words, we must remember, are "equal" and "protection." Impediments to preferential treatment do not deny equal protection. It is one thing to say that individuals have equal protection rights against political obstructions to equal treatment; it is quite another to say that individuals have equal protection rights against political obstructions to preferential treatment. While the Constitution protects against obstructions to equal treatment, it erects obstructions to preferential treatment by its own terms.

The alleged "equal protection" burden that Proposition 209 imposes on those who would seek race and gender preferences is a burden that the Constitution itself imposes. The Equal Protection Clause, parked at our most "distant and remote" level of government, singles out racial preferences for severe political burdens—it prohibits them in all but the most compelling circumstances. It is well-settled that "all governmental action based on race—a group classification long recognized as in most circumstances irrelevant and therefore prohibited—should be subject to detailed judicial inquiry to ensure that the personal right to equal protection of the laws has not been infringed." That is because "there is simply no way of determining what classifications are 'benign' or 'remedial' and what classifications are in fact motivated by illegitimate notions of racial inferiority or simple racial politics."

The Constitution permits the people to grant a narrowly tailored racial preference only if they come forward with a compelling interest to back it up. Section 708 of Title VII provides:

Nothing in this subchapter shall be deemed to exempt or relieve any person from any liability, duty, penalty, or punishment provided by any present or future law of any State or political subdivision of a State, other than any such law which purports to require or permit the doing of any act which would be an unlawful employment practice under this subchapter.

That is all Title VII pre-empts. Proposition 209 does not remotely purport to require the doing of any act which would be an unlawful employment practice under Title VII. Because Title VII by its plain language does not preempt Proposition 209, the district court relied on an erroneous legal premise in concluding that plaintiffs are likely to succeed on the merits of their pre-emption claims.

With no likelihood of success on the merits of their equal protection or pre-emption claims, plaintiffs are not entitled to a preliminary injunction.

Assuming all facts alleged in the complaint and found by the district court to be true, and drawing all reasonable inferences in plaintiffs' favor, we must conclude that, as a matter of law, Proposition 209 does not violate the United States Constitution. With no constitutional injury on the merits as a matter of law, there is no threat of irreparable injury or hardship to tip the balance in plaintiffs' favor.

For the foregoing reasons, we vacate the preliminary injunction, deny the motion to stay the injunction as moot, and remand to district court for further proceedings consistent with this opinion.

Preliminary injunction VACATED.
Judgment for Wilson.

Case Commentary

The Ninth Circuit held that granting preferential treatment based on race in school admissions, contracts with the state, and state jobs was prohibited by voter approved Proposition 209. The court further held that Proposition 209 does not violate the Equal Protection Clause of the Fourteenth Amendment.

Case Questions

1. Should the voters have the right to decide this issue or should it be left to the courts or the legislature?
2. Do you agree with the decision in this case?
3. Where does this decision leave women and minorities? Are they on an equal footing?
4. Is this the death knell for affirmative action?

CONCLUSION

In 1977, the *Bakke* decision cast doubt over the merits of affirmative action. These doubts were quickly set aside the following year by the United States Supreme Court's reaffirmation of affirmative action in *Weber*. In that case, criteria were set forth to justify the implementation of affirmative action programs: remedial purpose, limited duration, qualified applicants, and no adverse consequences to current employees. Since 1996, some affirmative action plans have been falling short of these requirements. The fifth circuit in the *Hopwood* case and the third circuit in the *Taxman* case both ruled against affirmative action programs, deciding they were not remedial in purpose, and that their implementation affected white people adversely. Both *Hopwood* and *Taxman* indicate that affirmative action plans will be subject to more intensive scrutiny in the future. As a result, more plans will fail to meet the requirements set forth in *Weber*. Whereas before many private employers, state and local governments, and federal agencies formulated affirmative action plans to avoid litigation, they will now have to reevaluate their plans to see if they are in strict compliance with *Weber* requirements. If the criteria have not been met, the affirmative action plan will have to be discontinued or these employers will risk litigation with the opposition, which will cite the courts' interpretation of the *Weber* requirements in the *Hopwood* and *Taxman* cases.

The United States Supreme Court agreed to hear the *Taxman* case; however, before they did, the case was settled for an amount greatly exceeding what Sharon Taxman originally requested. Proponents of affirmative action feared the Supreme Court might require strict scrutiny of the *Weber* criteria in all affirmative action cases. This would have been a death knell for affirmative action.

Meanwhile, California's voter-approved Proposition 209 went beyond strictly scrutinizing existing affirmative action plans to eliminating them for all state jobs, for all businesses contracting with the state, and for all state schools. Private employers were not affected, but this does not bode well for the future of affirmative action. Currently, other states are formulating referenda similar to California's Proposition 209, while some members of Congress are introducing bills designed to save affirmative action programs.

Affirmative action is in a state of transition. What the future holds is not entirely certain, but it appears the application of a strict scrutiny standard and the possibility of additional state voter referenda will make severe inroads into affirmative action programs.

❖ EMPLOYER LESSONS

- Understand the history of affirmative action.
- Appreciate the significance of the Equal Employment Opportunity Act.
- Conduct a voluntary self-audit of your business to determine if it has adequate representation of women and minorities.
- If it does not, determine how and why your company created this disparate impact.
- Recognize that affirmative action is in a state of transition.
- Familiarize yourself with the *Hopwood, Taxman,* and *Coalition* (Proposition 209) cases.
- Apprise yourself of the status of affirmative action in the state in which your business is located.

- Formulate an affirmative action plan only if it is remedial in purpose and does not have an adverse effect on the current workforce.
- Appreciate the difference between a quota and an affirmative action plan.
- Guard against instituting a plan that will result in reverse discrimination.

❖ EMPLOYEE LESSONS

- Take advantage of the opportunities afforded by affirmative action programs if you are a woman or a minority.
- Appreciate why these programs were instituted.
- Be aware of current decisions that may jeopardize the future of affirmative action.
- Understand that affirmative action programs must be remedial in their purpose.
- Be cognizant that affirmative action plans must not adversely affect current employees.
- Know that affirmative action plans must be discontinued once their purpose has been achieved.
- Recognize that you must be qualified to be hired under an affirmative action plan.
- Learn that if a quota system is employed, as in the *Bakke* case, it will result in reverse discrimination.
- Appreciate the argument that the existence of a disparate impact against a class of people because of race or sex can only be obliterated through an affirmative action program.
- Understand the opposing position that giving preferential treatment to people because of their race or sex is in violation of the Equal Protection Clause of the Fourteenth Amendment.

❖ SUMMARY

Whenever one group constitutes the majority of the population or has political, military, or economic control, there is going to be unequal discrimination; that is, one group which is in control is capable of affecting the employment of the other groups and, with it, their lifestyle. If all groups were equally represented in numbers as well as political, military, and economic strength, there would still be discrimination, but it would be equal. Group A would associate, work, and live predominantly with Group A people. Group B would do the same, and so on. It would be predominantly, not exclusively, because some people enjoy intermingling or may, in fact, prefer another group entirely. Group A employers would predominantly hire Group A people, assuming that the general abilities of the group were similar. Why? Because people usually feel more comfortable with people with whom they can identify—those similar to themselves. The main categories that create similarities are race, national origin, gender, religion, age, economic status or standard of living, domicile, education, and associations or clubs.

In the hypothetical situation of equal representation, the discrimination, while having societal drawbacks, would not have affected the employment and, as a result, the income, education, housing, and standard of living of any one of the groups. In the United States, where the white race has been the majority in population and the white male the dominant force in politics, the military, and business, the result has been an unequal discrimination against women and minorities. How does the United States measure up against other countries?

It may be true that other countries are doing the same, if not worse. They may be acting discriminatorily to their minority white populations. But the old adage "two wrongs don't make a right" rings clear. As proponents of human rights, Americans should be solving our own problems and teaching other nations through the good examples of promoting equality among peoples. To accomplish this, the majority does not have to give handouts to women and minorities. All that is required is to remove the obstacles in their path to job hiring and subsequent promotions. Let them be judged on their content rather than on their cover. Equal opportunity is the answer. The pendulum was stuck on one side. Swinging it to the other side is not the answer. Stopping it in the middle is. Giving women and minorities preference will only incite prejudices more and undermine their ability to perform. With multinationals downsizing work forces and relocating them to foreign countries, American jobs can only be saved by ability. Successful businesses will not survive by employing minimally qualified people; they must employ the most qualified people. The players in the National Football league are qualified, but the most successful teams are the ones who have employed the most qualified players. This is the philosophy which will rule in the world of global business. Helping women and minorities to be the most qualified they can be should be the philosophy adopted. The American business who will not hire women or minorities may end up losing business to a competitor who will hire women and what we call minorities overseas, *i.e.*, Pakistani women and Sri Lankan men. Discrimination will be phased out in favor of ability. The most qualified will rule.

❖ REVIEW QUESTIONS

1. What is affirmative action?
2. When did this concept first arise?
3. How is a quota different from an affirmative action plan?
4. Why would a company voluntarily institute an affirmative action plan?
5. What is meant by equal employment opportunity?
6. Explain the affirmative action plan guidelines for the private sector.
7. Explain the concept of reverse discrimination.
8. How can the EEOC enforce its ruling against an employer who refuses to comply?
9. Are affirmative action plans ethical?
10. Once an affirmative action plan is implemented, can it remain indefinitely?
11. Mr. Lawson served as coordinator for the security department of the Central Louisiana State Hospital (CLSH) for six months during the illness of the previous Police Chief. When applications for the vacancy were accepted, Mr. Lawson ranked first on the promotional certificate of eligibles issued by the Department of State Civil Service and third on the probational certificate.

Mr. Lawson also notes that he was interviewed by a five-member, all white committee appointed by the hospital's associate administrator and that the committee was not refereed according to the hospital's Affirmative Action Plan. It is undisputed that in the hospital's Affirmative Action Plan, the position of DHH Police Chief falls within Group 4-A, specialty staff consisting of one black male, one white female, and nine white males; the group bears the label: "underutilization of minority employees."

Acknowledging that the Affirmative Action Plan was not considered, the Commission, through its referee, concluded that appellant presented no evidence that racial bias or prejudice affected the results of the selection process for Police Chief. The referee pointed out that appellant neither alleged nor proved that the questions asked during the interview were designed to disadvantage a minority applicant such as himself, nor that any member of the selection committee exhibited a predisposition against him either before, during, or after the interview. What was the result? *Lawson v. Dept. of Health and Hospitals,* 618 So.2d 1002 (La.App. 1 Cir. 1993)

12. Miller, who was unfamiliar with the new AAP, interviewed Stock for the open position on September 9, 1991. Miller told Stock he was impressed with Stock's qualifications and arranged for Stock to be interviewed the next day by the plant manager, Allan Brethauer ("Brethauer"). After this second interview, Miller again told plaintiff that everything "looked good," and Miller began arranging for a physical examination for Stock.

It then came to the attention of Dennis Cassidy, the Assistant Plant Manager, that Miller had interviewed an applicant before the position had been publicly advertised. Cassidy contacted Miller and informed him of the AAP's requirements. Miller in turn told Stock that the company needed to advertise and interview more applicants to comply with its affirmative action plan, but that Miller was still very impressed by plaintiff's qualifications.

Tyrone Anderson ("Anderson") was interviewed and subsequently hired by Universal for the maintenance vacancy. Anderson, who is black, had vocational training from a respected school and had production line equipment experience. His former employer gave him an unqualified recommendation and expressed disappoint-ment that he was leaving. Despite his admitted prejudice against minorities, Miller was impressed by Anderson's qualifications and decided Universal should hire him. What was the result? *Stock v. Universal Foods Corp.,* 817 F.Supp. 1300 (D.Md. 1993)

13. Mr. Kelsay's statement of claim is repeated below in its entirety:

> As a Limited Term Employee at MATC (Milwaukee Area Technical College), I was entitled to retain the teaching position to which I had been appointed until such time as a permanent hiring took place. Instead, at the beginning of the second semester of the 1990-91 school year MATC transferred a black male NON-APPLICANT into this position in violation of the Collective Bargaining Agreement then in effect between the teachers, union AFT (of which I am a member) and the administration of MATC. I filed a grievance and was reinstated but lost wages as a result of this incident.

Mr. Kelsay is a white male. That addendum also states that Carol Brady, a black female, was hired by MATC on August 26, 1991, to fill the permanent paralegal instructor position that Mr. Kelsay had applied for on August 1, 1990, and was qualified for, and had filled for MATC as a limited term employee from August 1990 through May 1991. What was the result? *Kelsay v. Milwaukee Area Technical College,* 825 F. Supp. 215 (E.D. Wis. 1993)

❖ **WEB SITES**

www.dol.gov/dol/esa/public/regs/cfr/41cfr/toc_chapt60/60_1.40.htm
www.feminist.org/other/ccri/aafact2.html
www.now.org/nnt/08-95/affirmhs.html
www.affirmativeaction.com
www.washingtonpost.com/wp-srv/politics/special/affirm/affirm.htm
www.usnews.com/usnews/wash/affhigh.htm

RACIAL DISCRIMINATION

INTRODUCTION

Racial discrimination exists where employees of one race are favored by the employer over another. Usually it is the white race favored over the black race, but there are also many instances of Hispanics, Orientals, Asians, and American Indians being subjected to racial discrimination. There are even isolated instances of white people being victimized as well.

EMPLOYMENT PERSPECTIVE

Mary Jones, who is black, and Martha Thomas, who is white, were both salespersons for the Fashion Boutique, a women's apparel store. In concert, they stole over $4,000 worth of merchandise. Upon discovery, Martha was terminated, but Mary was not. Fashion Boutique felt that if Mary was terminated, she might file a complaint with the EEOC, claiming discrimination since she was the only black employee. Martha filed a claim for racial discrimination. Is she correct? Yes! Although both could be terminated for the theft, by choosing one race over the other, the employer racially discriminated against Martha. The argument that Title VII does not cover white people is without merit. It applies to *all* races. ◼

CHAPTER CHECKLIST

❖ Learn the meaning of race discrimination.

❖ Understand that white people can be the victims of race discrimination.

❖ Know the importance of treating all workers equally.

❖ Appreciate the fact that an employer usually invites litigation when it treats people differently.

❖ If you are white, imagine that you are of another race before forming an opinion on race discrimination.

❖ Be aware of what constitutes racial harassment.

❖ Be able to define color discrimination.

❖ Be apprised of the parameters of the Reconstruction Era Act.

EMPLOYMENT SCENARIO

The Long and the Short of It advertise for four new employees. Tim Jackson sees the ad and tells three of his friends, "Wouldn't it be great if we could all work together?" Tim and his friends are black. When Tom Long and Mark Short are confronted by four black men looking for employment, Tom abruptly responds that three of the positions have been filled, but they would be interested in considering one person for the fourth position. Tim is eventually selected. After gaining employment he learns that L & S is still interviewing for the three positions that were supposed to have been filled. Tim confronts Tom and Mark about this issue. Tom and Mark put Tim off until they can consult with their attorney Susan North. Tom explains they did not mind hiring a black person for one of four vacancies, but filling all four slots with black people would have been overwhelming. Susan asks Tom and Mark if all four black applicants were qualified. Mark responds, "Yes, but that's not the point." Susan interrupts Mark and informs him that that is exactly the point. She emphasizes that L&S must be colorblind and make hiring decisions based solely on qualifications. Susan advises Tom and Mark to instruct Tim to have his friends come back for a second interview. She counsels Tom and Mark to verify their qualifications, and if they meet L&S's standards, to hire all three men. Otherwise, L&S might end up facing an EEOC investigation or possible litigation involving compensatory and punitive damages, along with bad publicity.

In the following case, a black professor was denied tenure at a college. He brought a racial discrimination suit. The college claimed it was justified in denying tenure because of a failure to produce scholarly work. The professor claimed the college's argument was just a pretext in order to racially discriminate.

CASE

JIMINEZ v. MARY WASHINGTON COLLEGE

57 F.3d 369 (4th Cir. 1995)

HAMILTON, Circuit Judge.

Anthony Jiminez, a black professor from Trinidad, West Indies, instituted suit pursuant to Title VII of the Civil Rights Act of 1964, against Mary Washington College (MWC) and Philip Hall, Vice President of Mary Washington College, for alleged employment discrimination based on race and national origin. According to

Jiminez, he was impermissibly given a terminal contract instead of remaining in a tenure-track teaching position. Following a bench trial, the district court rendered judgment in favor of Jiminez, ruling that he had established a prima facie case of race and national origin discrimination, and he had demonstrated MWC's proffered reason for the adverse action was pretextual and unworthy of credence. MWC appeals, contending that the district court erred in ruling in favor of Jiminez, and Jiminez cross-appeals, asserting that the damages are inadequate. Concluding that the factual findings of the district court are clearly erroneous, we reverse.

Jiminez applied for an assistant professorship in the Department of Economics at MWC on March 4, 1989. In connection with his application, Jiminez represented that he would receive his doctorate degree in economics in June of 1989 from the University of New Mexico. A divided Economics Department extended Jiminez an offer, even though he was not the most qualified applicant; he only met MWC's minimal standards. The department was split in its decision to offer Jiminez a position since he garnered inauspicious evaluations at the University of New Mexico. Despite this knowledge, MWC offered Jiminez the position because the college was seeking to increase the number of blacks on its faculty. To a degree, therefore, Jiminez was hired because he was black. By letter dated August 3, 1989, William Anderson, President of MWC, notified Jiminez of MWC's offer, expressly explaining that Jiminez' appointment was "contingent upon his being granted his Ph.D. by August 16, 1989." This contingency reflected MWC's policy applicable to Jiminez that professors seeking tenure have terminal degrees, as reflected in the faculty handbook, which provided that for consideration for promotion to assistant professor "possession of the appropriate earned terminal degree, in most cases, the Doctorate in one's discipline in unusual circumstances, equivalent professional achievement" was necessary. Thus, on extension of the offer, Jiminez was aware that obtaining his Ph.D. was necessary for promotion. In this respect, Jiminez' offer differed from that of his colleague in the Economics Department, Professor Steve Greenlaw, because according to the 1982 faculty handbook in effect when

Greenlaw was hired, attaining a terminal degree was not a prerequisite for advancement. Thus, Greenlaw was given tenure even though he did not obtain a terminal degree until 1986.

As a nontenured professor seeking tenure, Jiminez was subject to a six-year probationary period after which he could be awarded tenure. Consistent with MWC's procedures, Jiminez initially was awarded a one-year contract as a newly-hired, tenure-track faculty member. Subsequent to his initial year, a tenure-track faculty member can be awarded a two-year contract, followed by a three-year contract, provided, of course, his performance satisfied MWC's standards. Following successful completion of the three-year contract, a faculty member could be considered for tenure. If a tenure-track professor is not considered for further advancement because of unsatisfactory performance, however, MWC grants him a one-year terminal contract, which expires at the termination of the academic year.

Tenure is based largely on teacher evaluations. The faculty at MWC is evaluated annually according to three criteria: (1) teaching effectiveness; (2) service to MWC; and (3) scholarship or professional activity. Of these criteria, teaching effectiveness is paramount and is based largely on evaluations from students, the department chairman, and other faculty within the department. Scholarship or professional activity includes publication or presentation of scholarly works.

After his first semester of teaching, MWC evaluated Jiminez' performance on February 22, 1990. This evaluation was a compendium of faculty observations, student course ratings, and the annual Faculty Activities Report. The gist of this initial evaluation was that Jiminez' skills as a professor were lacking, but his personal fortitude was commendable. Specifically with respect to the tenure criteria, this evaluation concluded: 1. Concerning teaching effectiveness, "students were critical of the clarity and loudness of his voice, his speaking to the chalk board instead of the class, poorly worded tests, and covering material too fast." These negative conclusions were countered by the generic observation that they were "shortcomings any new teacher is bound to have and are things easily corrected by experience. Additionally, Jiminez was "praised . . . for caring about his students, holding review sessions, encouraging questions, and taking the time to make sure students understand the material." 2. Regarding service to MWC, Jiminez was rated highly for his participation in college organizations. 3. Respecting scholarship, the evaluation admonished that Jiminez' major focus for the immediate future must be completion of this dissertation." Significantly, Jiminez neither protested nor contradicted the initial evaluation's conclusions.

On April 2, 1991, MWC again evaluated Jiminez' performance, this evaluation again being an amalgam of the faculty observations, student course ratings, and the annual Faculty Activities Report. Focusing on the three primary criteria for tenure, this second MWC evaluation concluded: 1. With respect to teaching effectiveness, the evaluation reported that while Jiminez was dedicated, his "student evaluation scores were below average for both the Economics Department and College-wide faculty," but expressing the hope that time would cure this failure. 2. With respect to service Jiminez again rated highly; and 3. With respect to scholarship, the evaluation observed that Jiminez had attended various meetings. As with the initial MWC evaluation, Jiminez conspicuously took no exception to the conclusions, nor did he request consideration for a merit award.

An example, a letter from former student Laura Kasley recited:

It is my understanding that several students have either given Mr. Jiminez poor evaluations, or have written negative letters of complaint concerning his teaching. . . . Last semester (Fall 1991), I . . . witnessed, on evaluation day, a collaborative effort on the part of the majority of students to give Mr. Jiminez poor evaluations. They have also written negative letters of complaint concerning his teaching. It is my opinion that the students in this class, who gave Mr. Jiminez poor evaluations, did not take the time required by the course to fully understand the material. Since the first day of classes, Mr. Jiminez forewarned us to ask him to

repeat himself if we couldn't understand his accent. . . . I have acclimated to his accent and find no trouble understanding him. Ultimately, Kasley opined that despite the fact that Jiminez was not the best qualified candidate, on hiring him MWC assumed particular or additional burdens "to protect Jiminez from racial and national origin animus." MWC's duty was only to refrain from taking adverse employment action against him because of invidious racial discrimination, and MWC's obligation did not extend to protecting Jiminez against any alleged racial and national origin animus by others in the employment community, nor to excusing derelictions in the job performance because the animus of others may have contributed to it.

Jiminez produced no scholarly work. While he was somewhat excused from this requirement while working on his Ph.D. he did not complete his Ph.D. in the prescribed time, nor by the time he was given a terminal contract: hence, he cannot take refuge in this safe harbor. Jiminez himself testified that during his entire stint at the college, he never published a single work in a peer-review publication. We note that Jiminez' failure to produce scholarly publications presents a legitimate rationale for issuing a terminal contract. (See *King v. Board of Regents of Univ. of Wis. Sys.* explaining that a Title VII plaintiff "was not qualified for tenure renewal," because she failed to produce "scholarly publications" and noting that scholarship is an integral factor in assessing tenure-type decisions.) As with the other evidence, the district court disregarded the fact that Jiminez had defaulted on this obligation and in so doing, clearly erred.

We hold that Jiminez failed to satisfy the obligations imposed on him in that he failed to prove that he was a victim of invidious discrimination.

The judgment of the district court, therefore, is reversed.

Judgment for Mary Washington College.

Case Commentary

The Fourth Circuit held that Professor Jiminez failed to meet the requirements for tenure in that during the time allotted, he did not receive his

Ph.D. nor did he publish any scholarly works. Therefore, Jiminez's Title VII race discrimination suit is without merit because he is not qualified.

Case Questions

1. Was the Fourth Circuit correct in reversing the District Court's decision?
2. Are the tenure requirements of this college a business necessity and job related?

3. Do you believe the college's reasoning was pretextual; in other words, was the real reason for not granting professor Jiminez tenure his race?

The issue in the following case is whether an African-American female did not receive her promotion to full professor because of race discrimination.

CASE

BICKERSTAFF v. VASSAR COLLEGE

196 F.3d 435 (2nd Cir. 1999)

McAVOY, Chief District Judge.

Plaintiff Joyce Bickerstaff appeals from a final judgment of the United States District Court for the Southern District of New York, Charles L. Brieant, Judge, dismissing her complaint alleging that defendant Vassar College ("Vassar") denied her request for promotion to full professor because of her race and sex, in violation of Title VII of the Civil Rights Act of 1964 ("Title VII"). The district court granted summary judgment dismissing the complaint on the ground that Vassar had presented a sufficiently supported nondiscriminatory reason for denying Bickerstaff promotion and Bickerstaff had not produced evidence that the reason advanced was pretextual. On appeal, Bickerstaff contends that summary judgment was improper because the district court overlooked and misconstrued a vast array of evidence establishing genuine issues of material fact as to whether Vassar's decision to deny her promotion to full professor was race and sex-based. Finding no basis for reversal, we affirm.

I. BACKGROUND

The facts of this case, taken in the light most favorable to Bickerstaff as the party against whom summary judgment was granted, are as follows.

Vassar is a private educational institution, chartered in 1863, and located in Poughkeepsie, New York. Dr. Bickerstaff, an African-American female, was hired by Vassar as a lecturer with a joint appointment in the Africana Studies Program and the Education Department in 1971. Her joint appointment was originally allocated two-thirds to the Department of Education and one-third to the Africana Studies Program. That allocation was later reversed. Upon earning a Ph.D. in 1975, Bickerstaff received the rank of Assistant Professor at Vassar. In 1978, Vassar promoted Bickerstaff to the rank of Associate Professor and granted her tenure.

In 1989, Bickerstaff sought promotion to full professor, which Vassar denied. Bickerstaff appealed to Vassar's Appeal Committee ("VAC"), which rejected her challenge. No litigation ensued. Between 1989 and 1994, Bickerstaff published no scholarly articles. Bickerstaff spent the entire 1990-91 and 1991-92 academic years on leave as a visiting professor at Berea College. In 1994, Bickerstaff again sought promotion to full professor, which Vassar denied. The present litigation ensued concerning the denial in 1994 only. We thus review Vassar's procedures for promotion and the events surrounding Bickerstaff's application in 1994 for full professor.

A. Vassar's Criteria and Procedures for Promotion to Full Professor

To achieve promotion to full professor, the Vassar Faculty Handbook requires a candidate to meet the following posted criteria:

Continued demonstration of sound scholarship or significant artistic activity and teaching of a high quality will be required. It is necessary that marked distinction will have been reached in scholarship or teaching, preferably in both.

An additional important consideration will be academic leadership, which may be evidenced by participation in professional activities outside the College, service on committees within the College, or contributions to educational innovation or policy making at both the departmental and college levels. Vassar's procedures for promotion are established in its bylaws and are set forth in the Faculty Handbook. For a candidate such as Bickerstaff with a joint appointment, the review is a diffusive process that involves several steps and multiple recommenders. First, "two members of rank higher than that of the member under consideration each from the home department (e.g., the chair and one other) and from the multidisciplinary program . . . meet to evaluate the professional qualifications of the candidate." Second, members of the program and the department confer and "make a written report of their deliberations," which is transmitted to the program, the department, the college-wide Faculty Appointments and Salary Committee ("FASC"), the Dean of the Faculty, and the President. Third, "the program and the department . . . take this report into consideration in making their own separate recommendations to FASC, the Dean and the President." Fourth, FASC and the Dean, upon consideration of the departmental and program recommendations, the teaching evaluation of the Student Advisory Committee ("SAC"), the committee reports of the department and the program, and the reports of the outside evaluators, make separate recommendations to the President. Lastly, the President submits her final recommendation to the Board of Trustees. In instances "when the department or the program has fewer than two members of rank higher then that of the person under consideration, an ad hoc committee is formed in each case." These procedures "are designed to accommodate recommendations from both the department and program." An appeal is available to VAC, comprised exclusively of members of the Vassar faculty.

B. Bickerstaff's Review for Promotion to Full Professor in 1994–1995

At issue is Bickerstaff's review for promotion to full professor over the 1994–95 academic year. On November 14, 1994, SAC, which is charged with reviewing student Course Evaluation Questionnaires ("CEQs") and issuing its analysis and recommendation on promotional applications, issued a 5-0 (with one abstention) recommendation against promotion for Bickerstaff. SAC stated that it was alarmed by Bickerstaff's recently "remarkably low" CEQs and that "the only identified trend is a steady decline in evaluations." SAC added that it "is so concerned at Bickerstaff's performance that it feels her present status as an associate Professor deserves reexamination by the College."

On November 28, 1994, a group consisting of the ad hoc Education Committee ("Education Committee") and the ad hoc Africana Studies Committee ("AS Committee") met to discuss Bickerstaff's qualifications for promotion. Vassar asserts that, in accordance with its bylaws, it convened the two ad hoc committees to review Bickerstaff for promotion because the Africana Studies Program and the Education Department each had fewer than two members of rank higher than hers. The meeting between the two committees was memorialized in a written report dated November 30, 1994, which generally discussed her candidacy, without reaching any firm conclusions, under the criteria of scholarship, teaching, and service.

On December 2, 1994, the three-member AS Committee unanimously recommended Bickerstaff for promotion to full professor. As past committees had done when reviewing other faculty for promotion, the AS Committee examined Bickerstaff's scholarship and teaching under a "broader" lens that it deemed more reflective of her real contributions, which included "nontraditional scholarship" and her role outside the classroom as an "educator." The AS Committee stated, in pertinent part, that: Bickerstaff more than any other faculty member in the Africana Studies Program provided the constant vision and guidance, regardless of whether she was the program director. The toll on her time and energy in establishing a new area of study at Vassar is another reason for viewing her scholarly contributions in a different light.

In terms of Bickerstaff's classroom teaching, however, the AS Committee did find "problems" as reflected in her CEQs. Thus, it urged her to "refocus and reinvigorate her efforts in the classroom." In the end, the AS Committee concluded that Bickerstaff had made "distinctive contributions to scholarship" and that she had "a constant and consistent educational vision through all of her work as educator, scholar, and consultant."

On December 5, 1994, the three-member Education Committee issued its report. In assessing her scholarship, it too viewed Bickerstaff's work in a "broader" context, and remarked positively on a number of Bickerstaff's specific achievements. But as to teaching, the Education Committee stated that Bickerstaff's CEQs placed her "considerably lower than what would be expected of a faculty member at Vassar in order to receive a marked distinction in teaching." In unanimously recommending against promotion, the Education Committee concluded that Bickerstaff's scholarly activities, while "creditable," did not exhibit "marked distinction" and that her teaching fell short of "marked distinction by a rather wide margin."

The three outside evaluators asked to assess Bickerstaff's scholarship and service (they were not asked to assess her teaching) unanimously recommended her for promotion to full professor. The outside evaluators commended Bickerstaff's commitment to the Africana Studies Program at Vassar and, more generally, recognized her as a national leader in her field.

On December 7, 1994, the three-member FASC issued its report unanimously recommending against Bickerstaff for promotion, stating that the members found that "she did not meet the stated criteria for promotion." With regard to Bickerstaff's scholarship, FASC noted that there was just one piece of traditional scholarship in her dossier. "Overall, it found Ms. Bickerstaff's scholarship to be exceptionally thin." With respect to her teaching, FASC noted that Bickerstaff's CEQs were declining and that, of recent, were "dismally low, among the very worst" that the FASC members had seen. It concluded that her teaching did not exhibit "high quality, much less . . . marked distinction." On January 23, 1995, a joint meeting was held in which FASC, the Dean and the President met with the AS Committee.

Dean Kalin recommended against promotion for Bickerstaff because she did not meet the posted criteria of marked distinction in teaching. In his affidavit, he states that "her teaching evaluations are among the poorest he has seen in a promotional review for full professor."

On February 8, 1995, the President of Vassar wrote to Bickerstaff and informed her that she would not be recommending her for promotion to the rank of full professor. While acknowledging Bickerstaff's contribution to the Africana Studies Program at Vassar, the President expressed concerns relating to her teaching and scholarship. The President wrote that her classroom teaching was "uneven" and that "the most recent reports indicate a significant decline in classroom effectiveness." The President also stated that while she agreed with the outside evaluators that Bickerstaff's service to the educational community and to Vassar has been significant, Vassar "requires the achievement of 'marked distinction' in at least teaching or scholarship, a standard which has not yet been met." The President concluded that "while service is certainly important, it cannot alone compensate for limitations in both these areas."

Bickerstaff filed an appeal of the denial of promotion to VAC, claiming that Vassar's appointment of two ad hoc committees violated its written procedures. VAC denied the appeal, stating that in the event of a joint appointment, its written procedures provide for a recommendation from both the Africana Studies Program and the Education Department.

In the academic year 1994-95, Vassar considered eight applications for promotion to full professor. Of the six successful candidates, five were women. At present, Bickerstaff continues to teach at Vassar as a tenured associate professor.

C. The Present Action

Following the denial of her request in 1994 for promotion to full professor, Bickerstaff filed charges of race and sex-based discrimination with the Equal Employment Opportunity Commission.

After receiving a right-to-sue letter, on November 29, 1996, Bickerstaff timely filed a complaint against Vassar in the United States District Court for the Southern District of New York. The complaint claimed that she was denied promotion to full professor in 1994 because of her race and sex, in violation of Title VII of the Civil Rights Act of 1964. It also alleged that Vassar denied her promotion in 1994 in retaliation for her internal appeal of the denial of her promotion to full professor; and that Vassar paid her less than male professors of comparable rank, in violation of the Equal Pay Act. The complaint sought monetary damages and an order granting her the rank of full professor at Vassar. After discovery, Vassar moved for summary judgment on all of Bickerstaff's claims. On January 26, 1998, the district court granted Vassar's motion for summary judgment and dismissed the complaint in its entirety.

II. DISCUSSION

A violation of Title VII can be shown by either direct, statistical or circumstantial evidence. Title VII suits fall into two basic categories: "single issue motivation" and "dual issue motivation" cases. In single issue motivation cases, "the single issue is whether an impermissible reason motivated the adverse action," which courts analyze under the framework first set forth in McDonnell Douglas Corp. v. Green. In dual issue motivation cases, the determination involves "both the issue of whether the plaintiff has proved that an impermissible reason motivated the adverse action and the additional issue of whether the defendant has proved that it would have taken the same action for a permissible reason."

In the instant matter, while Bickerstaff principally treats this as a single issue motivation case pursuant to McDonnell Douglas, she does make passing argument for dual issue motivation treatment under Price Waterhouse. If there had been "policy documents or evidence of statements or actions by decisionmakers at Vassar that may be viewed as directly reflecting the alleged discriminatory attitude," i.e., a "smoking gun," we would agree that this is a dual issue motivation case. But there is not.

As a single issue motivation case, we apply the three-step, burden-shifting paradigm set forth in McDonnell Douglas Applying the paradigm to the present case, we too shall assume in Bickerstaff's favor a prima facie case of sex and race discrimination. Vassar, in turn, has satisfied its burden of production by proffering admissible evidence of a legitimate, nondiscriminatory reason for denying Bickerstaff promotion to full professor—namely, that she did not meet the posted criteria. Thus, the central question presented on this appeal is whether Bickerstaff has presented sufficient admissible evidence from which a rational finder of fact could infer that more likely than not she was the victim of intentional discrimination. We now turn to consider whether Bickerstaff's evidence is sufficient to create an issue of material fact as to whether she was the victim of discrimination.

Statistical Evidence

Bickerstaff submitted to the district court a statistical report from Professor Mary Gray, which addressed two basic questions: whether salaries at Vassar varied due to race or sex, and whether Bickerstaff's CEQs varied based on the racial makeup of her classes. Without attempting to control for such other causes, her assumption that race bias affected the CEQs is untenable. In short, because Gray's statistical evidence does not make it more or less likely that Vassar discriminated against Bickerstaff because of her race or sex, the district court did not abuse its discretion in finding the statistical evidence of no probative value.

Shamba Donovan

She thus asserts that the unfavorable SAC Report, which formed part of the materials reviewed by Vassar's decision makers in evaluating her teaching, was impermissibly tainted with race bias. We recognize that the impermissible bias of a single individual at any stage of the promoting process may taint the ultimate employment decision in violation of Title VII. We find that there is insufficient evidence to raise a reasonable inference that such occurred in this case.

In short, given that Bickerstaff's evidence does not support the reasonable inference that Donovan harbored discriminatory bias, and the absence of evidence establishing any causal link between Donovan's alleged discriminatory bias and Vassar's decision to deny her promotion, we find Bickerstaff's allegation that Donovan infected the promotional review process with racism insufficient to raise a question of material fact.

Alleged Incidences of Disparate Treatment

Bickerstaff has not shown that the creation of two ad hoc committees in her case was a procedural irregularity or, more importantly, that it was either race-related or motivated by retaliation.

Bickerstaff has not presented evidence that an illegal discriminatory motive played a motivating role in Vassar's decision to deny her promotion. Instead, the evidence overwhelmingly supports Vassar's explanation that it denied Bickerstaff promotion for the legitimate, nondiscriminatory reason that she did not satisfy the posted criteria for promotion.

In the final analysis, in response to the evidence that Vassar denied Bickerstaff promotion to full professor because she did not satisfy the criteria for promotion, Bickerstaff does not present sufficient rebuttal evidence from which a rational finder of fact could infer that more likely than not Vassar intentionally discriminated against Bickerstaff because of her race or sex. The district court thus properly granted summary judgment to Vassar College and dismissed Bickerstaff's Title VII and section 1981 claims. Bickerstaff's Equal Pay Act claim, which relies on the statistical evidence that we have already discussed and found that the district court properly discounted, was also properly dismissed.

CONCLUSION

We have considered all of Bickerstaff's arguments on appeal and have found them to be without merit. The judgment of the district court dismissing the complaint is affirmed.

Case Commentary

The Second Circuit Court of Appeals concluded that Professor Bickerstaff did not meet Vassar's job-related requirements for promotion to full professor because student evaluations of her teaching were not of the high caliber required of a full professor. Furthermore, the court held that the alleged racial prejudice of one student on the Student Advisory Committee was not proven. Finally, the statistical evidence introduced by Bickerstaff was not probative of whether Vassar had discriminated against Bickerstaff and denied her equal pay.

Case Questions

1. Was Bickerstaff entitled to the full professorship?
2. What do you think about the differences in the student evaluations in the African Studies classes and the Education classes?

3. Was there evidence of race discrimination?
4. Did a violation of the Equal Pay Act exist?

EMPLOYMENT PERSPECTIVE

Fishers Oil Drilling Equipment prides itself on being an equal opportunity employer because it has numerous employees of all races. However, the minority employees are all factory workers. Each time a minority worker applies for a managerial position, he or she is rejected. Fisher feels that it is better that the minorities work among their own kind. Is this racial discrimination? Yes! Fisher Oil is prejudicing the ability and competence of its minority workers on the basis of the color of their skin or of their origin. Fisher Oil may know that its white managers may feel uncomfortable with minorities working with them rather than underneath them, but this privilege of racial dominance can no longer be sustained. Everyone must be given an equal opportunity. ■

The issue in the following case is whether the plaintiff may commence an action under the First, Fifth, and Fourteenth Amendments where he is time barred from suing under Title VII.

BELHOMME v. WIDNALL, SECRETARY OF THE AIR FORCE

127 F.3d 1214 (10th Cir. 1997)

EBEL, Circuit Judge.

The appellant challenges the dismissal of his statutory and constitutional claims arising out of his termination from a civilian position with the Air Force at Kirtland Air Force Base. Although we differ in some respects from the district court's rationale, we affirm the district court's judgment on all of the appellant's claims: Renaud Belhomme, a black of Haitian national origin, was hired by the Air Force to work as a front desk clerk in the billeting office at Kirtland Air Force Base. On December 16, 1988, less than two months after Mr. Belhomme began work, the Air Force fired him for insubordination. The record reflects that this insubordination consisted of Mr. Belhomme's failure to answer the phone when directed to do so, and his failure to come to his supervisor's office promptly upon being requested to do so, considered against a backdrop of other complaints against Mr. Belhomme.

Mr. Belhomme complained that his firing actually resulted from his supervisor's racial and national-origin discrimination. An internal investigation by the Air Force Civilian Appellate Review Agency confirmed Mr. Belhomme's characterization of his supervisor as rude and abrasive, and that Mr. Belhomme had been criticized for his French Caribbean accent. The investigation concluded, however, that Mr. Belhomme's termination was not motivated by illegal discrimination.

On June 21, 1991, the Air Force issued its proposed determination of no illegal discrimination in Mr. Belhomme's case. Mr. Belhomme requested a hearing, which was held before an administrative law judge of the EEOC on August 16, 1991. The judge issued her bench decision that Mr. Belhomme was not the victim of illegal discrimination, as its final agency action. On January 6, 1992, Mr. Belhomme appealed the Air Force's decision to the EEOC.

The EEOC issued its decision affirming the Air Force's conclusions on August 13, 1992. The notice informed Mr. Belhomme that he had thirty days from his receipt of the decision either to file a civil action in district court or to file a request under the Commission's regulations to reopen the case. Mr. Belhomme received his copy of the decision by certified mail on August 17, 1992, giving him until September 16, 1992, to respond. Two days after this deadline, on September 18, 1992, Mr. Belhomme filed a petition to reopen the EEOC case. On April 29, 1993, the Commission denied the petition as untimely. In this denial, the commission again informed Mr. Belhomme that he had a right to file a civil action in district court to challenge the underlying Air Force decision within thirty days.

Thirty-five days later, on June 2, 1993, Mr. Belhomme filed this action, denominated as a class action, alleging violations of his rights under Title VII and the First, Fifth and Fourteenth Amendment to the United States Constitution. The district court converted the motion of the Secretary of the Air Force for judgment on the pleadings into a motion for summary judgment and granted judgment in favor of the Secretary. The court found that Mr. Belhomme had not filed his petition to reopen the EEOC case within the time set.

A federal employee who claims that he was the victim of illegal employment discrimination may bring a claim in district court under Title VII.

As a prerequisite to his suit,(1) the federal employee must file an administrative complaint concerning his allegations, and he may not bring his suit more than ninety days after receiving a final decision from either his employing agency or from the EEOC. Under the EEOC's administrative rules, a complainant may file a petition to reopen his case within thirty days of receiving the EEOC's final action.

In this case, Mr. Belhomme's petition to reopen his EEOC case was filed two days after the EEOC's thirty-day administrative deadline. Thus, Mr. Belhomme's petition was not timely. The district court properly dismissed Mr. Belhomme's individual claim pursuant to Title VII.

The district court did not address Mr. Belhomme's claims under the Constitution, but we believe that these claims also are without merit. First, Mr. Belhomme's claims under the Constitution fail because the Supreme Court has clearly stated that a federal employee's only avenue for judicial relief from federal employment discrimination is through Title VII. As a result, Title VII preempts any constitutional cause of action that a court might find under the First or Fifth Amendments for discrimination in federal employment.

Judgment for Widnall,
Secretary of the Air Force.

Case Commentary

The Court held that Belhomme did not file a timely claim for discrimination under Title VII. Furthermore, it stated that Title VII was the only method by which a federal employee could file a discrimination claim.

Case Questions

1. Do you believe the Court treated Belhomme fairly?
2. Should federal employees be able to sue for discrimination under the First, Fifth, and Fourteenth Amendments?
3. Do you think the limits for filing should be extended?

EMPLOYMENT PERSPECTIVE

Marshall Jackson, who is black, has been a sales representative for Tucker Machinery Corp. for 20 years. His district has a predominantly black population. He has applied for promotion to sales manager. Although his credentials are superior to those of the other candidates, Jackson is overlooked because management feels that he will not command the respect of the sales force, which is overwhelmingly white. Is this employment discrimination? Yes! Tucker Machinery has violated Title VII because the sole reason that Jackson was not selected was because he was black. Jackson would be entitled to the promotion, together with the pay differential from the date when he should have been selected. ■

In the case that follows, a black male claimed he was discharged from his position as a disc jockey because of his race. He satisfied his initial burden under the McDonnell Douglas test. The employer, in turn, met its burden of justifiable action. The question presented is whether the employer's reason for discharge was a pretext.

THOMPSON v. PRICE BROADCASTING CO.

817 F. Supp. 1538 (D. Utah 1993)

ANDERSON, District Judge.

Wayne Thompson (hereafter "Thompson") brought this race discrimination action against his former employer, Price Broadcasting Company KCPX (hereafter referred to as "Price" or "KCPX"), for allegedly discharging him in violation of Title VII of the 1964 Civil Rights Act.

Thompson is a 36-year-old African male who has worked since 1980 in the broadcasting industry. During that time Thompson has worked in radio production, and has acted as a radio personality ("Jockey"). As a Disk Jockey, Thompson is aware that listeners develop listening habits and loyalty to radio stations because of the particular personalities involved. Thus, radio stations require their Disk Jockeys to make every effort possible to be at work in sufficient time to go "on the air" for assigned time slots.

On October 14, 1988, Thompson was hired by Price to work part time as a KCPX Jockey for the Sunday afternoon time slot 2:00 p.m. to 9:00 p.m. Prior to working for Price, Thompson worked as a Disk Jockey for Radio Station KDAB in Ogden, Utah, where Thompson resided. KCPX is located in Salt Lake City, Utah, and Thompson agreed to provide his own transportation to and from work on Sundays.

Shortly after going to work for Price, Thompson brought a Title VII lawsuit against his former employer KDAB for allegedly firing him because of his race. This lawsuit was publicized in the local newspapers, and a copy of an article relating to the suit was cut out by an unknown employee of Price, and placed on the desk of supervisor David Leppink, whose radio name is Morgan Evans (hereafter "Evans"). Evans acknowledged seeing the article, but testified that it played no part in his decision making with regard to Thompson.

A few days after the local newspapers publicized Thompson's suit against KDAB, a snow storm hit the northern parts of Utah. By 4:00 p.m., Mountain Standard Time, on Saturday, November 26, 1988, driving conditions in the Ogden area became hazardous as a result of snowy and icy roads. Thompson, being concerned about the driving conditions, telephoned Evans' home at 4:43 p.m. to inform Evans that he would not be coming into KCPX the next day for his radio slot. Evans was not home, and Thompson left a message on Evans' answering machine.

When Evans returned home at approximately 4:50 p.m. he listened to the telephone message from Thompson and telephoned Thompson's house. Mrs. Thompson answered the telephone, and informed Evans that her husband was not at home, and was at Lionel Playworld in Ogden where he had a second job. Evans informed Mrs. Thompson that roads in Salt Lake City were not too bad, and that he expected Thompson to be at work at 2:00 p.m. the next day. Evans further informed Mrs. Thompson that she should contact her husband to tell him that he was expected to report to work, and that if there was a problem Thompson should call Evans to talk about it.

Mrs. Thompson did as she was instructed and telephoned Evans' home thirty minutes later with her husband's reply. Evans had gone out, however, and Mrs. Thompson had to leave another message on Evans' answering machine. She stated that her husband still felt the same way, and that he would not be coming into work the next day. Five hours later, when Evans returned home and listened to his messages, Evans telephoned Mrs. Thompson to get Thompson's telephone number at Lionel Playworld.

When Evans spoke with Thompson at Lionel Playworld, he asked Thompson what the problem was. Thompson responded that KCPX did not pay him enough to risk his life driving down to Salt Lake City to do a shift. Evans responded that he needed someone he could count on every Sunday, regardless of the weather. When Thompson stated he would not be coming down to Salt Lake City the next day for the 2:00 p.m. shift, Evans fired him.

Following his firing by KCPX, Thompson brought race discrimination claims against Price before the Anti-Discrimination Division of the Industrial Commission of Utah ("ICU") and the Equal Opportunity Commission of the United States ("EEOC"). The ICU and EEOC found no basis for Thompson's discrimination charges.

There are two theories of employment discrimination under Title VII: disparate treatment and disparate impact. The disparate treatment theory focuses on the employer's intent to discriminate. Disparate impact, on the other hand, requires no proof of discriminatory intent. Rather, a plaintiff need only show that the employer's practices are "discriminatory in operation."

At trial, Thompson only sought relief for disparate treatment under Title VII, specifically, discriminatory discharge and retaliatory discharge. Consequently, Thompson needed to show discriminatory intent on the part of Price. Thompson failed to do so.

Title VII of the 1964 Civil Rights Act makes it unlawful for an employer to discharge any individual, or to otherwise discriminate against any individual . . . because of such individual's race.

To establish a prima facie case for discrimination under Title VII, the plaintiff must show that: (1) he belongs to a protected group; (2) he was qualified for his job; (3) he was terminated despite his qualifications; and (4) after his termination, the employer hired someone or sought applicants for the plaintiff's vacated position, whose qualifications were no better than the Plaintiff's.

The court is persuaded that Thompson met the burden of establishing a prima facie case of discriminatory discharge. In that regard, Thompson, an African-American, is a member of a protected class. Further, Price did not dispute that Thompson was qualified for the Disk Jockey job. Price conceded that Thompson has been involved in the radio broadcast industry for a number of years, and had performed his job at KCPX for six weeks without complaint from management as to his performance. Despite being qualified for the job, Thompson was discharged. Finally, while there

was a dispute between the parties as to who took over Thompson's radio time slot, there is no question that someone handled the air time.

The Court is also persuaded that Thompson met his burden to establish a prima facie cause of action for retaliatory discharge under Title VII of the 1964 Civil Rights Act. The Act provides:

> It shall be unlawful . . . for an employer to discriminate against any of his employees . . . because the employee has made a charge, testified, assisted, or participated in any manner in an investigation, proceeding, or hearing under this subchapter.

The Tenth Circuit Court of Appeals has held that in order for a plaintiff to establish a prima facie cause of action for retaliation, the plaintiff must show by a preponderance of the evidence that: (1) Plaintiff engaged in protected opposition to discrimination or participation in a proceeding arising out of discrimination; (2) adverse action by the employer subsequent to the protected activity; and (3) a causal connection between the employee's activity and the adverse action.

Thompson established that he was engaged in a protected activity at the time of his discharge from KCPX. In that regard, although there exists no business relationship between KDAB, the station against whom Thompson brought his discrimination suit and KCPX, the law does not require such a relationship. If a relationship between employers was required, claimants would be discouraged from filing discrimination claims against former employers because of the fear that their present employers, upon learning of the claims, would fire them. The purposes of Title VII would, therefore, be frustrated.

Thompson also established the second requirement of a retaliation claim, by showing that subsequent to his filing of a suit against KDAB, he was fired by Price. Termination of employment clearly constitutes an "adverse action by the employer subsequent to the protected activity."

Finally, Thompson established, as a result of the timing of his discharge by KCPX and the filing of the claim against KDAB, that a causal connection existed between the protected activity and the adverse action, at least for purposes of proving a prima facie case.

A "causal connection may be demonstrated by the proximity of the adverse action to the protected activity, provided, the employer . . . had knowledge of the plaintiff's protected activity."

Having found a prima facie case for Thompson's discriminatory discharge claim and retaliatory discharge claim, the burden of production shifts to Price to show "a legitimate non-discriminatory reason for terminating the employee."

In meeting its burden, Price need not prove that it was actually motivated by its non-discriminatory reason.

As noted by the United States Supreme Court:

> "The burden that shifts to the defendant, therefore, is to rebut the presumption of discrimination by producing evidence that the plaintiff was rejected . . . for a legitimate, nondiscriminatory reason. The defendant need not persuade the court that it was actually motivated by the proffered reasons. . . . It is sufficient if the defendant's evidence raises a genuine issue of fact as to whether it discriminated against the plaintiff. To accomplish this, the defendant must clearly set forth, through the introduction of admissible evidence the reasons for the plaintiff's rejection. The explanation must be legally sufficient to justify a judgment for the defendant.

The question of Price's actual motivation is only addressed after Price shows a legitimate nondiscriminatory reason for termination, and the burden of proof shifts back to Thompson under McDonnell Douglas.

At trial, Price presented credible evidence that on the day before Thompson was to report to work, Thompson telephoned his superior at KCPX, Morgan Evans, to inform Evans that he was not going to come to work because of adverse weather conditions. Evans informed Thompson that the weather was not that bad, and that he expected him to report to work. When Thompson continued to refuse to come to work, he was fired.

A refusal to work is a legitimate nondiscriminatory reason for terminating an employee. In *E.E.O.C. v. Wendy's of Colorado Springs, Inc.,* the reason for terminating the employee that Defendant articulated was that he "refused to work necessary time periods necessary to meet store needs." Refusal to work the time periods necessary to meet the demands of business demonstrates a lack of qualification for the job. Lack of qualifications is a legitimate, nondiscriminatory reason for terminating an employee.

In the radio broadcast industry, management is constantly concerned with the concept of "listener expectation." That concept is that listeners have expectations that when they tune to a certain radio station at a certain time, a particular music or news format will be in the process of being presented, and that a certain disk jockey will be on the air. By consistently fulfilling the listener's expectations, the radio station keeps the listener's loyalty, and can ask advertisers to pay for the privilege of broadcasting their messages to the listener. For this reason, broadcast employers legitimately expect their Disk Jockeys to make every effort possible to be on the air when scheduled. Thompson was unable to satisfy Price that he would make that effort. The Court determines, therefore, that Price had a legitimate reason to terminate Thompson.

Price did not discuss the KDAB suit with Thompson and did not look for an excuse to fire Thompson after finding out about the lawsuit. On the contrary, the evidence shows that when Evans was first informed by Thompson that Thompson was not coming in to work the next day, Evans did not fire Thompson but, rather, gave Thompson an opportunity to say that he would be coming into work. The Court is convinced that if Thompson had simply informed Evans on November 26, 1988, that he would be at the radio station for his assigned time slot on Sunday, Thompson would not have been fired. Even if Evans "had in mind" the KDAB lawsuit at the time that he fired Thompson, and there is no direct evidence that he did, Thompson's Title VII claim would still fail.

As noted by the Tenth Circuit Court of Appeals:

> Once a plaintiff in a Title VII case shows that an illegitimate reason played a motivating part in an employment decision, the defendant may avoid a finding of liability only by proving that it would have made the same decision even if it had not allowed the improper motive to play such a role.

The Court finds that Price would have discharged Thompson on November 21, 1988, even if no lawsuit had been filed by Thompson against his former employer, KDAB. Price needed Disk Jockeys that it could count on to make every reasonable effort possible to make their assigned shifts regardless of the weather. Thompson was not willing to make that effort.

While Thompson established a prima facie case under Title VII on both his retaliatory discharge and discriminatory discharge claims, he was unable to show by a preponderance of the evidence that Price's legitimate nondiscriminatory reason for discharge was a pretext. No violation of Title VII was shown and judgment will be entered for the defendant.

Judgment for Price Broadcasting.

Case Commentary

The District Court of Utah determined that Thompson's discharge for not arriving at work due to a snowstorm was not evidence of discrimination due to race.

Case Questions

1. Do you agree with the Court's decision?

2. Was the snowstorm a legitimate excuse?

RACIAL HARASSMENT

Racial harassment in the workplace exists when conduct by coworkers, superiors, or the company itself has created a hostile work environment in which the victimized employee's ability to do his or her job has been impaired. Evidence of the severity of the incidents is equally as important as the frequency.

When an employee claims that he or she is being racially harassed by a coworker, the employee must notify the employer. The employer must not condone this activity and must investigate the complaint in a timely fashion. If the employer finds a reasonable basis for believing that the harassment exists, it must take corrective action immediately, or otherwise it will be held liable. When the harassment originates with the employer itself, then no notification is needed. The employer will be held liable.

EMPLOYMENT SCENARIO

One day, Greg, Sam, and Bill, all white employees, were exchanging racial jokes during their break. Mark Short, while passing by, stopped to listen, then joined in, telling a few racial jokes of his own.

Tim Jackson, a black employee, overheard the laughter, and listened in. He became visibly upset and approached Mark with his concerns. Mark put his arm around Tim's shoulder and dismissed the jokes as harmless fun. Mark told Tim to ignore the jokes and to take a walk around the block. These episodes continued to occur and Tom and Mark continued to ignore Tim's complaints of a hostile work environment. Tim filed a racial harassment complaint with the EEOC. When they learned that the EEOC intended to investigate Tim's allegations, Tom and Mark sought Susan North's counsel. Susan responded that their cavalier attitude toward employment law had once again embroiled them in a conflict unrelated to the business of selling clothing. Susan recommended a full apology to Tim by those concerned; an educational seminar for all employees on race discrimination and harassment, which she would facilitate; and a company policy, which she would draft, defining discrimination and harassment affecting race and its prohibition during the scope of employment. Susan said she hoped this would appease Tim and the EEOC, and serve as a strong lesson to Tom, Mark, and the participating employees, that racial harassment would not be tolerated and that the consequences for any reoccurrence would be severe. Susan believed these steps would serve as an impetus for modifying the behavior of the participants.

EMPLOYMENT PERSPECTIVE

Todd Washington was hired as a management trainee in Bulls and Bears Brokerage House. He was the first black person in a managerial position in the Jackson, Mississippi, office. Towards the end of the first week, he found his desk covered by a white sheet with a burnt cross lying across it. Washington complained to his superiors, who told him that the boys just have a warped sense of humor. Similar incidents followed. Does this constitute racial harassment? Yes! Todd Washington was harassed by his coworkers. He made a timely complaint to his employer, which made no attempt to investigate and took no corrective action. For its failure to act, Bulls and Bears is liable. ■

The question presented in the following case is whether racial comments made by coworkers were severe and pervasive, thus rendering the employer guilty of condoning a hostile work environment based on racial harassment.

CASE

BROWN v. COACH STORES, INC.

163 F.3d 706 (2nd Cir. 1998)

PARKER, Circuit Judge.

Plaintiff-Appellant Marva Brown appeals from the judgment of the United States District Court for the Southern District of New York (Jed S. Rakoff, *Judge*), entered September 22, 1997, dismissing Brown's claims under Title VII of the Civil Rights Act of 1964 ("Title VII") that Defendant-Appellee Coach Stores, Inc. ("Coach") discriminated against her on the basis of her race. The district court held that Brown's second amended complaint failed to state a claim because Brown neglected to allege that she applied for, was qualified for and was rejected from, any specific position or positions at Coach. The court also held that Brown failed to adequately allege a claim of disparate impact.

I. BACKGROUND

Marva Brown is an African-American who has worked as a receptionist in Coach's Human Resource Department at its headquarters in Manhattan since 1988. In December 1996, Brown, through her attorney, filed a Notice of Charge of Discrimination with the Equal Employment Opportunity Commission ("EEOC"). In this charge, she claimed that despite repeated requests to be promoted, Coach had refused to promote her and had instead promoted dozens of non-minority employees and "scarcely any" minorities. She also claimed that one of her co-employees at Coach told her that she looked "black like a real nigger" when she returned from a vacation, a comment for which the employee was not sanctioned, and that she was routinely excluded from business meetings and holiday parties held by her department.

In January 1997, Brown filed a complaint in the district court asserting claims under Title VII. Specifically, Brown contended that in August 1995 and August 1996 she requested a promotion during her annual evaluation. According to the second amended complaint, during her employment with Coach she was qualified for promotion to "dozens to hundreds" of open positions including "secretary," "administrative assistant" and "human resources assistant." Brown asserted that she was told repeatedly by supervisors that she was "too valuable in her current position to promote."

Brown alleged that she was told by her supervisors that Coach "seeks to hire and promote people who have a 'Coach look'—the examples to whom her supervisors referred were young non-minority persons." Further, Brown alleged that one of her supervisors made several discriminatory remarks about minorities. The second amended complaint also made allegations which were not asserted in the original EEOC charge regarding Coach's employment practices toward minorities as a whole. Brown points to EEOC statistics which show a low proportion of minority employees in management positions at Coach. Thus, Brown claims that Coach's hiring and promotion practices have a discriminatory impact on minorities. The district court granted Coach's motion to dismiss, dismissing the second amended complaint with prejudice. The court found that Brown had failed to state a prima facie case of discrimination under *McDonnell Douglas Corp. v. Green* because "nowhere . . . does the Amended Complaint allege any specific position for which plaintiff applied, was qualified, and was rejected." The court noted that in the hearing on the motion to dismiss, Brown's counsel conceded that " 'there is no allegation that Ms. Brown asked at a specific time for a specific job.' "

As to Brown's disparate impact claim, the court found her statistics "very general," noting that they failed to take account of the various types of positions at Coach, the qualifications required for promotion and the relevant minority composition of the applicant pool. The court noted that even if the statistics were sufficient to establish disparities in the relevant workpools, Brown's case would fail because she has not alleged a causal relationship between a Coach policy or practice and the underrepresentation of minorities in certain jobs.

Brown filed a timely notice of appeal to this Court.

II. DISCUSSION

Brown argues on appeal that she has adequately pleaded four claims of discrimination: 1) failure to promote, 2) pattern and practice discrimination, 3) disparate impact and 4) hostile environment. We disagree. We hold that Brown's failure to apply and be rejected for a specific position or positions is fatal to her failure to promote and pattern and practice claims. Further, we find Brown's pleadings inadequate to state a disparate impact claim or a hostile environment claim.

Failure to Promote Claim

To establish a prima facie case of disparate impact, a plaintiff must show that a facially neutral employment policy or practice has a significant disparate impact. Allegations which contend only that there is a bottom line racial imbalance in the work force are insufficient.

Brown's allegations of disparate impact fail because they do not adequately allege a causal connection between any facially neutral policy at Coach and the resultant proportion of minority employees. Brown's complaint uses general reports of the EEOC to assert that from 1990 to 1995 the overall percentage of minority employees at Coach headquarters dropped from 30% to 11%, while in 1995 the New York City retail trade employed almost 25% minority employees. Further, the complaint contends that Coach did not employ any minority managers in its headquarters location from 1990-1994 and then in 1995 reported three minority managers.

Brown does not connect these general statistics to any Coach policy. Although Brown asserts that Coach's training and promotion policies deliberately keep minorities from being promoted, those alleged policies seem utterly disconnected from the fact that the overall percentage of minority employees as a whole at Coach dropped between 1990 and 1995 and is less than the percentage of minorities in the retail industry as a whole. The statistics shed no light on whether there is a disparity between the number of minorities in the higher positions at Coach and in the retail industry's higher positions which, if significantly different, could support an inference of discriminatory promotion practices at Coach. Brown fails to connect the statistics with any other policy. As a result, her complaint fails to adequately allege a disparate impact claim.

Hostile Work Environment Claim

On appeal, Brown also argues that she was subjected to a hostile work environment at Coach. This claim was apparently not considered by the district court as it is not plainly articulated in Brown's complaint. The complaint does contend that one Coach supervisor made, on occasion, racist remarks and one such comment was directed at Brown. Again, we find the allegations

in the complaint lacking. Although the alleged comments are despicable and offensive, they fail to constitute discriminatory behavior that is sufficiently severe or pervasive to cause a hostile environment Brown also failed to allege that the remarks unreasonably interfered with her job performance. As a result, she has not alleged a prima facie case of hostile work environment.

III. CONCLUSION

We hereby AFFIRM the decision of the district court dismissing Brown's complaint for failure to state a claim.

Case Commentary

The Second Circuit decided that a person alleging race discrimination who attempts to use statistical evidence to support her case must tie the statistics to the alleged discrimination. Here, Marva Brown asserted that the number of minorities employed in management at Coach was substantially below that in the retail industry, but never connected these sta-

tistics to a specific Coach policy. The Second Circuit also found against Marva Brown on her racial harassment complaint. Although the Court acknowledged the statements were offensive, it said they were not severe and pervasive. In addition, Marva Brown never proved that the statements interfered with the performance of her job.

Case Questions

1. Do you agree with the decision of the Court?
2. Do you understand how Marva Brown was supposed to tie her statistical evidence to her allegations of race discrimination?

3. Do you think the offensive statements were sufficient to constitute racial harassment?

The issue in the following case is whether an employee of Hawaiian ancestry was a victim of ethnic and racial harassment.

CASE

ALOIA v. EASTMAN KODAK COMPANY

No. 96-4113 (10th Cir. 1997)

Before PORFILIO, Circuit Judge, LUCERO, Circuit Judge, and McWILLIAMS, Senior Circuit Judge.
Patrick H. Aloia ("Aloia") was hired by Eastman Kodak Company ("Kodak") on August 8, 1988,

and, after training, was assigned to Kodak's Salt Lake City, Utah, office as a Customer Product Sales Representative. Kodak terminated Aloia's employment on April 29, 1993. On December 8, 1993, Aloia brought suit against Kodak in the United

States District Court for the District of Utah, charging Kodak with breach of contract, retaliatory termination, racial discrimination, intentional inflection of emotional distress, and defamation.

On May 22, 1996, the district court entered a formal order granting summary judgment in favor of Kodak and against Aloia on all of his claims. Aloia appeals. We affirm.

In his complaint, Aloia described himself as being "a person of Hawaiian/Pacific Island parentage and ancestry." In this connection, Aloia in his deposition stated that he was born in the United States, as were his parents, and that his mother was of Irish ancestry and his father of Italian ancestry. Further, according to Aloia, his paternal grandmother was Italian and his biological paternal grandfather was of Portuguese and Polynesian ancestry.

Aloia alleged that in terminating his employment Kodak was "motivated by reasons of race and national origin" in violation of Title VII for which he sought damages in an unspecified amount.

As indicated, Aloia's claim was a Title VII claim of racial harassment in the work place. In granting summary judgment the district court relied primarily on Bolden v. PRC, Inc.

In Bolden, we spoke as follows:

> For Mr. Bolden's harassment claim to survive summary judgment, his facts must support the inference of a racially hostile environment, and support a basis for liability. Specifically, it must be shown that under the totality of the circumstances (1) the harassment was pervasive or severe enough to alter the terms, conditions, or privilege of employment, and (2) the harassment was racial or stemmed from racial animus. General harassment if not racial or sexual is not actionable. The plaintiff must show " 'more than a few isolated incidents of racial enmity.' " Instead of sporadic racial slurs, there must be a steady barrage of opprobrious racial comments.

As indicated, in granting summary judgment on Aloia's claim of racial harassment, the district court, citing Bolden, held that the epithets directed to Aloia, such as "coconut head," the "throwin' Samoan," "Aloha," "Island Boy," and the like, were "occasional" and not pervasive, and that, in any event, the terms and conditions of his employment with Kodak were not in any wise altered by such name calling. In his de-

position, Aloia said that any name calling by his co-workers did not interfere with his job performance, that he did a good job for Kodak, and "enjoyed the hell out of his job with Kodak. It was a great job."

Aloia's termination "was not motivated by racial bias," notwithstanding the fact that in his complaint Aloia alleged that he was terminated "by reasons of race and national origin." The fact that it is now conceded that Aloia's termination was not the result of race or national origin takes much of the steam out of his Title VII claim. In any event, all things considered, the district court did not err in granting summary judgment for Kodak on Aloia's claim of racial harassment.

Aloia worked as a sales representative with Kodak from 1988 until his termination on April 29, 1993. Although there were occasional complaints about Aloia from customers and co-workers along the way, he apparently was a good salesman and his record of sales was good. As indicated, Aloia did have some "run-ins" along the road, he, at times, evidencing a rather short temper and was "confrontational" with co-workers and others. In this connection, Aloia had been given several warnings about his conduct.

The straw that broke the camel's back occurred on April 6, 1993, after a sales meeting which took place in Salt Lake City. Stanley Sukalski, a co-worker at Kodak in Salt Lake City, was 20 minutes late for the meeting, which, for some reason, extremely irritated Aloia, who was also attending the meeting. At the conclusion of the meeting, Aloia confronted Sukalski and publicly berated him, at length. Various obscenities were used, Aloia calling Sukalski, an ignorant SOB. Aloia, in his deposition, denied calling Sukalski a "dumb Polack," although Sukalski, when deposed, testified that Aloia had, indeed, called him a "dumb Polack," more than once. This confrontation resumed in the hallway outside Kodak's offices within earshot of Liberty Mutual, which had offices on the same floor as Kodak. Later, Aloia and Sukalski figuratively "shook hands" and agreed to drop the matter. However, Kodak later took statements from its employees, and conferred with both Aloia and Sukalski. The upshot of all this was that Kodak terminated Aloia on April 29, 1993.

Judgment affirmed.

Case Commentary

The Tenth Circuit ruled that Aloia was not the victim of racial harassment and was properly dismissed. The conduct Aloia complained of was not so severe and pervasive as to constitute a hostile work environment.

Case Questions

1. Do you agree with the Court's decision?
2. Do you consider the epithets directed at Aloia to be severe and pervasive?
3. If you say no, what would you consider to be severe and pervasive?
4. Do you believe Aloia instituted this lawsuit as a result of being terminated because of his conflict with Sukalski?

COLOR DISCRIMINATION

Title VII prohibits discrimination against color in addition to race. Color could apply to people of mixed races, as well as to the different color of pigmentation of people of the same race. In Europe, white people from southern Europe have darker pigmentation than white people from northern Europe. Black, Asian, and Hispanic people have different shades of pigmentation.

EMPLOYMENT PERSPECTIVE

Rachel Blake, who is a dark-skinned black woman, is employed as a teller in the Bank of Los Angeles. Dena Perry, a light-skinned black woman, is the bank manager. For eight years Rachel has been passed over for promotions by whites and light-skinned blacks. Rachel claims that she has been discriminated against by her superior. Dena disagrees, claiming that discrimination cannot exist where both parties are of the same race. Who is correct? Rachel! Dena has discriminated against Rachel because of the color of her skin and not because of her race. ▪

RECONSTRUCTION ACT

Following the abolition of slavery with the passage of the Thirteenth Amendment to the Constitution, Congress passed the Reconstruction Era Act in 1866. The Act provided blacks with the right "to make and enforce contracts . . . as enjoyed by white citizens." The right to make and enforce contracts includes employment contracts. The Civil Rights Act of 1991 has amended and incorporated this Act within it. There are several distinctions between bringing a claim under the Reconstruction Act and under Title VII.

Title VII applies to employers with 15 or more employees. The Reconstruction Act applies to all employees. Title VII has a statute of limitations for filing. The Reconstruction Act does not. Title VII places monetary limitations on the recovery of compensatory and punitive damages. The Reconstruction Act has no such limitations.

The availability of the Reconstruction Act is limited to race, color, and national origin. It does not apply to sex, religion, disability, or age. The reason that not all claims for racial discrimination are filed under the Reconstruction Act is that there is a more stringent requirement for proving intentional discrimination. Under Title VII, proving intentional discrimination is not required, only that a disparate impact exists.

EMPLOYMENT PERSPECTIVE

The Beanery, a cafeteria-style restaurant, required that all employees be clean-shaven and free of facial hair. Because Edward Jordan refused to shave his beard, he was discharged. Jordan sued under the Reconstruction Act. His claim was based on the fact that many black men have a facial skin condition that becomes very irritated when they shave. To require them to do so is discriminatory. Will he win? No! Jordan will be unable to prove that the Beanery's requirement was intended to discriminate purposely against black men. He would be better off instituting a claim for disparate impact under Title VII, where no intent on the part of the employer is required. If Jordan sued under Title VII, he would most likely win. However, if more than 180 days from the date of his discharge has elapsed, he will be barred from proceeding under Title VII because of its statute of limitations. ■

U.S. CONSTITUTION

The Fifth Amendment to the U.S. Constitution provides that no person shall be deprived of "life, liberty or property, without due process of the law." This Amendment, which originally applied only to the federal government, was later applied to the states through the Fourteenth Amendment. The Fourteenth Amendment also guarantees to all persons "the equal protection of the laws." Bringing an action under the Constitution does not relieve a party from the statute of limitations under Title VII. The amendments only embellish the validity of the argument against discrimination.

The following case addresses the question of whether the equal protection clause is applicable to black applicants who were equally qualified with the white applicants selected for the position in question.

CASE

SIMS v. MONTGOMERY COUNTY COM'N

887 F. Supp. 1479 (M.D.Ala. 1995)

THOMPSON, Chief Judge.

This litigation consists of two consolidated class-action lawsuits . . . a class of black employees sought relief from the Montgomery County Sheriff's Department's racially discriminatory employment practices.

On December 15 and 16, 1993, the Sheriff's Department made its selections for promotion to sergeant and lieutenant from among the candidates in band A, the highest band, certified for each rank. Ten white males, one African-American male, and one African-American female scored in the sergeant's band A certification, and two white males, one white female, and one African-American female scored in the lieutenant's band A certification. Because there were no court-approved guidelines to govern the choice of candidates considered equally qualified within a band, the department's selections "were made with consideration of any adverse impact as to race or gender and thereafter, based upon seniority first as to 'time in grade' and second as to time served as a deputy sheriff." The department selected two white males, Robert L. Ingram and Mark C. Thompson, for promotion to sergeant and lieutenant in the enforcement division.

On December 21, 1993, the Sims plaintiffs and the Scott intervenors objected to the selection of two white males, and moved to enjoin the selections. They alleged, among other things, that the Sheriff's Department's selections from within the bands was "unaided by any judicially approved guidelines and was based on seniority, as the determining factor . . . , thereby perpetuating the Department's proven policy and practice of discriminating against African-Americans, who were not even employed in the enforcement division until 1988 and remain woefully under-represented in the 'rank' positions of Sergeant and Lieutenant."

On October 20, 1994, the Sims plaintiffs, the Scott intervenors, and the defendants moved for approval of an agreement settling the Sims plaintiffs' and the Scott intervenors' objection to the 1993 selections for promotion to sergeant and lieutenant. Under the agreement, in addition to the two whites selected for promotion to sergeant and lieutenant, the department must select two African-Americans from the top scoring band of most qualified candidates.

Under the equal protection clause, this court must apply strict scrutiny to race conscious relief voluntarily implemented by a public employer. . . . The Sims plaintiffs, the Scott intervenors, and the defendants contend that strict scrutiny analysis is not required because all those in the sergeant and lieutenant bands from which the African-Americans are to be selected are equally qualified, that is, African-Americans were not selected over more qualified whites. The court agrees with the Sims plaintiffs, the Scott intervenors, and the defendants that African-Americans were not selected over more qualified whites. The record is clear that all those in band A for both the sergeant and lieutenant positions were equally qualified.

Judgment for Sims.

Case Commentary

In *Sims*, the Middle District Court of Alabama decided that the black employees selected were not less qualified than the white employees who were passed over. Therefore, the selection process was not in violation of the Equal Protection Clause of the Fourteenth Amendment.

Case Questions

1. Do you believe the court decided this case correctly?
2. Is the selection of equally qualified black candidates sufficient to satisfy the Equal Protection Clause?
3. How is it possible that all of the candidates in band A were equally qualified?

❖ EMPLOYER LESSONS

- Be cognizant of race in the selection, compensation, and promotion process.
- Apprise yourself of the proportion of minority groups in the area from which you hire your workers.
- Treat all workers equally.
- Do not discriminate because of race.
- Be color blind in making employment decisions.
- Judge applicants, employees, and independent contractors on their qualifications.

- Do not participate in, encourage, or condone racial harassment.
- Establish a company policy against race and color discrimination and racial harassment.
- Define each of these suspect classifications explicitly in your company policy.
- Teach employees to understand why race and color discrimination and racial harassment are hurtful to the victims as well as damaging to the company.

❖ Employee Lessons

- Know what constitutes race and color discrimination under the Civil Rights Act of 1964.
- Be aware of the requirements and usefulness of Reconstruction Era Act.
- Think before you speak, especially if your statement has racial overtones.
- Treat your coworkers equally.
- Guard against participating in, encouraging, or condoning racial harassment.
- Do not judge coworkers or superiors by their race or color lest they judge you in the same way.
- Be apprised of company policy dealing with race and color discrimination and racial harassment.

❖ Summary

When baseball finally opened its doors to blacks and Hispanics, their numbers proliferated. The same situation may be true in the future for Asian baseball players. Blacks have also flourished in basketball and football. The integration of minorities into sports has not caused a decline; instead, sports are growing at unprecedented rates because people want to see the best players compete. The same is true in the business arena. If businesses give minorities the opportunity to work but with their jobs contingent upon performance, then minorities will have the impetus to perform to the highest potential to which they are capable. Only opportunities can be guaranteed, not lifetime jobs. In sports, minorities must perform up to their potential or otherwise be released. It is rare to hear of a player suing for racial discrimination. In turn, businesses must act like sports teams and hire the most qualified. They must also be color blind.

The population of the United States is made up of approximately one-quarter minorities, a number too formidable in size to be ignored. This country must embrace the fact that it is racially diverse. There are strengths in this situation that must be recognized. People who come from different backgrounds and cultures have different viewpoints, work habits, traits, traditions, and decision-making methods that they bring to the workplace. These must be exploited, not suppressed. In addition, workers often rise to the level of an employer's expectations. If the expectation is low, the result will be, too. Employers need to present a common color-blind-gender-blind level for their workers.

Leading by example is very important. Businesses can do this, and so can successful business people in the minority community. Minorities that become successful must not abdicate their community in favor of white ones and then allege white people discriminate. They must do their part being role models. Communicating the message that education enables people to become the best that they can be is essential. Education, like a career, is something to be embraced for life.

In a global world, every country is a team, and every person on the team must be a player. There can be no benchwarmers. If there are, the team will be operating at a disadvantage in the global league. This will be the fault of the team for not giving these non-participatory members the opportunity and encouragement to become team players with the goal of enabling these individuals to make a significant contribution to the team's success. Teams that meet the challenge will have a successful quest in the global bowl.

❖ REVIEW QUESTIONS

1. Define racial discrimination.
2. What groups could be the subject of racial discrimination?
3. Explain the difference between color discrimination and racial discrimination.
4. Define racial harassment.
5. What impact has the Reconstruction Act had on racial discrimination?
6. Can a bona fide occupational qualification ever exist with regard to race?
7. What effect does the United States Constitution have with respect to race?
8. Why is it preferable to sue under Title VII rather than the Reconstruction Act?
9. In what situation must a victim of racial discrimination sue under the Reconstruction Act because Title VII is unavailable?
10. Are the tensions involving racial discrimination decreasing?
11. Plaintiff's employment discrimination claim is based on the denial of his applications for promotion to either Dean of the School of Engineering at TSU or Head of the Mechanical Engineering Department at TSU. Rather than include all of the bio-data from Plaintiff's personnel file, Defendant Rogers gave to the selection committee only Plaintiff's faculty profile on file with the university for accreditation purposes. After learning of the university's recommendation to offer the position to Dr. Okeke, Plaintiff filed an objection with the Tennessee Board of Regents, claiming that he was more qualified for the position and that his application was not given appropriate consideration. As a result of this objection, the recommendation was withdrawn. The following year, Defendant Rogers began a new search for the Head of the Mechanical Engineering Department. Defendant Rogers also altered the published requirements for the position. Initially, the job announcement required only a Ph.D. in Mechanical Engineering. The second job announcement included the requirement of a B.S. degree in Mechanical Engineering as well. Plaintiff does not have a B.S. degree in Mechanical Engineering but in another related field. Unfortunately, virtually all of the records regarding the selection of the Dean of the School of Engineering in 1988 cannot be found. Plaintiff contends that the very fact that these documents have been "lost" renders Defendants' promotion decision suspect. What was the result? *Chaudmuri v. State of Tennessee,* 886 F.Supp. 1374 (M.D. Tenn. 1995)
12. Is a white plaintiff entitled to the same inference of discrimination as a minority plaintiff? *Wilson v. Bailey,* 934 F.2d 301 (11th Cir. 1991)
13. Are pretexts often used to cover up discriminatory behavior?
14. When poor performance and racist behavior are both involved, what takes precedence?
15. Are minorities as racist as whites? In other words, if minorities had equal power as whites have, would they be equally racist?
16. Should white people be afforded the same protection under the Equal Protection Clause as minorities?
17. Based solely on her evaluation of their relative qualifications and respective races, Carr concluded that Jackson had been chosen for the manager's position over her because of racial prejudice. On July 28, 1990, she questioned Area Manager McCullen on her hiring decision. Although allegedly admitting having made a mistake, McCullen defended her initial choice, saying she had been impressed by Jackson's more recent sales experience, more extensive college education, management background, and more enthusiastic and outgoing attitude, which McCullen thought would benefit sales.

On August 28, 1990, McCullen informed Carr that she had spoken with Mildred Hodgin, Carr's former supervisor at Seymour

Johnson Federal Credit Union. Contrary to statements contained in her AfterThoughts application, Hodgin told McCullen that Carr had not been employed as a loan interviewer who occasionally filled in as a teller, but rather the reverse; Carr had worked primarily as a teller, but did loan interviews and collections work when needed. Hodgin also returned a reference form in which she rated Carr's performance as "fair," and indicated that she would not rehire Carr based on her spotty attendance and professed need for a better-paying job. After a brief argument concerning these revelations, McCullen dismissed Carr for falsifying her application and for poor references.

Carr proceeded to file Title VII charges against Woolworth's, accusing the corporation of racial discrimination in hiring and retaliatory discharge. What was the result? *Carr v. F.W. Woolworth Co.,* 883 F.Supp. 10 (E.D.N.C. 1992)

18. Plaintiff's claim ... is based on the promotion of Danny Mott, an African American, to the position of Deputy Director of Emergency Ambulance Bureau (EAB) of the DCFD in March of 1988. Plaintiff alleges that the selection was made on the basis of race. Plaintiff also alleges that defendants Barry, Coleman, and Thornton preselected Mott for the position in October 1987. Mott was "acting" Deputy Director at the time and remained in the "acting" position until the official announcement of his selection after a purported competitive selection process in March of 1988.

Defendants argue that the plaintiff's claim is time-barred because he alleges that the actual selection occurred in October 1987. Plaintiff's claim as to the March 1988 selection process was filed within the three year statute of limitations. What was the result? *Zervas v. District of Columbia,* 817 F.Supp. 148 (D.D.C. 1993)

19. To help Harriston increase her sales performance, Riordan removed her from the RECAS project in January 1989. Her sales did not improve. Revenue in her territory for the first four months of 1981 was down nearly $75,000.00. In May 1989, Riordan sent Harriston a memorandum expressing his displeasure with her sales performance and requested her to inform him how she planned to improve. Riordan did not threaten to fire Harriston. Harriston, however, failed to respond to the memorandum. Instead, she submitted a letter of resignation in June 1989. In the letter, she alleged age and race discrimination as well as retaliation against her both because she had filed complaints with the Equal Employment Opportunity Commission in the past concerning employment discrimination against her and because she had an employment discrimination lawsuit against the Defendants pending in federal district court. What was the result? *Harriston v. Chicago Tribune Co.,* 992 F.2d 697 (7th Cir. 1993)

❖ WEB SITES

www.naacp.org
www.discriminationattorney.com/race.html
www.aclu.org/news/n092795a.html
www.look4Law.com/topics/Race Discrim.asp
www.eeoc.gov/facts/fs-race.html
www.findlaw.com
www.yale.edu/ynhti/curriculum/units/1994/1/94.01.02.html
www.eeoc.gov/facts/fs-race.html

SEX DISCRIMINATION

INTRODUCTION

In the past, sex was considered a bona fide occupational qualification. Stereotypes ruled. Men were physicians, lawyers, construction workers, and policemen. Women were nurses, flight attendants, secretaries, and teachers. This arrangement had the effect of discriminating against men and women in certain job classifications. The effect on women, particularly with regard to higher-paying positions, was noticeable. Women and men must be treated equally in all aspects of employment, hiring, compensation, training, transfer and promotions. Prescribing limits for lifting or carrying weight or for working before or after childbirth is prohibited. Any provisions or benefits must be provided to both sexes. Job requirements must be the same for male and female candidates.

CHAPTER CHECKLIST

❖ Understand the need for a prohibition against sex discrimination to counteract historical stereotypes.

❖ Learn that men are also protected against sex discrimination.

❖ Appreciate that women are often discriminated against not solely because they are women, but also because they have small children, elderly parents, etc., *i.e.,* sex plus discrimination.

❖ Be aware of the limited exceptions for bona fide occupational qualifications.

❖ Be apprised of potential violations of the Equal Pay Act.

❖ Be familiar with the impracticability of comparable worth.

❖ Appreciate the wide latitude given to employers in setting dress codes and grooming standards.

❖ Understand that workers should be judged based on their qualifications.

❖ Be cognizant of the fact that women do not perform better than men and vice versa in certain jobs solely because they are of a particular sex; other attributes are involved.

❖ Learn that customer preferences are not a valid reason to discriminate on the basis of sex.

EMPLOYMENT SCENARIO

Meg Johnson and Stacy Roberts are friends who have children in the Grasmere Elementary School. They would both like to work part time during school hours. Meg and Stacy apply to The Long and the Short of It, which has advertised part time sales positions. Tom and Mark interview Meg and Stacy, but decide not to hire them. Mark says to Tom, "We don't want school moms who are looking to earn extra spending cash. They don't fit our image." Subsequently, Tom and Mark hire two men without experience for the positions. Two weeks later, Meg and Stacy tell Laurie, another mother with school children, that they were disappointed L&S did not hire them. Laurie seems surprised. She remarks that her brother-in-law, Fred, who has not worked in six months, was hired on the spot. Meg and Stacy inquire as to Fred's experience in sales and Laurie replies that he has none. Meg and Stacy visit four of the L&S stores and to their astonishment they find no women working in sales. Meg and Stacy file a claim for sex discrimination against L&S. Tom Long and Mark Short, copresidents of L&S, consult with their attorney, Susan North, Esq. They argue that hiring men exclusively to work as salespeople in a men's clothing store is a bona fide occupational qualification. Susan begs to differ. She explains men and women are equally qualified to sell the clothing of both sexes. There is nothing unique about a man that will better enable him to sell men's clothing. Susan advises Tom and Mark to reexamine their opposition to hiring Meg and Stacy and offer them employment as sales associates.

EMPLOYMENT PERSPECTIVE

Eric Freeman is a vice-president at Bulls and Bears, Inc., an investment banking firm. There is an opening for an assistant vice-president to work directly underneath Freeman. There are two in-house candidates: Tom Folino, a competent securities trader with two years of experience, and Mary Michaels, a senior bond trader with seven years of experience. Mary's experience and competence is clearly superior, but Freeman selects Tom because they have common interests. They go to the hockey games after work and have a few beers together. Eric and Tom are both single, whereas Mary is married with children. Eric and Mary have nothing in common outside of work. Does this qualify as sexual discrimination? Yes! Eric's decision is not based on job performance, but rather on personal interests he shares with one candidate. ■

The issue in this case is whether prohibiting women from admission to Virginia Military Institute is sex discrimination.

UNITED STATES v. VIRGINIA

518 U.S. 515 (1996)

JUSTICE GINSBURG delivered the opinion of the Court.

Virginia's public institutions of higher learning include an incomparable military college, Virginia Military Institute (VMI). The United States maintains that the Constitution's equal protection guarantee precludes Virginia from reserving exclusively to men the unique educational opportunities VMI affords. We agree.

Founded in 1839, VMI is today the sole single-sex school among Virginia's 15 public institutions of higher learning. VMI's distinctive mission is to produce "citizen-soldiers," men prepared for leadership in civilian life and in military service. VMI pursues this mission through pervasive training of a kind not available anywhere else in Virginia. Assigning prime place to character development, VMI uses an "adversative method" modeled on English public schools and once characteristic of military instruction. VMI constantly endeavors to instill physical and mental discipline in its cadets and impart to them a strong moral code. The school's graduates leave VMI with heightened comprehension of their capacity to deal with duress and stress, and a large sense of accomplishment for completing the hazardous course.

VMI attracts some applicants because of its reputation as an extraordinarily challenging military school, and "because its alumni are exceptionally close to the school." "Women have no opportunity anywhere to gain the benefits of the system of education at VMI."

In 1990, prompted by a complaint filed with the Attorney General by a female high-school student seeking admission to VMI, the United States sued the Commonwealth of Virginia and VMI, alleging that VMI's exclusively male admission policy violated the Equal Protection Clause of the Fourteenth Amendment.

In the two years preceding the lawsuit, the District Court noted, VMI had received inquiries from 347 women, but had responded to none of them. "Some women, at least," the court said, "would want to attend the school if they had the opportunity." The court further recognized that, with recruitment, VMI could "achieve at least 10% female enrollment"—"a sufficient 'critical mass' to provide the female cadets with a positive educational experience." And it was also established that "some women are capable of all of the individual activities required of VMI cadets." In addition, experts agreed that if VMI admitted women, "the VMI ROTC experience would become a better training program from the perspective of the armed forces, because it would provide training in dealing with a mixed-gender army."

The heightened review standard our precedent establishes does not make sex a proscribed classification. Supposed "inherent differences" are no longer accepted as a ground for race or national origin classifications. Physical differences between men and women, however, are enduring: "The two sexes are not fungible; a community made up exclusively of one sex is different from a community composed of both."

"Inherent differences" between men and women, we have come to appreciate, remain cause for celebration, but not for denigration of the members of either sex or for artificial constraints on an individual's opportunity. Sex classifications may be used to compensate women "for particular economic disabilities they have suffered," to "promote equal employment opportunity," to advance full development of the talent and capacities of our Nation's people. But such classifications may not be used, as they once were, to create or perpetuate the legal, social, and economic inferiority of women.

Measuring the record in this case against the review standard just described, we conclude that Virginia has shown no "exceedingly persuasive justification" for excluding all women from the citizen-soldier training afforded by VMI. We therefore affirm the Fourth Circuit's initial judgment, which held that Virginia had violated the Fourteenth Amendment's Equal Protection Clause. Because the remedy proffered by Virginia-the Mary Baldwin VWIL program—does not cure the constitutional violation, i.e., it does not provide equal opportunity, we reverse the Fourth Circuit's final judgment in this case.

Judgment for the United States.

Case Commentary

The United States Supreme Court decided that a renown military college such as VMI cannot discriminate against women by denying them admission.

Case Questions

1. Was the Court's decision correct?
2. Female colleges do exist. Why can't VMI be limited to males?
3. Has allowing women to serve in the armed forces been a good idea?

The issue in this case is whether there should be a presumption against discrimination where the person who is discharging the employee is the same person who hired her.

CASE

BUHRMASTER v. OVERNITE TRANSPORTATION COMPANY

61 F.3d 461 (6th Cir. 1995)

BROWN, Circuit Judge.

Plaintiff Mary E. Buhrmaster claims that defendant Overnite Transportation Company violated Title VII by firing her because of her sex. Her case went to trial, and the jury found for the defendant. Claiming several errors by the district court, the plaintiff brought the instant appeal.

I.

Mary Buhrmaster was initially hired in 1984 by Charles Littleton, the Manager of Overnite's Dayton Terminal. For the next seven and a half years, she had a relatively successful career there. She became a Customer Service Representative, and in May of 1989, she was promoted to Office Manager—the only woman with a supervisory position in the office.

As Office Manager, Buhrmaster admitted she served as Littleton's "right hand man." She also served as a dispatcher when necessary and performed myriad administrative functions. Finally, she admitted she was second in command at the Overnite Dayton Terminal in that all "supervisory" personnel reported to her. Throughout her employment, Buhrmaster was never written up for any workplace violations, and Littleton repeatedly complimented her competency and willingness to work hard.

The evidence presented at trial, however, showed that despite these laudations, Buhrmaster was not the perfect employee. Although married, she carried on a close personal relationship with Mike Southward, a subordinate who drove trucks for the Company. They would often eat breakfast and lunch in her office, and he regularly gave her flowers and gifts. Several employees complained to Buhrmaster and Littleton about this relationship, finding it offensive. Littleton counseled Buhrmaster to be more discreet, and Southward and Buhrmaster decided to suppress the relationship at work.

In addition, there was apparently widespread discontent among Overnite's employees concerning Buhrmaster's management style. The employees complained to Littleton about these problems several times both individually and en masse, but nothing was done. The employees then complained to the home office in Richmond, Virginia, precipitating a visit from Ray Laughrum, an executive with the Company. After meeting with various employees, Laughrum advised Littleton, and, according to Overnite, Littleton decided to fire Buhrmaster. Buhrmaster received the following reasons for her termination:

The fact that she had been unable to maintain the morale and provide the leadership to the office personnel, the fact that if she had been able to provide the leadership to the personnel, they wouldn't have been coming to me individually and en masse to complain about the way they felt about her as an office manager, and that the feelings were so strong that the office staff was in near revolt at the time and the only way to get the terminal operation at the administrative end of it back on an even keel was to remove her from the position as office manager.

Littleton replaced Buhrmaster with another woman.

Because there was no direct evidence of discrimination, Buhrmaster attempted to prove her case circumstantially by claiming that she had been treated differently from similarly situated men who had engaged in similar conduct. At trial, she produced evidence showing that a number of supervisors had also engaged in some form of misconduct and had *not* been fired. After deliberating for ten hours, the jury found for the defendant, and the plaintiff appealed.

II.

The most significant issue raised in this appeal is whether the district court was correct in giving the jury an instruction on the "same actor" inference, which allows one to infer a lack of discrimination from the fact that the same individual both hired and fired the employee. This instruction was based on the evidence that Littleton both hired and fired Buhrmaster. Thus far, two circuits have used the same actor inference in upholding the

dismissal of an age discrimination claim. No circuit has used the inference in the context of sex discrimination, and no circuit has approved any jury instructions on the same actor inference.

In the present case, the district court decided that the same actor inference could be applied in sex discrimination cases. It therefore gave the jury the following instruction:

You have heard that Mr. Chuck Littleton, the person who hired Ms. Buhrmaster, was also the person who discharged her. In addition, during her period of employment at Overnite's Dayton terminal, Mr. Littleton promoted Ms. Buhrmaster on more than one occasion, including making her the first female office manager for the Dayton terminal. He also approved periodic pay raises for her. Mr. Littleton also hired another woman, Marcia Walters, as office manager after he discharged Ms. Buhrmaster.

When the individual who hires a person is the same person who fires an employee, there is a strong inference that discrimination did not motivate the employment decision. You may, but are not required to, infer from this evidence that Mr. Littleton's decision to terminate Ms. Buhrmaster's employment was not motivated by sex.

Plaintiff contends that Ms. Buhrmaster was in effect fired by the home office, and not by Mr. Littleton. The question of who fired Ms. Buhrmaster is a question of fact for you, the jury, to decide.

The plaintiff objects to this instruction on a number of grounds.

First, she argues that there was insufficient evidence to show that Littleton made the ultimate discharge decision, and the instruction therefore should not have been given at all. Our recent decision rejected this very argument. In that case, we held that when a jury charge accurately states the law but is not supported by the facts, any error in giving the instruction is harmless as a matter of law. The jury will conclude for itself that there is insufficient evidence to support an application of the instruction, and thus reject it as "mere surplusage."

We agree with the plaintiff that the length of time between the hiring and firing of an employee affects the strength of the inference that discrimination was not a factor in the employee's discharge. Over the years, an individual may develop an animus towards a class of people that did not exist when the hiring decision was made. However, to say that time weakens the same actor inference is not to say that time destroys it. In discrimination cases where the employee's class does not change, it remains possible that an employer who has nothing against women *per se* when it hires a certain female will have nothing against women *per se* when it fires that female, regardless of the number of years that pass. Thus, a short period of time is not an essential element of the same actor inference, at least in cases where the plaintiff's class does not change. Accordingly, the district court did not misstate the law in giving the instruction.

Accordingly, the district court is AFFIRMED. Judgment for Overnite Transportation Company.

Case Commentary

The Sixth Circuit held that the instruction to the jury regarding the same actor rule was proper. The fact that she was employed for seven and one-half years does not weaken the presumption in favor of the same actor rule.

Case Questions

1. Was this case decided correctly?

2. Was the charge to the jury proper?

3. Is the application of the same actor rule appropriate in this case?

In the case that follows, the issue is whether United's motive for rejecting the employee's request to be promoted to line pilot/flight officer was motivated by disparate treatment, disparate impact, retaliation, or the statute of limitations.

CASE

BULLINGTON v. UNITED AIR LINES, INC.

186 F.3d 1301 (10th Cir. 1997)

BRORBY, Circuit Judge

United Airlines, Inc. ("United") interviewed and rejected Ms. Bullington for the position of line pilot/flight officer on three separate occasions. Ms. Bullington brought this action pursuant to Title VII of the Civil Rights Act of 1964, and the Age Discrimination in Employment Act ("ADEA"), claiming United refused to hire her because of her gender, her age and in retaliation for complaining about alleged discrimination during the interview process. Ms. Bullington further claims United breached an implied contract or an otherwise enforceable promise by refusing to hire her. The district court granted United's motion for partial dismissal and United's subse-

quent motion for summary judgment, and Ms. Bullington appeals. We affirm in part and reverse in part.

I. BACKGROUND

Ms. Bullington, a female over the age of forty, currently works for United as a ground school academic instructor. Over a two-year period, Ms. Bullington sought but was denied a position as line pilot with United on three occasions. United's application and selection process for flight officers involves three phases. In the initial phase, United accepts applications from individuals meeting certain minimum qualifications including 350 hours of flight experience, commercial pilot certification, a high school diploma, and other physical and medical requirements. United then ranks eligible applicants according to aeronautical experience. Those applicants ranked at the top of the list advance to the second phase of the selection process. Because female applicants typically have less aeronautical experience than male applicants, United ranks male and female applicants separately. United then selects a proportionate number of males and females to proceed to the second phase. At the second phase, applicants must complete a simulator flight and a formal interview. Based on the applicant's performance, a review board then decides whether to reject the applicant or to extend a conditional offer. If United extends a conditional offer, the candidate moves on to the third phase, which includes a medical exam and background check. Ms. Bullington objects to the formal interview portion of the selection process.

Two United employees conduct the formal interview, an employment representative and a flight operations representative. These individuals assess the applicant in seven broad categories or "dimensions" including: industry motivation, decision making/problem solving, compliance and conformity, leadership, interpersonal skills, technical evaluation, and appearance/presentation. Each dimension is broken down into a set of attributes or "anchors" United deems desirable in a flight officer. Interviewers ask applicants questions from a suggested list and, based on the applicant's response, evaluate whether the applicant meets United's set standards for each attribute.

Based on those attribute evaluations, the interviewers give the applicant a numerical score for each dimension, ranging from a low of "1" to a high of "5." The dimension scores are then averaged to arrive at the applicant's overall score. An applicant must have an overall score of "3" or better to be recommended for a flight officer position. However, if an applicant scores a "2" or lower on any one dimension, her overall score will also be a "2," and the interviewers will not recommend her for a flight officer position.

United interviewed Ms. Bullington for a flight officer position three times—January 1993, March 1995 and May 1995. Each time, Ms. Bullington received an overall score of "2,"

thereby disqualifying her from further consideration. After her first unsuccessful interview in January 1993, Ms. Bullington spoke with Ms. Nancy Stuke, United's Manager of Flight Officer Employment, and expressed her concerns that one of her interviewers was biased against her. Ms. Bullington claims Ms. Stuke failed to adequately address her complaints. After unsuccessfully interviewing a second and third time, Ms. Bullington filed suit alleging: (1) United failed to hire her on all three occasions because of her sex and age, (2) United failed to hire her in 1995 in retaliation for her complaints to Ms. Stuke in 1993, and (3) United's failure to hire her breached an implied contract or otherwise enforceable promise for career advancement.

United moved to dismiss Ms. Bullington's claims to the extent they were based on Ms. Bullington's January 1993 rejection because those claims were barred by the statute of limitations. The district court agreed and granted United's motion. United then moved for summary judgment on Ms. Bullington's remaining claims. The district court granted that motion as well, concluding Ms. Bullington failed to establish a *prima facie* case of age or sex discrimination under either a disparate impact or disparate treatment theory, failed to establish a *prima facie* case of retaliation, and failed to present sufficient evidence of an enforceable contract or promise.

II. STATUTE OF LIMITATIONS

In Colorado, ADEA and Title VII complainants must file a charge of discrimination with the Equal Employment Opportunity Commission ("EEOC") within 300 days after the alleged unlawful discriminatory practice occurred.

This filing is a prerequisite to a civil suit under either statute. In this case, United first rejected Ms. Bullington for the position of flight officer in January 1993. In March 1993, Ms. Bullington complained to Ms. Stuke that she suspected one of her interviewers discriminated against her. In order for a claim based on this conduct to be timely, Ms. Bullington was required to file an EEOC charge within 300 days after the March 1993 incident. However, Ms. Bullington waited almost three years, until February 6, 1996, to file her charge.

Ms. Bullington attempts to avoid this apparent untimeliness by invoking the continuing violation doctrine. Under that doctrine, a plaintiff may recover for incidents which occurred outside the statutory time limit if at least one instance of the alleged discriminatory practice occurred within the limitations period and the earlier acts are part of a "continuing pattern of discrimination." To determine whether alleged incidents of discrimination constitute a continuing violation, a court considers three factors: (i) subject matter—whether the violations constitute the same type of discrimination; (ii) frequency; and (iii) permanence—whether the nature of the violations should trigger an employee's awareness of the need to assert her rights and whether the consequences of the act would continue even in the absence of a continuing intent to discriminate.

Applying these factors, the district court determined that the events arising in 1993 and the later events in 1995 did not constitute a continuing violation. Instead, the court concluded the 1993 non-hire was an isolated event and, moreover, Ms. Bullington had reason to believe she was a victim of discrimination as early as 1993. As such, the court found application of the continuing violation doctrine inappropriate and Ms. Bullington's claims, to the extent they relied on the 1993 conduct, untimely. The court therefore dismissed those claims for failure to state a claim upon which relief may be granted. We review de novo the district court's dismissal for failure to state a claim upon which relief can be granted. We uphold a dismissal "only when it appears that the plaintiff can prove no set of facts in support of the claims that would entitle her to relief, accepting the well-pleaded allegations of the complaint as true and construing them in the light most favorable to the plaintiff."

The continuing violation doctrine "is premised on the equitable notion that the statute of limitations should not begin to run until a reasonable person would be aware that his or her rights have been violated." Thus, a continuing violation claim will likely fail if the plaintiff knew, or through the exercise of reasonable diligence would have known, she was being discriminated against at the time the earlier events occurred. We agree with the district court's conclusion that, although the 1993 conduct is of the same general type as the 1995 conduct, the 1993 deci-

sion was a discrete and salient event that put Ms. Bullington on notice that United violated her rights. The allegations contained in Ms. Bullington's Amended Complaint clearly indicate that after United declined to hire her in January 1993, she spoke to Ms. Stuke in March 1993 and expressed her opposition to "what she believed ... to have been sex and age discrimination by United in not selecting her for the position of line pilot." Because Ms. Bullington was, at the very least, on inquiry notice of the alleged discrimination as early as 1993, she had a duty to assert her rights at that time and she cannot rely on a continuing violation theory to avoid the statutory time bar.

Ms. Bullington also argues for a continuing violation based on her statistical evidence of a pattern and practice of discrimination. It is true that a continuing violation may be based on either a series of related acts taken against a single individual or the maintenance of a company-wide policy or practice of discrimination. However, Ms. Bullington's argument below focused entirely on the specific acts taken against her and did not contend that a company-wide policy of discrimination existed before and after the limitations period. Moreover, she did not present her statistical evidence until well after the district court issued its order granting partial dismissal. The district court properly dismissed Ms. Bullington's discrimination claims for events arising in 1992/1993 as time barred.

III. DISPARATE IMPACT

Ms. Bullington argues United's interview process caused a significant disparate impact on women. As is typical in disparate impact cases, Ms. Bullington relies on statistical evidence to establish her *prima facie* case. Her statistics compare the "pass rates" of male and female applicants who interviewed for United flight officer positions. The "pass rate," as defined by Ms. Bullington's expert, represents the number of applicants who received an overall score of "3" or better on the interview.

For interviews conducted after 1994, the pass rate for women was 27.9% while the pass rate for men was 46.6%. As such, the women's pass rate is equal to only 60% of the pass rate for men—a statistically significant disparity under EEOC guidelines (stating that a selection rate for a protected group which is less than 80% or 4/5 of the selection rate for the majority group is generally regarded as evidence of adverse impact). This disparity, Ms. Bullington argues, is significant enough to establish a *prima facie* case of disparate impact discrimination.

The district court disagreed. It determined Ms. Bullington's statistics did not establish a *prima facie* case because they failed to compare similarly situated individuals.

After examining the facts and circumstances of this case, we find Ms. Bullington's statistical data sufficiently reliable to raise a genuine issue of material fact regarding the existence of a statistical disparity. Her analysis identified a specific employment practice (the interview) and identified two relevant populations for impact comparison—persons who interviewed for flight officer positions and persons who received a passing score on the interview. Her analysis focused on the specific position at issue, namely flight officer. In addition, her applicant pool was appropriately limited to persons who sought out and were at least minimally qualified for the position of flight officer. In fact, each member of the applicant pool not only applied for the at-issue position, as is the usual case with applicant flow data, but actually interviewed for the at-issue position. Based on United's interview eligibility requirements, we can therefore assume each member of the applicant pool was, at the very least, a certified pilot with a high school diploma and at least 350 hours of flight experience. The relative homogeneity of the applicant pool reassures us that its members are not so diverse as to render her statistics totally meaningless.

This is not to say Ms. Bullington's statistics are without fault. As the district court noted, her analysis fails to account for differences in male and female interviewees' aeronautical experience—a potentially non-discriminatory explanation for the disparate impact. However, we do not believe that fault renders Ms. Bullington's statistics incapable of raising a genuine issue of material fact. We emphasize that Ms. Bullington's burden as the nonmovant is to set forth specific facts establishing a genuine issue for trial. The issue of material fact, here the existence of a significant statistical disparity, need not be resolved conclusively in Ms. Bullington's favor. We simply conclude the

district court's basis for granting summary judgment was insufficient, and United has not shown an absence of issues of material fact with respect to Ms. Bullington's *prima facie* case.

IV. DISPARATE TREATMENT

If she establishes a *prima facie* case, the burden shifts to United to articulate a legitimate, nondiscriminatory reason for the adverse employment decision. If United offers a legitimate, nondiscriminatory reason for its actions, the burden reverts to Ms. Bullington to show United's proffered reason was a pretext for discrimination.

The only remaining issue, then, is whether Ms. Bullington has shown "that there is a genuine dispute of material fact as to whether the employer's proffered reason for the challenged action is pretextual."

To establish pretext a plaintiff must show either that "a discriminatory reason more likely motivated the employer or … that the employer's proffered explanation is unworthy of credence." Plaintiff may accomplish this by demonstrating "such weaknesses, implausibilities, inconsistencies, incoherencies, or contradictions in the employer's proffered legitimate reasons for its action that a reasonable factfinder could rationally find them unworthy of credence." However, the plaintiff's "mere conjecture that her employer's explanation is a pretext for intentional discrimination is an insufficient basis for denial of summary judgment."

In this case, Ms. Bullington bases her pretext argument on the following evidence: disputes regarding things she said and did during the interview, the interviewers' use of gender and age stereotypes, a comparison of her qualifications with those of successful flight officer interviewees, and statistical evidence. We conclude that, even viewing this evidence in the light most favorable to Ms. Bullington, it fails to demonstrate a genuine issue of fact as to whether United's reasons for not hiring her were pretextual.

First, Ms. Bullington lists numerous disputes she has with the notes and summaries prepared by her interviewers. We disagree.

A review of the record shows that the vast majority of the "factual disputes" alleged by Ms. Bullington are in reality her opinion that the interviewers were wrong in their assessment of her qualifications.

However, her own opinions about her qualifications do not give rise to a material fact dispute.

Ms. Bullington's argument merely takes issue with what she believes is an incorrect assessment of her communication skills, goals, and motivation level. As discussed above, Ms. Bullington's opinion about the fairness or accuracy of the interviewers' evaluation is not evidence of pretext.

Next, Ms. Bullington offers a comparison of her qualifications with those of seven other male and/or younger individuals that United interviewed and hired as flight officers. She claims United hired these individuals despite the fact many were less qualified than her or, in many cases, had the same deficiencies identified during her interview. However, we emphasize that an employer does not violate Title VII by choosing between *equally* qualified candidates, so long as the decision is not based on unlawful criteria. Therefore, pretext cannot be shown simply by identifying minor differences between plaintiff's qualifications and those of successful applicants.

A comparison of Ms. Bullington's qualifications with those of the other interviewees in this case gives us no reason to question United's explanation for its hiring decision. Ms. Bullington's evidence does not show that she was overwhelmingly better qualified than the other candidates. At most, the seven other candidates were similarly qualified and the fact that United chose between them is not evidence of pretext.

V. RETALIATION

Ms. Bullington claims United retaliated against her based on a conversation she had in March 1993 with Ms. Stuke, United's Manager of Flight Officer Employment. During this conversation, Ms. Bullington allegedly informed Ms. Stuke of her "strong concerns" that one of her interviewers in the 1993 interview was biased against her. Because of this complaint, Ms. Bullington claims Ms. Stuke retaliated against her by influencing the interviewers' hiring decisions in her 1995 interviews. As proof of Ms. Stuke's animus towards her, Ms. Bullington points to a conversation which occurred shortly before her March 1995 interview between Ms. Stuke and Mr. H. Jeffery Bartels about a recommendation Mr. Bartels submitted in support of Ms. Bullington's flight officer application. In his affidavit, Mr. Bartels states that Ms. Stuke asked him if he was sure he wanted to submit a recommendation for Ms. Bullington and told him that Ms. Bullington acted like a "real airhead" and "held a troll doll for good luck" during her previous interview.

To establish a *prima facie* case of retaliation, Ms. Bullington must show: "1) she was engaged in protected opposition to Title VII or ADEA discrimination; 2) she was subjected to adverse employment action; and 3) a causal connection existed between the protected activity and the adverse employment action." The causal connection may be shown by producing "evidence of circumstances that justify an inference of retaliatory motive, such as protected conduct closely followed by adverse action." In other words, Ms. Bullington must present some evidence that her employer undertook the adverse employment action for the purpose of retaliation.

The district court concluded summary judgment in favor of United was appropriate because Ms. Bullington failed to establish a nexus or causal connection between her 1993 complaint to Ms. Stuke and the interviewers' hiring selections in 1995. We agree. The interviewers' decisions in 1995 were remote in time from Ms. Bullington's 1993 complaint, thus undercutting an inference of retaliatory motive.

Judgment for United Airlines.

Case Commentary

Ms. Bullington applied for line pilot once in 1993 and twice in 1995. The Tenth Circuit concluded Ms. Bullington's 1993 discrimination claim was not timely filed. Ms. Bullington's attempt to apply the continuous violation rule failed for lack of continuity. The Tenth Circuit concluded that Ms. Bullington's disparate impact claim was viable because the women's pass rate was only 60 percent of the men's pass rate in violation of the 80 percent rule. The Tenth Circuit dismissed the disparate treatment claim because there was no evidence of pretext on United's part. Ms. Bullington's retaliation claim was also dismissed because the retaliation occurred in 1995, while the alleged event leading to the retaliation happened in 1993. This was too remote.

Case Questions

1. Was the Court's decision correct?
2. Do you think the retaliation claim was too remote?
3. Do you think the women's 60 percent pass rate created a disparate impact?
4. If so, how do you think the Court will resolve this?

Men are also protected against gender discrimination under Title VII. Although it does not happen very often, there are occasions when men have been treated unfavorably because of their gender.

The following case addresses the question of whether a female superior could be found to have sexually discriminated against a male subordinate.

The issue in the following case is whether a superior who promotes a female lover has sexually discriminated against male employees who would otherwise have been in line for the promotion.

CASE

BECERRA v. DALTON, SECRETARY OF THE NAVY

94 F.3d 145 (4th Cir. 1996)

CHAPMAN, Senior Circuit Judge.

Appellant Francisco B. Becerra brought this Title VII action in the District Court for the District of Maryland. Becerra, a former civilian employee of the United States Navy, alleged that the Navy discriminated against him on the basis of sex and national origin. He also alleged that the Navy retaliated against him after he filed his EEO complaints by revoking his security clearance. The Navy moved for partial summary judgment claiming that the decision to revoke Becerra's security clearance was not subject to judicial review. The district court granted this motion. The defendants then moved for summary judgment as to plaintiff's other claims arguing that he failed to produce any evidence of discriminatory intent. The district court granted this motion. We affirm.

I.

Becerra began working for the Navy on September 12, 1983 as a civilian employee in the Office of Naval Intelligence ("ONI"), headquartered in Suitland, Maryland. Becerra, a United States born Hispanic, was fluent in several languages and had experience in military intelligence. He was an emigre debriefer for Task Force 168, a section of ONI, which is engaged in human source intelligence collection worldwide.

In August, 1984, Commander David Muller was appointed operations officer of Task Force 168 and also commander of the smaller Task Group 168.0, a division within Task Force 168 involved in domestic human intelligence gathering. As commander of Task Group 168.0, Commander Muller set up new field offices across the United States. Because of Becerra's fluency in Spanish and his familiarity with the Hispanic community, Muller chose Becerra to head the Miami, Florida office.

Maria Pallas was also a civilian employee of Task Force 168. She was hired as a Polish linguist, but rapidly advanced, eventually reaching the position of Overt Program Manager of Human

Intelligence. Becerra alleged that Pallas traded sexual favors with her superiors, especially Muller and Captain Roland Saenz, commander of Task Force 168, to achieve her success.

Muller's duties as both commander of Task Group 168.0 and operations officer of Task Force 168 became burdensome, and to give him some relief, the position of Deputy Commander of Task Group 168.0 was created and Pallas was named to this position. Muller soon realized that he could not remain commander of Task Group 168.0 and also fulfill his duties as operations officer of Task Force 168. The Navy was unable to provide an active duty military officer to fill the 168.0 position, and Captain Saenz decided to create the entirely new position of Supervisory Intelligence Specialist CTG 168.0, which could be held by a civilian, to head the Task Group's activities.

On July 1, 1988, Pallas entered this new position, replacing Muller as commander of Task Group 168.0. Pallas was detailed to the position, i.e., her appointment was temporary until this new position could be competed and a suitable candidate hired. Becerra maintains that no employees were informed that the position was temporary and that it would later be competed. He claims that the Navy had no intention of opening the position to competition until he complained. However, the personnel office at ONI issued a Notice of Personnel Action, the mechanism by which Pallas was transferred to the position, two months before Becerra made his first complaint. That document clearly indicated that Pallas was detailed to the position for a period not to exceed 120 days.

Saenz and Pallas visited Miami in early August, 1988. During the visit, Saenz, Pallas, and Becerra visited a local, high-ranking official. Becerra did not wear a coat and tie but instead wore a guayabera, an open-necked shirt often worn in the Hispanic community and, according to Becerra, acceptable business attire in Miami. After returning to Maryland, Pallas sent Becerra a letter pointing out problems that she had noticed on her visit. The letter covered the office's production, collections, personnel, telephone bills, and Becerra's personal appearance and professional etiquette. Pallas mentioned Becerra's style of dress, stating "I recommend you wear a jacket and tie when calling on the Admiral or the Chief

of Staff (Coast Guard). Miami is casual, but this still is a military organization."

On September 28, 1988, the Navy announced the vacancy for the position of commander of the Task Group, the position that Pallas was temporarily holding. After this announcement, Becerra sent a message to headquarters requesting clarification of the vacancy announcement because he felt that Pallas had been preselected for the position. Saenz replied that Pallas had been detailed to the position and that "all qualified applicants will be considered by a selection board."

Thirteen candidates applied for the position. A panel was selected to review the application packages, pick out the best qualified, and then rank them numerically for Captain Saenz, the selecting official.

The panel chose four finalists. The panel gave Pallas a perfect score of 56 and Becerra the second highest score of 55. Captain Saenz, relying on the panel's scores, the application packages, and his knowledge of the individual candidates, chose Pallas for the position.

Becerra claims that this selection was tainted in several ways. First, one of the panel members was Pallas' close friend; second, Muller, who Becerra claims was receiving sexual favors from Pallas lobbied Saenz on behalf of Pallas; third, Muller was the officer that drew up the crediting plan for the position. This crediting plan listed the experience criteria, and Becerra claims that it was tailored to match Pallas' experience.

After Pallas' appointment to the position, Becerra attempted to telephonically file an EEO complaint. He was told that he must travel to Washington to file a complaint in person, which he did. Becerra claims that the Navy retaliated against him because of his filing the EEO complaint in the following ways: Pallas' second-in-command told him that he better find another job, Pallas would not allow him time to process his complaint until she was told that she must, employees of Task Force 168 were instructed to provide headquarters with whatever negative details they could find on Becerra, and Pallas threatened to file an EEO complaint against him.

In November, 1988, the Navy began a security investigation on Becerra based on confidential information that Becerra claims the Navy knew or should have known was false. Becerra's security clearance was suspended on January 5, 1989. He was placed on administrative leave pending further investigation. On October 24, 1989, the Navy discharged Becerra based on his lack of security clearance. He appealed his discharge to the Merit Systems Protection Board which ordered Becerra reinstated to his position. The Navy discharged Becerra again on July 6, 1990; this prompted him to file his second EEO complaint on August 16, 1990.

II.

This court reviews a grant of a motion to dismiss and a grant of Summary judgment.

Becerra next argues that he was the victim of sexual discrimination and sexual harassment. Becerra claims that there is evidence of a sexually hostile environment wherein Pallas was trading sexual favors for promotional opportunities to Becerra's career detriment. Becerra relies on 29 C.F.R. § 1604.11(g) to establish this definition of sexual harassment:

Other related practices: Where employment opportunities or benefits are granted because of an individual's submission to the employer's sexual advances or requests for sexual favors, the employer may be held liable for unlawful sex discrimination against other persons who are qualified but denied that employment opportunity or benefit.

The district court relied on one case in a line of cases that holds that an employer who promotes his lover or paramour, or otherwise accords the lover or paramour preferential treatment, is not liable for sexual harassment under Title VII. The male plaintiffs claimed discrimination when a female who was engaged in a sexual relationship with the selecting official was promoted over them. The Second Circuit held that promotion of a paramour does not violate Title VII:

We find that even accepting as true the fact that the commanding officer was accepting sexual favors from Pallas, this conduct does not amount to sexual discrimination against Becerra under Title VII.

For the foregoing reasons, the decision of the district court is *AFFIRMED.*

Judgment for Dalton, Secretary of the Navy.

Case Commentary

The Fourth Circuit ruled that the promotion of a paramour does not constitute sex discrimination against those passed over.

Case Questions

1. Do you agree with the Court's decision?
2. How can one employee be favored over another for sexual reasons without this resulting in a violation of Title VII of the Civil Rights Act?
3. Is this behavior sex discrimination or sexual harassment?

The question presented in the next case is whether an employee can be entitled to both reinstatement and front pay under Title VII of the Civil Rights Act of 1964.

KERR SELGAS v. AMERICAN AIRLINES

104 F.3d 9 (1ˢᵗ Cir. 1997)

COFFIN, Senior Circuit Judge.

At issue in this case are the equitable remedies awarded to the plaintiff, Mary Jane Kerr Selgas ("Kerr Selgas"), in a sex discrimination suit against her employer, American Airlines ("American"). A jury awarded Kerr Selgas a lump sum award in that suit that included an unspecified amount for front pay. In an earlier appeal, this court affirmed the judgment. The district court subsequently ordered Kerr Selgas reinstated by American. American maintains in this appeal that front pay and reinstatement are mutually exclusive equitable remedies, and that the court therefore erred in allowing both to Kerr Selgas. It further claims that the district court erred in ordering reinstatement without conducting a hearing, without permitting American to conduct additional discovery, and in considering extra-record evidence submitted by Kerr Selgas. We affirm the court's legal judgment that both front pay and reinstatement are permissible, but we vacate the district court's order and remand for a hearing on whether reinstatement is an appropriate remedy here.

BACKGROUND

Mary Jane Kerr Selgas was fired by American Airlines in 1992 after 18 years with the company; she brought suit under federal and Puerto Rico law, alleging sex discrimination, harassment, and violation of her local law right to privacy. At the conclusion of a three week trial, a jury awarded her over $1 million in damages; under Puerto Rico law, this was doubled automatically to over $2 million. A remittitur and the rejection of punitive damages by this court in Kerr I resulted in a final damages award of $1.2 million.

While Kerr Selgas had requested reinstatement in her initial complaint, and also in subsequent motions, the district court set this issue aside during the course of the trial and during the pen-

dency of the Kerr I appeal. One month after this court's decision in Kerr I on November 13, 1995, the district court ordered American to reinstate Kerr Selgas. The court did so without holding a full hearing on this issue, and its order was based on the evidence received at trial and on additional materials submitted with motions by Kerr Selgas. American claims that this reinstatement order is improper for two reasons. First, it argues that reinstatement and front pay are alternative remedies and that Kerr Selgas was fully compensated by the jury award including front pay. Second, if reinstatement is permissible, it argues that it should not have been ordered here without first giving American additional discovery and an opportunity to be heard on the issue, particularly if evidence obtained after the trial was to be considered.

A. Equitable Remedies Under Title VII: Front Pay and Reinstatement.

The remedial scheme in Title VII is designed to make a plaintiff who has been the victim of discrimination whole through the use of equitable remedies. These remedies (which include reinstatement, back pay, and front pay) are accordingly intended to compensate a plaintiff for the effects of the discrimination, both past and future, and to bring the plaintiff to the position which s/he would have occupied but for the illegal acts. Under Title VII, the first choice is to reinstate the plaintiff at the original employer; this accomplishes the dual goals of providing full coverage for the plaintiff and of deterring such conduct by employers in the future.

Where reinstatement is not immediately available as a remedy, either due to the plaintiff's condition, or due to conditions at the employer that preclude the plaintiff's return (such as hostility of other employees, or the need for an innocent employee to be "bumped" in order to reinstate the plaintiff), front pay is available as an alternative to compensate the plaintiff from the conclusion of trial through the point at which the plaintiff can either return to the employer or obtain comparable employment elsewhere. It is this context, where the overarching preference is for reinstatement and front pay is an alternative for finite periods during which reinstatement is unavailable, which is the key to understanding the construction of remedial packages. In this context, it can be seen that front pay and reinstatement are not mutually exclusive. Front pay takes a plaintiff to the point of employability. Reinstatement at that point would, in effect, "perfect" the remedy because the plaintiff would be back in the very job she lost unlawfully.

Trial courts have discretion to fashion the awards in Title VII cases so as to fully compensate a plaintiff in a manner that suits the specific facts of the case; this discretion includes the selection of the elements which comprise the remedial recovery. Traditionally, the court determines the whole remedial package in one fell swoop. Hybrid awards combining front pay with other equitable elements, while rare, are not novel. This court, while it has not previously addressed this particular issue, has indicated a preference for a flexible approach in the construction of remedial awards. The district court therefore had the option here of combining an award of front pay with reinstatement. Its only limitation was to avoid duplication. Because courts typically consider all remedies at the same time, duplication most commonly would be avoided by denying front pay when an immediate reinstatement is ordered.

Although the district court was not explicit about what it was doing in this instance (allowing American to argue that reinstatement had been excluded as a prospective remedy), it appears to have bifurcated the traditional remedies analysis on the assumption that, since Kerr Selgas was unable to return to work at the time of trial, pay for some future time—i.e., front pay—was necessary to compensate Kerr Selgas, whether or not reinstatement would be an appropriate additional remedy. It therefore reserved the reinstatement issue for later resolution, and sent the compensatory elements (back pay, front pay, and damages) to the jury for determination. By including front pay in its lump sum award, the jury fully compensated Kerr Selgas for the discrimination she had suffered from the point of the initial illegal act to the point at which she

would once again be employable at her prior level. The court then took up post-trial whether American was required to take her back.

Due to the amorphous nature of the jury award—it was simply a lump sum with no distinctions made between the amounts allocated to back pay, front pay, or damages, and with no statement as to the time period which the front pay portion was intended to cover—it cannot be stated with any certainty which dates or figures the jurors determined were applicable to the front pay issue. In other words, it is not clear when they thought she would be ready to return to work. Testimony at trial, however, put the longest date at 18 months after trial, or October 1995. Furthermore, in its charge to the jury, the court specifically limited any damages to those caused by the defendants' wrongful conduct. Reinstatement was ordered in December 1995. The front pay and reinstatement awards thus seem most reasonably to cover separate and distinct periods of time. Because there is no duplication, the two equitable remedies of front pay and reinstatement could be used in concert to achieve Title VII's goal of fully compensating the plaintiff. This brings us to American's second point on appeal: whether the process used to reach the reinstatement decision was proper.

Accordingly, while we hold that reinstatement may properly be awarded in a Title VII case together with front pay as long as there is no duplication between the two awards, in this case we believe a hearing should have been held to determine whether reinstatement was appropriate. Therefore, we vacate the district court's reinstatement order and remand for proceedings consistent with this opinion to determine whether Kerr Selgas should be reinstated by American.

CONCLUSION

Courts may properly combine the equitable remedies of front pay and reinstatement in order to meet Title VII's goal of providing full compensation to the victims of illegal discrimination, as long as there is no economic or chronological duplication between the awards. However, the protections inherent in the adversarial system demand that full and complete hearings be provided on contested issues affecting these equitable remedies.

Vacated and remanded.
No costs to either party.

Case Commentary

The First Circuit held that reinstatement and front pay may be granted as long as the awards do not duplicate each other. Here, the First Circuit vacated the District Court's judgment for Kerr Selgas because of concerns over whether reinstatement was appropriate, and ordered the District Court to resolve this matter.

Case Questions

1. Was this case correctly decided?
2. Should Kerr Selgas be reinstated?

3. When would it be appropriate to grant both reinstatement and front pay?

SEX PLUS DISCRIMINATION

Discrimination may occur against an individual not solely because of his or her gender, but that fact coupled with another may be its cause. Women with small children, women in child-bearing years, and women taking care of elderly parents are all examples.

As part of their interview process, some companies endeavor to discover if a female applicant has small children. It has been their experience that mothers are preoccupied with worrying about their children. In addition, many employers believe if the child becomes ill or gets hurt, the mother will leave work immediately. This behavior can be disruptive to the workplace. For that reason, the company may nonchalantly ask the female applicant where her children go to school. The response will indicate whether the woman has children and, if so, what their ages are. The company can then generally refuse her or deny her for another reason. This is discriminatory behavior.

In the next case, a female worker told her employer she was going to marry and relocate to Atlanta. She asked the company whether they would relocate her. The company agreed to do so, but they later reneged. She claimed retaliation and constructive discharge based upon sex plus age discrimination.

CASE

WEST v. MARION MERRELL DOW, INC.

34 F.3d 493 (8th Cir. 1995)

LOKEN, Circuit Judge.
Myrna West commenced this employment discrimination suit against her former employer, Marion Laboratories, Inc., now Marion Merrell Dow, Inc. ("Marion"), alleging sex, age, and retaliation discrimination. After a six-day trial, the jury awarded West $350,000 in compensatory damages on her claim that Marion had retaliated after West filed a charge accusing Marion of sex and age discrimination. The district court awarded additional front-pay damages and attorney's fees, and Marion appealed.

West's retaliation claim is that Marion reneged on a promise that it would find her a position in Atlanta if she married and moved there. After West committed to the move, Marion advised that it had no openings in Atlanta, and West took the position she was constructively discharged. However, before West resigned, Marion reconsidered and offered her a choice of Atlanta-based positions. West nonetheless immediately resigned her employ with Marion. Because West unreasonably refused Marion's attempt to accommodate her desire to transfer, we conclude that there was insufficient evidence that Marion reneged on a promise, or that West was constructively discharged. Accordingly, we reverse.

The jury rejected West's claims of sex and age discrimination, so we limit our discussion to the facts relevant to her retaliation claim. We view the evidence in the light most favorable to West and give her the benefit of all reasonable inferences that may be drawn from that evidence.

Marion hired West in February 1978. In late 1986, she was promoted to district manager of the Wound Care Division, marketing products used in treating major wounds and burns. As District Manager, West was based in Dallas, Texas, and managed eight field sales representatives who covered the western half of the country.

In November 1988, West told her supervisor, James Laufenberg, that she was planning to marry an Atlanta resident in June 1989. West advised that she wanted to remain with Marion but, following the marriage, would need to relocate to Atlanta, or to Marion in Kansas City where her new husband could relocate. West hoped that she would be promoted to Regional Manager for the Wound Care Division in Kansas City, but Laufenberg was "not particularly positive" that she would attain that position.

On May 5, 1989, West again expressed concern about her upcoming wedding and need to relocate. Laufenberg assured her that she could remain with the Wound Care Division and transfer to Atlanta. At a minimum, Laufenberg explained, he would split an existing sales territory and give West an entry level field sales position until the division grew enough to justify creating a new district manager position in Atlanta.

On August 29, West met with both Laufenberg and Gianini. Laufenberg advised that there was no opening in the Wound Care Division in Atlanta. Gianini advised that he had looked but was unable to find her an Atlanta position elsewhere in the company. West then wrote a lengthy letter to Laufenberg on September 2, and she filed a charge of retaliation discrimination on September 5. In both documents, she asserted that Laufenberg had withdrawn his offer to find her a Wound Care Division position in Atlanta, that Gianini had made a perfunctory effort to find her an alternative opportunity in Atlanta and therefore that she was forced to leave Marion because the company refused to offer her "the same transfer opportunities that countless others had received."

On September 11, Laufenberg wrote West and asked that she provide the specific date of her move to Atlanta to "help me to start the process of interviewing for a district manager in Dallas."

Treating this as a request to resign, West again wrote to Laufenberg on September 20th, asserting that she had endured eleven years of sexual discrimination and harassment and concluding, "I am now forced to tender my resignation effective September 30, 1989. It is my belief that because I have protested the treatment I have received that the position you promised to make for me in Atlanta was withdrawn."

On September 21, apparently before he received West's September 20 resignation letter, Laufenberg responded to her September 2 letter. Expressing his surprise at this letter, Laufenberg commented, "You know very well that I sincerely want you to remain with Marion, in the Wound Care Division if possible." Laufenberg stated that the Wound Care Division's expansion plans were on hold, so he could not add a new Atlanta district manager. He suggested the following alternatives to permit West to remain with Marion:

"Remain in your District Manager position in Dallas pending resolution of these workforce scale-up issues." Apply for any of five executive positions then available at Marion's Kansas City headquarters. (None was a regional manager's position, the subject of West's discrimination charge.)

Although Marion has no open field sales positions in the Atlanta area, "You may take any of several territories open in the southeastern United States."

Alternatively, Marion's Prescription Products Division "will provide you with a rover position in Field Sales. . . . This will permit you to move to Atlanta and remain with Marion at no loss in base pay while we wait for a regular opening to develop" in Atlanta.

After receiving Laufenberg's September 21 letter, West declined all of the positions offered and resigned on September 30. She testified that, by late September 1989, she had committed to reside in Atlanta after her marriage. She rejected Laufenberg's offer of sales positions in Atlanta because they were "too little, too late," they were not bona fide offers but only invitations to "interview for a position" and she was not willing to accept an insulting demotion to a field sales position.

At trial, the parties differed as to why Laufenberg in May had assured West of at least a sales position with the Wound Care Division in Atlanta, but then in August told her that nothing was available. West argued this was retaliation for her May 16 discrimination charge. She presented evidence that Marion had specially accommodated many other employees who asked to relocate. On the other hand, Laufenberg testified that the Wound Care Division's business conditions changed dramatically between May 5 and August 8, 1989, eliminating his ability to offer West a Wound Care Division position in Atlanta. First, the Division encountered production problems with two significant products. Then, in mid-July, Marion agreed to merge with Merrell Dow Pharmaceuticals, Inc. The merger froze Laufenberg's expansion plans for the Wound Care Division. Laufenberg explained in October 1989 after West resigned that Marion decided to divest the entire Wound Care Division because its product line did not fit the post-merger company's global marketing strategy.

An employer may not retaliate against an employee for bringing charges of age or sex discrimination. To prove unlawful retaliation discrimination, a plaintiff must show "(1) statutorily protected participation in Title VII or ADEA process adverse employment action; and (2) a connection between the two." An employee is constructively discharged when an employer deliberately renders the employee's working condition intolerable and thus forces her to quit her job. The standard is an objective one. An employee may not be unreasonably sensitive to her working environment. A constructive discharge arises only when a reasonable person would find her working conditions intolerable.

Turning to the issue of constructive discharge, we note that West rejected Laufenberg's September 21 offers without any investigation and immediately resigned. She testified that Laufenberg's September 21 letter was not "a bona fide offer" because the Atlanta positions offered were simply, invitations to interview. But this is contrary to the plain meaning of Laufenberg's letter, which said that "You may take" any open Southeastern sales territory, and that the Prescription Products Division "will provide" a rover sales Position. West admitted that Laufenberg's prior plan to expand the Wound Care Division had been derailed by the recent merger. She could not continue to serve as District Manager for the Western United States while living in Atlanta. In these circumstances, her decision to quit one week after receiving the offers contained in Laufenberg's September 21 letter was unreadably precipitous.

"Part of an employee's obligation to be reasonable is an obligation not to assume the worst and not to jump to conclusions too fast." An employee who quits without giving the employer a reasonable chance to work out a problem is not constructively discharged. Indeed, even if Marion had made the decision to transfer West to a position she opposed, she would not necessarily have been constructively discharged.

Unless the transfer is, in effect, a discharge, the employee has no right simply to walk out. . . . The employee cannot recover damages for losses that he could have avoided without risk of substantial loss or injury.

Here, the problem was caused by West's desire to relocate for personal reasons, so she had an even greater obligation to be flexible and reasonable. West also testified that she rejected Laufenberg's September 21 offers because she considered them a "visible insult" and "another effort on Marion's part to humiliate me." Given West's belief that she had been the victim of long-standing sex and age discrimination, these subjective reactions were no doubt genuine. However, frustration and embarrassment at not being promoted do not make work conditions sufficiently intolerable to constitute constructive discharge.

Judgment for Marion Merrell Dow.

Case Commentary

The Eighth Circuit ruled a female employee's desire to relocate because of her impending marriage, and the subsequent refusal by her employer to relocate her due to the lack of an available opening, did not amount to sex discrimination.

Case Questions

1. Do you agree with the Eighth Circuit's decision?

2. How could the District Court have found in favor of Myrna West?

3. Must the company acquiesce in granting all transfer requests where the employee belongs to a suspect class out of fear of litigation?

4. Do you believe Myrna West knew she would not triumph in court, but attempted to use the lawsuit as leverage to force the company to grant her request?

BONA FIDE OCCUPATIONAL QUALIFICATION (BFOQ)

The bona fide occupational qualification (BFOQ) operates as a defense to a suit for discrimination with regard to religion, national origin, gender, and age. The first three defenses are found in Title VII, while the age BFOQ is found in the Age Discrimination in Employment Act. The courts have narrowly construed this defense, limiting it to job requirements that are essential to the job or are at the core purpose of the business. Mere job relatedness is not sufficient.

EMPLOYMENT PERSPECTIVE

Nancy Hartwick attended Podunk University where she was a star basketball player. She later became a women's basketball coach at Premier College where she won the national championship four times. When a vacancy arose for the men's basketball coach at her alma mater, she applied. Although Podunk's administration had fond affection for Hartwick, they refused her application after consulting the school's students, players, and alumni. The students and alumni said that they would boycott the games. The players said they would have no confidence in her ability. Nancy claimed sex discrimination. Podunk argued that requiring a man to fill the position of men's basketball coach is a BFOQ. Are they correct? No! The preference of the constituents of Podunk does not qualify as a BFOQ. Nancy Hartwick's qualification must be judged in its face alone. Gender preference may not play a part. ■

EMPLOYMENT PERSPECTIVE

Gail Dudack is a sports reporter for the Minnesota Moon, an evening daily newspaper. Gail had been covering women's sporting events, but now with the retirement of Charlie Scofield, she has been elevated to the major team sports. Her first assignment is a pro basketball game. During the game, Shorty Williams scores his 25,000th point. After the contest, all the reporters are rushing into the locker room to interview Shorty. Gail is refused entry because the men are changing and showering and she is a woman. Gail files a claim with the EEOC, alleging pro basketball is discriminating against women reporters. The team argues that the closed-door policy toward women is a BFOQ. Is her claim viable? Yes! The locker-room policy makes it impossible for a woman to be a first-rate reporter. Either the team must allow unrestricted entry or forbid all reporters from the locker room and conduct all interviews in the press room where equal access can be given. ■

EMPLOYMENT PERSPECTIVE

Roger Bishop is a registered nurse at Sumner County Hospital. Roger is on duty one evening when Mildred Dirkson calls for assistance. When Roger attempts to assist Mildred, she admonishes him that she called for a nurse. Roger explains that he is a nurse, but she wants no part of him. Roger queries Mildred about the fact that if he were a physician, she would have no problem having him touch her. The next day Mildred's family complains to the hospital administration, and Roger is assigned to an all-male ward. The hospital justifies its action by asserting it is a BFOQ. Roger claims that this behavior is discriminatory because female nurses are not confined to servicing exclusively female patients. Who is correct? Roger! The hospital's action was not justified. BFOQ's do not apply to one sex but not the other. Hospitals cannot discriminate in deference to their patients' preferences. The patients must accept the hospital staff as long as they are qualified. What if Mildred's request concerned applying medication to or washing the genital area? Every accommodation should be made in this regard if there are female nurses available. Respecting privacy is important. But patients who are hospitalized must have physicians on duty, who are predominantly male, view their private parts if the need arises and their private physician is not available. So, too, with nurses. ■

EQUAL PAY

The Equal Pay Act of 1963 is an amendment to the Fair Labor Standards Act, which regulates child labor, minimum wage, and overtime pay. The Equal Pay Act prohibits the payment of different wages to men and women who are performing the same job. This Act covers all types of job categories from clerical to executive. The jobs must be equal with regard to skill, knowledge, or experience, and the conditions under which the work is performed must be similar. For example, a person working overseas is entitled to a pay differential for the same job performed domestically.

The issue in the following case is whether the job of a prison guard requires a bona fide occupational qualification.

CARL v. ANGELONE

883 F.Supp. 1433 (D.Nev. 1995)

REED, Jr., District Judge.

Plaintiff alleges that Mr. Angelone is the director of Nevada Department of Prisons (NDOP). Plaintiffs are Correctional Officers (C/Os within NDOP). They allege that Mr. Angelone intentionally discriminated against them on the basis of their gender.

Plaintiffs allege that Mr. Angelone transferred Plaintiff male C/Os out of two women's correctional facilities and transferred plaintiff female C/Os from other correctional facilities to fill the vacancies. Mr. Angelone concedes that he did this and that he did so based on the plaintiff's gender: i.e., Mr. Angelone admits he made the transfers because he wanted female correctional officers at the women's correctional facilities and therefore transferred the male officers out because they were men and transferred the female officers in because they were women.

Qualified immunity protects government officials from civil liability for actions taken in the performance of discretionary functions when their actions do not violate clearly established statutory or constitutional rights of which a reasonable person should have known. However, no official can in good faith impose discriminatory burdens on a person or group by reason of a racial or ethnic animus against them. The constitutional right to be free from such invidious discrimination is so well established and so essential to the preservation of our constitutional order that all public officials must be charged with knowledge of it.

In cases involving intentional discrimination there can be no qualified immunity defense, and the dispositive issue of the defendant's intent merge. If the plaintiff fails to establish that the discrimination was intentional, the claim fails. If the plaintiff does establish such intent, there can be no qualified immunity. Thus, it seems simpler to say that qualified immunity is not a defense in such cases rather than that the defense prevails where proof of intentional discrimination is not established.

There is substantial evidence that the motivating factor for Mr. Angelone's actions was the gender of each of the individual plaintiffs. Mr. Angelone not only admits that he took the challenged actions solely on the basis of gender. Mr. Angelone contends that because he thought his actions were legal and appropriate responses, . . . his actions were non-discriminatory.

Mr. Angelone's belief that his actions were legal and appropriate . . . does not remove discriminatory intent from his actions. This raises the affirmative defense of bona fide occupational qualification (bfoq) in which a defendant admits the discriminatory intent motivating the actions, but claims that such actions were otherwise necessary.

The bfoq is an affirmative defense in itself. To allow defendants to elevate it into a qualified immunity appears improper for several reasons. First, the bfoq is an affirmative defense to liability. No good reason is presented why qualified immunity should flow from the assertion of an affirmative defense on which defendant has the burden of proof. This would in essence reverse the burden of proof, requiring plaintiff to demonstrate that defendant could not have reasonably believed the bfoq defense applied, even though the defendant would bear the burden of proving the bfoq defense.

Where discrimination on the basis of gender exists, the employer bears the burden of proving: 1) that the job qualification or function justifying the discrimination is reasonably necessary to the essence of the defendant's particular business; and 2) that gender is a legitimate proxy for the qualification or function because (a) there is a substantial basis for believing that all or nearly all employees of the affected gender lack the qualification or ability to perform that function, or (b) it is impossible or highly impractical for the defendant to insure by individual testing that its employees will have qualifications for the job.

A defendant Prison must demonstrate why it cannot reasonably rearrange job responsibilities within the prison to minimize the clash between the privacy interests of the inmates and the safety of the Prison employees on the one hand and the non-discriminatory requirement of Title VII on the other, before the prison will be entitled to the bfoq exception.

First, Mr. Angelone argues a per se rule making it illegal for male correctional officers to conduct routine or random body searches of female prisoners. If that were so, such a rule would be binding upon Mr. Angelone. . . .

. . . there is no per se rule upon which Mr. Angelone may rely which would permit him to take the challenged actions. There is no per se rule providing a substantial basis for believing that male C/Os lack the legal ability to perform random or routine body searches of female inmates.

Judgment for Carl.

Case Commentary

The District Court of Nevada decided that employing only female correction officers in a female prison is not a bona fide occupational qualification. This policy is discriminatory toward male correction officers.

Case Questions

1. Do you agree with the Court's decision?
2. Do you believe male correction officers should be employed in female prisons?
3. Should male correction officers be allowed to conduct body searches on female inmates if these inmates are uncomfortable with this procedure?
4. Should the BFOQ have been implemented in this case?

In the following case, a female veterinarian claimed that her employer paid her less than similarly experienced male colleagues. The issue is whether the employer discriminated against her in violation of the Equal Pay Act.

CASE

McMILLAN v. MASSACHUSETTS SOC. OF CRUELTY TO ANIMALS

880 F. Supp. 900 (D. Mass. 1995)

STEARNS, District Judge.

Dr. Marjorie McMillan began her career as Director of Radiology at Angell in 1981. She worked continuously until December of 1983, when she took a leave of absence lasting through 1985. Angell maintains some twenty veterinarians on staff who provide direct care as well as instructional guidance to interns and post-graduate residents. McMillan's salary complaint dates from her return as Director of Radiology in 1985.

Until 1989, Thornton served as Angell's Chief of Staff. In that position, he was responsible for setting salary levels for new employees and determining annual increases. In 1989, Thornton became President of the MSPCA and Gambardella designed and implemented a salary system which assigned a grade to every veterinarian and awarded annual increases in pay based on performance evaluations and ranges within each grade. In the year following the implementation of this new pay system, McMillan's salary jumped from $58,295 to $72,000. Notwithstanding this increase, it is undisputed that from 1985 until the termination of her employment on November 26, 1991, McMillan was paid less than any other Director/Department Head, while her job description was for all practical purposes indistinguishable from that of her male colleagues.

McMillan first discovered the pay disparity in August of 1989. She filed a gender discrimination claim with the MCAD in October of 1989. In January of 1990, McMillan entered into negotiations with Angell over the purchase of Windhover, a private aviary practice established by McMillan in Walpole, Mass. McMillan sought to rent space at Angell to carry on the new practice.

To establish a prima facie case under the Equal Pay Act, a plaintiff must show: 1. that her employer is subject to the Act; 2. that discrimination regarding wages occurred within the same working establishment; 3. that she performed work in a position requiring equal skill, effort and responsibility under similar working conditions; and 4. that she was paid less than a comparable employee of the opposite sex. The plaintiff is not required to show that the compared jobs are identical, only that they are "substantially equal." Once a prima facie case is made out under the Equal Pay Act, the employer must resort to the Act's statutory defenses, that is, that pay differentials can be explained by seniority, merit, quantity or quality of production or by "any other factor other than sex."

The affirmative defenses of the Equal Pay Act were incorporated by Congress into Title VII by way of the so-called Bennett Amendment. The Amendment is intended to prevent plaintiffs from using Title VII to circumvent the Equal Pay Act when the pay difference at issue can be justified by one or more of the Equal Pay Acts' affir-

mative defenses. However, as construed by the Supreme Court, the Amendment does not confine Title VII sex-based wage discrimination claims to the four corners of the Equal Pay Act. The Court's concern was with the "equal work" requirement of the Act. If strictly applied in the Title VII context, "this requirement would mean that a woman who is discriminatorily underpaid could obtain no relief—no matter how egregious the discrimination might be—unless her employer also employed a man in an equal job in the same establishment, at a higher rate of pay." Equal Pay Act litigation, therefore, has been structured to permit employers to defend against charges of discrimination where their pay differentials are based on a bona fide use of facts other than sex.

EQUAL PAY

The MSPCA argues that because McMillan as Director/Department Head of Radiology did not have the same supervisory, budgetary, or administrative responsibilities as did other Directors/Department Heads (that is, her job was not "substantially equivalent"), she cannot establish a prima facie case under the Equal Pay Act. Thornton and Gambardella also deny that gender formed the basis of any of their salary decisions. They justify the significant salary differential between McMillan and the others by asserting that her job was less time consuming, produced less revenue for the MSPCA, and involved fewer functions. Specifically, they point to the fact that Radiology had the smallest staff and no actual responsibility for interns or residents.

Because a material dispute of fact exists concerning the comparability of McMillan's position with that of other department heads, the defendant's motion for summary judgment must be denied with respect to a claim of a violation of the Equal Pay Act.

Judgment for McMillan.

Case Commentary

The District Court of Massachusetts held that the Equal Pay Act is at issue. McMillan will be given the opportunity to prove her case at trial.

Case Questions

1. Do you agree with the Court's decision?
2. Do you believe McMillan will triumph?

3. Are there any instances where women do not deserve equal pay?

This case presents the issue of whether the Equal Pay Act infringes upon the states' rights to sovereign immunity.

CASE

ANDERSON v. SUNY COLLEGE AT NEW PALTZ

169 F.3d117 (2d Cir. 1999)

Per Curiam.

Defendants State University of New York, College at New Paltz, et al., appeal from an order of the United States District Court for the Northern District of New York denying their motion to dismiss Plaintiff Dr. Janice W. Anderson's claim pursuant to the Equal Pay Act of 1963 ("EPA"), for lack of subject matter jurisdiction under the Eleventh Amendment. For the reasons that follow, we hold that the District Court has jurisdiction over the plaintiff's EPA claim because Congress abrogated the States sovereign immunity through a valid exercise of its powers under the Fourteenth Amendment.

BACKGROUND

Dr. Anderson brought this suit against various state entities and officers, alleging violations of the EPA, Title VII of the Civil Rights Act of 1964, and the New York Human Rights Law, N.Y. Exec. Law. When she filed her complaint, Dr. Anderson was employed as an Assistant Professor at the State University of New York, College at New Paltz (SUNY New Paltz). Dr. Anderson began teaching in the SUNY New Paltz Communications Department in 1984 and was granted a continuing appointment or tenure in 1991. She alleges that since 1984, she has been paid less than male faculty of similar rank at SUNY New Paltz despite her equivalent or superior qualifications, record, and workload. She began complaining to responsible officials at SUNY New Paltz in 1991, and she contends that she was denied a merit increase in salary in January 1993 as a result of such complaints. She

filed her complaint in this case in the Northern District of New York on July 19, 1995.

DISCUSSION

The EPA was passed in 1963 as an amendment to the Fair Labor Standards Act of 1938 ("FLSA"). As part of the FLSA, the EPA utilizes the FLSA's enforcement mechanisms and employs its definitional provisions. Thus, when the FLSA was amended in 1974 to allow for suit against any employer (including a public agency) in any Federal or State court of competent jurisdiction, the scope of the EPA was extended as well. The FLSA as amended in 1974 evinces a clear intent to abrogate the States sovereign immunity by allowing suit in federal courts. Therefore, we turn to the sole question raised by this appeal whether Congress enacted the EPA pursuant to a valid exercise of its remedial power under the Fourteenth Amendment.

Finally, the EPA's provisions are not out of proportion to the harms that Congress intended to remedy and deter. Since the EPA provides an employer with four affirmative defenses, including the ability to prove that the wage differential is based on any other factor other than sex, the EPA reaches only those wage disparities for which the employee's sex provides the sole explanation. Thus, the statute is remedial legislation reasonably tailored to remedy intentional gender-based wage discrimination and is sufficiently limited in scope.

CONCLUSION

For all of the foregoing reasons, the order of the District Court is affirmed.

Case Commentary

The Second Circuit ruled that the Equal Pay Act was designed to remediate wage dispari- ties where sex was the sole reason for the differential.

Case Questions

1. Was this case decided correctly?
2. Is the Equal Pay Act remedial in nature?

3. Does the Equal Pay Act infringe on the states' rights to sovereign immunity?

COMPARABLE WORTH

Comparable worth is an attempt to assign values to male-dominated and female-dominated jobs based on worth. Where the values are equated, equal pay would be required. The theory behind this doctrine was that most female-dominated jobs pay less than male-dominated jobs. This argument has not found favor with the courts because assigning values is arbitrary and interferes with payments based on supply and demand.

EMPLOYMENT PERSPECTIVE

Gary Josephson is a construction worker. Jessica Tremont is a stenographer. He earns $36,000. She earns $22,000. Jessica argues that both jobs have comparable worth and that she should earn the same as Gary. Is she correct? No! Although her argument is based on comparable worth, the courts have decided not to enforce this doctrine. ∎

GROOMING

When employers attempt to regulate grooming, *i.e.,* length of hair, beards, and mustaches, courts have usually found in favor of the employer. Their reasoning is that grooming codes are more closely related to the manner in which an employer decides to operate its business than to equal opportunity. Good grooming standards have always been required in the business world. Imagine walking into a bank and seeing a long-haired branch manager who has not shaved or showered, wearing jeans and a wrinkled shirt. This kind of appearance is not allowed because it would not be a good business policy. Customers may lose confidence in the bank and move their accounts elsewhere.

Arguments against grooming codes have come in the form of the First Amendment's rights of speech through personal expression, the Fourteenth Amendment Equal Protection Clause, and Title VII's provision regarding terms and conditions of employment.

EMPLOYMENT PERSPECTIVE

Richard Masters is 29, and he is becoming bald. He is very self-conscious, so he has started wearing a hat all the time. Richard works as a bond trader for Bulls and Bears, Inc. While his manager empathizes with Richard's dilemma, Richard is told to remove the hat while in the office. Richard objects, claiming that baldness is a disability, and files a claim with the EEOC. Will he win? Probably not! Richard is not being subjected to discrimination because of his disability. If Richard is harassed by coworkers, he may register a complaint for harassment. That is not the problem here, though. It revolves around Richard's vanity and his own perception of himself. This reasoning cannot outweigh Bulls and Bears' maintenance of dress codes as the way it conducts its business. ■

EMPLOYMENT PERSPECTIVE

Mary Jo Worthington, a longtime customer at Grasmere Bank, is informed by Felix Farnsworth that he will be leaving the branch for a new position. On Monday, his replacement will begin. When Mary Jo enters the bank on Monday, she is horrified to see a long-haired man who has neither showered nor shaved, wearing jeans, cowboy boots, and a T-shirt, sitting behind Felix's old desk. The scruffy man smiles, then introduces himself as Jesse Mickelson, new branch manager. Mary Jo dashed out of the bank and calls its customer service department reporting what she saw. Mickelson is informed of the bank's grooming policy and told never to be seen like that again. The next day, Mickelson looks the same and therefore is immediately terminated. He files a Title VII claim with the EEOC asserting that his actions are protected by freedom of speech through personal expression. Jesse also claims the grooming policy as a term and condition of employment is discrimination. Is he correct? Most likely not! Although there have been conflicting cases, the bank will be able to enforce its grooming policy because it is requiring of Mickelson only what is considered to be the norm in American business. He is not being deprived of an equal opportunity. He is only being asked to conform to the generally accepted standards of our society. ■

EMPLOYMENT PERSPECTIVE

Sonja Hendricks was a trader at First Financial in Buffalo. Their company dress code requires women to wear skirts, dresses, or suits with skirts. In the winter, the temperature is often below freezing. Sonja wore pants to keep her legs warm. First Financial dismissed her for being uncooperative. She claimed that the dress code manifested sex discrimination because it forced women to show their legs and to be subjected to the cold weather. Is she correct? Probably! This restriction places an undue burden on women in that it does not give them the choice to protect themselves from the cold during the winter months. First Financial's business reasons are not paramount to a woman's health. However, First Financial may suggest women wear leg warmers or tights under their skirts or dresses and then remove then upon arriving to work. There is no definitive answer to this scenario. ■

In the next case, a female contests an employer's dress code as being discriminatory in that the women's attire is demeaning as compared with the men's attire. The women were suspended when they wore the same business attire as the men.

O'DONNELL v. BURLINGTON COAT FACTORY WAREHOUSE

706 F. Supp. 263 (S.D.Ohio 1987)

SPIEGEL, District Judge.

In this sex discrimination action, plaintiffs, female sales clerks at defendants' retail store, challenge defendants' dress code as being violative of Title VII of the Civil Rights Act of 1964. The dress code in question requires female sales clerks to wear a "smock," while male sales clerks only are required to wear business attire consisting of slacks, shirt and a necktie. The smocks are supplied to the female sales clerks at no cost. After complaining that the smock requirement for women is discriminatory, plaintiffs refused to wear the smocks and instead wore regular business attire. Plaintiffs filed sex discrimination charges with the EEOC on August 18, 1983. Thereafter, plaintiffs reported for work wearing a blouse and tie and each day they were suspended. On August 30, 1983, plaintiffs were discharged when they refused to wear smocks. Plaintiffs filed charges with the EEOC claiming their discharge was sex discrimination and retaliation. Subsequently, the EEOC determined that there was reasonable cause to believe that the charge was true. After attempts at conciliation proved futile, plaintiffs commenced the present action in this Court. Both parties agree that the issue before this Court on summary judgment is whether defendants' dress code requiring female sales clerks to wear a smock while allowing male sales clerks to wear a shirt and tie is discriminatory under Title VII. The defendants' contend that distinctions between the sexes that do not adversely effect the terms and conditions of employment or employment opportunities do not violate Title VII. In Barker, the Court upheld an employer's grooming code which mandated shorter hair lengths for men than for women. Importantly, this grooming code set standards for both sexes: it regulated the length of men's hair and the styles for women's hair. According to defendants, the question we must decide is whether the differences in treatment created disadvantages for women in their compensation, terms, conditions or privileges of employment or employment opportunities. Because plaintiffs stipulated that wearing the smocks had no effect on their salary, benefits, hours of employment, raises, employment evaluations or any other term or condition of employment, defendants argue that the distinction in question is not discriminatory. Analogizing the dress requirement here to the grooming code in Barker, defendants claim both sexes had equal burdens with respect to their dress requirements: female employees had to wear a smock and male employees had to wear a shirt and tie. Plaintiffs acknowledge that Title VII does not prohibit all differences in treatment between the sexes but claim that a rule requiring only women to wear a smock does violate Title VII. In support of the position, plaintiffs claim that the instant case should not be governed by the "hair length/grooming" line of decisions cited by defendants. Rather, plaintiffs direct our attention to cases directly addressing "uniform" requirements that mandate different dress standards for male and female employees. In the lead case of *Carroll v. Talman Fed. Sav. & Loan,* a bank required its female tellers, officers and managerial employees to wear a uniform while male employees working in the same positions were required only to wear customary business attire. Unlike the case at bar, the female employees in Talman incurred the initial cost of their uniforms as well as subsequent cleaning and maintenance expenses. The employer expressly maintained that the purpose of the uniform requirement was to reduce fashion competition among women. Since men do not engage in such competition, they do not need a uniform requirement.

The Seventh Circuit held that personal appearance regulations with differing requirements for men and women do not violate Title VII as long as there is "some justification in commonly accepted social norms and are reasonably related to the employer's business needs." However, an employer who imposes separate dress requirements for men and women performing the same jobs will violate Title VII when one sex can wear regular business attire and the other must wear a uniform. Finding the uniform requirement demeaning to women, the Talman Court stated; "while there is nothing offensive about uniforms per se, when some employees are uniformed and others are not there is a natural tendency to assume that the uniformed women have lesser professional status than their colleagues." Even though defendants have expressed no discriminatory motive for the "smock" rule, we find that the blatant effect of such a rule is to perpetuate sexual stereotypes. We believe the cornerstone of the Talman decision is that it is demeaning for one sex to wear a uniform when members of the other sex holding the same positions are allowed to wear professional business attire. In contrast to the "hair length" standards for male employees, the smock requirement finds no justification in accepted social norms. Moreover, as plaintiffs point out, defendants have several non-discriminatory alternatives for achieving the goal of sales clerk identification: both sexes could wear the smock, a distinguishing blazer or identifying badges on their professional attire. Thus, we find that the smock rule creates disadvantages to the conditions of employment of females sales clerks and hence, is a violation of Title VII.

Judgment for O'Donnell.

Case Commentary

The Southern District of Ohio ruled that requiring women to wear smocks, while men wore business attire, constituted sex discrimination because the requirement was demeaning to women.

Case Questions

1. Do you agree with the Court's decision?
2. Why do you think the company had different requirements for men and women?
3. If you were representing the company, what argument would you make on its behalf?

CUSTOMER PREFERENCES

Although we are in an age in which customer service and satisfaction rules, acceding to customer preferences for service exclusively by one gender to the exclusion of the other is contradictory to Title VII's prohibition against gender discrimination.

EMPLOYMENT PERSPECTIVE

Tooters, a sports bar and restaurant chain, known for its voluptuous female servers, has recently received applications from Ken, Frank, and Nick, who seek employment as servers. Tooters polls its clientele, who resoundingly state that they will no longer frequent the premises if male servers appear. Tooters denies the position to Ken, Frank, and Nick because of their gender. Ken, Frank, and Nick sue for sex discrimination arguing as long as they were otherwise qualified, they cannot be refused employment on the basis of their gender. Is the customer always right and will they be toiling at Tooters? This issue has been left in doubt in light of the EEOC's recent decision not to pursue its case involving a similar situation against Hooters Restaurant. ■

Job selection cannot be based on customer preference for a particular gender; otherwise, it is discriminatory.

EMPLOYMENT PERSPECTIVE

Thomas Stockwell applies for a position with "Workouts for Women Only," a health club exclusively for women. He is denied employment because he is a man. The proprietors are concerned with respecting the privacy rights of women. They argue that requiring only women employees is a bona fide occupational qualification. Thomas argues that assisting women with fitness instruction, teaching aerobics, and performing desk duties do not qualify as a BFOQ. Besides, he adds there are female employees available for locker-room maintenance. Is he correct? Yes! The preference of women customers to refrain from working out in front of men does not qualify as a BFOQ sufficient enough to override perpetuating discrimination against men by requiring their exclusion from employment. ■

❖ EMPLOYER LESSONS

- Formulate grooming standards and dress codes.
- Treat men and women in a consistent manner.
- Eliminate stereotypes when employing and/or assigning men and women to particular jobs.
- Identify instances of sex plus discrimination.
- Pay women an amount equal to men when the qualifications needed and the work performed are similar.
- Know that bona fide occupational qualifications exist only in a very limited number of instances, such as for bathroom or locker room attendants.
- Realize that customer preferences cannot dictate your hiring selections with regard to sex.
- Learn that comparable worth has never been implemented in employment.
- Encourage women to realize their full potential in the workplace.
- Understand that men may also be victims of sex discrimination.

❖ EMPLOYEE LESSONS

- Know what constitutes sex discrimination.
- Learn the requirement for filing a sex discrimination claim.
- Ascertain whether as a woman you are being paid a salary comparable to a man with similar experience for the same job.
- Do not let stereotypes hinder your realization of your true potential.
- Appreciate why the enactment of the Equal Pay Act and the Civil Rights Act of 1964 was needed to protect women's rights.
- Understand that under certain limited circumstances, your sex may disqualify you from being hired because of a bona fide occupational qualification.
- Realize that the doctrine of comparable worth was never implemented because supply and demand renders it impractical.
- Demand that you be treated in a manner consistent with the opportunities afforded to employees of the opposite sex.

- Be cognizant of situations where you are discriminated against not only based on sex, but also because you have small children, are pregnant, or care for elderly parents, *i.e.*, sex plus discrimination.
- Be aware of grooming and dress code requirements and adhere to them where they are consistent and reasonable.

❖ SUMMARY

In the past, American society excluded women from many positions in the labor market because they could afford to. The American society was the most affluent in the world while its economy was flourishing almost exclusively at the hands of men. In today's global environment no brain can be left untapped. Women should be encouraged by men to realize their potential in the workplace. Some men fear that employing women in business will reduce the number of positions for them. Their fear is misdirected. "Us against them" should not mean men against women. It should mean keeping the jobs in the United States as opposed to losing them to foreign labor. If the power of each American male and female is not used to its fullest to become innovators and entrepreneurs to develop newer, faster, cheaper, and better products, services, and technologies, then the positions that men are trying to safeguard from women will be lost to overseas competitors. The key is that the number and quality of jobs are elastic and can expand or contract, depending upon how well we perform.

❖ REVIEW QUESTIONS

1. Define sex discrimination.
2. What is sex plus discrimination?
3. Explain the significance of the Equal Pay Act.
4. Define comparable worth.
5. Is comparable worth in effect today?
6. Are grooming standards permissible?
7. Can a man be discriminated against because of his gender?
8. Why is a BFOQ a defense to a gender discrimination suit?
9. Ethically, should women tennis players be paid the same as the men in the U.S. Open, even though the women play 2 out of 3 sets in comparison to the 3 out of 5 sets played by the men?
10. Are employers justified in practicing sex discrimination in hiring because of customer preferences?
11. Should grooming codes be the same for men as for women?
12. Is the Equal Pay Act helping women to achieve equality in pay?
13. Is there any reason why women should not be paid at the same rate as a man?
14. What must a plaintiff prove to establish a prima facie case under the Equal Pay Act?
15. Marilyn A. Doerter was hired as Assistant Dean at Bluffton College by Dean William Hawk. Less than a year later, she was terminated because of her lack of skills and her inability to communicate effectively with Dean Hawk. She was replaced by a woman. Doerter claimed sex discrimination, arguing Dean Hawk was unfriendly toward her and preferred the company of other men. Doerter acknowledged that a personality conflict existed that contributed to the communications problem. What was the result? *Doerter v. Bluffton College*, 647 N.E.2d 876 (Ohio App. 3 Dist. 1994)
16. King, a professor at the University of Wisconsin, applied for tenure. Her tenure review was not granted because she did not provide any scholarly publications. King claimed sex discrimination. What was the result? *King v. Board of Regents of Wisconsin System*, 898 F.2d 533 (7th Cir. 1990)
17. The crux of plaintiff's sex discrimination claim is a comparison of the treatment of her

and the treatment of Mr. Mann for the handling of the Hanlon Call. Plaintiff was eventually terminated for her actions while Mann did not receive discipline. Plaintiff also contends that Mann shared the responsibility and some degree of culpability for the alleged errors in the handling of the Hanlon call. Plaintiff admitted in her brief, and in her oral arguments before this court, that she had primary responsibility for the Hanlon call. An internal affairs investigation directed by John C. Driscoll determined that plaintiff's confusion as to Hanlon's location at the mall had caused her to commit several serious errors, including failure to ask any questions from the EMD protocol cards; failure to determine that the Hanlon call was an injury type call; an inappropriate delay of dispatch; and an inappropriate dispatch. Plaintiff argues that the fact that the dispatchers used a team concept and that Mann was involved with the Hanlon call created a shared responsibility and some degree of culpability on Mann's part for the errors in the handling of the Hanlon call. What was the result? *Sorensen v. City of Aurora,* 984 F.2d 349 (10th Cir. 1993)

18. In January 1990, Plaintiff asked the bank if she could work only in the afternoons and use accumulated sick leave to pay for the mornings that she would not be working. The bank granted her request, and plaintiff continued to receive the same salary even though she worked only afternoons.

   On May 4, 1990, plaintiff requested a one-year leave of absence for health reasons. The bank again granted plaintiff's request.

   Plaintiff contends that the bank created a hostile working environment for older employees, and that she suffered mental anguish and depression as a result. She claims that her depression caused and aggravated her physical ailments.

   Plaintiff . . . alleges claims of sex discrimination under the Minnesota Human Rights Act ("MHRA") and Title VII of the Civil Rights Act. What was the result? *Zelewski v. American Federal Sav. Bank,* 811 F.Supp. 456 (D.Minn. 1993)

19. Ezold was hired at Wolf by Seymour Kurland, then chairman of the litigation department.

The district court found that Kurland told Ezold during an interview that it would not be easy for her at Wolf because "she was a woman, had not attended an Ivy League law school, and had not been on law review."

   Kurland was at one time a decision maker and eventually supported Ezold's admission to the partnership; he took no part in the final votes or evaluation concerning Ezold's termination because he had by that time left the firm. What was the result? *Ezold v. Wolf, Block, Schorr and Solis-Cohen,* 983 F. 2d 509 (3rd Cir. 1992)

20. Until February 1983, Hastings' immediate, first line supervisor was Senior Surety Bond Officer Helen Edwards. Edwards was transferred to the Denver District Office after filing numerous complaints for sex and age discrimination against the SBA and several individuals, including Hastings.

   In February 1985, Edwards prevailed on portions of her sex discrimination case, and in May of that year she was transferred back to the Denver Regional Offices Surety Bond Division. Edwards once again became Hastings' first line supervisor and Berry was moved to Hastings' second line supervisor and Edwards' immediate supervisor. Hastings claims after Edwards' return to the bond surety program, she began subjecting him to various forms of hostile treatment, including delays in reviewing his work that caused his performance evaluations to suffer and public abuse of Hastings in the presence of his coworkers. What was the result? *Hastings v. Saiki,* 824 F. Supp. 969 (D. Colo. 1993)

21. Dr. Chance complained to Rice officials that her salary was not commensurate with that of her male colleagues, and that she was not given adequate consideration for two "endowed chairs," prestigious positions within the department that carry a title and increased compensation. She complained that these inequities resulted from the subjective determination of compensation and promotion within her department, a process controlled by males.

   In response to Dr. Chance's allegations, Rice officials reviewed her past internal evaluations and asked other scholars, both within and outside Rice, to critique her published works. Based upon this investigation, the officials concluded that Dr. Chance's salary was commensurate with her abilities, and that she was not a victim of sexual discrimination within the English Department. What was the result? *Chance v. Rice University,* 989 F. 2d 179 (5th Cir. 1993)

❖ WEB SITES

www.findlaw.com
www.westlaw.com
www.eeoc.gov/facts/fs-sex.html
http://workers.labor.net.au/26/news9_sex.html
www.pfc.org.uk/legal/sda-gr.htm
www.info.gov.hk/hab/sdo.htm
www.nationalpartnership.org/work and family/workplace/doublediscrim/rs_discrim.htm

Sexual Harassment

INTRODUCTION

Sexual harassment encompasses the request for sexual favors as well as touching, joking, commenting, or distributing material of a sexual nature that an employee has not consented to and finds offensive. The aggrieved individual may initiate a lawsuit against the individual personally or may proceed against the company. If there was unpermitted touching, this gives rise to the torts of civil assault and battery. If there were sexual comments made with a particular individual in mind, that would constitute slander. If sexual comments were written or sexual pictorials were drawn, it would be libel. If generic comments were made that degraded the gender, an individual could claim the tort of infliction of emotional distress.

REQUIREMENTS

There are six requirements that must be satisfied for sexual harassment to exist:

1. The victimizing employee alleging sexual harassment must be a member of a protected class, that is, a man or a woman.
2. The complaint must be gender related, for example, a female must assert there would have been no harassment if she were not a woman.
3. The employee must not have consented to the sexual advances or participated in the hostile work environment.
4. The harassment must be based on sex.
5. The conduct complained of must have had a deleterious effect on the employee's job.
6. *Respondeat superior* exists, that is, the harassment must have occurred during the scope of employment, thus making the employer liable for the sexual harassing conduct of its employees.

CHAPTER CHECKLIST

❖ Identify what constitutes sexual harassment.

❖ Learn the distinction between the two types of sexual harassment: *quid pro quo* and hostile work environment.

❖ Know that sexual harassment must be severe and pervasive to be actionable.

❖ Understand that terms such as babe, sweetheart, and honey are not severe, but may violate company policy.

❖ Appreciate that sexual harassment must be based on sex.

❖ Be aware that harassment that is neither sexual nor covered under any suspect classification is not protected under the Civil Rights Act of 1964.

❖ Be cognizant of the fact that victims of harassment may sue the perpetrator under tort law in state court.

❖ Be apprised of the fact that sexual harassment suits are brought only against the company.

❖ Understand that the sexual harassment must have occurred within the scope of employment.

❖ Know that employers are generally liable only where they have failed to investigate and/or take appropriate action.

❖ Become familiar with your employer's sexual harassment policy and conduct yourself accordingly.

The issues in this case are whether hostile work environment is an actionable form of sexual harassment and whether an employer is absolutely liable for sexual harassment whether it knows about it or not.

CASE

MERITOR SAVINGS BANK v. VINSON

477 U.S. 57 (1986)

JUSTICE REHNQUIST delivered the opinion of the Court.
This case presents important questions concerning claims of workplace "sexual harassment" brought under Title VII of the Civil Rights Act of 1964.

I

In 1974, respondent Mechelle Vinson met Sidney Taylor, a vice president of what is now petitioner Meritor Savings Bank (bank) and manager of one of its branch offices. When respondent asked whether she might obtain employment at the bank, Taylor gave her an application, which she completed and returned the next day; later that same day Taylor called her to say that she had been hired. With Taylor as her supervisor, respondent started as a teller-trainee, and thereafter was promoted to teller, head teller, and assistant branch manager. She worked at the same branch for four years, and it is undisputed that her advancement there was based on merit alone. In September 1978, respondent notified Taylor that she was taking sick leave for an indefinite period. On November 1, 1978, the bank discharged her for excessive use of that leave.

Respondent brought this action against Taylor and the bank, claiming that during her four years at the bank she had "constantly been subjected to sexual harassment" by Taylor in violation of Title VII. She sought injunctive relief, compensatory and punitive damages against Taylor and the bank, and attorney's fees.

At the 11-day bench trial, the parties presented conflicting testimony about Taylor's behavior during respondent's employment. Respondent testified that during her probationary period as a teller-trainee, Taylor treated her in a fatherly way and made no sexual advances. Shortly thereafter, however, he invited her out to dinner and, during the course of the meal, suggested that they go to a motel to have sexual relations. At first she refused, but out of what she described as fear of losing her job she eventually agreed. According to respondent, Taylor thereafter made repeated demands upon her for sexual favors, usually at the branch, both during and after business hours; she estimated that over the next several years she had intercourse with him some 40 or 50 times. In addition, respondent testified that Taylor fondled her in front of other employees, followed her into the women's restroom when she went there alone, exposed himself to her, and even forcibly raped her on several occasions. These activities ceased after 1977, respondent stated, when she started going with a steady boyfriend.

Taylor denied respondent's allegations of sexual activity, testifying that he never fondled her, never made suggestive remarks to her, never engaged in sexual intercourse with her, and never asked her to do so. He contended instead that respondent made her accusations in response to a business-related dispute. The bank also denied respondent's allegations and asserted that any sexual harassment by Taylor was unknown to the bank and engaged in without its consent or approval.

The District Court denied relief, but did not resolve the conflicting testimony about the existence of a sexual relationship between respondent and Taylor. It found instead that

"if respondent and Taylor did engage in an intimate or sexual relationship during the time of respondent's employment with the bank, that relationship was a voluntary one having nothing to do with her continued employment at the bank or her advancement or promotions at that institution.

The court ultimately found that respondent "was not the victim of sexual harassment and was not the victim of sexual discrimination" while employed at the bank. Although it concluded that respondent had not proved a violation of Title VII, the District Court nevertheless went on to address the bank's liability. After noting the bank's express policy against discrimination, and finding that neither respondent nor any other employee had ever lodged a complaint about sexual harassment by Taylor, the court ultimately concluded that "the bank was without notice and cannot be held liable for the alleged actions of Taylor."

The Court of Appeals for the District of Columbia Circuit reversed. The court stated that a violation of Title VII may be predicated on either of two types of sexual harassment: harassment that involves the conditioning of concrete employment benefits on sexual favors, and harassment that, while not affecting economic benefits, creates a hostile or offensive working environment.

As to the bank's liability, the Court of Appeals held that an employer is absolutely liable for sexual harassment practiced by supervisory personnel, whether or not the employer knew or should have known about the misconduct. The court relied chiefly on Title VII's definition of "employer" to include "any agent of such a person." The court held that a supervisor is an "agent" of his employer for Title VII purposes, even if he lacks authority to hire, fire, or promote, since "the mere existence—or even the appearance—of a significant degree of influence in vital job decisions gives any supervisor the opportunity to impose on employees."

We granted certiorari and now affirm but for different reasons.

II

In defining "sexual harassment," the EEOC Guidelines first describe the kinds of workplace conduct that may be actionable under Title VII. These include "unwelcome sexual advances, requests for sexual favors, and other verbal or physical conduct of a sexual nature." Relevant to the charges at issue in this case, the Guidelines provide that such sexual misconduct constitutes prohibited "sexual harassment," whether or not it is directly linked to the grant or denial of an economic quid pro quo, where "such conduct has the purpose or effect of unreasonably interfering with an individual's work performance or creating an intimidating, hostile, or offensive working environment."

Since the Guidelines were issued, courts have uniformly held, and we agree, that a plaintiff may establish a violation of Title VII by proving that discrimination based on sex has created a hostile or abusive work environment.

Of course, not all workplace conduct that may be described as "harassment" affects a "term, condition, or privilege" of employment within the meaning of Title VII ("mere utterance of an ethnic or racial epithet which engenders offensive feelings in an employee" would not affect the conditions of employment to sufficiently significant degree to violate Title VII). For sexual harassment to be actionable, it must be sufficiently severe or pervasive "to alter the conditions of the victim's employment and create an abusive working environment." Respondent's allegations in this case — which include not only pervasive harassment but also criminal conduct of the most serious nature — are plainly sufficient to state a claim for "hostile environment" sexual harassment.

In sum, we hold that a claim of "hostile environment" sex discrimination is actionable under Title VII, that the District Court's findings were insufficient to dispose of respondent's hostile environment claim, and that the District Court did not err in admitting testimony about respondent's sexually provocative speech and dress. As to employer liability, we conclude that the Court of Appeals was wrong to entirely disregard agency principles and impose absolute liability on employers for the acts of their supervisors, regardless of the circumstances of a particular case.

Accordingly, the judgment of the Court of Appeals reversing the judgment of the District Court is affirmed, and the case is remanded for further proceedings consistent with this opinion.

Case Commentary

The United States Supreme Court held in *Meritor* that an employer will be liable for a hostile work environment where the employer knew or should have known that the behavior complained of was severe and pervasive. This was the major case establishing hostile work environment as a form of sexual harassment under Title VII.

Case Questions

1. Do you agree with the Court's decision?
2. Why is the employer not absolutely liable for all severe and pervasive behavior of its employees which lead to a hostile work environment claim?

3. Do you believe Taylor's conduct was severe and pervasive?

The issue in the following case is whether an employee must have suffered harm to her psychological well-being in order for her to claim hostile work environment.

HARRIS v. FORKLIFT SYSTEMS, INC.

510 U.S. 17 (1993)

JUSTICE O'CONNOR delivered the opinion of the Court.

In this case, we consider the definition of a discriminatorily "abusive work environment" (also known as a "hostile work environment") under Title VII of the Civil Rights Act of 1964.

I

Teresa Harris worked as a manager at Forklift Systems, Inc., an equipment rental company, from April, 1985, until October, 1987. Charles Hardy was Forklift's president.

The Magistrate found that, throughout Harris' time at Forklift, Hardy often insulted her because of her gender and often made her the target of unwanted sexual innuendos. Hardy told Harris on several occasions, in the presence of other employees, "You're a woman, what do you know" and "We need a man as the rental manager"; at least once, he told her she was "a dumb ass woman." Again in front of others, he suggested that the two of them "go to the Holiday Inn to negotiate Harris' raise." Hardy occasionally asked Harris and other female employees to get coins from his front pants pocket. He threw objects on the ground in front of Harris and other women, and asked them to pick the objects up. He made sexual innuendos about Harris' and other women's clothing.

In mid-August, 1987, Harris complained to Hardy about his conduct. Hardy said he was surprised that Harris was offended, claimed he was only joking, and apologized. He also promised he would stop, and, based on this assurance Harris stayed on the job. But in early September, Hardy began anew: While Harris was arranging a deal with one of Forklift's customers, he asked her, again in front of other employees, "What did you do, promise the guy . . . some sex Saturday

night?" On October 1, Harris collected her paycheck and quit.

Harris then sued Forklift, claiming that Hardy's conduct had created an abusive work environment for her because of her gender. The United States District Court for the Middle District of Tennessee, adopting the report and recommendation of the Magistrate, found this to be "a close case," but held that Hardy's conduct did not create an abusive environment. The court found that some of Hardy's comments "offended Harris, and would offend the reasonable woman," but that they were not "so severe as to be expected to seriously affect Harris' psychological wellbeing." A reasonable woman manager under like circumstances would have been offended by Hardy, but his conduct would not have risen to the level of interfering with that person's work performance.

"Neither do I believe that Harris was subjectively so offended that she suffered injury. . . . Although Hardy may at times have genuinely offended Harris, I do not believe that he created a working environment so poisoned as to be intimidating or abusive to Harris."

In focusing on the employee's psychological wellbeing, the District Court was following Circuit precedent.

We granted certiorari to resolve a conflict among the Circuits on whether conduct, to be actionable as "abusive work environment" harassment (no quid pro quo harassment issue is present here), must "seriously affect an employee's psychological wellbeing" or lead the plaintiff to "suffer injury."

II

Title VII of the Civil Rights Act of 1964 makes it "an unlawful employment practice for an employer . . . to discriminate against any individual with respect to his compensation, terms, conditions, or privileges of employment, because of such individual's race, color, religion, sex, or national origin." As we made clear in Meritor Savings Bank v. Vinson, this language is not limited to "economic" or "tangible" discrimination. The phrase "terms, conditions, or privileges of employment" evinces a congressional intent "to strike at the entire spectrum of disparate treatment of men and women in employment," which includes requiring people to work in a discriminatorily hostile or abusive environment. When the workplace is permeated with "discriminatory intimidation, ridicule, and insult,"that is "sufficiently severe or pervasive to alter the conditions of the victim's employment and create an abusive working environment," Title VII is violated.

This standard, which we reaffirm today, takes a middle path between making actionable any conduct that is merely offensive and requiring the conduct to cause a tangible psychological injury. As we pointed out in Meritor, "mere utterance of an . . . epithet which engenders offensive feelings in a employee," does not sufficiently affect the conditions of employment to implicate Title VII. Conduct that is not severe or pervasive enough to create an objectively hostile or abusive work environment—an environment that a reasonable person would find hostile or abusive—is beyond Title VII's purview. Likewise, if the victim does not subjectively perceive the environment to be abusive, the conduct has not actually altered the conditions of the victim's employment, and there is no Title VII violation.

But Title VII comes into play before the harassing conduct leads to a nervous breakdown. A discriminatorily abusive work environment, even one that does not seriously affect employees' psychological wellbeing, can and often will detract from employees' job performance, discourage employees from remaining on the job, or keep them from advancing in their careers. Moreover, even without regard to these tangible effects, the very fact that the discriminatory conduct was so severe or pervasive that it created a work environment abusive to employees because of their race, gender, religion, or national origin offends Title VII's broad rule of workplace equality. The appalling conduct alleged in

Meritor, and the reference in that case to environments "so heavily polluted with discrimination as to destroy completely the emotional and psychological stability of minority group workers," merely present some especially egregious examples of harassment. They do not mark the boundary of what is actionable.

We therefore believe the District Court erred in relying on whether the conduct "seriously affected plaintiff's psychological wellbeing" or led her to "suffer injury." Such an inquiry may needlessly focus the factfinder's attention on concrete psychological harm, an element Title VII does not require. Certainly Title VII bars conduct that would seriously affect a reasonable person's psychological wellbeing, but the statute is not limited to such conduct. So long as the environment would reasonably be perceived, and is perceived, as hostile or abusive,there is no need for it also to be psychologically injurious.

This is not, and by its nature cannot be, a mathematically precise test. But we can say that whether an environment is "hostile" or "abusive" can be determined only by looking at all the circumstances. These may include the frequency of the discriminatory conduct; its severity; whether it is physically threatening or humiliating, or a mere offensive utterance; and whether it unreasonably interferes with an employee's work performance. The effect on the employee's psychological wellbeing is, of course, relevant to determining whether the plaintiff actually found the environment abusive. But, while psychological harm, like any other relevant factor, may be taken into account, no single factor is required.

III

Forklift, while conceding that a requirement that the conduct seriously affect psychological wellbeing is unfounded, argues that the District Court nonetheless correctly applied the Meritor standard. We disagree. Though the District Court did conclude that the work environment was not "intimidating or abusive to Harris," it did so only after finding that the conduct was not "so severe as to be expected to seriously affect plaintiff's psychological well-being," and that Harris was not "subjectively so offended that she suffered injury," The District Court's application of these incorrect standards may well have influenced its ultimate conclusion, especially given that the court found this to be a "close case."

We therefore reverse the judgment of the Court of Appeals, and remand the case for further proceedings consistent with this opinion.

Judgment for Harris.

Case Commentary

The United States Supreme Court held that an employee's psychological well-being does not have to be adversely affected for there to be grounds for her claim of hostile work environ-ment. It may be a factor to be considered, but it is enough if the conduct complained of is severe and pervasive.

Case Questions

1. Do you agree with the Court's decision?
2. Do you believe the conduct complained of was severe and pervasive?

3. Should there be a universal standard for what constitutes a hostile work environment?

EMPLOYMENT PERSPECTIVE

George Miles works as an insurance underwriter. In the office, he has openly stated his view that women are good only for sex and do not belong in the workplace because they are always crying about PMS. Susan cringes when she hears these remarks and tries to hide from George lest she become a target. George continues to fondle Amanda's backside when she has repeatedly admonished him. He photostated a caricature of Debbie, a coworker, as a naked woman with large breasts. George speaks about the pornographic films that he has viewed and describes them in detail. He also has commented that he is due for a promotion after having sex with Margaret, the vice president for operations. What recourse do these women have against George? Amanda may sue George for the tort of battery because the fondling was unpermitted touching that she has found offensive and embarrassing. Margaret may sue for slander because George's remarks are untrue and damaging to her reputation. Debbie may sue for libel because the sexually offensive drawing has been distributed. Susan may sue for infliction of emotional distress because his comments, although not directed at her personally, are degrading to her because she is a woman. ■

The majority of the victims who are harassed seek recovery from the company, the rule of thumb being to sue the deepest pocket.

The following case addresses the question of whether an employee can sue her supervisor individually for sexual harassment.

PARSONS v. NATIONWIDE MUTUAL INS. CO.

899 F. Supp. 465 (M.D. Fla. 1995)

KOVACHEVICH, Judge.

Plaintiffs (Parsons, Selph and MacDonald) were employed on the office staff at Nationwide Mutual Insurance. Defendant Walker was also employed by Nationwide, and during the scope of this employment Defendant Walker alleged orally published "rude and offensive remarks" about Plaintiffs sexual practices, gave detailed accounts of his own sexual exploits, made unwelcome sexually suggestive comments to Plaintiffs and generally created a sexually graphic and offensive work environment. After the occurrence of the alleged events, each of the Plaintiffs were discharged from employment at Nationwide. As a result of these supposed actions, Plaintiffs brought suit against Defendants Walker and Nationwide.

Plaintiffs allege that Defendants (hereinafter "Walker" and "Nationwide") are joint employers of Plaintiffs because of Nationwide's "exercise of substantial control of the business of Defendant Walker including ownership of accounts, equipment and contracts, the interrelationship of operations, and the centralized control of labor relations and common management." However, Plaintiffs fail to specifically allege in the complaint what Walker's role is within Nationwide. Further, there is no mention of Walker's official capacity or job title at Nationwide; it may only be inferred that Walker held some form of supervisory control over Plaintiffs.

Walker moves to dismiss the sexual harassment and retaliation claims against him because he alleges that he is being sued in his individual capacity as a result of his employment at Nationwide.

The court professed that, "The relief granted under Title VII is against the employer, not individual employees whose actions constitute a violation of the Act," and "the proper method for a plaintiff to recover under Title VII is by suing the employer, either by naming the supervisory employees, as agents of the employer or by naming the employer directly." The crux . . . is that, even though Congress defined "employer" to include any "agent" this provision does not impose individual liability but only holds the employer accountable for the acts of its individual agents. Even though such a definition might be construed so as to impose liability on individual employees as "agents" the Eleventh Circuit Court has held that agents of employers who violate Title VII provisions only trigger an action against the employer, and not an action against the individual agent/employee. Moreover, the law in the Eleventh Circuit has been settled that there is no individual liability under Title VII. "If Congress had envisioned individual liability under Title VII for compensatory or punitive damages, it would have included individuals in this litany of limitations and would have discontinued the exemption for small employers."

Judgment for Nationwide.

Case Commentary

The Florida Middle District Court ruled that Title VII does not provide for individual liability in cases of sexual harassment. Parsons could sue Walker individually under tort law in state court.

Case Questions

1. Do you agree with the Court's decision?
2. Why do you think Parsons sued Walker individually?
3. Do you believe individuals should be liable for sexual harassment?

The predominant number of instances of sexual harassment have been men harassing women, but there are occasions when men have been harassed by women or other men and when women have been harassed by other women. These instances are equally unacceptable.

The issue in the case that follows is whether a male employee can claim sexual harassment against his homosexual supervisor.

CASE

FREDETTE v. BVP MANAGEMENT ASSOCIATES

112 F.3d 1503 (11th Cir. 1997)

ANDERSON, Circuit Judge.

Appellant Robert Fredette brought this action against BVP Management Associates ("BVP"), alleging that Dana Sunshine, the male maitre d' or manager of BVP's restaurant, sexually harassed him in violation of Title VII of the Civil Rights Act of 1964 and in violation of the Florida Human Rights Act of 1977. BVP sought summary judgment, which the magistrate judge recommended be denied. The district court rejected the recommendation of the magistrate judge and granted summary judgment in favor of BVP, concluding that Fredette had not created an issue of fact regarding the causal element of his sexual harassment claim—i.e., that the harassment occurred "because of sex." On appeal, appellee BVP argues that we should affirm the summary judgment because same-sex harassment claims are wholly outside the purview of Title VII. Because we disagree with both the district court and the appellee, we reverse.

I. BACKGROUND

Fredette was a waiter in BVP's restaurant, and Mr. Sunshine, who is homosexual, was the maitre d' or manager. Fredette proffered evidence from which a factfinder could conclude that Fredette's supervisor, Mr. Sunshine, repeatedly propositioned him, offering employment benefits in exchange for Fredette's providing sexual favors to Mr. Sunshine, and when Fredette refused to comply and later reported the matter to management

that Mr. Sunshine retaliated against Fredette in various work-related ways. There was similar evidence with respect to other male victims, and there was evidence that Mr. Sunshine provided work-related benefits to another male waiter who did accede to Mr. Sunshine's propositions.

II. ISSUE

The single issue presented in this appeal is whether, under the circumstances of this case, the sexual harassment of a male employee by a homosexual male supervisor is actionable under Title VII.

III. DISCUSSION

We begin with the language of the statute. Title VII of the Civil Rights Act of 1964 reads in relevant part: It shall be an unlawful employment practice for an employer . . . to discriminate against any individual with respect to his compensation, terms, conditions, or privileges of employment, because of such individual's . . . sex. . . . We note first that the statute prohibits an "employer," whether male or female, from discriminating against "any individual," whether male or female. There is simply no suggestion in these statutory terms that the cause of action is limited to opposite gender contexts. Next we focus on the statute's causation requirement—i.e., that the discrimination occurs "because of such individual's . . . sex." In the paradigm harassment case, where a heterosexual male makes unwelcome advances toward a female, we have readily concluded that the harassment occurred "because of sex." The reasonably inferred motives of the homosexual harasser are identical to those of the heterosexual harasser—i.e., the harasser makes advances towards the victim because the victim is a member of the gender the harasser prefers. Fredette proffered evidence from which a reasonable factfinder could conclude that he was the victim of sexual advances to which members of the opposite gender were not subjected. This was sufficient to survive summary judgment as to causation.

The EEOC's interpretation of Title VII provides further support for appellant's argument that same-sex sexual harassment is actionable in the instant circumstances. The EEOC Compliance Manual states in relevant part: The victim does not have to be of the opposite sex from the harasser. Since sexual harassment is a form of sex discrimination, the crucial inquiry is whether the harasser treats a member or members of one sex differently from members of the other sex. The victim and the harasser may be of the same sex where, for instance, the sexual harassment is based on the victim's sex (*not* on the victim's sexual preference) and the harasser does not treat employees of the opposite sex the same way.

The Compliance Manual in fact uses as an example of actionable same-sex harassment a case identical to the one before us today:

Example 1—If a male supervisor of male and female employees makes unwelcome sexual advances toward a male employee because the employee is male but does not make similar advances toward female employees, then the male supervisor's conduct may constitute sexual harassment since the disparate treatment is based on the male employee's sex.

The only circuit court of appeals adopting a position inconsistent with holding in favor of Fredette is the Fifth Circuit in *Oncale v. Sundowner Offshore Servs., Inc.* The legal principle which apparently emerges from *Oncale* is that "all same-sex sexual harassment claims" are barred.

The law is well established that Title VII protects men as well as women, without regard to whether the workplace is male-dominated. This is most obvious in cases involving male plaintiffs' challenges to affirmative action plans enacted to promote the advancement of women. Because employers typically adopt such plans precisely because the environment is male-dominated, the paradigm reverse-discrimination plaintiff is one whose workplace is dominated by members of his own gender.

Finally, we address concerns raised by the appellee regarding the implications of this case for the law regarding discrimination based on sexual orientation. BVP argues that to hold in favor of the appellant is, in effect, to protect against discrimination on the basis of sexual orientation. The short but complete answer to this argument is to make clear the narrowness of our holding today. We do not hold that discrimination because of sexual orientation is actionable. Rather, we hold today that when a homosexual male supervisor solicits sexual favors from a male subordinate and conditions work benefits or detriment on receiving such favors, the male subordinate can state a viable Title VII claim for *gender* discrimination. We note that the EEOC has also drawn a distinction between the conduct at issue here, which is actionable as gender discrimination, and discrimination because of sexual orientation.

IV. CONCLUSION

In summary, we conclude that the plain language of Title VII provides protection against the conduct at issue here where a homosexual male superior has solicited sexual favors from a male subordinate and conditioned work benefits or detriment on receiving such favors. We find nothing to the contrary in the legislative history. Our holding is in accord with the interpretation of the EEOC, and is in accord with the weight of the case law and the better-reasoned cases.

For the foregoing reasons, the judgment of the district court is reversed with respect to both the claim of quid pro quo sexual harassment and the claim for hostile environment sexual harassment. REVERSED and REMANDED.

Judgment for Fredette.

Case Commentary

The Eleventh Circuit decided that same-sex sexual harassment is protected under Title VII where it involves a homosexual superior who is attempting to elicit sexual favors from a male subordinate. This court alluded to the Fifth Circuit's decision in *Oncale* barring same-sex sexual harassment claims. The United States Supreme Court reversed the Fifth Circuit when it heard the Oncale case thereafter.

Case Questions

1. Do you agree with the decision of the Court in this case?
2. Doesn't this give rise to sexual orientation protection?
3. What if Fredette's superior had been heterosexual?
4. What if the sexual orientations in this case had been reversed? Would the homosexual subordinate be entitled to protection from a hostile work environment?

EMPLOYMENT PERSPECTIVE

Phil Thomas is a construction worker who lives with his mother. After work every day he rushes home to tend to her needs. When he won't join them for a few beers, his coworkers taunt him continuously, claiming that he's a Momma's boy, a wimp tied to his mother's apron strings. This taunting happens continuously throughout the day. The coworkers leave notes, photostat caricatures, and openly make remarks. Is this sexual harassment? Probably not! Phil's coworkers are inflicting emotional distress upon him. But this isolated instance of teasing alone is not sufficient to constitute sexual harassment. ■

The question presented in the following case is whether the employer is liable even though it took the appropriate steps to address the hostile work environment.

CASE

FLEENOR v. HEWITT SOAP COMPANY

81 F.3d 48 (6th Cir. 1996)

MERRITT, Chief Judge.

Plaintiff, an employee of Defendant Hewitt Soap Company, appeals the District Court's dismissal of his claim for failure to state a cause of action. Plaintiff, a male, alleged that several male colleagues had taunted him with sexually explicit language and conduct, thereby creating a "hostile working environment." He sought relief under Title VII for discrimination on the basis of sex. The District Court dismissed the claim on the grounds that same-sex sexual harassment claims are not cognizable under Title VII.

We find that plaintiff failed to assert that his employer was responsible for the alleged discrimination as required by Title VII, and we therefore affirm the District Court's decision for this reason. We need not reach the question of whether Title VII prohibits same-sex sexual harassment.

I. FACTS

In April 1994, plaintiff, Roger Fleenor, filed a complaint against defendant Hewitt Soap Company and several other defendants who were employed by Hewitt. The complaint alleged that for a two-week period in August of 1992, he was subjected to "repeated and unwelcome sexual advances and harassment" by two co-workers, defendants Hatmaker and Wallet. He alleged specifically that defendant Hatmaker exposed his genitals to plaintiff, threatened to force plaintiff to engage in oral sex with him, and "stuck a ruler up Plaintiff's buttocks" against plaintiff's will. In September 1992, the company reprimanded Hatmaker for his behavior. The complaint also alleged harassment of a non-sexual nature, including the removal of plaintiff's timecard to prevent him from clocking in and out of work and threats to throw plaintiff over a fence, which created "an intimidating, hostile, and offensive work environment" until December 1993. Plaintiff's appeal is taken from the District Court's order dismissing with prejudice his Title VII claim and remanding to state court his state tort claims.

II. DISCUSSION

In order to prevail on a claim of hostile environment sexual harassment under Title VII, we have said that an employee must allege and prove that:

(1) the employee is a member of a protected class; (2) the employee was subject to unwelcomed sexual harassment . . .; (3) the harassment complained of was based on sex; (4) the charged sexual harassment had the effect of unreasonably interfering with the plaintiff's work performance and creating an intimidating, hostile, or offensive work environment . . .; and (5) *the existence of respondeat superior liability.*

While it is by no means clear that the plaintiff properly alleged the third and fourth elements of his case, he fails on the last element, and we affirm the District Court's dismissal of his claim on that basis.

The use of the term "respondeat superior" in this area has created a certain amount of confu-

sion that we wish to dispel before proceeding with our analysis. When the Supreme Court first recognized a cause of action for "hostile environment" sexual harassment in *Meritor Savings Bank v. Vinson,* it declined to define a precise standard for employer liability under Title VII. Instead, the Court stated simply that "Congress wanted courts to look to agency principles for guidance in this area" and that this "surely evinces an intent to place some limits on the acts of employees for which employers under Title VII are to be held responsible." In *Vinson,* the alleged harassment was inflicted by a supervisor on his subordinate. This court, therefore, has looked to traditional agency principles—such as scope of employment and foreseeability—to determine employer liability under Title VII when a supervisor harasses a subordinate.

We have defined the standard for sexual harassment by co-workers and supervisors in a similar way. When a plaintiff alleges harassment by co-workers, we have defined the test as whether the employer "knew or should have known of the charged sexual harassment and failed to implement prompt and appropriate corrective action."

Although we erroneously referred to it as "respondeat superior," we later realized that "the term 'respondeat superior'—which connotes derivative liability—is an incorrect label for co-worker harassment cases, where the employer is directly liable for its own negligence." This understanding, that the employer is directly not derivatively liable, and the underlying "knew or should have known" standard, are consistent with the law in other circuits. The standard is also consistent with the common law understanding of an employer's liability for the misconduct of employees.

In the case before us, the pleading is deficient with respect to defendant Wallet because it does not allege what he did to sexually harass plaintiff. The plaintiff appears to allege that one of his harassers, Mr. Wallet, is a supervisor and that therefore agency principles should apply. Mr. Wallet, however, was not plaintiff's supervisor, but a supervisor elsewhere in the company. Furthermore, regardless of whether we treat Mr. Wallet as a supervisor or a co-worker, the plaintiff's allegations with respect to him are not specific enough to satisfy even the loose requirements of notice pleading. The complaint does not attribute any specific statements or conduct to Mr. Wallet.

The plaintiff is capable of stating specific facts where he claims that wrongful conduct actually happened, as he does regarding defendant Hatmaker, but the pleading does not give any hint as to what specific conduct Mr. Wallet engaged in and whether he is responsible as a supervisor or co-worker. Thus, the pleading does not establish employer liability as to Wallet's conduct.

As noted, the plaintiff is capable of pleading with the requisite specificity, as he demonstrates with his allegations regarding defendant Hatmaker. Hatmaker is a fellow worker. The standard is whether the company failed to correct after notice or "knew or should have known of the charged sexual harassment and failed to implement prompt and appropriate corrective action." Here, the sexual conduct at issue occurred during a two-week period in August of 1992. The company reprimanded defendant Hatmaker in September of 1992, and, by plaintiff's own admission, the sexual conduct stopped. Even if the conduct alleged up to that time could support a claim under Title VII, the company's action was sufficient to stop it and to relieve itself of liability. The conduct alleged after that time does not state a set of facts that would establish sex discrimination under Title VII whether the employer knew about it or not. For these reasons, we AFFIRM the District Court's dismissal of the Title VII claim and the remand of the state claims to state court.

Judgment for Hewitt.

Case Commentary

The Sixth Circuit decided that an employer is liable for hostile work environment where a superior is guilty of conduct that is severe and pervasive. This was not the case here. The Court also held that an employer is not liable for a hostile work environment created by coworkers where the employer put an end to the sexual harassment immediately upon becoming aware of this conduct.

Case Questions

1. Did the Court come to the right conclusion?
2. How would you reconcile this case with the *Oncale* case that follows?
3. Should employer knowledge be a factor in determining hostile work environment involving coworkers?

The question presented in the following case is whether a victim of same-sex sexual harassment has a viable claim under Title VII of the Civil Rights Act.

CASE

ONCALE v. SUNDOWNER OFFSHORE SERVICES, INC.

523 U.S. 75 (1998)

JUSTICE SCALIA delivered the opinion of the Court.

This case presents the question whether workplace harassment can violate Title VII's prohibition against "discriminat[ion] . . . because of . . . sex," when the harasser and the harassed employee are of the same sex.

I

The District Court having granted summary judgment for respondent, we must assume the facts to be as alleged by petitioner Joseph Oncale. The precise details are irrelevant to the legal point we must decide, and in the interest of both brevity and dignity we shall describe them only generally. In late October 1991, Oncale was working for respondent Sundowner Offshore Services on a Chevron U. S. A., Inc., oil platform in the Gulf of Mexico. He was employed as a roustabout on an eight-man crew which included respondents John Lyons, Danny Pippen, and Brandon Johnson. Lyons, the crane operator, and Pippen, the driller, had supervisory authority. On several occasions, Oncale was forcibly subjected to sex related, humiliating actions against him by Lyons, Pippen and Johnson in the presence of the rest of the crew. Pippen and Lyons also physically assulted Oncale in a sexual manner, and Lyons threatened him with rape.

Oncale's complaints to supervisory personnel produced no remedial action; in fact, the company's Safety Compliance Clerk, Valent Hohen, told Oncale that Lyons and Pippen "picked on him all the time too," and called him a name suggesting homosexuality. Oncale eventually quit—asking that his pink slip reflect that he "voluntarily left due to sexual harassment and verbal abuse." When asked at his deposition why he left Sundowner, Oncale stated "I felt that if I didn't leave my job, that I would be raped or forced to have sex."

Oncale filed a complaint against Sundowner in the United States District Court for the Eastern District of Louisiana, alleging that he was discriminated against in his employment because of his sex. Relying on the Fifth Circuit's decision in Garcia v. Elf Atochem North America, the district court held that "Mr. Oncale, a male, has no cause of action under Title VII for harassment by male co-workers." On appeal, a panel of the Fifth Circuit concluded that Garcia was binding Circuit precedent, and affirmed. We granted certiorari.

II

Title VII's prohibition of discrimination "because of . . . sex" protects men as well as women and in the related context of racial discrimination in the workplace we have rejected any conclusive presumption that an employer will not discriminate against members of his own race. "Because of the many facets of human motivation, it would be unwise to presume as a matter of law that human beings of one definable group will not discriminate against other members of that group." In Johnson v. Transportation Agency, Santa Clara Cty. a male employee claimed that his employer discriminated against him because of his sex when it preferred a female employee for promotion. Although we ultimately rejected the claim on other grounds, we did not consider it significant that the supervisor who made that decision was also a man. If our precedents leave any doubt on the question, we hold today that nothing in Title VII necessarily bars a claim of discrimination "because of . . . sex" merely because the plaintiff and the defendant (or the person charged with acting on behalf of the defendant) are of the same sex. Courts have had little trouble with that principle in cases like Johnson, where an employee claims to have been passed over for a job or promotion. But when the issue arises in the context of a "hostile environment" sexual harassment claim, the state and federal courts have taken a bewildering variety of stances. Some, like the Fifth Circuit in this case, have held that same-sex sexual harassment claims are never cognizable under Title VII. Other decisions say that such claims are actionable only if the plaintiff can prove that the harasser is homosexual (and thus presumably motivated by sexual desire). Still others suggest that workplace harassment that is sexual in content is always actionable, regardless of the harasser's sex, sexual orientation, or motivations.

We see no justification in the statutory language or our precedents for a categorical rule excluding same-sex harassment claims from the coverage of Title VII. As some courts have observed, male-on-male sexual harassment in the workplace was assuredly not the principal evil Congress was concerned with when it enacted Title VII. But statutory prohibitions often go beyond the principal evil to cover reasonably comparable evils, and it is ultimately the provisions of our laws rather than the principal concerns of our legislators by which we are governed. Title VII prohibits "discriminat[ion] . . . because of . . . sex" in the "terms" or "conditions" of employment. Our holding that this includes sexual harassment must extend to sexual harassment of any kind that meets the statutory requirements.

We have emphasized, moreover, that the objective severity of harassment should be judged from the perspective of a reasonable person in the plaintiff's position, considering "all the circumstances." In same-sex (as in all) harassment cases, that inquiry requires careful consideration of the social context in which particular behavior occurs and is experienced by its target. A professional football player's working environment is not severely or pervasively abusive, for example, if the coach smacks him on the buttocks as he heads onto the field—even if the same behavior would reasonably be experienced as abusive by the coach's secretary (male or female) back at the office. The real social impact of workplace behavior often depends on a constellation of surrounding circumstances, expectations, and relationships which are not fully captured by a simple recitation of the words used or the physical acts performed. Common sense, and an appropriate sensitivity to social context, will enable courts and juries to distinguish between simple teasing or roughhousing among members of the same sex, and conduct which a reasonable person in the plaintiff's position would find severely hostile or abusive.

III

Because we conclude that sex discrimination consisting of same-sex sexual harassment is actionable under Title VII, the judgment of the Court of Appeals for the Fifth Circuit is reversed, and the case is remanded for further proceedings consistent with this opinion.

Judgment for Oncale.

Case Commentary

The United States Supreme Court stated that sexual harassment under Title VII encompasses a hostile work environment involving employees of the same sex.

Case Questions

1. Do you agree with the decision of this case?
2. Do you believe same-sex sexual harassment should apply only where one employee is a homosexual?
3. Should Oncale have been left to handle this himself?

EMPLOYMENT PERSPECTIVE

Steve Hart is a happily married man with three children. His superior, Linda Evert, finds him very attractive. She invites him to dinner, a show, and her apartment. Steve politely declines each time. Linda stresses to Steve that if he wants to get promoted, he must have a close, intimate relationship with her. Is this sexual harassment? Yes! It is an unwelcome sexual advance. ■

QUID PRO QUO

There are two distinct situations for which the company may be liable; *quid pro quo* and hostile work environment. *Quid pro quo* means "this for that." It involves situations in which a superior is eliciting sexual favors from a subordinate in return for some form of sexual activity.

EMPLOYMENT PERSPECTIVE

Clarence Conklin, a hospital administrator, approaches one of the nurse's aides and informs her that he can arrange a schedule change from nights, weekends, and holidays to day work if she is willing to sleep with him. Is this *quid pro quo*? Yes! The hospital is liable for the sexual harassment of its employee because a benefit was denied to the nurse's aide unless she agreed to have sex. ■

EMPLOYMENT SCENARIO

Tom Long has been walking on air since the arrival of Jenn Smiley, the new inventory control analyst. Jenn has been currying favor with Tom, hoping it pays off with a raise and promotion down the road. Tom sees things differently. He believes Jenn is infatuated with him. This makes Tom think that, at age 47, he still has what it takes. This could not be further from the truth. When Tom puts the moves on Jenn, inviting her for the weekend to his ski chalet, Jenn rebuffs his advances. Jenn's flirtatious behavior was just a façade. Tom was furious. His initial reaction was to fire Jenn on the spot. When he discussed this with coowner Mark Short, Mark suggested Tom talk this over with L&S's attorney, Susan North. After their consultation, Susan admonished Tom that if he fired Jenn, it would give her grounds for a *quid pro quo* sexual harassment suit, *i.e.,* that Jenn was fired for not spending the weekend with Tom. Susan informed Tom that he should limit his contact with Jenn and when speaking to her be nothing more than cordial. Susan contended if Jenn should broach the issue with Tom, he should discreetly inform her it was a misunderstanding that will not reoccur in the future.

There are also instances in which a person uses sex to gain advancement, sometimes called "sleeping the way to the top."

EMPLOYMENT PERSPECTIVE
Christine Wiley was an administrative assistant at Bay Ridge Publishing when she met Joe Flanagan, the president, at a company picnic. Joe immediately became infatuated with Christine, and they began an affair. During the next two years, she was promoted seven times, eventually to vice president of corporate affairs. Her skills were not particularly impressive. Every other vice president had been in a managerial position at least 14 years before attaining the position of vice president. Is this sexual harassment? Yes! In the opposite direction, though. The employees who were passed over for promotion have been sexually harassed because of the favoritism exhibited to Christine. ■

In some cases, sexual harassment can be used as a threat against management, in that an employee may demand a promotion or else will file a claim against the management.

EMPLOYMENT PERSPECTIVE
It was obvious to everyone at Parker Management Co. that Charlie Harris was very fond of Marie Copley, a marketing research assistant. He would compliment her every day and often bring her flowers. One day Marie learned of an opening for a sales representative within the company. Marie was tired of doing research—she wanted to earn commissions and work with people. This would be tantamount to a transfer and

promotion. Marie approached Charlie, who was vice president of marketing, and asked him to grant her request. Charlie informed Marie that although he was fond of her, he could not grant the request because she was not qualified. Marie told Charlie that unless he granted her wish, she would file a complaint against him, alleging that he demanded sex for the promotion. What should Charlie do? This action is blackmail. Charlie is in a delicate situation because his conduct, although not constituting sexual harassment, has laid the foundation for a false claim to be leveled against him. Charlie should seek the advice of upper management and legal counsel. Ethically, Marie's request should not be granted because it is false. Practically, it may be granted by Charlie or the company to avoid future public embarrassment and litigation. If Charlie adopts an ethical viewpoint and refuses Marie's request and the company is sued, Charlie must be prepared to be severely reprimanded at best or to lose his job at worst as a consequence of the damage done to the company. ■

HOSTILE WORK ENVIRONMENT

Hostile work environment is intimidating and offensive conduct perpetrated by a superior or coworker against an employee. The hostile action must be severe and pervasive so as to interfere with the performance of the employee's work. Touching, joking, commenting, and distributing material of a sexual nature all fall within the confines of a hostile work environment.

EMPLOYMENT PERSPECTIVE
Dawn West, an employee of Bull and Bear Stockbrokers, appeared one Monday morning with a new hairstyle and wearing a royal blue dress. Jack Olsen, a coworker, couldn't take his eyes off Dawn. Finally, he said, "Boy don't you look fantastic." Dawn, embarrassed in front of her coworkers, filed a claim for sexual harassment. Will she be successful? No! This incident was not severe nor did it reoccur. It was an isolated occurrence. What if Jack's behavior is repeated on a daily basis? The answer would depend upon whether Dawn communicated to Jack her distaste for his conduct or whether it was blatantly obvious from Dawn's reaction each day that she did not welcome Jack's behavior. ■

EMPLOYMENT PERSPECTIVE
Susan Jennings is speaking to Jessica Randolph in the latter's cubicle about the terrible cramps she is experiencing this month. John Woods, a coworker, happens to overhear their conversation and interjects, "Why don't you let Dr. John have a look down there and see what the problem is? You know I have magic fingers not to mention...." "No thanks, John, now take a walk," was their response. Later, they filed a sexual harassment claim against John. Will they win? Again, this is an isolated occurrence during which the women made clear to John that they did not appreciate his comments. By filing the complaint, they are putting the company on notice that they will not tolerate further harassment from John. The company should investigate their complaint and upon satisfying itself about its accuracy, notify John that future misbehavior will result in suspension or dismissal. ■

EMPLOYMENT PERSPECTIVE

Kay Stevens was 5 feet tall and weighed 250 pounds at the age of 32. She worked in a meat-packing plant, where she was subjected to constant criticisms by her coworkers: "You're eating the company's profits, no man would sleep with you because he could not fit in the bed," and "Your mother thought she was having twins, then you appeared." For many years Kay endured the belittling behavior because she was ashamed to repeat what had been said. She has been very depressed. Should Kay file a complaint? Yes! If she does not, the harassment will never stop. By filing a complaint, Kay is putting the onus on the company to stop what she cannot end herself. ▪

EMPLOYMENT SCENARIO

Edward Fantry, Chris Mendam, and Roy McDonald are all salespeople at the Long and the Short of It. One stormy Monday morning, while business is slow, they are conversing about their weekend sexual exploits. Their recounting of the details of their sexual relations is vivid and demeaning toward women. All this is transpiring within earshot of the cashier, Sandra Jacoby. Sandra is visibly upset by their language and she asks them to knock it off. They are unrelenting and reply in tandem to Sandra to buzz off. Sandra files a complaint with L&S for hostile work environment. Tom Long and Mark Short seek Susan North's advice on how to handle this. Susan counsels Tom and Mark to investigate expeditiously by speaking to Sandra, Edward, Chris, and Roy individually. If they believe Sandra's account of the facts is reasonable, then the men should be reprimanded. The investigation should be documented and a copy of its findings along with the resolution should be placed in each man's personnel file. In addition, the salesmen should be warned that if the hostile working environment continues due to actions on their part, they will be subject to suspension and/or dismissal.

The case that follows presents the question of whether the presentation of a sexual gift to a female employee for her birthday constitutes sexual harassment. Furthermore, the case addresses the issue of whether the complainant's acceptance of the gift and participation in the event preclude her from winning the lawsuit.

HANSEN v. DEAN WITTER REYNOLDS, INC.

887 F. Supp. 669 (S.D.N.Y. 1995)

BAER, District Judge.

PLAINTIFF'S HOSTILE WORK ENVIRONMENT CLAIM

Plaintiff focused primarily on three incidents in her effort to show that defendant maintained a hostile work environment. Two of them involved sexually explicit birthday cakes, while the other concerned what a female employee, Lynn Jerome, described as an "act of terrorism" perpetrated against her by a male Dean Witter manager. As explained below, I find that the birthday cake incidents are not attributable to defendant Dean Witter; the incident that Jerome called an act of "terrorism," meanwhile, is at best an exaggeration and at worst calls into question Jerome's judgment generally.

One of the birthday cakes in question was presented to plaintiff in 1986 by several co-workers. The cake was in the shape and color of a black man's penis, was filled with Devil Dog cream, and bore the dubious greeting, "Happy Birthday, Bitch." Hansen did not file a complaint or otherwise report this incident to management. In fact, there was testimony by a former co-worker that Hansen was so proud to receive the cake that she stored the remaining portion in her freezer and brought it to her parents' home for their July 4th barbecue.

While food for thought, it is unnecessary to decide whether Hansen considered the cake an insult or a joke. There was evidence that she partook enthusiastically in the event, and there was testimony that she was proud of being referred to as the "bitch" and that the name was in fact a self-professed title as she considered herself "a tough cookie." The fact is that she failed to inform any supervisory personnel, and thus there is nothing on which to base a determination that Dean Witter tolerated, prohibited, or encouraged such activity. There was, however, a similar situation that was reported to management; Dean Witter's

reaction left no doubt as to its stance towards such cakes. In 1982, Ms. Jerome received a cake from co-workers "in the shape of a man's anatomy." Upon being made aware of the nature of the cake, Dean Witter's Chairman issued a memorandum stating that such behavior would not be tolerated and that any persons involved in such activity would be terminated. In light of this response, there is hardly support that the birthday cake incident is indicative of a sanctioned hostile work environment for women at Dean Witter.

The same is true of the event that Jerome referred to at trial as an act of terrorism. Jerome stated during her initial testimony that she had complained about "sexual matters" in 1989 based on her being "called in and terrorized" at Dean Witter. When asked to provide greater detail, Jerome offered, "It's very strong male intimidation to the point of, without touching a person, there is a physical reaction by the strength of the words."

When asked to what she was referring regarding the 1989 complaint, Jerome testified to only one event, an incident where she and a male colleague were called into a conference room by Ray Anderson, a Dean Witter manager. Jerome and her colleague had been reading newspapers on the trading floor. According to Jerome, Anderson "rose himself up in an intimidating male stature." Jerome conceded that Anderson never got within three and one-half feet of her, nor did he make any sexist or off-color remarks. Finally, as Jerome acknowledged, no adverse personnel action resulted, notwithstanding Anderson's statement that if Jerome and her colleague "had nothing better to do than read the paper, he wanted their resignations." Jerome then pointed out that Anderson had made the statement "in an extremely loud tone of voice." It is beyond peradventure that one would be hard pressed to consider this an act of terrorism.

Judgment for Dean Witter.

Case Commentary

The Southern District of New York held that an employee who participates in what would normally constitute a hostile work environment will be precluded from instituting a claim.

Case Questions

1. Do you believe this decision is correct?
2. Why do you believe she brought the claim after participating?
3. Should an employee be precluded from suing because she participated?

The composition of sexual harassment will vary among different types of employment. Conduct and language which is accepted in certain manual labor jobs may be regarded as offensive in an office environment. Each employment environment will have a different set of standards. These will be determined by company policy and female employees themselves. If employees participate, encourage, or accept what would otherwise constitute sexual harassment, they will be precluded from claiming such behavior was intimidating and offensive to them.

In the next case, a female construction worker claimed her supervisor created a hostile work environment when he used profane language in her presence and directed some of it at her. The question presented is whether the profanity must contain language relating to the female gender to be actionable.

CASE

GROSS v. BURGGRAF CONSTRUCTION CO.

53 F.3d 1531 (10th Cir. 1995)

ANDERSON, Circuit Judge.

Gender discrimination can be based on sexual harassment or a hostile work environment. Gross has not asserted that she was subjected to sexual harassment, in the form of "unwelcome sexual advances, requests for sexual favors, and other verbal or physical conduct of a sexual nature." Therefore, there is only one issue on appeal: did the district court err in granting summary judgment because there is a genuine issue of material fact in dispute regarding whether Anderson's conduct and statements created a hostile work environment for Gross?

Burggraf is a road construction company. Most of Burggraf's employees are hired on a seasonal basis. The construction season generally runs from May to October of each year. Gross drove a water truck for Burggraf in 1989. Her employment was terminated on October 20, 1989.

Gross was hired again by Burggraf as a truck driver for the 1990 construction season. In mid-May, Gross was assigned to drive a water truck for the Jenny Lake Project in the Grand Teton National Park. Anderson was the supervisor of the Jenny Lake Project. He was responsible for supervising more than 100 individuals.

Gross was an hourly employee. She was subject to being released from work at any time that her services were no longer needed. Gross was initially paid $12.50 per hour for her work on the Jenny Lake Project. Toward the end of the summer, her salary was increased to $13.50 per hour. Gross worked more hours on the Jenny Lake Project than any other truck driver employed by Burggraf.

It is undisputed that Gross was laid off on October 2, 1990, because Burggraf no longer needed the services of a water truck driver on the Jenny Lake Project. Paving operations on the Jenny Lake project were commenced on September 10, 1990; the final paving was completed on October 3, 1990. As the paving operations began to wind down, the need for the water truck diminished. On September 30, 1990, Gross was sent home early because there was nothing for her to do. On October 2, 1990, Gross was informed that she was being laid off because the water truck was no longer needed for the Jenny Lake Project. The water truck was not used on the Jenny Lake Project after October 2, 1990.

On September 28, 1993, Gross filed this action against Burggraf and Anderson. In count one, Gross alleged that she was subjected to gender discrimination in violation of Title VII and retaliation because she contemplated filing a claim with the EEOC.

In *Meritor Sav. Bank, FSB v. Vinson,* the Supreme Court stated that "for sexual harassment to be actionable it must be sufficiently severe or pervasive to alter the conditions of the victim's employment and create an abusive working environment." The existence of sexual harassment must be determined "in light of the record as a whole 'and courts must examine the totality of the circumstances, such as the nature of the sexual advances and the context in which the alleged incidents occurred.'" The mere utterance of a statement which "engenders offensive feelings in an employee would not affect the conditions of employment to a sufficiently significant degree to violate Title VII."

Any harassment of an employee that would not occur but for the sex of the employee ... may, if sufficiently patterned or pervasive comprise an illegal condition of employment under Title VII. "If the nature of an employee's environment, however unpleasant, is not due to her gen-

der, she has not been the victim of sex discrimination as a result of that environment."

In determining whether Gross has established a viable Title VII claim, we must first examine her work environment. In the real world of construction work, profanity and vulgarity are not perceived as hostile or abusive. Indelicate forms of expression are accepted or endured as normal human behavior. As is clear from Gross' deposition testimony, she contributed to the use of crude language on the job site:

Q. As a construction worker, you had occasion to use profane or obscene language, didn't you?
A. [Gross] Yes.

Q. Can you describe for me or give me examples of the type of language that you would use?
A. Only to say that it was no different than the language that anyone else around here was using.

Q. So you basically could profane equally with the men who were on the job.
A. That's a difficult comparison. I wasn't in competition with anybody.

Q. And I understand that and I'm not calling it competition. I'm just indicating, you say that you used the same language that other people on the job—I guess I'm saying that when you say other people on the job, you're talking about the male construction workers in addition to the female construction workers, right?
A. Yes.

Q. You didn't have any reluctance on the construction job to use profanity, did you?
A. No.

Q. You were not offended by the use of profanity on the construction site, were you?
A. No.

Q. Did you in fact tell off-color jokes at the construction site?
A. I can't recall specifics, but I told jokes similar to the same jokes that I was hearing.

Q. And I understand you can't remember the same jokes. I can't remember the jokes

I told last week, Patty. So I don't expect you to remember the specific jokes, but you don't know that you would have told off-color jokes like they were telling on the construction site.

A. Yes.

Q. And probably if you heard one at the end of the construction site, when you got to the other end, you would tell it down there because that's—I mean, that's just part of the society on a construction job, isn't it?

A. Yes.

Clint Guthrie, another Burggraf employee who worked with Gross during the 1990 season on the Jenny Lake Project, testified that Gross used profanity in the workplace:

Q. Did Patty Gross use profanity on the job site?

A. Yes.

Q. Did she use profanity as much as George Anderson did or more or less?

A. Everybody was pretty equal on that aspect.

Accordingly, we must evaluate Gross' claim of gender discrimination in the context of a blue collar environment where crude language is commonly used by male and female employees. Speech that might be offensive or unacceptable in a prep school faculty meeting, or on the floor of Congress, is tolerated in other work environments. We agree with the following comment by the district court in *Rabidue v. Osceola Refining Co.*:

> The standard for determining sexual harassment would be different depending upon the work environment. Indeed, it cannot seriously be disputed that in some work environments, humor and language are rough hewn and vulgar. Sexual jokes, sexual conversations and girlie magazines may abound. Title VII was not meant to or can change this. It must never be forgotten that Title VII is the federal court mainstay in the struggle for equal employment opportunity for the female workers of America. But it is quite different to claim that Title VII was designed to bring about a magical transformation in the social mores of American workers.

Gross maintains that Anderson made several vulgar and "harassing" statements in her presence that demonstrate that she was subject to a hostile work environment. We discuss each allegation under separate headings.

1. Anderson's reference to a portion of Gross' body

One afternoon, at 4:00 p.m., Anderson yelled at Gross: "What the hell are you doing? Get your ass back in the truck and don't you get out of it until I tell you." It is undisputed that Gross was aware that compaction and density tests were being performed that afternoon. Further, Gross testified that she knew that some members of the roadcrew, of both genders, were needed to perform such tests and that Anderson insisted that the employees stay on the site until all of the tests were completed. The term "ass" is a vulgar expression that refers to a portion of the anatomy of persons of both sexes. Thus, the term is gender-neutral. Its usage on a construction site does not demonstrate gender discrimination.

2. Anderson's use of demeaning terms

Gross maintains that Anderson referred to her as "dumb." Gross did not present any evidence that he characterized her as "dumb" when she was present. The only evidence that Gross presented that Anderson referred to her in this manner, is the portion of Guthrie's deposition quoted in the section entitled "Alleged inflammatory sexual epithets." Guthrie's deposition testimony establishes that when Anderson was upset, he called Gross "dumb."

Guthrie's deposition, however, also establishes that Anderson used crude or harsh language in reprimanding each of his employees. The term "dumb" is gender-neutral. Guthrie's testimony does not demonstrate that Anderson subjected Gross to gender discrimination.

Gross argues that "she was not alone in finding Mr. Anderson's conduct intolerable." She maintains that we can infer that Anderson's treatment of women created a hostile work environment from the fact that only two women, out of the forty who worked under Anderson's supervision, completed the 1990 construction season.

The only evidence in the record concerning the reason that women left the Jenny Lake Project before the construction season ended is that most of them departed to return to college. No evidence was presented that any of them left early because of a hostile work environment. The mere fact that only two women employees remained on the job at the end of the season does not support an inference that Anderson created a hostile work environment for Gross and the other female employees at the Jenny Lake Project.

Gross maintains that "Anderson acknowledged that he hired Ms. Gross not because he wanted to, but in order to meet federal opportunity requirements on the Jenny Lake Project." According to Gross, the fact that Anderson hired her to comply with federal law is evidence that she was subjected to a hostile work environment. Gross submitted the following portion of Anderson's deposition testimony to support this theory:

Q. Would you explain to me what your relationship to Patricia Gross was during the 1990 construction season?
A. I was her supervisor.

Q. Had she ever worked for you before?
A. No.

Q. Had she ever worked for Burggraf before?
A. Yes, she had. She had worked for Burggraf, I think, the preceding summer under Richard Neff as supervisor.

Q. Was that the basis under which you hired her, that she had previous experience with the company?
A. No.

Q. Tell me why you hired her.
A. I hired her—I asked Richard Neff for some women truck drivers, so we could meet our women minor for the participation on the Jenny Lake Project. I asked Richard for some women that could drive trucks. Tracey, I forget her last name, and Patty.

Q. Did you hire Patty?
A. I contacted Tracey first because that was Richard's recommendation, that Tracey would be his first choice. Patty was second choice. I could not get ahold of Tracey, she had obtained employment elsewhere, so I got ahold of Patty.

This evidence establishes that Anderson hired Gross because he was required to do so under federal law. Thus, it demonstrates his compliance with a law that compels the hiring of women. It does not support an inference of gender discrimination. The record shows that Anderson approached Gross after work one day, and stated that he had heard that Rick had "chewed her out." Gross replied "yeah, I fucked up." Anderson stated that he would buy Gross a case of beer if she told Rick to "go fuck himself the next time he chewed her out." Although Anderson's comment is clearly offensive in certain settings, and to many persons, he merely repeated the same vulgar verb that had been previously used by Gross. Anderson's use of this term does not support Gross' contention that she was subject to discrimination because of her gender.

Gross alleges that Anderson embarrassed and humiliated her in the presence of employees when he told her that if she ruined the transmission on the truck she was driving, she would be fired because her truck would be inoperable. It is undisputed that the clutch in Gross' truck required extensive repairs.

In *Steiner*, a female blackjack dealer testified that her supervisor referred to her in her presence as a "dumb fucking broad," a "cunt," and a "fucking cunt." Additionally, the record showed that he yelled profanities at her in front of customers and other casino employees while moving toward her in a threatening manner. In reversing an order granting summary judgment, the Ninth Circuit held that while the evidence established that the Supervisor was "abusive to men and women alike; . . . his abusive treatment and remarks to women were of a sexual or gender-specific nature." In this action, Gross has failed to submit any admissible evidence that Anderson used a gender based vulgarity in reference to her or that he engaged in any physically threatening conduct. Instead, the admissible evidence in the record demonstrates that Anderson criticized her in the presence of others because of his belief that she had abused company equipment. She has not presented any evidence that his criticism of her driving was sexual or gender specific.

In *Huddleston*, the evidence showed that a supervisor yelled at Huddleston every day in front of her co-workers. On one occasion, her supervisor "grabbed her by the arm and forcibly moved her a few feet." She was called a "bitch" and a "whore" to her face and in front of her customers. Her appearance was frequently ridiculed, and she was told " 'we're going to take your pants off and put a skirt on you,' and 'we're going to take your clothes off to see if you are real.' "

The Eleventh Circuit concluded that this evidence was sufficient to demonstrate gender discrimination.

After reviewing the admissible evidence in the record, we conclude that Gross has failed to demonstrate that there is a genuine issue of material fact in dispute that she was subjected to a hostile work environment because of her gen-

der. None of the alleged instances cited by Gross to support her Title VII claim is sufficient on its own to establish that she was discriminated against because of her gender. We have examined the evidence as a whole to determine whether the totality of the circumstances supports a viable Title VII claim.

Therefore, after considering the totality of the circumstances we hold that Gross has failed to establish that there is a genuine issue of material fact to establish gender based harassment that was pervasive and severe enough to alter the terms, conditions or privileges of employment.

Judgment for Burggraf Construction Co.

Case Commentary

The Tenth Circuit ruled that Gross consented to and participated in the exchange of rough language and joke telling. The Court also noted the

language used was not sexual in nature. This is a requirement for hostile work environment.

Case Questions

1. Do you believe this case was decided in a fair manner?
2. Must language always be sexual to constitute sexual harassment?

3. Why does the use of gender neutral terms such as "ass" fall short of qualifying as sexual harassment?

SEVERE AND PERVASIVE

The sexual harassment complained of must be severe enough to create an abusive work environment and to disrupt the victim's employment. Casual comments or insignificant events that are isolated or happen only intermittently are not sufficient. In order to come to a determination, the accused's conduct must be viewed in light of all of the circumstances, including the victim's behavior. If the victim consented to, participated in, or initiated the hostile work environment, then that will severely mitigate the victim's claim. If the work environment becomes intolerable because the employer refuses to remedy the situation, thus forcing the victim to resign, the victim can claim constructive discharge. The victim must resign in response to the sexual harassment. If the resignation is for another reason, constructive discharge will not apply.

The issue in the case that follows is whether the plaintiff's allegations are severe and pervasive enough to warrant a determination that a hostile work environment exists.

SHOEMAKER v. NATIONAL MANAGEMENT RESOURCES CORP.

(10th Cir. 1997)

BALDOCK, EBEL, and MURPHY, Circuit Judges.

Appellant Carla Shoemaker brought this suit against her former employer, National Management Resources Corporation (NMRC), and former immediate supervisor, Gerald Matheny, alleging that she was sexually harassed by Matheny and discharged by NMRC in retaliation for complaining about the harassment, both in violation of Title VII. Plaintiff also asserted state law claims for intentional infliction of emotional distress, discrimination under the Oklahoma Discrimination in Employment Act, wrongful discharge in violation of Oklahoma public policy, and negligent hiring. She appeals from the district court's grant of summary judgment in favor of defendants on all of her claims. We have jurisdiction and reverse.

Plaintiff was employed by defendant NMRC from March 1994 until March 15, 1995. On February 5, 1995, defendant Matheny was hired as plaintiff's supervisor. He immediately began a campaign of sexual harassment against her. He asked her out to dinner on his first day at work, and gave her his motel room number and telephone number the next day, assuring her that nobody else had those numbers.

He repeatedly told her he wanted to develop a close 'working relationship' with her. He continuously called her at home to see if she wanted to go out with him, and when she told him she had a boyfriend, he repeated that he wanted only a close working relationship with her. He would sit in front of her desk and stare at her for perhaps fifteen minutes at a time, and moved the copy machine into his office so that she would have to stand with her back to him to make copies. He once slammed a book shut in her face while she was reading, barely missing her nose. Matheny cornered plaintiff in private to tell her a story about how big he thought his penis was until he unwrapped the complimentary condom in his motel room, and then realized the condom was actually a shower cap. He also privately told her a story about a friend of his having sex with a woman who was screaming, but it turned out she was having an asthma attack.

He privately told her about getting a blow job from a beautiful woman for only $10.00 at the motel where he was staying. Matheny admitted that he told a joke about getting a penguin job for $20.00; that is, he dropped his pants for a blow job, but the woman took off with his money. Plaintiff felt belittled and intimidated by Matheny's conduct, but was afraid of his temper and afraid to complain.

Matheny once cornered plaintiff against a wall for ten or fifteen minutes. She was so terrified that she could not even recall what was said.

Matheny once called her home and asked her boyfriend if she was upset about something that had happened at work.

Matheny asked plaintiff to do push-ups for him on at least two occasions. Once, when she was carrying aerobic tights through the office on her way to change clothes in the restroom, Matheny told her it looked like she needed Vaseline to help put her tights on and asked her if she needed any help.

He patted her on her behind once after asking her to get up and retrieve a file for him.

He also harassed another female employee by pulling on the breast pocket of her jacket where a button was missing and making a comment that he had one of those back in Wisconsin.

Plaintiff said that she suffered anguish, uneasiness, fear, belittlement, intimidation, depression, and stress due to Matheny's conduct.

She sometimes broke down crying at work, and changed from an outgoing, energetic, bubbly person to one who kept to herself, kept quiet, did her job; and barely spoke.

Plaintiff finally wrote a letter to the president of NMRC about Matheny's conduct. She asked for a paid leave of absence while the company investigated her complaint, but upper management's initial reaction was that she must not be doing her job. NMRC's president and Matheny's district manager discussed the matter and decided that plaintiff would be more easily replaced than Matheny.

NMRC management never interviewed the other employees plaintiff said she had confided in, and management gave her the option only to tolerate Matheny's conduct or quit her job. When she told NMRC management that she could no longer tolerate Matheny's harassment, they terminated her on the spot.

The district court erred in granting summary judgment to defendant NMRC on plaintiff's hostile work environment claim.

'For sexual harassment to be actionable, it must be sufficiently severe or pervasive to alter the conditions of the victim's employment and create an abusive working environment.

Moreover, except for the book-slamming incident, the incidents alleged by plaintiff are either overtly sexual or could reasonably be construed as sexual. Her allegations are considerably more than enough to create a triable factual dispute as to the existence of a hostile work environment due to sexual harassment. There is no need to go into the nuances in this case.

Therefore, plaintiff's retaliation claim must be reinstated for further proceedings.

The judgment of the United States District Court for the Western District of Oklahoma is REVERSED, and the case is REMANDED for additional proceedings consistent with this order and judgment.

Judgment for Shoemaker.

Case Commentary

The Tenth Circuit held that Carla Shoemaker's allegations of sexual harassment were more than sufficient to evidence a hostile work environment.

Case Questions

1. Do you agree with the decision in this case?
2. Were Matheny's actions severe and pervasive?

3. What do you think about upper management's reaction?

REASONABLE PERSON STANDARD

The standard by which sexual harassment will be judged is a reasonable person standard. A reasonable person must believe that the conduct complained of must have substantially interfered with the victim's ability to work or created an environment that was intimidating and offensive.

The issue in the following case is whether an employer is liable for a supervisor's threatening sexual advances where the employee has suffered no adverse effects to her job.

BURLINGTON INDUSTRIES, INC. v. ELLERTH

524 U.S. 742 (1998)

JUSTICE KENNEDY delivered the opinion of the Court.

We decide whether, under Title VII of the Civil Rights Act of 1964, as amended, an employee who refuses the unwelcome and threatening sexual advances of a supervisor, yet suffers no adverse, tangible job consequences, can recover against the employer without showing the employer is negligent or otherwise at fault for the supervisor's actions.

I

Summary judgment was granted for the employer, so we must take the facts alleged by the employee to be true. The employer is Burlington Industries, the petitioner. The employee is Kimberly Ellerth, the respondent. From March 1993 until May 1994, Ellerth worked as a salesperson in one of Burlington's divisions in Chicago, Illinois. During her employment, she alleges, she was subjected to constant sexual harassment by her supervisor, one Ted Slowik.

In the hierarchy of Burlington's management structure, Slowik was a mid-level manager. Burlington has eight divisions, employing more than 22,000 people in some 50 plants around the United States. Slowik was a vice president in one of five business units within one of the divisions. He had authority to make hiring and promotion decisions subject to the approval of his supervisor, who signed the paperwork. According to Slowik's supervisor, his position was "not considered an upper-level management position," and he was "not amongst the decision-making or policy-making hierarchy." Slowik was not Ellerth's immediate supervisor. Ellerth worked in a two-person office in Chicago, and she answered to her office colleague, who in turn answered to Slowik in New York.

Against a background of repeated boorish and offensive remarks and gestures which Slowik allegedly made, Ellerth places particular emphasis on three alleged incidents where Slowik's comments could be construed as threats to deny her tangible job benefits. In the summer of 1993, while on a business trip, Slowik invited Ellerth to the hotel lounge, an invitation Ellerth felt compelled to accept because Slowik was her boss. When Ellerth gave no encouragement to remarks Slowik made about her breasts, he told her to "loosen up" and warned, "you know, Kim, I could make your life very hard or very easy at Burlington."

In March 1994, when Ellerth was being considered for a promotion, Slowik expressed reservations during the promotion interview because she was not "loose enough." The comment was followed by his reaching over and rubbing her knee. Ellerth did receive the promotion; but when Slowik called to announce it, he told Ellerth, "you're gonna be out there with men who work in factories, and they certainly like women with pretty butts/legs."

In May 1994, Ellerth called Slowik, asking permission to insert a customer's logo into a fabric sample. Slowik responded, "I don't have time for you right now, Kim—unless you want to tell me what you're wearing." Ellerth told Slowik she had to go and ended the call. A day or two later, Ellerth called Slowik to ask permission again. This time he denied her request, but added something along the lines of, "are you wearing shorter skirts yet, Kim, because it would make your job a whole heck of a lot easier."

A short time later, Ellerth's immediate supervisor cautioned her about returning telephone calls to customers in a prompt fashion. In response, Ellerth quit. She faxed a letter giving reasons unrelated to the alleged sexual harassment we have described. About three weeks later, however, she sent a letter explaining she quit because of Slowik's behavior.

During her tenure at Burlington, Ellerth did not inform anyone in authority about Slowik's conduct, despite knowing Burlington had a policy against sexual harassment. In fact, she chose not to inform her immediate supervisor (not Slowik) because " 'it would be his duty as my supervisor to report any incidents of sexual harassment.' " On one occasion, she told Slowik a comment he made was inappropriate.

In October 1994, after receiving a right-to-sue letter from the Equal Employment Opportunity Commission (EEOC), Ellerth filed suit in the United States District Court for the Northern District of Illinois, alleging Burlington engaged in sexual harassment and forced her constructive discharge, in violation of Title VII. The District Court granted summary judgment to Burlington. The Court found Slowik's behavior, as described by Ellerth, severe and pervasive enough to create a hostile work environment, but found Burlington neither knew nor should have known about the conduct. There was no triable issue of fact on the latter point, and the Court noted Ellerth had not used Burlington's internal complaint procedures. Although Ellerth's claim was framed as a hostile work environment complaint, the District Court observed there was a *quid pro quo* "component" to the hostile environment. Proceeding from the premise that an employer faces vicarious liability for *quid pro quo* harassment, the District Court thought it necessary to apply a negligence standard because the *quid pro quo* merely contributed to the hostile work environment. The District Court also dismissed Ellerth's constructive discharge claim.

The Court of Appeals en banc reversed in a decision which produced eight separate opinions and no consensus for a controlling rationale. The judges were able to agree on the problem they confronted: Vicarious liability, not failure to comply with a duty of care, was the essence of Ellerth's case against Burlington on appeal. The judges seemed to agree Ellerth could recover if Slowik's unfulfilled threats to deny her tangible job benefits was sufficient to impose vicarious liability on Burlington.

At the outset, we assume an important proposition yet to be established before a trier of fact. It is a premise assumed as well, in explicit or implicit terms, in the various opinions by the judges of the Court of Appeals. The premise is: a trier of fact could find in Slowik's remarks numerous threats to retaliate against Ellerth if she denied some sexual liberties. The threats, however, were not carried out or fulfilled. Cases based on threats which are carried out are referred to often as *quid pro quo* cases, as distinct from bothersome attentions or sexual remarks that are sufficiently severe or pervasive to create a hostile work environment. The terms *quid pro quo* and hostile work environment are helpful, perhaps, in making a rough demarcation between cases in which threats are carried out and those where they are not or are absent altogether, but beyond this are of limited utility. Section 703(a) of Title VII forbids "an employer—

"(1) to fail or refuse to hire or to discharge any individual, or otherwise to discriminate against any individual with respect to his compensation, terms, conditions or privileges of employment, because of such individual's . . . sex." *Quid pro quo*" and "hostile work environment" do not appear in the statutory text. The terms appeared first in the academic literature; found their way into decisions of the Courts of Appeals; and were mentioned in this Court's decision in *Meritor Savings Bank, FSB* v. *Vinson.*

In *Meritor,* the terms served a specific and limited purpose. There we considered whether the conduct in question constituted discrimination in the terms or conditions of employment in violation of Title VII. We assumed, and with adequate reason, that if an employer demanded sexual favors from an employee in return for a job benefit, discrimination with respect to terms or conditions of employment was explicit. Less obvious was whether an employer's sexually demeaning behavior altered terms or conditions of employment in violation of Title VII. We distinguished between *quid pro quo* claims and hostile environment claims and said both were cognizable under Title VII, though the latter requires harassment that is severe or pervasive. The principal significance of the distinction is to instruct that Title VII is violated by either explicit or constructive alterations in the terms or conditions of employment and to explain the latter must be severe or pervasive.

We must decide, then, whether an employer has vicarious liability when a supervisor creates a hostile work environment by making explicit threats to alter a subordinate's terms or conditions of employment, based on sex, but does not fulfill the threat. We turn to principles of agency law, for the term "employer" is defined under Title VII to include "agents." In express terms, Congress has directed federal courts to interpret Title VII based on agency principles.

A

Section 219(1) of the Restatement sets out a central principle of agency law:

"A master is subject to liability for the torts of his servants committed while acting in the scope of their employment."

An employer may be liable for both negligent and intentional torts committed by an employee within the scope of his or her employment. Sexual harassment under Title VII presupposes intentional conduct. While early decisions absolved employers of liability for the intentional torts of their employees, the law now imposes liability where the employee's "purpose, however misguided, is wholly or in part to further the master's business."

The general rule is that sexual harassment by a supervisor is not conduct within the scope of employment.

B

Scope of employment does not define the only basis for employer liability under agency principles. In limited circumstances, agency principles impose liability on employers even where employees commit torts outside the scope of employment. The principles are set forth in the much-cited § 219(2) of the Restatement:

"(2) A master is not subject to liability for the torts of his servants acting outside the scope of their employment, unless:

"(a) the master intended the conduct or the consequences, or

"(b) the master was negligent or reckless, or

"(c) the conduct violated a non-delegable duty of the master, or

"(d) the servant purported to act or to speak on behalf of the principal and there was reliance upon apparent authority, or he was aided in accomplishing the tort by the existence of the agency relation."

Subsection (a) addresses direct liability, where the employer acts with tortious intent, and indirect liability, where the agent's high rank in the company makes him or her the employer's alter ego. None of the parties contend Slowik's rank imputes liability under this principle.

When a supervisor makes a tangible employment decision, there is assurance the injury could not have been inflicted absent the agency relation. A tangible employment action in most cases inflicts direct economic harm. As a general proposition, only a supervisor, or other person acting with the authority of the company, can cause this sort of injury. A co-worker can break a co-worker's arm as easily as a supervisor, and anyone who has regular contact with an employee can inflict psychological injuries by his or her offensive conduct. But one co-worker (absent some elaborate scheme) cannot dock another's pay, nor can one co-worker demote another. Tangible employment actions fall within the special province of the supervisor. The supervisor has been empowered by the company as a distinct class of agent to make economic decisions affecting other employees under his or her control.

Tangible employment actions are the means by which the supervisor brings the official power of the enterprise to bear on subordinates. A tangible employment decision requires an official act of the enterprise, a company act. The decision in most cases is documented in official company records, and may be subject to review by higher level supervisors. For these reasons, a tangible employment action taken by the supervisor becomes for Title VII purposes the act of the employer. Whatever the exact contours of the aided in the agency relation standard, its requirements will always be met when a supervisor takes a tangible employment action against a subordinate. In that instance, it would be implausible to interpret agency principles to allow an employer to escape.

An employer is subject to vicarious liability to a victimized employee for an actionable hostile environment created by a supervisor with immediate (or successively higher) authority over the employee. When no tangible employment action is taken, a defending employer may raise an affirmative defense to liability or damages, subject to proof by a preponderance of the evidence. The defense comprises two necessary elements: (a) that the employer exercised reasonable care to prevent and correct promptly any sexually harassing behavior, and (b) that the plaintiff employee unreasonably failed to take advantage of any preventive or corrective opportunities provided by the employer or to avoid harm otherwise. While proof that an employer had promulgated an anti-harassment policy with complaint procedure is not necessary in every instance as a matter of law, the need for a stated policy suitable to the employment circumstances may appropriately be addressed in any case when litigating the first element of the defense. And while proof that an employee failed to fulfill the corresponding obligation of reasonable care to avoid harm is not limited to showing any unreasonable failure to use any complaint procedure provided by the employer, a demonstration of such failure will normally suffice to satisfy the employer's burden under the second element of the defense. No affirmative defense is available, however, when the supervisor's harassment culminates in a tangible employment action, such as discharge, demotion, or undesirable reassignment.

IV

Relying on existing case law which held out the promise of vicarious liability for all *quid pro quo* claims, Ellerth focused all her attention in the Court of Appeals on proving her claim fit within that category. Given our explanation that the labels *quid pro quo* and hostile work environment are not controlling for purposes of establishing employer liability, Ellerth should have an adequate opportunity to prove she has a claim for which Burlington is liable.

Although Ellerth has not alleged she suffered a tangible employment action at the hands of Slowik, which would deprive Burlington of the availability of the affirmative defense, this is not dispositive. In light of our decision, Burlington is still subject to vicarious liability for Slowik's activity, but Burlington should have an opportunity to assert and prove the affirmative defense to liability.

For these reasons, we will affirm the judgment of the Court of Appeals, reversing the grant of summary judgment against Ellerth.

The judgment of the Court
of Appeals is affirmed.

Case Commentary

The United States Supreme Court decided that Kimberly Ellerth should have the opportunity to prove that Burlington Industries is vicariously liable for the sexually harassing actions of its supervisor.

Case Questions

1. Did Slowik's actions occur within the scope of employment?
2. Must sexual harassment result in adverse job consequences to the victim?
3. Was Ellerth at fault for not reporting Slowik's behavior to the company?

The question presented in the case that follows is whether an employer is vicariously liable for a supervisor's creation of a hostile work environment where the employer was unaware of such conduct.

FARAGHER v. CITY OF BOCA RATON

524 U.S. 775 (1998)

JUSTICE SOUTER delivered the opinion of the Court.

This case calls for identification of the circumstances under which an employer may be held liable under Title VII of the Civil Rights Act of 1964, for the acts of a supervisory employee whose sexual harassment of subordinates has created a hostile work environment amounting to employment discrimination. We hold that an employer is vicariously liable for actionable discrimination caused by a supervisor, but subject to an affirmative defense looking to the reasonableness of the employer's conduct as well as that of a plaintiff victim.

Between 1985 and 1990, while attending college, petitioner Beth Ann Faragher worked part time and during the summers as an ocean lifeguard for the Marine Safety Section of the Parks and Recreation Department of respondent, the City of Boca Raton, Florida (City). During this period, Faragher's immediate supervisors were Bill Terry, David Silverman, and Robert Gordon. In June 1990, Faragher resigned.

In 1992, Faragher brought an action against Terry, Silverman, and the City, asserting claims under Title VII and Florida law. So far as it concerns the Title VII claim, the complaint alleged that Terry and Silverman created a "sexually hostile atmosphere" at the beach by repeatedly subjecting Faragher and other female lifeguards to "uninvited and offensive touching," by making lewd remarks, and by speaking of women in offensive terms. The complaint contained specific allegations that Terry once said that he would never promote a woman to the rank of lieutenant, and that Silverman had said to Faragher, "Date me or clean the toilets for a year." Asserting that Terry and Silverman were agents of the City, and that their conduct amounted to discrimination in the "terms, conditions, and privileges" of her employment, Faragher sought a judgment against the City for nominal damages, costs, and attorney's fees.

Following a bench trial, the United States District Court for the Southern District of Florida found that throughout Faragher's employment with the City, Terry served as Chief of the Marine Safety Division, with authority to hire new lifeguards (subject to the approval of higher management), to supervise all aspects of the lifeguards' work assignments, to engage in counseling, to deliver oral reprimands, and to make a record of any such discipline. Silverman was a Marine Safety lieutenant from 1985 until June 1989, when he became a captain. Gordon began the employment period as a lieutenant and at some point was promoted to the position of training captain. In these positions, Silverman and Gordon were responsible for making the lifeguards' daily assignments, and for supervising their work and fitness training.

The lifeguards and supervisors were stationed at the city beach and worked out of the Marine Safety Headquarters, a small one-story building containing an office, a meeting room, and a single, unisex locker room with a shower. Their work routine was structured in a "paramilitary configuration," with a clear chain of command. Lifeguards reported to lieutenants and captains, who reported to Terry. He was supervised by the Recreation Superintendent, who in turn reported to a Director of Parks and Recreation, answerable to the City Manager. The lifeguards had no significant contact with higher city officials like the Recreation Superintendent.

In February 1986, the City adopted a sexual harassment policy, which it stated in a memorandum from the City Manager addressed to all employees. In May 1990, the City revised the policy and reissued a statement of it. Although the City may actually have circulated the memos and statements to some employees, it completely failed to disseminate its policy among employees of the Marine Safety Section, with the result that Terry, Silverman, Gordon, and many lifeguards were unaware of it.

From time to time over the course of Faragher's tenure at the Marine Safety Section, between 4 and 6 of the 40 to 50 lifeguards were women. During that 5-year period, Terry repeatedly touched the bodies of female employees without invitation, would put his arm around Faragher, with his hand on her buttocks, and once made contact with another female lifeguard in a motion of sexual simulation. He made crudely demeaning references to women generally, and once commented disparagingly on Faragher's shape. During a job interview with a woman he hired as a lifeguard, Terry said that the female lifeguards had sex with their male counterparts and asked whether she would do the same.

Silverman behaved in similar ways. He once tackled Faragher and remarked that, but for a physical characteristic he found unattractive, he would readily have had sexual relations with her. Another time, he pantomimed an act of oral sex. Within earshot of the female lifeguards, Silverman made frequent, vulgar references to women and sexual matters, commented on the bodies of female lifeguards and beachgoers, and at least twice told female lifeguards that he would like to engage in sex with them.

Faragher did not complain to higher management about Terry or Silverman. Although she spoke of their behavior to Gordon, she did not regard these discussions as formal complaints to a supervisor but as conversations with a person she held in high esteem. Other female lifeguards had similarly informal talks with Gordon, but because Gordon did not feel that it was his place to do so, he did not report these complaints to Terry, his own supervisor, or to any other city official. Gordon responded to the complaints of one lifeguard by saying that "the City just doesn't care."

In April 1990, however, two months before Faragher's resignation, Nancy Ewanchew, a former lifeguard, wrote to Richard Bender, the City's Personnel Director, complaining that Terry and Silverman had harassed her and other female lifeguards. Following investigation of this complaint, the City found that Terry and Silverman had behaved improperly, reprimanded them, and required them to choose between a suspension without pay or the forfeiture of annual leave.

On the basis of these findings, the District Court concluded that the conduct of Terry and Silverman was discriminatory harassment sufficiently serious to alter the conditions of Faragher's employment and constitute an abusive working environment. The District Court then ruled that there were three justifications for holding the City liable for the harassment of its supervisory employees. First, the court noted that the harassment was pervasive enough to support an inference that the City had "knowledge, or constructive knowledge" of it. Next, it ruled that the City was liable under traditional agency principles because Terry and Silverman were acting as its agents when they committed the harassing acts. Finally, the court observed that Gordon's knowledge of the harassment, combined with his inaction, "provides a further basis for imputing liability on the City." The District Court then awarded Faragher one dollar in nominal damages on her Title VII claim.

A panel of the Court of Appeals for the Eleventh Circuit reversed the judgment against the City. Although the panel had "no trouble concluding that Terry's and Silverman's conduct . . . was severe and pervasive enough to create an objectively abusive work environment," it overturned the District Court's conclusion that the City was liable. The panel ruled that Terry and Silverman were not acting within the scope of their employment when they engaged in the harassment, that they were not aided in their actions by the agency relationship, and that the City had no constructive knowledge of the harassment by virtue of its pervasiveness or Gordon's actual knowledge.

A "master is subject to liability for the torts of his servants committed while acting in the scope of their employment." Restatement §219(1). This doctrine has traditionally defined the "scope of employment" as including conduct "of the kind a servant is employed to perform," occurring "substantially within the authorized time and space limits," and "actuated, at least in part, by a purpose to serve the master," but as excluding an intentional use of force "unexpectable by the master."

The rationale for placing harassment within the scope of supervisory authority would be the fairness of requiring the employer to bear the burden of foreseeable social behavior, and the same rationale would apply when the behavior was that of co-employees. The employer generally benefits just as obviously from the work of common employees as from the work of supervisors; they simply have different jobs to do, all aimed at the success of the enterprise. As between an innocent employer and an innocent employee, if we use scope of employment reasoning to require the employer to bear the cost of an actionably hostile workplace created by one class of employees (*i.e.,* supervisors), it could appear just as appropriate to do the same when the environment was created by another class (*i.e.,* co-workers).

We therefore agree with Faragher that in implementing Title VII it makes sense to hold an employer vicariously liable for some tortious conduct of a supervisor made possible by abuse of his supervisory authority. The agency relationship affords contact with an employee subjected to a supervisor's sexual harassment, and the victim may well be reluctant to accept the risks of blowing the whistle on a superior. When a person with supervisory authority discriminates in the terms and conditions of subordinates' employment, his actions necessarily draw upon his superior position over the people who report to him, or those under them, whereas an employee generally cannot check a supervisor's abusive conduct the same way that she might deal with abuse from a co-worker. When a fellow employee harasses, the victim can walk away or tell the offender where to go, but it may be difficult to offer such responses to a supervisor, whose "power to supervise—which may be to hire and fire, and to set work schedules and pay rates—does not disappear . . . when he chooses to harass through insults and offensive gestures rather than directly with threats of firing or promises of promotion." Recognition of employer liability when discriminatory misuse of supervisory authority alters the terms and conditions of a victim's employment is underscored by the fact that the employer has a greater opportunity to guard against misconduct by supervisors than by common workers; employers have greater opportunity and incentive to screen them, train them, and monitor their performance.

The requirement to show that the employee has failed in a coordinate duty to avoid or mitigate harm reflects an equally obvious policy imported from the general theory of damages, that a victim has a duty "to use such means as are reasonable under the circumstances to avoid or minimize the damages" that result from violations of the statute.

Applying these rules here, we believe that the judgment of the Court of Appeals must be reversed. The District Court found that the degree of hostility in the work environment rose to the actionable level and was attributable to Silverman and Terry. It is undisputed that these supervisors "were granted virtually unchecked authority" over their subordinates, "directly controlling and supervising all aspects of Faragher's day-to-day activities." It is also clear that Faragher and her colleagues were "completely isolated from the City's higher management."

While the City would have an opportunity to raise an affirmative defense if there were any serious prospect of its presenting one, it appears from the record that any such avenue is closed. The District Court found that the City had entirely failed to disseminate its policy against sexual harassment among the beach employees and that its officials made no attempt to keep track of the conduct of supervisors like Terry and Silverman. The record also makes clear that the City's policy did not include any assurance that the harassing supervisors could be bypassed in registering complaints. Under such circumstances, we hold as a matter of law that the City could not be found to have exercised reasonable care to prevent the supervisors' harassing conduct. Unlike the employer of a small workforce, who might expect that sufficient care to prevent tortious behavior could be exercised informally, those responsible for city operations could not reasonably have thought that precautions against hostile environments in any one of many departments in far-flung locations could be effective without communicating some formal policy against harassment, with a sensible complaint procedure.

> The judgment of the Court of Appeals for the Eleventh Circuit is reversed, and the case is remanded for reinstatement of the judgment of the District Court.

Case Commentary

The United States Supreme Court ruled that the City of Boca Raton was liable for the sexual harassment perpetrated by its supervisors against Beth Ann Faragher. The City failed to apprise the supervisors concerning its sexual harassment policy and to train them to act in accordance with this policy. Faragher's com- plaint to Gordan, a supervisor, went unheeded. The City's argument that it lacked knowledge of the sexual harassment was due in part to the City's failure to monitor its supervisors. Employers cannot expect that all instances of sexual harassment will be reported because of employee's justifiable fear of reprisal.

Case Questions

1. Should Faragher have reported the sexual harassment to a higher authority in the City?
2. Do you agree with the decision of the Court?

3. Should an employer be liable for sexually harassing conduct of which it is unaware?

The incidents of sexual harassment must be at the workplace or otherwise work related. If the sexual harassment has no connection with work, then action against the employer is without merit. A criminal harassment complaint against the accused may be more appropriate.

Economic dependence has long placed women in vulnerable positions with their fathers, husbands, and employers. A feeling of inferiority has long caused women to have inadequate self-esteem. On the job, verbal and physical sexual abuse are rampant. Almost every woman will be subject to an incident of this during her working career. Most women accept this conduct begrudgingly because they have felt powerless in an employment environment where men are powerful. They fear reporting sexual harassment because of subtle reprisals. Instances of sexual harassment at work often make women feel anxious, embarrassed, and insecure. Their emotional distress and mental anguish interfere with their ability to perform well at work.

In an age in which women are exercising greater freedom in the control of their bodies, they should not submit to unwarranted sexual comments and advances. Women should stand firm in their refusal to accept this treatment and be proactive in seeking a resolution from the company. However, this will happen only when women feel more secure in protecting themselves. Men must be admonished that they have no right to mistreat women, expect sexual gratification at work, and use their positions to extort sex from women in return for promotions, raises, easier work schedules, or just allowing them to keep their jobs. Companies should be educated that permitting the harassment of women results in their decreased performance on the job and the possibility of a long, protracted, and expensive law suit.

Respect for women means more than just paying lip service to them. It means speaking to them as a man would speak to his mother, sister, wife, or daughter. Building women's self-esteem on the job will enable women to become more productive in the work environment.

Sexual harassment complaints are no longer confined to the workplace. Children also face harassment from other students and teachers at school. It is important that schools investigate these incidents as soon as they come to their attention. Schools are usually not liable where they lack knowledge of the sexual harassment.

The issue in the following case involves whether a student is entitled to money damages from a Board of Education because of their indifference to her pleas for the Board to take action against another student who had been sexually harassing her.

CASE

DAVIS v. MONROE COUNTY BOARD OF EDUCATION

526 U.S. 629 (1999)

JUSTICE O'CONNOR delivered the opinion of the Court.

Petitioner brought suit against the Monroe County Board of Education and other defendants, alleging that her fifth-grade daughter had been the victim of sexual harassment by another student in her class. Among petitioner's claims was a claim for monetary and injunctive relief under Title IX of the Education Amendments of 1972 (Title IX). The District Court dismissed petitioner's Title IX claim on the ground that "student-on-student," or peer, harassment provides no ground for a private cause of action under the statute. The Court of Appeals for the Eleventh Circuit, sitting en banc, affirmed. We consider here whether a private damages action may lie against the school board in cases of student-on-student harassment. We conclude that it may, but only where the funding recipient acts with deliberate indifference to known acts of harassment in its programs or activities. Moreover, we conclude that such an action will lie only for harassment that is so severe, pervasive, and objectively offensive that it effectively bars the victim's access to an educational opportunity or benefit.

I

A

Petitioner's minor daughter, LaShonda, was allegedly the victim of a prolonged pattern of sexual harassment by one of her fifth-grade classmates at Hubbard Elementary School, a public school in Monroe County, Georgia. According to petitioner's complaint, the harassment began in December 1992, when the classmate, G. F., attempted to touch LaShonda's breasts and genital area and made vulgar statements such as " 'I want to get in bed with you' " and " 'I want to feel your boobs.' " Similar conduct allegedly occurred on or about January 4 and January 20, 1993. LaShonda reported each of these incidents to her mother and to her classroom teacher, Diane Fort. Petitioner, in turn, also contacted Fort, who allegedly assured petitioner that the school principal, Bill Querry, had been informed of the incidents. Petitioner contends that, notwithstanding these reports, no disciplinary action was taken against G. F.

G. F.'s conduct allegedly continued for many months. In early February, G. F. purportedly placed a door stop in his pants and proceeded to act in a sexually suggestive manner toward LaShonda during physical education class. LaShonda reported G. F.'s behavior to her physical education teacher, Whit Maples. Approximately one week later, G. F. again allegedly engaged in harassing behavior, this time while under the supervision of another classroom teacher, Joyce Pippin. Again, LaShonda allegedly reported the incident to the teacher, and again petitioner contacted the teacher to follow up.

Petitioner alleges that G. F. once more directed sexually harassing conduct toward LaShonda in physical education class in early March, and that LaShonda reported the incident to both Maples and Pippen. In mid-April 1993, G. F. allegedly rubbed his body against LaShonda in the school hallway in what LaShonda considered a sexually suggestive manner, and LaShonda again reported the matter to Fort.

The string of incidents finally ended in mid-May, when G. F. was charged with, and pleaded guilty to, sexual battery for his misconduct. The complaint alleges that LaShonda had suffered during the months of harassment, however; specifically, her previously high grades allegedly dropped as she became unable to concentrate on her studies, and, in April 1993, her father discovered that she had written a suicide note. The complaint further alleges that, at one point, LaShonda told petitioner that she " 'didn't know how much longer she could keep G. F. off her.' "

Nor was LaShonda G. F.'s only victim; it is alleged that other girls in the class fell prey to G. F.'s conduct. At one point, in fact, a group composed of LaShonda and other female students tried to speak with Principal Querry about G. F.'s behavior. According to the complaint, however, a teacher denied the students' request with the statement, " 'If Querry wants you, he'll call you.' "

Petitioner alleges that no disciplinary action was taken in response to G. F.'s behavior toward LaShonda. In addition to her conversations with Fort and Pippen, petitioner alleges that she spoke with Principal Querry in mid-May 1993. When petitioner inquired as to what action the school intended to take against G. F., Querry simply stated, " 'I guess I'll have to threaten him a little bit harder.' " Yet, petitioner alleges, at no point during the many months of his reported misconduct was G. F. disciplined for harassment. Indeed, Querry allegedly asked petitioner why LaShonda " 'was the only one complaining.' "

Nor, according to the complaint, was any effort made to separate G. F. and LaShonda. On the contrary, notwithstanding LaShonda's frequent complaints, only after more than three months of reported harassment was she even permitted to change her classroom seat so that she was no longer seated next to G. F. Moreover, petitioner alleges that, at the time of the events in question, the Monroe County Board of Education (Board) had not instructed its personnel on how to respond to peer sexual harassment and had not established a policy on the issue.

B

On May 4, 1994, petitioner filed suit in the United States District Court for the Middle District of Georgia against the Board, Charles Dumas, the school district's superintendent, and Principal Querry. The complaint alleged that the Board is a recipient of federal funding for purposes of Title IX, that "the persistent sexual advances and harassment by the student G. F. upon LaShonda interfered with her ability to attend school and perform her studies and activities," and that "the deliberate indifference by Defendants to the unwelcome sexual advances of a student upon LaShonda created an intimidating, hostile, offensive and abusive school environment in violation of Title IX." The complaint sought compensatory and punitive damages, attorney's fees, and injunctive relief.

As for the Board, the court concluded that Title IX provided no basis for liability absent an allegation "that the Board or an employee of the Board had any role in the harassment." Petitioner appealed the District Court's decision dismissing her Title IX claim against the Board, and a panel of the Court of Appeals for the Eleventh Circuit reversed.

We granted certiorari in order to resolve a conflict in the Circuits over whether, and under what circumstances, a recipient of federal educational funds can be liable in a private damages action arising from student-on-student sexual harassment There is no dispute here that the Board is a recipient of federal education funding for Title IX purposes. Nor do respondents support an argument that student-on-student harassment cannot rise to the level of "discrimination" for purposes of Title IX. Rather, at issue here is the question whether a recipient of federal education funding may be liable for damages under Title IX under any circumstances for discrimination in the form of student-on-student sexual harassment.

Petitioner urges that Title IX's plain language compels the conclusion that the statute is intended to bar recipients of federal funding from permitting this form of discrimination in their programs or activities. She emphasizes that the statute prohibits a student from being "subjected to discrimination under any education program or activity receiving Federal financial assistance." Here, however, we are asked to do more than define the scope of the behavior that Title IX proscribes. We must determine whether a district's failure to respond to student-on-student harassment in its schools can support a private suit for money damages

Here, petitioner attempts to hold the Board liable for its own decision to remain idle in the face of known student-on-student harassment in its schools. We thus conclude that recipients of federal funding may be liable for "subjecting" their students to discrimination where the recipient is deliberately indifferent to known acts of student-on-student sexual harassment and the harasser is under the school's disciplinary authority.

We stress that our conclusion here—that recipients may be liable for their deliberate indifference to known acts of peer sexual harassment—does not mean that recipients can avoid liability only by purging their schools of actionable peer harassment or that administrators must engage in particular disciplinary action. We thus disagree with respondents' contention that, if Title IX provides a cause of action for student-on-student harassment, "nothing short of expulsion of every student accused of misconduct involving sexual overtones would protect school systems from liability or damages."

While it remains to be seen whether petitioner can show that the Board's response to reports of G. F.'s misconduct was clearly unreasonable in light of the known circumstances, petitioner may be able to show that the Board "subjected" LaShonda to discrimination by failing to respond in any way over a period of five months to complaints of G. F.'s in-school misconduct from LaShonda and other female students.

The most obvious example of student-on-student sexual harassment capable of triggering a damages claim would thus involve the overt, physical deprivation of access to school resources. Consider, for example, a case in which male students physically threaten their female peers every day, successfully preventing the female students from using a particular school resource—an athletic field or a computer lab, for instance. District administrators are well aware of the daily ritual, yet they deliberately ignore requests for aid from the female students wishing to use the resource. The district's knowing refusal to take any action in response to such behavior would fly in the face of Title IX's core principles, and such deliberate indifference may appropriately be subject to claims for monetary damages. It is not necessary, however, to show physical exclusion to demonstrate that students have been deprived by the actions of another student or students of an educational opportunity on the basis of sex. Rather, a plaintiff must establish sexual harassment of students that is so severe, pervasive, and objectively offensive, and that so undermines and detracts

from the victims' educational experience, that the victim-students are effectively denied equal access to an institution's resources and opportunities. Indeed, at least early on, students are still learning how to interact appropriately with their peers. It is thus understandable that, in the school setting, students often engage in insults, banter, teasing, shoving, pushing, and gender-specific conduct that is upsetting to the students subjected to it. Damages are not available for simple acts of teasing and name-calling among school children, however, even where these comments target differences in gender. Rather, in the context of student-on-student harassment, damages are available only where the behavior is so severe, pervasive, and objectively offensive that it denies its victims the equal access to education that Title IX is designed to protect.

The drop-off in LaShonda's grades provides necessary evidence of a potential link between her education and G.F.'s misconduct, but petitioner's ability to state a cognizable claim here depends equally on the alleged persistence and severity of G. F.'s actions, not to mention the Board's alleged knowledge and deliberate indifference.

Applying this standard to the facts at issue here, we conclude that the Eleventh Circuit erred in dismissing petitioner's complaint. Petitioner alleges that her daughter was the victim of repeated acts of sexual harassment by G. F. over a 5-month period, and there are allegations in support of the conclusion that G. F.'s misconduct was severe, pervasive, and objectively offensive. The harassment was not only verbal; it included numerous acts of objectively offensive touching, and, indeed, G. F. ultimately pleaded guilty to criminal sexual misconduct. Moreover, the complaint alleges that there were multiple victims who were sufficiently disturbed by G. F.'s misconduct to seek an audience with the school principal. Further, petitioner contends that the harassment had a concrete, negative effect on her daughter's ability to receive an education. The complaint also suggests that petitioner may be able to show both actual knowledge and deliberate indifference on the part of the Board, which made no effort whatsoever either to investigate or to put an end to the harassment.

Accordingly, the judgment of the United States Court of Appeals for the Eleventh Circuit is reversed, and the case is remanded for further proceedings consistent with this opinion.

Case Commentary

The United States Supreme Court held that a student may recover from a school board for their deliberate indifference to her sexual harassment complaint.

Case Questions

1. Do you agree with the decision in this case?
2. What was the reason for the inaction on the part of the principal and teachers?

3. Do you think G. F.'s actions created a severe and pervasive environment?

The question presented in the following case is whether a school district will be liable when a teacher sexually harasses a student where the school district lacks knowledge of the harassment.

CASE

GEBSER AND McCULLOUGH v. LAGO VISTA INDEPENDENT SCHOOL DISTRICT

524 U.S. 274 (1998)

JUSTICE O'CONNOR delivered the opinion of the Court.

The question in this case is when a school district may be held liable in damages in an implied right of action under Title IX of the Education Amendments of 1972 for the sexual harassment of a student by one of the district's teachers. We conclude that damages may not be recovered in those circumstances unless an official of the school district who at a minimum has authority to institute corrective measures on the district's behalf has actual notice of, and is deliberately indifferent to, the teacher's misconduct.

I

In the spring of 1991, when petitioner Alida Star Gebser was an eighth-grade student at a middle school in respondent Lago Vista Independent School District (Lago Vista), she joined a high school book discussion group led by Frank Waldrop, a teacher at Lago Vista's high school. Lago Vista received federal funds at all pertinent times.

During the book discussion sessions, Waldrop often made sexually suggestive comments to the students. Gebser entered high school in the fall and was assigned to classes taught by Waldrop in both semesters. Waldrop continued to make inappropriate remarks to the students, and he began to direct more of his suggestive comments toward Gebser, including during the substantial amount of time that the two were alone in his classroom. He initiated sexual contact with Gebser in the spring, when, while visiting her home ostensibly to give her a book, he kissed and fondled her. The two had sexual intercourse on a number of occasions during the remainder of the school year. Their relationship continued through the summer and into the following school year, and they often had intercourse during class time, although never on school property.

Gebser did not report the relationship to school officials, testifying that while she realized Waldrop's conduct was improper, she was uncertain how to react and she wanted to continue having him as a teacher. In October 1992, the parents of two other students complained to the high school principal about Waldrop's comments in class. The principal arranged a meeting, at which, according to the principal, Waldrop indicated that he did not believe he had made offensive remarks but apologized to the parents and said it would not happen again. The principal also advised Waldrop to be careful about his classroom comments and told the school guidance counselor about the meeting, but he did not report the parents' complaint to Lago Vista's superintendent, who was the district's Title IX coordinator. A couple of months later, in January 1993, a police officer discovered Waldrop and Gebser engaging in sexual intercourse and arrested Waldrop. Lago Vista terminated his employment, and subsequently, the Texas Education Agency revoked his teaching license. During this time, the district had not promulgated or distributed an official grievance procedure for lodging sexual harassment complaints; nor had it issued a formal anti-harassment policy.

Gebser and her mother filed suit against Lago Vista and Waldrop in state court in November 1993, raising claims against the school district under Title IX, and state negligence law, and claims against Waldrop primarily under state law. They sought compensatory and punitive damages from both defendants. After the case was removed, the United States District Court for the Western District of Texas granted summary judgment in favor of Lago Vista on all claims, and remanded the allegations against Waldrop to state court. In rejecting the Title IX claim against the school district, the court reasoned that the statute "was enacted to counter policies of discrimination . . . in federally funded education programs," and that "only if school administrators have some type of notice of the gender discrimination and fail to respond in good faith can the discrimination be interpreted as a policy of the school district." Here, the court determined, the parents' complaint to the principal concerning Waldrop's comments in class was the only one Lago Vista had received about Waldrop, and that evidence was inadequate to raise a genuine issue on whether the school district had actual or constructive notice that Waldrop was involved in a sexual relationship with a student.

Unquestionably, Title IX placed on the Gwinnett County Public Schools the duty not to discriminate on the basis of sex, and 'when a supervisor sexually harasses a subordinate because of the subordinate's sex, that supervisor "discriminates" on the basis of sex.' We believe the same rule should apply when a teacher sexually harasses and abuses a student.

Applying those principles here, we conclude that it would "frustrate the purposes" of Title IX to permit a damages recovery against a school district for a teacher's sexual harassment of a student based on principles of respondeat superior or constructive notice, i.e., without actual notice to a school district official. Because Congress did not expressly create a private right of action under Title IX, the statutory text does not shed light on Congress' intent with respect to the scope of available remedies.

As a general matter, it does not appear that Congress contemplated unlimited recovery in damages against a funding recipient where the recipient is unaware of discrimination in its programs. When Title IX was enacted in 1972, the principal civil rights statutes containing an express right of action did not provide for recovery of monetary damages at all, instead allowing only injunctive and equitable relief. It was not until 1991 that Congress made damages available under Title VII, and even then, Congress carefully limited the amount recoverable in any individual case, calibrating the maximum recovery to the size of the employer.

That contractual framework distinguishes Title IX from Title VII, which is framed in terms not of a condition but of an outright prohibition. Title VII applies to all employers without regard to federal funding and aims broadly to "eradicate discrimination throughout the economy." Thus, whereas Title VII aims centrally to compensate victims of discrimination, Title IX focuses more on "protecting" individuals from discriminatory practices carried out by recipients of federal funds. If a school district's liability for a teacher's sexual harassment rests on principles of constructive notice or respondeat superior, it will likewise be the case that the recipient of funds was unaware of the discrimination. It is sensible to assume that Congress did not envision a recipient's liability in damages in that situation.

The number of reported cases involving sexual harassment of students in schools confirms that harassment unfortunately is an all too common aspect of the educational experience. No one questions that a student suffers extraordinary harm when subjected to sexual harassment and abuse by a teacher, and that the teacher's conduct is reprehensible and undermines the basic purposes of the educational system. The issue in this case, however, is whether the independent misconduct of a teacher is attributable to the school district that employs him under a specific federal statute designed primarily to prevent recipients of federal financial assistance from using the funds in a discriminatory manner. Our decision does not affect any right of recovery that an individual may have against a school district as a matter of state law or against the teacher in his individual capacity under state law or under 42 U.S.C. § 1983. Until Congress speaks directly on the subject, however, we will not hold a school district liable in damages under Title IX for a teacher's sexual harassment of a student absent actual notice and deliberate indifference.

We therefore affirm the judgment of the Court of Appeals.

Case Commentary

The United States Supreme Court reasoned that under Title IX school districts should be liable for the conduct of their teachers only where the School District has knowledge of the behavior. This decision is contrary to *Faragher v. City of Boca Raton.*

Case Questions

1. Do you agree with the Court's decision?
2. How do you reconcile this case with *Faragher?*
3. If school districts are not liable for their teachers' conduct absent knowledge, what incentive is there for them to monitor the behavior of their teachers?

Companies and schools should draft a sexual harassment policy and have it well publicized throughout the workplace. The policy should clearly define the types of sexual harassment as well as set forth examples of verbal and physical abuse that will not be tolerated. Investigations will be thorough and the consequences severe.

A MODEL SEXUAL HARASSMENT POLICY

Sexual harassment is defined as (1) a sexual advance or request for sexual favor made by one employee to another which is unwelcome and not consented to; and (2) touching, joking, commenting, or distributing material of a sexual nature that an employee has not consented to and finds offensive.

Sexual advance may be defined as embracing, touching, cornering, or otherwise restricting an individual's freedom to move with the intent of pursuing sexual intimacy.

Request for sexual favors may be defined as asking an individual to engage in some type of sexual behavior such as but not limited to sexual intercourse, oral sex, intimate touching, and kissing.

Touching may be defined as placing hands on or rubbing against some part of another individual's body that is unwelcome and not consented to. The part of the person's body includes not only the breast, genitals, and buttocks, but also leg, knee, thigh, arm, shoulder, neck, face, and hair.

Joking may be defined as encouraging, participating, or telling sexual jokes which are offensive and demeaning.

Commenting may be defined as passing remarks of a sexual nature about an individual's anatomy, sex life, or personality or about that individual's gender, which is offensive and demeaning.

Distributing material of a sexual nature encompasses pornography, photostatic sheets which depict sexual cartoons or sexual jokes, or libelous statements about an individual's sex life.

Although the court appointed test for determining what constitutes sexual harassment is a reasonable person standard and what is reasonable may vary depending on the work environment, it is the purpose of this policy on sexual harassment to avoid litigation, not to win lawsuits. Therefore, employees are forewarned that the use of the terms "babe, broad, bitch, and chick" when spoken either alone or coupled with hot, foxy, dumb, stupid, and like words may give rise to a woman filing a sexual harassment complaint and are therefore prohibited.

If a complaint is filed with the company's human resources department on any of the above allegations, it will be investigated immediately. The investigation shall consist of questioning the complainant, alleged perpetrator, co-workers, superiors, and subordinates. If a determination is made that a valid complaint had been issued against an employee, that employee will be entitled to a hearing to which he or she may be assisted by outside counsel. If a conclusion is reached that the conduct complained of meets one of the above criteria, then the employee shall be dismissed forthwith.

Furthermore, the victim will be afforded counseling services if needed. Every effort will be made by the company to aid the victimized employee in overcoming the emotional trauma of the unfortunate ordeal.

Finally, the company will sponsor in-house workshops explaining this policy on sexual harassment, cautioning employees against engaging in it and encouraging those affected by sexual harassment to come forward with the details of their encounter with it in order for the company to investigate and resolve the dilemma and service the needs of the victimized employee.

The following case presents the settlement agreement reached in the Mitsubishi case.

Mitsubishi Motor Company has agreed to settle a claim June 10, 1998, which was brought against them by the Equal Employment Opportunity Commission. Mitsubishi agreed to pay $34 million in compensation for at least 350 women who were employed at a Normal, Ill., plant since 1990. The women were allegedly subjected to a pattern of sexual harassment which led to the filing of a civil class action prior to the EEOC suit.

EQUAL EMPLOYMENT OPPORTUNITY COMMISSION v. MITSUBISHI MOTOR MANUFACTURING OF AMERICA

Case No. 96-1192 (C.Dist. Ill. 1998)

McDADE, Judge.

CONSENT DECREE

1. This Consent Decree (the "Decree") is made and entered into by and between Plaintiff United States Equal Employment Opportunity Commission (hereinafter referred to as the "Commission" or "EEOC") and Defendant Mitsubishi Motor Manufacturing of America, Inc., formerly known as "Diamond Star Motors," (hereinafter referred to as "MMMA") (EEOC and MMMA are collectively referred to herein as "the Parties").

Now, therefore, the Court having carefully examined the terms and provisions of this Consent Decree, and based on the pleadings, record and stipulations of the Parties, it is ordered, adjudged and decreed that.

General Injunctive Provisions

15. Sexual Harassment. MMMA and its officers, agents, management (including supervisory employees), successors and assigns, and all those in active concert or participation with them, or any of them, are hereby enjoined from: (i) discriminating against women on the basis of sex; (ii) engaging in or being a party to any action, policy or practice that is intended to or is known to them to have the effect of harassing or intimidating any female employee on the basis of her gender; and/or (iii) creating, facilitating or permitting the existence of a work environment that is hostile to female employees.

16. Retaliation. MMMA and its officers, agents, management (including supervisory employees), successors and assigns, and all those in active concert or participation with them, or any of them, are hereby enjoined from engaging in, implementing or permitting any action, policy or practice with the purpose of retaliating against any current or former employee of MMMA because he or she opposed any practice of sex discrimination, sexual harassment or sex-based harassment made unlawful under Title VII; filed a Charge of Discrimination alleging any such practice; testified or participated in any manner in any investigation (including, without limitation, any internal investigation undertaken by MMMA), proceeding, or hearing in connection with this case and/or relating to any claim of sex discrimination, sexual harassment or sex-based harassment; was identified as a possible witness in this action; asserted any rights under this Decree; or sought and/or received any monetary and/or nonmonetary relief in accordance with this Decree.

Monetary Relief

Establishment of Settlement Fund

17. MMMA shall pay the gross sum of thirty-four million dollars ($34,000,000.00) (hereinafter referred to as the "Settlement Fund") to be distributed among all "Eligible Claimants" (as that term is defined in paragraph 20 herein), all in accordance with the provisions of this Decree. None of the amounts paid to Eligible Claimants shall be for back pay.

22. Eligible Claimants shall include only those claimants who satisfy each and all of the following criteria:

(i) the claimant was either: (a) employed by MMMA at any time between January 1, 1987 and the date of entry of this Decree; or (b) worked at MMMA's Normal, Illinois facility pursuant to a contract between MMMA and her direct employer at any time during such time period and has been identified by EEOC, prior to entry of this Decree, as a potential victim.

(ii) EEOC timely received from such claimant, in accordance with the procedures set forth in this Decree, a Claim Form and a Release in the form of Exhibits B and D attached to this Decree; and (iii) EEOC received evidence credible to EEOC that the individual was (a) subjected to sexual harassment or sex-based harassment, or (b) retaliated against because she opposed sexual harassment or participated in any proceeding relating to a complaint of sexual harassment, sex-based harassment or retaliation.

Non-Monetary Relief

43. MMMA affirms the following "Statement of Zero-Tolerance Policy and Equality Objectives": Mitsubishi Motor Manufacturing of America, Inc. is firmly committed to developing and maintaining a zero-tolerance policy concerning sexual harassment, sex-based harassment and retaliation against individuals who report harassment in the company's workplace; to swiftly and firmly responding to any acts of sexual or sex-based harassment or retaliation of which the company becomes aware; to implementing a disciplinary system that is designed to strongly deter future acts of sexual or sex-based harassment or retaliation; to eradicating any vestiges of a work environment that is hostile to women; and to actively monitoring its workplace in order to ensure tolerance, respect and dignity for all people. This paragraph does not create any contractual causes of action or other rights that would not otherwise exist.

Specific Non-Monetary Relief

44. In order to effectuate the objectives embodied in MMMA's Statement of Zero Tolerance Policy and Equality Objectives and this Decree, MMMA shall make whatever specific modifications are necessary to its existing policies, procedures and practices in order to ensure that the following policies, procedures and practices are in effect:

(a) Sexual Harassment Policy. MMMA agrees that it shall revise its sexual harassment policy, as necessary, in order to: (i) provide examples to supplement the definitions of sexual harassment and sex-based harassment; (ii) include strong non-retaliation language with examples to supplement the definition of retaliation, and provide for substantial and progressive discipline for incidents of retaliation; (iii) eliminate the "false accusation" provision contained in its current sexual harassment policy; (iv) provide that com-

plaints of sexual harassment, sex-based harassment and/or retaliation will be accepted by MMMA in writing and orally; (v) provide a timetable for reporting harassment, for commencing an investigation after a complaint is made or received and for remedial action to be taken upon conclusion of an investigation; and (vi) indicate that, promptly upon the conclusion of its investigation of a complaint, MMMA will communicate to the complaining party the results of the investigation and the remedial actions taken or proposed, if any.

(b) Complaint Procedures.

(i) MMMA agrees that it shall revise its complaint procedure as necessary in order to ensure that it is designed to encourage employees to come forward with complaints about violations of its sexual harassment policy. As part of this policy, MMMA agrees that it shall provide its employees with convenient, confidential and reliable mechanisms for reporting incidents of sexual harassment, sex-based harassment and retaliation. MMMA agrees that it shall designate at least two employees from the department charged with investigating such issues as persons who may be contacted, and their names, responsibilities, work locations and telephone numbers shall be routinely and continuously posted. Also as part of its procedure, MMMA agrees that it shall keep its 24-hour Complaint hotline in place, and shall take seriously anonymous complaints received on the hotline. Additionally as part of its complaint procedure, MMMA agrees that it shall maintain in the plant the presence of personnel charged with handling complaints of sexual harassment, sex-based harassment and retaliation.

(ii) MMMA agrees that it shall revise its policies as necessary to enable complaining parties to be interviewed by MMMA about their complaints in such a manner that permits the complaining party, at such party's election, to remain inconspicuous to all of the employees in such party's work area. MMMA agrees that its complaint procedure shall not impose upon individuals seeking to make a complaint alleging sexual harassment, sex-based harassment and/or retaliation any requirements that are more burdensome than are imposed upon individuals who make other complaints of comparable gravity. (iii) MMMA agrees that it shall revise its complaint handling and disciplinary procedures as necessary to ensure that all complaints of sexual harassment, sex-based harassment and/or retaliation are investigated and addressed promptly. Specifically, MMMA agrees that it shall make best efforts to investigate all complaints of sexual harassment, sex-based harassment and/or retaliation promptly and to complete investigations within three (3) weeks. MMMA will further make best efforts to prepare its written findings of the results of each investigation and the remedial actions proposed within seven (7) days after completion of the investigation, and shall thereupon promptly communicate to the complaining party the results of the investigation and the remedial actions taken or proposed, if any.

(iv) MMMA agrees that it shall make best efforts to ensure that appropriate remedial action is taken to resolve complaints and to avoid the occurrence of further incidents of sexual harassment, sex-based harassment and/or retaliation. MMMA specifically agrees that its complaint procedure shall include the power, in MMMA's sole discretion, to order, during the pendency of the investigation, the immediate transfer of persons accused of having violated MMMA's sexual harassment policy or of persons who claim to have been victims of such violations, as well as the power to order the permanent transfer of employees found to have violated such policy, and, upon the request of the complaining party, the permanent transfer of any complaining party who is found to have been the victim of a violation of MMMA's sexual harassment policy. Where possible, transfer will be in line with seniority. MMMA further agrees that it shall revise its progressive discipline policy to provide for substantial discipline short of termination—including, but not limited to, suspensions without pay—as a possible consequence for violations of its sexual harassment policy.

(c) Policies Designed To Promote Supervisor Accountability.

(i) MMMA agrees that it shall impose substantial discipline—up to and including termination, suspension without pay or demotion—upon any supervisor or manager who engages in sexual harassment or sex-based harassment or permits any such conduct to occur in his or her work area or among employees under his or her supervision, or who retaliates against any person who complains or participates in any investigation or proceeding concerning any such conduct. MMMA

shall communicate this policy to all of its supervisors and managers.

(ii) MMMA agrees that it shall continue to advise all managers and supervisors of their duty to actively monitor their work areas to ensure employees' compliance with the company's sexual harassment policy, and to report any incidents and/or complaints of sexual harassment, sex-based harassment and/or retaliation of which they become aware to the department charged with handling such complaints.

(iii) MMMA agrees that it will complete its current revision of the supervisor appraisal process to include performance evaluations for the handling of equal employment opportunity ("EEO") issues as an element in supervisor appraisals, and to link such evaluations directly to supervisor salary/bonus structure.

(iv) MMMA agrees that it shall include "commitment to equal employment opportunity" as a criterion for qualification for supervisory positions.

(d) Sexual Harassment Training.

(i) MMMA agrees that it shall continue to provide mandatory annual sexual harassment training to all supervisors; to provide mandatory sexual harassment training to all new employees during employee orientation; to provide mandatory sexual harassment training to all senior management officials; to provide mandatory sexual harassment training for all employees of Mitsubishi Motors Corporation who are assigned to work at MMMA's facility in Normal, Illinois, prior to their commencing employment at MMMA's facility in Normal, Illinois; and to provide training to all persons charged with the handling of complaints of sexual harassment, sex-based harassment and/or retaliation related thereto conducted by experienced sexual harassment educators and/or investigators to educate them about the problems of sexual harassment in the workplace and the techniques for investigating and stopping it.

(ii) MMMA agrees that it shall require a senior management official to introduce all sexual harassment training to communicate MMMA's commitment to its Statement of Zero-Tolerance Policy and Monitoring of Complaints.

58. In addition to the functions and purposes described above, the Decree Monitors shall also have the responsibility for overseeing the investiga-

tion of all sexual and sex-based harassment and related retaliation complaints reported to MMMA. The Chairperson shall be initially designated as the person who will be responsible for monitoring such complaints (such designated person is hereinafter referred to as the "Complaint Monitor").

59. MMMA shall transmit to the Complaint Monitor a copy of each such written complaint reported to MMMA as soon as practicable and, in any event, no later than the close of the next business day after MMMA receives any such complaint.

60. The Complaint Monitor will oversee the investigation and, where appropriate, may make recommendations to MMMA concerning the conduct of the investigation of each such complaint. MMMA shall make a good faith best effort to follow any recommendations made by the Complaint Monitor concerning the conduct of the investigation. The Complaint Monitor may also interview the complaining party, if the Complaint Monitor deems it appropriate.

61. Upon completion of the investigation, MMMA shall promptly prepare and provide the Complaint Monitor with a copy of a written report summarizing the investigation undertaken and any remedial actions taken or proposed by MMMA, and shall also promptly communicate to the complaining party the results of the investigation and the remedial actions taken or proposed, if any, and shall further inform the complaining party of her right to appeal MMMA's finding to the Complaint Monitor.

62. If, upon receiving and reviewing an appeal from an individual complainant or upon its own initiative, the Complaint Monitor believes that the remedial action proposed by MMMA is inconsistent with MMMA's Statement of Zero-Tolerance Policy and Equality Objectives or with the terms of this Decree, the Complaint Monitor shall first attempt to resolve the disagreement with MMMA. If MMMA and the Complaint Monitor are unable to reach a resolution of their disagreement to the satisfaction of the Complaint Monitor, the Complaint Monitor shall report to EEOC any such inconsistency.

Case Commentary

The Central District Court of Illinois presided over the settlement agreement reached in the Mitsubishi case. Mitsubishi agreed to pay $34 million in settlement of the female employees's sexual harassment claims. Mitsubishi was enjoined from retaliating against any of the victims of sexual harassment. It agreed to start a sexual harassment training program for its managers and employees. Mitsubishi also agreed to provide a complaint monitor to oversee the workplace.

Case Questions

1. Does this consent decree adequately address the injustices perpetrated upon the female employees?

2. Can you think of anything else that should have been included?
3. Why do you think Mitsubishi management allowed these conditions to continue?

DAMAGES

The 1991 Amendment to the Civil Rights Act has now made compensatory and punitive damages available to Title VII plaintiffs including those victimized by sexual harassment.

❖ EMPLOYER LESSONS

- Draft a sexual harassment policy.
- Educate managers and employees about what constitutes sexual harassment.
- Understand the difference between *quid pro quo* and hostile work environment.
- Investigate complaints expeditiously and thoroughly.

- Determine how you will deal with employees who are guilty of harassment.
- Instruct managers to avoid favoritism, since this may lead to the perception of harassment.
- Acknowledge that harassment may be perpetrated against employees of the same sex.
- Appreciate that a comment, joke, or pictorial must be sexual in nature.
- Realize that sexual harassment must be severe and pervasive.
- Address only those instances of sexual harassment committed during the scope of employment.

❖ EMPLOYEE LESSONS

- Realize that the harassment must be sexual.
- Understand that as a victim of harassment, you must not have consented to or participated in the hostile work environment.
- Do not engage in sexual joke telling, using sexual language, or distributing sexual pictorials.
- Appreciate that the sexual harassment must occur within the scope of employment.
- Guard against giving the perception of creating a hostile work environment.
- Realize that although sweetheart, babe, and honey are not sexually harassing terms, they may be against company policy.
- Learn that the harassing behavior must make it difficult for you to perform your job.
- Realize that men can be victims of sexual harassment.
- Know that people of the same sex may be victims of sexual harassment.
- Report instances of sexual harassment to human resources in a timely fashion.

❖ SUMMARY

In the competitive global environment in which businesses operate, employees should be instructed that their work hours should be spent productively, not taking time for idle chatter, much less for abusing coworkers and subordinates. The team concept should be promoted, and personal favoritism should be discarded for the success of the team. Encouragement and a willingness to help one another should displace personal aggrandizement at the expense of demeaning one's coworkers. Employees who embrace these concepts will make positive contributions to the firm in a future in which employees will be judged not only on their positive contributions but also on what their negative actions are likely to cost the company.

❖ REVIEW QUESTIONS

1. Define sexual harassment.
2. Explain hostile work environment.
3. Define the concept of *quid pro quo*.
4. What should be included in a company policy on sexual harassment?
5. Can sexual harassment be directed against management?
6. Is it possible for a man to be a victim of sexual harassment?
7. Can sexual harassment occur outside the work environment?
8. Does using the term "babe" constitute sexual harassment?
9. Can sexual harassment involve an aggressor and a victim from the same sex?
10. In situations involving sexually harassing comments, is truth an absolute defense?

11. A female employee sued her employer for sexual harassment, claiming that a supervisor referred to her as a "worthless broad." The employer argued that the supervisor's alleged abuse was not gender-oriented in that he treated men the same way. What was the result? *Steiner v. Showboat Operating Co.,* 25 F.3d 1459 (9th Cir. 1994)

12. The workplace was permeated with discriminatory intimidation, ridicule, and insult that is sufficiently severe or pervasive to alter the conditions of the victim's employment and create an abusive working environment. The employer argued that this was not sufficient unless the employee had suffered psychological distress. What was the result? *Harris v. Forklift Systems, Inc.,* 114 S. Ct. 367 (1994)

13. This case involved the display and posting of pornographic photographs, and the use of derogatory language directed at women. Does this qualify as a hostile work environment? What was the result? *Jenson v. Eveleth Taconite Co.,* 824 F.Supp. 847 (D.Minn. 1993)

14. Sparks sued the Northeast Alabama Regional Medical Center, her employer, claiming to be sexually harassed by Dr. Garland. Sparks alleged that Dr. Garland joked about her breast size and sex life and cursed at her for being late in front of her coworkers. The hospital claimed that this was outside the scope of Dr. Garland's employment. What was the result? *Sparks v. Regional Medical Center Bd.,* 792 F.Supp. 735 (N.D. Ala. 1992)

15. Byron Brown, a senior counselor at a drug rehabilitation facility engaged in sexual intercourse with Kimberly Bunce, a patient. This happened several times with her consent. Thereafter, she sued Brown in civil court for sexual assault, battery, and malpractice. Brown argued that consent is a defense. What was the result? *Bunce v. Parkside Lodge of Columbus,* 596 N.E. 2d 1106 (Ohio App. 10 Dist. 1991)

16. Should the plaintiff's acquiescence in a relationship preclude him from recovery?

17. If off-color jokes are acceptable to everyone, should an employer still prohibit this type of behavior?

18. If an employee has participated in the offensive behavior, can he or she later claim hostile work environment?

19. Was a company ethical for being indifferent to the employee's affair until such time as the female employee became pregnant, at which time both she and her lover were discharged?

20. Within a two to three week period approximately six separate incidents occurred in which Mr. Strauss's conduct could be considered abusive. The most severe of these incidents included Mr. Strauss leaning or rubbing himself against Plaintiff. In fact, according to Plaintiff, she may have been encountering Mr. Strauss's alleged abusive conduct as frequently as every other day during her first few weeks of employment. Is this *Quid Pro Quo*? *Canada v. Boyd Group Inc.* 809 F.Supp. 771 (D.Nev. 1992)

21. Plaintiff testified that after she began working on the main floor of the factory Oslac, the 65-year-old owner, talked to her about sex, showed her pictures from Penthouse magazine, tried to get her to go out with him, and invited her to his apartment on the top floor of the factory to watch pornographic movies. She said that she did not say "no" outright because she was afraid of losing her job. Rather, she would decline his advances with one reason or another and try to change the subject.

    In the spring of 1982, plaintiff appeared nude in *Easy Riders* "In the Wind" magazine. In April 1983, she appeared nude in *Easy Riders* magazine. The magazine circulated throughout the plant, and employees saw them. In these photographs she had ornaments or earrings attached to her nipples. One picture revealed a tattoo in the pelvic region. Her father had pierced her nipples and had taken the photographs in her brother's presence.

    On July 19, 1984, plaintiff walked off the job following a work dispute with Eugene Ottaway. Plaintiff testified she got upset, left, and that weekend decided to quit her job.

    Plaintiff did not see Oslac in the plant during the last four to six weeks of her employment with McGregor Electronics. What was the result? *Burns v. McGregor Electronic Industries, Inc.,* 807 F.Supp. 506 (N.D.Iowa 1992)

22. At the time of the incidents complained of, plaintiff was receiving a pension from the Veterans Administration based on 100% disability. He is a reformed alcoholic and former

substance abuser, divorced with at least one adult child. Defendant, Dr. Janet Foy, is a psychologist practicing in the City of Peekskill, who specializes in marital counseling. She also is divorced with at least one adult child.

A consensual sexual relationship developed between Mr. Carter and Dr. Foy in about September 1989.

The path of true love seldom runs smoothly. Mr. Carter testified that he first attempted to "break-off" the relationship with Dr. Foy in November of 1989, and again in December of 1989, because he felt that Dr. Foy was "very controlling and critical" of his participation in support groups and AA.

Mr. Carter testified, and defendant Foy concedes, that on June 5, 1990 at 10:00 a.m., Dr. Foy called Mr. Carter at work, and asked him to meet over dinner that evening to reconsider their relationship. After Mr. Carter declined the invitation, Dr. Foy then suggested that he resign from his position at Jan Peek House "as a personal consideration" to her and asked him to take a one-week vacation to consider his options.

Mr. Carter acknowledged during his direct and cross-examination that he was assured immediately and directly by Ms. Quinn, the Director of Jan Peek House, and also by the Board of Directors of the corporate defendant, that his job was not in jeopardy. Did Dr. Foy sexually harass Carter? *Carter v. Caring for the Homeless of Peekskill,* 821 F. Supp. 225 (S.D.N.Y. 1993)

23. Gary Showalter and Nenh Phetosomphone alleged that they were sexually harassed while employed at Techni-Craft Plating Company, a jewelry plating firm located in Cranston, Rhode Island. Essentially, they both claim that defendant Noel Smith, the General Manager of Techni-Craft, forced them to engage in various sexual activities with his secretary, defendant Carol Marsella, by threatening them with the loss of their jobs if they did not acquiesce in his demands. What was the result? *Showalter v. Allison Reed Group, Inc.,* 767 F. Supp. 1205 (D.R.I. 1991)

24. The Employment Security Board denied Plaintiff unemployment benefits because before quitting her job, she did not give notice to her employer's business manager or someone in similar authority that she was being sexually harassed by her supervisor. Plaintiff appealed. We reverse and remand. What was the result? *Allen v. Dept. of Employment Training,* 618 A.2d 1317 (Vt. 1992)

25. A female employee and her male superior conducted an open affair for many years. The employer did not discourage this until she became pregnant for the second time. At this point, both were discharged. The company claimed that the termination was necessary to prevent potential sexual harassment suits by the female employee involved for quid pro quo and the coworkers for hostile work environment. What was the result? *Cumpiano v. Banco Santander Puerto Rico,* 902 F.2d 148 (1st Cir. 1990)

26. Because a female employee was forcibly restrained by her employer in an attempt to kiss and touch her, she resigned from her job. The question is whether this conduct substantially interferes with her employment by creating a hostile work environment. What was the result? *Radtke v. Everett,* 501 N.W.2d 155 (Mich. 1993)

27. Kerr-McGee contends that Lord's complaints do not constitute an "intimidating, hostile, or offensive working environment" as a matter of law. Kerr-McGee urges that Lord has failed to articulate sufficient evidence to refute the reason that she was demoted, *i.e.,* poor job performance.

In contrast, Lord alleges she was unlawfully harassed based on her gender. To wit, supervisors never said nice things to her, supervisor Keithan called her "dumb" and talked about her behind her back; male employees were treated better than she was at the warehouse area; foremen were not nice to her, and supervisor Elliot treated her as "mentally retarded" by virtue of the test Elliot administered to her regarding her job skill level. Lord argues that the real reason she was demoted from her job in the toolroom was due to gender discrimination against her. She seeks back-wages and desires to be returned to her toolroom job. What was the result? *Lord v. Kerr-McGee Coal Corp.,* 809 F.Supp 87 (D.Wyo. 1992)

28. Evidence was presented that defendant Carpenter forcefully placed his foot in plaintiff's

crotch and wiggled it, pulled the waistband on her pants and exposed her undergarments on at least two occasions, slapped her on the buttocks, and pushed her in a threatening manner. Plaintiff complained to John

Schmidt, her supervisor, that Carpenter had been mean to her and frequently used sexual language in her presence. Was this conduct severe and pervasive? *Dombeck v. Milwaukee Valve Co.*, 823 F.Supp. 1473 (W.D. 1993)

❖ WEB SITES

www.matriarch.com/sexual_harassment.htm
www.aclu.org/news/w111097d.html
www.jri-inc.com/sexharr.htm
www.nydailynews.com/archive/97_05/051897/news/22177.htm
www.vix.com/pub/men/harass/commentary/white-fault.html
http://headlines.yahoo.com/eonline/stories/8690967523.html
www://vix.com/pub/men/harass/commentary/white-fault.html
www.eeoc.gov/facts/fs-sex.html

11

FAMILY LEAVE AND PREGNANCY DISCRIMINATION

INTRODUCTION

Pregnancy most often leads to the birth of child. Although a child is precious, its birth may temporarily halt the employment of the mother and the father because of the love and care required by the newborn. This raises two issues.

First, a woman must not be discriminated against because of her desire to become pregnant, her pregnancy, or because she has a child. The Pregnancy Discrimination Act of 1978 protects women against these forms of discrimination. There is no doubt that an employee's pregnancy may be disruptive to the workplace. But with regard to employment, pregnancy is a temporary disability and, as such, is no more disruptive to the workplace than disability due to sickness, accident, or injury.

Second, to accommodate the parents' desire to bond with their newborn, 12 weeks of unpaid family leave must be granted to the mother and father if they have worked for a company with 50 or more employees for one year and have accrued at least 1,250 hours of work time during that year. The Family and Medical Leave Act of 1991 guarantees this. The Act also extends that guarantee when a serious health condition befalls a spouse, child, or parent.

CHAPTER CHECKLIST

❖ Learn the requirements for taking family and medical leave.

❖ Define serious health condition.

❖ Understand that health benefits are maintained during family and medical leave.

❖ Appreciate that certification of the serious health condition by a health care provider may be required.

❖ Know that medical leave may be granted on an intermittent or consecutive basis.

❖ Realize that family leave applies to fathers as well as mothers for the birth of a child.

❖ Be aware that adoptive parents are entitled to family leave.

❖ Understand the purpose of the Pregnancy Discrimination Act.

❖ Be apprised of why some employers do not want to employ pregnant workers.

❖ Be cognizant of the existence of fetal protection policies.

FAMILY LEAVE

The Family and Medical Leave Act of 1991 permits an employee in any 12-month period to take up to 12 weeks of unpaid leave for the birth or adoption of a child; for the care of a spouse, child, or parent who has a serious health condition; or because of a serious health problem that makes the employee unable to work.

The issue in the case that follows is whether a biological father who is seeking to adopt his own child is entitled to family leave.

CASE

KELLEY v. CROSFIELD CATALYSTS

135 F.3d 1202 (7th Cir. 1998)

FLAUM, Circuit Judge.

Dwayne Kelley allegedly received authorization from his employer, Crosfield Catalysts ("Crosfield"), to travel to New York in order to "seek custody of a young girl for foster care or adoption." Kelley's trip for this purpose caused him to miss four days of scheduled work. Crosfield terminated Kelley on his next work day on account of this four-day absence; Kelley claims that the dismissal was pretextual and in violation of the Family and Medical Leave Act (FMLA). The district court dismissed Kelley's Second Amended Complaint. We disagree with the district court's characterization of the Second Amended Complaint, and we therefore reverse the dismissal and remand the case for further proceedings.

I. BACKGROUND

Dwayne Kelley began working for Crosfield as a laboratory technician on August 1, 1992. This position required Kelley to work twelve-hour shifts for four consecutive days followed by three consecutive "off" days. Kelley was scheduled to begin a four-day work rotation on October 22, 1993, when he unexpectedly received a phone call from his mother. His mother informed him that the Brooklyn Bureau of Child Welfare was preparing to take custody of Shaneequa Forbes, an eleven-year-old girl. Shaneequa was born into the marriage of Barbara and Michael Forbes, but—although this information was not contained in his Second Amended Complaint—Kelley had reason to believe that he might be the girl's biological father. He told his supervisors at Crosfield that Shaneequa was his daughter. Kelley missed four scheduled workdays while attending to this matter in New York. On his first day back at work, October 29, Crosfield terminated Kelley's employment.

The parties' pleading maneuvers constitute the focus of this appeal. Kelley filed a pro se complaint on October 26, 1995, which alleged that his termination violated the FMLA because he took leave from work in order to "obtain custody of my kids." Crosfield filed a motion to dismiss this complaint arguing that seeking custody of one's own children was not covered by the FMLA. Before the district court ruled on Crosfield's motion, Kelley filed an amended pro se complaint on April 25, 1996. The amended complaint stated only that the child "grew up" with Kelley, and it referenced Shaneequa's birth certificate on which Barbara and Michael Forbes are listed as the girl's biological parents.

The parties discussed the matter of Shaneequa's parentage at a status hearing regarding the amended complaint five days after it was filed. Kelley admitted there was some confusion about whether he was Shaneequa's father. He stated, "Your Honor, I was told—there is nothing in any records showing that I am the father. I was told that I was the father. So I took this as I'm being the father. But as of late, I found out that I might not even be the father. On record, I am not the father." Based on this colloquy, Crosfield moved to dismiss the amended complaint for failure to state a claim, arguing that obtaining custody of one's own child was not a protected activity under the FMLA.

II. DISCUSSION

The Family and Medical Leave Act of 1993 affords flexibility in employment for medical or family emergencies to anyone working at least 1250 hours per year at a business employing fifty or more people for at least twenty weeks of the year. Congressional hearings revealed that the FMLA was needed to help balance the demands of work and family, as well as to ease the burden of caretaking among individual family members. The provision of the FMLA most relevant to the instant appeal is 29 U.S.C. sec. 2612(a)(1)(B), which provides that eligible employees may receive twelve weeks of excused leave per year "because of the placement of a son or daughter with the employee for adoption or foster care."

Kelley's Second Amended Complaint did not make any reference to Shaneequa's biological parentage. It only stated that he traveled to New York to "seek custody of Shaneequa for foster care or adoption." Thus, based on the allegations of the Second Amended Complaint alone, the issue of Kelley's biological connection to Shaneequa was not before the district court. It is apparent, however, that the court considered

Shaneequa's biological parentage by concluding that Kelley's emergency trip to New York did not fit within the meaning of the FMLA.

The same principle applies in the instant case. Any facts that Kelley had pleaded in his first two complaints were effectively nullified for 12(b)(6) purposes when he filed his Second Amended Complaint, which did not reference those facts.

In addition, we think it is important to note that Kelley could have stated a viable FMLA claim even if his Second Amended Complaint had declared that he was the biological father of Shaneequa. The district court believed that the "usual sense" of the relevant FMLA terms "adoption" and "foster care" did not encompass a situation in which a biological father takes custody of his own child. Indeed, the Department of Labor has defined the term "adoption" as used in the FMLA as the "legal process in which an individual becomes the legal parent of another's child." The court seemed to fear that allowing one to adopt one's own child or to take the child into foster care would grant FMLA coverage to run-of-the-mill custody disputes.

This is not just another custody case, though, and we believe that Kelley could state a valid claim under the FMLA. The FMLA defines "son or daughter" as "a biological, adopted, or foster child, a stepchild, a legal ward, or a child of a person standing in loco parentis." Thus, in light of this definition, the FMLA expressly protects leaves taken "because of the placement of a biological child with an employee for adoption or foster care." Furthermore, Kelley was not Shaneequa's father of record—unlike the usual situation in custody disputes—and he would have sought leave to take custody of a child who (according to public record) was "another's child."

It will indeed be unusual to encounter a situation in which a biological parent takes a leave from work in order to adopt or take into foster care his own child. This situation may be rare, but Kelley has proven that it is not entirely impossible. In a case such as this in which a biological parent has no custodial rights over a child and is not listed as the child's parent as a matter of record, it may be possible for that parent to adopt his own child. Thus, regardless of whether he was the biological father, Kelley could state a claim under the FMLA.

III. CONCLUSION

Discovery may reveal Kelley's claim⋯ itless. The face of the ⋯ not ⋯

would entitle Kelley to relief. Dismissal, therefore, was unwarranted. For the foregoing reasons, we reverse the district court's dismissal of Kelley's Second Amended Complaint and remand the cause for further proceedings.

Judgment for Kelly.

FMLA even if it turns out that he is the biological father.

3. Why should the FMLA protect him in these unusual circumstances?

⋯vorked for the employer for at least one ⋯vice during the previous 12 months. The ⋯ to employers who have *50* or more ⋯g 20 weeks of the current or preceding

⋯company with less than 50 employees ⋯e of its employees under the FMLA.

G. BALDWIN

ROSEN, ⋯

⋯and representations, modified its at-will employment relationship with Plaintiff by effectively adopting the terms of the Act and the corresponding obligations, thereby exposing Baldwin to potential liability for breach of contract. Although not raised by the parties, the threshold question raised by this appeal is whether federal question jurisdiction exists where an employer who does not employ a sufficient number of employees to come within the ambit of the Family and Medical Leave Act has nevertheless explicitly adopted its policies as its own. For the following reasons, we find that it

INTRODUCTION

Plaintiff Sheila R. Douglas initiated this action against her employer, Defendant E. G. Baldwin and Associates Baldwin, claiming she was not offered an equivalent position when she returned from her maternity leave, in violation of the Family and Medical Leave Act. Although Baldwin did not employ the requisite number of employees to fall with the ambit of the Act itself, the District Court ruled that Baldwin had, through its con-does not, and that the District Court erred by failing to recognize that because Baldwin did not fall within the statutory definition of employer under the Family and Medical Leave Act, federal question jurisdiction over the case did not exist. Therefore, we dismiss the case for lack of subject matter jurisdiction.

FACTS

Defendant E. G. Baldwin & Associates, Inc. is an Ohio corporation which sells and services medical diagnostic imaging equipment and supplies. Baldwin's corporate headquarters are located in Cleveland, Ohio, and it has several division offices, including one in Holland, Ohio. On August 3, 1992, Plaintiff Sheila R. Douglas began working at Baldwin's Holland office as a sales secretary. At the time the events giving rise to this action occurred, Baldwin employed 29 people in its Holland office. When Baldwin hired Mrs. Douglas, she was given an Employee Handbook that set forth personnel policy statements and outlined performance requirements. After Congress enacted the Family and Medical Leave Act FMLA, Baldwin formally adopted the provisions of the FMLA by adding a new policy to its Employee Handbook, effective January 1, 1994. The policy stated:

Employees who have worked for the Company for at least twelve (12) months and at least 1,250 hours during the prior twelve (12) months may take up to twelve (12) weeks of unpaid Family and Medical Leave (hereinafter leave).

On December 19, 1994, Mrs. Douglas, having by this time been promoted to the position of image processing coordinator, requested a leave of absence from work due to her impending child birth. Upon Douglas' return from leave, Defendant Baldwin informed her that the image processing coordinator position had been eliminated pursuant to a corporate restructuring, and offered her three alternative positions: sales secretary, receptionist, and customer service representative. Plaintiff claimed that none of these positions were equivalent to the position she held at the commencement of her leave, as required by the Act.

DISTRICT COURT'S DECISION

The District Court determined that although Defendant did not technically come within the statutory ambit of the Act, Defendant had voluntarily agreed to abide by the terms of the Act in its employment contract with Plaintiff.

ANALYSIS

In this case, the FMLA specifies that the Act shall only apply to companies that employ 50 or more employees. Consequently, Congress specifically defined the coverage of the Act to exclude coverage for any employee of an employer who is employed at a worksite at which such employer employs less than 50 employees if the total number of employees employed by that employer within 75 miles of that worksite is less than 50. In this case, although Baldwin employed far more than 50 employees nationwide, it only employed 29 employees at or within 75 miles of the Holland office at the time the events giving rise to this suit took place. Therefore, the plain language of the FMLA excludes Baldwin's Holland office from coverage under the Act.

Whatever the rationale behind this limitation, be it Congress' desire not to burden small businesses by requiring them to operate without employees for an extended period of time or their determination that the effect upon commerce from the small companies is de minimis, is not for us to question and, in any event, is immaterial to our jurisdictional determination. For a federal court to exercise subject matter jurisdiction in a statutory scheme such as the FMLA, the defendant-company must meet the statutory definition of employer.

If the Court were to exercise jurisdiction where the employer does not meet the statutory prerequisite, it would effectively be expanding the scope of the Act, and the scope of our limited jurisdiction as defined by Congress, by judicial decree. This we do not have the power to do.

The fact that the parties contracted to incorporate the terms and responsibilities of the FMLA into their employment relationship does not bring them within the Act itself.

Judgment for Baldwin.

Case Commentary

The Sixth Circuit held that an employer who lacks the requisite number of employees for the FMLA to be applicable cannot voluntarily agree to provide leave under the Act.

Case Questions

1. Do you agree with the Court's decision?
2. Why can't an employer voluntarily agree to cover its employees under the FMLA?
3. Do you believe it was Congress's intent to prohibit a large company like Baldwin from granting its employees FMLA coverage at one of its work sites where there are fewer than 50 employees?

SERIOUS HEALTH CONDITION

Serious health condition means that the person is in a hospital, hospice, or nursing home or requires continuous medical treatment. Biological, adopted, foster, and stepchildren are covered by the Act.

The issue presented in the case that follows is whether the diagnosis of the plaintiff's son qualified as a serious health condition under the Family and Medical Leave Act.

CASE

MARTYSZENKO v. SAFEWAY, INC.

120 F.3d 120 (8th Cir. 1997)

LAY, Circuit Judge.

This is an action brought under the Family and Medical Leave Act of 1993 (FMLA). Vivian Martyszenko was working as a cashier at Safeway grocery store in Ogallala, Nebraska, when she received a call indicating that police believed her two children may have been sexually molested. On the basis of this information, Dennis Davis, Martyszenko's supervisor at Safeway, permitted Martyszenko two weeks' vacation leave to care for her children.

Dr. Randall Sullivan, a psychiatrist, examined Martyszenko's seven-year-old son, Kyle, on August 4, 1995, and found he had no behavior problems. Dr. Sullivan found no evidence of distractibility, psychosis or hallucinations. He concluded that "it would be premature to make a diagnosis of sexual abuse." Dr. Sullivan suggested Kyle should be supervised, but did not believe he needed to be observed continuously.

After the August 4 appointment, Martyszenko returned to Safeway and spoke with her supervisor.

She informed Davis that the visit with Dr. Sullivan was inconclusive and that Kyle was scheduled for additional appointments at about two-week intervals. Davis offered to schedule Martyszenko around Kyle's appointments. Martyszenko then left Safeway permanently. She did not report to work as scheduled and she did not contact Davis.

Dr. Sullivan evaluated Kyle on August 14. He reported:

Kyle is not expressing any issues that he has been sexually abused or had any sexual contact. The family reports that his behavior at home is essentially normal with no behavior problems. He had no behavior problems at school last year.

Dr. Sullivan observed that his final interview with Kyle was "essentially unremarkable."

In October 1995, Safeway twice wrote Martyszenko and advised her that she could return to her position at Safeway with full reinstatement of benefits and no loss in seniority. In January 1996, Safeway provided Martyszenko a check in the amount she would have received as compensation had she remained at work. Martyszenko rejected the offer to return but cashed the check.

In her suit in district court, Martyszenko asserts that Safeway fired her after she requested time off from work and that Safeway failed to inform her of leave available under the FMLA. The district court granted Safeway's summary judgment motion on the basis that Kyle did not have a "serious health condition," which is necessary to trigger the FMLA. Martyszenko appeals.

DISCUSSION

We affirm.

Family and Medical Leave Act

In relevant part, the FMLA entitles an eligible employee to twelve workweeks' leave per year to care for a child with a serious health condition. This leave generally may be unpaid. An employer violates the FMLA if it denies the employee leave or reinstatement following the leave.

A "serious health condition" is any physical or mental condition that involves inpatient care or continuing treatment by a health care provider. This case does not concern inpatient care. The FMLA does not define what medical attention constitutes "continuing treatment" by a health care provider, nor does it further define "serious health condition." However, Congress directed the Secretary of Labor to promulgate regulations to effectuate the Act.

Under the governing regulations, to constitute a serious health condition premised upon continuing treatment by a health care provider, the condition at a minimum will include either: a period of incapacity of more than three consecutive days together with subsequent multiple treatments or related periods of incapacity; a period of incapacity due to pregnancy or for prenatal care; a period of incapacity or treatment for the incapacity due to a chronic serious health condition; a permanent or long-term period of incapacity due to ineffective treatment; or a period of absence to receive or recover from multiple treatments by a health care provider for restorative surgery or for a condition likely to result in incapacity if no treatment is received.

"Serious Health Condition"

The district court interpreted these regulations as requiring incapacity. It is difficult to fault this as-

sessment. In construing regulations of the Secretary, we were recently reminded that "where Congress has not 'directly spoken to the precise question at issue,' we must sustain the Secretary's approach so long as it is 'based on a permissible construction of the statute.'" Martyszenko argues that incapacity is not required to trigger the FMLA. She contends that even if incapacity is required, Kyle's three consultations with Dr. Sullivan qualify as a period of incapacity. We find no error in the district court's interpretation. In addition to the standards set forth in the regulations, the legislative history of the FMLA supports the district court's construction. The Act was designed to permit a parent to tend to her child where the child is "unable to participate in school or in his or her regular daily activities." The Act was "not intended to cover short-term conditions for which treatment and recovery are very brief."

Uniformly, courts applying the FMLA expressly or impliedly have required a showing of incapacity.

Here, the alleged molestation did not create a mental condition that hindered Kyle's ability to participate in any activity at all. From the outset, Dr. Sullivan did not report any psychological disorder or mental condition and found Kyle to be worry free and undistracted. He did not restrict any of Kyle's daily activities. The record does not establish the existence of any health condition, let alone a "serious health condition" as contemplated by the FMLA.

Although periodic examinations may constitute treatment, by the FMLA's express terms such treatment must be "continuing" to require extended leave. That is, consistent with the aim of the statute to permit reasonable leave "for eligible medical reasons . . . and for compelling family reasons," examinations and evaluations concerning serious health conditions will implicate the FMLA only to the extent their importance, duration and frequency require absence from work.

Safeway accommodated Kyle's first examination immediately by permitting Martyszenko a full two weeks' leave, and offered not to schedule her to work at any time during Kyle's subsequent examinations. While the accusation of molestation led Dr. Sullivan to suggest that Kyle should be supervised, he at no time found any support for the uncorroborated molestation accusation, and in any event did not order Kyle to be observed continuously. We hold that Safeway met its obligation to Martyszenko under the FMLA by releasing her from work for an extended period up through the first examination and by offering to schedule her to work around the two subsequent examinations.

ing Dr. Sullivan's interviews could be deemed examinations to determine the existence of a serious health condition, Safeway met its FMLA-leave obligation by permitting Martyszenko's leave initially and by offering to schedule her around any examinations. The judgment of the district court is affirmed.

Judgment for Safeway.

CONCLUSION

In sum, we hold that Kyle did not have a "serious health condition" under the FMLA. Even assum-

Case Commentary

The Eighth Circuit concluded that Safeway met its obligation under the FMLA by initially permitting Martyszenko to take two weeks, vacation to attend to her son's needs. When it was deter-

mined that her son did not have a serious health condition, Martyszenko lost her right to unpaid leave under the FMLA. Since Martyszenko failed to return to work, Safeway terminated her.

Case Questions

1. Do you agree with the Court's decision?
2. Do you believe Martyszenko's son had a serious health condition?
3. Should Martyszenko's personal belief concerning her son's condition be taken into account?

In cases of birth or adoption, the employee is required to provide the employer with at least 30 days' notice of his or her intent to request family leave. When a serious health condition is foreseeable, the employee must provide 30 days' notice and take into consideration the employer when scheduling treatment, if this is practicable.

EMPLOYMENT PERSPECTIVE

Joseph Woodward is an accountant with Bean, Brower and Boseman, CPA firm. In early December, his father had been advised to undergo a cataract operation within the next six months. The recovery period is up to three months. Joseph, dreading the upcoming tax season, schedules his father's operation for mid-January and gives the required 30 days' notice of his intent to take 12 weeks leave. Is Joseph acting in good faith? No! He has violated the provision of making a reasonable effort to schedule the leave with his employer in mind. Moreover, the operation could have been scheduled in April, thus being in accord with the physician's directive and lessening the burden on his employer. ■

If the employee has unused paid leave in the form of vacation, personal days, or sick time, he or she may elect, or the employer may require, that time be used toward the 12-week family and medical leave. Use of sick time would apply only to medical leave for the employee himself or herself or for a family member.

EMPLOYMENT PERSPECTIVE

Henry Marceni's five-year-old daughter has been diagnosed with leukemia and has to be hospitalized immediately. Henry informs his employer, Apple Valley Bank, that he must take twelve weeks leave. Henry currently has ten vacation days, four personal days, and five sick days remaining. He asks Apple Valley to apply those nineteen days of paid leave to the twelve weeks. Apple Valley agrees except for the sick time, asserting that this may only be used when he is sick. Is Apple Valley's reasoning correct? No! The use of sick time may be applied when leave is taken for a serious health condition of a family member. ■

The question presented in the following case is whether the plaintiff was terminated for taking medical leave or for poor performance.

CASE

CLAY v. CITY OF CHICAGO DEPT. OF HEALTH

143 F.3d 1092 (7th Cir. 1998)

CUMMINGS, Circuit Judge.

Plaintiff Dorothy Clay was employed as Director of Human Resources in Chicago's Department of Health in November 1992. Defendant Jackie Kean, who was then Assistant Commissioner for the Department of Health, interviewed Clay for the position and explained at length the duties that plaintiff would be performing, including the distribution of paychecks, recruitment and hiring of Department employees and management of its personnel. Plaintiff was an at-will employee. Kean spent much time with Clay explaining her duties and answering any of her questions. Other personnel also explained to Clay the duties of Director of Human Resources.

Clay has a degenerative disk disease causing severe back pain which required her to take several medical leaves. She took her last medical leave from July 7, 1994, through August 8, 1994, receiving hospital treatment and then convalescing at home. On her August 9th return, defendant Erlinda Tzirides, Deputy Commissioner of Administration for the Department of Health, and Kean met with her and told her they wanted Michael Sulewski, who had replaced Clay during her leave, to continue as Acting Director of Human Resources because he had worked so effectively during Clay's absence. They told Clay that they would have her work on special projects until she found employment elsewhere.

On December 19, 1994, after having given Clay five months' notice to find another job,

Tzirides advised Clay that her discharge would be effective December 31, 1994. Because of many observed deficiencies in her performance, Tzirides, Kean and Commissioner Lyne had earlier decided to terminate Clay.

In June 1996, Clay filed a complaint against the City of Chicago, its Department of Health, Commissioner Sheila Lyne, Erlinda Tzirides and Jackie Kean. Count I alleged a violation of the Family and Medical Leave.

In April 1997, in a third and final opinion, the district court granted defendants' motion for summary judgment because plaintiff had not shown that she was meeting defendants' legitimate expectations and had failed to show that her discharge for unsatisfactory performance was pretextual. We affirm.

The evidence shows that Clay was discharged for poor performance. The hiring forms prepared by her office were defective, and she did not submit request to hire forms with screening criteria under official City job requirements. Consequently vacancies remained unfilled, and Clay was unable to get along with the staff of the City Deputy Budget Director. In June 1994, Commissioner Lyne received a memorandum from the City Budget Director describing a number of shortcomings in the Human Resources unit.

Because of Clay's inattention, hiring for vacant positions in the Department of Health was delayed. She also promised employees various positions for which they were not qualified.

Christine Kosmos, Director of Division of Health Protection and Regulations of the Department of Health, advised Clay how to implement cutbacks but a month later Clay still did not have an appropriate plan.

During Clay's tenure, many Department of Health employees filed grievances, but Clay was unable to provide documentation showing compliance. In addition, she rarely returned the telephone calls of Patrick Ward, Personnel Analyst for the Department of Personnel, concerning hiring process issues. She also failed to follow his instructions about advertisements for positions and repeatedly failed to get paychecks out on time. According to Assistant Health Commissioner Jackie Kean, Clay adopted uncompromising positions in labor management negotiations and had personnel difficulties with her own staff. For example, Johanna Ryan left her position as supervisor of personnel under Clay because of Clay's micro-management.

While Clay's first rating was "very good," it was reduced to "good" because of her hands-on management style and the lack of autonomy given to her staff. At the time of the second rating, Kean told Clay where she needed to improve her performance. In June 1994, after receiving complaints and negative feedback about Clay from various officials, Deputy Commissioner Tzirides concluded that Clay's job performance was deficient and, in August 1994, informed Clay that Sulewski would remain as Director of Human Resources.

Discussion

The evidence summarized above shows that Clay was discharged at the end of 1994 for poor performance. Indeed when she returned to work in August 1994, she was told she must find work elsewhere in view of her work deficiencies. Plaintiff has not shown that her discharge was for having taken medical leave. Indeed there is voluminous evidence that she was replaced solely because of her work deficiencies known to defendants prior to her leave. Therefore we disagree with plaintiff and the Secretary of Labor that the district court's judgment be reversed.

Judgment affirmed.

Judgment for City of Chicago Dept. of Health.

Case Commentary

The Seventh Circuit determined that Clay was terminated for her poor performance on the job. The Court cited numerous instances where she did not discharge her duties in good faith. The medical leave she had taken had no bearing on her termination.

Case Questions

1. Do you agree with the decision of the Court?
2. Do you believe retaliation played a part in the employer's decision?
3. How would you determine whether the employer's actions were retaliatory?

MAINTENANCE OF HEALTH BENEFITS

When an employee takes family and medical leave, he or she is entitled to the maintenance of health benefits while on leave. If an employee does not return, he or she may be charged by the employer for the health care premiums while on leave, unless it is due to a continuation of the serious health problem. With regard to pension, life insurance, and other employment benefits, these may be suspended during the period of the leave but must be restored immediately upon the return of the employee.

EMPLOYMENT PERSPECTIVE

Two months before giving birth, Jessica McCormick applied for family leave for the 12-week period after the birth of her child. At the expiration of the 12-week period, Jessica has decided to resign her position and stay home with her child. Can she be charged for the health care premiums paid on her behalf? Yes! In not returning to work, it was as though she resigned when she gave birth. There is no indication in the Act for how long a period of time she must return. ∎

EMPLOYMENT PERSPECTIVE

Christie Wesley, a financial analyst with Magnificent Mutual Funds, was a senior member of her department. While Christie was on family leave, Kurt Walker was promoted to department manager on the basis of being the senior member at the time that the promotion was made. Christie claimed that she did not forfeit her position of seniority while on family leave. Is she correct? Yes! Although she did not accrue time toward seniority while on leave, she must be accorded her status as senior member even though she is not there. ■

Certification of a serious health problem may be required by an employer. The health care provider shall provide the date when the condition began, its likely duration, and a medical explanation of the condition. If the request for leave is to care for a spouse, child, or parent, then a statement by the health care provider is required, stating that the employee's services are needed and indicating the amount of time likely to be expended. If the employer doubts the validity of the certification, it can, at its own expense, require the employee to get a second opinion. If that opinion is in conflict, the employer may again, at its own expense, request a third opinion, which shall be the final arbitrator.

If the employee requests intermittent leave, then a certification of the medical necessity must be presented. The employer may temporarily transfer the employee to another position of equal pay and benefits that is less disruptive to the employer's work environment.

EMPLOYMENT PERSPECTIVE

Pamela Whalen's daughter Julia has cancer. She is required to go for treatments three days a week during the afternoon. Pamela requests medical leave on an intermittent basis for three afternoons a week. In this manner, her 12-week unpaid leave can be taken over a much longer period. Is this situation acceptable? Yes! ■

PREGNANCY DISCRIMINATION

In 1978, discrimination on the basis of pregnancy became illegal in the United States, with passage of the Pregnancy Discrimination Act, an amendment to Title VII of the 1964 Civil Rights Act.

Pregnant women must be treated the same as other applicants or employees. They must be judged by their ability to perform rather than on their physical condition.

PREGNANT WOMEN IN THE WORKPLACE

One-half of all women who give birth each year return to their jobs before the child is one year old. An increasing number of women choose to remain at their jobs until they give birth. These women are working well into their ninth month.

In the next case, an unmarried teacher in a religiously affiliated school became pregnant. The church discharged her because that behavior was not in accord with its theology. She claimed that the church discriminated against her because of her pregnancy.

BOYD v. HARDING ACADEMY OF MEMPHIS, INC.

887 F. Supp. 157 (W.D. Tenn. 1995)

McCALLA, District Judge.

Plaintiff, who is unmarried, was employed by defendant Harding Academy of Memphis, Inc., ("Harding Academy"), in January of 1992 as a teacher in a preschool facility known as Little Harding. Harding Academy is a religious school affiliated with the Church of Christ, and as such, expects that its teachers will adhere to the religious tenets it supports. All faculty members are required to be Christians with a preference given to Church of Christ members. Harding Academy uses as its religious tenets the teachings of the New Testament, and one of the religious principles embodied therein is that sex outside of marriage is proscribed. Plaintiff knew that Harding Academy was a church-related school and indicated on her employment application that she had a Christian background and believed in God.

In early February, 1993, Brenda Rubio, the director of the Little Harding program, was told by her assistant Sharon Cooper that plaintiff may be pregnant. That information, if true, would inequivocally establish that plaintiff had engaged in sex outside of marriage. Upon receiving this information, Brenda Rubio reported the information through her superior to Dr. Harold Bowie, the President and Chief Executive Officer of Harding Academy. Dr. Bowie required that the information be confirmed by direct conversation with plaintiff, and further directed that plaintiff be terminated if the information was true. At trial, Dr. Bowie testified that he determined to terminate plaintiff if it were verified that plaintiff was pregnant and unmarried, not because of the pregnancy per se, but because the facts would indicate that plaintiff engaged in sex outside of marriage.

At Dr. Bowie's instruction, a meeting was scheduled between plaintiff, Brenda Rubio, and Sharon Cooper. At that meeting, plaintiff admitted that she was pregnant. Plaintiff was then informed that she would be terminated but that she would be eligible for re-employment if she were to marry the father of the child. During this meeting, Brenda Rubio used words to the effect that plaintiff was being terminated because she was "pregnant and unwed." Plaintiff relies on the statements made by Brenda Rubio at this meeting in support of her allegations that her discharge from Harding Academy under the circumstances of her out of wedlock pregnancy constitutes impermissible gender discrimination. However, Brenda Rubio's testimony at trial also indicates that in explaining the reason for plaintiff's termination, Brenda Rubio used the phrase "pregnant and unwed" to mean plaintiff engaged in sex outside of marriage in violation of the religious principles subscribed to by Harding Academy. It is not disputed that Brenda Rubio did not have the power or authority to terminate plaintiff or any other employee of Harding Academy.

It is also undisputed that Dr. Bowie is the only person with the authority to terminate the employment of teachers at Harding Academy. Throughout Dr. Bowie's tenure as the chief administrative officer of Harding Academy, Dr. Bowie has discharged teachers, both male and female, for engaging in acts of sex outside of marriage, whether or not pregnancy resulted from the proscribed sexual conduct. No deviation from this doctrine-based policy was shown to the Court under circumstances where knowledge of an employee's sexual activity outside of marriage was made known to Dr. Bowie. Furthermore, it was not shown that women employees at Harding Academy are terminated solely on the basis of pregnancy. In fact, the testimony at trial demonstrated that many married women have become pregnant while working at Harding Academy and have remained employed during and after their pregnancies.

CONCLUSIONS OF LAW

Title VII of the Civil Rights Act of 1964 prohibits employment discrimination based on sex. Section 2000e-2 (a) states that:

[i]t shall be an unlawful employment practice for any employer—

(1) to fail or refuse to hire or to discharge any individual, or otherwise to discriminate against any individual with respect to his compensation, terms, conditions, or privileges of employment, because of such individual's race, color, religion, sex or national origin.

Title VII further defines sex discrimination as follows:

The terms "because of sex" or "on the basis of sex" include, but are not limited to, because of or on the basis of pregnancy, childbirth, or related medical conditions; and women affected by pregnancy, childbirth, or related medical conditions shall be treated the same for all employment-related purposes. . . . Section 2000e (k), referred to as the Pregnancy Discrimination Act, makes clear that sex discrimination includes any adverse employment decision based upon pregnancy.

(a) Inapplicability of subchapter to certain aliens and employees of religious entities

This subchapter shall not apply to . . . a religious corporation, association, educational institution, or society with respect to the employment of individuals of a particular religion to perform work connected with the carrying on by such corporation, association, educational institution, or society of its activities.

Although this provision permits religious organizations to discriminate based on religion, religious employers are not immune from liability for discrimination based on race, sex, or national origin. In order for the religious entities exemption in Title VII to apply, a religious employer must make its employment decision upon a religious basis or criteria. In the present case, defendant Harding Academy asserts that plaintiff's termination was based on her violation of the religious tenet proscribing sex outside of marriage, which was evidenced by the fact of her out of wedlock pregnancy. Plaintiff, however, contends that the religious reason cited by defendant for her termination is simply a pretext for sex discrimination.

If the defendant can show a legitimate nondiscriminatory reason for its employment decision, the plaintiff must then show that the defendant's proffered reason is just a pretext for discrimination. In the present case, plaintiff asserts that she was terminated because she was pregnant, not because she violated Harding Academy's proscription against sex outside of marriage and that defendant's proffered reason for her termination is merely pretext for unlawful gender discrimination.

In support of this contention, plaintiff relies upon statements made to her by her supervisor, Brenda Rubio, on February 10, 1993, when plaintiff was terminated. During this meeting, Brenda Rubio used words to the effect that plaintiff was being terminated because she was "pregnant and unwed." Plaintiff asserts that such statements by Brenda Rubio demonstrate that her discharge from Harding Academy was based solely on her pregnancy and therefore constitutes impermissible gender discrimination.

At trial, Dr. Bowie's testimony clearly established that he did not receive information regarding plaintiff's prior miscarriage and that if he had received such information and it was confirmed then plaintiff would have been terminated according to Harding Academy's doctrine-based policy. Dr. Bowie also testified that plaintiff was terminated not because of her pregnancy per se, but because her pregnancy indicated that plaintiff engaged in sex outside of marriage as proscribed by Harding Academy. Dr. Bowie was a very credible witness and was not materially impeached in any respect. Based on Dr. Bowie's testimony, the fact that Dr. Bowie was the only person with the authority to terminate plaintiff, and the fact that Harding Academy has consistently discharged both male and female employees who engaged in sex outside of marriage, whether or not pregnancy resulted from the conduct, the Court finds that plaintiff has failed to show that defendant's proffered nondiscriminatory reason for plaintiff's termination was mere pretext for gender discrimination. Plaintiff having failed to sustain her burden of proof in this case, plaintiff's claim of gender discrimination under Title VII must be DENIED, and a judgment must be entered in favor of the defendant.

Judgment for Harding Academy of Memphis.

Case Commentary

The Western District Court of Tennessee ruled that the decision to terminate Boyd was based on the fact that she had engaged in sex outside of marriage, not on the fact that she was pregnant.

Case Questions

1. Do you agree with the Court's decision?
2. Are female employees at Harding Academy being treated as equals with their male counterparts?
3. How would Harding Academy know if men were engaging in sex outside of marriage?
4. Would Harding Academy have preferred that Boyd have an abortion to eliminate the pregnancy before it became recognizable?

The issue in the following case is whether a club designed to provide positive role models for teenage girls may bar single pregnant workers. The employee in this case was dismissed because of her pregnancy. The club maintained that it was justified in doing so.

CASE

CHAMBERS v. OMAHA GIRLS CLUB, INC.

840 F.2d 583 (8th Cir. 1988)

LAY, Chief Judge

The Omaha Girls Club's termination of its arts and crafts teacher because of her pregnancy is the most blatant form of sex discrimination that can exist. In my judgment the Girls Club's pregnancy-based discrimination constitutes a per se violation of Title VII of the Civil Rights Act of 1964. The proffered reasons for the discharge of Crystal Chambers are entirely inconsistent with Congress' avowed intent to "ensure that working women are protected against *all* forms of employment discrimination" and with its "unmistakable reaffirmation that sex discrimination includes discrimination based on pregnancy."

The action of the Girls Club is contrary to the letter of the law under the Pregnancy Discrimination Act of 1978 (PDA), the spirit of equal treatment for pregnant women intended by Congress under that Act, and decisions both of this court and of the Supreme Court of the United States.

The district court found that Chambers "was fired solely because of her pregnancy," but did not discuss the enactment of the PDA in 1978. Even prior to passage of the PDA such a finding was sufficient in this circuit to establish a prima facie violation of Title VII.

The district court found that the Girls Club had articulated a neutral reason for its rule barring single pregnant workers: to provide positive role models for the teenagers with whom the Girls Club worked. The court then shifted the burden back to the plaintiff to show that "the rule was a pretext for discriminating against *black women or single black women.*" The difficulty I have with this analysis is that when a court finds as a fact, as the district court did, that a plaintiff was fired "solely" because of membership in a protected class, the inquiry should be ended, unless the employer can establish that non-membership in the protected class is a BFOQ. There can be no issue of pretext — whether an alleged nondiscriminatory reason masks a discriminatory reason—when the employer openly admits the reason for the discharge was solely because of the employee's membership in a protected class. The issue of pretext is not involved. When this occurs we mistakenly substitute our judgment for that of the district court and attempt to make such judgment under standards the district court did not even consider.

In its discussion of Chambers's disparate *impact* claim, the district court stated that because the Girls Club "met its burden on the basis of business necessity, it was not necessary to determine whether the evidence would satisfy a BFOQ, although presumably it would." Nonetheless the panel decides, based on the district court's findings with respect to the business necessity defense, that a BFOQ was shown. The Girls Club raised the business necessity defense to Chambers's *race* discrimination claim, however, which was not based on the disparate impact of the Girls Club role model rule on blacks. I respectfully submit that a business necessity defense to a race-based disparate impact claim is simply not equivalent to a BFOQ defense to a sex-based disparate treatment claim; the factual findings relevant to one defense are not necessarily relevant to or sufficient to sustain the other defense.

The BFOQ defense in a pregnancy discrimination case thus invokes only an extremely narrow inquiry: (1) what are the requirements of the *particular* job in question; and (2) is there objective and compelling proof that the excluded woman is unable to perform the duties that constitute the essence of that job because of her pregnancy.

The PDA and its legislative history contain numerous indications that Congress intended pregnancy to be a relevant consideration in an employer's decision to fire a worker only when the pregnancy affects the woman's physical capabilities such that the employer would fire *anyone* who was similarly physically affected. The language of the PDA itself suggests that Congress so intended:

The terms "because of sex" or "on the basis of sex" include, but are not limited to, because of or on the basis of pregnancy, childbirth, or *related medical conditions;* and women *affected by* pregnancy, childbirth, or related medical conditions shall be treated the same for all employment-related purposes, including receipt of benefits under fringe benefit programs, as other persons not so affected *but similar in their ability or inability to work.* Its use of the terms "related medical conditions" and "affected by" suggests that Congress thought of pregnancy as a physical condition that, like gender, is unrelated to job capabilities except in the narrowest of circumstances.

Moreover, by requiring employers to treat pregnant employees the same as other employees "not so affected but similar in their ability or inability to work," Congress must have been referring to *physical* ability to work; there is no other ability-to-work basis on which all pregnant women as a class can be compared to all non-pregnant persons. Congress clearly stated that pregnant women must be treated the same as those similarly situated, which presupposes that there are other workers who are in some sense similarly situated. Yet by treating pregnancy as a distasteful component of a negative "role model" rather than as a physical condition that may or may not affect one's ability to work, the employer here has relegated pregnant women to a class by themselves, incapable of being "similarly situated" to anyone. Such segregation is exactly the type of invidious discrimination that Congress intended to eradicate when it enacted the PDA.

As one commentator has stated:

"Accidents of the body," such as one's female sex and thus one's capacity to become pregnant, are not to be criteria for differentiation. Instead all employees, regardless of bodily differences, shall be judged on their ability to perform on the job. That the cause of disability is pregnancy becomes, like one's race or eye color, irrelevant to how one is treated.

Judgment for Chambers.

Case Commentary

The Eight Circuit held that discharging a female employee who is pregnant because she represents a poor role model for the teenage girls in the club amounts to pregnancy discrimination.

Case Questions

1. Do you agree with the Court's decision?
2. Are role models important?
3. Can Chambers be a positive role model even though she is pregnant and unwed?
4. Who should make the determination of what constitutes a positive role model, and what standards should he or she use?
5. How do you reconcile this case with the *Boyd v. Harding Academy* case?

FETAL PROTECTION POLICIES

Companies that research, manufacture, warehouse, transport, and use hazardous chemicals and toxic waste are concerned from a liability standpoint about the effect these chemicals may have on their workers, particularly female workers in their childbearing years. While no adult is immune from the harmful effects of hazardous chemicals and toxic waste, exposure of a fetus to toxic waste could result in deformities, diseases, brain dysfunction, and cancer. The fetus's future quality of life may be severely jeopardized.

From an ethical viewpoint, companies should not want this to happen. From a liability perspective, companies do not want to become embroiled in expensive, time-consuming lawsuits that they will not win and that will result in a public-relations nightmare. To resolve this dilemma, fetus protection policies have been adopted by certain companies that prohibit women in their childbearing years from working in an environment with hazardous chemicals and toxic waste. This places an economic burden on women who cannot find another position paying the same wages. Some companies will arrange transfers, but often the compensation is lower or without the benefit of overtime. This arrangement is not an adequate accommodation. Women claim that this action is discriminatory because their childbearing state has no impact on their job performance and therefore should not be a reason for exclusion.

In the next case, an employer attempted to exclude fertile women from the workplace to avoid damage to fetuses. Female employees claimed this policy was an attempt to discriminate against pregnant women and women who potentially could become pregnant.

CASE

UAW v. JOHNSON CONTROLS, INC.

499 U.S. 187 (1991)

JUSTICE BLACKMUN delivered the opinion of the Court.

In this case we are concerned with an employer's genderbased fetal-protection policy. May an employer exclude a fertile female employee from certain jobs because of its concern for the health of the fetus the woman might conceive?

Before the Civil Rights Act of 1964 became law, Johnson Controls did not employ any woman in a battery-manufacturing job. In June

1977, however, it announced its first official policy concerning its employment of women in lead-exposure work:

"Protection of the health of the unborn child is the immediate and direct responsibility of the prospective parents. While the medical profession and the company can support them in the exercise of this responsibility, it cannot assume it for them without simultaneously infringing their rights as persons."

I

". . . Since not all women who can become mothers wish to become mothers (or will become mothers), it would appear to be illegal discrimination to treat all who are capable of pregnancy as though they will become pregnant."

Consistent with that view, Johnson Controls "stopped short of excluding women capable of bearing children from lead exposure," but emphasized that a woman who expected to have a child should not choose a job in which she would have such exposure. The company also required a woman who wished to be considered for employment to sign a statement that she had been advised of the risk of having a child while she was exposed to lead. The statement informed the woman that although there was evidence "that women exposed to lead have a higher rate of abortion," this evidence was "not as clear . . . as the relationship between cigarette smoking and cancer," but that it was, "medically speaking, just good sense not to run that risk if you want children and do not want to expose the unborn child to risk, however small. . . ."

Five years later, in 1982, Johnson Controls shifted from a policy of warning to a policy of exclusion. Between 1979 and 1983, eight employees became pregnant while maintaining blood lead levels in excess of 30 micrograms per deciliter. This appeared to be the critical level noted by the Occupational Health and Safety Administration (OSHA) for a worker who was planning to have a family. The company responded by announcing a broad exclusion of women from jobs that exposed them to lead: " . . . It is Johnson Controls' policy that women who are pregnant or who are capable of bearing children will not be placed into jobs involving lead exposure or which could expose them to lead through the ex-

ercise of job bidding, bumping, transfer or promotion rights."

The policy defined "women . . . capable of bearing children" as "all women except those whose inability to bear children is medically documented." It further stated that an unacceptable work station was one where, "over the past year," an employee had recorded a blood lead level of more than 30 micrograms per deciliter or the work site had yielded an air sample containing a lead level in excess of 30 micrograms per cubic meter.

II

In April 1984, petitioners filed in the United States District Court for the Eastern District of Wisconsin a class action challenging Johnson Controls' fetal-protection policy as sex discrimination that violated Title VII of the Civil Rights Act of 1964. Among the individual plaintiffs were petitioners Mary Craig, who had chosen to be sterilized in order to avoid losing her job, Elsie Nason, a 50-year-old divorcee, who had suffered a loss in compensation when she was transferred out of a job where she was exposed to lead, and Donald Penney, who had been denied a request for a leave of absence for the purpose of lowering his lead level because he intended to become a father. Upon stipulation of the parties, the District Court certified a class consisting of "all past, present and future production and maintenance employees" in United Auto Workers bargaining units at nine of Johnson Controls' plants "who have been and continue to be affected by the employer's Fetal Protection Policy implemented in 1982."

The District Court granted summary judgment for defendant-respondent Johnson Controls. Applying a three-part business necessity defense derived from fetal-protection cases in the Courts of Appeals for the Fourth and Eleventh Circuits, the District Court concluded that while "there is a disagreement among the experts regarding the effect of lead on the fetus," the hazard to the fetus through exposure to lead was established by "a considerable body of opinion"; that although "expert opinion has been provided which holds that lead also affects the reproductive abilities of men and women . . . and that these effects are as great as the effects of exposure of the fetus . . . a great body of experts are of the opinion that the fetus is more vulnerable to levels of lead that would not affect adults"; and that petitioners had "failed to establish that there is an acceptable alternative policy which would protect the fetus." The court stated that, in view of this disposition of the business necessity defense, it did not "have to undertake a bona fide occupational qualification's (BFOQ) analysis."

The Court of Appeals for the Seventh Circuit, sitting en banc, affirmed the summary judgment by a 7-to-4 vote. The majority held that the proper standard for evaluating the fetal-protection policy was the defense of business necessity; that Johnson Controls was entitled to summary judgment under that defense; and that even if the proper standard was a BFOQ, Johnson Controls still was entitled to summary judgment.

The Court of Appeals, first reviewed fetal-protection opinions from the Eleventh and Fourth Circuits. Those opinions established the three-step business necessity inquiry: whether there is a substantial health risk to the fetus; whether transmission of the hazard to the fetus occurs only through women; and whether there is a less discriminatory alternative equally capable of preventing the health hazard to the fetus. The Court of Appeals agreed with the Eleventh and Fourth Circuits that "the components of the business necessity defense the courts of appeals and the EEOC have utilized in fetal protection cases balance the interests of the employer, the employee and the unborn child in a manner consistent with Title VII." The court further noted that, under *Wards Cove Packing Co. v. Atonio,* the burden of persuasion remained on the plaintiff in challenging a business necessity defense, and—unlike the Fourth and Eleventh Circuits—it thus imposed the burden on the plaintiffs for all three steps.

Applying this business necessity defense, the Court of Appeals ruled that Johnson Controls should prevail. Specifically, the court concluded that there was no genuine issue of material fact about the substantial health-risk factor because the parties agreed that there was a substantial risk to a fetus from lead exposure. The Court of Appeals also concluded that, unlike the evidence of risk to the fetus from the mother's exposure, the evidence of risk from the father's exposure, which petitioners presented, "is, at best, speculative and unconvincing."

The en banc majority ruled that industrial safety is part of the essence of respondent's business, and that the fetal-protection policy is reasonably necessary to further that concern.

III

The bias in Johnson Controls' policy is obvious. Fertile men, but not fertile women, are given a choice as to whether they wish to risk their reproductive health for a particular job. Section 703 (a) of the Civil Rights Act of 1964, 42 U.S.C. 2000e-2(a), prohibits sexbased classifications in terms and conditions of employment, in hiring and discharging decisions, and in other employment decisions that adversely affect an employee's status. Respondent's fetal-protection policy explicitly discriminates against women on the basis of their sex. The policy excludes women with childbearing capacity from lead-exposed jobs and so creates a facial classification based on gender. Respondent assumes as much in its brief before this Court.

First, Johnson Controls' policy classifies on the basis of gender and childbearing capacity, rather than fertility alone. Respondent does not seek to protect the unconceived children of all its employees. Despite evidence in the record about the debilitating effect of lead exposure on the male reproductive system, Johnson Controls is concerned only with the harms that may befall the unborn offspring of its female employees.

Our conclusion is bolstered by the Pregnancy Discrimination Act of 1978 (PDA), Congress explicitly provided that, for purposes of Title VII, discrimination "on the basis of sex" includes discrimination "because of or on the basis of pregnancy, childbirth, or related medical conditions." "The Pregnancy Discrimination Act has now made clear that, for all Title VII purposes, discrimination based on a woman's pregnancy is, on its face, discrimination because of her sex." In its use of the words "capable of bearing children" in the 1982 policy statement as the criterion for exclusion, Johnson Controls explicitly classifies on the basis of potential for pregnancy. Under the PDA, such a classification must be regarded, for Title VII purposes, in the same light as explicit sex discrimination. Respondent has chosen to treat all its female employees as potentially pregnant; that choice evinces discrimination on the basis of sex.

We concluded above that Johnson Controls' policy is not neutral because it does not apply to the reproductive capacity of the company's male employees in the same way as it applies to that of the females. Moreover, the absence of a malevolent motive does not convert a facially discriminatory policy into a neutral policy with a discriminatory effect. Whether an employment practice involves disparate treatment through explicit facial discrimination does not depend on why the employer discriminates but rather on the explicit terms of the discrimination.

In sum, Johnson Controls' policy "does not pass the simple test of whether the evidence shows 'treatment of a person in a manner which but for that person's sex would be different.' " We hold that Johnson Controls' fetal-protection policy is sex discrimination forbidden under Title VII unless respondent can establish that sex is a "bona fide occupational qualification."

IV

Under Title VII, an employer may discriminate on the basis of "religion, sex, or national origin in those certain instances where religion, sex, or national origin is a bona fide occupational qualification reasonably necessary to the normal operation of that particular business or enterprise." 42 U.S.C. 2000e-2 (e) (1). We therefore turn to the question whether Johnson Controls' fetal-protection policy is one of those "certain instances" that come within the BFOQ exception.

The BFOQ defense is written narrowly, and this Court has read it narrowly.

The wording of the BFOQ defense contains several terms of restriction that indicate that the exception reaches only special situations. The statute thus limits the situations in which discrimination is permissible to "certain instances" where sex discrimination is "reasonably necessary" to the "normal operation" of the "particular" business. Each one of these terms—certain, normal, particular—prevents the use of general subjective standards and favors an objective, verifiable requirement. But the most telling term is "occupational"; this indicates that these objective, verifiable requirements must concern job-related skills and aptitudes.

The unconceived fetuses of Johnson Controls' female employees, however, are neither customers nor third parties whose safety is essential to the business of battery manufacturing. No

one can disregard the possibility of injury to future children; the BFOQ, however, is not so broad that it transforms this deep social concern into an essential aspect of batterymaking.

Our case law, therefore, makes clear that the safety exception is limited to instances in which sex or pregnancy actually interferes with the employee's ability to perform the job. This approach is consistent with the language of the BFOQ provision itself, for it suggests that permissible distinctions based on sex must relate to ability to perform the duties of the job. Johnson Controls suggests, however, that we expand the exception to allow fetal-protection policies that mandate particular standards for pregnant or fertile women. We decline to do so. Such an expansion contradicts not only the language of the BFOQ and the narrowness of its exception but the plain language and history of the Pregnancy Discrimination Act.

The PDA's amendment to Title VII contains a BFOQ standard of its own: unless pregnant employees differ from others "in their ability or inability to work," they must be "treated the same" as other employees "for all employment related purposes." 42 U.S.C. 2000e(k). This language clearly sets forth Congress' remedy for discrimination on the basis of pregnancy and potential pregnancy. Women who are either pregnant or potentially pregnant must be treated like others "similar in their ability . . . to work." In other words, women as capable of doing their jobs as their male counterparts may not be forced to choose between having a child and having a job.

We conclude that the language of both the BFOQ provision and the PDA which amended it, as well as the legislative history and the case law, prohibit an employer from discriminating against a woman because of her capacity to become pregnant unless her reproductive potential prevents her from performing the duties of her job.

V

We have no difficulty concluding that Johnson Controls cannot establish a BFOQ. Fertile women, as far as appears in the record, participate in the manufacture of batteries as efficiently as anyone else. Johnson Controls' professed moral and ethical concerns about the welfare of the next generation do not suffice to establish a BFOQ of female sterility. Decisions about the welfare of future children must be left to the parents who conceive, bear, support, and raise them rather than to the employers who hire those parents. Congress has mandated this choice through Title VII, as amended by the Pregnancy Discrimination Act. Johnson Controls has attempted to exclude women because of their reproductive capacity. Title VII and the PDA simply do not allow a woman's dismissal because of her failure to submit to sterilization.

VI

Our holding today that Title VII, as so amended, forbids sex-specific fetal-protection policies is neither remarkable nor unprecedented. Concern for a woman's existing or potential offspring his-

torically has been the excuse for denying women equal employment opportunities. Congress in the PDA prohibited discrimination on the basis of a woman's ability to become pregnant. We do no more than hold that the Pregnancy Discrimination Act means what it says.

It is no more appropriate for the courts than it is for individual employers to decide whether a woman's reproductive role is more important to herself and her family than her economic role. Congress has left this choice to the woman as hers to make.

The judgment of the Court of Appeals is reversed and the case is remanded for further proceedings consistent with this opinion.

It is so ordered.
Judgment for UAW.

Case Commentary

The United States Supreme Court decided that Johnson Controls's attempt to exclude pregnant women from certain jobs that could have poten-

tially damaged their fetuses amounted to sex discrimination.

Case Questions

1. Do you agree with the decision in this case?
2. Why do women have the right to work in a job that may damage their fetuses?

3. Should the company close the plant if it cannot be made safe?

In *United Auto Workers v. Johnson Controls, Inc.,* the Supreme Court ruled that fetal protection policies were a form of gender discrimination. This decision places companies in a catch-22 situation. If they exclude women, they are guilty of sex discrimination. If they permit women to work and their offspring are born defective or with a life-threatening illness, they will be held strictly liable for the injuries. A possible benefit could occur if exposure to the hazardous chemicals and toxic waste is minimized or eliminated as a result of the development of protective equipment and gear or the modification of the plant and working environment.

If that solution is impossible or not economically feasible, companies will either close down the plants or move them offshore where there will be no resulting liability for damage to the fetus. While the latter may be unethical, it is a realistic and practical solution. In any event, both actions will result in a loss of jobs for all workers, something that the women were initially trying to guard against.

The following case addresses the question of whether an employee's termination was based on her pregnancy. The employer argued that it was based on her competency. She retorted that it was a pretext used to disguise the discriminatory intent of her employer.

HANSEN v. DEAN WITTER REYNOLDS, INC.

887 F. Supp. 669 (S.D.N.Y. 1995)

BAER, District Judge.

Plaintiff Michele Hansen brought this action under Title VII of the Civil Rights Act of 1964, The Pregnancy Discrimination Act, 42 U.S.C. #2000e (k), and the New York Human Rights Law, claiming sex and pregnancy discrimination by her former employer, defendant Dean Witter Reynolds, Inc. ("Dean Witter") in the termination of her employment as Dean Witter's Assistant Vice President/Intermediate Mortgage-Backed "Repo" Trader.

I find that plaintiff has failed to establish that (1) Dean Witter terminated her on the basis of her sex and/or her pregnancy, or that (2) Dean Witter's reasons for terminating her employment were pretextual. Plaintiff's complaint must therefore be dismissed.

THE LAW

Relevant Statutes

Title VII of the Civil Rights Act of 1964 42 U.S.C. #2000e-2(a) (1), provides that it is unlawful for "an employer to fail or refuse to hire or to discharge any individual . . . with respect to his or her compensation, terms, conditions or privileges of employment, because of such individual's race, color, religion, sex or national origin." In 1978, pregnancy discrimination was also expressly prohibited as constituting impermissible discrimination on the basis of sex. The New York State equivalent of the federal Title VII protections are found in the New York Human Rights Law.

One manner of establishing a prima facie case of sex discrimination under Title VII involves plaintiff showing that she was treated less favorably than comparable male employees in circumstances from which a gender based motive could be inferred.

Once plaintiff has established her prima facie case, the burden shifts to the defendant to show that unlawful discrimination did not cause the subject's employment action. If the employer has articulated a legitimate reason for the challenged employment decision, plaintiff must establish that the proffered reason is a pretext for discrimination.

The ultimate burden of persuasion, as always, rests with the plaintiff to persuade the factfinder that the defendant intentionally discriminated against her. This may be accomplished "either directly by persuading the court that a discriminatory reason more likely motivated the employer or indirectly by showing that the employer's proffered explanation is unworthy of credence."

At trial, plaintiff's claim that her discharge from Dean Witter resulted from sex and pregnancy discrimination relied heavily on Dean Witter's decision to retain Melvin Relova, a man, on its TFU desk at the time of plaintiff's discharge. Plaintiff attempted in her case-in-chief to show that Relova was less qualified than she, and therefore, that her termination from Dean Witter must have been discriminatory. For the reasons stated below, I find plaintiff's argument unpersuasive.

At the outset, I find that Hansen has not put forth sufficient evidence of pregnancy discrimination. Plaintiff proffered as evidence of her pregnancy discrimination claim isolated statements made by Ian Bernstein, a Dean Witter manager, about how difficult it was to raise children in New York. I find credible Bernstein's assertion that these comments were conversational in nature. His testimony included the fact that he himself had twins. I can find nothing in Berstein's testimony to suggest that his comments evidenced a discriminatory attitude toward pregnant women in that workplace. This is made especially clear by juxtaposing Bernstein's comments with Dean Witter's consistent policy that permitted pregnant employees to retain their position at Dean Witter following their pregnancies, including plaintiff herself following her 1987 pregnancy. While Dean

Witter's treatment of other pregnant women, as well as Hansen in 1987, cannot preclude a finding of discrimination in the instant case, it does appear inconsistent with plaintiff's claim and therefore militates against that finding. I turn now to Hansen's sex discrimination claim.

Bernstein testified that Relova was the best qualified to staff the TFU desk. He based that assessment on "having worked with those individuals for several years in the capital markets area, as well as having supervised them for a period of time." Bernstein testified that his assessment was also based on reviews from the sales force that were generally much more favorable towards Melvyn's. . . .

In view of the findings, I conclude that plaintiff has not met her burden of proving that sex and/or pregnancy discrimination caused her termination. The record contains ample testimony supporting Dean Witter's position that Relova was better qualified for the position than Hansen. Indeed, the law provides that, in discrimination actions, the court is not to second-guess the defendant's judgment; the factfinder should not assess "whether the employer's decision was erroneous or even rational, so long as the employer's actions were not taken for a discriminatory reason."

CONCLUSION

For the reasons stated above, I find that plaintiff has failed to satisfy her burden of proof that Dean Witter's decision to retain Melvyn Relova and terminate plaintiff was motivated by the plaintiff's sex and/or pregnancy. The complaint is dismissed.

Judgment for Dean Witter.

Case Commentary

The Southern District Court of New York concluded that Michele Hansen was terminated based on reasons relating to her competency, not due to the fact that she was pregnant.

Case Questions

1. Are you in agreement with the Court's decision?
2. Do you believe her employer's comments were evidence of an intent to discriminate against her because of her pregnancy?
3. Do you think Dean Witter's decision to retain a man because of his superior credentials was a pretext?

Pregnancy disability must not be viewed any differently than any other disability. Pregnant women must be viewed based on their ability to perform the essential functions of the job.

The question in the next case is whether protection is afforded against pregnancy discrimination under the state statute.

CASE

BADIH v. MYERS

43 Cal. Rptr.2d 229 (Cal. App. 1 Dist. 1995)

DOSSEE, Associate Justice.
On June 25, 1990, Badih filed a complaint against Myers alleging, among other things, that Myers had discriminated against her on the basis of race and pregnancy. The complaint also alleged that Badih had attempted to file a complaint with the

Department of Fair Employment and Housing (FEHA) but that the department had refused to accept the complaint because Myers employed less than five people.

At trial, Badih gave the following testimony: In January 1987, Badih, a recent immigrant from the West African nation of Sierra Leone, began working as a medical assistant in the offices of Myers, a medical doctor. About nine months later, she started dating Constantine Kalaveras. Myers, who disapproved of interracial relationships, referred to Kalaveras as "the White guy."

In December 1988, Badih married Kalaveras. When Badih told Myers about the marriage, "he slapped on the table, stood up, and started yelling and hollering about what a mistake I've made, how much I'm going to regret this, and how disappointed he is in me, that he's never seen an African that . . . came to this country and started, you know, doing things I did, you know, hanging—marrying my husband and all that, having a White boyfriend and finally marrying him. And he gave me long lectures how marriages like that don't last and how they end up in tragedy and it's very bad, especially if children get involved and all that, and he just got so upset."

On September 6, 1989, Badih told Myers that she was pregnant. According to Badih, Myers replied, "'I just can't believe you. I just don't know what to say to you anymore. It seems like everything I ever told you just went right in vain. First you introduce me to this White guy, and then you marry him, and then you're having his baby. What's next? I can't take this anymore. If you told me you were going to get married and have babies, I wouldn't have hired you in the first place. I need an office girl when I need her, not a person that has responsibilities the way you do now. And . . . I am just so sorry, but I don't think I can take this anymore. You're going to have to go.'" Badih asked Myers whether he was serious. He told her that he was and that her last day would be September 15. On September 13, Myers threatened to call security if Badih did not leave immediately. Badih complied.

Myers denied that he had fired Badih because she was pregnant. According to Myers, Badih quit her job.

Following its deliberations, the jury found that Myers had not terminated Badih's employment on the basis of race but that he had terminated her employment on the basis of pregnancy.

The jury awarded $20,226 in damages to Badih. The trial court subsequently granted Badih's motion for attorney fees. Myers has filed timely notices of appeal from both the judgment and the attorney fees order.

Badih argues that pregnancy discrimination in employment is a form of sex discrimination and, as such, is prohibited not only by the FEHA but also by article I, section 8 of the California Constitution. For the reasons discussed below, we agree.

The question of whether pregnancy discrimination in employment is a form of sex discrimination is not without controversy. In *Geduldig v. Aiello* the United States Supreme Court, in the context of the equal protection clause of the United States Constitution, concluded that "while it is true that only women can become pregnant, it does not follow that every legislative classification concerning pregnancy is a sex-based classification. . . . Normal pregnancy is an objectively identifiable physical condition with unique characteristics. Absent a showing that distinctions involving pregnancy are mere pretexts designed to effect an invidious discrimination against the members of one sex or the other, lawmakers are constitutionally free to include or exclude pregnancy from the coverage of legislation such as this on any reasonable basis, just as with respect to any other physical condition. The lack of identity between the excluded disability pregnancy and gender as such under this insurance program becomes clear upon the most cursory analysis. The program divides potential recipients into two groups—pregnant women and nonpregnant persons. While the first group is exclusively female, the second includes members of both sexes. The fiscal and actuarial benefits of the program thus accrue to members of both sexes." In *General Electric Co. v. Gilbert,* the court extended the reasoning of *Geduldig* to employment discrimination cases brought under Title VII of the Civil Rights Act of 1964.

Both the California Legislature and the United States Congress reacted swiftly to the *Gilbert* decision. In 1978, the California Legislature amended the Fair Employment Practices Act (later recodified as the FEHA) to add a provision specifically prohibiting pregnancy discrimination in employment. The provision states that it "shall not be construed to affect any other provision of law relating to sex discrimination or pregnancy." Also in 1978, the United States Congress amended Title VII to provide that "the terms 'because of sex' or 'on the basis of sex' include, but are not limited to, because of or on the basis of pregnancy, childbirth, or related medical conditions." "When Congress amended Title VII in 1978, it unambiguously expressed its disapproval of both the holding and the reasoning of the Court in the *Gilbert* decision."

With this background in mind, we turn to the question at hand—namely, whether pregnancy discrimination is a form of sex discrimina-

tion under article I, section 8 of the California Constitution.

In short, we conclude that pregnancy discrimination is a form of sex discrimination under article I, section 8 of the California Constitution. Since article I, section 8 expresses a fundamental public policy against sex discrimination in employment, Badih was properly allowed to maintain her cause of action for wrongful discharge in contravention of public policy.

Judgment for Badih.

Case Commentary

The California Appellate Court held that pregnancy discrimination is protected under Title VII as well as California state law.

Case Questions

1. Do you agree with the decision in this case?
2. Why was Badih successful when Myers only had five employees?
3. Should employers have the right to involve themselves in the personal lives of their employees?

Some employers have instituted prenatal counseling programs to give medical and emotional assistance. This reduces absenteeism, minimizes complications during the pregnancy, and otherwise helps a woman to work longer and more productively during the pregnancy.

With employer sponsored programs, women are learning morning sickness and fatigue are ailments common to pregnant women. They are adjusting their work days to perform their most important tasks at the time of the day when they are most likely going to feel well.

Some companies have nurses and counselors on call to respond to their pregnant employees' needs. The results of these programs mean better health for pregnant women employees and their babies and minimal loss of employee efficiency. Some employers are contributing a portion of the increased savings to more comprehensive obstetrics care coverage.

The plight of pregnant women and mothers with small children, which in past times had been neglected, has now received the attention it deserves. Attitudes concerning their employment capability are changing with time. Whereas before it can be said that they needed the companies, as the labor shortage increases, it is turning out that companies need them. The greatest thing that can happen to these women is to be needed, wanted, and employed.

❖ EMPLOYER LESSONS

- Realize that some employees may try to take advantage of the medical leave policy.
- Determine whether an employee has a serious health condition.
- Require certification of the serious health condition by a health care provider.
- Be aware of when your company reaches the 50 employee threshold.

- Demand 30 days' notice for family leave definitely, and for medical leave where practical.
- Refrain from discouraging eligible employees from taking family and medical leave.
- Do not ask women if they intend to become pregnant.
- Do not discourage women from becoming pregnant.
- Treat pregnant women the same as other employees.
- Refrain from instituting a fetal protection policy.
- Reassign women whose fetuses may be in danger to positions with comparable pay, overtime, and promotion opportunities.

❖ EMPLOYEE LESSONS

- Discover whether your employer grants family and medical leave.
- Learn what is meant by a serious health condition.
- Appreciate that health benefits will be continued during family and medical leave.
- Realize that fathers are entitled to family leave as well as mothers.
- Understand that a 30-day notice is required for family leave and for medical leave when the condition is foreseeable.
- Know that an employer may require certification of a serious health condition by a health care provider.
- Become familiar with the protection afforded by the Pregnancy Discrimination Act.
- Be aware of any questions asked by an employer regarding your intentions of having children.
- Be cognizant of your rights when your employer has adopted a fetal protection policy.

❖ SUMMARY

Under the Pregnancy Discrimination Act, pregnant women cannot be refused employment or be removed from employment due to their temporary disability unless they are unable to perform the essential functions of the job. Pregnant women should not be looked down upon; they should be revered, since procreation enables society to flourish through the birth of children, who will become future workers.

The birth of a child is a life-changing event. A newborn requires a great amount of time. Indefinite unpaid leave is not practical, but family leave is guaranteed for three months in companies with 50 or more employees. Smaller companies are not required to provide family leave because the burden of adjusting to the employee's lengthy absence may be too great. Medical leave is also available to employees who must care for a family member with a serious health condition.

Addressing the family and medical concerns of employees is a huge undertaking for employers. But it is another step forward in the advancement of working conditions where employees are treated as worthwhile human beings who have problems that need solutions other than resignation or termination.

❖ REVIEW QUESTIONS

1. Explain the significance of the Family Medical Leave Act.
2. What are the eligibility requirements?
3. For what duration may family or medical leave be taken?
4. Define serious health condition.

5. Is the employee entitled to health benefits while on leave?

6. What percentage of women return to the job within one year of giving birth?

7. Is pregnancy a disability?

8. Explain the significance of the Pregnancy Disability Act.

9. With whom should pregnant women file complaints of discrimination?

10. Can pregnancy ever be considered a bona fide occupational qualification?

11. Should an employer have to accommodate a pregnant worker even though the accommodation is disruptive to the workplace?

12. Must an applicant disclose the fact that she is pregnant?

13. Is it acceptable for an employer to ask all female applicants if they are pregnant?

14. Is there any justifiable reason to deny a pregnant employee maternity leave?

15. Defendant is a church-affiliated social services agency.

In October 1988, Savage became a part-time salaried employee, working as an Overnight Awake Residential Counselor I at Woodhouse.

Savage submitted a written request to Scott for a leave of two months pursuant to her doctor's order. Savage indicated to Scott in her request that she would like to apply her accrued sick and vacation time—then totalling 21 days—to her leave of absence.

Although she had not received the needed authorization for an extended leave without pay from either Larry Paul, defendant's Area Director, or William Brittain, defendant's President, Savage began her leave on October 28, 1991.

In a letter, Paul informed Savage that her request for accrued vacation and sick leave pay would not be honored because Savage gave defendant only two days' notice of her intent to take leave, instead of the four week notice required by defendant's policies. In conclusion, Paul informed Savage that, because she would not tender her resignation as requested, he would proceed with her termination. What was the result? *E.E.O.C. v. Lutheran Family Services,* 884 F. Supp. 1022 (E.D.N.C. 1994)

16. The gist of the United States' complaint is the CBA provisions and the practices of District 230 prohibiting pregnant teachers from taking sick leave for pregnancy-related disability and then taking maternity leave at the expiration of the sick leave, and the Collective Bargaining Agreement (CBA) provision excluding maternity benefits from the sick leave bank ("SLB"), violate Title VII. What was the result? *U.S. v. Bd. of Educ. of Consol. High Sch. D. 230,* 761 F. Supp. 524 (N.D.Ill. 1990)

17. The plaintiff testified that, after being interviewed on February 20, 1987, by William Zammer, the defendant's president, she was employed by the defendant as its marketing director beginning March 23, 1987. On April 24, 1987, she told Zammer that she was pregnant. Zammer was extremely upset by that revelation. He told her that the situation was "untenable" and that she could not continue in the position for which she had been employed. He said that he felt "personally betrayed." Zammer told her that she had lied to him about being career oriented. What was the result? *Lysak v. Seiler Corp.,* 614 N.E.2d 991 (Mass. 1993)

❖ WEB SITES

www.opm.gov/hrss/html/fmla96.htm

www.nationalpartnership.org/workandfamily/fmleave/statelaw.htm

www.findlaw.com

www.dol.gov/dol/esa/fmla.htm

www.unlv.edu/Human_Resources/Benefits/fmla.html

www.babybag.com/articles/laws.htm

CHAPTER

12

SEXUAL ORIENTATION

INTRODUCTION

The Civil Rights Act does not prohibit employers from refusing to hire or subsequently firing someone because he or she is a homosexual. Although there is no federal law, state and local laws do exist in select jurisdictions. The term most commonly used is sexual orientation. Many cities also disallow discrimination, but only a few of them extend it to employment.

There is also no federal law protecting transsexuals and those undertaking gender corrective surgery.

CHAPTER CHECKLIST

❖ Know that protection under the Civil Rights Act does not extend to sexual orientation.

❖ Learn that certain states and cities do provide sexual orientation protection.

❖ Realize that homosexuals with AIDS or sexually transmitted diseases will be safeguarded under the Americans with Disabilities Act.

❖ Appreciate that homosexuals can cover their partners under their health plan in a small but growing number of companies.

❖ Understand that gays and lesbians may serve in the military.

❖ Recognize that schoolteachers should not be judged by their sexual orientation, but on their ability to teach and follow the course curriculum.

❖ Be cognizant of the arguments presented for those advocating gay rights in employment and those against it.

❖ Be careful about judging others whose lifestyle may not conform to yours, lest they judge you in the same way.

AVAILABLE PROTECTION

Gays and lesbians working pursuant to employment contracts or employee handbooks may be protected by a clause in the agreement requiring that an employee may be discharged only for cause. In such a case, sexual orientation would not qualify as cause, and the homosexual employee could not be terminated. Some courts have overruled the dismissal based on public policy considerations. Other courts have stated that dismissing an individual because of sexual orientation violates the implied covenant of good faith and fair dealing which exists between employer and employee.

The issue in the next case is whether an amendment overriding a city ordinance protecting sexual orientation is unconstitutional.

The issue in the case that follows is whether homosexuals should be an identifiable class protected from discrimination.

CASE

EQUALITY FOUNDATION v. CITY OF CINCINNATI

54 F.3d 261 (6th Cir. 1995)

KRUPANSKY, Circuit Judge.
On March 13, 1991, the Cincinnati City Council (the "Council") enacted ordinance No. 79-1991, commonly known as the "Equal Employment Opportunity Ordinance." This measure provided that the City could not discriminate in its own hiring practices on the basis of classification factors such as race, color, sex, handicap, religion, national or ethnic origin, age, sexual orientation, HIV status, Appalachian regional ancestry, and marital status.

Subsequently, Council on November 25, 1992 adopted Ordinance No. 490-1992 (commonly referred to as the "Human Rights Ordinance") which prohibited, among other things, private discrimination in employment, housing, or public accommodation for reasons of sexual orientation. The opening paragraph of the Human Rights Ordinance expressed the purpose of the legislation as:

Prohibiting unlawful discriminatory practices in the City of Cincinnati based on race, gender, age, color, religion, disability status, sexual orientation, marital status, or ethnic, national or Appalachian regional origin, in employment, housing, and public accommodations by ordaining Chapter 914, Cincinnati Municipal Code.

Among other things, the new law created complaint and hearing procedures for purported victims of sexual orientation discrimination and exposed offenders to potential civil and criminal penalties.

ERNSR was organized for the purpose of eliminating special legal protection accorded to persons based upon their sexual orientation pursuant to the Human Rights Ordinance. ERNSR campaigned to rescind the Human Rights Ordinance by enacting a proposed City Charter amendment (Issue 3), which was to be submitted directly to the voters on the November 2, 1993 local ballot. On July 6, 1993, plaintiff Equality Foundation of Greater Cincinnati, Inc. ("Equality Foundation") was incorporated by the opponents, of the ERNSR agenda. A vigorous political contest between ERNSR and Equality Foundation, involving aggressive campaigning by both sides and high media exposure, ensued over Issue 3.

The ERNSR-sponsored proposed charter amendment ultimately appeared on the November 2, 1993 ballot as:

NO SPECIAL CLASS STATUS MAY BE GRANTED BASED UPON SEXUAL ORIENTATION CONDUCT OR RELATIONSHIPS.

The City of Cincinnati and its various Boards and Commissions may not enact, adopt, enforce or administer any ordinance, regulation, rule or policy which provides that homosexual, lesbian, or bisexual orientation, status, conduct, or relationship constitutes, entitles, or otherwise provides a person with the basis to have any claim of minority or protected status, quota preference or other preferential treatment. This provision of the City Charter shall in all respects be self-executing. Any ordinance, regulation, rule or policy enacted before this amendment is adopted that violates the foregoing prohibition shall be null and void and of no force or effect.

Issue 3 passed by a popular vote of approximately 62% in favor and 38% opposed and became Amendment XII to the Cincinnati City Charter.

On November 8, 1993, plaintiffs Equality Foundation, several individual homosexuals (Richard Buchanan, Chad Bush, Edwin Greene, Rita Mathis, and Roger Asterino), and Housing Opportunities Made Equal, Inc. ("H.O.M.E.") (a housing rights organization), filed a complaint against the City under 42 U.S.C. 1983 which alleged that their constitutional rights had been, or would potentially be, violated by the adoption of Issue 3, and sought temporary and permanent injunctive relief, a declaration that the Amendment was unconstitutional, and an award of costs (including attorneys' fees). It concluded that the Amendment infringed the plaintiffs' purported "fundamental right to equal access to the political process," as well as First Amendment rights of free speech and association and the right to petition the government for redress of grievances, which violations of constitutional rights subjected the Amendment to a "strict scrutiny" constitutional evaluation. Additionally, the district court posited that, because homosexuals collectively comprise a "quasi-suspect class," the Amendment was alternatively reviewable under the intermediate "heightened scrutiny" constitutional standard. The constitutional guarantee of equal protection insulates citizens only from unlawfully discriminatory state action; it constructs no barrier against private discrimination, irrespective of the degree of wrongfulness of such private discrimination (1972). The Equal Protection Clause of the Fourteenth Amendment to the United States Constitution did not compel the

City of Cincinnati to enact legislation to protect homosexuals from discrimination, and accordingly the City, through its ordinary legislative processes, was at liberty to rescind any previous enactments which had fashioned such safeguards. Accordingly, the mere repeal of certain sections of the Human Rights Ordinance which had previously protected homosexuals, lesbians, and bisexuals was not itself constitutionally assailable. However, the district court ruled that the Amendment not only nullified the previously-enacted special legal protection for homosexuals; rather, it assertedly prevented a distinct class of citizens from exercising certain equal protection and First Amendment rights in the future, which, in the lower court's analysis, triggered constitutional review of the Amendment. In declaring this novel ruling, the lower court in the instant case misconstrued *Bowers v. Hardwick,* wherein the Court mandated that homosexuals possess no fundamental right to engage in homosexual conduct and consequently that conduct could be criminalized. The Bowers Court further directed that the courts should resist tailoring novel fundamental rights. Since *Bowers,* every circuit court which has addressed the issue has decreed that homosexuals are entitled to no special constitutional protection, as either a suspect or a quasi-suspect class, because the conduct which places them in that class is not a constitutionally protected categorization. The trial court found that gays, lesbians, and bisexuals are not identified by any particular conduct; to the contrary, they are distinguished by their "sexual orientation," which references an innate and involuntary state of being and set of drives. From this perspective, the Amendment uniquely affected individuals belonging to a discrete segment of society on the basis of their status as persons oriented towards a particular sexual attraction or lifestyle.

Assuming arguendo the truth of the scientific theory that sexual orientation is a "characteristic beyond the control of the individual" as found by the trial court, the reality remains that no law can successfully be drafted that is calculated to burden or penalize, or to benefit or protect, an unidentifiable group or class of individuals whose identity is defined by subjective and unapparent characteristics such as innate desires, drives, and thoughts. Those persons having a homosexual "orientation" simply do not, as such, comprise an identifiable class. Many homosexuals successfully conceal their orientation. Because homosexuals generally are not identifiable "on sight" unless they elect to be so identifiable by conduct (such as public displays of homosexual affection or self-proclamation of homosexual tendencies), they cannot constitute a suspect class or a quasi-suspect class because "they do not necessarily exhibit obvious, immutable, or distinguishing characteristics that define them as a discrete group."

Therefore, *Bowers v. Hardwick* and its progeny command that, as a matter of law, gays, lesbians, and bisexuals cannot constitute either a "suspect class" or a "quasi-suspect class," and, accordingly, the district court's application of the intermediate heightened scrutiny standard to the constitutional analysis of the Amendment was erroneous.

The lower court also invalidated the Amendment by theorizing that it was unconstitutionally vague, because it affected only special legal protection for "gays, lesbians and bisexuals," whereas the Human Rights Ordinance had erstwhile protected all persons based upon their sexual orientation. The district court found that plaintiff H.O.M.E. and other private employers in the City were confronted by a hiring dilemma,

a result of a purported ambiguity inherent in the Amendment. Initially, it is noted that plaintiff H.O.M.E. is without standing to assert its argument because it has suffered no actual or imminent injury by the implementation of the Amendment, nor do its assertions present a case in controversy. Rather, H.O.M.E. has merely asserted an abstract hypothetical scenario and conjectured that it was unable to determine if the employment of a homosexual, lesbian, or bisexual because of his or her sexual orientation would be civilly or criminally actionable under the Human Rights Ordinance as anti-heterosexual discrimination. Moreover, even if H.O.M.E. had standing below, the vagueness issue has been rendered moot by Council's March 8, 1995 amendment to the Human Right Ordinance (per Ordinance No. 66-1995), which struck all references to "sexual orientation" from the legislation. At the present time, the City's municipal ordinances provide no protection against private discrimination to any citizen by reason of sexual orientation, irrespective of whether that orientation is heterosexual, homosexual, lesbian, or bisexual.

Accordingly, the judgment below in favor of the plaintiffs is hereby REVERSED.

Judgment for the City of Cincinnati.

Case Commentary

The Sixth Circuit ruled that it is within the providence of the City of Cincinnati to ask its citizens to decide by referendum whether a special class shall be created for homosexuals against whom no one may discriminate. Since the vote was against the creation of a special class, no protection is afforded to homosexuals prohibiting discrimination against them. The Court concluded homosexuals are not an identifiable class.

Case Questions

1. Do you agree with the Court's determination in this case?
2. Should the citizens be able to decide the rights of homosexuals by referendum?

3. Do homosexuals belong to an identifiable class?

In the case that follows, a municipality granted special protection for sexual orientation. This action was in direct contravention of a state statute. The issue is whether both laws may coexist.

DEPARRIE v. STATE

893 P.2d 541 (OR. App. 1995)

DEITS, Presiding Judge.

These are appeals by the plaintiffs in two consolidated declaratory judgment actions that were brought, respectively, by plaintiff deParrie and by plaintiffs Mahon, Neet, Graham and No Special Rights Committee, PAC. In both actions, the plaintiffs sought a declaration that ORS 659.165 is invalid. That statute provides:

"(1) A political subdivision of the state may not enact or enforce any charter provision, ordinance, resolution or policy granting special rights, privileges or treatment to any citizen or group of citizens on account of sexual orientation, or enact or enforce any charter provision, ordinance, resolution or policy that singles out citizens or groups of citizens on account of sexual orientation."

We turn to the merits of plaintiffs' appeal. Their principal argument is that ORS 659.165 is not a "valid preemptive statute" and that it cannot be used, consistently with the Home Rule Amendments to the Oregon Constitution, to prevent "municipalities from establishing substantive policy on the issue of sexual orientation."

Plaintiffs state that, "until the legislature establishes statewide standards on the issue of sexual orientation, it is without authority to preclude the local governments from establishing their own."

We do not agree that, in order to rise to the level of a policy choice, a statute must regulate particular persons or subjects in either a positive or negative manner; it is just as much a substantive policy of the state if the legislature prohibits any regulation of particular persons or matters, or defines the extent to which they may be regulated, as if the legislature itself regulates the persons or matters in a particular manner. In both situations, the legislature has established a state policy concerning the regulation of a subject. To the extent that plaintiffs' argument is that the statute fails to establish a state policy because it does not say enough, we again disagree.

We conclude that ORS 659.165 validly and effectively preempts local legislation of the kind that it declares. Such local legislation is ipso facto in conflict with the statute, because the statute prohibits the legislation. For the same reason, the defined local legislation "cannot operate concurrently" with the statute. It is also clear that "the legislature meant its law to be exclusive"; the entire purpose of the statute is exclusionary.

As the emphasis we have added to plaintiffs' text shows, their argument is misfocused. We might agree that the legislature cannot prevent the people of the state as a whole from exercising initiative and referendum rights to enact or reject state statutes. However, that is not what ORS 659.165 does. It preempts the enactment or enforcement of certain local legislation. Its preemptive effect does and may apply to all local legislation on the subject, whether it is adopted by the local legislative body or the local voters.

Judgment for the State.

Case Commentary

The Oregon Appellate Court held that a state statute prohibiting the granting of special rights to protect homosexuals is valid. The court stated this statute can be overruled by referendum, but not by local legislation.

Case Questions

1. Do you agree with the Court's decision in this case?
2. Should local legislatures have the right to determine whether homosexuals should be accorded special class status?
3. How do you reconcile this Oregon case with the Colorado case that follows?

The question presented in the following case is whether a state amendment prohibiting protection from being granted to homosexuals in employment, housing, etc., is in violation of the Fourteenth Amendment's Equal Protection Clause.

CASE

ROY ROMER, GOVERNOR OF COLORADO v. EVANS

116 S.Ct. 1620 (1996)

JUSTICE KENNEDY delivered the opinion of the Court.

The enactment challenged in this case is an amendment to the Constitution of the State of Colorado, adopted in a 1992 statewide referendum. The parties and the state courts refer to it as "Amendment 2," its designation when submitted to the voters. The impetus for the amendment and the contentious campaign that preceded its adoption came in large part from ordinances that had been passed in various Colorado municipalities. For example, the cities of Aspen and Boulder and the City and County of Denver each had enacted ordinances which banned discrimination in many transactions and activities, including housing, employment, education, public accommodations, and health and welfare services. What gave rise to the statewide controversy was the protection the ordinances afforded to persons discriminated against by reason of their sexual orientation Amendment 2 repeals these ordinances to the extent they prohibit discrimination on the basis of "homosexual, lesbian or bisexual orientation, conduct, practices or relationships."

Yet Amendment 2, in explicit terms, does more than repeal or rescind these provisions. It prohibits all legislative, executive or judicial action at any level of state or local government designed to protect the named class, a class we shall refer to as homosexual persons or gays and lesbians. The amendment reads: "No Protected Status Based on Homosexual, Lesbian, or Bisexual Orientation. Neither the State of Colorado, through any of its branches or departments, nor any of its agencies, political subdivisions, municipalities or school districts, shall enact, adopt or enforce any statute, regulation, ordinance or policy whereby homosexual, lesbian or bisexual orientation, conduct, practices or relationships shall constitute or otherwise be the basis of or entitle any person or class of persons to have or claim any minority status, quota preferences, protected status or claim of discrimination. This Section of the Constitution shall be in all respects self executing."

Soon after Amendment 2 was adopted, this litigation to declare its invalidity and enjoin its enforcement was commenced in the District Court for the City and County of Denver. Among the plaintiffs (respondents here) were homosexual persons, some of them government employees. They alleged that enforcement of Amendment 2 would subject them to immediate and substantial risk of discrimination on the basis of their sexual orientation. Other plaintiffs (also respondents here) included the three municipalities whose ordinances we have cited and certain other governmental entities which had acted earlier to protect homosexuals from discrimination but would be prevented by Amendment 2 from continuing to do so. Although Governor Romer had been on record opposing the adoption of Amendment 2, he was named in his official capacity as a defendant, together with the Colorado Attorney General and the State of Colorado.

The trial court granted a preliminary injunction to stay enforcement of Amendment 2, and an appeal was taken to the Supreme Court of Colorado. Sustaining the interim injunction and remanding the case for further proceedings, the State Supreme Court held that Amendment 2 was subject to strict scrutiny under the *Fourteenth Amendment* because it infringed the fundamental right of gays and lesbians to participate in the political process. On remand, the State advanced various arguments in an effort to show that Amendment 2 was narrowly tailored to serve compelling interests, but the trial court found none sufficient. It enjoined enforcement of Amendment 2, and the Supreme Court of Colorado, in a second opinion, affirmed the ruling. We granted certiorari and now affirm the judgment, but on a rationale different from that adopted by the State Supreme Court.

The State's principal argument in defense of Amendment 2 is that it puts gays and lesbians in the same position as all other persons. So, the State says, the measure does no more than deny homosexuals special rights. This reading of the amendment's language is implausible. We rely not upon our own interpretation of the amendment but upon the authoritative construction of Colorado's Supreme Court. The state court, deeming it unnecessary to determine the full extent of the amendment's reach, found it invalid even on a modest reading of its implications. The critical discussion of the amendment is as follows: "The immediate objective of Amendment 2 is, at a minimum, to repeal existing statutes, regulations, ordinances, and policies of state and local entities that barred discrimination based on sexual orientation."

Homosexuals, by state decree, are put in a solitary class with respect to transactions and relations in both the private and governmental spheres. The amendment withdraws from homosexuals, but no others, specific legal protection from the injuries caused by discrimination, and it forbids reinstatement of these laws and policies.

We have attempted to reconcile the principle with the reality by stating that, if a law neither burdens a fundamental right nor targets a suspect class, we will uphold the legislative classification so long as it bears a rational relation to some legitimate end.

Amendment 2 fails, indeed defies, even this conventional inquiry. First, the amendment has the peculiar property of imposing a broad and undifferentiated disability on a single named group, an exceptional and, as we shall explain, invalid form of legislation. Second, its sheer breadth is so discontinuous with the reasons offered for it that the amendment seems inexplicable by anything but animus toward the class that it affects; it lacks a rational relationship to legitimate state interests.

The primary rationale the State offers for Amendment 2 is respect for other citizens' freedom of association, and in particular the liberties of landlords or employers who have personal or religious objections to homosexuality. Colorado also cites its interest in conserving resources to fight discrimination against other groups. The breadth of the Amendment is so far removed from these particular justifications that we find it impossible to credit them. We cannot say that Amendment 2 is directed to any identifiable legitimate purpose or discrete objective. It is a status based enactment divorced from any factual context from which we could discern a relationship to legitimate state interests; it is a classification of persons undertaken for its own sake, something the Equal Protection Clause does not permit.

We must conclude that Amendment 2 classifies homosexuals not to further a proper legislative end but to make them unequal to everyone else. This Colorado cannot do. A State cannot so deem a class of persons a stranger to its laws.

Amendment 2 violates the Equal Protection Clause, and the judgment of the Supreme Court of Colorado is affirmed.

JUSTICE SCALIA, with whom THE CHIEF JUSTICE and JUSTICE THOMAS join, dissenting.

In holding that homosexuality cannot be singled out for disfavorable treatment, the Court contradicts a decision, unchallenged here, pronounced only 10 years ago and places the prestige of this institution behind the proposition that opposition to homosexuality is as reprehensible as racial or religious bias. Whether it is or not is *precisely* the cultural debate that gave rise to the Colorado constitutional amendment (and to the preferential laws against which the amendment was directed). Since the Constitution of the United States says nothing about this subject, it is left to be resolved by normal democratic means, including the democratic adoption of provisions in state constitutions. This Court has no business imposing upon all Americans the resolution favored by the elite class from which the Members of this institution are selected, pronouncing that "animosity" toward homosexuality is evil. I vigorously dissent.

But though Coloradans are, as I say, *entitled* to be hostile toward homosexual conduct, the fact is that the degree of hostility reflected by Amendment 2 is the smallest conceivable. The Court's portrayal of Coloradans as a society fallen victim to pointless, hate filled "gay bashing" is so false as to be comical. Colorado not only is one of the 25 States that have repealed their antisodomy laws, but was among the first to do so. But the society that eliminates criminal punishment for homosexual acts does not necessarily abandon the view that homosexuality is morally wrong and socially harmful; often, abolition simply reflects the view that enforcement of such criminal laws involves unseemly intrusion into the intimate lives of citizens.

There is a problem, however, which arises when criminal sanction of homosexuality is eliminated but moral and social disapprobation of homosexuality is meant to be retained. The Court cannot be unaware of that problem; it is evident in many cities of the country, and occasionally bubbles to the surface of the news, in heated political disputes over such matters as the introduction into local schools of books teaching that homosexuality is an optional and fully acceptable "alternate life style." The problem (a problem, that is, for those who wish to retain social disapprobation of homosexuality) is that, because those who engage in homosexual conduct tend to reside in disproportionate numbers in certain communities, have high disposable income, and of course care about homosexual rights issues much more ardently than the public at large, they possess political power much greater than their numbers, both locally and statewide. Quite understandably, they devote this political power to achieving not merely a grudging social toleration, but full social acceptance, of homosexuality.

By the time Coloradans were asked to vote on Amendment 2, their exposure to homosexuals' quest for social endorsement was not limited to newspaper accounts of happenings in places such as New York, Los Angeles, San Francisco, and Key West. Three Colorado cities—Aspen, Boulder, and Denver—had enacted ordinances that listed "sexual orientation" as an impermissible ground for discrimination, equating the moral disapproval of homosexual conduct with racial and religious bigotry. The phenomenon had even appeared statewide: the Governor of Colorado had signed an executive order pronouncing that "in the State of Colorado we recognize the diversity in our plu-

ralistic society and strive to bring an end to discrimination in any form," and directing state agency heads to "ensure non discrimination" in hiring and promotion based on, among other things, "sexual orientation." I do not mean to be critical of these legislative successes; homosexuals are as entitled to use the legal system for reinforcement of their moral sentiments as are the rest of society. But they are subject to being countered by lawful, democratic countermeasures as well.

That is where Amendment 2 came in. It sought to counter both the geographic concentration and the disproportionate political power of homosexuals by (1) resolving the controversy at the statewide level, and (2) making the election a single issue contest for both sides. It put directly, to all the citizens of the State, the question: Should homosexuality be given special protection? They answered no. The Court today asserts that this most democratic of procedures is unconstitutional. Lacking any cases to establish that facially absurd proposition, it simply asserts that it *must* be unconstitutional, because it has never happened before.

Amendment 2 identifies persons by a single trait and then denies them protection across the board. The resulting disqualification of a class of persons from the right to seek specific protection from the law is unprecedented in our jurisprudence. The absence of precedent for Amendment 2 is itself instructive . . . .

The United States Congress, by the way, *required* the inclusion of these anti polygamy provisions in the constitutions of Arizona, New Mexico, Oklahoma, and Utah, as a condition of their admission to statehood I cannot say that this Court has explicitly approved any of these state constitutional provisions; but it has approved a territorial statutory provision that went even further, depriving polygamists of the ability even to achieve a constitutional amendment, by depriving them of the power to vote.

It remains to be explained how sect. 501 of the Idaho Revised Statutes was not an "impermissible targeting" of polygamists, but (the much more mild) Amendment 2 is an "impermissible targeting" of homosexuals. Has the Court concluded that the perceived social harm of polygamy is a "legitimate concern of government," and the perceived social harm of homosexuality is not?

I strongly suspect that the answer to the last question is yes.

Today's opinion has no foundation in American constitutional law, and barely pretends to. The people of Colorado have adopted an entirely reasonable provision which does not even disfavor homosexuals in any substantive sense, but merely denies them preferential treatment.

Amendment 2 is designed to prevent piecemeal deterioration of the sexual morality favored by a majority of Coloradans, and is not only an appropriate means to that legitimate end, but a means that Americans have employed before. Striking it down is an act, not of judicial judgment, but of political will. I dissent.

Case Commentary

The United States Supreme Court ruled that the Colorado Amendment violated the Equal Protection Clause of the Fourteenth Amendment because it specifically treated homosexuals in a way that was not equal. The dissenting opinion focused upon the fact that many people believe homosexuality is morally wrong. The dissent reasoned that the fact homosexuals have to be tolerated does not mean that they have to be accepted.

Case Questions

1. Do you agree with the decision of the Court?
2. Should homosexuals be a suspect classification entitled to be protected from discrimination?
3. Who should decide this: courts or the people? In this case, the people decided this issue and lost.

The following case addresses the question of whether a male transsexual may come to work dressed as a female. The employer argued that a transsexual is not a member of a protected class.

CASE

JAMES v. RANCH MART HARDWARE, INC.

881 F. Supp. 478 (D. Kan. 1995)

VRATIL, District Judge.

Barbara Renee James, an anatomically male transsexual, alleges sex discrimination under Title VII of the Civil Rights Act of 1991, and the Kansas Act Against Discrimination (KAAD). More specifically, plaintiff claims that Ranch Mart Hardware, Inc. ("Ranch Mart"), terminated her employment under circumstances in which "a similarly situated male, living and working full time as a male," would not have been terminated.

The undisputed facts are as follows:

On September 1, 1992, Ranch Mart hired Glenn Wayne James as a sales clerk in its electrical department. James M. Bays, the store manager who hired James, made no inquiry regarding the applicant's sexual orientation and had no knowledge before August 19, 1993, that James was a transsexual. From September 1, 1992, through August 19, 1993, James worked in the Ranch Mart hardware store "as a man," using the name Glenn Wayne James. James did not wear women's clothing, a wig or makeup.

James was not scheduled to work on August 19, 1993. On that date, however, James went to the store to speak with Bays. James told Bays that she wanted to start dressing and trying to appear as a woman and to use the name Barbara Renee James. James also told Bays that she wanted to wear a wig and makeup to work. James does not recall telling Bays what her dress would be, but Bays remembers James saying that she wanted to wear a dress to work.

In response to James's statements, Bays told her that he preferred that James not come to work in a wig and makeup and that he did not want James wearing a dress at the store. When James protested, Bays agreed to discuss the matter with Vic Regnier, the president of Ranch Mart, and get back in touch with James. James apparently assumed that Bays would call her on August 20, 1993, to report the outcome of that discussion.

Bays talked to Regnier on August 19, 1993, and they agreed to make no final decision until James appeared for work the next day, so they could see what James was wearing and decide whether it was appropriate for work in a hardware store. Bays did not call James to report this decision.

James was scheduled to work on August 20 and 21, 1993, but did not report to work, call in, or inquire why she had not heard from Bays. As a result, as of August 21, 1993, Ranch Mart assumed that James had quit her job without notice. Ranch Mart subsequently terminated James' employment for the stated reason that James "did not show up for scheduled work shift."

The Court has previously determined that James cannot state an actionable claim under Ti-tle VII or the KAAD for employment discrimination based upon transsexualism. To proceed on her claim that Ranch Mart terminated her employment when it would not have terminated "a similarly situated female, living and working full time as a male," James must establish a prima facie case of employment discrimination. The four elements of a prima facie employment discrimination case are (1) plaintiff must be a member of a protected class, (2) plaintiff must have been discharged, (3) plaintiff must have been qualified, and (4) plaintiff must show that non-class members in the same or similar circumstances were treated more favorably.

The first element presents the defeating hurdle for plaintiff. If plaintiff claims that Ranch Mart discriminated against her as a male, then this case must be viewed in the reverse discrimination context. As such, the first element becomes a question whether the plaintiff has shown the "existence of background circumstances which support the suspicion that the defendant is that unusual employer who discriminates against the majority." James makes no allegations and provides no facts to support any assertion that Ranch Mart discriminates against males. Thus, under this reverse discrimination analysis, James has failed to show membership in a protected class under Title VII.

Thus, regardless of whether James can prevail on the three remaining elements of the prima facie case, she fails to demonstrate the existence of the first element. Because James fails to meet this primary burden, Ranch Mart is entitled to summary judgment.

Judgment for Ranch Mart.

Case Commentary

The District Court of Kansas decided that transsexuals are not protected under Title VII or the Kansas Act Against Discrimination. However, in this case, Barbara Renee James's failure to show for work precluded the Court from having to rule on the issue of transsexualism.

Case Questions

1. Do you agree with the Court's determination in this case?
2. Do you believe the Court should have ruled on the issue of transsexualism?

3. Do you believe that, if someone has an operation to change his or her sex, he or she should be afforded protection from discrimination?

A woman discharged because she is a lesbian may argue that her sexual orientation was a mere pretext. The real reason for her dismissal was because of her gender. Arguing gender discrimination places a lesbian in a protected class, but she will be protected only as far as her womanhood is the issue and not her homosexuality. Gays and lesbians have been trying to have sex discrimination enlarged to encompass sexual orientation, but so far most courts and legislatures do not agree.

Homosexuals who have the AIDS virus or other sexually transmitted diseases will be protected under the Americans with Disabilities Act because they are operating under a disability. Homosexuals who are promoting gay rights may not be discharged in some states for espousing their political beliefs.

Gays and lesbians have been fired for flaunting their relationships. While this may sound egregious, it is no different from a heterosexual speaking about his or her amorous relationship. Treatment should be similar. If heterosexuals may display pictures of loved ones, so should homosexuals. Buttons espousing political beliefs such as "Support Gay Rights" or "It's OK to Be Gay" may be disallowed if the company has a policy disallowing the visible expression of political viewpoints at the workplace.

The issue in the next case is whether a male employee may have long hair and wear facial jewelry. The employee argued that the company's imposition was discriminatory. The company claimed it had the right to uphold its image.

CASE

LOCKHART v. LOUISIANA-PACIFIC CORP.

795 P.2d 602 (OR. App. 1990)

RICHARDSON, Presiding Judge.

Plaintiff was discharged by Louisiana-Pacific Corporation (employer), after he refused to comply with the requirement of a dress and grooming rule that male employees not wear facial jewelry while on the job. The rule allows female employees to wear jewelry that is not "unusual or overly-large." Plaintiff contends that the rule is sexually discriminatory, and that he was discharged for "resisting" the discriminatory policy. He brought this action for wrongful discharge against his employer and for interference with contractual relations against his supervisor, Montel Work (Work). The trial court dismissed the wrongful discharge claim for failure to state a claim and allowed Work's motion for summary judgment on the interference claim. Plaintiff appeals and assigns error to both rulings. We affirm.

"The recent federal cases hold that a private employer's promulgation and enforcement of reasonable grooming regulations that restrict the hair length of male employees only is not forbidden by the sex discrimination provisions of the federal act. Only those distinctions between the sexes which are based on immutable, unalterable, or constitutionally protected personal characteristics are forbidden."

"... The federal statute was never intended to prohibit sex-based distinctions inherent in a private employer's personal grooming code for employees which do not have a significant effect on employment and which can be changed easily by the employee. ... The enforcement of a reasonable hair length policy is permissible since such a policy is not used to inhibit equal access to employment opportunities between males and females, is not an employer's attempt to deny employment to a particular sex, and is not a significant employment advantage to either sex."

Perhaps no facet of business life is more important than a company's place in public estimation. That the image created by its employees dealing with the public when on company assignment affects its relations is so well known that we may take judicial notice of an employer's proper desire to achieve favorable acceptance. Good grooming regulations reflect a company's policy in our highly competitive business environment. Reasonable requirements in furtherance of that policy are an aspect of managerial responsibility. Congress has said that no exercise of that responsibility may result in discriminatory deprivation of equal opportunity because of immutable race, national origin, color, or sex classification.

It is not a purpose of the federal statute to accommodate a male employee's desire to wear his hair longer than a private employer's appearance policy allows.

It is unnecessary in this case for us to address the full sweep of the Washington court's reasoning. Plaintiff advances the argument that employer may not prohibit him from wearing an earring, if it allows female employees to wear jewelry. As his argument is cast, plaintiff cannot demonstrate impermissible discrimination unless every difference in dress or grooming requirements for men and women under an employer's rules is impermissibly discriminatory. We reject that argument. The trial court was correct in dismissing the wrongful discharge claim.

Judgment for Louisiana-Pacific Corp.

Case Commentary

The Oregon Appellate Court concluded that the First Amendment of the United States Constitution does not protect male employees who wish to wear facial jewelry in violation of company dress and grooming rules.

Case Questions

1. Do you agree with the Court's decision?
2. Why does the First Amendment's freedom of speech protection not extend to an employee who wishes to wear facial jewelry?

3. Do you think the rules regarding the right to wear jewelry and makeup as well as the right to wear skirts, dresses, and long hair should apply equally to men and women?

HOMOSEXUAL PARTNERS

Currently, gays and lesbians do not have the right to include their partners under their health coverage. Since homosexual marriages are not legally sanctioned except in Vermont, which permits two people of the same sex to enter into a civil union, partners are considered mere friends who are not qualified for coverage. Family leave policies for sickness and death do not extend to gays and lesbians. A Hawaii Circuit Court was the first to legitimize same sex marriages, but this was quickly overruled by the Hawaii State Legislature and subsequently affirmed by the Hawaii Supreme Court. A few states have passed and a number of states are attempting to pass anti-gay marriage bills.

EMPLOYMENT PERSPECTIVE

Bruce Wagner's gay partner, Paul, has passed away. Bruce asks for time off to attend Paul's wake and funeral. The firm is amenable as long as Bruce uses his personal days or takes a leave without pay. Bruce argues that if he were married, he would be entitled to leave with pay. The company asserts that neither it nor state law recognizes homosexual marriages. Does Bruce have any recourse? No! Sexual orientation is not included under the Family Leave Act. ▪

The issue in the following case is whether individuals of the same sex should have the right to marry.

BAEHR v. LAWRENCE MIKE, DIRECTOR OF THE DEPARTMENT OF HEALTH, STATE OF HAWAII

910 P.2d 112 (Hi 1996)

SUMMARY DISPOSITION ORDER

Pursuant to Hawaii Rules of Evidence (HRE) Rules 201 and 202 (1993), this court takes judicial notice of the following: On April 29, 1997, both houses of the Hawaii legislature passed, upon final reading, House Bill No. 117 proposing an amendment to the Hawaii Constitution (the marriage amendment). See 1997 House Journal at 922; 1997 Senate Journal at 766. The bill proposed the addition of the following language to article I of the Constitution: "Section 23. The legislature shall have the power to reserve marriage to opposite-sex couples." See 1997 Haw. Sess. L. H.B. 117 § 2, at 1247. The marriage amendment was ratified by the electorate in November 1998.

In light of the foregoing, and upon carefully reviewing the record and the briefs and supplemental briefs submitted by the parties and amicus curiae and having given due consideration to the arguments made and the issues raised by the parties, we resolve the defendant-appellant Lawrence Mike's appeal as follows:

On December 11, 1996, the first circuit court entered judgment in favor of plaintiffs-appellees Ninia Baehr, Genora Dancel, Tammy Rodrigues, Antoinette Pregil, Pat Lagon, and Joseph Melillo (collectively, "the plaintiffs") and against Mike, ruling (1) that the sex based classification in Hawaii Revised Statutes (HRS) § 572-1 (1985) was "unconstitutional" by virtue of being "in violation of the equal protection clause of article I, section 5 of the Hawaii Constitution," (2) that Mike, his agents, and any person acting in concert with or by or through Mike were enjoined from denying an application for a marriage license because applicants were of the same sex, and (3) that costs should be awarded against Mike and in favor of the plaintiffs. The circuit court subsequently stayed enforcement of the injunction against Mike. The passage of the marriage amendment placed HRS § 572-1 on new footing.

The marriage amendment validated HRS § 572-1 by taking the statute out of the ambit of the equal protection clause of the Hawaii Constitution, at least insofar as the statute, both on its face and as applied, purported to limit access to the marital status to opposite-sex couples. Accordingly, whether or not in the past it was violative of the equal protection clause in the foregoing respect, HRS § 572-1 no longer is. (1) In light of the marriage amendment, HRS § 572-1 must be given full force and effect.

The plaintiffs seek a limited scope of relief in the present lawsuit, i.e., access to applications for marriage licenses and the consequent legally recognized marital status. Inasmuch as HRS § 572-1 is now a valid statute, the relief sought by the plaintiffs is unavailable. The marriage amendment has rendered the plaintiffs' complaint moot. Therefore, IT IS HEREBY ORDERED that the judgment of the circuit court be reversed and that the case be remanded for entry of judgment in favor of Mike and against the plaintiffs.

IT IS FURTHER ORDERED that the circuit court shall not enter costs or attorneys' fees against the plaintiffs.

DATED: Honolulu, Hawaii, December 9, 1999.

Case Commentary

The Hawaii Supreme Court decided that the legislative amendment restricting marriages to persons of the opposite sex was constitutional, and

Case Questions

1. Do you agree with the Court's decision?
2. Do you believe the Hawaii legislature acted appropriately in limiting marriages to individuals of the opposite sex?

not in violation of the Hawaii equal protection clause. The United States Supreme Court elected not to hear this case.

3. How do you reconcile the Hawaii decision with the Vermont case that follows?

The issue in the case that follows is whether persons of the same sex should be entitled to marry, thereby granting unto them all of the rights afforded to married couples.

CASE

BAKER v. STATE OF VERMONT

Supreme Court of Vermont No. 98-032 1999

AMESTOY, Chief Judge

May the State of Vermont exclude same-sex couples from the benefits and protections that its laws provide to opposite-sex married couples? That is the fundamental question we address in this appeal, a question that the Court well knows arouses deeply-felt religious, moral, and political beliefs. Our constitutional responsibility to consider the legal merits of issues properly before us provides no exception for the controversial case. The issue before the Court, moreover, does not turn on the religious or moral debate over intimate same-sex relationships, but rather on the statutory and constitutional basis for the exclusion of same-sex couples from the secular benefits and protections offered married couples.

We conclude that under the Common Benefits Clause of the Vermont Constitution, which, in pertinent part, reads,

That government is, or ought to be, instituted for the common benefit, protection, and security of the people, nation, or community, and not for the particular emolument or advantage of any single person, family, or set of persons, who are a part only of that community, plaintiffs may not be deprived

of the statutory benefits and protections afforded persons of the opposite sex who choose to marry. We hold that the State is constitutionally required to extend to same-sex couples the common benefits and protections that flow from marriage under Vermont law. Whether this ultimately takes the form of inclusion within the marriage laws themselves or a parallel "domestic partnership" system or some equivalent statutory alternative, rests with the Legislature. Whatever system is chosen, however, must conform with the constitutional imperative to afford all Vermonters the common benefit, protection, and security of the law.

Plaintiffs are three same-sex couples who have lived together in committed relationships for periods ranging from four to twenty-five years. Two of the couples have raised children together. Each couple applied for a marriage license from their respective town clerk, and each was refused a license as ineligible under the applicable state marriage laws. Plaintiffs thereupon filed this lawsuit against defendants — the State of Vermont, the Towns of Milton and Shelburne, and the City of South Burlington — seeking a declaratory judgment that the refusal to issue them a license violated the marriage statutes and the Vermont Constitution.

The State, joined by Shelburne and South Burlington, moved to dismiss the action on the ground that plaintiffs had failed to state a claim for which relief could be granted. The trial court granted the State's and the Town of Milton's motions and dismissed the complaint. The court ruled that the marriage statutes could not be construed to permit the issuance of a license to same-sex couples. The court further ruled that the marriage statutes were constitutional because they rationally furthered the State's interest in promoting "the link between procreation and child rearing." This appeal followed.

Vermont's marriage statutes are set forth in Chapter 1 of Title 15, entitled "Marriage," which defines the requirements and eligibility for entering into a marriage, and Chapter 105 of Title 18, entitled "Marriage Records and Licenses," which prescribes the forms and procedures for obtaining a license and solemnizing a marriage. Although it is not necessarily the only possible definition, there is no doubt that the plain and ordinary meaning of "marriage" is the union of one man and one woman as husband and wife. This understanding of the term is well rooted in Vermont common law. The legislative understanding is also reflected in the enabling statute governing the issuance of marriage licenses, which provides, in part, that the license "shall be issued by the clerk of the town where either the bride or groom resides." "Bride" and "groom" are gender-specific terms.

These statutes, read as a whole, reflect the common understanding that marriage under Vermont law consists of a union between a man and a woman. Plaintiffs essentially concede this fact. They argue, nevertheless, that the underlying purpose of marriage is to protect and encourage the union of committed couples and that, absent an explicit legislative prohibition, the statutes should be interpreted broadly to include committed same-sex couples. Plaintiffs rely principally on our decision in In re B.L.V.B. There, we held that a woman who was co-parenting the two children of her same-sex partner could adopt the children without terminating the natural mother's parental rights. Although the statute provided generally that an adoption deprived the natural parents of their legal rights, it contained an exception where the adoption was by the

"spouse" of the natural parent. Technically, therefore, the exception was inapplicable. We concluded, however, that the purpose of the law was not to restrict the exception to legally married couples, but to safeguard the child, and that to apply the literal language of the statute in these circumstances would defeat the statutory purpose and "reach an absurd result."

Contrary to plaintiffs' claim, B.L.V.B. does not control our conclusion here. We are not dealing in this case with a narrow statutory exception requiring a broader reading than its literal words would permit in order to avoid a result plainly at odds with the legislative purpose. Unlike B.L.V.B., it is far from clear that limiting marriage to opposite-sex couples violates the Legislature's "intent and spirit." Rather, the evidence demonstrates a clear legislative assumption that marriage under our statutory scheme consists of a union between a man and a woman. Accordingly, we reject plaintiffs' claim that they were entitled to a license under the statutory scheme governing marriage.

With these general precepts in mind, we turn to the question of whether the exclusion of same-sex couples from the benefits and protections incident to marriage under Vermont law contravenes Article 7. The first step in our analysis is to identify the nature of the statutory classification. As noted, the marriage statutes apply expressly to opposite-sex couples. Thus, the statutes exclude anyone who wishes to marry someone of the same sex.

Next, we must identify the governmental purpose or purposes to be served by the statutory classification. The principal purpose the State advances in support of the excluding same-sex couples from the legal benefits of marriage is the government's interest in "furthering the link between procreation and child rearing." The State has a strong interest, it argues, in promoting a permanent commitment between couples who have children to ensure that their offspring are considered legitimate and receive ongoing parental support. The State contends, further, that the Legislature could reasonably believe that sanctioning same-sex unions "would diminish society's perception of the link between procreation and child rearing . . . and advance the notion that fathers or mothers . . . are mere surplusage to the functions of procreation and child rearing." The State argues that since same-sex couples cannot conceive a child on their own, state-sanctioned same-sex unions "could be seen by the Legislature to separate further the connection between procreation and parental responsibilities for raising children." Hence, the Legislature is justified, the State concludes, "in using the marriage statutes to send a public message that procreation and child rearing are intertwined."

Do these concerns represent valid public interests that are reasonably furthered by the exclusion of same-sex couples from the benefits and protections that flow from the marital relation? It is beyond dispute that the State has a legitimate and long-standing interest in promoting a permanent commitment between couples for the security of their children. It is equally undeniable that the State's interest has been advanced by extending formal public sanction and protection to the union, or marriage, of those couples considered capable of having children, i.e., men and women. And there is no doubt that the overwhelming majority of births today continue to result from natural conception between one man and one woman.

It is equally undisputed that many opposite-sex couples marry for reasons unrelated to procreation, that some of these couples never intend to have children, and that others are incapable of having children. Therefore, if the purpose of the statutory exclusion of same-sex couples is to "further the link between procreation and child rearing," it is significantly under-inclusive. The law extends the benefits and protections of marriage to many persons with no logical connection to the stated governmental goal.

Furthermore, while accurate statistics are difficult to obtain, there is no dispute that a significant number of children today are actually being raised by same-sex parents, and that increasing numbers of children are being conceived by such parents through a variety of assisted-reproductive techniques (citing estimates that between 1.5 and 5 million lesbian mothers resided with their children in United States between 1989 and 1990, and that thousands of lesbian mothers have chosen motherhood through donor insemination or adoption); (estimating that numbers of children of either gay fathers or lesbian mothers range between six and fourteen million).

Thus, with or without the marriage sanction, the reality today is that increasing numbers of same-sex couples are employing increasingly ef-

ficient assisted-reproductive techniques to conceive and raise children. The Vermont Legislature has not only recognized this reality, but has acted affirmatively to remove legal barriers so that same-sex couples may legally adopt and rear the children conceived through such efforts. The State has also acted to expand the domestic relations laws to safeguard the interests of same-sex parents and their children when such couples terminate their domestic relationship. Therefore, to the extent that the State's purpose in licensing civil marriage was, and is, to legitimize children and provide for their security, the statutes plainly exclude many same-sex couples who are no different from opposite-sex couples with respect to these objectives. If anything, the exclusion of same-sex couples from the legal protections incident to marriage exposes their children to the precise risks that the State argues the marriage laws are designed to secure against. In short, the marital exclusion treats persons who are similarly situated for purposes of the law, differently.

The question thus becomes whether the exclusion of a relatively small but significant number of otherwise qualified same-sex couples from the same legal benefits and protections afforded their opposite-sex counterparts contravenes the mandates of Article 7. While the laws relating to marriage have undergone many changes during the last century, largely toward the goal of equalizing the status of husbands and wives, the benefits of marriage have not diminished in value. On the contrary, the benefits and protections incident to a marriage license under Vermont law have never been greater. They include, for example, the right to receive a portion of the estate of a spouse who dies intestate and protection against disinheritance through elective share provisions; preference in being appointed as the personal representative of a spouse who dies intestate; the right to bring a lawsuit for the wrongful death of a spouse; the right to bring an action for loss of consortium; the right to workers' compensation survivor benefits; the right to spousal benefits statutorily guaranteed to public employees, including health, life, disability, and accident insurance; the opportunity to be covered as a spouse under group life insurance policies issued to an employee; the opportunity to be covered as the insured's spouse under an individual health insurance policy; the right to claim an evidentiary privilege for marital communications; homestead rights and protections; the presumption of joint ownership of property and the concomitant right of survivorship; hospital visitation and other rights incident to the medical treatment of a family member; and the right to receive, and the obligation to provide, spousal support, maintenance, and property division in the event of separation or divorce.

While other statutes could be added to this list, the point is clear. The legal benefits and protections flowing from a marriage license are of such significance that any statutory exclusion must necessarily be grounded on public concerns of sufficient weight, cogency, and authority that the justice of the deprivation cannot seriously be questioned. Considered in light of the extreme logical disjunction between the classification and the stated purposes of the law—protecting children and "furthering the link between procreation and child rearing"—the exclusion falls substantially short of this standard. The laudable governmental goal of promoting a commitment between married couples to promote the security of their children and the community as a whole provides no reasonable basis for denying the legal benefits and protections of marriage to same-sex couples, who are no differently situated with respect to this goal than their opposite-sex counterparts.

We hold only that plaintiffs are entitled under Chapter I, Article 7, of the Vermont Constitu-

tion to obtain the same benefits and protections afforded by Vermont law to married opposite-sex couples.

CONCLUSION

The past provides many instances where the law refused to see a human being when it should have. The future may provide instances where the law will be asked to see a human when it should not (noting concerns that genetically engineering humans may threaten very nature of human individuality and identity). The challenge for future generations will be to define what is most essentially human. The extension of the Common Benefits Clause to acknowledge plaintiffs as Vermonters who seek nothing more, nor less, than legal protection and security for their avowed commitment to an intimate and lasting human relationship is simply, when all is said and done, a recognition of our common humanity.

The judgment of the superior court upholding the constitutionality of the Vermont marriage statutes under Chapter I, Article 7 of the Vermont Constitution is reversed. The effect of the Court's decision is suspended, and jurisdiction is retained in this Court, to permit the Legislature to consider and enact legislation consistent with the constitutional mandate described herein.

Case Commentary

Through this decision, the Vermont Supreme Court provided an impetus to the legislature to validate civil unions between persons of the same sex. Their reasoning was based upon the

right of homosexuals who maintain permanent relationships to be afforded security through the legal protection granted to married couples.

Case Questions

1. Do you believe this case was correctly decided?
2. How is it possible to marry someone of the same sex?
3. Are same sex married couples no different than parents who adopt?

4. Should marriage be based on love and devotion, not the procreation of children?
5. Should all of the rights and privileges granted to married couples be afforded to couples of the same sex?

FEDERAL GOVERNMENT'S POLICY

The federal government's treatment of homosexuals is divided. Some agencies discriminate, while others do not. The Civil Service Commission was charged with actively implementing the Equal Employment Opportunity Act of 1972. On December 21, 1973, the Commission issued a directive in its Civil Service Bulletin to supervisors in the employ of the federal government regarding the treatment of homosexuals. It provided that, with respect to employment, no action should be taken against a person because he or she is a homosexual.

The military has long had a policy of refusing to enlist homosexuals. Early in his tenure as president, Bill Clinton took an opposing viewpoint to the military's rigidness on the exclusion of gays. After being adjudicated in federal court, the ban on gays was lifted to the extent that the military will not inquire into the sexual preference of enlisted persons nor will it discharge someone who is gay on that basis alone. But if the homosexual engages in any overt acts ranging from hand holding to sexual conduct, the homosexual will be discharged from the military.

Professional license requirements often mandate good moral character as a criterion for acceptance. This often barred homosexuals from being admitted to a practice. Over time this obstacle has fallen into disuse because homosexual behavior is not evidence of a person's lack of morality. Furthermore, sexual orientation has nothing to do with the practice of a trade or profession.

EMPLOYMENT PERSPECTIVE

Wilson Fredericks, who is gay, has just learned he has passed the bar exam. He is given an appointment before members of the character and fitness committee. During the interview, one member asks Wilson about his sexual orientation. Wilson refuses to answer on the grounds of his right to privacy. Has Wilson addressed this matter appropriately? Yes! Wilson's homosexuality is a private matter. The fact that he prefers men to women does not mean he is unethical and therefore any less qualified to practice law. ■

TEACHING IN SCHOOLS

Perhaps the most heated debate is over whether gays and lesbians should be allowed to teach in the public school system and work in day care centers. The fear persists among many that gays and lesbians will indoctrinate the children into the homosexual way of life and possibly persuade children into having homosexual acts with them. First, teachers must submit a plan book detailing their course content for each day. This must parallel the course curriculum. If a teacher substantially deviates from this requirement, appropriate disciplinary measures may be taken. The fact that a homosexual teacher may interject subtle references to the benefits of an alternative lifestyle is a given. However, there is no evidence that these remarks, if made, are enough to change a child's sexual orientation involuntarily. Second, homosexuality is not synonymous with pedophilia. Homosexuals usually engage in relationships with other adults, not little children. Being a homosexual is not indicative of being a pedophile. Within the pedophile constituency exist both homosexual and heterosexual adults. Allowing a homosexual to work in a day care center is no more dangerous for fear of pedophilia than allowing a heterosexual to work there. Pedophilia is a sickness unrelated to sexual orientation.

The important criterion for a teacher or a day care worker is job performance capability. A teacher or day care worker should be dismissed if the person is unfit to teach or unfit to exhibit care and concern, not on the basis of having chosen an alternative lifestyle. In most cultures, one dominant party has ruled; that party has been men. Where there have been different races, religions, and national origins present, the group having the greatest wealth, military strength, or political power is in control. In the United States, white Anglo Saxon Protestant (WASP) men have long held the power.

The next case deals with denial of employment as a public school teacher to a man because of his sexual tendencies.

CASE

JANTZ v. MUCI

759 F. Supp. 1543 (D.Kan. 1991)

KELLY, District Judge.

Plaintiff Vernon Jantz has brought the present action under 42 U.S.C. 1983 alleging a violation of his right to equal protection. The plaintiff alleges that he was denied by the defendant, then school principal Cleofas Muci, employment as a public school teacher on the basis of Muci's perception that Jantz had "homosexual tendencies."

Jantz graduated from high school in Newton, Kansas in 1963. He graduated cum laude from Wichita State University, receiving a bachelor's degree from Wichita State University in 1972 and a master's degree in 1978. After serving in the United States Air Force, Jantz completed course work in secondary education at Western New Mexico State University, and obtained a New Mexico secondary school teaching permit in 1985.

During the 1985–86 school year, Jantz taught social studies in the New Mexico schools. Jantz and his wife moved to Wichita, Kansas in the summer of 1986. Obtaining Kansas certification in September, 1986, Jantz took employment with Unified School District No. 259 and began substitute teaching for the district in early 1987. Jantz substituted at several middle and elementary schools in the district, including Wichita North High School.

During this time, Jantz did no coaching. In his interviews with school administrators, including an interview conducted by a Wichita North administrative officer on behalf of Muci, Jantz did not volunteer to perform coaching activities. By the same token, Jantz was not asked whether he was able and willing to assume coaching responsibilities. Jantz, who had experience in basketball,

baseball, soccer, and tennis, was able to coach, and would have done so had he been asked.

In May, 1987, Jantz contacted the district's Director of Secondary Personnel, Frank Crawford, and inquired about the possibility of obtaining a teacher's position for the 1987–88 school year. Despite his talk with Crawford, it remained uncertain whether there were any openings for the upcoming school year. Jantz interviewed at Wichita South and at Wichita North (with associate principal Milford Johnson). However, as it turned out, no positions were open for the 1987–88 school year at the schools where Jantz interviewed. As with the previous year, Jantz provided substitute teaching services during the 1987–88 school year.

Jantz met with Crawford's successor, Jane Ware, in February, 1988. Due to the upcoming merger of ninth grade students into the Wichita high schools, a combined social studies teacher and coach position was created at Wichita North for the 1989 school year. Jantz applied for the position.

The contentions of fact presented by the parties establish that the principals of the individual schools in the district exercise de facto the predominant role in hiring decisions, with some input by the district personnel office. The principal usually conducts the job interview with any applicant and his determination is normally decisive.

Jantz's application was turned down and Matthew Silverthorne was selected to fill the new position. The parties dispute the reason for this decision by Wichita North's principal, Cleofas Muci. Muci was principal of Wichita North for the 1986–87 and 1987–88 school years. Muci retired in November, 1988.

According to Muci, he hired Silverthorne because he was the best candidate. Silverthorne had student taught and coached at Wichita North. In Muci's opinion, Silverthorne had done a good job while coaching. Silverthorne was certified to teach social studies (with the exception of world geography, in which he had only a provisional certification).

Jantz disputes this version of the decision to hire Silverthorne. Jantz cites the testimony of Sharon Fredin (Muci's secretary) and William Jenkins (the coordinator of social studies at Wichita North). Fredin has acknowledged in her deposition that during the 1987–88 school year she "made the offhand comment" to Muci that Jantz reminded her of her husband, whom she believed to be a homosexual. Jenkins has testified that when he asked why Jantz was not hired for the new position, Muci told him it was because of Jantz's "homosexual tendencies."

After being denied the social sciences position at Wichita North, Jantz worked during the 1989–90 school year as a (half-time) social studies teacher and a (half-time) facilitator for gifted students at the middle school. Jantz currently is employed full-time as a facilitator for gifted students at Hadley Intermediate School. Jantz is a 45-year-old white male. He is married with two children.

In *Bowers v. Hardwick,* the Supreme Court held that the due process clause of the Fourteenth Amendment does not prohibit the states from criminalizing homosexual sodomy. That case, cited by defendant Muci, is not directly relevant here. The Bowers Court only addressed the respondent's claim that the Georgia statute was a violation of due process; equal protection was not an issue. The case presented the limited issue of whether homosexual conduct could be regulated by the states. Whether a state or its agents may discriminate among citizens on the basis of their sexual orientation was not at issue.

The distinction between conduct and orientation is both proper and useful in analyzing the constitutional rights of homosexuals. Due process, which was at issue in *Bowers,* serves as a limitation of majoritarian restrictions of traditionally favored and sanctioned activities and rights; it necessarily focuses on historical practice and tradition. Equal protection, on the other hand, protects disadvantaged groups of individuals from governmental discrimination,

even where the discrimination is enshrined in a deep historical tradition. Bowers merely established that homosexual conduct was not a recognized historical liberty. The case does not deal with the issue of whether societal bigotry against private homosexual orientation or tendencies legitimizes governmental discrimination against homosexuals under equal protection.

The strength of the historical tradition of discrimination against homosexuals documented by the Supreme Court in Bowers, while supporting the denial of the due process claim in that case, in fact supports the view that governmental discrimination on the basis of sexual orientation may represent a violation of equal protection considerations. It is perfectly consistent to say that homosexual sodomy is not a practice so deeply rooted in our traditions as to merit due process protection, and at the same time to say, for example, that because homosexuals have historically been subject to invidious discrimination, laws which burden homosexuals as a class should be subjected to heightened scrutiny under the equal protection clause. Indeed, the two propositions may be considered complementary: In all probability, homosexuality is not considered a deeply-rooted part of our traditions precisely because homosexuals have historically been subjected to invidious discrimination.

Bowers, however, provides no bar to the use of heightened scrutiny when analyzing governmental discrimination based upon sexual orientation. However, in identifying which governmental classifications require heightened scrutiny analysis, the Supreme Court, in a series of cases, has identified several considerations which are relevant. The discrimination must be invidious and unjustifiable, that is, discrimination based upon an obvious, immutable, or distinguishing trait which frequently bears no relation to ability to perform or contribute to society. A second factor is whether the class historically has suffered from purposeful discrimination. Third and finally, the class must lack the political power necessary to obtain protection from the political branches of government.

According to that information, sexual orientation (whether homosexual or heterosexual) is generally not subject to conscious change. Sexual orientation becomes fixed during early childhood, "it is not a matter of conscious or controllable choice." If the government began to discriminate against heterosexuals, how many heterosexuals "would find it easy not only to abstain from heterosexual activity but also shift the object of their desires to persons of the same sex"?

Aside from the available scientific evidence, which strongly supports the view that sexual orientation is not easily mutable, complete and absolute immutability simply is not a prerequisite for suspect classification. Race, gender, alienage, and illegitimacy can all be changed, yet discrimination on the basis of any of these categories compels heightened scrutiny by the courts. Aliens may obtain citizenship, gender may be altered by surgery, lighter-skinned blacks may pass as white. Discrimination on the basis of race would not become permissible merely because a future scientific advance permits the change in pigmentation.

While traits such as race, gender, or sexual orientation may be altered or concealed, that change can only occur at a prohibitive cost to the average individual. Immutability therefore defines traits which are central, defining traits of personhood, which may be altered only at the expense of significant damage to the individual's sense of self.

In this context, classification on the basis of orientation fulfills the concern that the identifying trait of the class be immutable. Sexual orientation is a trait which is not subject to voluntary control or change. More importantly, to discriminate against individuals who accept their given sexual orientation and refuse to alter that orientation to conform to societal norms does significant violence to a central and defining character of those individuals.

Discrimination on the basis of sexual orientation is invidious. In addition to the immutable nature of the trait, homosexual individuals have been and are the subject of incorrect stereotyping. Homosexual orientation "implies no impairment in judgment, stability, reliability or general social or vocational capabilities." Nor does homosexual orientation alone impair job performance, including the job of teaching in public schools.

Yet homosexuals remain the subject of significant and virulent stereotyping in modern society. Homosexuals are believed to be effeminate (if gay) or masculine (if lesbian), they are believed to proselytize children to homosexuality or indeed seek out children to molest, they are believed to be mentally ill; stereotypes which are all demonstrably false. In truth, the sexual orientation of the vast majority of homosexuals is not identifiable on the basis of mannerism alone. Homosexuals are no more likely to molest children than are heterosexuals. "The National Association for Mental Health, the American Psychiatric Association, and the Surgeon General now agree that homosexuality, in and of itself, is not a mental illness."

Widespread discrimination against homosexuals exists in both public and private employment. Homosexuals must also face discrimination in many other facets of modern life. In finding jobs, securing housing, in nearly every aspect of social existence, discrimination on the basis of sexual orientation has been a persistent facet of life in America. The prejudice against homosexuals is "so severe and pervasive that homosexuals are often forced to hide their identities as homosexuals." Unfortunately, the deep-seated societal prejudice against homosexuals also evidences itself in widespread violence against homosexuals. One study has found that homosexuals probably face victimization more frequently than any other minority group. Law enforcement officials report that violence against homosexuals is both significant, and, perhaps due to the AIDS epidemic, increasing. "Unfortunately, very little legislation protects gay men and lesbians from discrimination in the private sector. No federal statute bars discrimination by private citizens or organizations on the basis of sexual orientation. Nor do the states provide such protection: only Wisconsin has a comprehensive statute barring such discrimination in employment." The Harvard study concludes that discrimination against homosexuals is pervasive, and recent changes in the law too inadequate to provide adequate protection. Unless more is done, the study found, "gay men and lesbians will remain unable to conduct their lives free from discrimination."

The existence of isolated, local anti-discrimination successes is insufficient to deprive homosexuals of the status of a suspect classification. Compare the situation with that of blacks, who clearly constitute a suspect category for equal protection purposes. Blacks are protected by three federal constitutional amendments, major federal Civil Right Acts as well as anti-discrimination laws in 48 of the states. By that comparison, and by absolute standards as well, homosexuals are politically powerless.

In reality, homosexuals face severe limitations on their ability to protect their interest by means of the political process. As Justice Brennan has observed, "because of the immediate and severe opprobrium often manifested against homosexuals once so identified publicly, members of this group are particularly powerless to pursue their rights openly in the political arena."

There are several factors which limit effective political action by homosexuals. Due to the harsh penalties imposed by society on persons identified as homosexual, many homosexual persons conceal their sexual orientation. Silence, however, has its cost. It may allow a given individual to escape from the discrimination, abuse, and even violence which is often directed at homosexuals, but it ensures that homosexuals as a group are unheard politically. Moreover, the prejudice that compels many homosexuals to refrain from open political activity also limits access to political power in other ways. By diminishing contact between the heterosexual majority and avowed homosexuals, the majority loses any perspective on concerns in the homosexual community and is deprived of the resulting sensitivity to those concerns. Politicians seeking to limit the impact of anti-homosexual prejudices through legislation are themselves the target of prejudice.

There is, the court believes, no way to analyze the present issue under the guidelines set down by the Supreme Court and reach any conclusion other than that discrimination based on sexual orientation is inherently suspect. Sexual orientation is not a matter of choice; it is a central and defining aspect of the personality of every individual. Homosexuals have been and remain the subject of invidious discrimination. No other identifiable minority group faces the dilemma dealt with every day by the homosexual community—the combination of active and virulent prejudice with the lack of an effective political voice. Only by abandoning the established tests of suspectness, and retreating to some other formulation is it possible to achieve some other result. This court cannot join in such a retreat. Accordingly, the court finds that a governmental classification based on an individual's sexual orientation is inherently suspect.

Judgment for Jantz.

Case Commentary

The District Court of Kansas ruled that Jantz could not be prohibited from being employed as a schoolteacher because of his sexual orientation. The court added that homosexuals have met with invidious discrimination and because of that sexual orientation will now be treated as a suspect class.

Case Questions

1. Do you agree with this decision?
2. How do you reconcile this case with the *James v. Ranch Mart* case, both of which were decided by the same court?
3. Why do some states offer protection for sexual orientation while other states and the federal government do not?

COMPARISON TO OTHER DISCRIMINATION VICTIMS

Over time, significant inroads have been made by Jews and Catholics and others with European ancestry. All of them are white males. It is difficult, at times, to determine religion or national origin by someone's demeanor. Intermarriage has also resulted in fewer homogeneous groups. The distinction for women and minorities remains because it cannot be disguised. Racial and gender differences are obvious. Although age, pregnancy, and disabilities are often obvious, sexual orientation may not be so. It can be evidenced through the display of overt acts such as exhibiting feminine mannerisms and speech, cross dressing, hand holding, and exhibiting other characteristics of the opposite sex. For the most part, homosexuality is not readily identifiable unless the individual chooses to speak about it. Many gays and lesbians want their lifestyles to be tolerated to the point where people will not be shocked to learn of their choice, snide remarks and jokes will not be made, and discrimination will not take place. Is this asking too much? No!

The prejudices of the white male should not have a deleterious effect on the rights of others, who for some particular reason are different because of their sex, race, religion, age, disability, pregnancy, sexual orientation, personality, hobbies, standard of living, social connections, or vices (drinking, smoking, gambling). Tolerance of differences should be preached. In diversity there is strength. Economic livelihood through the deprivation of employment opportunities should not be affected. Job qualifications and performance should rule. All other unrelated suspect classifications should not be considered. It is time for individuals to be judged on the merits of what they do rather than on the personal characteristics they cannot change.

A strong argument has been made to grant homosexuals Title VII protection under gender discrimination because they have the right to work. Equal employment opportunities should not be denied to them, as it is not denied to single and married heterosexuals who sleep around. Sexual orientation is a private matter that is not job related. As long as conduct such as hand holding, kissing, touching, and incessantly preaching the virtues of homosexuality is not displayed on the job, an employee's private affinity for members of his or her gender should be tolerated. A gay or lesbian should be held to the same standards as a so-called straight male or female, no more, no less.

ACCEPTANCE OR TOLERANCE

Acceptance of gays and lesbians may never take place, but tolerance must. Acceptance means confirming a personal conviction in the person in question. Tolerance means keeping any personal hostility to oneself and refraining from causing harm to the individual because of his or her difference. This applies to race, religion, gender, national origin, age, pregnancy, and disability as well. We cannot delude ourselves into thinking someday everyone will accept everyone else. There have been a lot of somedays that have come and gone. Personal prejudices and traditions stand in the way. They have been instilled from generation to generation in family life, the community, the educational system, and the media. Personal prejudices exist on both sides. There are many minorities and people of foreign extraction who despise whites. Many women have hostile feelings toward men. Many claim justification because of past atrocities. Many white males feel resentful because of what they perceive to be favorable dispositions given to others.

❖ EMPLOYER LESSONS

- Discover whether state or local protection for sexual orientation exists.
- Choose whether to allow homosexuals to cover their partners under the health plan you provide.
- Decide whether you will take sexual orientation into account in your employment decisions.
- Be cognizant of the power of the gay and lesbian lobby.
- Learn from the judicial overruling of the Colorado referendum outlawing protection for homosexuals.

- Distinguish between homosexuals, transsexuals, and transvestites in determining company policy.
- Realize that the Americans with Disabilities Act extends to homosexuals with AIDS or sexually transmitted diseases.
- Be aware of the trend to provide more protection to gays and lesbians by public and private employers.

❖ EMPLOYEE LESSONS

- Check to see if your state or city affords protection on the basis of sexual orientation.
- Realize that federal protection under the Civil Rights Act does not encompass sexual orientation.
- Familiarize yourself with support groups and political organizations advocating employment rights on the basis of sexual orientation.
- Understand the reasoning behind opponents of sexual orientation protection.
- Inquire as to whether your employer covers or would consider covering homosexual partners under its health plan.
- Appreciate that if you are a homosexual with AIDS or a sexually transmitted disease, you will be covered under the Americans with Disabilities Act.
- Be aware that the military may not stop you from serving because of your sexual orientation.
- Recognize that your ability to work in a school or day care center should not be compromised because of your sexual orientation.

❖ SUMMARY

The bottom line is there will never come a day where there will be complete acceptance. Some feel we are losing ground rather than gaining it. After Rodney King and O.J. Simpson, it may be true in the racial arena. The practical solution is to mandate tolerance. Society would like you to love everybody, but society cannot make you. However, society can require you to tolerate everyone. In your mind, if you choose to hate someone, that is up to you. It is subjective, and although society may try, society cannot enforce that because it is your state of mind. But any objective manifestation of your state of mind that results in harm to another can be disciplined. Society can judge people's objective actions, and it should where it results in unfair treatment of another. Political correctness is an example of this. People who are politically correct may hate their neighbor, but they do not show it. They keep their prejudices to themselves or amongst people who have the same feelings. Politically correct people do not offend anyone. They tolerate the behavior of others. Whether they accept it or not will never be known. Society may have a higher goal acceptance, but realistically, it should be looking to achieve removal of discrimination from the workplace and everyday life.

❖ REVIEW QUESTIONS

1. Is the Civil Rights Act applicable to homosexuals?
2. Are there any laws prohibiting discrimination against gays and lesbians?
3. Why is sexual-orientation discrimination not covered under gender discrimination?
4. Is it ethical to discriminate against people of alternative lifestyles?

5. Can a homosexual wear a button saying "Support Gay Rights" at the workplace?

6. Are there any homosexuals protected against discrimination?

7. Do Family Medical Leave policies extend to homosexual partners?

8. What is the policy with regard to gays and lesbians in the military?

9. Should gays and lesbians be allowed to teach in the schools?

10. Can a homosexual be denied a professional license because he or she is lacking good moral character?

11. Plaintiffs' first amendment complaint alleges only a single cause of action: sex discrimination. This complaint alleges the following:

    Supervisors Jennings and Daniel, and other coemployees of Plaintiffs, in an open and notorious manner, engaged in the sexual harassment of plaintiffs by means of writing, drawing, and explicitly discussing homosexual acts, excrement, urine, and other topics in a depraved manner which created for Plaintiffs a harmful and oppressive work environment and which materially interfered with plaintiffs' ability to perform their work-related duties. Jennings's and Daniel's depraved comments and conduct were done openly, and Jennings's and others' drawings were posted openly and near his office. What was the result? *Fox v. Sierra Development Co.,* 876 F.Supp.1169–D.Nev. (1995)

12. Address these issues: first, whether homosexuals could qualify as adoptive parents, and second, whether homosexuals could operate a day care center. What was the result?

13. Carreno complained that his coworkers were harassing him because of his sexual orientation. He claimed that he was afforded protection from this situation under Title VII. What was the result? *Carreno v. Local Union No. 226, International Brotherhood of Electrical Workers,* 54 FEP 81 (D. Kan. 1990)

14. Ethically, should homosexuals be protected against discrimination under Title VII?

15. Should transsexuals be entitled to dress as they please?

16. Should a company be allowed to dictate what jewelry its male and female employees may wear?

17. Is it ethical for a school to refuse to hire a homosexual as a teacher?

18. Plaintiff names Frank Vaughn, Food Service manager at the Western Missouri Correctional Center, as defendant in this action. According to plaintiff, defendant removed plaintiff from his job as a bakery worker at the Western Missouri Correctional Center solely because of the fact that plaintiff is a homosexual. Plaintiff asserts that this action was discriminatory and that it infringed upon his personal liberty. For relief, plaintiff seeks $50,000.00 in damages. What was the result? *Kelley v. Vaughn* 760 F.Supp. 161 (W.D.Mo.1991)

❖ WEB SITES

www.findlaw.com
www.westbuslaw.com
www.religioustolerance.org/hom-empl.htm
www.law.cornell.edu/topics/employment_discrimination.html
www.aclu.org/issues/gay/hmgl.html
www.lager.dircon.co.uk/
www.ibiblio.org/gaylaw/issue3/mison.html

CHAPTER

B

RELIGIOUS DISCRIMINATION

INTRODUCTION

The First Amendment to the United States Constitution provides for freedom of religion. It also states that Congress shall not establish a national religion, thus ensuring the right of individuals to engage in whatever religious practices they wish. These practices must not, however, violate other laws such as criminal laws prohibiting sacrificial offerings. The First Amendment applies directly to the federal government and to the states through the Fourteenth Amendment.

While the Constitution protects individuals from governmental infringement, Title VII protects them from employment discrimination. Religious affiliation is one of the classes protected under Title VII from invidious discrimination. Employers may not refuse to hire an individual because he or she is a member of a particular religion.

CHAPTER CHECKLIST

❖ Become familiar with the religious implications of the First Amendment to the United States Constitution.

❖ Understand that employers must reasonably accommodate the religious beliefs of their employees.

❖ Appreciate that religious accommodation may not extend to situations creating an undue burden on the employer.

❖ Recognize that a bona fide occupational qualification exists for religious institutions wishing to hire members of their own faith.

❖ Realize that religious practices cannot compromise food safety, *i.e.*, dreadlocks, long hair and beards, or seniority under collective bargaining agreements.

❖ Know that employers generally cannot tell employees where to live.

❖ Learn that employers do not have to permit employees to promote their religious beliefs at the workplace.

❖ Be aware that employers do not have to allow religious services in the workplace.

❖ Be cognizant of the fact that employers do not have to accommodate an employee beyond what the religion itself requires.

❖ Recognize that religious discrimination is one of the suspect classifications under the Civil Rights Act.

EMPLOYMENT SCENARIO

Arafa Habib is employed in the shipping and receiving department of the Long and Short of It. He begins work before sunrise. At sunrise during a break and at noon during lunch he prays to Allah. One morning a huge shipment of suits arrives and Arafa, is told to work through his break. He refuses because of his prayer ritual. His supervisor informs Mark Short, copresident of L&S. Mark informs Arafa, in no uncertain terms, that his job comes before his religious practices. Furthermore, Mark stipulates that engaging in religious prayer at the workplace is disruptive. From now on Arafa must discontinue it. Arafa explains that he is Muslim. Mark is unrelenting. Arafa resigns immediately and files a claim with the EEOC. Arafa stipulates that his accommodation request was reasonable and that L&S discriminated against him because of his religious beliefs. Mark consults with Susan North, L&S's attorney. Susan divides Arafa's request for accommodation into two parts: first, his religious belief requires him to pray at sunrise and noon and, second, he wishes to fulfill his religious practice by praying on the premises. While these issues certainly can be litigated, Susan believes L&S should agree to Arafa's first request, but not his second. Susan agrees that the performance of a religious practice at the workplace can be disruptive to other workers and customers.

EMPLOYMENT PERSPECTIVE

Herman Tuffle, an atheist, is the owner of bookstores called "The Classics." Shamus O'Neill applies for a position in the bookstore. During the course of the interview, Shamus mentions that one of the priests of his parish saw the Classic's employment advertisement in the local paper. Herman, who never questioned Shamus about his religion, refused to hire him. Shamus, uncertain as to why he was not hired, relates the story to one of his friends. The friend tells him that Herman is a confirmed atheist. Shamus files a claim with the EEOC. Will he win? Yes! As long as Shamus was otherwise qualified for the position, Herman will have no valid defense for refusing to hire him. What if Herman had hired him and then, upon learning of Shamus's religious affiliation, terminated him? The result would be the same. ■

The issue in the following case is whether an employer is guilty of religious discrimination for adversely affecting a worker's employment by failing to investigate an anti-Semitic hate letter.

BERNSTEIN v. BOARD OF ED. OF SCHOOL DISTRICT 200

203 F.3d 1056 (7th Cir. 1999)

ORDER

Rhoda G. Bernstein, a tenured psychologist and teacher at Oak Park-River Forest High School ("OPRF"), appeals the district court's dismissal of her Title VII religious discrimination claim. Ms. Bernstein, who is Jewish, alleged in her complaint that OPRF intentionally discriminated against her on the basis of her religion by failing to adequately investigate an anti-Semitic hate letter she received, and then subjecting her to several adverse personnel decisions. The district court dismissed Ms. Bernstein's claim, holding that because none of the actions complained of rose to the level of materially adverse employment actions, she failed to state a claim of religious discrimination. Because we conclude that the district court erred in its determination, we **REVERSE** and **REMAND** for further proceedings.

FACTS

Ms. Bernstein began working at OPRF in 1982 as a school psychologist. On January 30, 1991, she received an anti-Semitic hate letter at her home which referenced administration and employees at OPRF, leading her to believe that it had been written by a fellow OPRF employee. Consequently, she immediately informed OPRF's associate superintendent, Donald Offerman, as well as the Oak Park police about the letter. While the Oak Park police investigated the matter and eventually pinpointed a couple of OPRF employees as the prime suspects, Ms. Bernstein alleges in her complaint that OPRF, through its agent Mr. Offerman, conducted an "intentionally ineffective and/or negligently indifferent inquiry into the incident."

Neither the letter, nor a copy thereof, was included in the record. However, Ms. Bernstein asserts that the letter contained "swastikas and threats along religious lines," characterizations OPRF does not refute.

After complaining about the inadequate investigation, Ms. Bernstein asserts, OPRF began to treat her unfavorably. First, for the 1991/1992 school year, OPRF assigned her to a psychologist position in which she would be supervised by one of the suspected perpetrators of the hate letter. After protesting, she was eventually transferred to another department. However, in June 1993, her new supervisor, Maryanne Kelly, allegedly told other employees at OPRF that she knew who authored the hate letter. But when questioned by the Oak Park police, Ms. Kelly refused to provide any information, except for labeling Ms. Bernstein a "trouble-maker." During Ms. Bernstein's review in March 1994, then, Ms. Kelly rated her performance as "unsatisfactory." Prior to that time, Ms. Bernstein had consistently received "superior" or "excellent/superior" ratings. As a result of the "unsatisfactory" rating, and pursuant to its policy, OPRF informed Ms. Bernstein that she would be placed on a remediation plan, and notified members of the State Board of Education of the negative rating. However, Ms. Bernstein appealed the "unsatisfactory" rating internally, and in June, 1994, OPRF upgraded her rating to "satisfactory."

Although on various occasions in 1995 and 1996, Ms. Bernstein continued to press OPRF to further investigate the hate letter, OPRF refused to do so. Consequently, she filed several charges with the EEOC, obtained a right to sue letter, and commenced suit in federal court.

In her complaint brought under Title VII of the Civil Rights Act of 1964, Ms. Bernstein alleges that she received less favorable treatment than similarly situated non-Jewish employees. Specifically, she asserts that OPRF violated its duty to conduct investigations and implement personnel decisions without regard to religion by (1) conducting an inadequate investigation of the hate letter; (2) refusing to transfer her from a department in which she was supervised by one of the prime suspects in the hate letter incident; (3) allowing another supervisor who claimed knowledge about the hate letter's perpetrator, but refused to divulge that information, to give her an "unsatisfactory" performance rating; and (4) threatening to subject her to a disciplinary measure because of the "unsatisfactory" rating.

OPRF filed a motion to dismiss, arguing that Ms. Bernstein failed to state a claim for religious discrimination because the conduct she complained of did not amount to actionable materially adverse actions. The district court agreed and dismissed the claim.

Furthermore, on a motion to dismiss, all reasonable inferences are also to be drawn in the plaintiff's favor. It is implicit within the failure to investigate claim that Ms. Bernstein's employment conditions were adversely affected as she was forced to work in an environment where an unknown coworker or coworkers so intensely hated her that the perpetrator(s) prepared a vicious letter, complete with threats and swastikas, and mailed it to her home. Consequently, the district court erred in holding that the inadequate investigation allegations did not amount to a viable adverse action. On that basis alone, the district court improperly dismissed the religious discrimination claim.

Next, the complaint alleges that although there were other psychologist positions available, and in spite of her protests, in June of 1991,

OPRF assigned Ms. Bernstein to a position where her supervisor was "an outspoken anti-Semite and prime suspect in connection with the hate crime." The district court held that this claim did not rise to the level of an adverse action because Ms. Bernstein "does not allege any adverse effect from working under that supervisor," or "harm resulting from the failure to transfer."

As we previously emphasized, however, it is highly conceivable, and reasonable to infer, that being assigned to work under a person considered one of the "prime suspects" in connection with a hateful anti-Semitic letter would affect the conditions of Ms. Bernstein's employment. The fact that she does not explicitly say so, then, does not defeat her claim. Consequently, the district court's holding to the contrary is erroneous.

Although it may ultimately be determined that Ms. Bernstein's claims of adverse action here are not in fact actionable, it would be difficult to conclude at this juncture, based solely on the complaint before us, that the "unsatisfactory" rating and threat of remediation cannot constitute adverse actions.

The district court acted prematurely in concluding that the complaint failed to allege adverse employment actions. Accordingly, the judgment of the district court is **REVERSED,** and this matter is **REMANDED** for further proceedings consistent with this opinion.

Judgment for Bernstein.

Case Commentary

The Seventh Circuit ruled that Bernstein's claim of religious discrimination was prematurely dismissed. Bernstein should be permitted to establish that the high school did not adequately investigate the anti-Semitic hate letter and that its actions toward Bernstein had an adverse impact on her employment.

Case Questions

1. Was this case decided correctly?
2. Do you believe Bernstein's employment was adversely affected?

3. Why should the high school be responsible for investigating further than it has already done?

ACCOMMODATING RELIGIOUS BELIEFS

To require an employer to accommodate an employee's religious beliefs, the employee must first explain to the employer what his or her religious beliefs are and how they are being compromised by the employer because of the task at hand. The employer must acquiesce if such accommodation would not cause the employer undue hardship, compromise the rights of others, or does not require more than minimal cost. If the employee resigns or is terminated for failing to perform the job because of religious beliefs, then the question of religious discrimination will be decided on the basis of the criteria of reasonable accommodation.

Many claims of religious discrimination relate to religious observance. Employers have a duty to make reasonable accommodations for the employee as long as it does not present an undue hardship for the employer.

EMPLOYMENT PERSPECTIVE

John Edwards, a Catholic, is employed as an intern at Bay Ridge Hospital. At times, John must be physically present at the hospital for thirty-six hours. When this occurs mid-Saturday to Sunday evening, it conflicts with John's religious belief in attending Mass. When John informs the hospital, his plea is ignored. Is the hospital guilty of religious discrimination? Yes! Bay Ridge Hospital could make a reasonable accommodation for John to allow him one hour to attend Mass, either on Saturday evening or on Sunday. This provision does not present an undue hardship to the hospital which could either rearrange his work hours or give him a one-hour break.

Suppose that the hospital is able to rearrange John's work hours to allow him to have all Saturday evenings off. Some time ago, the Catholic Church permitted its members to attend a service after 4:00 p.m. on Saturdays to fulfill the Sunday obligation. John insists that he must attend Mass on Sunday because that is the way he was raised. He does not accept this Saturday night exception. Has Bay Ridge Hospital made a reasonable accommodation? Yes! After John advised Bay Ridge Hospital that he was a Catholic, it worked out a schedule to permit him to attend Mass on Saturday afternoon or evening, which is acceptable to the Catholic Church. John is being unreasonable in insisting that he be permitted to attend Mass on Sunday. He is asking for an exception on religious grounds that is not required by the religion itself. ■

The issue in this case is whether an employer must make a good faith effort to try to accommodate an employee's Sabbath where the accommodation would place the employer in violation of the collective bargaining agreement.

IN THE MATTER OF NEW YORK TRANSIT AUTH. v. NEW YORK, EXECUTIVE DEP'T, DIV. OF HUMAN RIGHTS

89 N.Y.2d 79 (1996).

TITONE, Judge.

Our State's Human Rights Law prohibits employers from discriminating against their employees because of their religiously-motivated Sabbath observance. Recognizing that there may be circumstances in which the mandate of the statute conflicts with the strictures of a collective bargaining agreement, we have previously held that an employer caught in such a conflict is obligated only to make a "good faith" effort to accommodate a Sabbath observing employee. The present appeal requires us to apply that principle and to delineate some of the contours of what a "good faith" effort is.

Respondent Mary Myers is a practicing Seventh Day Adventist. The tenets of her religion forbid her from engaging in any form of work on the Sabbath, which extends from sundown on Friday to sundown on Saturday. In June of 1988, Myers was hired as a full-time bus operator trainee by the New York City Transit Authority, which operates its buses on a seven-day per week, twenty-four-hour per day basis. From the outset, Myers made it clear to her supervisors that her religious commitments would prevent her from working between sundown on Friday and sundown on Saturday. During her training period and the first week of her regular employment, Myers' Sabbath observance presented little conflict with the demands of her job. However, a problem arose shortly thereafter because she was assigned Wednesdays and Thursdays as her days off, a schedule requiring her regularly to work on her Sabbath. Under the terms of the collective bargaining agreement between the Authority and the Transport Workers Union, the privilege of selecting weekly

days off was allocated in accordance with a strict seniority system. Ordinarily, employees were not able to choose weekend days as their days off under this system until they had accumulated as much as five years of seniority.

According to the testimony, Myers spoke with several of her employer's representatives in an effort to obtain some accommodation for her Sabbath observance. Her request for "split" days off was rebuffed on the ground that the practice was forbidden by the collective bargaining agreement. Her request to be permitted to work an early shift on Friday was initially granted, but the Authority denied her request to postpone her Saturday service until after sundown because there were no bus run shifts that began after 5:00 and because respondent had not been trained for other available work. After a few weeks, even her Friday afternoon accommodation was withdrawn. The only solution suggested to Myers was to find another worker in her depot who would be willing to trade shifts with her. However, the Authority did not offer to assist her in locating a willing co-worker. Instead, a supervisor told her that she would have to stand at the door as the bus drivers were leaving and ask each of them if they would consider an exchange of shifts. Having failed to obtain an accommodation or to locate a co-worker who was willing to "swap" shifts, Myers began taking unauthorized days off. Although she called in on several occasions to report her plans to absent herself, she did not think it necessary to call in each time, since her employers knew that she was unwilling to work on her Sabbath. Myers was ultimately discharged on October 10, 1988 because of her unexcused absences.

Following her discharge, Myers filed a complaint with the State Human Rights Division, alleging that the Transit Authority and the Transport Workers Union had violated Executive Law § 296(10)(a). The Division found probable cause to believe that a violation had occurred and directed that a hearing be held. At the hearing, a labor relations specialist for the Authority testified that the Authority had a policy to accommodate Sabbath observers only if it could be accomplished without additional cost, disruption of scheduled runs or risk of labor strife. He acknowledged that a Sabbath observers such as respondent were caught in a Catch-22 situation, since they would have difficulty securing accommodations unless they had seniority and they could not obtain seniority without working on weekends for several years.

On the basis of the evidence adduced at the hearing, the Human Rights Division concluded that both the Authority and the union had violated the statutory provisions prohibiting discrimination against Sabbath observers. The Division found that both parties had failed to make good faith efforts to accommodate respondent, despite a statutorily imposed duty to do so. The Division noted that there had been no efforts by either the Authority or the Union to make arrangements for a voluntary exchange of shifts, that the parties' collective bargaining agreement did not preclude such a voluntary exchange and that the Authority had not shown that accommodating Myers would result in economic hardship or serious labor difficulties. Accordingly, the Authority was directed to reimburse Myers, with interest, for her lost back pay. Additionally, the Authority and the union were each directed to compensate her for her mental anguish, and both were ordered to accommodate her Sabbath observance in the future.

On transfer from the Supreme Court, the Appellate Division annulled the agency's order, concluding that the seniority provisions of the Authority's collective bargaining agreement foreclosed any realistic possibility of accommodating Myers. Since the Division had erroneously ignored the effect of these provisions, the Appellate Division held, its ruling was not supported by substantial evidence. We now reverse the Appellate Division's order insofar as it exonerated the Transit Authority.

Before discussing the Transit Authority's duty, we turn briefly to the application of that statute to the collective bargaining agent, the Transport Workers Union. Executive Law § 296(10)(a), the sole predicate for this Human Rights Law proceeding, makes it unlawful "for any employer to prohibit, prevent or disqualify any person from, or otherwise to discriminate against any person in, obtaining or holding employment, because of his observance of any particular day or days * * * as a Sabbath * * * in accordance with the requirements of his religion." By its terms, the prohibition is aimed only at employers, a class that plainly does not include the Transport Workers Union in this situation.

Respondent Myers' contention that Executive Law § 296(10) should be construed to encompass union conduct is not convincing. "Labor organizations" and "employers" are defined separately in the Human Rights Law and their substantive obligations are also. Separately, this Court held that the State Human Rights Division had not erred in adjudging the employer guilty of violating Executive Law § 296(10)(a) under these circumstances, since the employer had made no efforts to accommodate the complainant's religious observance by at least trying to find an existing day-shift employee willing to exchange shifts for the critical Friday evening Sabbath. In so ruling, the Court was careful to note that an employer is not obligated to assist a Sabbath-observing worker to arrange a voluntary shift swap where "clearly prohibited from doing so by nondiscriminatory provisions of its collective bargaining agreement."

In this connection, we deem it significant that the disputed collectively bargained provision in this case involved a bona fide, nondiscriminatory system for distributing days off according to the public transportation employees' longevity of service. Where there is no prior history of invidious discrimination within the particular business or industry, such seniority systems often operate to promote anti-discriminatory values by providing a neutral and fair method for allocating scarce benefits and privileges among employees. Given the utility of these seniority systems, it would be unreasonable to construe and apply our State Human Rights Law in such a way as to compel employers to challenge a union's rational interpretation of the shop's existing seniority plan. There is no proof, for example, that the Authority's managers had approached the union in an effort either to negotiate an overall plan to accommodate Sabbath observers or to secure a specific waiver of seniority rules for Myers individually.

In the final analysis, what the "good faith" standard requires is that the employer show that it exerted reasonable efforts to accommodate its Sabbath observing employees. This standard does not require proof that an accommodation was ac-

tually found, but rather that a genuine search for reasonable alternatives was undertaken. Since there was no showing that such a search was conducted here and since it is undisputed that Myers was discharged only because of her inability to work a normal weekend shift, the finding of the Human Rights Division that the Authority violated § 296(10) was supported by substantial evidence and its determination should be upheld.

Judgment for Myers.

Case Commentary

The New York Court of Appeals held that although an employer does not have to violate a collective bargaining agreement to accommodate an employee's religious accommodation

request, it must make a good faith effort to seek alternative means that do not place it in violation of the agreement.

Case Questions

1. Do you agree with the Court's decision?
2. Why should the onus be on the employer to seek out alternative ways to accommodate?
3. Are employees asking too much when they apply for a job in an organization that requires weekend work and then stipulate that they cannot work for what amounts to a day and a half on the weekend?

EMPLOYMENT PERSPECTIVE

Sidney Green, who is Jewish, responds to an advertisement for a position as a manager in a Food King store. During the interview, Sidney is informed that the position is for weekend work. Sidney tells Food King that his religion does not permit him to work on Saturdays. Food King says that that is the only position open and the hours cannot be altered with the weekday manager. Sidney argues that the advertisement did not specify weekend work and files a religious discrimination claim with the EEOC. Will he win? No! The advertisement does not have to specify every detail of the job. Sidney asked for an accommodation, and Food King recounted that the accommodation would impose an undue hardship on it because it would leave no managerial coverage for Saturdays. Sidney claims that once Food King learned he was Jewish, it informed him that the position was for weekend work, knowing that he would have to decline because of his religious beliefs. If Sidney could prove this, he would win. But there is no evidence that Food King knew Sidney was Jewish when it told him that the opening was for a weekend job. Under the facts as stated, Sidney's claim would most likely fail. ■

BONA FIDE OCCUPATIONAL QUALIFICATION

Religious organizations are permitted to discriminate as long as the position relates to the promotion of the religion. Religious belief is considered a bona fide occupational qualification.

EMPLOYMENT PERSPECTIVE
St. John's Lutheran Church has a position available as administrative assistant to the minister. MaryBeth Luciano, a Catholic, is refused the position because she is not Lutheran. Is this religious discrimination? No! St. John's Lutheran may discriminate in favor of its own parishioners because the position is involved with the operation of the Church. ▊

EMPLOYMENT PERSPECTIVE
Mount Franklin United Methodist Church runs a summer soccer camp for children aged six through twelve. It is open to children of all faiths. Al Kaplan, who is Jewish, applies for the position of soccer instructor. Al played four years as starting forward for the state university, and he is well qualified. Mount Franklin refuses to hire Al because he is not Methodist. Al claims that religious beliefs are not a bona fide occupational qualification of a soccer instructor. Who would win? Most likely Al! The determination would hinge upon whether Mount Franklin is trying to promote the Methodist Religion to young children through their participation in the soccer camp. As the camp is open to children of all faiths, this is not the case. ▊

The term *religion* refers to religious practice as well as religious belief. There is often a conflict as to whether a group qualifies as a religion or is secular in nature. One test to apply would be to find whether its members belong to an organized religion in addition to the group.

EMPLOYMENT PERSPECTIVE
During an interview for a supervisory position in the auto plant of Prestige Motors, Tom Westfield, the applicant, was asked whether he could start to work the evening shift every Tuesday night. Tom responded that on Tuesday nights, he was obligated to attend a Ku Klux Klan meeting but that he would be available every other evening. Tom was rejected because he was unavailable on Tuesday nights. Tom filed a claim with the EEOC under Title VII, claiming that Prestige would not make a reasonable accommodation for his religious practices. Prestige argued that the Ku Klux Klan is not a religious organization. Will Tom win? No! The Ku Klux Klan has been determined to be a political rather than a religious organization and that as such no accommodation has to be made. ▊

Religious practices that require its members to wear certain clothing or to groom themselves in certain ways are protected unless they present an undue hardship to the employer.

In the next case, a worker wore a button having controversial religious overtones. The employer prohibited her from wearing the button. She cited religious discrimination, claiming that she was not reasonably accommodated.

WILSON v. U.S. WEST COMMUNICATIONS

58 F.3d 1337 (8th Cir. 1995)

GIBSON, Senior Circuit Judge.

Christine L. Wilson appeals from judgment entered in favor of U.S. West Communications on her religious discrimination claim under Title VII of the Civil Rights Act of 1964. Wilson's wearing of a graphic anti-abortion button caused immediate and emotional reactions from co-workers, and U.S. West asked Wilson to cover the button during work. She refused, and U.S. West ultimately fired her.

Wilson worked for U.S. West for nearly 20 years before U.S. West transferred her to another location as an information specialist assisting U.S. West engineers in making and keeping records of the location of telephone cables. This facility had no dress code.

In late July 1990, Wilson, a Roman Catholic, made a religious vow that she would wear an anti-abortion button "until there was an end to abortion or until she could no longer fight the fight." The button was two inches in diameter and showed a color photograph of an eighteen to twenty-week old fetus. The button also contained the phrases "Stop Abortion," and "They're Forgetting Someone." Wilson chose this particular button because she wanted to be an instrument of God like the Virgin Mary. She believed that the Virgin Mary would have chosen this particular button. She wore the button at all times, unless she was sleeping or bathing. She believed that if she took off the button she would compromise her vow and lose her soul.

Wilson began wearing the button to work in August 1990. Another information specialist asked Wilson not to wear the button to a class she was teaching. Wilson explained her religious vow and refused to stop wearing the button. The button caused disruptions at work. Employees gathered to talk about the button. U.S. West identified Wilson's wearing of the button as a "time rob-

bing" problem. Wilson acknowledged that the button caused a great deal of disruption. A union representative told Wilson's supervisor, Mary Jo Jensen, that some employees threatened to walk off their jobs because of the button. Wilson's co-workers testified that they found the button offensive and disturbing for "very personal reasons," such as infertility problems, miscarriage, and death of a premature infant, unrelated to any stance on abortion or religion.

In early August 1990, Wilson met with her supervisors, Jensen and Gail Klein, five times. Jensen and Klein are also Roman Catholics against abortion. Jensen and Klein told Wilson of co-workers' complaints about the button and an anti-abortion T-shirt Wilson wore which also depicted a fetus. Jensen and Klein told Wilson that her co-workers were uncomfortable and upset and that some were refusing to do their work. Klein noted a 40 percent decline in the productivity of the information specialists since Wilson began wearing the button. Wilson told her supervisors that she should not be singled out for wearing the button because the company had no dress code. She explained that she "just wanted to do [her] job," and suggested that co-workers offended by the button should be asked not to look at it. Klein and Jensen offered Wilson three options: (1) wear the button only in her work cubicle, leaving the button in the cubicle when she moved around the office; (2) cover the button while at work; or (3) wear a different button with the same message but without the photograph. Wilson responded that she could neither cover nor remove the button because it would break her promise to God to wear the button and be a "living witness." She suggested that management tell the other information specialists to "sit at their desk[s] and do the job U.S. West was paying them to do."

On August 22, 1990, Wilson met with Klein, Jensen, and the union's chief steward. During the meeting, Klein again told Wilson that she could either wear the button only in her cubicle or cover the button. Klein explained that, if Wilson continued to wear the button to work, she would be sent home until she could come to work wearing proper attire.

In an August 27, 1990 letter, Klein reiterated Wilson's three options. He added that Wilson could use accrued personal and vacation time instead of reporting to work. Wilson filed suit but later dismissed the action when U.S. West agreed to allow her to return to work and wear the button pending an investigation by the Nebraska Equal Opportunity Commission.

Wilson returned to work on September 18, 1990, and disruptions resumed. Information specialists refused to go to group meetings with Wilson present. The employees complained that the button made them uneasy. Two employees filed grievances based on Wilson's button. Employees accused Jensen of harassment for not resolving the button issue to their satisfaction. Eventually, U.S. West told Wilson not to report to work wearing anything depicting a fetus, including the button or the T-shirt. U.S. West told Wilson again that she could cover or replace the button or wear it only in her cubicle. U.S. West sent Wilson home when she returned to work wearing the button and fired her for missing work unexcused for three consecutive days. Wilson sued U.S. West, claiming that her firing constituted religious discrimination.

An employee establishes a prima facie case of religious discrimination by showing that: (1) the employee has a bona fide religious belief that conflicts with an employment requirement; (2) the employee informed the employer of this belief; (3) the employee was disciplined for failing to comply with the conflicting employment requirement. The parties stipulated that Wilson's "religious beliefs were sincerely held," and the district court ruled that Wilson made a prima facie case of religious discrimination. The court then considered whether U.S. West could defeat Wilson's claim by demonstrating that it offered Wilson a reasonable accommodation. An employer is required to "reasonably accommodate" the religious beliefs or practices of employees unless doing so would cause the employer undue hardship.

The court considered the three offered accommodations and concluded that requiring Wilson to leave the button in her cubicle or to replace the button were not accommodations of Wilson's sincerely held religious beliefs because: (1) removing the button at work violated Wilson's vow to wear the button at all times; and (2) replacing the button prohibited Wilson from wearing the particular button encompassed by her vow. However, the court concluded that requiring Wilson to cover the button while at work was a reasonable accommodation. The court based this determination on its factual finding that Wilson's vow did not require her to be a living witness. The court reasoned that covering the button while at work complied with Wilson's vow but also reduced office turmoil. The court also concluded that, even if Wilson's vow required her to be a living witness, U.S. West could not reasonably accommodate Wilson's religious beliefs without undue hardship. The court entered judgment for U.S. West, and Wilson appeals.

The employer violates the statute unless it "demonstrates that [it] is unable to reasonably accommodate . . . an employee's . . . religious observance or practice without undue hardship on the conduct of the employer's business." When the employer reasonably accommodates the employee's religious beliefs, the statutory inquiry ends. The employer need not show that the employee's proposed accommodations would cause an undue hardship. Undue hardship is at issue "only where the employer claims that it is unable to offer any reasonable accommodation without such hardship." Because we hold that U.S. West offered Wilson a reasonable accommodation, our inquiry ends, we need not consider Wilson's argument that her suggested accommodations would not cause undue hardship.

We recognize that this case typifies workplace conflicts which result when employees hold strong views about emotionally charged issues. We reiterate that Title VII does not require an employer to allow an employee to impose his religious views on others. The employer is only required to reasonably accommodate an employee's religious views.

We affirm the district court's judgment. Judgment for U.S. West Communications.

Case Commentary

The Eighth Circuit ruled that an employee does not have the right to promote his or her religious belief through the wearing of a button advocating his or her religious belief.

Case Questions

1. Do you agree with the Eighth Circuit's decision?

2. Why was the button so harmful?

3. What about the employee's freedom of speech argument?

EMPLOYMENT PERSPECTIVE

Morris Gold was hired as a teller for Mid-Island Savings Bank. He wore his yarmulke for work the first day and was told to remove it as it was not proper attire. Because he refused, he was terminated. Morris filed a claim with the EEOC, stating that it was a recognized religious practice of the Jewish faith. Will he win? Yes! The practice of wearing a yarmulke is protected as it does not present an undue hardship to the employer. ■

In the following case, an employee selected the town in which he wished to relocate on the basis of its having an active religious community of his faith. His employer objected because it was too far from the place of employment. The first issue is whether an employee's residence may be determined by an employer. The second is, if so, then may an exception be carried out to accommodate this employee because of his religious beliefs.

CASE

VETTER v. FARMLAND INDUSTRIES, INC.

884 F. Supp. 1287 (N.D. Iowa 1995)

BENNETT, District Judge.

The summary judgment record reveals that the following facts are undisputed: Vetter and his wife are adherents of the Jewish faith. Although Mrs. Vetter had been born into the Jewish faith, Vetter had converted to Judaism in a ceremony only about four months prior to Vetter's employment with Farmland. Prior to his employment with Farmland, Vetter and his family were living in Muscatine, Iowa, a town without a significant Jewish community. While living in Muscatine, the Vetters travelled approximately thirty miles to attend regular religious services. Farmland is an agricultural products company that sells supplies to the farming community. Farmland is a corporation owned by its member farm cooperatives. In its Webster City trade area, Farmland works with United Co-op, a member farm cooperative, to sell farming supplies to farmers in the area.

Vetter applied for a job with Farmland as a Livestock Production Specialist (LPS) in July of 1992. The principal job duties of an LPS are to work in conjunction with the management of the assigned cooperative to sell Farmland livestock feed and animal health products within the cooperative's trade territory. Vetter had an initial telephone interview with George Gleckler, Farmland's Area Feed Sales Manager. In-person interviews with Farmland officials followed in early and mid-August.

Vetter's mid-August interview was with Gleckler, Dave Engstrom, who was Farmland's LPS Supervisor, Al Jorth, the General Manager for the United Co-op, and Ken Bever, a Supervisor for the United Co-op. During this interview, Mr. Jorth asked how soon Vetter could start, and also asked about Vetter's interest in purchasing or renting housing. Mr. Jorth suggested that rental housing would be difficult to find. Following the interview, in a separate conversation, Gleckler informed Vetter that he "could live where he could find a house," which Vetter understood to mean anywhere within a reasonable distance of Webster City. The evening following the interview, Vetter and his wife drove around Webster City for approximately forty-five minutes looking for appropriate housing.

Gleckler offered Vetter the job in Webster City by telephone on August 21, 1992. In a follow-up telephone call on August 24, Vetter indicated that they had been looking for housing in Ames, approximately 35 miles from Webster City, because it had an active synagogue. Gleckler responded that Ames might be "a little far," but that he would check on it. Later that evening, Gleckler called Vetter back to inform him that he had found out that there was a synagogue in Fort Dodge, Iowa. Vetter began working for Farmland on September 1, 1992, by attending a sales meeting in Des Moines, at which he again raised the issue of living in Ames with Gleckler. Gleckler reiterated that he thought that Ames would not be acceptable. Again during meetings in Kansas City on September 9th and 10th, 1992, Vetter discussed the possibility of living in Ames with Terry Allen, Farmland's regional Feed Manager. Allen also indicated that Ames would not be an acceptable place for Vetter to live. Gleckler and Allen suggested that Vetter look further in Webster city and Fort Dodge. The Vetters rejected Fort Dodge after learning that the synagogue there was essentially "inactive," providing services only every few months, and that there was no Jewish community of significant size or activity. The Vetters also considered the only housing they had found in Webster city that was large enough to accommodate their whole family inadequate on the grounds that they believed it was in a government subsidized complex for which they would not qualify and which they did not think was adequate.

On September 21, 1992, Gleckler told Vetter that the had learned that Vetter was planning to rent housing in Ames. Vetter explained that he had put a small deposit on one residence in Ames. Vetter was therefore terminated effective September 21, 1992. Vetter asserts that he was not given any reason for his termination at the time he was discharged. The employee separation form filled out by Terry Allen has checked as the reason for discharge "other," and in the space provided for explanation "Relocation within trade territory was condition of employment. Employee refused to locate as required." Gleckler, Vetter's supervisor, testified in deposition that Vetter was terminated for "insubordination." In answer to interrogatories from Vetter, Farmland identified as the reason for his discharge that Vetter "apparently was not willing to live within the trade territory he was responsible for servicing after having been informed as to the requirement and after having agreed to do so."

There are a number of factual disputes raised by the Parties, some of which are material to disposition of this case. A key dispute in this matter is whether Farmland officials ever specifically told Vetter that Ames was an unacceptable place for him to live. Farmland asserts that Vetter was told on a number of occasions that Ames would not be acceptable. Vetter asserts that he was never told Ames was unacceptable, just that various people doubted that it would be acceptable, and that every time he raised the issue, it was apparent that Farmland officials preferred that he live closer to Webster City, because he was encouraged to keep looking in the surrounding area.

Juxtaposed to this dispute over the genuineness of Farmland's interest in where Vetter lives is the dispute of the parties over whether Vetter's desire to live in Ames was based on his religious beliefs or merely on personal preference. Vetter has provided the affidavit of Rabbi Stanley Hernan, who affirms that "living in an active Jewish community with an active synagogue is essential to the sustenance of one's faith as a Jew, so much so that it rises to the level of being a niitzvah (Jewish law)." However, Farmland points out that Vetter formerly lived in a community that had no such active Jewish community, and the court observes that a great many Jews in this area of the country do not live in such an "active Jewish community."

The parties also dispute the availability and definition of "suitable" housing in the Webster City trade area. Vetter has found little housing of any kind available either for sale or rent in Webster City, Vetter said that he doubted that his family would be qualified for housing suggested by Farmland because it was government subsidized. Vetter admits that he considered the housing complex in question otherwise unacceptable for personal reasons. Farmland asserts that Vetter was unduly selective in his definition of suitable housing and made inadequate efforts to find housing within the trade territory.

Vetter's complaint alleges discrimination on the basis of religion on two theories. First, Vetter alleges that he was subjected to disparate treatment, because other LPSs have been allowed to live either outside of their trade areas or at greater distances from cooperatives that they serve than he would have been if allowed to live in Ames, and further that other LPSs were not terminated, whereas he was, for desiring to live or living outside of their trade areas. Second, Vetter alleges that Farmland refused to make reasonable accommodations to his religious observances or practices by refusing to allow him to live in Ames, or to allow him to live in Webster City while his family lived in Ames. The court will consider whether Farmland is entitled to summary judgment on either of these claims.

A disparate treatment case based on religion requires the plaintiff to show that he or she is, or was, treated less favorably than others because of the plaintiff's religion. Thus, the plaintiff in a disparate case based on religion must prove he or she is a member of a protected class and must compare his or her treatment to that of a similarly situated member of a non-protected class in his complaint.

Vetter argues that Farmland refused to make reasonable accommodations to his religious beliefs because Farmland refused to consider his suggestion that he maintain a residence for himself in Webster City while his family lived in Ames. Vetter has since argued that he also suggested as a reasonable accommodation that he bear any additional costs of his travel to his trade

area that might result if he and his family were to live in Ames. Farmland argues that nothing about Vetter's religion required him to live in Ames, or outside of the trade area, therefore it was under no obligation to provide any accommodation. Farmland has also, at least implicitly, suggested that by pointing out that Fort Dodge had a synagogue and that Vetter could live there, they offered a reasonable accommodation.

To reiterate, Vetter must make the following prima facie showing in support of his claim of failure to accommodate his religion: (1) Vetter has a bona fide belief that compliance with an employment requirement is contrary to his religious faith; (2) Vetter informed Farmland about the conflict; and (3) Vetter asserts that a religious belief is incompatible with a requirement of employment. On this issue: Vetter was a recent convert to Judaism, and his children were endeavoring to pursue religious training in that faith. Thus, the growth of the family's faith during the period in question is uncontradicted. Because Vetter was a recent convert to Judaism, the court finds that his prior conduct in Muscatine is of little relevance to the question of the sincerity of his belief in a need to live in a Jewish community. To the extent that is relevant, the court finds that Vetter's uncontradicted testimony is that even had Vetter not taken the job with Farmland, they would have attempted to move to the Quad Cities area, because of its active Jewish community. Their evidence, again uncontroverted, is that their plans to move to the Quad Cities for this reason before Vetter was offered the job with Farmland were thwarted by floods in the area. Furthermore, the sincerity of Vetter's belief is reinforced by his conduct of asserting the belief in the face of opposition from his employer, and in his offers to provide for that belief at some personal cost in his offers either to pay for extra travel costs or to live in Webster City while his family lives in Ames. Thus, the court finds as a matter of law that Vetter's religious beliefs in question here were indeed sincerely held. As to the third element, there is no dispute that Vetter was discharged because of noncompliance with the employment requirement that he live within his trade area. Vetter has established at least a genuine issue of material fact in each element of his prima facie case of disparate treatment because of religion and on the question of whether Farmland's proffered legitimate reason for his discharge is pretextual. The court concludes that the elements of a prima facie case of disparate treatment because of religion are as follows: (1) the plaintiff was a member of a protected class because of the plaintiff's religious affiliation or beliefs; (2) the employee informed the employer of his or her religious beliefs; (3) the plaintiff was qualified for the position; (4) despite plaintiff's qualifications, the plaintiff was fired or denied an employment benefit; and (5) similarly situated employees, outside of the plaintiff's protected class were treated differently or there is other evidence giving rise to an inference of discrimination.

Examining these elements in this light the court finds that there is no significant dispute that Vetter was a member of a protected class on the basis of his adherence to the Jewish faith, he informed his employer of his adherence to that faith, he was qualified for the position in which he was employed, and he was fired from that position. Vetter has generated a genuine issue of material fact to go with the final element of his prima facie case because, although he was hired and fired essentially by the same person, there is no presumption that the termination was not discriminatory, because it was only after he was hired that Farmland officials learned of his religious affiliation, and because of evidence of more favorable treatment of similarly situated LPSs who were not members of his faith.

Judgment for Vetter.

Case Commentary

The Northern District of Iowa decided that an employer has no right to determine where its employees live especially if the employees have chosen a community for religious reasons.

Case Questions

1. Are you in agreement with the Court's decision?
2. Why do you think the employer cared where Vetter lived?
3. Under what circumstances should an employer be able to require a worker to live at or near the job?

EMPLOYMENT PERSPECTIVE

Mustafa Darey, a Rastafarian, wore his hair in dreadlocks. When he was hired by Faster Food Service, he was told he would have to cut them. He refused. Mustafa filed a claim with the EEOC citing the wearing of dreadlocks were part of his religion. Faster Food maintained it was unsanitary in violation of Health Department regulations. Will Mustafa prevail? It may be possible to accommodate Mustafa by having him enclose his hair in a plastic cap. If Mustafa refuses, then his religious practice will be overridden for public health reasons. ■

FIRST AMENDMENT PROTECTION

The First Amendment to the United States Constitution addresses religion in two respects. First, it prohibits the government from establishing a national religion. Freedom from religious persecution is an important reason why many immigrants came to this country. Permitting people the freedom to choose how, when, and where to worship is an important consideration in this country. Allowing others to discriminate because of religion not only compromises this First Amendment right but also promotes the economic advantages of belonging to one religion. The latter factor violates the Establishment Clause.

The First Amendment also promotes the freedom to associate. If a person chooses to associate socially only with members of his or her own religion, that is a protected choice. Employment, however, is not social; it is economic. It is unfair for an employer to choose its employees on the basis of their religious preference. How is this characteristic job related? It is not. Employers should respect the right of employees to worship as they please on their own time and, if possible, should reasonably accommodate their employees to enable them to do so.

❖ EMPLOYER LESSONS

- Decide what religious accommodations to provide for your employees.
- Realize that you cannot discriminate in making an employment decision because of the religion of an applicant or an employee.
- Recognize that food safety is paramount to religious practices involving facial hair or hair length.
- Learn the significance of the First Amendment of the United States Constitution for religion.
- Know that religion is a suspect class under Title VII of the Civil Rights Act.
- Understand that you do not have to permit religious services to be conducted at the workplace.
- Be aware that you do not have to allow employees to promote their religious or political beliefs at the workplace.
- Be cognizant of the fact that religious institutions may employ members of their own faith to promote their religion.
- Acknowledge the fact that a person's religion has no bearing on their ability to perform a job.

❖ EMPLOYEE LESSONS

- Familiarize yourself with the protections afforded your religious beliefs by the First Amendment.
- Be aware that you cannot be discriminated against in employment because of your religion.
- Be cognizant of the fact that if you choose to live in a certain area because of your religious affiliation, your employer cannot tell you otherwise.
- Know that an employer must accommodate your religious belief if it is reasonable.
- Learn that you may not promote your religious and political beliefs in the workplace.
- Understand that religious institutions have the right to refuse employment to those not of the same faith in positions where knowledge or belief in that religion is necessary.
- Realize that you cannot conduct a religious service at the workplace.
- Appreciate that your seniority under a collective bargaining agreement will not be compromised by another employee's request for religious accommodation.
- Be aware that religious practices can never take precedence over food safety.
- Know that an employer may never have to grant a request for accommodation if that which is required exceeds what the religion itself requires of its members.

❖ CONCLUSION

Employers should not pry into the personal lives of their employees any more than they would like their employees seeking personal information about them or their top executives. If everyone converted to a particular religion, their job performance would not therefore improve. Thus, employers have no right to discriminate because of religion.

Employers need only consider global trade. It would be a foolish thought for an employer to trade only with countries having the same religion as the employer. More so, if an employer establishes a subsidiary overseas or otherwise employs foreign people to work on its behalf, it would be nearly impossible to discriminate on the basis of religion, race, or national origin. Religious discrimination is rendered impracticable in a global environment. The same philosophy should apply domestically. The practice of any form of discrimination weakens the employer by narrowing the pool of qualified candidates available for the job.

❖ REVIEW QUESTIONS

1. Define religious discrimination.
2. Explain the significance of the First Amendment with respect to religious discrimination.
3. Define reasonable accommodation for religious observances.
4. Can an employer refuse to accommodate an employee's religious belief because it imposes a hardship?
5. How can an employer discern whether a group to which an employee claims membership qualifies as a religion?
6. Can religious belief qualify as a bona fide occupational qualification?
7. May an employee dress in his or her religious garb at work?
8. Must an employer allow the wearing of a button saying "Stop Abortion Now"?
9. Is religious grooming an acceptable practice in the workplace?
10. May an employer question the authenticity and genuineness of an employee's religion?
11. Plaintiff has brought suit under 42 U.S.C. 1983, contending that Defendants deprived him of his civil rights by offering Christian prayers at university-sponsored functions that he is required to attend. Plaintiff also complains that Defendant Onwubiko holds Bible study classes at the Engineering School. Plaintiff alleges that the promotion of these religious activities in such a manner violates the Establishment Clause of the First Amendment. He further contends that requiring students and faculty to attend such events violates their rights under the Free Exercise Clause of the First Amendment. What was the result? *Chaudmuri v. State of Tennessee,* 886 F.Supp. 1374 (M.D. Tenn. 1995)
12. An action was brought by two members of the Native American Church who had been denied unemployment compensation by the State of Oregon. Compensation had been denied because the two workers had been discharged by their private employer for "misconduct." The "misconduct" was the ingestion of peyote at a religious ceremony. Oregon law made the possession of peyote a crime and provided no exception for religious use. The two church members claimed that the denial of unemployment benefits on that ground violated their First Amendment right to free exercise of their religion. Was this an act of religious discrimination? *Employment Division, Dept. of Human Resources of Oregon v. Smith,* 494 U.S. 872 (1990)
13. The facts as found show that Mary E. Schumaker, a member of the United Pentecostal Church, was employed by the District as an interpreter and tutor for deaf students. Schumaker would not take God's name in vain nor use everyday swear words. She interpreted the line in *Gone With the Wind,* "Frankly my dear, I don't give a damn," as "Frankly, I don't care."

    The District board then adopted the committee's guidelines, including the requirement of literal word for word interpretation to the deaf students. Because she would not work at the District's high school under the new guidelines, she was terminated. What was the result? *Sedalia School Dist. v. Commission on Human Rights,* 843 S.W.2d 928 (Mo.App. W.D. 1992)

14. Should religious beliefs be accorded reasonable accommodation in the workplace?

15. Should an employer be allowed to dictate where an employee lives in regard to his or her proximity to the workplace?

16. Should employees be allowed to express their religious beliefs through the wearing of buttons at the workplace?

❖ WEB SITES

www.eeoc.gov/facts/fs-relig.html
www.findlaw.com
www.chicagolegalnet.com/religion.htm
http://hydra.gsa.gov/eeo/newpage110.htm
http://prairielaw.com/articles/chnl20/artcl1116.asp
www.multifaithnet.org/religdiscrim/reports.htm
www.davislevin.com/facts/fs-relig.html
www.westbuslaw.com

CHAPTER

14

NATIONAL ORIGIN

INTRODUCTION

Individuals are protected from discrimination based on national origin under Title VII of the Civil Service Rights Act and the Immigration Reform and Control Act of 1986. National origin refers to a person's roots, that is, the country in which the person or the person's ancestors were born. The four-step test for national origin discrimination is as follows:

1. Employee belongs to the protected class.
2. Employee wanted to retain or obtain the position.
3. Employee was terminated or applicant was refused employment.
4. Termination or refusal to hire occurred because of employee's or applicant's national origin.

CHAPTER CHECKLIST

❖ Define national origin.

❖ Know what rights to employment are afforded to resident aliens.

❖ Learn that discrimination against an applicant or employee because of his or her spouse's national origin is a violation of Title VII.

❖ Appreciate that discrimination against people because of the national origin of their surname is impermissible.

❖ Be aware of the documentation required to work in this country.

❖ Understand that national origin is a suspect class covered under Title VII of the Civil Rights Act.

❖ Be apprised of the purpose of the Immigration Reform and Control Act.

❖ Be familiar with the number of employees required for the application of each act.

❖ Recognize that the Immigration Reform and Control Act applies to all workers employed in the United States, but it has no application to American workers employed abroad.

❖ Realize what is required to bring a disparate treatment case for national origin discrimination.

EMPLOYMENT SCENARIO

Faruq Salio and Mohammed Khad, both Pakistani immigrants, apply for a job as sales associates at the Long and the Short of It (L&S) men's clothing store. Both have three years' experience in the importation and sale of women's clothing. During an interview with Faruq and Mohammad, Tom Long discovers that their three years of experience is in women's clothing. Tom explains to the candidates that L&S was looking for experience in the sale of men's clothing. Faruq and Mohammed state that the skills are similar. Tom begs to differ. Tom explains that he has been in the business for 25 years, so he knows what is best for L&S. Faruq and Mohammed leave feeling disgruntled. Tom brags to his partner, Mark, about how easily he got rid of those "Towel Heads." Mark agrees and tells Tom that that is why Tom is such a valuable partner. Meanwhile, Faruq asks his neighbor, Jim Byrnes, to visit L&S the next day and request an interview. As a favor, Jim does as Faruq requests. Jim is hired on the spot although he has no sales experience. Tom Long assures Jim that L&S will train him for the sales associate position. When they learn about this, Faruq and Mohammed file a claim with the EEOC. Upon being apprised of this Susan North, Esq. is livid. She is adamant about impressing Tom and Mark with the fact that this is the twentieth century—no ethnic discrimination is allowed. Tom and Mark argue that this is their business; why can't they choose to hire those individuals who fit the image L&S is seeking to project? Susan responds that Title VII, ADEA, and ADA override L&S's rights, in that these laws protect all groups of people. Tom and Mark do not want to hire Faruq and Mohammed. Susan concludes by reiterating that the days of businesses with exclusively white male employees are gone.

EMPLOYMENT PERSPECTIVE

Manolo Fuentes is a Spanish-American; his ancestors came from Spain. When Manolo applies for a position as a stockbroker with Bull and Bear after graduating at the top of his university class, he is offered a job in the mail room. When he questions this offer, a manager from Bull and Bear informs him that "this is where you Puerto Ricans belong." Manolo corrects Bull and Bear about his heritage, but the manager retorts, "You are all the same." Manolo argues that it should not matter whether he is from Spain, Puerto Rico, Latin America, or Mexico and that he should be judged on the basis of his qualifications, not regional or ethnic stereotypes. Will Manolo win? Yes! Offering a person a low-level position solely because he or she is from Spain, Puerto Rico, Latin America, or Mexico is in violation of Title VII's prohibition against national origin discrimination. ▪

The issue in the following case is whether the plaintiff was subject to national origin discrimination due to the employer's unfavorable treatment toward those physicians who had trained in Mexico.

MUZQUIZ, JR., M.D. v. W.A. FOOTE MEMORIAL HOSPITAL, INC.

70 F.3d 422 (6th Cir. 1995)

JONES, Circuit Judge.

Plaintiff Dr. Moses Muzquiz appeals the judgment for Defendant W.A. Foote Memorial Hospital, Inc. ("Hospital") in this action. The Hospital cross-appeals, arguing that this court should assess attorney fees and costs pursuant to the Health Care Quality Improvement Act ("HCQIA"). For the reasons that follow we affirm the decision of the district court, and we deny the Hospital's request for attorney fees and costs for this appeal.

BACKGROUND

Dr. Muzquiz was born in Texas in 1932, is of Hispanic origin (Mexican-Indian), and graduated from a Mexican medical school in 1963. Dr. Muzquiz completed his residency in internal medicine/cardiology in 1968 and has performed invasive cardiology, including heart catheterizations, since that time.

In 1985, Dr. Muzquiz moved from Texas to Michigan and commenced a cardiology practice. From 1985-89, Dr. Muzquiz performed no cardiac catheterizations in Michigan, but did travel to Mexico for several weeks each year where he performed that procedure.

In January 1989, Dr. Muzquiz became a member of the provisional staff of Defendant Hospital, which is a not for profit institution. In late 1990, the Hospital was in the process of establishing a cardiac catheterization laboratory, which opened on January 1, 1991.[1] In November 1990, Dr. Muzquiz, along with ten other cardiologists, applied for invasive cardiology privileges at the Hospital, which would become available upon the opening of the cardiac catheterization laboratory. Dr. Muzquiz was the only applicant of Mexican-Indian extraction, and he was also the oldest applicant. At the time Muzquiz applied, the Hospital had adopted "Guidelines for Credentialling in Invasive Cardiology," that had been promulgated by the American College of Cardiology. As relevant to the instant case, the Guidelines state the following:

a. In addition to meeting the basic qualifications (above), a physician who seeks to independently perform invasive cardiology procedures shall meet the following specific requirements:

b. A favorable review of medical charts and films of patients for whom the physician served as primary physician for diagnostic catheterizations in the past year selected at random. The number of charts, the manner of random selection, and the reviewers shall be determined by the Service Director. If there is an expense of such review, it shall be borne by the physician seeking privileges. A physician who is board certified or an active board candidate, or whose skills are known on a firsthand basis by the Service Director may be exempted from this requirement in the discretion of the Service Director.

At the core of the instant dispute is the difficulty Dr. Muzquiz encountered in trying to meet requirement 3b. Dr. Muzquiz had performed all of his recent cardiac catheterizations during his trips to Mexico. Consequently, to comply with requirement 3b, it was necessary to obtain the films and charts of the catheterizations he had performed in the past year from the hospital in Mexico. The Internal Medicine Executive Committee determined that ten films and charts needed to be reviewed. On September 18, 1991, already almost a year after Dr. Muzquiz had applied for catheterization privileges, Dr. Frank Morales, Administrator and CEO of the hospital in Mexico forwarded the English translation of ten patient charts.

The Credentials Committee then sent all of Dr. Muzquiz's information to an outside consultant, Dr. Fierens, for a review and recommendation regarding Dr. Muzquiz's request for catheterization privileges. Dr. Fierens recommended review of properly authenticated catheterization films of Dr. Muzquiz's past four years experience prior to making a final assessment of Dr. Muzquiz's qualifications.

On December 11, 1991, the Credentials Committee informed Dr. Muzquiz that they needed (1) a written explanation from Dr. Morales as to why the actual case logs and copies of the films corresponding to the ten translated charts sent were not available, and (2) copies of the actual medical records that had been translated. Upon receipt and review of that documentation, the Committee was prepared to recommend Dr. Muzquiz for provisional cardiac catheterization privileges conditioned on a favorable evaluation of his first ten catheterization procedures. In a letter dated December 31, 1991, Dr. Morales explained that the requested films were unavailable because the hospital followed a policy of giving the films to the patients at the time of discharge. With respect to the original Spanish records of the charts, Dr. Morales explained that it was the policy of the hospital not to release the records. He stated, however, that he had prepared the English translations himself, and that they were exact translations of the Spanish records. The Credentials Committee determined that this was a satisfactory explanation and went forward with its recommendation.

On January 15, 1992, however, the Medical Executive Committee voted to reject the recommendation of the Credentials Committee with respect to the ten proctored cases, and instead recommended proctoring Muzquiz' first twenty-five cases. As noted in the minutes of that committee meeting, this recommendation is based on

information from the Journal of the American College of Cardiology, November 1, 1991, Volume 18, Number 5, Page 1166:

"If the time away from the cardiac catheterization has been 1-3 years, the physician should undergo a period of preceptorship, working under the direct observation of the laboratory director until the director can certify the competence of that individual. This work should include at least 25 cases with a variety of diagnoses." Meanwhile, Dr. Muzquiz and the Credentials Committee were engaging in increasingly disharmonious correspondence over the nature of the ten-proctored cases arrangement.

On January 22, 1992, the Board of Trustees met and voted to approve the Medical Executive Committee's recommendation. On February 4, 1992, Tejada, the President of the Hospital, informed Dr. Muzquiz that his request for catheterization privileges had been granted in accordance with the recommendation of the Medical Executive Committee. Tejada also forwarded the curricula vitae of three independent physicians proposed by the hospital to be proctors for Dr. Muzquiz's first twenty-five cases.

On February 11, 1992, Dr. Muzquiz expressed disapproval of the selected proctors because he considered them to be direct competitors for consultations and other cardiovascular procedures. He thus again recommended "someone or some group from well beyond the same or contiguous geographical area to insure objectivity in the review process," and offered to help in the selection process. He also expressed reservations about the number of cases that were to be proctored. On February 13, 1992, Dr. Muzquiz registered his strong objection to the twenty-five proctored cases requirement, and asked for reconsideration of the ten-proctored cases arrangement as initially recommended by the Credentials Committee. On March 17, Dr. Muzquiz met with representatives of the Hospital and refused to accept the terms of the provisional grant of catheterization privileges. On March 25, 1992, the Board of Trustees deemed the provisional grant of privileges withdrawn, and determined that if Dr. Muzquiz still wished to seek privileges that he would have to reapply.

Dr. Muzquiz then brought suit in federal court. As originally filed by Dr. Muzquiz on September 21, 1992, and as amended on May 27,

1993, the complaint alleged seven counts, including claims for breach of contract, violations of Title VII.

After two days of deliberation, the jury concluded that Dr. Muzquiz had not been discriminated against due to his age or national origin.

Discriminatory Impact Theory

Starting from the facially neutral requirement of the Credentialling Guidelines of providing films and charts, the most Dr. Muzquiz could show with respect to disparate impact would be a negative effect on those who trained in Mexico, and not those who were of Mexican heritage. Those who receive training in Mexico are simply not a protected class for purposes of discrimination analysis under Title VII. The district court did not err in rejecting the disparate impact theory presented by Dr. Muzquiz below; nor is Dr. Muzquiz entitled to a rehearing on the new disparate impact theory he presents to this court.

Although ultimately the law was not in Dr. Muzquiz's favor, his appeal had legal foundation. The district court made certain discretionary determinations to exclude evidence at trial, and Dr. Muzquiz sought to reverse those rulings through appropriate, although ultimately unsuccessful, legal arguments. Dr. Muzquiz sought to challenge the district court's interpretation of Michigan law with respect to his breach of contract claim. Overall, his arguments before this court, although ultimately unsuccessful, were not completely without legal foundation. We thus hold that the Hospital is not entitled to attorney fees for this appeal.

CONCLUSION

For the reasons just stated, we affirm the decision of the district court and we deny the request for attorney fees and costs on appeal.

Case Commentary

The Sixth Circuit concluded that Muzquiz was not discriminated against due to his national origin because Title VII protection extends to those of Mexican heritage, not to physicians trained in Mexico.

Case Questions

1. Do you agree with the Court's decision?
2. Should the Court distinguish between training in Mexico and being of Mexican heritage?
3. Why do you think the hospital wanted copies of the Mexican records in Spanish?

The issue presented in the case that follows is whether the plaintiff was subject to national origin discrimination by university professors who refused to allow the plaintiff to sit in a particular row in their classrooms.

SALEHPOUR v. UNIVERSITY OF TENNESSEE

159 F.3d 199 (6th Cir. 1998)

CLAY, Circuit Judge.

Plaintiff, Samad Salehpour, appeals from the order entered by the United States District Court for the Western District of Tennessee granting Defendant, the University of Tennessee's motion for summary judgment in this case arising Title VI of the Civil Rights Act of 1964, 42 U.S.C. § 2000d; § 504 of the Rehabilitation Act of 1973, 29 U.S.C. § 794, and Title II of the Americans with Disabilities Act ("ADA"), 42 U.S.C. § 12131 et seq.; 42 U.S.C. § 1983; and ancillary state law claims of intentional and negligent infliction of emotional distress. For the reasons stated herein, the district court's order is AFFIRMED.

STATEMENT OF FACTS

Plaintiff (who was forty-three years old at the time he filed this appeal) is a native of Iran and has been a citizen of the United States since 1979. Because of his Iranian ethnicity, Plaintiff is dark complected and speaks with an accent. Plaintiff was admitted to the College of Dentistry ("College") at the University of Tennessee ("University") as a first-year dental student on August 12, 1994, after a twelve-year career as a mechanical engineer in the aerospace industry.

Dr. William F. Bowles (Chair of the Department of Prosthodontics, Professor in the Department of Prosthodontics, and a Member of the Academic Status Committee (the "Committee") at the University), as well as Dr. Victor A. Fletcher (Associate Professor in the Department of Prosthodontics at the University), have a policy of barring first-year dental students from sitting in the last row of their classrooms. Dr. Bowles informed Plaintiff and his classmates on the first day of class of this policy. On January 31, 1995, Dr. Bowles and Dr. Lynch (Associate Dean of the College and a Professor in the Department of Orthodontics at the University) met with Plaintiff, at his request, regarding the "last row rule" and other matters of concern, such as Dr. Bowles classroom dress code. At the meeting, Dr. Lynch informed Plaintiff that Dr. Bowles had every right to tell his students where he wished them to sit in his classroom, and that by accepting admission into the College, Plaintiff agreed to abide by all of the rules, not just the ones that suited his temperament.

Less than one week later, Plaintiff wrote a letter to Dr. Bowles reiterating the same concerns addressed at the meeting, including Plaintiff's displeasure with the "last row rule." The next day, February 7, 1995, Plaintiff sat in the last row of Dr. Bowles' class. Dr. Bowles allowed Plaintiff to remain seated in the last row, so as not to disturb the class. However, in a letter dated February 9, 1995, addressed to Plaintiff, Dr. Bowles expressed his displeasure with Plaintiff's decision to sit in the last row (despite the numerous requests not to do so), and warned Plaintiff that he would be instructed to leave the classroom if he violated the "last row rule" again.

Plaintiff alleged that he desired to sit in the last row because he could see and hear better in that location, and that he found sitting elsewhere to be disruptive to his thinking process. Plaintiff stated that he perceived the dispute over his decision to sit in the last row as a "power struggle" between him and the professors, and refused to comply with rule, especially since he had informed the professors how he felt about the issue.

The Committee decided that a letter of severe reprimand would be sent to Plaintiff and that the letter would be incorporated into his academic record. In addition, it was decided that Plaintiff would be required to apologize in a timely fashion to his professors and classmates for the disruptive episodes during educational periods. Finally, it was decided that Plaintiff would be placed on disciplinary probation for the entirety of his matriculation at the College, and warned that he would be dismissed if found guilty of other academic infractions.

Plaintiff appeared at the appeal and was allowed to speak out of the presence of Dr. Lynch. Thereafter, the Appeals Committee affirmed the decision against Plaintiff with modifications, and Slagle informed Plaintiff of the outcome of his appeal by way of letter dated May 4, 1995. Four days later, Plaintiff sent Dr. Slagle a letter informing him that Plaintiff was voluntarily withdrawing from the College. Despite his voluntary withdrawal from the College, Plaintiff still submitted appeals to Joseph E. Johnson (President of the University) and William R. Rice (Chancellor of the University), which were subsequently denied.

Plaintiff filed suit against Defendants alleging ethnic discrimination.

On March 10, 1997, the district court entered an "Order Granting Defendants' Motion for Summary Judgment on Plaintiff's Federal Claims and Dismissing Without Prejudice Plaintiff's State Law Claims." Plaintiff filed a motion for reconsideration of the district court's order, which was denied. This appeal ensued.

DISCUSSION

Indeed, the First Amendment right to freedom of expression of political, social, religious, and other such views may be most precious in an educational setting. However, as in the instant case, where the expression appears to have no intellectual content or even discernable purpose, and amounts to nothing more than expression of a personal proclivity designed to disrupt the educational process, such expression is not protected and does violence to the spirit and purpose of the First Amendment. The rights afforded to students to freely express their ideas and views without fear of administrative reprisal, must be balanced against the compelling interest of the academicians to educate in an environment that is free of purposeless distractions and is conducive to teaching. Under the facts of this case, the balance clearly weighs in favor of the University.

Accordingly, Plaintiff's claim fails to present a constitutional violation because Plaintiff's conduct did not constitute protected speech. As such, the issue of qualified immunity need not be further explored, and it may be concluded that the district court properly granted Defendants' motion for summary judgment.

CONCLUSION

For the above stated reasons, we AFFIRM the district court's order granting summary judgment in favor of Defendants.

Case Commentary

The Sixth Circuit ruled that the "last row rule," which prohibited first year students such as Salehpour from sitting in the last classroom row, was not predicated on national origin or on any other federal statute. The court added that selection of class seating is not protected by the First Amendment either.

Case Questions

1. Do you agree with the Court's decision?
2. Why would someone drop out of dental school to argue over a policy regarding classroom seating?
3. Do you think the professors were enforcing this policy against Salehpour because of his national origin?

Not only is discrimination against a person for his or her own national origin prohibited, but the issue can also be raised by a person who is discriminated against because of

1. his or her spouse's national origin;
2. membership in an association of a particular national origin;

3. attendance at a school or religious institution identified with people of a specific national origin; or

4. the association of his or her name with persons of a particular national origin.

The Immigration Reform and Control Act requires that employers discern whether their employees are citizens or immigrants. If they are immigrants, the employer must verify the documentation of the employee to determine whether he or she has legal immigration status.

A passport, Certificate of U.S. citizenship, a Certificate of Naturalization, or a resident alien card is sufficient. A Social Security Card or Certificate of U.S. Birth, when combined with a driver's license, are also appropriate. The employer must photocopy these documents for verification. The individual must attest that either he or she is a U.S. citizen or an alien lawfully admitted for permanent residence.

ETHNIC HARASSMENT

Joke telling, disparaging remarks, and slang epithets about people's ethnic origins may create a hostile work environment if they are severe and pervasive.

The questions presented in the following case are whether the plaintiff's claim of national origin harassment was severe and pervasive, and whether his claims for discrimination as well as harassment were time barred.

CASE

FILIPOVIC v. K & R EXPRESS SYSTEMS, INC.

176 F.3d 390 (7th Cir. 1999)

COFFEY, Circuit Judge.
On July 19, 1993, the plaintiff-appellant, Momcilo Filipovic ("Filipovic"), filed charges with the Equal Employment Opportunity Commission ("EEOC"), alleging that his employer, the defendant-appellee K&R Express Systems, Inc., ("K&R") discriminated against him because of his Yugoslavian origin and in retaliation for prior complaints of discrimination. Specifically, Filipovic contended that he was denied a promotion, was "harassed and subjected to derogatory language," and was given written warnings for various rule infractions. On December 20, 1993, Filipovic filed additional charges with the EEOC, this time complaining of retaliation based on K&R's denial of overtime and vacation requests. Some seven months later, on July 19, 1994, Fil-

ipovic filed other charges with the EEOC, alleging that, on the basis of his age, he was "rejected for a promotion." The EEOC issued findings of no cause on all three filings, and Filipovic filed suit in the United States District Court for the Northern District of Illinois, alleging discrimination based on national origin under Title VII of the Civil Rights Act of 1964. Filipovic did not pursue the age discrimination charge. K&R filed a motion for summary judgment which the trial court granted, ruling that certain allegedly discriminatory actions suffered by the plaintiff were time-barred under Illinois law and that the remaining actions did not create a hostile work environment. The plaintiff appeals, contending that he properly stated a claim of discrimination based on national origin under Title VII. We affirm.

I. BACKGROUND

Filipovic was born in Yugoslavia on July 10, 1939. In 1973, he emigrated to the United States, obtained citizenship, and took up residence in Illinois. On January 26, 1982, Filipovic was hired by K&R as a full-time dockman and joined the International Brotherhood of Teamsters, Local Union No. 710 ("union"). Beginning in 1984 and throughout his employment with K&R, Filipovic contends that he was subjected to a "continuing violation" of discrimination based upon his national origin. The centerpiece of his charge of discrimination is Filipovic's allegation that he was repeatedly called names and subjected to vulgar language by his coworkers for the eleven years of his employment prior to his filing suit. For example, coworkers referred to him as "scumbag," "pyromaniac," "piece of ass," "piece of shit," "stupid asshole," "sheep fucker," and "Russian dick head." According to Filipovic, K&R supervisory personnel also engaged in coarse language directed toward him at work. Sometime prior to 1990, Filipovic was called a "dirty Commie" by a former supervisor, and in 1993, another K&R supervisor called him a "fucking foreigner," and commented, with respect to the civil war in Yugoslavia, that "it seems to me all Serbians are barbarians." The undisputed facts at trial establish that Filipovic engaged in similar behavior, often calling his coworkers names in response.

Filipovic also contends that he was singled out for unfair treatment by K&R's management as a result of his national origin. On April 17, 1984, Filipovic went to lunch with dockman Bill Bartuch ("Bartuch"). Bartuch was well known around the company as having a "big" drinking problem. Intoxication during working hours is a terminable offense at K&R. If management has probable cause to suspect an employee is intoxicated, that employee is sent to a clinic for a blood alcohol test. Furthermore, a blood alcohol test is required under union work rules. Filipovic's supervisor, Jeffery Epstein ("Epstein") was told that Bartuch and Filipovic were seen entering a bar during their lunch break. In accordance with K&R's policies and union rules, Epstein sent Bartuch and Filipovic to submit to a blood alcohol test upon their return from lunch. Filipovic refused because of religious reasons and was discharged. Bartuch, who was not Yugoslavian, took the blood test. The afternoon of his discharge, Fil-

ipovic went to a hospital and submitted to a urine alcohol test, which yielded a negative result for alcohol. After receiving the results, K&R reinstated Filipovic with no disciplinary action.

In 1985, Filipovic contends that he was discriminated against when he was investigated for possibly stealing company property. After freight is reported missing, K&R policy requires all persons who came in contact with the freight, as well as any persons who management believes might have information about the missing freight, to be interviewed by a private investigator. In this case, the investigator asked Filipovic whether he had stolen fifteen calculators from the company, and Filipovic responded that he had not. The investigator went on to interview all other dockworkers as well as Filipovic's supervisor, Epstein.

Filipovic also claims that he was discriminated against for being Yugoslavian when he was denied a promotion to the position of "spotter." Filipovic acknowledges that K&R is bound to follow union-imposed seniority rules in allocating spotter positions to workers. Filipovic admits that he is eleven places lower on the seniority list than the last worker in Filipovic's position who became a spotter. Furthermore, spotter positions are not available frequently; the last time a full-time dockman, such as Filipovic, was trained as a spotter occurred in 1993.

In response to all of these incidents of perceived discrimination against him, Filipovic filed three charges with the EEOC in 1993 and 1994. In each case, the EEOC concluded that Filipovic had not established violations of Title VII. On November 20, 1995, Filipovic filed suit in the U.S. District Court for the Northern District of Illinois, accusing K&R of discrimination based on national origin. The complaint provided that the objectionable conduct of his coworkers and supervisors had created a hostile work environment. K&R filed a motion for summary judgment, and the district court granted the same on December 16, 1997, and dismissed the case, finding that some of the discriminatory acts alleged by Filipovic were time barred under Illinois law and that the remaining acts did not constitute discrimination on the basis of national origin.

II. ISSUES

On appeal, we consider whether the district court erred in failing to find that: (1) allegedly discriminatory acts constituted a "continuing violation" which became cognizable as discrimination based on national origin only after the 300-day period of limitation imposed by 42 U.S.C. sec. 2000e-5(e) had elapsed; (2) a hostile work environment resulted from discrimination based on national origin directed at Filipovic; and (3) Filipovic had produced sufficient evidence of a prima facie case of retaliation by K&R beginning after he filed charges of discrimination with the EEOC.

III. DISCUSSION

According to the Federal Rules of Civil Procedure, a motion for summary judgment must be granted when "there is no genuine issue as to any material fact and … the moving party is entitled to a judgment as a matter of law." In determining whether a genuine issue of material fact exists, "a trial court must view the record and all reasonable inferences drawn therefrom in the light most favorable to the non-moving party." To defeat a motion for summary judgment, the non-moving party cannot rest on the mere allegations or denials contained in his pleadings, but "must present sufficient evidence to show the existence of each element of its case on which it will bear the burden at trial." An appellate court will review de novo the district court's grant of summary judgment.

A. Continuing Violation

Initially, we consider whether the district court erred in failing to find that Filipovic's allegedly discriminatory acts constituted a "continuing violation" which became cognizable as discrimination based on national origin only after the 300-day period of limitation had elapsed. In Illinois, a complainant must file a charge with the EEOC within 300 days of the alleged discriminatory act and failure to do so renders the charge untimely. Because Filipovic filed the first of his three charges of discrimination based on national origin with the EEOC on July 18, 1993, any discriminatory acts which occurred prior to September 21, 1992, would be time-barred, unless Filipovic can show that these acts were "related closely enough" to the acts occurring within the established time frame "to be considered one ongoing violation." The continuing violation doctrine allows a complainant to obtain relief for a time-barred act of discrimination by linking it with acts that fall within the statutory limitations period.

Courts will then treat the series of acts as one continuous act ending within the limitations period. See id. Courts will consider three factors in making this determination: (1) whether the acts involve the same subject matter; (2) the frequency at which they occur; and (3) the degree of permanence of the alleged acts of discrimination, "which should trigger an employee's awareness of and duty to assert his or her rights." The continuing violation doctrine is applicable only if it would have been unreasonable to expect the plaintiff to sue before the statute ran on the conduct, as in a case in which the conduct could constitute, or be recognized, as actionable harassment only in the light of events that occurred later, within the period of the statute of limitations.

By contrast, many of the discriminatory acts which Filipovic has alleged occurred up to thirteen years prior to September 21, 1992, and of those incidents, many involve name-calling by eight fellow dockworkers. This Court has previously held that when "it is evident long before the plaintiff sues that he was the victim of actionable harassment, he cannot reach back and base his suit on conduct that occurred outside the statute of limitations. While a single comment may not be harassment, if the comment is repeated over a period of years, its cumulative effect likely precludes invocation" of the continuing violation doctrine.

With respect to the allegations of disparate treatment by K&R management, to establish a continuing violation, Filipovic must, as discussed earlier, demonstrate that the allegedly discriminatory acts which occurred outside the limitations period were "related closely enough to constitute a continuing violation" with those occurring within the limitations period and not "merely discrete, isolated, and completed acts" which must be regarded as individual violations. Furthermore, in making this determination, courts consider whether the acts involve the same subject matter, the frequency at which they occur, and the degree of permanence of the alleged acts of discrimination.

With respect to the third factor, Filipovic has not shown that these acts were either closely related or motivated by animus against Yugoslavians. Three incidents occurring over a nine year period "cannot reasonably be linked together into a single chain, a single course of conduct, to defeat the statute of limitations."

B. Hostile Work Environment

In determining the existence of a hostile work environment, the district court considered only those incidents that occurred within the statutory time frame, thus on or after September 21, 1992. This included some of the name-calling incidents by both coworkers and supervisors and one incident during which Filipovic was given the undesirable job of unloading a trailer full of rancid food. On this basis, the district court ruled that the conduct of Filipovic's supervisors and coworkers was insufficient to constitute a hostile work environment and that the comments were few in number, were not physically threatening, were spread out over more than a year, and were relatively mild compared to epithets that can be lodged against other racial, ethnic, and religious groups.

As a threshold matter, the district court ruled that Filipovic had shown that he had faced harassment "because of" his national origin, due to the ethnic content of the comments that had been made to him. However, "relatively isolated instances of nonsevere misconduct will not support a claim of a hostile environment." Furthermore, the ethnic slurs at issue were simply part of the normal dock environment and were too infrequent to constitute the "concentrated or insistent barrage" necessary to render Filipovic's claim actionable. Thus, the district court did not err in concluding that the harassment suffered by Filipovic was not severe or pervasive enough to create a hostile work environment.

IV. CONCLUSION

Filipovic has failed to establish that a genuine issue of material fact exists in his employment discrimination claim. In our opinion, the district court properly concluded that incidents of workplace harassment occurring prior to the statutory limitations period were time-barred and that the continuing violation doctrine is inapplicable to his claims of discrimination based on national origin. Further, we agree that Filipovic failed to demonstrate that the harassment he endured was sufficient to create a hostile work environment under Title VII. Finally, the district court correctly ruled that Filipovic fell short of establishing a prima facie case of retaliation by K&R since he offered no direct evidence of a causal connection between his filing charges of discrimination with the EEOC and his subsequent termination.

Affirmed.

Judgment for K&R Express Systems

Case Commentary

The Seventh Circuit ruled that Filipovic's claims of national origin discrimination and harassment were disconnected and time barred.

Case Questions

1. Do you think this case was decided correctly?
2. Why did the Court believe Filipovic's claims were disconnected?
3. Was the language directed at Filipovic severe and pervasive?
4. Should the location where the harassing language was uttered make a difference?

The issues in the following case are whether the ethnic epithets the plaintiff was exposed to were severe and pervasive enough to constitute harassment and so intolerable as to warrant constructive discharge.

AMIRMOKRI v. BALTIMORE GAS AND ELECTRIC COMPANY

60 F.3d 1126 (4th Cir. 1995)

MICHAEL, Circuit Judge.

Homi Amirmokri appeals the district court's grant of summary judgment in favor of Baltimore Gas and Electric Co. (BG&E) on his Title VII claims stemming from alleged mistreatment due to his Iranian national origin. Amirmokri asserts three claims: discriminatory failure to promote, harassment, and constructive discharge. We affirm summary judgment for BG&E on the claim of failure to promote.

However, because genuine issues of material fact exist regarding Amirmokri's constructive discharge claim and because equitable relief may be available to him ultimately on his harassment claim, we reverse the district court's grant of summary judgment on these two claims and remand for further proceedings.

I.

Amirmokri, an Iranian immigrant, interviewed for an engineering position with BG&E in August 1989. During his interview he told BG&E that he was interested in a Senior Engineer position. In October 1989 Amirmokri accepted BG&E's offer for an Engineer position at the Calvert Cliffs nuclear power plant. He says he understood that he would be promoted to Senior Engineer within six months.

Amirmokri alleges the following sequence of events. At the end of March 1990 a Senior Engineer position opened up at Calvert Cliffs. Douglas Lenker, another BG&E employee, was chosen to fill the slot. Amirmokri believed that this was the position he had been promised at the time of his offer and sought an explanation from his supervisors. He first met with Al Thornton, the General Supervisor, in April 1990 to discuss the unrealized promotion. The following month he met with Larry Tucker, who had replaced Thornton as the General Supervisor, about the promo-

tion issue and the way he was being treated by Michael Polak, his engineering work group leader. Tucker, who was new, told Amirmokri that he didn't know anything about the situation but said he would talk to Polak.

Around the time of Amirmokri's meetings with Thornton and Tucker, Polak began to harass Amirmokri by making derogatory references to his Iranian national origin, calling him "the local terrorist," a "camel jockey," "the ayatollah," and "the Emir of Waldorf" (Amirmokri lived in Waldorf, Maryland). Polak encouraged others to do the same thing. He also intentionally embarrassed Amirmokri in front of other employees by saying Amirmokri did not know what he was talking about. Finally, Polak withheld company benefits, like meal money, from Amirmokri.

By late July 1990 the harassment had not ceased. Frustrated, Amirmokri complained to Charlie Cruse, the Department Manager, who arranged for Amirmokri to meet with Bill Dunson, the Employee Grievance Coordinator, in August. Dunson told Amirmokri that he would investigate and get back to him. Dunson claims that he spoke to Polak and several of Polak's superiors, none of whom provided support for Amirmokri's allegations. In September 1990 Amirmokri began to suffer from severe gastric pain. His doctor told him that he was developing an ulcer caused by work-related stress and that he should quit his job if the harassment and stress did not end. By October Amirmokri had not heard back from Dunson, and he went to George Creel, a Vice President of BG&E. Amirmokri requested a transfer to a different job so he would not have to report to Polak.

Creel told him he would investigate and get back to him. Creel also arranged for Amirmokri to see BG&E's clinical psychologist. By November 1990 Amirmokri felt his situation was hopeless, so he resigned. Shortly thereafter he filed complaints with the Equal Employment Opportunity Commission (EEOC) and the Maryland Commission on Human Relations. In September 1992 the EEOC issued a determination that Title VII had not been violated. Amirmokri then sued BG&E in federal court, asserting three claims: (1) discriminatory failure to promote, (2) harassment based on national origin, and (3) constructive discharge. The court then granted BG&E's motion for summary judgment on all three claims.

II.

A. Failure to promote

The district court found that Amirmokri made out a prima facie case of discriminatory failure to promote, and we agree. Amirmokri is of Iranian national origin, placing him in a protected class. He produced evidence that he applied for, and was qualified for, the Senior Engineer position to which Lenker was ultimately promoted. Finally, the fact that the person selected (Lenker) was not of foreign origin gives rise to an inference of unlawful discrimination.

However, the district court also found that (1) BG&E produced evidence that Lenker was better qualified for the Senior Engineer position and (2) Amirmokri failed to rebut this with evidence showing BG&E's asserted reason for promoting Lenker was merely pretext.

Again, we agree with both of these determinations. BG&E claimed it promoted Lenker because he had hands-on experience as an engineer operating a nuclear submarine and had worked at Calvert Cliffs for two and one-half years with outstanding performance ratings. Amirmokri, on the other hand, had worked at Calvert Cliffs for only three months with mediocre performance ratings.

B. National origin harassment

To make out a claim of national origin harassment, Amirmokri must show (1) that the acts of BG&E employees were severe and pervasive enough to create a hostile working environment and (2) that some basis exists to impute liability to his employer. Liability may be imputed to the employer if the employer had actual or constructive knowledge of the existence of a hostile working environment and took no prompt and adequate remedial action.

Whether harassment is sufficiently severe or pervasive to create an abusive work environment is "quintessentially a question of fact." To show that harassment was severe or pervasive, a plaintiff must show that he perceived, and a reasonable person would perceive, the work environment to be abusive.

The district court found that Amirmokri produced sufficient evidence to show that harassment occurred and that it was severe and pervasive. He testified that for six months Polak and other co-workers abused him almost daily, calling him names like "the local terrorist," a "camel jockey" and "the Emir of Waldorf." He also asserted that Polak intentionally tried to embarrass him by giving him impossible tasks and by saying in front of co-workers that Amirmokri did not know what he was doing. He testified that this abuse led to his ulcer and his ultimate resignation. A reasonable person could easily find this atmosphere to be hostile.

BG&E may be liable for Polak's harassment if it knew or should have known of the harassment and failed to take "prompt remedial action reasonably calculated to end the harassment." The adequacy of BG&E's response once it was aware of the harassment is a factual issue.

Here, BG&E's response was even less decisive than that in Paroline. To begin with, it is not clear whether anyone at BG&E ever investigated Amirmokri's complaint, even after Amirmokri complained to Dunson, the Employee Grievance Coordinator, in August 1990. Dunson claims that he spoke to Polak and several other members of the Calvert Cliffs supervisory staff, Richard Honaker (Employment Recruiter), Thornton, Creel (a company Vice President), and a Mr. Denton. However, Polak testified that he never heard about Amirmokri's allegations until after Amirmokri resigned and filed his EEOC complaint.

C. Constructive discharge

To prove constructive discharge, Amirmokri must show that BG&E deliberately made his working conditions "intolerable" in an effort to induce him to quit. He must prove two elements: (1) the "deliberateness of BG&E's actions" and (2) the "intolerability of the working conditions."

Amirmokri's testimony is sufficient to raise a factual issue about whether his working conditions were intolerable. He testified that Polak and other co-workers subjected him to epithets about his Iranian origin almost daily and tried to embarrass him in public. The constant stress created by this atmosphere caused him to get an ulcer and eventually to resign. A reasonable trier of fact could find these conditions intolerable.

The more difficult question is whether Amirmokri has shown that BG&E deliberately attempted to force his resignation. Intent may be shown by evidence that an employee's resignation was the reasonably foreseeable consequence of the employer's conduct. For example, intent may be inferred from a failure to act in the face of known intolerable conditions. A complete failure to act by the employer is not required; an employer may not insulate itself entirely from liability by taking some token action in response to intolerable conditions. The reasonably foreseeable consequence of token action by the employer would still be that the employee resign. In other words, the employer's response must be reasonably calculated to end the intolerable working environment.

As discussed above, when an employee suffers from discriminatory treatment, claims for workplace harassment and constructive discharge are both governed by two-part tests. The first prong of each test weighs the severity of the conditions the employee faces. For a harassment claim the conduct must be "severe and pervasive," whereas for a constructive discharge claim

the environment must be "intolerable." The second prong examines the employer's response. For a harassment claim the employer must fail to take "prompt and adequate" remedial action, and for a constructive discharge claim the employer must intend for the employee to quit.

We hold that Amirmokri has produced evidence sufficient to allow a reasonable factfinder to conclude that BG&E's response was not reasonably calculated to end Amirmokri's intolerable working conditions and that Amirmokri's ultimate resignation was a reasonably foreseeable consequence of BG&E's insufficient response. Therefore, we reverse the district court's grant of summary judgment on Amirmokri's constructive discharge claim.

III.

For the above reasons, we affirm the grant of summary judgment on Amirmokri's claim for failure to promote and reverse the summary judgment on Amirmokri's claims for national origin harassment and constructive discharge. We remand to the district court for further proceedings consistent with this opinion.

Judgment for Amirmokri

Case Commentary

The Fourth Circuit held that Amirmokri had presented evidence sufficient to prove that he had

been subject to ethnic harassment and constructive discharge.

Case Questions

1. Do you agree with the Court's decision?

2. Was the harassment Amirmokri complained of severe and pervasive?

IMMIGRATION REFORM AND CONTROL ACT

The Immigration Reform and Control Act of 1986, which applies to employers with four or more employees, prohibits discrimination for national origin or for citizenship when the latter is an alien lawfully admitted for permanent residence. Whereas Title VII affords no protection against discrimination for citizenship or against employers of four to fourteen employees, the Immigration Reform and Control Act does. However, The Immigration Reform and Control Act makes no provision for the disparate impact that occurs unintentionally, as does Title VII. Intent to discriminate is mandated by the

Immigration and Control Act. The Immigration Reform and Control Act has been amended by the Immigration Act of 1990.

The Immigration Reform and Control Act applies to foreign and domestic companies who employ people within the United States. It has no application to American workers who are employed by foreign or domestic companies abroad.

The following case addresses the question of whether Title VII's protection against discrimination because of national origin applies to those American citizens who are working for American companies abroad.

CASE

EEOC v. ARAMCO

111 S. Ct. 1227 (1991)

CHIEF JUSTICE REHNQUIST delivered the opinion of the Court.
These cases present the issue whether Title VII applies extraterritorially to regulate the employment practices of United States employers who employ United States citizens abroad. The United States Court of Appeals for the Fifth Circuit held that it does not, and we agree with that conclusion.

Petitioner Boureslan is a naturalized United States citizen who was born in Lebanon. The respondents are two Delaware corporations, Arabian American Oil Company (ARAMCO), and its subsidiary, ARAMCO Service Company (ASC). Aramco's principal place of business is Dhahran, Saudi Arabia, and it is licensed to do business in Texas. ASC's principal place of business is Houston, Texas.

In 1979, Boureslan was hired by ASC as a cost engineer in Houston. A year later he was transferred, at his request, to work for ARAMCO in Saudi Arabia. Boureslan remained with ARAMCO in Saudi Arabia until he was discharged in 1984. After filing a charge of discrimination with the Equal Employment Opportunity Commission (EEOC), he instituted this suit in the United States District Court for the Southern District of Texas against ARAMCO and ASC. He sought relief under both state law and Title VII of the Civil Rights Act of 1964, 42 U.S.C. 2000a–2000h6, on the ground that he was harassed and ultimately discharged by respondents on account of his race, religion, and national origin.

Respondents filed a motion for summary judgment on the ground that the District Court lacked subject matter jurisdiction over Boureslan's claim because the protections of Title VII do not extend to United States citizens employed abroad by American employers. The District Court agreed, and dismissed Boureslan's Title VII claim. . . .

Both parties concede, as they must, that Congress has the authority to enforce its laws beyond the territorial boundaries of the United States. Whether Congress has in fact exercised that authority in this case is a matter of statutory construction. It is our task to determine whether Congress intended the protections of Title VII to apply to United States citizens employed by American employers outside of the United States.

It is a long-standing principle of American law "that legislation of Congress, unless a contrary intent appears, is meant to apply only within the territorial jurisdiction of the United States." This "canon of construction . . . is a valid approach whereby unexpressed congressional intent may be ascertained." It serves to protect against unintended clashes between our laws and those of other nations which could result in international discord.

In applying this rule of construction, we look to see whether "language in the relevant act gives any indication of a congressional purpose to extend its coverage beyond places over which the United States has sovereignty or has some measure of legislative control." We assume that Congress legislates against the backdrop of the presumption against extraterritoriality. Therefore, unless there is "the affirmative intention of the Congress clearly expressed," we must presume it "is primarily concerned with domestic conditions."

Title VII prohibits various discriminatory employment practices based on an individual's race, color, religion, sex, or national origin. See 42 U.S.C. 2000e-2, 2000e-3. An employer is subject to Title VII if it has employed 15 or more employees for a specified period and is "engaged in an industry affecting commerce." An industry affecting commerce is "any activity, business, or industry in commerce or in which a labor dispute would hinder or obstruct commerce or the free flow of commerce and includes any activity or industry 'affecting commerce' within the meaning of the Labor-Management Reporting and Disclosure Act of 1959." (LMRDA) (42 U.S.C. 2000e(h). "Commerce," in turn, is defined as "trade, traffic, commerce, transportation, transmission, or communication among the several States; or between a State and any place outside thereof; or within the District of Columbia, or a possession of the United States; or between points in the same State but through a point outside thereof." (See 42 U.S.C. 2000e(g)).

Petitioners argue that by its plain language, Title VII's "broad jurisdictional language" reveals Congress's intent to extend the statute's protections to employment discrimination anywhere in the world by a U.S. employer who affects trade "between a State and any place outside thereof." More precisely, they assert that since Title VII defines "States" to include States, the District of Columbia, and specified territories, the clause "between a State and any place outside thereof" must be referring to areas beyond the territorial limit of the United States.

Similarly, Congress failed to provide any mechanisms for overseas enforcement of Title VII. For instance, the statute's venue provisions, U.S.C. 2000e-5(f)(3), are ill-suited for extraterritorial application as they provide for venue only in a judicial district in the state where certain matters related to the employer occurred or were located. And the limited investigative authority

provided for the EEOC, permitting the Commission only to issue subpoenas for witnesses and documents from "anyplace in the United States or any Territory or possession thereof," U.S.C. 2000e-9, suggests that Congress did not intend for the statute to apply abroad.

It is also reasonable to conclude that had Congress intended Title VII to apply overseas, it would have addressed the subject of conflicts with foreign laws and procedures. In amending the Age Discrimination in Employment Act of 1967, (ADEA), to apply abroad, Congress specifically addressed potential conflicts with foreign law by providing that it is not unlawful for an employer to take any action prohibited by the ADEA "where such practices involve an employee in a workplace in a foreign country, and compliance with the ADEA would cause such employer . . . to violate the laws of the country in which such workplace is located." Title VII, by contrast, fails to address conflicts with the laws of other nations.

Our conclusion today is buttressed by the fact that "when it desires to do so, Congress knows how to place the high seas within the jurisdictional reach of a statute." Congress's awareness of the need to make a clear statement that a statute applies overseas is amply demonstrated by the numerous occasions on which it has expressly legislated the extraterritorial application of a statute. Finally, the EEOC, as one of the two federal agencies with primary responsibility for enforcing Title VII, argues that we should defer to its "consistent" construction of Title VII, first formally expressed in a statement issued after oral argument but before the Fifth Circuit's initial decision in this case, "to apply to discrimination against American citizens outside the United States." Citing a 1975 letter from the EEOC's General Counsel, 1983 testimony by its Chairman, and a 1985 decision by the Commission, it argues that its consistent administrative interpretations "reinforce" the conclusion that Congress intended Title VII to apply abroad.

In *General Electric Co. v. Gilbert,* we addressed the proper deference to be afforded the EEOC's guidelines. Recognizing that "Congress, in enacting Title VII, did not confer upon the EEOC authority to promulgate rules or regulations," we held that the level of deference afforded "will depend upon the thoroughness evident in its consideration, the validity of its reasoning, its consistency with earlier and later pronouncements, and all those factors which give it power to persuade, if lacking power to control."

The EEOC's interpretation does not fare well under these standards. As an initial matter, the position taken by the Commission "contradicts the position which it had enunciated at an earlier date, closer to the enactment of the governing statute." The Commission's early pronouncements on the issue supported the conclusion that the statute was limited to domestic application. ("Title VII . . . protects all individuals, both citizen and noncitizens, domiciled or residing in the United States, against discrimination on the basis of race, color, religion, sex, or national origin.") While the Commission later intimated that the statute applied abroad, this position was not expressly reflected in its policy guidelines until some 24 years after the passage of the statute. The

EEOC offers no basis in its experience for the change. The EEOC's interpretation of the statute here thus has been neither contemporaneous with its enactment nor consistent since the statute came into law. As discussed above, it also lacks support in the plain language of the statute. While we do not wholly discount the weight to be given to the 1988 guideline, its persuasive value is limited. We are of the view that, even when considered in combination with petitioners' other arguments, the EEOC's interpretation is insufficiently weighty to overcome the presumption against extraterritorial application.

Petitioners have failed to present sufficient affirmative evidence that Congress intended Title VII to apply abroad. Accordingly, the judgment of the Court of Appeals is

Affirmed.

Judgment for ARAMCO.

Case Commentary

The United States Supreme Court ruled that Title VII's protection against employment discrimination does not cover American citizens who are working for American companies outside the United States.

Case Questions

1. Are you in accord with the Court's resolution?
2. Should Title VII protection follow American citizens wherever they work?
3. Why should American companies be allowed to discriminate against American workers outside the United States, but not within?

EMPLOYMENT PERSPECTIVE

The law firm of Knapp and Schultz has 12 employees. Knapp and Schultz makes it their policy never to hire anyone who is not a U.S. citizen. Prasait Theesowatt, a permanent resident alien from Thailand, applies for a job with Knapp and Schultz, only to be informed of their policy. Prasait claims that Knapp and Schultz are in violation of the Immigration Reform and Control Act. Is he correct? Yes! The Immigration Reform and Control Act prohibits discrimination against permanent resident aliens and applies to employers with at least four employees. ▪

Discriminating against people who are not citizens is permissible under the Civil Rights Act, but not under the Immigration Reform and Control Act if they have a Certificate of Naturalization or a resident alien card.

In the next case, an applicant was denied a position at a pizza franchise after an in-person interview. The applicant claimed that the denial was due to his national origin because others were hired after he had applied. The issue is whether the franchisor or the franchisee is ultimately responsible for the discriminatory acts.

BAHADIRLI v. DOMINO'S PIZZA

873 F. Supp. 1528 (M.D.Ala. 1995)

ALBRITTON, District Judge.

On April 12, 1993, Mehrnet Bahadirli sought employment as a pizza delivery person at the Westgate Parkway store, a Domino's pizza franchise in Dothan, Alabama. According to the plaintiff, he visited the store and was told that he was well qualified for the position, but he never received word regarding the job. The plaintiff alleges that on his return to the store around April 25, 1993, he was told that he would not receive the position. According to the plaintiff, in the interim four other individuals were hired at the Westgate Parkway store.

Clarkfinn asserts that plaintiff returned to the store after approximately one month from his initial visit to inquire as to the status of his application. According to Clarkfinn, plaintiff was told that the application had been misfiled, that the Westgate Parkway store did not have any openings, but perhaps another location in Dothan did. Defendants allege that they contacted another store and that plaintiff said that he would pick up an application there.

Bahadirli contends that on learning he would not be hired, he went directly home and asked his wife to call the shop and inquire about employment. Plaintiff alleges his wife was offered a position over the phone.

As stated above, both Clark and Clarkfinn have filed Motions to Dismiss. Clarkfinn is the corporate entity that owns the Domino's Pizza franchise at issue here. Mr. Clark owns 75% of Clarkfinn's stock and serves as the corporation's president.

Until very recently, Eleventh Circuit law was very clear in holding that Title VII claims against a person in his individual capacity were "inappropriate." Accordingly, Clark may not be sued in his individual capacity. As stated above, in order to make out a case, plaintiff must show the plaintiff is of different nationality, plaintiff applied for a position, was qualified for that position; that the

plaintiff was rejected for the position despite his qualifications; and that the defendant continued to accept applications for the position following the rejection of the plaintiff.

However, in addition to establishing a prima facie case, the plaintiff must show that the defendants named are properly before the court on these claims. Domino's argues that it is entitled to summary judgment on plaintiff's Title VII claims because it is not the employer in this case. The defendant Reams contends that he cannot be sued under Title VII in his individual capacity and that, because the employer is named in the suit, naming him in his official capacity is repetitive. The court agrees with the argument of both Domino's and Reams.

Reams is the individual who served as manager at the Domino's franchise that plaintiff is suing. According to plaintiff, Reams turned him down for a position at the Westgate Parkway store because of plaintiff's national origin. Reams no longer works for Clarkfinn.

Plaintiff admits that Reams cannot be sued in his individual capacity, but argues that the court should not grant summary judgment as to Reams in his official capacity. The Court disagrees. As stated above, a suit under Title VII brought against an employee as agent of the employer is properly regarded as a suit against the employer. Domino's contends that it did not have control over the day to day operations or over hiring and firing that would allow a finding of liability should Bahadirli prove his claim. In support of its argument, Domino's has submitted affidavits from Linda Popevich, a Divisional Vice President of Franchise Services for Domino's. According to these affidavits, the Westgate Parkway store was, and is, a franchise, operated by an independent contractor—Clarkfinn. Popevich also avers that "persons who work at a store operated by a franchisee, including the Westgate Parkway Store, are employees of the Franchisee Clarkfinn and not DPI Domino's." In her supplemental affidavit, Popevich stated that Domino's has no knowledge of individuals who apply for positions at Domino's franchises. In this case, the plaintiff has presented no evidence that the defendant Domino's had any control over the employees' day to day activities, or control over hiring and firing at the Westgate Parkway store. Accordingly, Domino's Motion for Summary Judgment is due to be granted.

Judgment for Domino's.

Case Commentary

The Middle District of Alabama decided that a franchisor is not liable for the discriminatory actions of its franchisee. Here, Bahadirli was re- fused employment by Clarkfinn, the Domino's franchisee, because of his national origin.

Case Questions

1. Are you in accord with the Court's decision?
2. Do you believe Clarkfinn should be held liable?
3. Why do you think Clarkfinn refused Bahadirli employment?

❖ EMPLOYER LESSONS

- Treat all applicants and employees the same regardless of their national origin.
- Know what employment rights are given to resident aliens.
- Guard against employing illegal aliens.
- Learn what documentation is required before hiring aliens.
- Do not advocate or tolerate ethnic harassment in the workplace.
- Understand that a person's surname, spouse's national origin, and affiliation with an ethnic school or association should not be considered in any employment decision.
- Develop an expertise in the Immigration Reform and Control Act.
- Appreciate why the Civil Rights Act includes national origin as a suspect class.
- Refrain from asking candidates for employment what country they were born in.
- Recognize that Title VII and the Immigration Reform and Control Act do not apply to Americans working outside the United States.

❖ EMPLOYEE LESSONS

- Recognize that you are protected from national origin discrimination under Title VII of the Civil Rights Act.
- Realize that this protection extends to your school, ethnic associations, surname, and spouse's national origin.
- Be aware when an employer asks the country in which you were born.
- Do not initiate or participate in ethnic harassment in the workplace.
- Be familiar with the Immigration Reform and Control Act.
- Inquire as to the applicability of this Act as well as the Civil Rights Act to your employer.
- Provide the necessary documentation for your employer if you are a resident alien.
- Understand you may not be protected against national origin discrimination when working abroad.
- Be aware of the reasons for national origin discrimination.
- Apprise yourself of the requirements needed to file a disparate treatment case for national origin.

❖ **SUMMARY**

The United States of America is a melting pot and is probably the most integrated country in the world. America derives its strength from the attributes of a population diverse in culture and tradition. Excluding individuals because of their national origin goes against the grain of American heritage; individuals should be judged only on the basis of their merit. Most immigrants have taken their lumps upon entering this country. One hundred years ago, the Irish and Germans were not well received. Seventy-five years ago, the Italians and Polish were resented. Twenty-five years ago, the Spanish and Latin Americans were not wanted. Today, Indians and Koreans are looked upon with contempt.

Many Americans want immigration laws tightened up to the point of restricting most nonwhite immigrants. What these Americans are forgetting is the work ethic that their ancestors brought with them in building the infrastructure that exists today. Most immigrants are not freeloaders but rather are people seeking opportunities to put their talents to work to build a future for their families and themselves, a goal that everyone should encourage.

Immigrants are often used to performing the routine ministerial tasks that Americans refuse to do. Hard labor, assembly line factory work, janitorial maintenance, and gas pumping are a few occupations serviced by a significant number of immigrants. On the other side of the coin, as immigrants mesh themselves into our society and have children, those children will eventually compete with Americans for better-paying positions. Also, as the population grows, pollution and garbage increases proportionately. Development causes overuse of the land, natural resources, and water; erosion occurs; disease proliferates; and quality of life deteriorates. For America to maintain a sustainable quality of life, immigration cannot run rampant. In areas of technology, communications, and product development, our innovation is unparalleled, but in purifying our air, water, and food supply, we are underachievers. Therefore, the number of people that can adequately be supported by America's vital resources is an issue to be seriously considered.

This problem pertains to the number of immigrants in the future. For those immigrants already here, America should embrace them into our society and encourage them to utilize their talents to their greatest potential for the benefit of all of us. Discrimination against immigrants serves no purpose, since they rarely leave involuntarily; it serves only to delay their inevitable amalgamation into American employment and society.

Thoughtful planning with regard to supporting future immigrants with the vital resources available to us is an intelligent policy, but purposeful discrimination against the ones among us is not. They should be treated as our own.

❖ **REVIEW QUESTIONS**

1. Define national origin discrimination.
2. Explain the significance of the Immigration Reform and Control Act.
3. Can a person claim to be discriminated against because of his or her spouse's national origin?
4. Does discrimination because of membership in an association of a particular national origin qualify as national origin discrimination?
5. When a student is discriminated against because he or she is attending a school of a particular national origin, does Title VII apply?
6. Does the Civil Rights Act extend to a person's claiming discrimination because his or her surname is associated with a particular national origin?

7. Can an employer discriminate against someone on the basis of the person's lacking United States citizenship?

8. Does the Immigration Reform and Control Act apply to all employers?

9. Can national origin ever be considered a bona fide occupational qualification?

10. Must an employee be 100 percent of a particular national origin to qualify for protection under Title VII?

11. Rys once heard Lehman say that Adolf Hitler did not finish his job because he did not kill all the Polish and Jewish people. Lehman also said that he should shove those people into the ovens. Lehman once saw a woman having lunch and asked her what were "all those dumb Polacks" doing in the hallway. When Lehman fired the crew, Rys complained that Palka should be present. Lehman then said that he would fire "that dumb Polack, too." Are these events sufficient to constitute a claim for national origin discrimination? *ISS Intern. Service v. Human Rights Commission,* 651 N.E.2d 592 (Ill. App. 1 Dist. 1995)

12. Cruz alleged as follows in her EEOC complaint: Respondent stated that "since my employment with him I have been unable to get a decent letter out of my typewriter." Respondent stated that this might be attributed to her language barrier. In these circumstances, Cruz charged Ecolab with unlawful discrimination "by denying the equal terms, conditions and privileges of employment and terminating me because of my national origin." When editing letters typed for Vice President Mosh by Cruz, Mosh would on occasion comment "that plaintiff did not understand English because she was Puerto Rican." What was the result? *Cruz v. Ecolab,* 817 F.Supp. 388 (S.D. N.Y. 1993)

13. To reduce costs, Philippine Airlines (PAL) closed ten of its U.S. District Sales offices. Nine managers were discharged as follows: four non-Filipinos, two Filipinos, and three U.S. citizens of Filipino origin. Two non-Filipinos sued PAL, claiming reverse discrimination on the basis of national origin. What was the result? *Lemnitzer v. Philippine Airlines, Inc.,* 816 F.Supp. 1441 (N.D. Cal. 1992)

14. The Immigration Reform and Control Act (IRCA) requires employers to verify the legal immigration status of their employees. Catholic nuns challenged the civil and criminal sanctions for noncompliance. Their reasoning is their belief that they cannot refuse to aid their fellow brothers and sisters. To comply with this statute would mean they would have to do so. What was the result? *Inter-community Center for Justice and Peace v. INS,* 910 F.2d 42 (2nd Cir. 1990)

15. A Chinese and an African-American, both employees of Spun Steak Co., complained that two Hispanic coworkers made abusive racial remarks about them in Spanish. Spun Steak adopted a rule permitting only the English language to be used at work. Buitrago and Garcia, the alleged harassers, claimed that an English-language-only rule was an act of discrimination perpetrated by the company against them because of their national origin. What was the result? *Garcia v. Spun Steak Co.,* 988 F.2d 1980 (9th Cir. 1993)

16. Dr. Smith sent Ms. Hong a memorandum stating that her term of employment in the Clinical Chemistry Laboratory was at an end. The memo indicated that staff are obliged to conduct laboratory work reliably and quickly for the benefit of patients and that Ms. Hong's poor performance record over the previous year and a half was simply unsatisfactory. According to the plaintiff, Dr. Smith told her brother-in-law that Ms. Hong "should move back to Korea." Second, the plaintiff claims that her supervisor, Marina Barrientos, told her repeatedly at work to "learn to speak English" despite the absence of evidence that the plaintiff spoke anything other than English. What was the result? *Hong v. Children's Memorial Hospital,* 993 F.2d 1257 (7th Cir. 1993)

17. On three different occasions, Appellee, a Hispanic male, applied for an entry level sales position with Philip Morris. The Appellants hired one Caucasian male and two Caucasian females for the three sales positions.

   While it is clear from the record that Appellee was in fact considered for three positions to which he applied, other applicants were hired because according to the Appellants they were better qualified. What was the result? *Sanchez v. Philip Morris, Inc.* 992 F.2d 244 (10th Cir. 1993)

18. In December of 1991, Neely discovered that Jean had used the override system to enter lower prices for over-the-counter children's medicine she had purchased for her son. Neely also discovered that Jean had used the override system to order drugs for Dr. Alix Charles that were available in the warehouse, but could be ordered from an outside supplier at a cheaper price. Plaintiff purchased these drugs as a gift for the relief effort in Haiti.

Jean's complaint alleges that Walgreen illegally terminated her because of her national origin. What was the result? *Jean v. Walgreen Co.,* 887 F. Supp. 1007 (N.D. Ill. 1994)

19. The AFSC is a Quaker organization, whose activities include charitable and relief work. The employer sanction provisions of IRCA apply to the AFSC's employment of approximately 400 persons. Those provisions prohibit an employer from hiring, or continuing to employ, an alien who the employer knows is not authorized to work in the United States. Failure to comply with these provisions can result in civil and criminal sanctions.

AFSC has not complied with these provisions of IRCA because it believes that to do so would violate the religious beliefs and practices of its members. Those beliefs require that AFSC and its members "welcome—that they help and not show hostility to—the sojourner, the stranger, the poor, and the dispossessed in their midst." What was the result? *American Friends Service Committee v. Thornburgh,* 941 F.2d 808 (9th Cir. 1991)

20. Should Title VII be extended to cover American citizens working abroad? Was the plaintiff treated in an ethical manner?

21. Should a franchisor be responsible for the unethical conduct of the franchisee?

❖ WEB SITES

www.eeoc.gov/facts/fs-nator.html

www.dol.gov/dol/esa/public/regs/compliance/whdfs26.htm

www.freevillage.org/grids/ethnicmonitoring_definition.htm

www.ilo.org/public/english/protection/migrant/papers/usempir/ch6.htm

http://preview.biblioalerts.com/info/com.biblioalerts_biblioalerts_SOC000185.html?se=ink

www.civiljustice.com/empnews2.htm#raceandethnic-baseddiscrimination

www.findlaw.com

15

AGE DISCRIMINATION

INTRODUCTION

The Age Discrimination in Employment Act of 1967 (ADEA) was enacted to promote the employment of individuals over 40 years of age. Later, it was amended to discontinue mandatory retirement, thereby shifting the requirement for employment from age to ability. There are exceptions. Companies can force executives in high policy-making positions to retire at 65 and universities can require tenured professors to retire at 70.

CHAPTER CHECKLIST

❖ Appreciate the ramifications of the Age Discrimination in Employment Act.

❖ Learn that age discrimination applies to employees 40 years old or older.

❖ Know that the mandatory retirement age has been eliminated.

❖ Consider that age discrimination usually occurs when an employer chooses to discharge an older employer because of his or her higher salary.

❖ Realize that older employees are often replaced by younger ones who earn far less.

❖ Be aware that executives can be forced to retire when they attain age 65.

❖ Be concerned that forcing older employees to accept early retirement packages is age discrimination.

❖ Understand that an employer's justification for layoffs cannot be motivated by age discrimination.

❖ Appreciate that elderly people have the right to work.

EMPLOYMENT SCENARIO

Beatrice McCormick has been a cashier for The Long and Short of It since they opened six years ago. Beatrice is approaching 70. Tom Long and Mark Short have been urging her to retire, but so far they have had no luck. It seems Beatrice's life revolves around her work. Her children live far away and she has no hobbies. Tom and Mark ask Susan North, their attorney, if there is any way they can force Beatrice into retirement.

Susan asks them about Beatrice's job performance. Tom and Mark explain that Beatrice is extremely competent. However, Beatrice's age and appearance do not fit the youthful and up-to-date image that L&S wishes to project. They recently hired 19-year-old Tanya, who they describe as being really "hot." Beatrice is training Tanya. Tom and Mark plan to make the switch in two weeks, on Beatrice's birthday. Susan apologizes for bursting their birthday balloon surprise for Beatrice, and then rebukes them for being inconsiderate of Beatrice and self-centered. Legally, Beatrice has excellent grounds for an age discrimination suit, since there is no mandatory retirement age, and she is being replaced by someone much younger. Tom and Mark appear steadfast in their belief that given her age, Beatrice will not want to embroil herself in a costly and emotionally wrenching lawsuit. They explain to Susan that although they may be heartless, they are acting in the best interests of their business. Susan is distraught, but all she can do is offer her wisdom.

EMPLOYMENT PERSPECTIVE

Lawrence Wright is the chief financial officer for Code Blue Medical Supplies, Inc. Miriam Hodges is a quality control analyst. Both will be 70 in March. Code Blue has a policy of compulsory retirement at age 70. Will Lawrence and Miriam both have to retire? Under the ADEA, Miriam can continue to work as long as she is able to do the job. Lawrence will be forced to retire as CFO because he is a high policy-making executive. However, he will not be prevented from doing consulting work for the company. ■

EMPLOYMENT PERSPECTIVE

Professor Martin Ryan has been teaching mathematical statistics, differential equations, and complex variables at Moran University for 35 years. At the end of this academic year, he will turn 70. Martin is still highly competent, revered by his colleagues, and a favorite of the students. But, University policy mandates retirement of tenured professors at age 70. Martin implores Dean Margaret Stokes to make an exception. But Dean Stokes bellows that once Moran University makes one exception, it will set a precedent that will undermine University policy. Moran University may then be forced to permit scholars much less competent than Martin Ryan to continue working beyond age 70. The school may become stale, full of old codgers, and lose its stellar reputation. Does Professor Martin Ryan have any recourse? Unfortunately, No! The ADEA does not afford protection to tenured professors who reach 70. ■

DISCRIMINATION REQUIREMENTS

The initial test for determining age discrimination has four prongs:

1. Employee was qualified.
2. Employee was terminated.
3. Employee was a member of a protected class.
4. Employee was replaced by someone younger or was otherwise discharged because of age.

The employer must then provide a legitimate nondiscriminatory reason for the discharge. After satisfying this burden, the employee must prove that the employer's reasoning was false and that the real reason was to discriminate.

The issue in this case is whether an employee alleging age discrimination must be replaced by someone under 40 years of age.

CASE

O'CONNOR v. CONSOLIDATED COIN CATERERS

517 U.S. 308 (1996)

JUSTICE SCALIA delivered the opinion of the Court.

This case presents the question whether a plaintiff alleging that he was discharged in violation of the Age Discrimination in Employment Act of 1967 (ADEA) must show that he was replaced by someone outside the age group protected by the ADEA to make out a prima facie case under the framework established by McDonnell Douglas Corp. v. Green.

Petitioner James O'Connor was employed by respondent Consolidated Coin Caterers Corporation from 1978 until August 10, 1990, when, at age 56, he was fired. Claiming that he had been dismissed because of his age in violation of the ADEA, petitioner brought suit in the United States District Court for the Western District of North Carolina. After discovery, the District Court granted respondent's motion for summary judgment and petitioner appealed. The Court of Appeals for the Fourth Circuit stated that petitioner could establish a prima facie case under McDonnell Douglas only if he could prove that (1) he was in the age group protected by the

ADEA; (2) he was discharged or demoted; (3) at the time of his discharge or demotion, he was performing his job at a level that met his employer's legitimate expectations; and (4) following his discharge or demotion, he was replaced by someone of comparable qualifications outside the protected class. Since petitioner's replacement was 40 years old, the Court of Appeals concluded that the last element of the prima facie case had not been made out. Finding that petitioner's claim could not survive a motion for summary judgment without benefit of the McDonnell Douglas presumption, the Court of Appeals affirmed the judgment of dismissal. We granted O'Connor's petition for certiorari.

As the very name "prima facie case" suggests, there must be at least a logical connection between each element of the prima facie case and the illegal discrimination for which it establishes a "legally mandatory, rebuttable presumption." The element of replacement by someone under 40 fails this requirement. The discrimination prohibited by the ADEA is discrimination "because of an individual's age," though the prohibition is "limited to individuals who are at least 40 years of age." This language does not ban discrimination against employees because they are aged 40 or older; it bans discrimination against employees because of their age, but limits the protected class to those who are 40 or older. The fact that one person in the protected class has lost out to another person in the protected class is thus irrelevant, so long as he has lost out because of his age. Or to put the point more concretely, there can be no greater inference of age discrimination (as opposed to "40 or over" discrimination) when a 40 year-old is replaced by a 39 year-old than when a 56 year-old is replaced by a 40 year-old. Because it lacks probative value, the fact that an ADEA plaintiff was replaced by someone outside the protected class is not a proper element of the McDonnell Douglas prima facie case.

Perhaps some courts have been induced to adopt the principle urged by respondent in order to avoid creating a prima facie case on the basis of very thin evidence - for example, the replacement of a 68 year-old by a 65 year-old. While the respondent's principle theoretically permits such thin evidence (consider the example above of a 40 year-old replaced by a 39 year-old), as a practical matter it will rarely do so, since the vast majority of age-discrimination claims come from older employees. In our view, however, the proper solution to the problem lies not in making an utterly irrelevant factor an element of the prima facie case, but rather in recognizing that the prima facie case requires "evidence adequate to create an inference that an employment decision was based on an illegal discriminatory criterion. . . ." In the age-discrimination context, such an inference can not be drawn from the replacement of one worker with another worker insignificantly younger. Because the ADEA prohibits discrimination on the basis of age and not class membership, the fact that a replacement is substantially younger than the plaintiff is a far more reliable indicator of age discrimination than is the fact that the plaintiff was replaced by someone outside the protected class. The judgment of the Fourth Circuit is reversed, and the case is remanded for proceedings consistent with this opinion.

It is so ordered.

Judgment for O'Connor.

Case Commentary

The United States Supreme Court decided that an older person who was discharged does not have to be replaced by someone under 40 years of age in order to allege age discrimination. The disparity in age is key.

Case Questions

1. Are you in agreement with the decision of the United States Supreme Court?
2. If the age discrimination threshold is 40 years of age, why would the court allow an employee to sue when his or her replacement is over 40?
3. Should the requirement for age discrimination be the age of the replacement, disparity in age, or both?

MANDATORY RETIREMENT

The mandatory retirement age was originally 65. In 1978, it was adjusted to 70, and more recently, it has been eliminated. Age discrimination can begin at 40.

EMPLOYMENT PERSPECTIVE

Big Mac Kowalski is the quarterback for the Raleigh Rainbows. In the past year, he was ranked among the upper half of all quarterbacks in the league. Before the beginning of the season, Chubby Shelten, coach of the Rainbows, informs Kowalski that he is being discharged. Chubby explains that the team will be committing itself to younger players and that the younger players would prefer someone of similar age to be quarterback rather than an old man whom they cannot relate to. Kowalski is 38 years of age. He sues the Rainbows for age discrimination. Will he score? No. Big Mac is under 40. The protection of the Age Discrimination in Employment Act does not apply to him. Big Mac will become an armchair quarterback. ■

DAMAGES

Damages recoverable for age discrimination include reinstatement, back pay, differential in pay due to seniority, and pension-benefit contributions. Where the employer's motivation for discharge was intentional, double lost wages may be assessed as a form of liquidated damages. Interest and attorney's fees may also be awarded at the discretion of the court.

A victim of age discrimination must file a claim with the EEOC within two years of the incident. This statute of limitations is extended to three years if the employer acted with intent. After filing with the EEOC, the complainant may proceed in state or federal court himself or herself. It is possible for two corresponding suits, one brought by the EEOC and the other brought by the complainant, to take place at the same time.

Under Title VII, a separate suit may be commenced only when EEOC's determination is not to proceed. If the complaining party has not yet filed a separate suit and the EEOC has decided not to pursue the claim, the complainant has 90 days to bring a lawsuit from the receipt of the said notice.

The question presented in the case that follows is whether the employer's age discrimination toward an employee is mitigated by the fact that the employer later discovered the employee misappropriated company documents.

CASE

McKENNON v. NASHVILLE BANNER PUBLISHING CO.

513 U.S. 352 (1995)

JUSTICE KENNEDY delivered the opinion of the Court.

The question before us is whether an employee discharged in violation of the Age Discrimination in Employment Act of 1967 is barred from all relief when, after her discharge, the employer discovers evidence of wrongdoing that, in any event, would have led to the employee's termination on lawful and legitimate grounds.

I

For some 30 years, petitioner Christine McKennon worked for respondent Nashville Banner Publishing Company. She was discharged, the Banner claimed, as part of a work force reduction plan necessitated by cost considerations. McKennon, who was 62 years old when she lost her job, thought another reason explained her dismissal: her age. She filed suit in the United States District

Court for the Middle District of Tennessee, alleging that her discharge violated the Age Discrimination in Employment Act of 1967 (ADEA). The ADEA makes it unlawful for any employer: "to discharge any individual or otherwise discriminate against any individual with respect to his compensation, terms, conditions, or privileges of employment, because of such individual's age."

McKennon sought a variety of legal and equitable remedies available under the ADEA, including backpay. In preparation of the case, the Banner took McKennon's deposition. She testified that, during her final year of employment, she had copied several confidential documents bearing upon the company's financial condition. She had access to these records as secretary to the Banner's comptroller. McKennon took the copies home and showed them to her husband. Her motivation, she averred, was an apprehension she was about to be fired because of her age. When she became concerned about her job, she removed and copied the documents for "insurance" and "protection." A few days after these deposition disclosures, the Banner sent McKennon a letter declaring that removal and copying of the records was in violation of her job responsibilities and advising her again that she was terminated. The Banner's letter also recited that had it known of McKennon's misconduct it would have discharged her at once for that reason.

For purposes of summary judgment, the Banner conceded its discrimination against McKennon. The District Court granted summary judgment for the Banner, holding that McKennon's misconduct was grounds for her termination and that neither backpay nor any other remedy was available to her under the ADEA. We granted certiorari to resolve conflicting views among the Courts of Appeals on the question whether all relief must be denied when an employee has been discharged in violation of the ADEA and the employer later discovers some wrongful conduct that would have led to discharge if it had been discovered earlier. We now reverse.

II

We shall assume, as summary judgment procedures require us to assume, that the sole reason for McKennon's initial discharge was her age, a discharge violative of the ADEA. Our further premise is that the misconduct revealed by the deposition was so grave that McKennon's immediate discharge would have followed its disclosure in any event. The District Court and the Court of Appeals found no basis for contesting that proposition, and for purposes of our review we need not question it here. We do question the legal conclusion reached by those courts that after-acquired evidence of wrongdoing which would have resulted in discharge bars employees from any relief under the ADEA. That ruling is incorrect.

The Court of Appeals considered McKennon's misconduct, in effect, to be supervening grounds for termination. That may be so, but it does not follow, as the Court of Appeals said in citing one of its own earlier cases, that the misconduct renders it " 'irrelevant whether or not McKennon was discriminated against.' " We conclude that a violation of the ADEA cannot be so altogether disregarded.

The ADEA, enacted in 1967 as part of an ongoing congressional effort to eradicate discrimination in the workplace, reflects a societal condemnation of invidious bias in employment decisions. The ADEA is but part of a wider statutory scheme to protect employees in the workplace nationwide. The ADEA incorporates some features of both Title VII and the Fair Labor Standards Act, which has led us to describe it as "something of a hybrid." The substantive, antidiscrimination provisions of the ADEA are modeled upon the prohibitions of Title VII. Its remedial provisions incorporate by reference the provisions of the Fair Labor Standards Act of 1938. When confronted with a violation of the ADEA, a district court is authorized to afford relief by means of reinstatement, backpay, injunctive relief, declaratory judgment, and attorney's fees. In the case of a willful violation of the Act, the ADEA authorizes an award of liquidated damages equal to the backpay award. The Act also gives federal courts the discretion to "grant such legal or equitable relief as may be appropriate to effectuate the purposes of the Act."

The ADEA and Title VII share common substantive features and also a common purpose: "the elimination of discrimination in the workplace." Congress designed the remedial measures in these statutes to serve as a "spur or catalyst" to cause employers "to self-examine and to self-evaluate their employment practices and to endeavor to eliminate, so far as possible, the last vestiges" of discrimination. Deterrence is one object of these statutes. Compensation for injuries caused by the prohibited discrimination is another. The ADEA, in keeping with these purposes, contains a vital element found in both Title VII and the Fair Labor Standards Act: it grants an injured employee a right of action to obtain the authorized relief. The private litigant who seeks redress for his or her injuries vindicates both the deterrence and the compensation objectives of the ADEA. The private litigant in Title VII not only redresses his own injury but also vindicates the important congressional policy against discriminatory employment practices.

As we have said, the case comes to us on the express assumption that an unlawful motive was the sole basis for the firing. McKennon's misconduct was not discovered until after she had been fired. The employer could not have been motivated by knowledge it did not have and it cannot now claim that the employee was fired for the nondiscriminatory reason. Mixed motive cases are inapposite here, except to the important extent they underscore the necessity of determining the employer's motives in ordering the discharge, an essential element in determining whether the employer violated the federal antidiscrimination law.

The proper boundaries of remedial relief in the general class of cases where, after termination, it is discovered that the employee has engaged in wrongdoing must be addressed by the judicial system in the ordinary course of further decisions, for the factual permutations and the equitable considerations they raise will vary from case to case. We do conclude that here, and as a general rule in cases of this type, neither reinstatement nor front pay is an appropriate remedy. It would be both inequitable and pointless to order the reinstatement of someone the employer would have terminated, and will terminate, in any event and upon lawful grounds.

The proper measure of backpay presents a more difficult problem. Resolution of this question must give proper recognition to the fact that an ADEA violation has occurred which must be deterred and compensated without undue infringement upon the employer's rights and prerogatives. The object of compensation is to restore the employee to the position he or she would have been in absent the discrimination, but that principle is difficult to apply with precision where there is after-acquired evidence of wrongdoing that would have led to termination on legitimate grounds had the employer known about it. Once an employer learns about employee wrongdoing that would lead to a legitimate discharge, we cannot require the employer to ignore the information, even if it is acquired during the course of discovery in a suit against the employer and even if the information might have gone undiscovered absent the suit. The beginning point in the trial court's formulation of a remedy should be calculation of backpay from the date of the unlawful discharge to the date the new information was discovered. In determining the appropriate order for relief, the court can consider taking into further account extraordinary equitable circumstances that affect the legitimate interests of either party. An absolute rule barring any recovery of backpay, however, would undermine the ADEA's objective of forcing employers to consider and examine their motivations, and of penalizing them for employment decisions that spring from age discrimination.

Where an employer seeks to rely upon after-acquired evidence of wrongdoing, it must first establish that the wrongdoing was of such severity that the employee in fact would have been terminated on those grounds alone if the employer had known of it at the time of the discharge. The concern that employers might as a routine matter undertake extensive discovery into an employee's background or performance on the job to resist claims under the Act is not an insubstantial one, but we think the authority of the courts to award attorney's fees, mandated under the statute, will deter most abuses.

The judgment is reversed, and the case is remanded to the Court of Appeals for the Sixth Circuit for further proceedings consistent with this opinion.

It is so ordered.

Judgment for McKennon

Case Commentary

The United States Supreme Court ruled that the employer's subsequent discovery of the employee's theft of documents does not excuse its discharge of the employee due to age discrimination.

Case Questions

1. Are you in agreement with the Court?
2. Is the employer vindicated by the subsequent disclosure of the employee's document theft?

3. If the employer and the employee are both at fault, how can the case be resolved?

EMPLOYMENT PERSPECTIVE

Myrtle Eldridge has been working for Marvin Wilson as his personal secretary for 35 years. Their employer is Seacrest Shipping. Marvin retired recently. His replacement is Buddy Johnson, who is 27. After one look at Myrtle, he has decided that he would prefer someone who is more youthful. Buddy replaces Myrtle with Rhonda, a 22-year-old whose office skills barely measure up to Myrtle's. Myrtle files a claim with EEOC. Before its determination, she sues Seacrest Shipping in state court. Seacrest argues that her suit cannot be brought until the EEOC determination has been made, as in Title VII cases. Are they correct? No! After the filing of the EEOC claim, Myrtle is free to pursue her own suit in state court, unlike under Title VII, which requires an EEOC dismissal before suing. With regard to the issue in her case, Seacrest claims that incompatibility was the reason why Buddy wanted her replaced. Is this a sufficient reason? No! Since Buddy had Myrtle dismissed immediately, there is no basis on which to draw a conclusion of incompatibility. Myrtle will win and will be reinstated in the secretarial position. Naturally, it would be ludicrous for Buddy and Myrtle to work together, given the EEOC investigation and the lawsuit. Myrtle will be entitled to double back pay. The doubling is a form of liquidated damages because Buddy's actions were intentional: He did not want her because of her age. In addition, she will receive compensation for lost benefits, loss of seniority, and possibly attorney fees and interest. ∎

EMPLOYER'S JUSTIFICATION FOR LAYOFFS

Many firms lay off older workers for financial reasons. They can save money by replacing older workers with young workers, who are willing to do the same work for an entry level salary. For layoffs not to be in violation of the Age Discrimination in Employment Act, they must be made across the board.

In the next case, the issue is whether economic factors dictated the company's decision to downsize or whether they serve as a pretext for the company to discriminate.

JONES v. UNISYS CORP.

54 F.3d 624 (10th Cir. 1995)

LOGAN, Circuit Judge.

The district court found that plaintiffs failed to establish a prima facie case of age discrimination because they did not produce evidence from which a factfinder might reasonably conclude that Unisys made employment decisions with intent to discriminate on the basis of age. Alternatively, the district court found that plaintiffs failed to raise a genuine issue of material fact as to whether Unisys' proffered explanation was pretextual. We assume, for purposes of this opinion, that plaintiffs established a prima facie case of age discrimination. Therefore, we proceed to the district court's determination that Unisys provided evidence of legitimate, nondiscriminatory reasons for the decisions.

The district court summarized the reasons for laying off plaintiffs: Unisys was losing billions of dollars, facing economic disaster, and had to implement drastic cost-cutting measures. The district court thus found that Unisys articulated a legitimate nondiscriminatory reason for the reduction in force. We agree. Although the district court did not specifically address the reasons Unisys offered for its decisions to lay off or deny transfers to specific plaintiffs, the record reveals that Unisys articulated legitimate nondiscriminatory reasons for these decisions.

Of the sixty-three employees at the distribution center, forty-nine were laid off, one voluntarily retired, eight were transferred, and four were retained by the residual shipping and receiving group. Nineteen of the plaintiffs, all but Cole, were laid off from the Salt Lake distribution center. Unisys articulated legitimate nondiscriminatory reasons for retaining the four employees in the residual group.

Cole was laid off from the procurement group which was reduced from thirteen to five employees. Unisys produced evidence that his buying and contract negotiation skills and other qualifications did not meet the needs of the group as well as the five employees retained.

Many of the plaintiffs also asserted that decisions to transfer younger employees was evidence of age discrimination. However, only six plaintiffs applied for transfer; thus we need address only their situation.

Plaintiff Duncan requested a transfer to the defense division in Salt Lake only, but did not demonstrate she was qualified for the position to which she sought to be transferred. She made out no prima facie case of age discrimination on the adverse transfer decision. Cantrell did not identify specific jobs to which he claims he should have been transferred nor present evidence he was qualified for such jobs. Thus, we need not consider whether Unisys presented legitimate reasons for not transferring these plaintiffs because the burden of production never shifted to Unisys as to these individuals.

Plaintiffs Hall, Jones, Lowther, and Sturgeon each asserted that their transfers to San Jose engineer positions were denied because of age discrimination. Assuming plaintiffs produced evidence that younger employees were given those jobs for which plaintiffs arguably were qualified, Unisys articulated legitimate nondiscriminatory reasons for granting those transfers.

Because Unisys produced evidence of legitimate reasons for the challenged decisions, plaintiffs then had the burden to produce evidence of age discrimination or to show that the reasons given were a pretext for age discrimination.

Plaintiffs utterly failed to show direct evidence of age discrimination: they offer the "telling" statistic that "historically, 33.3% of the employees within the protected class were terminated in any given reduction in force. In the 1991 reduction in force which affected the plaintiffs, 62.5% of the employees in the protected class were terminated." However, as Unisys outlined in the 1991 layoffs a slightly higher percentage of employees outside the protected age group were terminated compared with those in the protected group. Indeed, the percentage of employees in the age group before and after the reduction force was almost the same—about sixty-nine percent. Statistics taken in isolation are generally not probative of age discrimination, and the statistics here do not support a finding of intent to discriminate.

The only other purported case of age discrimination was a double heresay comment by a Unisys employee responsible for job posting, that "It's about time we unloaded some of this old driftwood." This stray remark by someone not in a decision-making position does not establish intent to discriminate. Further, plaintiffs admitted they had not experienced negative treatment or discriminatory remarks based on age before the challenged decisions.

Because plaintiffs failed to produce direct evidence of intent to discriminate we have carefully reviewed the record for rebuttal evidence on which a finder of fact could conclude that Unisys' explanations for the challenged decisions were actually a pretext for age discrimination. "A plaintiff demonstrates pretext by showing either 'that a discriminatory reason more likely motivated the employer or . . . that the employer's proffered explanation is unworthy of credence.' " Plaintiff need not disprove defendant's reasons or demonstrate that age was the factor motivating the decision, but they "must show that age actually played a role in the employees decision-making process had a determinative influence" on the decision. In opposing summary judgment a plaintiff must be given an opportunity to show by competent evidence that the presumably valid reasons for the layoffs were really a pretext for a discriminatory decision. In evaluating plaintiffs' evidence, we must determine whether the evidence interpreted in the light most favorable to the plaintiffs "could persuade a reasonable jury that the employer had discriminated against the plaintiffs." If no material facts are in dispute concerning the pretextuality of defendants' actions, summary judgment is appropriate.

As the district court pointed out, plaintiffs conceded that "Unisys was facing an economic disaster," and that economic problems were "an adequate reason to declare a reduction in force." Thus, plaintiffs do not appear to argue that the reduction in force itself was a pretext for discrimination. Rather, plaintiffs argued that Unisys' failure to use the historical seniority-based layoff approach showed an intent to discriminate. The district court correctly found that a change of policy from seniority-based to skills-based evaluations does not establish pretext. Failure to base layoffs on seniority is not necessarily related. The district court also stated that "Unisys had a written policy of skills-based layoffs which plaintiffs concede is age-neutral."

Plaintiffs also alleged, however, that the policy of skills-based layoffs was not consistently followed and that the transfer decisions were improperly based on age. Plaintiffs failed to counter Unisys' evidence supporting the legitimacy of the reasons supporting the challenged layoffs. Summary judgment for Unisys on the ADEA claims was appropriate.

Affirmed.
Judgment for Unisys.

Case Commentary

The Tenth Circuit held that Unisys's economic disaster was justification for its decision to implement a skills-based layoff rather than a seniority-based layoff, which it had traditionally used.

Case Questions

1. Are you in agreement with the Court's resolution?
2. Do you believe Unisys should have been required to use a seniority-based layoff program?
3. Why should employers be bound by their prior actions?
4. Should not an employer be free to do what it believes is in the best interests of the business?

EMPLOYMENT PERSPECTIVE

Michael Ryan has worked as a driver for Yukon Bus Company for 35 years. He is 62 years old; his salary is $47,000. Ryan is laid off and then replaced by 22-year-old Jude West. West is paid $25,000. Ryan sues, citing age discrimination. Does he win? Yes! Unless Yukon can show cause, then it intentionally terminated Ryan because of his age and correspondingly higher salary. Ryan will be entitled to back pay, loss of pension benefits, as well as liquidated damages in the form of doubling the back pay that is owed. ■

RETIREMENT PACKAGES

Forcing older employees to accept retirement packages is another form of age discrimination. Retirement must not be mandatory; otherwise, the employer will be in violation of the Act. The retirement package must be accepted voluntarily, without coercion.

The issue in the following case is whether the release executed in return for severance pay was done so in accordance with the terms of the Older Workers Benefit Protection Act.

CASE

OUBRE v. ENTERGY OPERATIONS, INC.

522 U.S. 422(1998)

JUSTICE KENNEDY delivered the opinion of the Court.

An employee, as part of a termination agreement, signed a release of all claims against her employer. In consideration, she received severance pay in installments. The release, however, did not comply with specific federal statutory requirements for a release of claims under the Age Discrimination in Employment Act of 1967 (ADEA). After receiving the last payment, the employee brought suit under the ADEA. The employer claims the employee ratified and validated the nonconforming release by retaining the monies paid to secure it. The employer also insists the release bars the action unless, as a precondition to filing suit, the employee tenders back the monies received. We disagree and rule that, as the release did not comply with the statute, it cannot bar the ADEA claim.

I

Petitioner Dolores Oubre worked as a scheduler at a power plant in Killona, Louisiana, run by her employer, respondent Entergy Operations, Inc. In 1994, she received a poor performance rating. Oubre's supervisor met with her on January 17, 1995, and gave her the option of either improving her performance during the coming year or accepting a voluntary arrangement for her severance. She received a packet of information about the severance agreement and had 14 days to consider her options, during which she consulted with attorneys. On January 31, Oubre decided to accept. She signed a release, in which she "agreed to waive, settle, release, and discharge any and all claims, demands, damages, actions, or causes of action ... that I may have against Entergy ...." In exchange, she received six installment payments over the next four months, totaling $6,258.

The Older Workers Benefit Protection Act (OWBPA) imposes specific requirements for releases covering ADEA claims. In procuring the release, Entergy did not comply with the OWBPA in at least three respects: (1) Entergy did not give Oubre enough time to consider her options. (2) Entergy did not give Oubre seven days after she signed the release to change her mind. And (3) the release made no specific reference to claims under the ADEA.

Oubre filed a charge of age discrimination with the Equal Employment Opportunity Commission, which dismissed her charge on the merits but issued a right-to-sue letter. She filed this suit against Entergy in the United States District Court for the Eastern District of Louisiana, alleging constructive discharge on the basis of her age in violation of the ADEA and state law. Oubre has not offered or tried to return the $6,258 to Entergy, nor is it clear she has the means to do so. Entergy moved for summary judgment, claiming Oubre had ratified the defective release by failing to return or offer to return the monies she had received. The District Court agreed and entered summary judgment for Entergy. The Court of Appeals affirmed, and we granted certiorari.

II

The employer rests its case upon general principles of state contract jurisprudence. As the employer recites the rule, contracts tainted by mistake, duress, or even fraud are voidable at the option of the innocent party. The employer maintains, however, that before the innocent party can elect avoidance, she must first tender back any benefits received under the contract. If she fails to do so within a reasonable time after learning of her rights, the employer contends, she ratifies the contract and so makes it binding. The employer also invokes the doctrine of equitable estoppel. As a rule, equitable estoppel bars a party from shirking the burdens of a voidable transaction for as long as she retains the benefits received under it. Applying these principles, the employer claims the employee ratified the ineffective release (or faces estoppel) by retaining all the sums paid in consideration of it. The employer, then, relies not upon the execution of the release but upon a later, distinct ratification of its terms.

These general rules may not be as unified as the employer asserts. And in equity, a person suing to rescind a contract, as a rule, is not required to restore the consideration at the very outset of the litigation. Even if the employer's statement of the general rule requiring tender back before one files suit were correct, it would be unavailing. The rule cited is based simply on the course of negotiation of the parties and the alleged later ratification. The authorities cited do not consider the question raised by statutory standards for releases and a statutory declaration making nonconforming releases ineffective. It is the latter question we confront here.

In 1990, Congress amended the ADEA by passing the OWBPA. The OWBPA provides: "An individual may not waive any right or claim under the ADEA unless the waiver is knowing and voluntary. . . . A waiver may not be considered knowing and voluntary unless at a minimum" it satisfies certain enumerated requirements, including the three listed above.

The statutory command is clear: An employee "may not waive" an ADEA claim unless the waiver or release satisfies the OWBPA's requirements. The policy of the Older Workers Benefit Protection Act is likewise clear from its title: It is designed to protect the rights and benefits of older workers. The OWBPA implements Congress' policy via a strict, unqualified statutory stricture on waivers, and we are bound to take Congress at its word. Congress imposed specific duties on employers who seek releases of certain claims created by statute. Congress delineated these duties with precision and without qualification: An employee "may not waive" an ADEA claim unless the employer complies with the statute. Courts cannot with ease presume ratification of that which Congress forbids. The OWBPA sets up its own regime for assessing the effect of ADEA waivers, separate and apart from contract law. The statute creates a series of prerequisites for knowing and voluntary waivers and imposes affirmative duties of disclosure and waiting periods. The OWBPA governs the effect under federal law of waivers or releases on ADEA claims and incorporates no exceptions or qualifications. The text of the OWBPA forecloses the employer's defense, notwithstanding how general contract principles would apply to non-ADEA claims.

Oubre's cause of action arises under the ADEA, and the release can have no effect on her ADEA claim unless it complies with the OWBPA. In this case, both sides concede the release the employee signed did not comply with the requirements of the OWBPA. Since Oubre's release did not comply with the OWBPA's stringent safeguards, it is unenforceable against her insofar as it purports to waive or release her ADEA claim. As a statutory matter, the release cannot bar her ADEA suit, irrespective of the validity of the contract as to other claims.

In further proceedings in this or other cases, courts may need to inquire whether the employer has claims for restitution, recoupment, or setoff against the employee, and these questions may be complex where a release is effective as to some claims but not as to ADEA claims. We need not decide those issues here, however. It suffices to hold that the release cannot bar the ADEA claim because it does not conform to the statute. Nor did the employee's mere retention of monies amount to a ratification equivalent to a valid release of her ADEA claims, since the retention did not comply with the OWBPA any more than the original release did. The statute governs the effect of the release on ADEA claims, and the employer cannot invoke the employee's failure to tender back as a way of excusing its own failure to comply.

We reverse the judgment of the Court of Appeals and remand for further proceedings consistent with this opinion.

It is so ordered.

Judgment for Oubre.

Case Commentary

The United States Supreme Court held that Oubre's signing of the release was not conducted according to the Older Workers Benefit Protection Act. The fact that Oubre did not return the severance pay does not preclude her ADEA claim.

Case Questions

1. Do you agree with the decision of the United States Supreme Court?
2. Why do you think Oubre did not make restitution?
3. What do you think Oubre is trying to achieve in trying to set aside her agreement to the severance package?

EMPLOYMENT PERSPECTIVE

Mildred Greene is 58 years old. Her employer, Suds & Bubbles, a soap manufacturer, has offered her an attractive retirement package. Mildred, who has no family, would rather continue working in public relations, where she is able to meet new people. Suds & Bubbles informs Mildred that if she does not retire, she will be transferred to back-office bookkeeping work, where she will not be able to interact with anyone. Mildred files a claim with the EEOC and later brings an action in state court. Will she win? Of course! There is no reasonable basis for transferring her. The prospect of a transfer is being used as a threat to force her to retire. ■

COMPARATIVE TREATMENT OF THE ELDERLY

In many cultures, the elderly are looked upon as having much wisdom and are revered. In the United States, the elderly were often forced into retirement unless they were executives or politicians. Although under the Age Discrimination in Employment Act, mandatory retirement is gone, certain prejudices remain. Some prejudices are understandable in economic terms. For example, the performance of routine office work by a person with 24 years' seniority making a salary of $42,000 could easily be replaced by a young person for a salary of $28,000. With age often comes seniority, and with seniority often comes greater wages and benefits and sometimes greater knowledge. While in telecommunications and software development that may not be so, in many other cases it is. To automatically discount an older worker's skill, knowledge, and experience would not be prudent because it would not be utilizing the talents of all American workers.

The following case addresses the question of whether an older employee was terminated because of his age, with his work then reassigned to younger employees.

CASE

KERN v. KOLLSMAN

885 F. Supp. 335 (D.N.H. 1995)

DIVINE, Senior District Judge.

Kollsman is a defense, avionics and medical equipment manufacturer with its principal place of business located in Merrimack, New Hampshire. Plaintiff, having attained a masters degree in electrical engineering, was originally hired by Kollsman on July 18, 1966, to fill the position of Principal Engineer, Electronics. In 1977, plaintiff was promoted to Project Engineer, and in 1978 to Program Manager, a position he held until 1990. In 1990, plaintiff was transferred from Engineering to Marketing, where he was employed as a Manager of International Marketing. On April 8, 1993, Kern, then 60 years of age and earning an annual salary of $79,542, was terminated by Kollsman after nearly 27 years of continuous employment.

"Kollsman's business has traditionally been in the defense area," with the military systems division comprising approximately "70 percent" of all business. Due to a variety of reasons, both global and domestic, "it became clear that defense expenditures around the world would decline and that the defense business would become more difficult."

As an alleged result of such reduced defense expenditures, Kollsman experienced a 50 percent drop in sales between 1990 and 1992, posting a loss of over $23 million in 1991.

"Consistent with such decreasing sales, defendant began to reduce the number of Kollsman employees in order to save the business and save jobs. . . ." Between November 1989 and April 1993, when Kern was terminated, Kollsman reduced its work force by approximately 1100 employees on five separate occasions. It was understood by Kollsman employees, and Kern in particular, that the reason for such reductions was declining sales in the defense business.

Despite such fiscal belt-tightening, sales and prospective orders "in the military area for 1993 were way behind budget."

Determining that further cuts in manufacturing and engineering were no longer feasible, Ronald Wright, President of Kollsman, targeted marketing as the area for further appropriate downsizing. Wright then asked Charles Bernhardt, Vice President of Marketing and Kern's direct supervisor, to prepare a list of individuals recommended for elimination.

Bernhardt returned to Wright with a list of five individuals whose average age was 57.2. Wright agreed with Bernhardt in part, but chose to keep two of the five—Herb Sandberg, then aged 69, and Al Friedrich, then age 65—since they "both performed important functions for Kollsman." Kern claims that he was not dismissed pursuant to a reduction in force because many of his previous responsibilities were not eliminated with his position, but rather were allocated to younger employees. Such a redistribution of responsibilities, Kern argues, proves that his position was not "eliminated" and thus Kollsman's purported work force reduction is merely a pretext for age discrimination. In the alternative, Kern argues that his position was subject to a job combination rather than a job elimination and, as such, a peer ranking should have been performed. The failure of Kollsman to conduct such a ranking, according to Kern, is further evidence of discriminatory animus.

DISCRIMINATORY PRETEXT

Kern initially proffers the following deposition testimony of Bernhardt to establish pretext:

Q. In terms of the thinking that went into deciding who to put on the layoff list, was their impact on the payroll a consideration?

A. Yeah.

Q. . . . A person's cost to the company was figured by reference not only to his salary, but by reference to other things, as well; would you agree?

A. That's correct.

Q. Okay. And some of those other things would be his employee benefits?

A. Yes.

Q. Secretary?

A. Yes.

Q. Expense accounts?

A. Yes.

Q. Going back to the employee benefits, how close they'd be to retirement, that is when the pension would have to be paid?

A. I would assume that's a consideration, because under the new laws, you have to reserve for that type of thing.

And I think that is a factor, and it could be a very large factor.

Q. And in terms of the pensions, Kollsman had a so-called defined benefit.

A. Yes.

Q. Defined benefit type of plan; is that correct?

A. Yes, that's correct.

Q. And the longer a person served at Kollsman, the higher his pension benefits would be once he retired?

A. That's correct.

However, the mere reference to a correlation between pension and age, standing alone, is insufficient to sustain plaintiff's burden of demonstrating pretext.

Plaintiff contends that on several occasions defendants promulgated literature which either expressly or implicitly served to modify his status as an at-will employee. More specifically, Kern asserts that, based on alleged oral and written representations from Kollsman, he developed "an expectation of continued employment unless the application of peer ranking procedures and other objective criteria indicated that my termination was warranted." Defendant's employment handbook contains the following disclaimer:

EMPLOYMENT-AT-WILL STATEMENT

It is understood that nothing contained in the employment application, in the granting of an interview, or in this handbook is intended to create an employment contract between Kollsman and the individual either for employment or for providing any benefit. It is understood that no employment guarantee is binding upon Kollsman unless the terms and conditions are specified in writing. If an employment relationship is established, it is understood that the employee has the right to terminate his/her employment at any time and that Kollsman retains a similar right.

Defendant asserts that the clear meaning of said disclaimer is that it "did not alter the at-will relationship of the parties. It created no employment contract."

This conclusion, however, does not end the matter. Kern further submits that certain documents promulgated by Kollsman regarding reduction in force procedures lack any disclaiming language, can be found to be contractual promise equivalents, and are thus valid and enforceable modifications to his at-will status.

Plaintiff's case similarly rests on too frail or thin a reed. The court therefore finds and rules that plaintiff's breach of express or implied contract claim based on materials promulgated by his employer is insufficient as a matter of law. In consequence thereof, defendant's motion for summary judgment with respect to said breach of contract claim must be and is herewith granted.

Judgment for Kollsman.

Case Commentary

The District Court of New Hampshire decided that Kern was discharged because of a decline in the defense industry. Certain individuals older than Kern were retained because their contribution to Kollsman was determined to be more important than Kern's.

Case Questions

1. Do you agree with the Court's reasoning?
2. Do you believe Kollsman's retention of some senior workers was just a pretext to let others go?
3. Can a skills-based layoff that results in the discharge of predominantly older workers be justified?

❖ EMPLOYER LESSONS

- Do not take age into account in employment decisions.
- Understand the purpose of the Age Discrimination in Employment Act.
- Know that protection against age discrimination begins at 40.
- Consider that there is no longer mandatory retirement.
- Realize that employees may work so long as they are competent to do so.
- Refrain from coercing employees to accept early retirement packages.
- Be careful when downsizing not to discharge an inordinate number of older workers.
- Learn that the desire to project a more youthful and up-to-date image might have to give way to the rights of older workers.
- Be aware that company policy may dictate the mandatory retirement age of high-level executives.
- Learn that tenured professors may be forced into retirement at age 70.

❖ EMPLOYEE LESSONS

- Know what protections you are afforded under the Age Discrimination in Employment Act.
- Consider whether age may have been a factor in your termination if you are 40 years of age or older.
- Realize that you may work indefinitely so long as you are performing the essential functions of the job.
- Appreciate that if you are in your 30s and are replaced by someone 10 to 15 years younger, you are not protected under the ADEA.
- Be aware that you cannot be coerced into accepting an early retirement package.
- Be careful when an employer downsizes that its motivation is not based on age.
- Understand that age discrimination may occur when your position is terminated because of your high salary and age.
- Be aware that age discrimination exists when an older employee is replaced by someone significantly younger even where the younger person is over 40 years of age.
- Be apprised that policy-making executives may be forced to retire at 65 years of age.
- Be aware that tenured professors have no ADEA protection beyond 70.

❖ SUMMARY

In years gone by, most people worked either until they became disabled or until they died. Disabled workers were usually cared for by family members. There was no such thing as retirement unless a person was independently wealthy and could therefore live off the income from his or her investments. With the advent of Social Security, those aged 65 years or older are entitled to a small amount of income. As pensions became more prevalent, workers were guaranteed a defined benefit. The income from Social Security and the pension enabled people to survive after mandatory retirement. How well they survived depended upon the size of their pension and of their investment income. Pensions remained fixed because they were not adjusted for inflation. Social Security recipients received cost-of-living adjustments. Investment income has a built-in guard against inflation.

As life expectancies increased, the majority of Americans now live beyond 65. Surreptitiously prohibiting people from continuing to work because of their age when they are perfectly capable of doing so is discriminatory. The purpose of the Age Discrimination in Employment Act is to dispel this conduct and to give free access to the workplace to those people over the age of 65. Workers will be able to continue in their present job or to seek new employment elsewhere, thus broadening the pool of workers for companies to select from. As was stated, many older workers have special skills, knowledge, and experience. The freedom to employ these people is certainly a bonus for employers, especially those involved in the growing competitiveness of the global marketplace.

❖ REVIEW QUESTIONS

1. What is the significance of the Age Discrimination in Employment Act?
2. At what age may an employee claim age discrimination?
3. Is there a mandatory retirement age?
4. Are there any exceptions?
5. Is an advertisement which specifies "recent college graduate" discriminatory?
6. Can age be considered a bona fide occupational qualification?
7. What must be the determining factor in the dismissal of an older worker?
8. Can a young person who is not hired because of his or her youth claim age discrimination?
9. Does the Civil Rights Act encompass those discriminated against because of age?
10. In many cultures, age is a sign of wisdom. Why is that not generally the case in the United States?
11. At the time of his termination, Naas, then age 60, was employed as a "Senior Systems Consulting Analyst." On October 29, 1991, Naas timely filed a Charge of Discrimination with the Equal Employment Opportunity Commission, alleging that his termination violated the Age Discrimination in Employment Act (ADEA), 29 U.S.C. 621. Thereafter, plaintiff filed a complaint in this Court against Westinghouse, alleging violation of the ADEA. What was the result? *Naas v. Westinghouse Elec. Corp,* 818 F. Supp. 874 (W.D.Pa. 1993)
12. Gilmer filed an age discrimination lawsuit against Interstate/Johnson Lane Corp. The company argued that all employment matters were subject to arbitration. Gilmer retorted that an ADEA claim was exempt from that requirement. What was the result? *Gilmer v. Interstate/Johnson Lane Corp.,* 111 S. Ct 1647 (1991)
13. The Hazens hired respondent Walter F. Biggins as their technical director in 1977. They fired him in 1986, when he was 62 years old.
    Respondent brought suit against petitioners in the United States District Court for the District of Massachusetts, alleging a

violation of the ADEA. He claimed that age had been a determinative factor in petitioners' decision to fire him. Petitioners contested this claim, asserting instead that respondent had been fired for doing business with competitors of Hazen Paper. What was the result? *Hazen Paper Company, et al. v. Walter F. Biggins,* 113 S. Ct. 1701 (1993)

14. The following case concerns a 53-year-old employee who was terminated due to poor performance. He alleged that his evaluations were purposely lowered to effectuate his dismissal and that the underlying reason was his age. His replacement was 10 years younger.

    Martin alleges that no reason was given for his termination; that he had never been reprimanded, counseled, or disciplined in any way during his employment; that his evaluations were always "satisfactory"; and that he met all of the goals and objectives set by Ryder. Martin also alleges that after his termination Levering directed Eaves to lower Martin's performance to a level below satisfactory as a pretext for Martin's termination. What was the result? *Martin v. Ryder Distributions Resources, Inc.,* 811 F. Supp. 658 (1992)

15. Donald Pilot, a member of Local 350, retired in 1983. After retirement, he paid retired members' dues. In 1984, he decided to return to work, and signed onto the out of work list. Local 350 removed his name from the list, stating he was not eligible. In a letter dated April 20, 1984, Local 350 informed Pilot that, "as a retiree, having applied for and been granted pension, you are not presently eligible for dispatch through the UA Local 350 Hiring Hall." Local 350 informed Pilot that to be eligible to sign up for referral, he would have to cease receiving his pension. What was the result? *E.E.O.C. v. Local 350, Plumbers and Pipefitters,* 982 F.2d 1305 (9th Cir. 1992)

16. Plaintiff began her leave on May 21, 1990.

    Plaintiff claims that after Worwa became president, the bank instituted a program of eliminating employees over 40 years of age and replacing them with younger employees.

    Plaintiff filed a charge of age discrimination with the Equal Employment Opportunity Commission ("EEOC") on August 2, 1991. Under the ADEA, a plaintiff is required to file a charge with the EEOC "within 300 days after the alleged unlawful practice occurred." What was the result? *Zelewski v. American Federal Savings Bank,* 811 F. Supp. 456 (D. Minn. 1993)

17. His registration application, entitled "Uniform Application for Securities Industry Registration or Transfer," provided, among other things, that Gilmer "agreed to arbitrate any dispute, claim or controversy" arising between him and Interstate "that is required to be arbitrated under the rules, constitutions or by-laws of the organizations with which I register." NYSE Rule 347 provides for arbitration of "any controversy between a registered representative and any member or member organization arising out of the employment or termination of employment of such registered representative."

    Interstate terminated Gilmer's employment in 1987, at which time Gilmer was 62 years of age. Gilmer subsequently brought suit in the United States District Court for the Western District of North Carolina, alleging that Interstate had discharged him because of his age, in violation of the ADEA. In response to Gilmer's complaint, Interstate filed in the District Court a motion to compel arbitration of the ADEA claim. What was the result? *Gilmer v. Interstate/Johnson Lane Corp.,* 111 S. Ct. 1647 (1991)

18. Cowan submitted a proposal, dated January 19, 1990, recommending that Anchor transfer Bay Ridge branch of the Records Management Department to Albion to eliminate the cost of overhead in the Bay Ridge office and the duplication of certain verification duties in both offices. Cowan also suggested that Conroy, Wilson, and Kissoon be transferred to Albion to continue to perform their assigned duties. This proposal specifically stated that Conroy play a supervisory role at Albion, New York. Conroy sued under the ADEA. What was the result? *Conroy v. Anchor Sav. Bank, FSB.* 810 F. Supp 42 (E.D.N.Y. 1993)

19. At a January 1990 meeting, Burke refused to get Stetson a new job. Burke said Stetson had three options: continue to work at NSC, use the formal transfer process to seek a job in another NYNEX unit, or apply for early retirement under the SRI. According to

Stetson, Burke said, "Don't you feel like you have slowed down? I know I have."

On March 21, 1990, Stetson submitted his application for early retirement under the SRI.

After Fisher learned of Stetson's March 21 application, he sent Stetson a letter dated May 24, 1990, inviting Stetson to rescind his retirement decision and remain with NSC. He retired effective May 31.

In August 1990, Stetson commenced the present action, alleging that his early retirement decision was not voluntary but rather was a response to intolerable working conditions. He asserted that NYNEX and NSC executives had been pressured to force employees to participate in the early retirement plan, and that Fisher and Burke imposed the intolerable working conditions on him solely because of his age and with the intent of forcing him to retire. What was the result? *Stetson v. Nynex Service Co.,* 995 F.2d 355 (2nd Cir. 1993)

20. Hickman and McCann had been working at a refinery owned by Texas City Refining, Inc. (TCR). When that refinery was sold to Hill Petroleum, Inc. (Hill), Hickman and McCann were not offered jobs by the new owners. Subsequently Hickman and McCann sued Hill, TCR, and TCR's parent corporations (collectively Agway) for violations of the Age Discrimination in Employment Act (ADEA).

As a part of this restructuring, Hickman was laid off and her position as shift clerk was filled by younger employees, and McCann's position as a confidential secretary and personnel administrator was eliminated. Both Hickman and McCann had been long-time employees of TCR and were within the protected class of the ADEA. What was the result? *McCann v. Texas City Refining, Inc.,* 984 F.2d 667 (5th Cir. 1993)

21. Is it possible to claim age discrimination even though the individual opted for early retirement?

22. Is it ethical for a supervisor to discharge an employee, when he or she knows that the employer's motivation is age?

23. Are economic factors a justifiable defense to a suit based on age discrimination?

❖ WEB SITES

www.aoa.gov/factsheets/ageism.html
www.eeoc.gov/facts/age.html
www.hightechcareers.com/docs/agediscr.html
www.aristotle.net/~hantley/hiedlegl/statutes/agedis67.htm
www.cornell.edu/topics/employment_discrimination.html
www.aarp.org/ontheissues/issueagedisc.html
www.agerights.com

DISABILITY DISCRIMINATION

INTRODUCTION

In 1990, Congress passed the Americans with Disabilities Act (ADA). The ADA has a profound effect on the many millions of Americans who live with some type of disability. The Americans with Disabilities Act (ADA) requires employers with 15 or more employees to refrain from discriminating against any individual who has an impairment that limits major life activities, such as an impairment to sight, speech, hearing, walking, and learning. Also included are people with cancer, heart conditions, AIDS, and disfigurement, as well as people recovering from substance abuse.

The four largest categories of disabilities are physical (prosthetic, wheelchair, carpal tunnel), disease (heart, lung, cancer, AIDS), sensory (sight, speech, hearing) and mental (retarded, emotionally disabled, chemical dependency). The examples given are not all inclusive. Physical and disease represent a much larger proportion than sensory or mental.

CHAPTER CHECKLIST

❖ Be familiar with the intricacies of the Americans with Disabilities Act.

❖ Learn the four major categories of disabilities.

❖ Know that anyone perceived as having a disability will be covered under the ADA even if they would not otherwise be covered.

❖ Realize that reasonable accommodations must be made if an employee is disabled.

❖ Consider that employees may seek ADA coverage for many ailments, injuries, and conditions, but not all of these qualify as disabilities.

❖ Understand that AIDS is covered under the ADA as a disease.

❖ Be aware that applicants should not be asked if they are disabled.

❖ Be apprised that disabled employees must be able to perform the essential functions of the job.

❖ Be concerned that if the accommodation requested amounts to an undue burden, the employer does not have to grant it.

❖ Appreciate that disabled individuals have the right to be gainfully employed.

EMPLOYMENT SCENARIO

One day, Louise Fredricks enters the flagship store of the Long and Short of It in a wheelchair. She encounters Tom Long and informs him that she is responding to L&S's advertisement for a sales associate. Tom responds in amazement, "You're kidding." Louise reiterates her intent to gain employment. Tom begins laughing uncontrollably and opens the exit door. Louise, visibly upset, departs in despair. After composing herself, Louise becomes infuriated over the treatment she endured. She contacts the EEOC, which notifies L&S that they will be investigating. Susan North, Esq., L&S's attorney, recites a brief lesson on the Americans with Disabilities Act for Tom Long and Mark Short, copresidents of the Long and the Short of It. Susan states that Louise was entitled to be treated as any other applicant and judged based on her ability, not her disability. Susan rebuked Tom for his treatment of Louise, which amounted to disability discrimination. Susan stated that now L&S will be subject to an EEOC investigation, a possible lawsuit, and the payment of compensatory damages for the emotional upset endured by Louise, as well as possible punitive damages for intentional discrimination.

REASONABLE ACCOMMODATIONS

The ADA requires employers to make reasonable accommodations to enable the disabled to work. This includes making the worksite accessible, modifying equipment, and changing work schedules. Those businesses providing a service to the public must make their establishments accessible to the handicapped. This includes but is not limited to stores, restaurants, hotels, museums, theatres, historical landmarks, visitor centers, sports arenas, health and fitness facilities, and night clubs. The disabled person must be qualified to do the job; that is, he or she must be able to perform the essential functions with reasonable accommodation. The ADA was not designed to force employers to hire disabled workers who are not qualified. The qualifications required, however, must be necessary to do the job. If someone is more qualified than the disabled individual, the employer is not required to give the disabled individual preferential treatment.

The issue in the following case is whether twin sisters with severe myopia, which has been corrected with eyewear, are covered under the ADA.

SUTTON v. UNITED AIR LINES, INC.

527 U.S. 471 (1999)

JUSTICE O'CONNOR delivered the opinion of the Court.

The Americans with Disabilities Act of 1990 (ADA or Act), prohibits certain employers from discriminating against individuals on the basis of their disabilities. Petitioners challenge the dismissal of their ADA action for failure to state a claim upon which relief can be granted. We conclude that the complaint was properly dismissed. In reaching that result, we hold that the determination of whether an individual is disabled should be made with reference to measures that mitigate the individual's impairment, including, in this instance, eyeglasses and contact lenses. In addition, we hold that petitioners failed to allege properly that respondent "regarded" them as having a disability within the meaning of the ADA.

I

Petitioners are twin sisters, both of whom have severe myopia. Each petitioner's uncorrected visual acuity is 20/200 or worse in her right eye and 20/400 or worse in her left eye, but "with the use of corrective lenses, each . . . has vision that is 20/20 or better." Consequently, without corrective lenses, each "effectively cannot see to conduct numerous activities such as driving a vehicle, watching television or shopping in public stores," but with corrective measures, such as glasses or contact lenses, both "function identically to individuals without a similar impairment."

In 1992, petitioners applied to respondent for employment as commercial airline pilots. They met respondent's basic age, education, experience, and FAA certification qualifications. After submitting their applications for employment, both petitioners were invited by respondent to an interview and to flight simulator tests. Both were told during their interviews, however, that a mistake had been made in inviting them to interview because petitioners did not meet respondent's minimum vision requirement, which was uncorrected visual acuity of 20/100 or better. Due to their failure to meet this requirement, petitioners' interviews were terminated, and neither was offered a pilot position.

In light of respondent's proffered reason for rejecting them, petitioners filed a charge of disability discrimination under the ADA with the Equal Employment Opportunity Commission (EEOC). After receiving a right to sue letter, petitioners filed suit in the United States District Court for the District of Colorado, alleging that respondent had discriminated against them "on the basis of their disability, or because respondent regarded petitioners as having a disability" in violation of the ADA. Specifically, petitioners alleged that due to their severe myopia they actually have a substantially limiting impairment or are regarded as having such an impairment, and are thus disabled under the Act.

The District Court dismissed petitioners' complaint for failure to state a claim upon which relief could be granted. Because petitioners could fully correct their visual impairments, the court held that they were not actually substantially limited in any major life activity and thus had not stated a claim that they were disabled within the meaning of the ADA. The court also determined that petitioners had not made allegations sufficient to support their claim that they were "regarded" by the respondent as having an impairment that substantially limits a major life activity. The court observed that "the statutory reference to a substantial limitation indicates . . . that an employer regards an employee as handicapped in his or her ability to work by finding the employee's impairment to foreclose generally the type of employment involved."

But petitioners had alleged only that respondent regarded them as unable to satisfy the requirements of a particular job, global airline pilot. Consequently, the court held that petitioners had not stated a claim that they were regarded as substantially limited in the major life activity of working. Employing similar logic, the Court of Appeals for the Tenth Circuit affirmed the District Court's judgment.

The Tenth Circuit's decision is in tension with the decisions of other Courts of Appeals. We granted certiorari and now affirm.

II

The ADA prohibits discrimination by covered entities, including private employers, against qualified individuals with a disability. Specifically, it provides that no covered employer "shall discriminate against a qualified individual with a disability because of the disability of such individual in regard to job application procedures, the hiring, advancement, or discharge of employees, employee compensation, job training, and other terms, conditions, and privileges of employment." ("The term 'covered entity' means an employer, employment agency, labor organization, or joint labor-management committee.") A "qualified individual with a disability" is identified as "an individual with a disability who, with or without reasonable accommodation, can perform the essential functions of the employment position that such individual holds or desires." In turn, a "disability" is defined as:

"(A) a physical or mental impairment that substantially limits one or more of the major life activities of such individual;
"(B) a record of such an impairment; or
"(C) being regarded as having such an impairment."

Accordingly, to fall within this definition one must have an actual disability (subsection (A)), have a record of a disability (subsection (B)), or be regarded as having one (subsection (C)).

The parties agree that the authority to issue regulations to implement the Act is split primarily among three Government agencies. According to the parties, the EEOC has authority to issue regulations to carry out the employment provisions in Title I of the ADA. The Attorney General is granted authority to issue regulations with respect to Title II, which relates to public

services. Finally, the Secretary of Transportation has authority to issue regulations pertaining to the transportation provisions of Titles II and III.

No agency, however, has been given authority to issue regulations implementing the generally applicable provisions of the ADA, which fall outside Titles I-V. Most notably, no agency has been delegated authority to interpret the term "disability." The EEOC has, nonetheless, issued regulations to provide additional guidance regarding the proper interpretation of this term. After restating the definition of disability given in the statute, the EEOC regulations define the three elements of disability: (1) "physical or mental impairment," (2) "substantially limits," and (3) "major life activities." Under the regulations, a "physical impairment" includes "any physiological disorder, or condition, cosmetic disfigurement, or anatomical loss affecting one or more of the following body systems: neurological, musculoskeletal, special sense organs, respiratory (including speech organs), cardiovascular, reproductive, digestive, genito-urinary, hemic and lymphatic, skin, and endocrine." The term "substantially limits" means, among other things, "unable to perform a major life activity that the average person in the general population can perform;" or "significantly restricted as to the condition, manner or duration under which an individual can perform a particular major life activity as compared to the condition, manner, or duration under which the average person in the general population can perform that same major life activity." Finally, "major life activities means functions such as caring for oneself, performing manual tasks, walking, seeing, hearing, speaking, breathing, learning, and working." Because both parties accept these regulations as valid, and determining their validity is not necessary to decide this case, we have no occasion to consider what deference they are due, if any.

III

With this statutory and regulatory framework in mind, we turn first to the question whether petitioners have stated a claim under subsection (A) of the disability definition, that is, whether they have alleged that they possess a physical impairment that substantially limits them in one or more major life activities. Because petitioners allege that with corrective measures their vision "is 20/20 or better," they are not actually disabled within the meaning of the Act if the "disability" determination is made with reference to these measures. Consequently, with respect to subsection (A) of the disability definition, our decision turns on whether disability is to be determined with or without reference to corrective measures.

Looking at the Act as a whole, it is apparent that if a person is taking measures to correct for, or mitigate, a physical or mental impairment, the effects of those measures—both positive and negative—must be taken into account when judging whether that person is "substantially limited" in a major life activity and thus "disabled" under the Act.

Three separate provisions of the ADA, read in concert, lead us to this conclusion. The Act defines a "disability" as "a physical or mental impairment that *substantially limits* one or more of the major life activities" of an individual. Because the phrase "substantially limits" appears in the Act in the present indicative verb form, we think the language is properly read as requiring that a person be presently—not potentially or hypothetically—substantially limited in order to demonstrate a disability. A "disability" exists only where an impairment "substantially limits" a major life activity, not where it "might," "could," or "would" be substantially limiting if mitigating measures were not taken. A person whose physical or mental impairment is corrected by medication or other measures does not have an impairment that presently "substantially limits" a major life activity. To be sure, a person whose physical or mental impairment is corrected by mitigating measures still has an impairment, but if the impairment is corrected it does not "substantially limit" a major life activity.

The definition of disability also requires that disabilities be evaluated "with respect to an individual" and be determined based on whether an impairment substantially limits the "major life activities of such individual." Thus, whether a person has a disability under the ADA is an individualized inquiry.

The agency guidelines' directive that persons be judged in their uncorrected or unmitigated state runs directly counter to the individualized inquiry mandated by the ADA.

It explained that the estimates of the number of disabled Americans ranged from an over-inclusive 160 million under a "health conditions approach," which looks at all conditions that impair the health or normal functional abilities of an individual, to an underinclusive 22.7 million under a "work disability approach," which focuses on individuals' reported ability to work.

Regardless of its exact source, however, the 43 million figure reflects an understanding that those whose impairments are largely corrected by medication or other devices are not "disabled" within the meaning of the ADA.

Because it is included in the ADA's text, the finding that 43 million individuals are disabled gives content to the ADA's terms, specifically the term "disability." Had Congress intended to include all persons with corrected physical limitations among those covered by the Act, it undoubtedly would have cited a much higher number of disabled persons in the findings. That it did not is evidence that the ADA's coverage is restricted to only those whose impairments are not mitigated by corrective measures. The use of a corrective device does not, by itself, relieve one's disability. Rather, one has a disability under subsection A if, notwithstanding the use of a corrective device, that individual is substantially limited in a major life activity. For example, individuals who use prosthetic limbs or wheelchairs may be mobile and capable of functioning in society but still be disabled because of a substantial limitation on their ability to walk or run. The same may be true of individuals who take medicine to lessen the symptoms of an impairment so that they can function but nevertheless remain substantially limited. Alternatively, one whose high blood pressure is "cured" by medication may be regarded as disabled by a covered entity, and thus disabled under subsection C of the definition. The use or nonuse of a corrective device does not determine whether an individual is disabled; that determination depends on whether the limitations an individual with an impairment *actually* faces are in fact substantially limiting.

Applying this reading of the Act to the case at hand, we conclude that the Court of Appeals correctly resolved the issue of disability in respondent's favor. As noted above, petitioners allege that with corrective measures, their visual acuity is 20/20, and that they "function identically to individuals without a similar impairment," In addition, petitioners concede that they "do not argue that the use of corrective lenses in itself demonstrates a substantially limiting impairment." Accordingly, because we decide that disability under the Act is to be determined with reference to corrective measures, we agree with the courts below that petitioners have not stated a claim that they are substantially limited in any major life activity.

IV

Under subsection (C), individuals who are "regarded as" having a disability are disabled within the meaning of the ADA. Subsection (C) provides that having a disability includes "being regarded as having," "a physical or mental impairment that substantially limits one or more of the major life activities of such individual." There are two apparent ways in which individuals may fall within this statutory definition: (1) a covered entity mistakenly believes that a person has a physical impairment that substantially limits one or more major life activities, or (2) a covered entity mistakenly believes that an actual, nonlimiting impairment substantially limits one or more major life activities. In both cases, it is necessary that a covered entity entertain misperceptions about the individual—it must believe either that one has a substantially limiting impairment that one does not have or that one has a substantially limiting impairment when, in fact, the impairment is not so limiting. These misperceptions often "result from stereotypic assumptions not truly indicative of . . . individual ability." ("By amending the definition of 'handicapped individual' to include not only those who are actually physically impaired, but also those who are regarded as impaired and who, as a result, are substantially limited in a major life activity, Congress acknowledged that society's accumulated myths and fears about disability and disease are as handicapping as are the physical limitations that flow from actual impairment.")

There is no dispute that petitioners are physically impaired. Petitioners do not make the obvious argument that they are regarded due to their impairments as substantially limited in the major life activity of seeing. They contend only that respondent mistakenly believes their physical impairments substantially limit them in the major life activity of working. To support this claim, petitioners allege that respondent has a vision requirement, which is allegedly based on myth and stereotype. Further, this requirement substantially limits their ability to engage in the major life activity of working by precluding them from obtaining the job of global airline pilot, which they argue is a "class of employment." In reply, respondent argues that the position of global airline pilot is not a class of jobs and therefore petitioners have not stated a claim that they are regarded as substantially limited in the major life activity of working.

Standing alone, the allegation that respondent has a vision requirement in place does not establish a claim that respondent regards petitioners as substantially limited in the major life activity of working. By its terms, the ADA allows employers to prefer some physical attributes over others and to establish physical criteria. An employer runs afoul of the ADA when it makes an employment decision based on a physical or mental impairment, real or imagined, that is regarded as substantially limiting a major life activity. Accordingly, an employer is free to decide that physical characteristics or medical conditions that do not rise to the level of an impairment—such as one's height, build, or singing voice—are preferable to others, just as it is free to decide that some limiting, but not *substantially* limiting, impairments make individuals less than ideally suited for a job.

Assuming without deciding that working is a major life activity and that the EEOC regulations interpreting the term "substantially limits" are reasonable, petitioners have failed to allege adequately that their poor eyesight is regarded as an impairment that substantially limits them in the major life activity of working. An otherwise valid job requirement, such as a height requirement, does not become invalid simply because it *would* limit a person's employment opportunities in a substantial way *if* it were adopted by a substantial number of employers. Because petitioners have not alleged, and cannot demonstrate, that respondent's vision requirement reflects a belief that petitioners' vision substantially limits them, we agree with the decision of the Court of Appeals affirming the dismissal of petitioners' claim that they are regarded as disabled.

For these reasons, the decision of the Court of Appeals for the Tenth Circuit is affirmed.

Judgment for United Airlines,

Case Commentary

The United States Supreme Court resolved that the twins were not covered under the ADA because their vision problem was corrected with eyewear. Therefore they no longer had a disability that limited a major life activity.

Case Questions

1. Do you agree with the United States Supreme Court's decision?

2. Should people with correctable disabilities still be covered under the ADA?

3. If the twins had argued that United Airlines regarded them as having a disability, do you believe they would have prevailed?

The question presented in the case that follows is whether an employer may incorporate a federal safety standard into a job qualification that, in effect, bars a disabled person from employment.

CASE

ALBERTSONS, INC. v. KIRKINGBURG

527 U.S. 555 (1999)

JUSTICE SOUTER delivered the opinion of the Court.

The question posed is whether, under the Americans with Disabilities Act of 1990, an employer who requires as a job qualification that an employee meet an otherwise applicable federal safety regulation must justify enforcing the regulation solely because its standard may be waived in an individual case. We answer no.

I

In August 1990, petitioner, Albertsons, Inc., a grocery-store chain with supermarkets in several States, hired respondent, Hallie Kirkingburg, as a truckdriver based at its Portland, Oregon, warehouse. Kirkingburg had more than a decade's driving experience and performed well when Albertsons' transportation manager took him on a road test.

Before starting work, Kirkingburg was examined to see if he met federal vision standards for commercial truckdrivers. For many decades the Department of Transportation or its predecessors has been responsible for devising these standards for individuals who drive commercial vehicles in interstate commerce. Since 1971, the basic vision regulation has required corrected distant visual acuity of at least 20/40 in each eye and distant binocular acuity of at least 20/40. Kirkingburg, however, suffers from amblyopia, an uncorrectable condition that leaves him with 20/200 vision in his left eye and monocular vision in effect. Despite Kirkingburg's weak left eye, the doctor erroneously certified that he met the DOT's basic vision standard, and Albertsons hired him.

In December 1991, Kirkingburg injured himself on the job and took a leave of absence. Before returning to work in November 1992, Kirkingburg went for a further physical as required by the company. This time, the examining physician correctly assessed Kirkingburg's vision and explained that his eyesight did not meet the basic DOT standards. The physician, or his nurse, told Kirkingburg that in order to be legally qualified to drive, he would have to obtain a waiver of its basic vision standards from the DOT. The doctor was alluding to a scheme begun in July 1992 for giving DOT certification to applicants with deficient vision who had three years of recent experience driving a commercial vehicle without a license suspension or revocation, involvement in a reportable accident in which the applicant was cited for a moving violation, conviction for certain driving-related offenses, citation for certain serious traffic violations, or more than two convictions for any other moving violations. A waiver applicant had to agree to have his vision checked annually for deterioration, and to report certain information about his driving experience to the Federal Highway Administration, the agency within the DOT responsible for overseeing the motor carrier safety regulations. Kirkingburg applied for a waiver, but because he could not meet the basic DOT vision standard Albertsons fired him from his job as a truckdriver. In early 1993, after he had left Albertsons, Kirkingburg received a DOT waiver, but Albertsons refused to rehire him.

Kirkingburg sued Albertsons, claiming that firing him violated the ADA. Albertsons moved for summary judgment solely on the ground that Kirkingburg was "not 'otherwise qualified' to perform the job of truck driver with or without reasonable accommodation." The District Court granted the motion, ruling that Albertsons had reasonably concluded that Kirkingburg was not qualified without an accommodation because he could not, as admitted, meet the basic DOT vision standards. The court held that giving Kirkingburg time to get a DOT waiver was not a required reasonable accommodation because the waiver program was "a flawed experiment that has not altered the DOT vision requirements."

A divided panel of the Ninth Circuit reversed. In addition to pressing its claim that Kirkingburg was not otherwise qualified, Albertsons for the first time on appeal took the position that it was entitled to summary judgment because Kirkingburg did not have a disability within the meaning of the Act. The Court of Appeals considered but rejected the new argument, concluding that because Kirkingburg had presented "uncontroverted evidence" that his vision was effectively monocular, he had demonstrated that "the *manner* in which he sees differs significantly

from the *manner* in which most people see." That difference in manner, the court held, was sufficient to establish disability.

II

Though we need not speak to the issue whether Kirkingburg was an individual with a disability in order to resolve this case, that issue falls within the first question on which we granted certiorari, and we think it worthwhile to address it briefly in order to correct three missteps the Ninth Circuit made in its discussion of the matter. Under the ADA:

"The term 'disability' means, with respect to an individual—

"(A) a physical or mental impairment that substantially limits one or more of the major life activities of such individual;

"(B) a record of such an impairment; or

"(C) being regarded as having such an impairment."

We are concerned only with the first definition. There is no dispute either that Kirkingburg's amblyopia is a physical impairment within the meaning of the Act, (defining "physical impairment" as "any physiological disorder, or condition . . . affecting one or more of the following body systems: . . . special sense organs"), or that seeing is one of his major life activities. The question is whether his monocular vision alone "substantially limits" Kirkingburg's seeing.

This is not to suggest that monocular individuals have an onerous burden in trying to show that they are disabled. On the contrary, our brief examination of some of the medical literature leaves us sharing the Government's judgment that people with monocular vision "ordinarily" will meet the Act's definition of disability, and we suppose that defendant companies will often not contest the issue. We simply hold that the Act requires monocular individuals, like others claiming the Act's protection, to prove a disability by offering evidence that the extent of the limitation in terms of their own experience, as in loss of depth perception and visual field, is substantial.

III

Albertsons' primary contention is that even if Kirkingburg was disabled, he was not a "qualified" individual with a disability, because Albertsons merely insisted on the minimum level of visual acuity set forth in the DOT's Motor Carrier Safety Regulations. If Albertsons was entitled to enforce that standard as defining an "essential job function of the employment position," that is the end of the case, for Kirkingburg concededly could not satisfy it.

Under Title I of the ADA, employers may justify their use of "qualification standards . . . that screen out or tend to screen out or otherwise deny a job or benefit to an individual with a disability," so long as such standards are "job-related and consistent with business necessity, and . . . performance cannot be accomplished by reasonable accommodation. . . ."

In sum, the regulatory record made it plain that the waiver regulation did not rest on any final, factual conclusion that the waiver scheme would be conducive to public safety in the manner of the general acuity standards and did not purport to modify the substantive content of the general acuity regulation in any way. The waiver program was simply an experiment with safety, however well intended, resting on a hypothesis whose confirmation or refutation in practice would provide a factual basis for reconsidering the existing standards.

Nothing in the waiver regulation, of course, required an employer of commercial drivers to accept the hypothesis and participate in the Government's experiment. The only question, then, is whether the ADA should be read to require such an employer to defend a decision to decline the

experiment. Is it reasonable, that is, to read the ADA as requiring an employer like Albertsons to shoulder the general statutory burden to justify a job qualification that would tend to exclude the disabled, whenever the employer chooses to abide by the otherwise clearly applicable, unamended substantive regulatory standard despite the Government's willingness to waive it experimentally and without any finding of its being inappropriate? If the answer were yes, an employer would in fact have an obligation of which we can think of no comparable example in our law. The employer would be required in effect to justify *de novo* an existing and otherwise applicable safety regulation issued by the Government itself. The employer would be required on a case-by-case basis to reinvent the Government's own wheel when the Government had merely begun an experiment to provide data to consider changing the underlying specifications. And what is even more, the employer would be required to do so when the Government had made an affirmative record indicating that contemporary empirical evidence was hard to come by. It is simply not credible that Congress enacted the ADA (before there was any waiver program) with the understanding that employers choosing to respect the Government's sole substantive visual acuity regulation in the face of an experimental waiver might be burdened with an obligation to defend the regulation's application according to its own terms.

The judgment of the Ninth Circuit is accordingly reversed.

Judgment for Albertsons, Inc

Case Commentary

The United States Supreme Court decided that employers who use federal safety standards in determining whether an applicant is qualified for a position do not have to justify the validity of the standard under the ADA.

Case Questions

1. Are you in agreement with the Court's resolution?
2. Should all tests have to pass muster under the ADA before implementation?

3. Why are government standards immune from scrutiny?

The issue in the case that follows is whether an employee who controls his high blood pressure with medication is considered to be disabled under the ADA.

MURPHY v. UNITED PARCEL SERVICE, INC.

527 U.S. 516 (1999)

JUSTICE O'CONNOR delivered the opinion of the Court.

Respondent United Parcel Service, Inc. (UPS), dismissed petitioner Vaughn L. Murphy from his job as a UPS mechanic because of his high blood pressure. Petitioner filed suit under Title I of the Americans with Disabilities Act of 1990 (ADA or Act), in Federal District Court. The District Court granted summary judgment to respondent, and the Court of Appeals for the Tenth Circuit affirmed. We must decide whether the Court of Appeals correctly considered petitioner in his medicated state when it held that petitioner's impairment does not "substantially limit" one or more of his major life activities and whether it correctly determined that petitioner is not "regarded as disabled." In light of our decision in *Sutton* v. *United Air Lines, Inc.,* we conclude that the Court of Appeals' resolution of both issues was correct.

I

Petitioner was first diagnosed with hypertension (high blood pressure) when he was 10 years old. Unmedicated, his blood pressure is approximately 250/160. With medication, however, petitioner's "hypertension does not significantly restrict his activities and . . . in general he can function normally and can engage in activities that other persons normally do."

In August 1994, respondent hired petitioner as a mechanic, a position that required petitioner to drive commercial motor vehicles. Petitioner does not challenge the District Court's conclusion that driving a commercial motor vehicle is an essential function of the mechanic's job at UPS. To drive such vehicles, however, petitioner had to satisfy certain health requirements imposed by the Department of Transportation (DOT). ("A person shall not drive a commercial motor vehicle unless he/she is physically qualified to do so and . . . has on his/her person . . . a medical examiner's certificate that he/she is physically qualified to drive a commercial motor vehicle.") One such requirement is that the driver of a commercial motor vehicle in interstate commerce have "no current clinical diagnosis of high blood pressure likely to interfere with his/her ability to operate a commercial vehicle safely."

At the time respondent hired him, petitioner's blood pressure was so high, measuring at 186/124, that he was not qualified for DOT health certification. Nonetheless, petitioner was erroneously granted certification, and he commenced work. In September 1994, a UPS Medical Supervisor who was reviewing petitioner's medical files discovered the error and requested that petitioner have his blood pressure retested. Upon retesting, petitioner's blood pressure was measured at 160/102 and 164/104. On October 5, 1994, respondent fired petitioner on the belief that his blood pressure exceeded the DOT's requirements for drivers of commercial motor vehicles.

Petitioner brought suit under Title I of the ADA in the United States District Court for the District of Kansas. The court granted respondent's motion for summary judgment. It held that, to determine whether petitioner is disabled under the ADA, his "impairment should be evaluated in its medicated state." Noting that when petitioner is medicated he is inhibited only in lifting heavy objects but otherwise functions normally, the court held that petitioner is not "disabled" under the ADA. The court also rejected petitioner's claim that he was "regarded as" disabled, holding that respondent "did not regard Murphy as disabled, only that he was not certifiable under DOT regulations."

The Court of Appeals affirmed the District Court's judgment. Citing its decision in *Sutton* v.

United Air Lines, Inc., that an individual claiming a disability under the ADA should be assessed with regard to any mitigating or corrective measures employed, the court held that petitioner's hypertension is not a disability because his doctor had testified that when petitioner is medicated, he " 'functions normally doing everyday activity that an everyday person does.' " The court also affirmed the District Court's determination that petitioner is not "regarded as" disabled under the ADA. It explained that respondent did not terminate petitioner "on an unsubstantiated fear that he would suffer a heart attack or stroke," but "because his blood pressure exceeded the DOT's requirements for drivers of commercial vehicles." We granted certiorari, and we now affirm.

II

The first question presented in this case is whether the determination of petitioner's disability is made with reference to the mitigating measures he employs. We have answered that question in *Sutton* in the affirmative. Given that holding, the result in this case is clear. The Court of Appeals concluded that, when medicated, petitioner's high blood pressure does not substantially limit him in any major life activity. Petitioner did not seek, and we did not grant, certiorari on whether this conclusion was correct. Because the question whether petitioner is disabled when taking medication is not before us, we have no occasion here to consider whether petitioner is "disabled" due to limitations that persist despite his medication or the negative side effects of his medication. Instead, the question granted was limited to whether, under the ADA, the determination of whether an individual's impairment "substantially limits" one or more major life activities should be made without consideration of mitigating measures. Consequently, we conclude that the Court of Appeals correctly affirmed the grant of summary judgment in respondent's favor on the claim that petitioner is substantially limited in

one or more major life activities and thus disabled under the ADA.

III

The second issue presented is also largely resolved by our opinion in *Sutton*. Petitioner argues that the Court of Appeals erred in holding that he is not "regarded as" disabled because of his high blood pressure. As we held in *Sutton,* a person is "regarded as" disabled within the meaning of the ADA if a covered entity mistakenly believes that the person's actual, nonlimiting impairment substantially limits one or more major life activities. Here, petitioner alleges that his hypertension is regarded as substantially limiting him in the major life activity of working, when in fact it does not. To support this claim, he points to testimony from respondent's resource manager that respondent fired petitioner due to his hypertension, which he claims evidences respondent's belief that petitioner's hypertension—and consequent inability to obtain DOT certification—substantially limits his ability to work. In response, respondent argues that it does not regard petitioner as substantially limited in the major life activity of working but, rather, regards him as unqualified to work as a UPS mechanic because he is unable to obtain DOT health certification.

Consequently, in light of petitioner's skills and the array of jobs available to petitioner utilizing those skills, petitioner has failed to show that he is regarded as unable to perform a class of jobs. Rather, the undisputed record evidence demonstrates that petitioner is, at most, regarded as unable to perform only a particular job. This is insufficient, as a matter of law, to prove that petitioner is regarded as substantially limited in the major life activity of working. Accordingly, the Court of Appeals correctly granted summary judgment in favor of respondent on petitioner's claim that he is regarded as disabled. For the reasons stated, we affirm the decision of the Court of Appeals for the Tenth Circuit.

It is so ordered.

Judgment for UPS.

Case Commentary

The United States Supreme Court ruled that Murphy was not disabled under the ADA because he was under medication for his high blood pressure. Furthermore, the court held that UPS did not regard Murphy as having a disability.

Case Questions

1. Are you in agreement with the Court's decision?

2. Should a person with a disability lose ADA protection because the disability is being corrected by medication?

3. Do you believe UPS regarded Murphy as being disabled when it determined he was not certifiable under DOT regulations?

EMPLOYMENT PERSPECTIVE

Lisa Conroy applied for a position as a paralegal with the law firm of Moran, Holochwost, and Mullins. Lisa is a paraplegic confined to a wheelchair. The firm is located on the second floor of an office building with no elevator. The firm employs 18 individuals. What must the law firm do? The law firm has to refuse to hire Lisa. Existing businesses are not required to install elevators. If the law firm occupied the first floor as well, it would be required to make a reasonable accommodation for Lisa on the first floor. If the law firm was going to construct its own office building, an elevator would be required if the building was three stories or more.

If the law firm was located on the first floor but had two steps inside and a bathroom entrance that was not wide enough for a wheelchair, what would the law firm have to do? It would have to install a ramp and make the bathroom entrance wider. These are modifications that are reasonable. To do otherwise would be to refuse to hire Lisa solely because her disability. ■

The issue presented in the case that follows is whether a person who suffers with carpal tunnel syndrome is covered under the ADA.

CASE

McKAY v. TOYOTA MOTOR MANUFACTURING, U.S.A., INC.

110 F.3d 369 (6th Cir. 1997)

NORRIS, Circuit Judge.

Plaintiff Pamela McKay appeals the district court's order granting summary judgment to defendant Toyota Motor Manufacturing, U.S.A. Plaintiff alleged that she was terminated from her assembly-line position with Toyota in violation of the Americans with Disabilities Act of 1990 ("ADA"), because of a physical disability caused by carpal tunnel syndrome. We affirm the judgment of the district court because we conclude that plaintiff's impairment disqualified her from only a narrow range of repetitive-motion positions and not from working in the broader class of manufacturing jobs. She was therefore not an individual with a disability who qualified for protection under the Act.

Plaintiff began working in Toyota's Georgetown, Kentucky, plant in March 1992, shortly before her twenty-third birthday. She initially worked in the body-weld division, but reported to the company's health service after just ten days on the production line.

The health service placed her on a modified work program consistent with company policy. She was restricted to lifting weights of less than ten pounds, was to avoid pushing or pulling, and was told to avoid vibrating tools. Despite an attempt to re-introduce her to the line, she suffered pain in her right forearm and was sent home for rest on April 22. She returned to work on May 11, but complained of pain and swelling after one day of restricted duty. After another furlough, she returned to modified duty in the body-weld department on June 8.

On September 22, an orthopedic surgeon diagnosed plaintiff with carpal tunnel syndrome and muscle inflammation. After undergoing a physical therapy program in December, plaintiff returned to work on a modified duty assignment in the plastics department. Eventually, plaintiff began working full-time in the plastics department with some physical restrictions: maximum lifting of twenty pounds; no vibrating tools; and no repetitive use of her right hand. Nonetheless, on May 24, 1993, plaintiff advised her group leader that she continued to have considerable pain in her arm and was sent home for rest by the in-house health service. On June 4, Toyota terminated her for excessive absences, pursuant to its medical leave of absence policy. In her complaint, plaintiff alleged she is a "qualified individual with a disability" and that defendant discharged her "because of her disability."

The ADA empowers the Equal Employment Opportunity Commission ("EEOC") to promulgate regulations that will further define the scope and reach of the statute. The EEOC has defined "major life activity" to include both caring for oneself and working. Plaintiff contends that her disability limits both of these activities. In reaching its decision as to whether plaintiff was in fact a disabled person, the district court held:

In order to show that she is substantially limited in the major life activity of working, McKay must prove that she is "significantly restricted in ability to perform either a class of jobs or a broad range of jobs in various classes as compared to the average person with comparable training, skills, and abilities. The inability to perform a single, particular job does not constitute a substantial limitation in the major life activity of working."

At the time of her termination from Toyota, McKay was a 24 year old college graduate, working on earning her teaching certificate. Given her educational background and age, she is qualified for numerous positions "not utilizing" the skills she learned as an automobile assembler. Merely because she can no longer perform repetitive factory work does not render her significantly limited under the ADA. . . . McKay has not established that she is significantly restricted in her ability to perform a class of jobs or a broad range of jobs in various classes as compared to similarly-situated persons with comparable training, skills and abilities. Therefore, she is not substantially limited in the major life activity of working.

The court also concluded that plaintiff was not limited in the "major life activity" of caring for herself because "the only household function McKay claims to be substantially limited in is mopping." Finally, the court concluded that a diagnosis of carpal tunnel syndrome, by itself, was insufficient to raise a genuine issue of material fact concerning whether plaintiff was disabled within the contemplation of the ADA.

On appeal, plaintiff contends that genuine issues of material fact concerning whether she is an individual with a disability precluded summary judgment. The EEOC, as amicus curiae, joins the argument on her side of the table, contending that:

The ADA and its implementing regulations require the court to look at the class of jobs from which McKay is *disqualified,* not the class of jobs that she can perform. Because of her carpal tunnel syndrome, McKay is disqualified from performing any manual labor exceeding light duty. She therefore cannot perform (without accommodation) the job at issue with Toyota. She also cannot perform (without accommodation) manual labor for any other employer. Accordingly, McKay is disqualified from an entire class of jobs. Her ability to perform completely unrelated work has no bearing on whether she is "disabled" with respect to manual labor. . . .

. . . .

. . . The court should have looked at the extent to which McKay's impairment disqualifies her from the type of job at issue, not the extent to which she can do other work.

This court reviews the award of summary judgment, using the same standard as the district court. Having conducted such a review, we now affirm the judgment below.

Under the terms of the ADA, all parties agree that carpal tunnel syndrome constitutes a "physical impairment." The next question, then, is whether plaintiff's condition "substantially limits" a major life activity. As already noted, working falls within the definition of major life activity. According to the relevant regulation, "The term *substantially limits* means significantly restricted in the ability to perform either a class of jobs or a broad range of jobs in various classes as compared to the average person having comparable training, skills and abilities. The inability to perform a single, particular job does not constitute a substantial limitation in the major life activity of working." Plaintiff appears to contend that the district court based its ruling upon a holding that her carpal tunnel syndrome only rendered her unable to perform a single, particular job. The EEOC, on the other hand, argues the district court's holding is predicated on the jobs plaintiff *could* perform, rather than those she *could not* perform. We think both read the district court's opinion too narrowly.

As the regulations make clear, the question before the district court concerned whether plaintiff had carried her burden of establishing that her physical impairment significantly restricted her ability to perform "either a class of jobs or a broad range of jobs in various classes." In making this determination, a court should consider:

(i) The nature and severity of the impairment;
(ii) The duration or expected duration of the impairment; and
(iii) The permanent or long term impact, or the expected permanent or long term impact of or resulting from the impairment.

In addition, courts may consider several other factors:

(A) The geographical area to which the individual has reasonable access;

(B) The job from which the individual has been disqualified because of an impairment, and the number and types of jobs utilizing similar training, knowledge, skills or abilities, within that geographical area, from which the individual is also disqualified because of the impairment (class of jobs); and/or

(C) The job from which the individual has been disqualified because of an impairment, and the number and types of other jobs not utilizing similar training, knowledge, skills or abilities, within that geographical area, from which the individual is also disqualified because of the impairment (broad range of jobs in various classes).

Essentially, plaintiff in this case says the evidence regarding her physical impairment compels a conclusion that she is significantly restricted in her ability to perform any medium or heavy work. While she did present expert testimony to that effect, the same expert, when pressed, acknowledged that the positions she held at Toyota did not involve medium or heavy work. He also conceded that there were a broad range of jobs that she could perform. Since plaintiff's work history at Toyota involved only light work, and she made no showing that she ever was able to perform medium or heavy work, one is hard pressed to comprehend how she could have been regarded as a "qualified individual" with respect to medium and heavy work.

In light of the regulatory framework of the ADA, we hold that the physical restrictions caused by plaintiff's disability do not significantly restrict her ability to perform the class of jobs at issue, manufacturing jobs; at best, her evidence supports a conclusion that her impairment disqualifies her from only the narrow range of assembly line manufacturing jobs that require repetitive motion or frequent lifting of more than ten pounds. It follows that her limited impairment would not significantly restrict her ability to perform a broad range of jobs in various classes.

Finally, we agree with the district court that plaintiff has failed to show that her disability substantially limits her ability to care for herself.

For the foregoing reasons, the judgment of the district court is affirmed.

Judgment for Toyota.

Case Commentary

The Sixth Circuit resolved that McKay, who was suffering from carpal tunnel syndrome, was precluded from working in a narrow range of jobs.

Therefore, the carpal tunnel did not restrict a major life activity, which was a requirement to be considered disabled under the ADA.

Case Questions

1. Are you in accord with the Court's judgment?
2. Do you believe carpal tunnel should be considered a disability under the ADA?

3. Do you think carpal tunnel restricts a major life activity in most cases?

EMPLOYMENT PERSPECTIVE

Patricia Krakowski is 52 years old. She applied for a position as a high school history teacher with the Monroe Township Academy. Although her credentials were superior, she was passed over for a younger applicant. Patricia had had a cancerous kidney removed. The Academy feared that she might be a candidate for dialysis, which could cause its health costs to increase. Since the Academy was operating within a tight budget, Patricia posed a potential financial risk that it did not want to take. Has Patricia been discriminated against? Yes! Were it not for her disability, Patricia would have been hired. The Academy must give Patricia the position or reimburse her until she finds another suitable one. ■

The issue in the following case is whether a firefighter is capable of performing the essential functions of the job in spite of being a paraplegic.

CASE

STONE v. CITY OF MOUNT VERNON

118 F.3d 893 (2nd Cir. 1996)

KEARSE, Circuit Judge.

Plaintiff Matthew T. Stone, a firefighter employed by defendant City of Mount Vernon (the "City"), appeals from a judgment of the United States District Court for the Southern District of New York, dismissing his complaint alleging that defendants City and Fire Commissioner James Gleason (collectively the "Fire Department" or "Department") violated his rights under the Americans with Disabilities Act ("ADA"), and the Rehabilitation Act of 1973) ("Rehabilitation Act") (collectively the "federal disability

statutes"), principally by refusing to assign him to a light-duty position after an off-duty accident that left him a paraplegic. The district court granted summary judgment dismissing the complaint on the ground that no rational trier of fact could conclude that Stone was able to perform the essential functions of the job of firefighter, and therefore he was not qualified within the meaning of the federal disability statutes. On appeal, Stone contends principally that summary judgment was improper because there were genuine issues of fact to be tried as to whether fire suppression is an essential function of a position in certain of the Department's specialized bureaus, and whether the Department could reasonably accommodate his disability by assigning him to such a position. For the reasons that follow, we agree, and we therefore vacate the judgment of the district court and remand for further proceedings.

I. BACKGROUND

A. The Events

The City's Fire Department employs 109 firefighters. It has mutual-aid agreements with neighboring towns for assistance during multi-alarm fires. To the extent pertinent here, the Department has two "light-duty" bureaus: the Fire Alarm Bureau ("FAB") and the Fire Prevention Bureau ("FPB"). The duties of employees assigned to FAB include receiving and transmitting alarms of fires, answering telephones, and performing related paperwork; firefighters assigned to FAB assist non-firefighter dispatchers in dispatching firefighters to calls for service. The principal duties of employees assigned to FPB are enforcing the New York State Uniform Fire Prevention and Building Code and the Department's Fire Prevention Code, reviewing architectural plans and designs, meeting with builders, and performing inspections of buildings. Firefighters assigned to FPB may also be called upon to serve as guides to assist mutual-aid fire companies by meeting them at the City's border and leading them to the site of the fire; the guide travels either in the visiting fire rig or in a separate car.

Stone was hired by the Department in January 1990 and entered service as an active firefighter; he was assigned to fire-suppression duties, which principally include extinguishing fires, entering burning buildings, and performing rescues. In December 1992, while off-duty, he was helping friends to remove from a house a tree that had been uprooted by a storm; the tree suddenly sprang upright, throwing Stone to the ground. He sustained injuries inducing paraplegia, and was initially paralyzed from the waist down. After undergoing physical rehabilitation, Stone is able, with the assistance of leg braces, to walk for a few hours at a time. He also uses a wheelchair, in which he can negotiate curbs and ramps; and he has a car that is outfitted with spe-

cial hand controls that enable him to drive. Stone can get into and out of his car and his wheelchair without assistance. He is also able to climb and descend stairs out of his wheelchair while pulling the chair along with him.

Since his accident, Stone has remained an employee of the Department, on leave of absence with pay, thanks to contributions of accrued paid leave by his fellow firefighters. During this time, he has served as an instructor at the Westchester County Career Chiefs' Fire Academy, where he teaches fire-and-rescue-related courses to probationary firefighters from Westchester County. As an adjunct instructor at the New York State Fire Academy, he has taught a similar course to probationary firefighters from around New York State.

In November 1994, Stone, who passed an examination qualifying him for promotion to lieutenant, requested that he be returned to active duty and assigned a position in which his disability could be accommodated. His request identified FAB as one possible assignment. Stone received no response to his request. After attempting unsuccessfully to get a response, he wrote to Commissioner Gleason in January 1995, renewing his requests. In May 1995, Stone was informed that he would not be accommodated and that he could not return to work.

B. The Present Litigation

Stone commenced the present action in October 1995, alleging principally that defendants' refusal to accommodate his disability by giving him a light-duty assignment, such as to FAB, violated his rights under the federal disability statutes. The complaint alleged that a February 1994 Department order stated (a) that Department members who were hired after July 1993 or who were injured in the line of duty and assigned to light duty were to be assigned to FAB as needed, and (b) that other Department firefighters not within those categories could request assignment to FAB; such requests would be granted at the discretion of the commissioner. The complaint alleged that Stone was qualified to perform the essential functions of a position in FAB and other light-duty positions.

Judgment was entered dismissing the complaint in its entirety, including a state law claim that was dismissed without prejudice. This appeal followed.

II. DISCUSSION

A. The Federal Disability Statutes

The regulatory schemes of the ADA and the Rehabilitation Act are similar. The ADA prohibits covered employers from discriminating against an otherwise qualified employee "because of the disability of such individual in regard to job application procedures, the hiring, advancement, or discharge of employees, employee compensation, job training, and other terms, conditions, and privileges of employment." The statute defines "qualified individual with a disability" to mean "an individual with a disability who, *with or without reasonable accommodation,* can perform the *essential functions* of the employment position that such individual holds or desires." The ADA defines the term "discriminate" to include not making *reasonable accommodations* to the known physical or mental limitations of an otherwise qualified individual with a disability who is an applicant or employee, unless ... the employer can demonstrate that the accommodation would impose an *undue hardship* on the operation of the ... employer's business.

The Rehabilitation Act prohibits disability-based discrimination by government agencies and other recipients of federal funds. Section 504(a) of that Act provides that no otherwise qualified individual with a disability ... shall, solely by reason of her or his disability, be excluded from the participation in, be denied the benefits of, or be subjected to discrimination under any program or activity receiving Federal financial assistance ... Regulations promulgated by the Department of Health and Human Services under this statute define a "qualified" person with a disability as one "who, *with reasonable accommodation,* can perform the *essential functions* of the job in question." These regulations require recipients of federal funds to "make *reasonable accommodation* to the known physical or mental limitations of an otherwise qualified handicapped ... employee unless the recipient can demonstrate that the accommodation would impose an *undue hardship* on the operation of its program."

In the present case, the questions center on the meanings of "essential job functions," "reasonable accommodation," and "undue hardship."

1. "Essential Functions"

The term "essential functions," which is not defined in the statutes themselves, is generally defined in ADA regulations promulgated by the Equal Employment Opportunity Commission ("EEOC") to mean the "fundamental" duties to be performed in the position in question, but not functions that are merely "marginal." The regulations also provide illustrations of the reasons that a given function may be found to be fundamental to the position and examples of evidence that may be considered in making that finding:

Essential functions—(1) *In general.* The term *essential functions* means the fundamental job duties of the employment position the individual with a disability holds or desires. The term "essential functions" does not include the marginal functions of the position.

(2) A job function may be considered essential for any of several reasons, including but not limited to the following:

  (i) The function may be essential because the reason the position exists is to perform that function;

  (ii) The function may be essential because of the limited number of employees available among whom the performance of that job function can be distributed; and/or

  (iii) The function may be highly specialized so that the incumbent in the position is hired for his or her expertise or ability to perform the particular function.

(3) Evidence of whether a particular function is essential includes, but is not limited to:

  (i) The employer's judgment as to which functions are essential;

  (ii) Written job descriptions prepared before advertising or interviewing applicants for the job;

  (iii) The amount of time spent on the job performing the function;

  (iv) The consequences of not requiring the incumbent to perform the function;

  (v) The terms of a collective bargaining agreement;

  (vi) The work experience of past incumbents in the job; and/or

  (vii) The current work experience of incumbents in similar jobs.

Plainly, the considerations set out in this regulation are fact-intensive. Usually no one listed factor will be dispositive, and the regulations themselves state that the evidentiary examples provided are not meant to be exhaustive.

2. "Reasonable Accommodation"

With respect to the term "reasonable accommodation," the ADA sets out a nonexclusive list of different methods of accommodation encompassed by the term "reasonable accommodation," stating that

[t]he term "reasonable accommodation" *may include—*

    . . . .

    (i) *job restructuring,* part-time or modified work schedules, *reassignment to a vacant position,* . . . and other similar accommodations for individuals with disabilities.

The ADA regulations state that the employer is required to provide

    (ii) Modifications or adjustments to the work environment, or to the manner or circumstances under which the position held or desired is customarily performed, that enable a qualified individual with a disability to perform the essential functions of that position; or

    (iii) Modifications that enable a[n] . . . employee with a disability to enjoy equal benefits and privileges of employment as are enjoyed by its other similarly situated employees without disabilities.

As to the requirement that the requested accommodation be reasonable, "we have held that the plaintiff bears only a burden of production." This burden "is not a heavy one. . . . It is enough for the plaintiff to suggest the existence of a plausible accommodation, the costs of which, facially, do not clearly exceed its benefits." Having accomplished this, a plaintiff will have made a *prima facie* showing that a reasonable accommodation is available and the burden of nonpersuasion will shift to the defendant. The defendant must then show that the accommodation is not reasonable, or that it imposes an undue hardship, which "in practice . . . amount to the same thing."

3. "Undue Hardship"

In providing that discrimination includes an employer's failure to make a reasonable accommodation "unless such [employer] can demonstrate that the accommodation would impose an undue hardship on the operation of the business of such employer," the ADA defines "undue hardship" as follows:

(A) In general

The term "undue hardship" means an action requiring significant difficulty or expense, when considered in light of the factors set forth in subparagraph (B).

(B) Factors to be considered

In determining whether an accommodation would impose an undue hardship on a covered entity, factors to be considered include—

    (i) the nature and cost of the accommodation needed under this chapter;

    (ii) the overall financial resources of the facility or facilities involved in the provision of the reasonable accommodation; the number of persons employed at such facility; the effect on expenses and resources, or the impact otherwise of such accommodation upon the operation of the facility;

    (iii) the overall financial resources of the covered entity; the overall size of the business of a covered entity with respect to the number of its employees; the number, type, and location of its facilities; and

    (iv) the type of operation or operations of the covered entity, including the composition, structure, and functions of the workforce of such entity; the geographic separateness, administrative, or fiscal relationship of the facility or facilities in question to the covered entity.

We have noted that " 'undue' hardship, like 'reasonable' accommodation, is a relational term; as such, it looks not merely to the costs that the employer is asked to assume, but also the benefits to others that will result."

The burden on the employer, then, is to perform a cost/benefit analysis. In a sense, of course, that is what the plaintiff also had to do to meet her burden of making out a *prima facie* case that a reasonable accommodation existed. But while the plaintiff could meet her burden of production by identifying an accommodation that facially achieves a rough proportionality between costs and benefits, an employer seeking to meet its burden of persuasion on reasonable accommodation and undue hardship must undertake a more refined analysis. And it must analyze the hardship sought to be imposed through the lens of the factors listed in the regulations, which include consideration of the industry to which the employer belongs as well as the individual characteristics of the particular defendant-employer. If the employer can carry this burden, it will have shown both that the hardship caused by the proposed accommodation would be undue in light of the enumerated factors, and that the proposed accommodation is unreasonable and need not be made. However, we have "not at all intended to suggest that employers . . . must analyze the costs and benefits of proposed accommodations with mathematical precision."

Plainly, therefore, it cannot be said that the reason the FAB and FPB positions exist is to perform the fire-suppression function, or that the incumbents are assigned to those positions because of their ability to perform a fire-suppression function.

A function is, by definition, not "essential" to a position if that function is "marginal," and the evidence that neither the past nor the incumbent firefighters assigned to those bureaus have ever been requested to engage in a fire-suppression activity suggests that it would be entirely permissible for a factfinder to infer that the ability to engage in fire-suppression activities is marginal to the positions in FAB and FPB.

Nor do we see in the present record any basis on which it could be held as a matter of law that assignment of Stone to FAB or FPB would be an accommodation that was not "reasonable." The record indicates that in 1992-1996 some 15-20 firefighters were assigned to one of these bureaus following injuries. Though most of these assignments apparently were temporary, plainly the 10- and 20-year assignments of Koch and

Ionta, respectively, suggest that career placement in those bureaus is not unprecedented.

Further, in order to establish *prima facie* that the accommodation requested was reasonable, Stone need show only that the cost of assigning him to one of those bureaus would not clearly exceed its benefits. The present record plainly would support a finding that the assignment would benefit Stone; and the testimony of operations chief Campbell clearly indicated that Stone's productivity in such a position would benefit not only society, but the Department itself as well: I don't think there's a finer young person I ever met than Matt Stone and I think he would be an asset up there. . . Can we accommodate Matt Stone up there? I certainly can. I certainly can. And do we need him up there? Yeah, we need him.

In sum, while it surely is not unreasonable for the Department to distinguish between temporary and permanent assignments, the present record equally surely does not permit the conclusion that making a permanent assignment to Stone would be an accommodation that was unreasonable as a matter of law. We conclude that the evidence of record sufficed to show that Stone presented a *prima facie* case under the federal disability statutes.

CONCLUSION

In sum, on the basis of the present record, a reasonable factfinder could infer that, for a Department that (a) has periodically assigned disabled employees to FAB or FPB, and (b) so far as the record shows, has never once asked any employee, of either of those bureaus, whether disabled or not, and whether assigned temporarily or permanently, to engage in fire-suppression activity, the assignment to either bureau of a single disabled employee whose only limitation is that he cannot engage in fire-suppression activity is neither an accommodation that would be unreasonable nor a hardship that would be undue. We therefore vacate the judgment dismissing the complaint and remand for further proceedings not inconsistent with this opinion.

Costs to plaintiff.

Judgment for Stone

Case Commentary

The Second Circuit decided that assigning Stone to the Fire Alarm Bureau or the Fire Prevention Bureau where he would be able to perform the essential functions of the job was neither an accommodation nor a hardship.

Case Questions

1. Are you in agreement with the Court's decision?
2. Do you really believe Stone can perform the essential functions of the job?
3. Do you believe Fire Commissioner Gleason's argument that all firefighters should be capable of suppressing fires is reasonable?

AIDS DISCRIMINATION

Employers' concerns are many with regard to AIDS. Whenever an employee is questioned concerning whether he or she has the disease or whenever that information is related to other employees, an invasion of privacy may occur. If an assertion is made that an employee has the AIDS virus turns out to be unfounded, defamation may occur. If an applicant is refused employment because he or she has the AIDS virus, employment discrimination may be asserted. When an existing employee who is capable of working is discharged because he or she has the AIDS virus, a violation of the Federal Rehabilitation Act, Americans with Disabilities Act, or state law protecting the handicapped may result. Under the circumstances, how can an employer maintain harmony in the workplace? Employers must develop policies regarding the treatment afforded existing employees who have AIDS regarding the fringe benefits given, including absences, dental care, and medical benefits, alternative work location, and reassurance of support by the company. Applicants for positions who have AIDS must be treated on an equal basis. As long as a person who has AIDS is capable of performing the work, he or she should be treated no differently from any other employee. Employers are encouraged to develop an educational program designed to ease the fears of coworkers who worry about catching the virus. The key is successful planning.

The issue in the case that follows is whether a person with HIV is a covered person under the ADA.

BRAGDON v. ABBOTT

524 U.S. 624 (1998)

JUSTICE KENNEDY delivered the opinion of the Court.

We address in this case the application of the Americans with Disabilities Act of 1990 (ADA), to persons infected with the human immunodeficiency virus (HIV). We granted certiorari to review, first, whether HIV infection is a disability under the ADA when the infection has not yet progressed to the so-called symptomatic phase; and, second, whether the Court of Appeals, in affirming a grant of summary judgment, cited sufficient material in the record to determine, as a matter of law, that respondent's infection with HIV posed no direct threat to the health and safety of her treating dentist.

I

Respondent Sidney Abbott has been infected with HIV since 1986. When the incidents we recite occurred, her infection had not manifested its most serious symptoms. On September 16, 1994, she went to the office of petitioner Randon Bragdon in Bangor, Maine, for a dental appointment. She disclosed her HIV infection on the patient registration form. Petitioner completed a dental examination, discovered a cavity, and informed respondent of his policy against filling cavities of HIV-infected patients. He offered to perform the work at a hospital with no added fee for his services, though respondent would be responsible for the cost of using the hospital's facilities. Respondent declined.

Respondent sued petitioner under state law and §302 of the ADA, alleging discrimination on the basis of her disability. The state law claims are not before us. Section 302 of the ADA provides:

"No individual shall be discriminated against on the basis of disability in the full and equal enjoyment of the goods, services, facilities, privileges, advantages, or accommodations of any place of public accommodation by any person who ... operates a place of public accommodation."

The term "public accommodation" is defined to include the "professional office of a health care provider." A later subsection qualifies the mandate not to discriminate. It provides:

"Nothing in this subchapter shall require an entity to permit an individual to participate in or benefit from the goods, services, facilities, privileges, advantages and accommodations of such entity where such individual poses a direct threat to the health or safety of others."

The United States and the Maine Human Rights Commission intervened as plaintiffs. After discovery, the parties filed cross-motions for summary judgment. The District Court ruled in favor of the plaintiffs, holding that respondent's HIV infection satisfied the ADA's definition of disability. The court held further that petitioner raised no genuine issue of material fact as to whether respondent's HIV infection would have posed a direct threat to the health or safety of others during the course of a dental treatment. The court relied on affidavits submitted by Dr. Donald Wayne Marianos, Director of the Division of Oral Health of the Centers for Disease Control and Prevention (CDC). The Marianos affidavits asserted it is safe for dentists to treat patients infected with HIV in dental offices if the dentist follows the so-called universal precautions described in the Recommended Infection-Control Practices for Dentistry issued by CDC in 1993.

The Court of Appeals affirmed. It held respondent's HIV infection was a disability under the ADA, even though her infection had not yet progressed to the symptomatic stage. The Court of Appeals also agreed that treating the respondent in petitioner's office would not have posed a direct threat to the health and safety of others.

Unlike the District Court, however, the Court of Appeals declined to rely on the Marianos affidavits. Instead the court relied on the 1993 CDC Dentistry Guidelines, as well as the Policy on AIDS, HIV Infection and the Practice of Dentistry, promulgated by the American Dental Association in 1991.

II

We first review the ruling that respondent's HIV infection constituted a disability under the ADA. The statute defines disability as:

"(A)a physical or mental impairment that substantially limits one or more of the major life activities of such individual;"(B)a record of such an impairment; or "(C)being regarded as having such impairment."

We hold respondent's HIV infection was a disability under subsection (A) of the definitional section of the statute. In light of this conclusion, we need not consider the applicability of subsections (B) or (C).

Our consideration of subsection (A) of the definition proceeds in three steps. First, we consider whether respondent's HIV infection was a physical impairment. Second, we identify the life activity upon which respondent relies (reproduction and child bearing) and determine whether it constitutes a major life activity under the ADA. Third, tying the two statutory phrases together, we ask whether the impairment substantially limited the major life activity. In construing the statute, we are informed by interpretations of parallel definitions in previous statutes and the views of various administrative agencies which have faced this interpretive question.

A

The ADA's definition of disability is drawn almost verbatim from the definition of "handicapped individual" included in the Rehabilitation Act of 1973, and the definition of "handicap" contained in the Fair Housing Amendments Act of 1988. Congress' repetition of a well-established term carries the implication that Congress intended the term to be construed in accordance with pre-existing regulatory interpretations. In this case, Congress did more than suggest this construction; it adopted a specific statutory provision in the ADA directing as follows:

"Except as otherwise provided in this chapter, nothing in this chapter shall be construed to apply a lesser standard than the standards applied under title V of the Rehabilitation Act of 1973 or the regulations issued by Federal agencies pursuant to such title."

The directive requires us to construe the ADA to grant at least as much protection as provided by the regulations implementing the Rehabilitation Act.

1

The first step in the inquiry under subsection (A) requires us to determine whether respondent's condition constituted a physical impairment. The Department of Health, Education and Welfare (HEW) issued the first regulations interpreting the Rehabilitation Act in 1977. The regulations are of particular significance because, at the time, HEW was the agency responsible for coordinating the implementation and enforcement of §504. The HEW regulations, which appear without change in the current regulations issued by the Department of Health and Human Services, define "physical or mental impairment" to mean:

"(A)any physiological disorder or condition, cosmetic disfigurement, or anatomical loss affecting one or more of the following body systems: neurological; musculoskeletal; special sense organs; respiratory, including speech organs; cardiovascular; reproductive, digestive, genito-urinary; hemic and lymphatic; skin; and endocrine;" or "(B)any mental or psychological disorder, such as mental retardation, organic brain syndrome, emotional or mental illness, and specific learning disabilities."

In issuing these regulations, HEW decided against including a list of disorders constituting physical or mental impairments, out of concern that any specific enumeration might not be comprehensive. The commentary accompanying the regulations, however, contains a representative list of disorders and conditions constituting physical impairments, including "such diseases and conditions as orthopedic, visual, speech, and hearing impairments, cerebral palsy, epilepsy, muscular dystrophy, multiple sclerosis, cancer, heart disease, diabetes, mental retardation, emotional illness, and . . . drug addiction and alcoholism." In 1980, the President transferred responsibility for the implementation and enforcement of §504 to the Attorney General. The regulations issued by the Justice Department, which remain in force to this day, adopted verbatim the HEW definition of physical impairment quoted above. In addition, the representative list of diseases and conditions originally relegated to the commentary accompanying the HEW regulations were incorporated into the text of the regulations.

HIV infection is not included in the list of specific disorders constituting physical impairments, in part because HIV was not identified as the cause of AIDS until 1983. HIV infection does fall well within the general definition set forth by the regulations, however. The disease follows a predictable and, as of today, an unalterable course. Once a person is infected with HIV, the virus invades different cells in the blood and in body tissues. Certain white blood cells, known as helper T lymphocytes or CD4+ cells, are particularly vulnerable to HIV. The virus attaches to the CD4 receptor site of the target cell and fuses its membrane to the cell's membrane. HIV is a retrovirus, which means it uses an enzyme to convert its own genetic material into a form indistinguishable from the genetic material of the target cell. The virus' genetic material migrates to the cell's nucleus and becomes integrated with the cell's chromosomes. Once integrated, the virus can use the cell's own genetic machinery to replicate itself. Additional copies of the virus are released into the body and infect other cells in turn. Although the body does produce antibodies to combat HIV infection, the antibodies are not effective in eliminating the virus.

The virus eventually kills the infected host cell. CD4+ cells play a critical role in coordinating the body's immune response system, and the decline in their number causes corresponding deterioration of the body's ability to fight infections from many sources. Tracking the infected individual's CD4+ cell count is one of the most accurate measures of the course of the disease.

The initial stage of HIV infection is known as acute or primary HIV infection. In a typical case, this stage lasts three months. The virus concentrates in the blood. The assault on the immune system is immediate. The victim suffers from a sudden and serious decline in the number of white blood cells. There is no latency period. Mononucleosis-like symptoms often emerge between six days and six weeks after infection, at times accompanied by fever, headache, enlargement of the lymph nodes (lymphadenopathy), muscle pain (myalgia), rash, lethargy, gastrointestinal disorders, and neurological disorders. Usually these symptoms abate within 14 to 21 days. HIV antibodies appear in the bloodstream within 3 weeks; circulating HIV can be detected within 10 weeks.

After the symptoms associated with the initial stage subside, the disease enters what is referred to sometimes as its asymptomatic phase. The term is a misnomer, in some respects, for clinical features persist throughout, including lymphadenopathy, dermatological disorders, oral lesions, and bacterial infections. Although it varies with each individual, in most instances this stage lasts from 7 to 11 years. The virus now tends to concentrate in the lymph nodes, though low levels of the virus continue to appear in the blood. It was once thought the virus became inactive during this period, but it is now known that the relative lack of symptoms is attributable to the virus' migration from the circulatory system into the lymph nodes. The migration reduces the viral presence in other parts of the body, with a corresponding diminution in physical manifestations of the disease. The virus, however, thrives in the lymph nodes, which, as a vital point of the body's immune response system, represents an ideal environment for the infection of other CD4+ cells. Studies have shown that viral production continues at a high rate. CD4+ cells continue to decline an average of 5% to 10% (40 to 80 cells/mm 3) per year throughout this phase.

A person is regarded as having AIDS when his or her CD4+ count drops below 200 cells/mm 3 of blood or when CD4+ cells comprise less than 14% of his or her total lymphocytes. During this stage, the clinical conditions most often associated with HIV, such as pneumocystis carninii pneumonia, Kaposi's sarcoma, and non-Hodgkins lymphoma, tend to appear. In addition, the general systemic disorders present during all stages of the disease, such as fever, weight loss, fatigue, lesions, nausea, and diarrhea, tend to worsen. In most cases, once the patient's CD4+ count drops below 10 cells/mm 3 , death soon follows.

In light of the immediacy with which the virus begins to damage the infected person's white blood cells and the severity of the disease, we hold it is an impairment from the moment of infection. As noted earlier, infection with HIV causes immediate abnormalities in a person's blood, and the infected person's white cell count continues to drop throughout the course of the disease, even when the attack is concentrated in the lymph nodes. In light of these facts, HIV infection must be regarded as a physiological disorder with a constant and detrimental effect on the infected person's hemic and lymphatic systems from the moment of infection. HIV infection satisfies the statutory and regulatory definition of a physical impairment during every stage of the disease.

2

The statute is not operative, and the definition not satisfied, unless the impairment affects a major life activity. Respondent's claim throughout this case has been that the HIV infection placed a substantial limitation on her ability to reproduce and to bear children.

From the outset, however, the case has been treated as one in which reproduction was the major life activity limited by the impairment. It is our practice to decide cases on the grounds raised and considered in the Court of Appeals and included in the question on which we granted certiorari. We ask, then, whether reproduction is a major life activity.

We have little difficulty concluding that it is. Reproduction falls well within the phrase "major life activity." Reproduction and the sexual dynamics surrounding it are central to the life process itself. While petitioner concedes the importance of reproduction, he claims that Congress intended the ADA only to cover those aspects of a person's life which have a public, economic, or daily character. Nothing in the definition suggests that activities without a public, economic, or daily dimension may somehow be regarded as so unimportant or insignificant as to fall outside the meaning of the word "major."

As we have noted, the ADA must be construed to be consistent with regulations issued to implement the Rehabilitation Act. The Rehabilitation Act regulations support the inclusion of reproduction as a major life activity, since reproduction could not be regarded as any less important than working and learning. We agree

with the Court of Appeals' determination that reproduction is a major life activity for the purposes of the ADA.

3

The final element of the disability definition in subsection (A) is whether respondent's physical impairment was a substantial limit on the major life activity she asserts. The Rehabilitation Act regulations provide no additional guidance.

Our evaluation of the medical evidence leads us to conclude that respondent's infection substantially limited her ability to reproduce in two independent ways. First, a woman infected with HIV who tries to conceive a child imposes on the man a significant risk of becoming infected. The cumulative results of 13 studies collected in a 1994 textbook on AIDS indicates that 20% of male partners of women with HIV became HIV-positive themselves, with a majority of the studies finding a statistically significant risk of infection.

Second, an infected woman risks infecting her child during gestation and childbirth, i.e., perinatal transmission. Petitioner concedes that women infected with HIV face about a 25% risk of transmitting the virus to their children. Published reports available in 1994 confirm the accuracy of this statistic.

The Act addresses substantial limitations on major life activities, not utter inabilities. Conception and childbirth are not impossible for an HIV victim but, without doubt, are dangerous to the public health. This meets the definition of a substantial limitation. The decision to reproduce carries economic and legal consequences as well. There are added costs for antiretroviral therapy, supplemental insurance, and long-term health care for the child who must be examined and, tragic to think, treated for the infection. The laws of some States, moreover, forbid persons infected with HIV from having sex with others, regardless of consent.

In the end, the disability definition does not turn on personal choice. When significant limitations result from the impairment, the definition is met even if the difficulties are not insurmountable. For the statistical and other reasons we have cited, of course, the limitations on reproduction may be insurmountable here. Testimony from the respondent that her HIV infection controlled her decision not to have a child is unchallenged. In the context of reviewing summary judgment, we must take it to be true. We agree with the District Court and the Court of Appeals that no triable issue of fact impedes a ruling on the question of statutory coverage. Respondent's HIV infection is a physical impairment which substantially limits a major life activity, as the ADA defines it. In view of our holding, we need not address the second question presented, i.e., whether HIV infection is a per se disability under the ADA.

> "5.Did petitioner, Randon Bragdon, D. M. D., raise a genuine issue of fact for trial as to whether he was warranted in his judgment that the performance of certain invasive procedures on a patient in his office would have posed a direct threat to the health or safety of others?"

Notwithstanding the protection given respondent by the ADA's definition of disability, petitioner could have refused to treat her if her infectious condition "posed a direct threat to the health or safety of others." The ADA defines a direct threat to be "a significant risk to the health or safety of others that cannot be eliminated by a modification of policies, practices, or procedures or by the provision of auxiliary aids or services."

The ADA's direct threat provision stems from the recognition in School Bd. of Nassau Cty. v. Arline, of the importance of prohibiting discrimination against individuals with disabilities while protecting others from significant health and safety risks, resulting, for instance, from a contagious disease. In Arline, the Court reconciled these objectives by construing the Rehabilitation Act not to require the hiring of a person who posed "a significant risk of communicating an infectious disease to others." Congress amended the Rehabilitation Act and the Fair Housing Act to incorporate the language (excluding individuals who "would constitute a direct threat to the health or safety of other individuals"); it later relied on the same language in enacting the ADA. (ADA's direct threat provision codifies Arline.) Because few, if any, activities in life are risk free, Arline and the ADA do not ask whether a risk exists, but whether it is significant.

The existence, or nonexistence, of a significant risk must be determined from the standpoint of the person who refuses the treatment or accommodation, and the risk assessment must be based on medical or other objective evidence. As a health care professional, petitioner had the duty to assess the risk of infection based on the objective, scientific information available to him and others in his profession. His belief that a significant risk existed, even if maintained in good faith, would not relieve him from liability. To use the words of the question presented, petitioner receives no special deference simply because he is a health care professional. It is true that Arline reserved "the question whether courts should also defer to the reasonable medical judgments of private physicians on which an employer has relied." At most, this statement reserved the possibility that employers could consult with individual physicians as objective third-party experts. It did not suggest that an individual physician's state of mind could excuse discrimination without regard to the objective reasonableness of his actions.

Nor can we be certain, on this record, whether the 1991 American Dental Association Policy on HIV carries the weight the Court of Appeals attributed to it. The Policy does provide some evidence of the medical community's objective assessment of the risks posed by treating people infected with HIV in dental offices. It indicates:

> "Current scientific and epidemiologic evidence indicates that there is little risk of transmission of infectious diseases through dental treatment if recommended infection control procedures are routinely followed. Patients with HIV infection may be safely treated in private dental offices when appropriate infection control procedures are employed. Such infection control procedures provide protection both for patients and dental personnel."

We note, however, that the Association is a professional organization, which, although a respected source of information on the dental profession, is not a public health authority. It is not clear the extent to which the Policy was based on the Association's assessment of dentists' ethical and professional duties in addition to its scientific assessment of the risk to which the ADA refers. Efforts to clarify dentists' ethical obligations and to encourage dentists to treat patients with HIV infection with compassion may be commendable, but the question under the statute is one of statistical likelihood, not professional responsibility. Without more information on the manner in which the American Dental Association formulated this Policy, we are unable to determine the Policy's value in evaluating whether petitioner's assessment of the risks was reasonable as a matter of law.

We conclude the proper course is to give the Court of Appeals the opportunity to determine whether our analysis of some of the studies cited by the parties would change its conclusion that

petitioner presented neither objective evidence nor a triable issue of fact on the question of risk. In remanding the case, we do not foreclose the possibility that the Court of Appeals may reach the same conclusion it did earlier. A remand will permit a full exploration of the issue through the adversary process.

The determination of the Court of Appeals that respondent's HIV infection was a disability under the ADA is affirmed. The judgment is vacated, and the case is remanded for further proceedings consistent with this opinion.

It is so ordered.

Case Commentary

The United States Supreme Court ruled that HIV substantially inhibits the right to procreate, and that procreation qualifies as a major life activity. As such, an individual with HIV is covered

under the ADA. The court sent the case back for reconsideration on the issue of whether a dentist who works on a patient with HIV is exposing himself to the risk of contracting the disease.

Case Questions

1. Are you in accord with the Court's determination?
2. Do you believe HIV and/or AIDS should be covered under the ADA?

3. Do you believe Bragdon's refusal to perform dental work on Abbott for fear of exposing himself to the HIV virus was reasonable?

WORKERS WITH CONTAGIOUS DISEASES

THE QUESTION OF DISCLOSURE

To disclose or not to disclose—that has been the question for employees who have AIDS. Disclosure may be necessary to obtain excessive absences and to explain poor performance on the job, which may result from a weakened physical condition. Although a person with AIDS has little choice, disclosure has generally compounded the problems. Once notified, many employers have fired or coaxed employees who have AIDS into leaving quietly, promising to retain confidentiality and not to tell the world. Many panic-stricken fellow employees react negatively upon learning the news. They refuse to share drinking fountains, pens, telephones, and toilets. There are even some who refuse to breathe the same air as a fellow employee who has AIDS in a confined work environment. As a result, employees who have AIDS become isolated in much the same way as did lepers. However, unlike leprosy, AIDS cannot be transmitted through touching or any of the other unfounded ways which are responsible for the mass hysteria in the workplace. AIDS is communicable, but only through the exchange of body fluids, which allow for the AIDS virus to enter the bloodstream. AIDS cannot be transmitted by casual contact because the AIDS virus dies shortly after it is exposed to the air.

PREVENTATIVE PLANNING

Preventative planning will diminish the worry over lawsuits involving discrimination, defamation, and invasion of privacy. It will also bolster the company's public image concerning the treatment of an employee with a life-threatening disease. Planning is the key. Developing a sound AIDS policy now will prepare companies for the AIDS cases that are sure to follow.

A company's first priority is to protect the privacy of an employee who has AIDS, thus shielding itself from an invasion of privacy or defamation suit. Employees should be encouraged, but not required, to inform their managers that they have AIDS. By advocating that employees who have AIDS discuss their illness with the human resource department, the employees are assured that medical benefits and other accommodations, such as flexible work hours, may be arranged. The company may also place employees who have AIDS in contact with community groups that are concerned with the welfare of people who have AIDS and that provide counseling or medical assistance.

The implementation by companies of effective planning and educational programming will result in more humane treatment of employees who have AIDS.

A MODEL FOR A COMPANY
POLICY ON AIDS

Employers should take heed to educate themselves concerning the legal and medical issues and then develop a company policy to deal with employees who have AIDS, incorporating an educational program such as the one set forth below.

1. Equal treatment will be accorded to employees who have AIDS with regard to their right to work and to seek promotion and raises and their right to be protected from discrimination and harassment by managers and coworkers.
2. An employee suspected of having AIDS will not be approached and no statement will be made regarding the suspected illness to coworkers. This guards against an invasion of privacy suit as well as a defamation action should the hunch turn out to be false.
3. A well-informed human resource staff will be provided, which will be trained in dealing with all aspects of the AIDS dilemma. Employees who have AIDS will be encouraged to confide in the human resource staff. The staff will help employees who have AIDS cope with unfriendly coworkers and protect the employees from harassment and/or discrimination through education and then disciplinary action, if necessary. The human resource staff will explore the possibility of flexible work hours or permitting the employee who has AIDS to work at home through a computer terminal and modem. The future course of the AIDS virus will be discussed with the employee by explaining the medical and disability benefits available. A counselor will be employed to help the AIDS victim cope with the psychological trauma he or she will be dealing with. The AIDS victim will be placed in contact with community service programs which are geared to helping the needs of the AIDS victim outside the workplace.
4. Confidentiality will be extended to information received by the company from the AIDS employee. This information will not be placed in the AIDS employee's

personnel file, but may be documented in the employee's medical file with consent. This procedure guards against an invasion of privacy.

5. An educational program will be implemented consisting of booklets and other printed information on the causes of AIDS, working with AIDS or with someone who has AIDS. Seminars may be set up where a physician and psychologist are invited to discuss the physical and emotional consequences of AIDS and how to deal with them. The theory behind the program will be to create a comfortable atmosphere in which both AIDS employees and their coworkers can function productively.

6. Coworkers will be educated and counseled to dispel their fear of catching the AIDS virus from casual contact. An employee's refusal to work with an AIDS victim will not be given preferential treatment beyond the normal request for a transfer.

7. Those employees who hold positions of leadership in the community will be encouraged to espouse their concern for the need for AIDS awareness.

8. An employer's right to dismiss an AIDS employee is restricted to evaluating the employee's caliber of work. If the quality of the AIDS victim's work has suffered due to excessive absences and/or a weakened physical condition, the employer may legally exclude the employee from the workplace by placing him or her on disability. Prior to this, the employer will sit down with the AIDS victim and discuss the health benefits the company will provide.

THE FUTURE FOR DISABLED WORKERS

With the increase in information service type positions, the computer and the telephone become great equalizers for the disabled. Couple this with the decline in the number of young people entering the job market, and the future for disabled workers looks promising. Disabled individuals represent the largest pool of potential workers. This is but another group of productive and dedicated workers, whose abilities have remained untapped. They will prove to be useful resources to many companies in the future and will integrate themselves into the work force similar to those other groups who had previously been unwanted. McDonald's McJobs program hires individuals with mental and physical disabilities. It began in the early 1980s and has proven to be a sound business solution to McDonald's need for dedicated and loyal employees with low turnover ratio.

❖ EMPLOYER LESSONS

- Understand the provisions of the Americans with Disabilities Act.
- Treat disabled workers as you would treat other employees.
- Know what ailments, conditions, or sicknesses are covered under the ADA.
- Learn the four major categories of disabilities.
- Attempt to accommodate disabled workers if their requests are reasonable.
- Refrain from questioning applicants about whether they are disabled.

- Know that if the accommodation requested is an undue burden, then it does not have to be granted.
- Safeguard the confidentiality of the medical records of disabled employees.
- Do not speak to coworkers about an employee's disability.
- Be aware that the ADA does not mandate special treatment for the disabled; they must be able to perform the essential functions of the job.

❖ EMPLOYEE LESSONS

- Be familiar with the rights afforded to you under the Americans with Disabilities Act.
- Know that you have the right to be accommodated so long as the accommodation is reasonable and does not create an undue burden on the employer.
- Understand that you must be able to perform the essential functions of the job, albeit with accommodation.
- Be aware that employers should not query you regarding whether you have any disabilities.
- Be apprised that if an employer perceives you as having a disability, even though you do not, you are covered under the ADA.
- Appreciate the fact that if an employer divulges information about your disability that is not readily apparent, it may be an invasion of your privacy.
- Consider that AIDS is a protected disability.
- Realize that if someone falsely accuses you of harboring a loathsome disease, it is defamation.
- Learn what disabilities are protected under the ADA.
- Recognize that disabled workers have as much right to employment as anyone else.

❖ SUMMARY

The percentage of disabled workers who are unemployed is much greater than that of the general population. Public access and specific job accommodations have gone a long way to aid the gainful employment of many of the disabled. Encouraging a change in the mind-set of employers remains a formidable task. Many employers view disabled applicants as inferior to others. They represent an additional worry employers do not need. However, with reasonable accommodation, many disabled employees have proven to work as effectively as other workers because their handicap has been alleviated. They are operating on a level playing surface with the rest of the work population.

❖ REVIEW QUESTIONS

1. Explain the importance of the Americans with Disabilities Act of 1990.
2. What is the significance of the Rehabilitation Act of 1973?
3. Define disability.
4. Are disabled people covered under Title VII?
5. Explain the changes made to better accommodate the disabled in our society.
6. What types of reasonable accommodations have to be made for the disabled employee?
7. Can a disability ever preclude employment because it is considered a bona fide occupational qualification?
8. When can a request for disability accommodation be denied?
9. Are alcoholism and drug addiction disabilities?
10. How should the employer deal with these conditions?
11. Define AIDS.
12. Is AIDS a contagious disease?

13. Can a person having a contagious disease be discriminated against?
14. Is AIDS considered to be a disability?
15. Can a coworker refuse to work with an employee who has AIDS?
16. Do coworkers have a right to know if an employee has AIDS?
17. If management discloses that an employee has AIDS, what recourse does the employee have?
18. Is harassing an employee who has AIDS actionable?
19. If false rumors are spread stating that an employee has AIDS, on what principle of law would the employee sue?
20. A worker suffered from a knee injury that prevented him from working for several days in July. He requested reassignment to a position having a lighter workload. The company refused, claiming that the injury was only temporary. What was the result?
21. Aucutt claimed that Six Flags refused to accommodate his handicap by reassigning him to a less stressful position. Six Flags argued that high blood pressure and coronary artery disease do not qualify Aucutt as being handicapped. What was the result? *Aucutt v. Six Flags Over Mid America,* 869 F. Supp. 736 (E.D. Mo. 1994)
22. Paegle injured his back on two occasions, the second of which necessitated light-duty work status for nearly one year. He requested an accommodation but was refused by his employer. Is this disability discrimination? *Paegle v. Department of Interior,* 813 F. Supp. 61 (D.D.C. 1993)
23. In November 1987, a worker became ill and had gallbladder surgery. She did not work from November 16, 1987, through February 1, 1988. On February 3, 1988, after returning to her position with the Election Board, she reinjured her back because of continued heavy lifting. Upon the advice of a medical doctor, plaintiff did not work for two days. Upon her return to work she requested a transfer to a job with lighter duties. No transfer was offered. What was the result?
24. In July 1993, the plaintiff was diagnosed as having high blood pressure. His treating physician, Dr. Edmund Miller, stated that he authorized the plaintiff to remain out of work for nearly the entire month of July while his body adjusted to his high blood pressure medication. During this time, the plaintiff failed to report directly to his supervisor at Bryant Foods regarding his condition. After one of the supervisors reported seeing the plaintiff's car parked at his shop during the lunch hour, two members of management drove to the plaintiff's shop, whereupon they found the plaintiff standing in the hot sun, appearing to supervise work on automobiles. When the plaintiff returned to work on July 27, he was placed on 90 days probation for failing to communicate properly with his supervisor as to his medical condition and for working at his shop when he was supposedly unable to work at Bryant Foods. The plaintiff returned to work on August 11, after an absence of five working days, with a medical excuse for only one day. The defendant fired the plaintiff, effective August 12, 1993. The stated reason for the plaintiff's discharge was his failure to provide a doctor's excuse for the days he missed and his false statement about his medical treatment. Is this a violation of the ADA? *Oswalt v. Sara Lee Corp.,* 889 F. Supp. 253 (N.D. Miss. 1995)
25. The issue in this case is whether an employee's injury qualifies as a disability. The employee, who is a truck driver, injured his shoulder and could no longer perform his job. The company refused to place him on disability because it claimed that his injury was not debilitating. What was the result? *Mowat v. Transportation Unlimited, Inc.* 984 F.2d 230 (8th Cir. 1992)
26. An employee who had claimed to be totally disabled asked for a temporary, part-time employment accommodation, but this was refused. The employee was terminated for failure to return to work. He claimed disability discrimination for a failure to accommodate reasonably his clinical depression. What was the result? *August v. Offices Unlimited, Inc.,* 981 F.2d 576 (1st Cir. 1992)
27. Can an individual who became handicapped, and as a result was reasonably accommodated with light-duty work, be demoted in rank? The employer argued that the employee's function now qualified as a lower position than the one he previously held and that as a

consequence he should be paid accordingly. The employee claimed that such action would be discriminatory against the disabled. What was the result? *Gaither v. Anne Arundel County*, 618 A.2d 244 (Md. App. 1993)

28. Two school-van drivers were demoted because of their diabetes. They proposed carrying snacks and self-administered blood tests. The school district claimed that this action would not overcome the substantial risk of harm if they continued driving. The issue is whether their request amounts to a reasonable accommodation. What was the result? *Wood v. Omaha School Dist.*, 985 F.2d 437 (8th Cir. 1993)

29. Is it ethical to demote an employee who has become disabled?

30. What are the limits to which an employer must go in order reasonably to accommodate an employee?

31. Is the request for part-time work unreasonable when an employee becomes disabled?

32. How severe would a plaintiff's injury have to be to qualify as disabled?

33. Are the accommodations public establishments have been forced to make under the ADA reasonable or an undue burden?

34. Ronald Senter tested HIV positive in May 1986. In March 1991, he was diagnosed with AIDS. He died in January 1993. As owner of Car Parts Distribution Center, Senter participated in the Automotive Wholesaler's Association of New England Health Benefits Plan (Association). In October 1990, the Association amended its plan to limit the amount a person with AIDS could collect to $25,000. All other illnesses remained capped at $1 million. Senter contended that the Association limited its AIDS benefits after he began submitting claims in 1989. He felt this action amounted to discrimination based on his disability. What was the result? *Car Parts Distribution Center, Inc. v. Automotive Wholesaler's Association*, 37 F.3d 112 (1st Cir. 1994)

35. The law firm of Kohn, Nast & Graf searched the office of one of its employees, Doe, and found a letter from an AIDS organization discussing his condition. Is this an invasion of privacy? *Doe, Esquire, v. Kohn, Nast, & Graft, P.C.*, 862 F. Supp. 1310 (E.D. Pa. 1994)

36. Leckelt was a male hospital nurse. After he had undergone an HIV test, the hospital insisted that he disclose the result. Leckelt refused. The hospital fired him because his refusal prevented the hospital from having the information it felt necessary to ensure the safety of its patients and staff. Leckelt claimed that he was discriminated against because of the perception that he might be HIV positive. What was the result? *Leckelt v. Board of Commissioners*, 909 F.2d 820 (5th Cir. 1990)

37. Should people with AIDS be classified as victims deserving of accommodation, or should they be treated as alcoholics and drug addicts who are responsible for their actions?

38. Should the tort of invasion of privacy have been extended to AIDS victims?

39. Is it ethical to spend so much money on research for one illness—AIDS—rather than spreading the money around?

❖ WEB SITES

www.cyberscribe.com/talklaw/disabil.shtml
www.columbus.bcentral.com/columbus/stories/2001/02/19/daily11.html
www.cyberscribe.com/talklaw/disabil.shtml
www.mackinac.org/article.asp?ID=1848
www.findarticles.com/cf_dis/g2699/0003/2699000370/pl/article.jhtml
www.hmso.gov.uk/acts/acts1995/1995050.htm
www.infoxchange.net.au/ddlas/

CHAPTER 17

UNIONS AND COLLECTIVE BARGAINING AGREEMENTS

INTRODUCTION

The first unions were organized during the economic depression of the 1820s. The unions were against excessive taxation, prison labor as competition, and debtors' prisons. Unions stood for public schools and mechanics' liens, which tie up assets of those who refuse to pay their bills. Unions became politically active in their fight to limit the workday to 10 hours. They argued that the government, instead of protecting the poor and middle-class workers, protected the upper class, employers, and management by allowing them to maintain and at times increase their economic advantage.

In 1833, the general trade union was formed from 20 to 30 percent of Manhattan's workforce. Skilled and unskilled workers became members. By 1836, two-thirds of New York City workers and 15 percent of the entire American labor force were union members. Strikes were the unions' main weapon against employers. Strikes involved women as well as men—female bookbinders as well as male shoemakers. The general trade union admitted women to membership. Many other trade unions did not extend membership to women and blacks. Nonadmittance into unions impeded any rise in economic stature and public recognition of women and blacks.

CHAPTER CHECKLIST

❖ Understand that the right of workers to organize and participate in unions is viable.

❖ Appreciate that in certain parts of the country unions have flourished, whereas in other parts their existence has waned.

❖ Realize that the Norris LaGuardia Act revoked the power of federal courts to end strikes through injunctive relief.

❖ Be aware that nonunion membership cannot be a condition of employment.

❖ Learn that the National Mediation Board encourages voluntary mediation between management and labor.

❖ Recognize the deleterious effect that GATT and NAFTA have had on unions.

❖ Know that a collective bargaining agreement is a binding contract between management and labor.

❖ Become familiar with the terms included in a collective bargaining agreement.

❖ Be apprised of the history and purpose of unions.

❖ Incorporate an arbitration clause in collective bargaining agreements to avoid protracted litigation.

EMPLOYMENT SCENARIO

The Long and the Short of It is now in its seventh year of operation, with eight stores and over 175 employees. A large number of employees have become disenchanted with the autocratic management style of Tom Long and Mark Short. These employees want to form a union. When Tom and Mark learn of this through their spies, they decide to nip this "subversive activity" in the bud by requiring all employees to sign off on an agreement not to participate in the formation of a union. Those employees who refuse to sign will be immediately terminated to set an example. Thirty-five employees refuse to sign L&S's yellow-dog contract requiring nonunion membership as a condition to continued employment. They are discharged. When Susan North, company attorney, learns of this mass firing and the justification for it, she immediately reprimands Tom and Mark. She berates them by querying whether L&S is in the business of selling men's clothing or of litigating employment issues. Susan informs Tom and Mark that a signed agreement pledging nonunion membership as a condition of employment is called a yellow-dog contract, and that these contracts were outlawed in 1926. Susan criticizes Tom and Mark's employee relations as being dictatorial and passe. Susan advises L&S to rehire those 35 discharged workers immediately, and offers to mediate between Tom and Mark and L&S's employees to arrive at a compromise on compensation and related issues. Susan chides Tom and Mark into adopting a more conciliatory attitude to their employees. She concludes with the saying that you get more bees with honey than with vinegar.

SHERMAN ACT

Back in the early 1900s, monopolistic companies totally dominated labor. This trend was accepted more in Great Britain than in America, where it led to some unrest. Wage differences widened between skilled and unskilled workers. Employers exhibited a weak sense of responsibility and began to hoard their wealth. Single women worked, while married women stayed home.

The Sherman Antitrust Act, enacted in 1890, was initially applied to any activity that interrupted the free flow of commerce. The term "every business combination" came into use to include the unions. Whereas citizens had hoped that the Sherman Act would be used to lessen the power of monopolies, instead it became a tool for big business to use against its employees.

CLAYTON ACT

The Clayton Act, enacted in 1914 with good intent toward labor, exacerbated the problem by strengthening the application of the Sherman Act against labor. Whereas before, applications for injunctive relief rested only with the federal courts, under the Clayton Act employers themselves could file applications against their employees.

The language of Sections 6 and 20 of the Clayton Act seemed to invalidate the use of injunctive relief under the Sherman Act with regard to labor. Section 6 provided that employees' work is not goods available in commerce and that labor unions and their members are not illegal combinations acting in restraint of free trade. Section 20 went on to provide that injunctive relief is not to be granted in a labor dispute unless damage to property was intended. The language could not be clearer that Congress's intent was that the Sherman Act and its remedy of injunctive relief should not apply to labor. However, the courts carved many exceptions by claiming the Clayton Act does not apply to individuals who strike because they are no longer employees, to union organizers because they are not employees, and to employees who sign yellow-dog contracts.

YELLOW-DOG CONTRACT

A yellow-dog contract is a stipulation mandated by the employer that the employee will not join a union, as a condition of continued employment. Yellow-dog contracts were upheld by the courts in strict opposition to the legal principle of noninterference with contractual business relations. Interference with contracts is an actionable tort, which means that an individual can sue for money damages. In any event, this doctrine was overlooked and yellow-dog contracts were in effect until the passage of the Railway Labor Act of 1926 and the Federal Anti-Injunction Act of 1932.

RAILWAY LABOR ACT

The Railway Labor Act of 1926 outlawed yellow-dog contracts by prohibiting an agreement of nonunion membership as a condition to employment. It strengthened the right of unions to strike as long as the work stoppage and related protest were peaceful. The Act instituted the National Mediation Board (NMB) to encourage voluntary mediation between management and labor. If no resolution could be reached, then the NMB would propose binding arbitration. If agreed, both sides would be bound by its decision.

NORRIS LAGUARDIA ACT

This activity against labor continued until 1932, when the Federal Anti-Injunctive Act, more commonly known as the Norris LaGuardia Act, was passed. Its first section relieved federal courts of the power to grant injunctions in labor disputes, with limited exceptions, thus marking the end of the use of the Sherman and Clayton Acts' injunctive relief against labor.

NATIONAL LABOR RELATIONS ACT

The National Labor Relations Act (NLRA) was enacted in 1935 to ensure the right of employees to organize and participate in unions without fear of reprisals from employers.

In 1935, with the passage of the NLRA, also known as the Wagner Act, unions organized with the power of enforcement. Certified bargaining agreements were forthcoming. Company attempts at domination were stymied with the creation of the National Labor Relations Board, with investigatory and enforcement power being placed at its discretion.

TAFT HARTLEY ACT

The Taft Hartley Act, also known as the Labor Management Relations Act of 1947, declared the closed shop illegal. Workers who did not want to join the union could not be discriminated against. This Act delineated unfair labor practices by unions. One such practice prohibited was the use of coercion by unions to force workers to join.

THE FUTURE FOR UNIONS

The struggle waged by unions was certainly profitable for their members. From the 1940s until recently, skilled laborers have enjoyed a relatively high standard of living. However, many businesses have now taken advantage of lower living costs and cheaper office space outside the United States. With the emergence of the General Agreement on Tariffs and Treaties (GATT) and the North American Free Trade Agreement (NAFTA), more jobs, especially those in manufacturing, are moving to Mexico and overseas. The power of the unions has been crippled. In the past, unions were a major political force in the Democratic party. Now that is no longer true. Ironically, it was Democratic President Bill Clinton who signed off on the GATT, which signaled the death knell for unions.

In the global marketplace, comparative advantage will prevail. If goods can be manufactured somewhere cheaper with no loss in quality, then a company will move its operation there, and high-paying union jobs will be lost. The result will be the lowering of the standard of living for skilled, semiskilled, and unskilled laborers. The same phenomenon is happening even in the service sector with regard to certain data entry positions. Communications and computers are making this trend possible. Location is no longer a key factor. As a result, American office workers are working harder, lunch hours have been given up, longer hours are becoming the norm, and taking work home or coming into the office on weekends is commonplace. Workers had believed that using the computer to link their office with their home would cut their commuting time to three days a week. Instead, the office worker will still work a standard five-day week at the office. The computer link will enable the worker to work at home in the evenings and on the weekend.

Office workers and laborers are also being forced continually to reeducate and retrain themselves. Developing skills that cannot be easily and efficiently replicated overseas is vital to keeping one's job and maintaining a comfortable standard of living.

The issue in the case that follows is whether an investigator employed in NASA's Office of Inspector General is considered to be a representative of NASA.

CASE

NATIONAL AERONAUTICS AND SPACE ADMINISTRATION v. FEDERAL LABOR RELATIONS AUTHORITY

527 U.S. 229 (1999)

JUSTICE STEVENS delivered the opinion of the Court.

On October 12, 1978, Congress enacted the Inspector General Act (IGA), which created an Office of Inspector General (OIG) in each of several federal agencies, including the National Aeronautics and Space Administration (NASA). The following day, Congress enacted the Federal Service Labor-Management Relations Statute (FSLMRS), which provides certain protections, including union representation, to a variety of federal employees. The question presented by this case is whether an investigator employed in NASA's Office of Inspector General (NASA—OIG) can be considered a "representative" of NASA when examining a NASA employee, such that the right to union representation in the FSLMRS may be invoked. Although certain arguments of policy may support a negative answer to that question, the plain text of the two statutes, buttressed by administrative deference and Congress' countervailing policy concerns, dictates an affirmative answer.

In January 1993, in response to information supplied by the Federal Bureau of Investigation (FBI), NASA's OIG conducted an investigation of certain threatening activities of an employee of

the George C. Marshall Space Flight Center in Huntsville, Alabama, which is also a component of NASA. A NASA—OIG investigator contacted the employee to arrange for an interview and, in response to the employee's request, agreed that both the employee's lawyer and union representative could attend. The conduct of the interview gave rise to a complaint by the union representative that the investigator had improperly limited his participation. The union filed a charge with the Federal Labor Relations Authority (Authority) alleging that NASA and its OIG had committed an unfair labor practice.

The Administrative Law Judge (ALJ) ruled for the union with respect to its complaint against NASA—OIG. The ALJ concluded that the OIG investigator was a "representative" of NASA, and that certain aspects of the investigator's behavior had violated the right to union representation under that section. On review, the Authority agreed that the NASA—OIG investigator prevented the union representative from actively participating in the examination and (1) ordered both NASA and NASA—OIG to cease and desist (a) requiring bargaining unit employees to participate in OIG interviews without allowing active participation of a union representative, and (b) likewise interfering with, coercing, or restraining employees in exercising their rights under the statute; and (2) directed NASA to (a) order NASA—OIG to comply, and (b) post appropriate notices at the Huntsville facility.

NASA and NASA—OIG petitioned for review, asking whether the NASA—OIG investigator was a "representative" of NASA, and whether it was proper to grant relief against NASA as well as its OIG. The Court of Appeals upheld the Authority's rulings on both questions and granted the Authority's application for enforcement of its order. Because of disagreement among the Circuit Courts, we granted certiorari.

The FSLMRS provides, in relevant part,

"(2) An exclusive representative of an appropriate unit in an agency shall be given the opportunity to be represented at–

. . . . .

"(B) any examination of an employee in the unit by a representative of the agency in connection with an investigation if–

"(i) the employee reasonably believes that the examination may result in disciplinary action against the employee; and

"(ii) the employee requests representation."

In this case it is undisputed that the employee reasonably believed the investigation could result in discipline against him, that he requested union representation, that NASA is the relevant "agency," and that, if the provision applies, a violation of §7114(a)(2)(B) occurred. The contested issue is whether a NASA—OIG investigator can be considered a "representative" of NASA when conducting an employee examination covered by §7114(a)(2)(B).

NASA and its OIG argue that, when §7114(a)(2)(B) is read in context and compared with the similar right to union representation protected in the private sector by the National Labor Relations Act, the term "representative" refers only to a representative of agency management–"*i.e.,* the entity that has a collective bargaining relationship with the employee's union." Neither NASA nor NASA—OIG has such a relationship with the employee's union at the Huntsville facility (exclud-

ing certain agency investigators and auditors from "appropriate" bargaining units), and so the investigator in this case could not have been a "representative" of the relevant "entity."

By its terms, §7114(a)(2)(B) is not limited to investigations conducted by certain "entities" within the agency in question. It simply refers to representatives of "the agency," which, all agree, means NASA. §7114(a)(2) (referring to employees "in the unit" and an exclusive representative "of an appropriate unit in an agency"). Thus, relying on prior rulings, the Authority found no basis in the FSLMRS or its legislative history to support the limited reading advocated by NASA and its OIG. The Authority reasoned that adopting their proposal might erode the right by encouraging the use of investigative conduits outside the employee's bargaining unit, and would otherwise frustrate Congress' apparent policy of protecting certain federal employees when they are examined and justifiably fear disciplinary action.

In any event, the right Congress created in §7114(a)(2)(B) vindicates obvious countervailing federal policies. It provides a procedural safeguard for employees who are under investigation by their agency, and the mere existence of the right can only strengthen the morale of the federal workforce. The interest in fair treatment for employees under investigation is equally strong whether they are being questioned by employees in NASA's OIG or by other representatives of the agency. And, representation is not the equivalent of obstruction. In many cases the participation of a union representative will facilitate the factfinding process and a fair resolution of an agency investigation–or at least Congress must have thought so.

Whenever a procedural protection plays a meaningful role in an investigation, it may impose some burden on the investigators or agency managers in pursuing their mission. We must presume, however, that Congress took account of the policy concerns on both sides of the balance when it decided to enact the IGA and, on the heels of that statute, §7114(a)(2)(B) of the FSLMRS.

The judgment of the Court of Appeals is Affirmed.

Case Commentary

The United States Supreme Court ruled that an NASA-OIG inspector is a representative of NASA. The court rejected NASA's argument that the FSLMRS protection extended only to the private industry where a collective bargaining agreement was involved.

Case Questions

1. Are you in agreement with the Court's decision?
2. Why do you think Congress created the FSLMRS immediately after it established the Inspector General Act (IGA)?
3. What was NASA's motive in refusing to allow the employee's union representative to be present during the OIG's investigation?

COLLECTIVE BARGAINING

Collective bargaining is the negotiation process undertaken by a union on behalf of its members with the management of an organization with the intent of entering into a contract after the resolution of labor issues. The contract, known as the *collective bargaining agreement,* is binding on all union members. The advantage of collective bargaining is that the union has greater bargaining strength than an individual employee would have in attempting to negotiate the best possible deal.

KEY TERMS

The key terms to be negotiated in a collective bargaining agreement include full time wages, minimum number of hours required for full time status, overtime pay, vacation time, personal days, pension benefits, health care coverage for the employees and their dependents, description and classification of jobs, work schedules, rules regarding employee behavior, cost of living adjustments in pay, determination of promotion, policy termination committee to handle grievances, and procedure for arbitration to handle contract disputes.

The question presented in the case that follows is whether an employee who is asserting a violation of the Americans with Disabilities Act (ADA) must arbitrate this dispute in accordance with the arbitration provision of the collective bargaining agreement.

CASE

WRIGHT v. UNIVERSAL MARITIME SERVICE CORP.

525 U.S. 70 (1998)

JUSTICE SCALIA delivered the opinion of the Court.

This case presents the question whether a general arbitration clause in a collective-bargaining agreement (CBA) requires an employee to use the arbitration procedure for an alleged violation of the Americans with Disabilities Act of 1990 (ADA).

In 1970, petitioner Ceasar Wright began working as a longshoreman in Charleston, South Carolina. He was a member of Local 1422 of the International Longshoremen's Association, AFL-CIO (Union), which uses a hiring hall to supply workers to several stevedore companies represented by the South Carolina Stevedores

Association (SCSA). Clause 15(B) of the CBA between the Union and the SCSA provides in part as follows: "Matters under dispute which cannot be promptly settled between the Local and an individual Employer shall, no later than 48 hours after such discussion, be referred in writing covering the entire grievance to a Port Grievance Committee…." If the Port Grievance Committee, which is evenly divided between representatives of labor and management, cannot reach an agreement within five days of receiving the complaint, then the dispute must be referred to a District Grievance Committee, which is also evenly divided between the two sides. The CBA provides that a majority decision of the District Grievance Committee "shall be final and binding." If the District Grievance Committee cannot reach a majority decision within 72 hours after meeting, then the committee must employ a professional arbitrator.

Clause 15(F) of the CBA provides as follows:

> "The Union agrees that this Agreement is intended to cover all matters affecting wages, hours, and other terms and conditions of employment and that during the term of this Agreement the Employers will not be required to negotiate on any further matters affecting these or other subjects not specifically set forth in this Agreement. Anything not contained in this Agreement shall not be construed as being part of this Agreement. All past port practices being observed may be reduced to writing in each port."

Finally, Clause 17 of the CBA states: "It is the intention and purpose of all parties hereto that no provision or part of this Agreement shall be violative of any Federal or State Law."

Wright was also subject to the Longshore Seniority Plan, which contained its own grievance provision, reading as follows: "Any dispute concerning or arising out of the terms and/or conditions of this Agreement, or dispute involving the interpretation or application of this Agreement, or dispute arising out of any rule adopted for its implementation, shall be referred to the Seniority Board." The Seniority Board is equally divided between labor and management representatives. If the board reaches agreement by majority vote, then that determination is final and binding. If the board cannot resolve the dispute,

then the Union and the SCSA each choose a person, and this "Committee of two" makes a final determination.

On February 18, 1992, while Wright was working for respondent Stevens Shipping and Terminal Company (Stevens), he injured his right heel and his back. He sought compensation from Stevens for permanent disability under the Longshore and Harbor Workers' Compensation Act, and ultimately settled the claim for $250,000 and $10,000 in attorney's fees. Wright was also awarded Social Security disability benefits.

In January 1995 Wright returned to the Union hiring hall and asked to be referred for work. (At some point he obtained a written note from his doctor approving such activity.) Between January 2 and January 11, Wright worked for four stevedoring companies, none of which complained about his performance. When, however, the stevedoring companies realized that Wright had previously settled a claim for permanent disability, they informed the Union that they would not accept Wright for employment, because a person certified as permanently disabled (which they regarded Wright to be) is not qualified to perform longshore work under the CBA. The Union responded that the employers had misconstrued the CBA, suggested that the ADA entitled Wright to return to work if he could perform his duties, and asserted that refusing Wright employment would constitute a "lock-out" in violation of the CBA.

When Wright found out that the stevedoring companies would no longer accept him for employment, he contacted the Union to ask how he could get back to work. Wright claims that instead of suggesting the filing of a grievance, the Union told him to obtain counsel and file a claim under the ADA. Wright hired an attorney and eventually filed charges of discrimination with the Equal Employment Opportunity Commission (EEOC) and the South Carolina State Human Affairs Commission, alleging that the stevedoring companies and the SCSA had violated the ADA by refusing him work. In October 1995, Wright received a right-to-sue letter from the EEOC.

In January 1996, Wright filed a complaint against the SCSA and six individual stevedoring companies in the United States District Court for the District of South Carolina. Respondents' answer asserted various affirmative defenses, including Wright's failure to exhaust his remedies under the CBA and the Seniority Plan. After discovery, respondents moved for summary judgment and Wright moved for partial summary judgment with respect to some of respondents' defenses. A Magistrate Judge recommended that the District Court dismiss the case without prejudice because Wright had failed to pursue the grievance procedure provided by the CBA. The District Court adopted the report and recommendation and subsequently rejected Wright's motion for reconsideration. The United States Court of Appeals for the Fourth Circuit affirmed. We granted certiorari.

In this case, the Fourth Circuit concluded that the general arbitration provision in the CBA governing Wright's employment was sufficiently broad to encompass a statutory claim arising under the ADA, and that such a provision was enforceable.

In asserting the existence of an agreement to arbitrate the ADA claim, respondents rely upon the presumption of arbitrability this Court has found in the Labor Management Relations Act, 1947 (LMRA). In collective bargaining agreements, we have said, "there is a presumption of arbitrability in the sense that 'an order to arbitrate the particular grievance should not be denied unless it may be said with positive assurance that the arbitration clause is not susceptible of an interpretation that covers the asserted dispute.' " The dispute in the present case, however, ultimately concerns not the application or interpretation of any CBA, but the meaning of a federal statute. The cause of action Wright asserts arises not out of contract, but out of the ADA, and is distinct from any right conferred by the collective-bargaining agreement. To be sure, respondents argue that Wright is not qualified for his position as the CBA requires, but even if that were true he would *still* prevail if the refusal to hire violated the ADA.

Not only is petitioner's statutory claim not subject to a presumption of arbitrability; we think any CBA requirement to arbitrate it must be particularly clear.

The CBA in this case is very general, providing for arbitration of "matters under dispute," App. 43a—which could be understood to mean matters in dispute under the contract. And the remainder of the contract contains no explicit incorporation of statutory antidiscrimination requirements.

Finally, we do not find a clear and unmistakable waiver in the Longshore Seniority Plan. Like the CBA itself, the Plan contains no antidiscrimination provision; and it specifically limits its grievance procedure to disputes related to the agreement.

We hold that the collective-bargaining agreement in this case does not contain a clear and unmistakable waiver of the covered employees' rights to a judicial forum for federal claims of employment discrimination. We do not reach the question whether such a waiver would be enforceable. The judgment of the Fourth Circuit is vacated, and the case is remanded for further proceedings consistent with this opinion.

It is so ordered.

Case Commentary

The United States Supreme Court decided that the collective bargaining agreement's general arbitration provision does not extend to issues of employment discrimination.

Case Questions

1. Are you in accord with the United States Supreme Court in this case?
2. If the collective bargaining agreement's arbitration clause specifically provided for employment discrimination complaints, would the Court's decision have been different?
3. Do you believe Wright should be entitled to work after being certified as permanently disabled?

PURPOSE

Collective bargaining serves a useful purpose in allowing management to negotiate with one union rather than the hundreds or thousands of individual employees that the union represents. In most cases, it is an expeditious and inexpensive method of resolving labor issues.

UNLAWFUL PRACTICES

Where there is a valid collective bargaining agreement, it would be an unlawful practice to compromise employees' contracted rights, such as seniority and shift preference, in order to accommodate the religious beliefs of a particular employee. This would present an undue hardship for the employer.

EMPLOYMENT PERSPECTIVE

Mitchell Feldstein, an Orthodox Jew, has been employed at the Giant Motors Lexington, Kentucky, plant where he has seniority. Mitchell is granted a transfer to the Flint, Michigan, plant. According to the collective bargaining agreement, seniority is determined by years at the plant, not at the company. At Flint, Mitchell, having no seniority, is required to work Saturdays. Mitchell asserts that this requirement is against his religious beliefs. Giant Motors refuses to accommodate him, claiming undue hardship in that the accommodation will compromise the seniority rights of other employees as determined by the collective bargaining agreement. Mitchell is subsequently discharged for excessive absenteeism on Saturdays. Mitchell files an EEOC claim for religious discrimination. Will he be successful? No! To accommodate Mitchell would be a breach of the collective bargaining agreement and an unlawful employment practice. It is an undue hardship for Giant Motors. ■

The issue in the case that follows is whether an employer with a good faith doubt that the union has majority status prior to approval of the collective bargaining agreement may wait till after the collective bargaining agreement has been accepted before raising the issue of lack of majority status.

AUCIELLO IRON WORKS, INC. v. NATIONAL LABOR RELATIONS BOARD

517 U.S. 781 (1996)

JUSTICE SOUTER delivered the opinion of the Court.

The question here is whether an employer may disavow a collective-bargaining agreement because of a good-faith doubt about a union's majority status at the time the contract was made, when the doubt arises from facts known to the employer before its contract offer had been accepted by the union. We hold that the National Labor Relations Board reasonably concluded that an employer challenging an agreement under these circumstances commits an unfair labor practice.

I.

Petitioner Auciello Iron Works of Hudson, Massachusetts, had 23 production and maintenance employees during the period in question. After a union election in 1977, the NLRB certified Shopmen's Local No. 501, a/w International Association of Bridge, Structural, and Ornamental Iron Workers, AFL-CIO, as the collective-bargaining representative of Auciello's employees. Over the following years, the company and the Union were able to negotiate a series of collective-bargaining agreements, one of which expired on September 25, 1988. Negotiations for a new one were unsuccessful throughout September and October 1988, however, and when Auciello and the Union had not made a new contract by October 14, 1988, the employees went on strike. Negotiations continued, nonetheless, and, on November 17, 1988, Auciello presented the Union with a complete contract proposal. On November 18, 1988, the picketing stopped, and nine days later, on a Sunday evening, the Union telegraphed its acceptance of the outstanding offer. The very next day, however, Auciello told the Union that it doubted that a majority of the bargaining unit's employees supported the Union, and for that reason disavowed the collective-bargaining agreement and denied it had any duty to continue negotiating. Auciello traced its doubt to knowledge acquired before the Union accepted the contract offer, including the facts that 9 employees had crossed the picket line, that 13 employees had given it signed forms indicating their resignation from the Union, and that 16 had expressed dissatisfaction with the Union.

In January 1989, the Board's General Counsel issued an administrative complaint charging Auciello with violation of the NLRA. An administrative law judge found that a contract existed between the parties and that Auciello's withdrawal from it violated the Act. The Board affirmed the administrative law judge's decision; it treated Auciello's claim of good-faith doubt as irrelevant and ordered Auciello to reduce the collective-bargaining agreement to a formal written instrument. But when the Board applied to the Court of Appeals for the First Circuit for enforcement of its order, the Court of Appeals declined on the ground that the Board had not adequately explained its refusal to consider Auciello's defense of good-faith doubt about the Union's majority status. On remand, the Board issued a supplemental opinion to justify its position, and the Court of Appeals thereafter enforced the order as resting on a "policy choice both . . . reasonable and . . . quite persuasive." We granted certiorari, and now affirm.

II.

A.

The object of the National Labor Relations Act is industrial peace and stability, fostered by collective-bargaining agreements providing for the orderly resolution of labor disputes between workers and employees. To such ends, the Board has adopted various presumptions about the existence of majority support for a union within a bargaining unit, the precondition for service as its exclusive representative. The first two are conclusive presumptions. A union "usually is entitled to a conclusive presumption of majority status for one year following" Board certification as such a representative. A union is likewise entitled under Board precedent to a conclusive presumption of majority status during the term of any collective-bargaining agreement, up to three years. "These presumptions are based not so much on an absolute certainty that the union's majority status will not erode," as on the need to achieve "stability in collective-bargaining relationships." They address our fickle nature by "enabling a union to concentrate on obtaining and fairly administering a collective-bargaining agreement" without worrying about the immediate risk of decertification and by "removing any temptation on the part of the employer to avoid good-faith bargaining" in an effort to undermine union support.

There is a third presumption, though not a conclusive one. At the end of the certification year or upon expiration of the collective-bargaining agreement, the presumption of majority status becomes a rebuttable one. Then, an employer may overcome the presumption (when, for example, defending against an unfair labor practice charge) "by showing that, at the time of its refusal to bargain, either (1) the union did not in fact enjoy majority support, or (2) the employer had a 'good-faith' doubt, founded on a sufficient objective basis, of the union's majority support." Auciello asks this Court to hold that it may raise the latter defense even after a collective-bargaining contract period has apparently begun to run upon a union's acceptance of an employer's outstanding offer.

B.

The same need for repose that first prompted the Board to adopt the rule presuming the union's majority status during the term of a collective-bargaining agreement also led the Board to rule out an exception for the benefit of an employer with doubts arising from facts antedating the contract. The Board said that such an exception

would allow an employer to control the timing of its assertion of good-faith doubt and thus to "'sit' on that doubt and . . . raise it after the offer is accepted." The Board thought that the risks associated with giving employers such "unilateral control over a vital part of the collective-bargaining process," would undermine the stability of the collective-bargaining relationship, and thus outweigh any benefit that might in theory follow from vindicating a doubt that ultimately proved to be sound.

The Board's judgment in the matter is entitled to prevail. The Board's approach generally allows companies an adequate chance to act on their preacceptance doubts before contract formation, just as Auciello could have acted effectively under the Board's rule in this case. Auciello knew that the picket line had been crossed and that a number of its employees had expressed dissatisfaction with the Union at least nine days before the contract's acceptance, and all of the resignation forms Auciello received were dated at least five days before the acceptance date. During the week preceding the apparent formation of the contract, Auciello had at least three alternatives to doing nothing. It could have withdrawn the outstanding offer and then, like its employees, petitioned for a representation election. "If the Board determines, after investigation and hearing, that a question of representation exists, it directs an election by secret ballot and certifies the result." Following withdrawal, it could also have refused to bargain further on the basis of its good-faith doubt, leaving it to the Union to charge an unfair labor practice, against which it could defend on the basis of the doubt. and, of course, it could have withdrawn its offer to allow it time to investigate while it continued to fulfil its duty to bargain in good faith with the Union. The company thus had generous opportunities to avoid the presumption before the moment of acceptance.

We hold that the Board reasonably found an employer's precontractual, good-faith doubt inadequate to support an exception to the conclusive presumption arising at the moment a collective-bargaining contract offer has been accepted. We accordingly affirm the judgment of the Court of Appeals for the First Circuit.

It is so ordered.

Judgment for NLRB.

Case Commentary

The United States Supreme Court ruled that Auciello, having prior knowledge, committed an unfair labor practice by waiting until the collective bargaining agreement had been accepted before questioning the majority status of the union.

Case Questions

1. Are you in agreement with the Court's determination?

2. Why should it matter when Auciello raised the issue of lack of majority status?

3. Was the union at fault for not knowing whether it had majority status before approving the collective bargaining agreement?

❖ EMPLOYER LESSONS

- Determine the propensity for workers to organize unions in your business field and in your region.
- Refrain from mandating that employees promise not to organize or participate in a union.
- Familiarize yourself with the various labor laws.
- Be cognizant of the movement of manufacturing outside the country.
- Realize the impact GATT and NAFTA have had on unions.
- Evaluate whether it is best to relocate to another region of the country or overseas if your employees are forming a union.
- Fulfill employees' demands when reasonable, rather than be forced to relocate or to confront a union.
- Hire a specialist to negotiate collective bargaining agreements.
- Appreciate the significance of the National Labor Relations Board.
- Know that the National Mediation Board is available to negotiate labor disputes.

❖ EMPLOYEE LESSONS

- Be aware of the history and purpose of unions.
- Develop an understanding of the various labor laws.
- Determine the likelihood your employer will remain at its present location before purchasing a home or becoming entrenched in the community.
- Evaluate whether you will search for other employment or remain with your employer if it decides to relocate.
- Recognize that mediation is available to settle disputes.
- Become knowledgeable concerning the terms and conditions in a collective bargaining agreement.
- Appreciate that unions have, on occasion, secured higher wages and benefits for their members, only to have employers as a result relocate.
- Acknowledge the impact of GATT and NAFTA on employment.
- Realize that many manufacturing jobs have been replaced by lower paying nonunion service jobs.
- Understand that arbitration clauses are incorporated into many employment contracts, thereby eliminating the opportunity to have your case heard before a jury.

❖ REVIEW QUESTIONS

1. Why did workers have so much difficulty organizing?
2. How was the Sherman Antitrust Act used against workers?
3. When was the first union formed?
4. What is beneficial about unions?
5. How have the GATT and NAFTA affected unions?
6. Why did unions switch their political support from the Labor Party to the Democratic party?
7. Why was the American Federation of Labor successful?
8. Explain the significance of the Homestead strike.
9. Define yellow-dog contract.
10. Explain the function of the National Labor Relations Board.
11. A union shop mandates that the employer hire only union members. Is a union shop legal?
12. Can an individual be paid as a union representative without forgoing his rights under the NLRA?
13. Define collective bargaining.
14. What is a collective bargaining agreement?
15. Is a collective bargaining agreement binding on all union members?
16. Explain the terms in the agreement.
17. What is the method for dispute resolution?
18. Explain the purpose served by collective bargaining.
19. Give an example of when contract rights secured through collective bargaining conflict with civil rights.
20. How is this conflict resolved?
21. Explain the advantage of collective bargaining from an employer's perspective.
22. What is the law which secured the right of workers to bargain collectively?
23. Can provisions of a collective bargaining agreement survive its termination?
24. Is a ban on smoking in the workplace ethical?
25. Is it ethical to compel a nonunion member to pay union dues as a condition of his or her employment?
26. Six employees were discharged after signing union authorization cards. They claim that the company's action of mass firing was antiunion and constituted an unfair labor practice. What

was the result? *Davis Supermarkets, Inc. v. N.L.R.B.,* 2 F.3d 1162 (D. C. Cir. 1993)
27. A nonunion employee must pay union dues as a condition of his employment. The nonunion employee claimed his constitutional rights would be violated by the collective bargaining unit's service fee. What was the result? *James P. Lehnent v. Ferris Faculty Association,* 500 U.S. 507 (1991)
28. Petitioner, American Hospital Association, brought this action challenging the facial validity of the rule on three grounds: First, petitioner argues that Section 9(b) of the National Labor Relations Act requires the Board to make a separate bargaining unit determination "in each case" and therefore prohibits the Board from using general rules to define bargaining units; second, petitioner contends that the rule that the Board has formulated violates a congressional admonition to the Board to avoid the undue proliferation of bargaining units in the health care industry; and, finally, petitioner maintains that the rule is arbitrary and capricious. What was the result? *American Hospital Association v. National Labor Relations Board,* 499 U.S. 606 (1991)
29. A company required employees who intended on transferring to its new plant to pass a test. When only a few employees passed the test, the employer filled its slots from nonunion individuals. The employees claimed that this action was in breach of the collective bargaining agreement.

    The company negotiated a plant-closing agreement with its employees. The agreement provided for transfer opportunities to its new plant. When the employees applied for the transfer, they were required to take a test. This was not provided for in the agreement. The employees maintained that the test was not job-related. What was the result? *Jones v. Pepsi Cola Bottling Co., Inc.,* 822 F. Supp. 396 (E.D. Mich. 1993)
30. This case deals with the issue of whether a proposed ban on smoking should be compelled by the Federal Labor Relations Authority or should be bargained for with the local union chapters. The Department of Health

and Human Services has sought the mandate, while the Federal Labor Relations Authority has argued for collective bargaining. What was the result? *Dept. of Health & Human Serv. v. FLRA*, 920 F.2d 45 (D.C. Cir. 1990)

31. An employer did not give an employee her severance pay upon discharge. The state labor commissioner argued that the employee's right to pursue this is governed by a collective bargaining agreement that provides for arbitration. The employee retorted that the collective bargaining agreement is overridden by state law. What was the result? *Karen Livadas v. Victoria Bradshaw, California Labor Commissioner,* 114 S. Ct. 2068 (1994)

32. A dispute arose after the expiration of a collective bargaining agreement. The issue is whether the parties to the contract intended any of its provisions to be binding beyond the expiration of the contract. What was the result? *Litton Financial Printing Division, v. National Labor Relations Board,* 501 U.S. 190 (1991)

❖ WEB SITES

www.findlaw.com
www.busineesweek.lycos.com/smallbiz/content/may2000/ma3678033.htm
www.feedmag.com/templates/default.php3?a_id=1530
www.unionmuscle.com
http://kids.infoplease.lycos.com/spot/laborl.html
www.nrtw.org/legal.htm
http://stats.bls.gov/news.release/wkstp.toc.htm

18

WAGE AND HOUR REGULATION

INTRODUCTION

Wage and hour regulation has a two-fold purpose: first, to set an hourly subsistence wage for workers; and second, to regulate the number of hours individuals have to work before becoming entitled to overtime compensation of one and one-half times their regular wage. In reality, minimum wage workers must work overtime to support themselves, unless their spouse is also working or they are being subsidized in part by another family member. Arguments are often made that eliminating the minimum wage would stop manufacturers from relocating to Mexico or overseas. But, realistically, it is difficult to imagine anyone, except possibly newly arrived immigrants or illegal aliens, working for less than the minimum wage.

CHAPTER CHECKLIST

❖ Learn the significance of the Fair Labor Standards Act.

❖ Know what the minimum wage is.

❖ Appreciate why wage and hour laws exist.

❖ Be aware when overtime pay is required.

❖ Be apprised of the minimum wage and maximum hours exemptions.

❖ Realize that children may not be employed during school hours or in certain hazardous jobs.

❖ Understand that the number of hours worked cannot be averaged over several weeks to avoid overtime pay.

❖ Evaluate the argument that eliminating the minimum wage would keep more companies from relocating abroad.

❖ Recognize that children under 14 may work for their parents.

❖ Be apprised that court approval of entertainment and athletic contracts is required for children under 14 years of age.

EMPLOYMENT SCENARIO

The Long and the Short of It employs several newly arrived legal immigrants. L&S pays them a flat $4 per hour off-the-books for stocking inventory, cleaning the store and its bathrooms, and performing general maintenance work. Hours tallied by these workers usually exceed 60 hours per week. Regina Matthews, the new bookkeeper at L&S, discovers the scam. She relays this information to Susan North, L&S's attorney. Susan calls Tom Long and Mark Short, copresidents of L&S, to her office. She admonishes Tom and Mark violating the Fair Labor Standards Act by paying subminimum wages and for failing to withhold taxes from their paychecks. Tom and Mark adopt a cavalier attitude and assure Susan that no one will know. Susan is speechless. Finally, she rebukes them and asks if it's really worth sacrificing a successful enterprise with a stellar reputation to save a few bucks illegally. Susan demands that L&S eliminate this ill-conceived plan. Tom and Mark reluctantly agree to pay minimum wage and withhold income and social security taxes. The immigrant employees resign in protest to search for other work, which is off-the-books.

FAIR LABOR STANDARDS ACT

In 1938, Congress enacted the Fair Labor Standards Act to regulate both the minimum compensation that could be given to a worker on an hourly basis and the maximum number of hours an employee could be required to work before being compensated at an overtime rate of one and one-half times the normal rate of pay. The minimum wage has risen through the years but is not indexed to the cost of living. Since October 1, 1996, the minimum wage rate was $4.75. On September 1, 1997, the minimum wage will be increased to $5.15. The maximum number of hours before the overtime is required is 40 hours per work week. The regular rate of pay, which is used to determine the maximum wage, may include the reasonable cost of room, board, and other facilities; gifts; bonuses; days compensated for vacation, illness, or personal reasons; reimbursed expenses for meals, lodging, and travel expenses; contributions toward pensions; premiums for life, disability, and health insurance; and extra compensation for work performed on a Saturday or Sunday.

EMPLOYMENT PERSPECTIVE

Brittany Robinson works at the Baked Cake Shop in Vernon. She is a full-time employee who works Wednesday through Sunday, eight hours a day. Brittany's gross pay per week is $190.00. The Baked Cake pays $6.50 per hour on Saturday and Sunday. Is the Baked Shop in violation of the minimum wage law established in the Fair Labor Standard Act? Yes! The extra compensation Brittany received for Saturday and Sunday work cannot be used in determining the regular rate of hourly pay. Subtracting her Saturday and Sunday wages of $104 ($6.50 per hour times 16 hours), Brittany is paid $86.00 for the 24 hours of work. This amounts to $3.58 per hour, which is below the minimum wage. ▦

EMPLOYMENT PERSPECTIVE

Hector Jiminez is a Mexican farmworker in Southern California. Pine Valley Farm pays Hector $3.50 per hour throughout the year and then makes up the difference between that rate and the minimum wage rate at the end of the year. Is Pine Valley in violation of the minimum wage standard? Yes! The minimum wage is determined on the basis of each work week. The year-end payment must be looked on as extra compensation or a bonus and may not be factored in. Pine Valley is in violation of the minimum wage requirement. The first week it paid Hector at the rate of $3.50 per hour. Pine Valley is not given a grace period of an entire year to make up the difference. ■

The issue in the following case is whether an employer may designate limits on the accrual of comp time.

CASE

MOREAU v. HARRIS COUNTY, TEXAS

158 F.3rd 241 (5th Cir. 1998)

HIGGINBOTHAM, Circuit Judge.

Harris County appeals a grant of summary judgment in favor of a certified class of employees, finding that the County's policy requiring the use of accrued compensatory time by its employees contravened the Fair Labor Standards Act (FLSA). We are persuaded that the 1985 Amendments to the FLSA do not grant public employees a right to choose when they will use accrued comp time. We reverse.

The members of the class are employees of the Sheriff's Department of Harris County. The class asserted claims for wrongful refusal of compensatory time off, retaliation and involuntary use of compensatory time.

The parties have stipulated to the essential facts. By County policy the accrued comp time for non-exempt employees must be kept below a predetermined level, set by each bureau commander. This level is based on the personnel requirements of each bureau.

An employee reaching the maximum allowable hours of comp time authorized by the FLSA is requested to take steps to reduce the number of accrued hours. A supervisor is authorized to or-

der the employee to reduce accumulated comp time at a time suitable to the bureau. An employee dissatisfied with his supervisor's order may informally complain to higher levels of supervisory authority within the department.

Based upon the stipulation of facts, the district court ordered the parties to move for summary judgment and to address whether the County policy requiring the involuntary use of comp time by its employees contravened the FLSA.

Then, on July 28, 1997, the district court issued an order entitled "Final Judgment" which stated the following:

Final Judgment

1. Harris County may not force employees to use their accumulated compensatory time without violating the Fair Labor Standards Act.
2. The parties plaintiff are awarded attorneys' fees of $21,360 from Harris County.

Plaintiffs did not ask the district court to rule on their claims for wrongful refusal of the use of comp time and for retaliation and it did not do so. This appeal followed.

This dispute centers around Harris County's policy of not permitting accrued comp time for non-exempt employees to rise above a predetermined level by directing employees to reduce the number of hours of accrued comp time. The district court held that accumulated comp time and salary must be treated the same way and that employees have a right to use comp time when they choose. Granting summary judgment for the class, the district concluded that Harris County's policy of controlling the amount of accrued comp time violated the FLSA. More precisely put, we must decide whether Harris County violates the FLSA when it involuntarily shortens an employee's workweek with pay.

The relevant FLSA statute states:

(5) An employee of a public agency which is a State, political subdivision of a State, or an interstate governmental agency -

(A) who has accrued compensatory time off authorized to be provided under paragraph (1), and

(B) who has requested the use of such compensatory time, shall be permitted by the employee's employer to use such time within a reasonable period after making the request if the use of the compensatory time does not unduly disrupt the operations of the public agency.

The County urges that Congress must have intended for public employers to control the accrual of comp time because Congress contemplated a circumstance in which a public employer may elect to reduce or eliminate accrued comp time by making a cash payment. They point to 29 U.S.C. §207(o)(3)(B) which states that "if compensation is paid to an employee for accrued compensatory time off, such compensation shall be paid at the regular rate earned by the employee at the time the employee receives such payment." Since this statute permits a public employer to reduce accrued comp time with cash payments, Harris County asserts that reductions in comp time must be at the employer's option.

The class contends that Congress vested the employee, rather than the employer, with the right to determine the use of accrued comp time off. They urge that 29 U.S.C. §207(o)(5) imposes only one limitation on this right — that the use of the comp time not unduly disrupt the operations of the public agency. The plaintiffs maintain since no other limitation on this right was im-

posed by Congress, they could choose to use or to bank their comp time as they see fit. In their view, employers do not have the right to control employees' use of their accrued comp time, so long as their use does not unduly disrupt their operations.

The economic incentives at stake are clear. In an era of tight public budgets, state employers like Harris County wish to control the accrual of comp time in order to avoid paying cash overtime wages when the amount of accrued comp time for any employee reaches the statutory maximum of 240 or 480 hours. The state employees, on the other hand, want to accumulate accrued comp time up to the statutory maximum in order to receive cash payments at an overtime rate of time and one-half or at least retain the ability to "bank" comp time for later use at their behest.

Congress wanted to balance competing interests and intended for both public employers or employees to retain some control over accrued comp time.

Congress amended the FLSA in 1985 to ease the cost to state and local governments of complying with the FLSA, particularly its overtime payment provisions. During the debates, Congress considered proposals for an amendment exempting governmental agencies from the FLSA. Rather than completely excluding agencies from the reach of the FLSA, Congress balanced the burden of complying with the FLSA's overtime provisions with protection for the worker. The 1985 Amendments accomplished this dual purpose by allowing public employers to agree with employees to award comp time in lieu of monetary payments at a rate not lower than one and one-half hour for every overtime hour an employee works. Under this scheme, employees working overtime would receive additional time off from the job with pay but not cash at the higher overtime rates. In sum, Congress did not consider or resolve the question that we face here. Because the legislation reflected a compromise, it is impossible to determine how Congress would have legislated had it confronted the question. Before devising our own solution, we must of course look to precedent.

In general, allowing an employer to establish uniform employment policies with respect to questions not previously negotiated seems preferable to allowing each employee to establish his or her own policy, and it is certainly preferable to a regime in which the courts determine which default rule is best to apply one policy at a time.

Our holding here is thus merely an application of the general principle that the employer can set workplace rules in the absence of a negotiated agreement to the contrary.

While this default may not achieve the optimal solution in every case, it promotes justice writ large. In establishing this approach, we expect to promote the interests of employers and employees alike by minimizing the need for future litigation concerning policies not addressed by Congress or employer-employee agreements. And, of course, this general interpretive approach is itself a default, and the parties may select a different rule governing the construal of their agreements if they choose.

We REVERSE the district court's grant of summary judgment in favor of the class and enter judgment for Harris County and all other defendants.

Case Commentary

The Fifth Circuit resolved that the Fair Labor Standards Act does not preclude employers from mandating the use of accrued comp time by employees.

Case Questions

1. Are you in agreement with the Court's decision in this case?
2. Why do you think the County wanted to force its employees to use the comp time?

3. Why do you believe the employees wanted to save the comp time?

EMPLOYMENT PERSPECTIVE

Angela Montalbano is a Floral Arranger for Violets and Roses Flower Shop. She is a full-time employee. During Valentine's Day week Angela worked 50 hours, and the following week Angela worked 30 hours. Angela is paid every two weeks. In her paycheck, she was compensated at her regular rate of pay for 80 hours. Is Violets And Roses in violation of the overtime pay provision of the maximum hours requirement of the Fair Labor Standards Act? Yes! Each workweek must be looked at unto itself. One cannot offset against the other. The fact that Violets and Roses does not have enough work for Angela the week following Valentine's Day is immaterial. Angela is entitled to the hours of overtime pay for Valentine's week at the rate of one and one-half times the regular rate of pay. In the second week Angela will receive her regular rate of pay for 30 hours unless she was hired with the proviso that she would be guaranteed a 40-hour work week. Then she must be paid for the additional hours even if there is no work to do. ◼

Overtime pay is not required when the employee is receiving up to 10 hours per week of remedial education that is not specific job training. Overtime would be required in excess of the 10 hours if this remediation is mandated by the company. If it were a voluntary after-work program, no pay at all would be required.

EMPLOYMENT PERSPECTIVE

Rufus Buttonwod is an employee at Maple Woods Convention Center. At times, Rufus is asked to fill in as a customer service representative. Rufus's grammar is poor. Maple Woods provides him with remedial tutoring one hour per day, in addition to his normal eight hour day. Rufus's attendance is mandatory. He is paid at his regular rate for

> 45 hours. Is Maple Woods adhering to the provisions of the maximum-hour laws? Yes! The five hours' remediation is compensable at the regular rate of pay. ■

The issue in the case that follows is whether on-call time should be compensated as working time.

CASE

ANDREWS v. TOWN OF SKIATOOK, OKLAHOMA

123 F.3d 1327 (10th Cir. 1997)

EBEL, Circuit Judge.
The parties consented to trial before a United States Magistrate Judge.

The magistrate judge expressed his decision in well-reasoned Findings of Fact and Conclusions of Law with which we substantially agree. We thus attach the Findings of Fact and Conclusions of Law as an Appendix and AFFIRM for substantially the reasons stated therein.

Findings of Fact

1. Plaintiff, Michael Andrews, is a resident of the town of Skiatook, State of Oklahoma, and was employed by the Town of Skiatook as an Emergency Medical Technician (EMT) from February 28, 1993 to January 6, 1995.
2. Defendant, Town of Skiatook, is a political subdivision of the State of Oklahoma, existing under the laws of the State of Oklahoma, and was engaged in the business of managing, maintaining and operating an emergency ambulance service at all times relevant to this litigation.
3. During his employment as an EMT with the Town of Skiatook, Plaintiff was required to work four regular twelve-hour shifts per week and four twelve-hour on-call shifts per week which immediately followed his regular twelve-hour shift. Every third week Plaintiff was required to work one additional twelve-hour on-call shift. EMTs were permitted to trade their on-call shifts with another EMT and would then be expected to pay back the other EMT by covering an on-call shift for him/her.
4. The Town of Skiatook operated two emergency ambulances. One ambulance was staffed by two EMTs who remained at the ambulance station. The second ambulance was staffed by two "on-call EMTs" who were required to respond to calls in the second ambulance when an emergency call was received while the first ambulance was on another run. A call serviced by the second ambulance staffed by on-call EMTs is called a "second run."
5. While on-call, Plaintiff was required to monitor a pager which could be utilized to summon him for a second run. In addition to summoning the on-call personnel, the pager would advise the on-call personnel when the first ambulance had gone on a run. On-call EMTs could also monitor a police radio, which would advise them when the first ambulance had completed its run and returned to the ambulance station. Thus, the on-call EMTs would be aware when the first ambulance was on a run and there was an increased likelihood they could be summoned to make a second run.

6. While on-call, the EMTs were required to remain clean and appropriately attired, although not required to report in uniform, to refrain from drinking alcohol, and to respond to an on-call page within a reasonable period of time.

7–8. Omitted

9. Plaintiff was not compensated for the time spent on-call unless he was called back to make a second run, in which case, Plaintiff was compensated for a minimum of two hours at time and one/half pay. Of the 76 second runs Plaintiff made, none lasted more than two hours.

10. In 1993, the Town of Skiatook ambulance service made a total of 1,071 runs, 115 of which were second runs. Plaintiff made 28 second runs.

11. In 1994, the Town of Skiatook ambulance service made a total of 1,171 runs of which 140 were second runs. Plaintiff made 48 second runs.

12. Plaintiff worked ten months in 1993. At four on-call shifts per week and one extra on-call shift every three weeks, Plaintiff would have worked a total of 173 on-call shifts in 1993. Considering that Plaintiff went on 28 second runs in 1993, the Court calculates that Plaintiff was actually called back to service during 16.18% of his on-call shifts in 1993.

13. Plaintiff worked a full twelve months in 1994. At four on-call shifts per week and one extra on-call shift every three weeks, Plaintiff would have worked a total of 209 on-call shifts. Considering that Plaintiff went on 48 second runs in 1994, the Court calculates that Plaintiff was called back to service during 22.96% of his on-call shifts in 1994.

Conclusions of Law

This Court has jurisdiction of this matter pursuant to the Fair Labor Standards Act. Defendant Town of Skiatook is a public agency and employer within the meaning of the Fair Labor Standards Act, is located within the jurisdiction of this Court, and is subject to the provisions of the Fair Labor Standards Act.

The test to determine whether an employee's on-call time constitutes working time is whether the time is spent predominantly for the employer's benefit or for the employee's. That test requires consideration of the agreement between the parties, the nature and extent of the restrictions, the relationship between the services rendered and the on-call time and all surrounding circumstances. The sole 10th Circuit authority finding on-call time compensable is Renfro. Plaintiff argues that his case is controlled by the decision in Renfro. This Court disagrees.

In Renfro the firefighters, although not required to remain on the premises while on-call, were required to report to the station within twenty minutes of being called back, were called back as many as 13 times in one shift, and averaged 3 to 5 callbacks per on-call shift. In Renfro, the 10th Circuit affirmed the district court which found:

The frequency with which Emporia firefighters are subject to call-backs readily distinguishes this case from cases which have held that on-call time is non-compensable. In many of those cases, the probability of an employee being called in, and thus, the probability of disruption of the employee's personal activities, was minimal.

The infrequency of callbacks in this case distinguishes it from Renfro.

Instead of being called back to work on average between 3 to 5 times per on-call shift, Plaintiff was only called back 16.18% of the time during his on-call shifts in 1993 and 22.96% of the time for his on-call shifts in 1994. On the facts before this Court, it is clear that Plaintiff's on-call time was predominantly for his personal benefit. While on-call, Plaintiff was free to engage in any activity of his choosing as long as he remained clean, did not drink alcohol and could respond to the ambulance station within five to ten minutes. The five to ten minute requirement gave Plaintiff access to all of the small town of Skiatook. Further, the fact that Plaintiff was notified when the first ambulance had gone on a run enabled Plaintiff to prepare for the possibility of a second run and to structure his activities so his on-call time would be as least restrictive as possible. In this regard it is fair to conclude that Plaintiff felt only slight restrictions on his personal activities while the first ambulance was not out on a call. It was only when the first ambulance was out on a call that Plaintiff had any significant chance of having to respond to a second run call and, based upon actual experience, Plaintiff knew that the percentage of time when a second run call would be required was small. Thus, Plaintiff was predominantly free to pursue his personal activities during his on-call time.

Based upon the above FINDINGS OF FACT AND CONCLUSIONS OF LAW, the Court finds that Plaintiff has failed to prove by a preponderance of the evidence that his on-call time was spent predominantly on behalf of Defendant employer. THE COURT, THEREFORE, FINDS IN FAVOR OF DEFENDANT.

Judgment will be entered accordingly.

Case Commentary

The Tenth Circuit ruled that Andrews did not spend his on-call time predominantly for his employer; therefore he was not entitled to compensation for his time.

Case Questions

1. Are you in agreement with the Court's determination?
2. How did the Court determine whether Andrews spent the on-call time for his employer's benefit or for his own personal benefit?
3. Should on-call employees be entitled to some remuneration?

EXEMPTIONS

Certain employees are exempted from the minimum wage and the maximum hour requirements. These include executives, administrators, professionals, salespeople, elementary and secondary schoolteachers, domestic helpers who reside in the household, baby-sitters, and people who provide companionship and care to the elderly. Camp counselors are also exempted if the camp is not in operation for more than seven months in the calendar year.

EMPLOYMENT PERSPECTIVE

Tiffany O'Toole works as a camp counselor for three months each summer at Camp Fooey. The camp operates 13 weeks each year. She often works eight hours a day, seven days a week. Tiffany is paid a flat rate of $3,000 plus room and board, which has a reasonable value of $1,000. Is Camp Fooey in violation of the minimum wage and maximum hour requirement? No! Camp counselors are exempt even though Tiffany's cumulative compensation of $4,000 is less than the $4,284.80 minimum wage including overtime required by the Fair Labor Standards Act. The $4,284.80 figure is arrived at as follows: 13 weeks times 40 hours times $5.15 equals $2,678.00 plus 13 weeks times 16 hours (Saturday and Sunday) times $7.725 equals $1,606.80 for a total of $4,284.80. ■

The issue in the following case is whether the plaintiffs are salaried employees and thus exempt from overtime pay.

CARPENTER v. CITY & COUNTY OF DENVER, COLORADO

115 F.3d 765 (10th Cir. 1996)

PORFILIO, Circuit Judge.

In this appeal, we are asked to decide whether plaintiffs, lieutenants, captains, and division chiefs in the Denver Police Department, are salaried employees exempt from the overtime requirement of the Fair Labor Standards Act (FLSA). This resolution pivots on our reading of 29 C.F.R. 541.118(a), which states an employee whose salary is "subject to reduction because of variations in the quality or quantity of the work performed," is not exempt from payment of overtime. Because we read the language of the regulation to mean what it says, that the possibility of reduction defeats salaried status, we conclude plaintiffs are not exempt from the FLSA's overtime requirement. We reverse.

I.

Generally, the FLSA requires all employers, including state and local governments, to pay their employees a minimum wage for a 40-hour work week. Hours worked over the 40-hour week must be compensated at an overtime rate of time and a half. However, payment of overtime does not apply to "any employee employed in a bona fide executive, administrative, or professional capacity...." Congress delegated fleshing out this status to the Department of Labor (DOL), which devised a "short test," providing:

The term "employee employed in a bona fide executive * * * capacity ... shall mean any employee:

(a) Whose primary duty consists of the management of the enterprise in which he is employed....

(b) Who customarily and regularly directs the work of two or more other employees therein; and

(c) Who has the authority to hire or fire other employees or whose suggestions and rec-

ommendations as to the hiring or firing and as to the advancement and promotion or any other change of status of other employees will be given particular weight; and

(d) Who customarily and regularly exercises discretionary powers; and

(e) Who does not devote more than 20 percent ... of his hours of work in the workweek to activities which are not directly or closely related to the performance of the work described in paragraphs (a) through (d) ...; and

(f) Who is compensated for his services on a salary basis at a rate of not less than ... $250 per week ... and whose primary duty consists of the management of the enterprise in which the employee is employed or of a customarily recognized department or subdivision thereof, and includes the customary and regular direction of the work of two or more other employees therein, shall be deemed to meet all the requirements of this section."

The employer bears the burden of showing "the employee fits 'plainly and unmistakenly within the exemption's terms'— under both the 'salary' test and the 'duties' test."

Exempt employees receive straight-time overtime compensation. The City classifies plaintiffs as falling within the executive exemption.

Challenging this status, plaintiffs sued the City for declaratory relief, contending they are not exempt from coverage of the FLSA overtime requirements and seeking back pay for each hour of overtime worked at time and a half for approximately three years from 1990 through 1993, in addition to liquidated damages authorized by the FLSA. Their complaint attacked their exempt status solely on the basis of the salary test, alleging the City's practice of fining certain plaintiffs for violations of minor safety rules and docking pay for military leave after 15 days defeated its claim to the exemption. The City responded the executive, administrative, and professional exemptions barred plaintiffs' claims.

Finding no factual issues in dispute, the district court concluded plaintiffs are exempt employees, rejecting the Second, Seventh, and District of Columbia Circuits' interpretation and aligning itself with the Eighth, Eleventh, and Fifth Circuits which hold that absent an actual deduction from salary, the practice of offsetting leave with leave will not defeat an employee's exempt status.

The only material issue presented in this case is whether plaintiffs are paid on a salary basis as defined by DOL's regulations.

DOL's definition of salaried status, 29 C.F.R. 541.118(a), which states:

An employee will be considered to be paid "on a salary basis" within the meaning of the regulations if under his employment agreement he regularly receives each pay period on a weekly, or less frequent basis, a predetermined amount constituting all or part of his compensation, which amount is not subject to reduction because of variations in the quality or quantity of the work performed. Subject to the exceptions provided below, the employee must receive his full salary for any week in which he performs any work without regard to the number of days or hours worked. This policy is also subject to the general rule that an employee need not be paid for any workweek in which he performs no work.

It is the phrase, "subject to reduction" which the parties challenge, each citing those factual allegations which serve its partisan interpretation.

Plaintiffs maintain salaried employees are paid a fixed amount for doing a job. That is, they "are paid on a job function basis," in contrast to non-salaried employees "whose compensation depends on the number of hours they put in." The opposite of payment on a salary basis, then, is payment on an hourly basis. Consequently, plaintiffs contend the City's express policies on disciplinary infractions, military leave, and leave for jury duty, which require "fining" the employee by deducting leave days from their "leave banks" or other leave offsets, render their fixed salaries "subject to reduction" because ultimately these contingent deductions reflect the "quality or quantity" of the work performed.

The City counters no plaintiff has had a reduction in salary as a consequence of any City policy or practice. Further, only a plaintiff's leave bank, the repository of all accumulated leave inuring to each plaintiff's position, is tapped, the City maintains; and, even then, only leave is offset against leave.

We believe if we are to construe exceptions to the FLSA narrowly, giving substantial deference to DOL's interpretation of its own rules, we must conclude the City's express policy on discipline does not conform to DOL's parameters. Its "safety rules," in fact, are more often rules of behavior involving an officer's daily conduct on the force. Because the rules fall short, the City's punishing an errant officer by removing leave time from the officer's leave repository creates the potential for reducing pay. When leave is exhausted, the record makes clear a plaintiff's salary is "subject to reduction." That is, then, the quality of the officer's work may ultimately reduce the predetermined amount of salary the officer receives. Reading the regulations narrowly, we cannot say that employee is salaried.

Reversed.
Judgment for Carpenter

Case Commentary

The Tenth Circuit resolved that lieutenants, captains, and chiefs of the Denver Police Force are not salaried employees exempt from overtime, because they are subject to salary deduction.

Case Questions

1. Are you in accord with the Court's resolution in this case?
2. Do you believe the plaintiffs are paid on a wage basis rather than on a salary basis?
3. Did not the Court use the term "salary" in discussing the plaintiff's compensation?
4. Can the plaintiffs be compared to managers in business who are not paid overtime?

There are many exceptions to the maximum hours requirement, a few of which include domestic helpers, taxicar drivers, and movie theater employees.

EMPLOYMENT PERSPECTIVE

Myrtle Dover is a domestic helper who resides with the Remingtons. At times, she works more than eight hours per day and always works on Saturdays and Sundays unless the family is vacationing. Myrtle is paid a set fee each week in accordance with the minimum wage law, but she is not paid overtime. Are the Remingtons in violation of the maximum hour laws? No! There is an exception for domestic helpers. ◼

CHILD LABOR

Children who are at least 16 years of age may work in any occupation as long as it has not been deemed hazardous by the Secretary of Labor. Children who are 14 or 15 years of age shall not be permitted to work in manufacturing, mining, and other occupations that interfere with their schooling and/or their health and well-being. Children under 14 are not permitted to work unless it is for their parents or approved by the court for entertainment or athletic contracts.

EMPLOYMENT PERSPECTIVE

Robby Landry, who is 17, was hired by Major Waste Materials Corp. to load hazardous and radioactive containers for shipment. Is this permissible? No! The transport of hazardous and radioactive waste is a dangerous activity. Therefore, children may not work in this occupation. ◼

EMPLOYMENT PERSPECTIVE

Lawrence Connery is an attorney with his own practice. He employs his 12-year-old daughter, Tiffany, to work for him two hours after school each day. Her responsibilities include photocopying, stapling, dusting, and making coffee. Is this permissible? Yes! Parents may employ the services of their children as long as it is not in a hazardous occupation. ◼

EMPLOYMENT PERSPECTIVE

Michele Goldsmith is a 14-year-old freshman at Richmond Hill High. She works the 2-to-10 shift at Foodway three days a week. In order to get to work on time, she has to cut her last class, which, because of a rotating schedule, changes each day and is not particularly noticeable. Is this permissible? No! The Fair Labor Standards Act would prohibit Michele's current employment because it interferes with her schooling in that it forces her to leave school early and leaves her no time to do her homework. ◼

EMPLOYMENT PERSPECTIVE

Cindy Masterson is a four-year-old model of children's clothes. She also performs in a television commercial occasionally and is employed by various manufacturers and retail clothing stores. Is this employment permissible? Yes! Cindy's contracts must be court-approved. If the court determines this action is in Cindy's best interest, she will be allowed to perform. ◼

❖ EMPLOYER LESSONS

- Understand the provisions of the Fair Labor Standards Act.
- Pay at least the minimum wage.
- Compensate employees with overtime pay after a 40-hour workweek.
- Recognize that averaging hours worked over several weeks to avoid time and a half pay for overtime is illegal.
- Know the occupations exempted from minimum wage and maximum hours laws.
- Avoid hiring illegal aliens who will work for less than the minimum wage.
- Refrain from paying workers off-the-books.
- Appreciate that children may not be employed during school hours or in certain jobs deemed hazardous.
- Learn that children under 14 may work for their parents.
- Be aware that children under 14 who engage in athletics and entertainment must have their contracts approved by the court.

❖ EMPLOYEE LESSONS

- Become familiar with the Fair Labor Standards Act.
- Be apprised of what the minimum wage is currently.
- Learn that overtime pay begins after 40 hours, not 35 hours, which is the usual workweek.
- Understand that payroll deductions are necessary.
- Ascertain if the amount withheld from your check is accurate.
- Do not accept payments which are off-the-books.
- Know which occupations are exempted from the minimum wage and maximum hours laws.
- Be aware that your children may not work during school hours or in certain jobs deemed to be hazardous.
- Recognize that your children under the age of 14 may work for you.
- Be cognizant that children under 14 who participate for compensation in entertainment or athletics must have court approval.

❖ REVIEW QUESTIONS

1. Explain the significance of the Fair Labor Standards Act.
2. Is the current minimum wage adequate?
3. Explain the purpose of the minimum wage law.
4. What is the rule regarding maximum hours and overtime?
5. Why is there a need to cap the number of hours worked?
6. Explain the child labor laws.
7. What are the exceptions to the child labor laws?
8. Explain what would happen if there was no Fair Labor Standards Act.
9. Is it ethical to employ illegal immigrants at a wage below the minimum?
10. What effect will the GATT (General Agreement on Tariffs and Treaties) and NAFTA (North American Free Trade Agreement) have on wage and hour regulation?
11. What is the test to determine whether an employee is on the job and entitled to compensation? *Armour & Co. v. Wantock,* 323 U.S. 126 (1994)
12. Mireles, an employee for Frio Foods, was required to be on call. Frio Foods refused to compensate him for this time. Mireles brought suit, alleging that he was entitled to

be paid wages for time on call according to the Fair Labor Standards Act. What was the result? *Armour & Co. v. Wantock,* 323 U.S. 126 (1994)

13. Skidmore was required by his employer, Swift Co., to be "on call." His hours exceeded the 40-hour-workweek. Skidmore was not paid overtime. Swift argued Skidmore was not entitled to compensation. Whether "waiting time" is "working time" depends on the particular case and is a question of fact to be resolved by the trial court. The FLSA requires the payment of time and one-half of an employee's regular rate of pay for each hour worked in excess of 40 hours in any workweek. What was the result? *Skidmore v. Swift Co.,* 323 U.S. 134 (1994)

14. Did California violate the minimum wage provisions of the Fair Labor Standards Act ("FLSA"), by paying wages 14 to 15 days late because there was no state budget, and thus no funds appropriated for the payment of salaries, on payday? *Biggs v. Wilson* 1 F.3d 1537 (9th Cir. 1993)

15. Can a state labor agency automatically give its employees time off in lieu of overtime pay when the employees have designated a union representative to bargain for them? *Lynwood Moreau v. Johnny Klevenhagen, Sheriff, Harris County, Texas,* 113 S. Ct. 1905 (1993)

16. Police officers' overtime pay was calculated on the basis of a different number of hours from other city workers. The city argued that as long as all police officers were treated equally, the formula was acceptable. The officers complained that it violated the Fair Labor Standards Act in that one class of employees was treated differently from the others. What was the result? *Marie v. City of New Orleans,* 612 So.2d 244 (La. App. 4 Cir. 1992)

17. Should an employee who is "on call" be compensated for those hours in excess of 40 hours per week at the overtime rate? The employees argued they could not effectively use the waiting time for their own personal purposes. What was the result? *Casserly v. State,* 844 P.2d 1275 (Colo. App. 1992)

❖ WEB SITES

www.britannica.com/seo/f/fair-labor-standards-act/
www.findlaw.com
www.hrnext.com/content/view.cfm?subs_articles_id=1876
www.opm.gov/flsa/overview.htm
www.bna.com/bnabooks/publications/details/d_flsa.htm
www.dol.gov/elaws/flsa.htm
www.2mediate.com/articles/federal_fair_labor_standards_act.html

Occupational Safety and Health Act

The Occupational Safety and Health Act of 1970 (OSHAct) was designed to set forth a standard which would provide for the safety and health of employees while on the job. Employers are required to provide a place of employment free of occupational hazards. Employees are required to follow rules and regulations established to promote their safety and to use equipment designed to ensure their safety.

CHAPTER CHECKLIST

❖ Recognize the significance of the Occupational Safety and Health Act.

❖ Understand the purpose of the Occupational Safety and Health Administration.

❖ Appreciate the function of the Occupational Safety And Health Review Commission.

❖ Know that the National Institute of Occupational Safety and Health recommends health and safety measures. Learn that the Secretary of Labor establishes safety and health standards.

❖ Be cognizant of when emergency standards can be implemented.

❖ Define permanent disability.

❖ Acknowledge the extent of work-related injuries that occur each year.

❖ Discover the major causes of work-related injuries.

❖ Realize the meaning of the greater hazard defense.

EMPLOYMENT SCENARIO

In the Long and Short of It's Woodmere store, the bathroom ceiling's plaster is loose and cracking. It also leaks, which makes the floor extremely slippery. Sylvia Norton contacted OSHA, informing them of the unsafe working conditions. She also informed OSHA that there was no heat in the stockroom and employee lounge. An OSHA inspector arrived at the L&S store two weeks later. The inspector found the conditions to be as Sylvia had suggested. L&S's attorney, Susan North, was notified of the fine and was served with a 10-day notice to cure the defect before reinspection. She asked Tom Long and Mark Short why they neglected the repairs. Mark responded that they believed no one would complain, but now they stand ready to remedy the violations. Susan reminded Tom and Mark that an ounce of prevention is worth a pound of cure. She suggested L&S be more proactive in maintaining its stores in order to improve the morale of its employees.

ADMINISTRATIVE AGENCIES

The OSHAct created three administrative agencies. The first is the Occupational Safety and Health Administration, also known as OSHA. Its purpose is to set health and safety standards and see to it that these standards are implemented by employers through plant and office inspections. If an employer is in violation, OSHA seeks corrective action voluntarily by the employer through a hearing conducted by the Occupational Safety and Health Review Commission (OSHRC). If OSHRC rules against an employer, it may impose fines or other penalties against the employer. The employer has the right of appeal to the Circuit Court. OSHRC is the enforcement arm created by the Occupational Safety and Health Act. Finally, the National Institute of Occupational Safety and Health (NIOSH) was created to conduct research and make health and safety recommendations to OSHA for consideration.

The Occupational Safety and Health Act (OSHAct) was enacted to reduce safety and health hazards, thereby preventing injuries, loss of wages, lost production, and incurrence of medical and disability expenses. Employees must be provided with a safe environment free of toxic substances, asbestos dust, and cotton dust. Precautions must be taken for first aid, eye and face protection, and safety at excavation sites to prevent cave-ins. Employees must be accorded a work environment with adequate lighting, ventilation, and heat, as well as tools and equipment that are in proper working order. The Department of Labor has the right to inspect the work environment to insure adherence to the OSHA requirements. The Occupational Safety and Health Review Commission is the initial review body for violations of the act.

SECRETARY OF LABOR

The addition of or deletion of occupational health and safety standards is promulgated by the Secretary of Labor. Interested parties may submit written comments regarding a proposal. If the Secretary reiterates a proposal, an objection can be entered and a hearing held, after which the Secretary will submit the final document.

In establishing standards, the Secretary of Labor must set forth standards to prevent employees from suffering substantial harm to their health even if the employee worked at this job for most of his or her adult life. The Secretary of Labor must rely on research and experiments to establish reliable standards, which will be set forth objectively. The specific actions and the desired results must be set forth.

Employees may request a temporary variance from the Secretary of Labor if they do not have the technical know-how or materials and/or equipment needed to comply or the plant or equipment cannot be altered by the required date. Employers must make every effort to comply as soon as possible. The time limit is one year, which can be renewed twice.

Although it was thought that employers would have enough incentive to ensure a safe working environment because of the absolute liability imposed upon them under Worker's Compensation, Congress did not feel employers were doing all that they could do, so they created OSHAct.

Before OSHAct was enacted, most employees who were injured on the job were not successful in suing their employers if they were injured by a coworker, were negligent themselves, or were held to have assumed the risk. This situation was not a sufficient impetus for employers to improve the workplace, knowing that they would not have to compensate most employees for their injuries. The purpose of OSHAct was to insure that employees would not sustain the injuries in the first place.

Employers are required to comply with certain mandates of the Department of Labor regarding safety and health. Furthermore, the employment environment must be a safe and healthy place in which to work without hazards.

PERMANENT STANDARDS

Permanent standards are the standards originally introduced when OSHA was created as well as standards promulgated thereafter. The latter are referred to as National Consensus Standards. When OSHA develops a new standard, it is published in the *Federal Register.* The public, especially employees, has 30 days to request a hearing. If requested, notice of a public hearing will be made. After the hearing, OSHA must publish the standard incorporating the changes, if any, and the date of its commencement, within 60 days. The Secretary of Labor must explain the need for the new standard, or else it will be null and void. He or she may delay the date of its commencement. In one case, a delay of four years was imposed. An employer may file an appeal in the Circuit Court of Appeals within 60 days from OSHA's final announcement. If there is an appeal, the Secretary of Labor must demonstrate for the Court that the standard mitigates a significant health risk. If the Circuit Court is convinced that the Secretary of Labor has provided sufficient evidence, the standard will become permanent.

EMPLOYMENT PERSPECTIVE

Veggie King has just begun irradiating fruits and vegetables for a longer shelf life. OSHA has promulgated a standard that all workers who are subjected to the low levels of radiation used on the fruits and vegetables must wear radiation-proof jumpsuits and headwear. These suits are very expensive. Veggie King asks for a hearing, but OSHA's final determination is unchanged. On appeal before the Circuit Court, Veggie King proclaims that low levels of radiation have no impact on humans. The Secretary of Labor counters that studies have shown that subjecting a human to low levels of radiation for 20 years or longer will cause cancer. What is the likely result? If the Circuit

▌ Court believes that the studies introduced by the Secretary of Labor have merit, then
▌ the standard of requiring radiation-protective garments will become permanent. ▪

The occupational safety and health standard requires the employer to adopt
appropriate practices necessary to ensure that the place of employment is a safe and
healthy environment.

The national consensus standard is an occupational safety and health standard
designated by the Secretary of Labor after its formulation by a nationally recognized
safety and/or health organization which has conducted hearings.

The issue in the following case is whether the new standard for respiratory protection in the workplace is legal.

CASE

AMERICAN IRON v. OSHA

182 F.3d 1261 (11th Cir.1999)

ANDERSON, Chief Judge:
These consolidated cases seek judicial review of
the Occupational Safety and Health Administration's ("OSHA") new standard for respiratory
protection in the workplace. The separate challenges are brought by the American Iron and
Steel Institute ("Industry") and the American
College of Occupational and Environmental
Medicine ("Doctors") and relate to different aspects of the new standard. For the reasons that
follow, we conclude that OSHA correctly applied
the law and that its factual determinations were
supported by substantial evidence, and therefore
the petitions for review are DENIED.

I. BACKGROUND

The Occupational Safety and Health Act of 1970
was enacted to ensure safe and healthy working
conditions for employees. The OSH Act empowers
OSHA to promulgate standards "dealing with
toxic materials or harmful physical agents . . . which
most adequately assure, to the extent feasible, on
the basis of the best available evidence, that no employee will suffer material impairment of health or
functional capacity even if such employee has regular exposure to the hazard dealt with by such
standard for the period of his working life." One

such hazard is caused by harmful dusts, fumes,
gases, and the like that contaminate the atmospheres in many workplaces. OSHA began to regulate employee exposure to such contaminants as
early as 1971. In January 1998, OSHA issued a new
regulatory standard representing a comprehensive revision of those portions of the old standard
which addressed the manner and conditions of respirator use ("Standard"). It is the Standard that is
at issue in this case.

Highlights of the Standard

The Standard retains the Hierarchy-of-Controls
Policy, which as a general matter prefers engineering controls over respirators worn by individual employees. However, the employer is required to provide respirators for its employees
when respirators are necessary to protect their
health. The Standard requires certain employers
to develop and implement a written respiratory
protection program that includes several mandatory items. Employers are required to select particular types of respirators based on certain criteria, such as the nature of harmful contaminants
and workplace and user factors. In this regard, atmospheres in workplaces are classified into two
categories: "immediately dangerous to life and
health" ("IDLH"), and non-IDLH. Only certain

highly effective types of respirators may be used in IDLH atmospheres. With respect to non-IDLH atmospheres, the Standard permits an employer to choose between atmosphere-supplying respirators (i.e., those with a self-equipped oxygen tank) and the less burdensome air-purifying respirators (i.e., those which merely filter the incoming air). However, air-purifying respirators are usable only if certain specified steps are taken to ensure that the filtering device is working and maintained properly. The medical evaluation provisions of the Standard require the employer "to provide a medical evaluation to determine the employee's ability to use a respirator, before the employee is fit tested or required to use the respirator in the workplace." The medical evaluation provisions spell out the procedures in this regard much more specifically than the prior standard. In addition, whereas licensed physicians were responsible for such medical evaluations under the prior standard, the Standard allows non-physician "licensed health care professionals" to perform such evaluations to the extent allowed under state law. The new Standard also contains detailed provisions relating to initial and periodic fit-testing to ensure respirators fit an employee-user's face properly, proper day-to-day use of respirators, maintenance and care of respirators, the required quality of the breathing gases used in conjunction with an air-supplying respirator, proper identification and labeling of filters, cartridges, and canisters, provision of training and information to employees, periodic self-evaluations of an employer's written respiratory protection program to ensure that it continues to work properly, and appropriate record-keeping regarding medical evaluations and fit-testing.

Provisions Under Attack and Alignment of the Parties

The instant petitions for review are brought by the Industry and the Doctors. The Industry challenges three particular aspects of the Standard. First, it challenges the retention of the Hierarchy-of-Controls Policy, and OSHA's failure even to consider revising or abrogating that policy in light of its revision of the rest of the regulation. Second, it challenges the conditions placed upon the use of air-purifying respirators, as opposed to air-supplying respirators. Third, it challenges the requirements regarding, respectively, annual fit-testing and annual retraining, contending that less frequent fit-testing and retraining would have sufficed.

The Doctors, on the other hand, challenge only one aspect of the Standard: the provision enabling non-physician licensed health care professionals (e.g., nurses, physician's assistants, etc.) to perform the medical evaluation services that were previously conducted only by physicians ("Non-Physician Involvement Provision"). They contend that the Non-Physician Involvement Provision is defective because OSHA failed to notify interested parties that it was considering the elimination of mandatory physician involvement, that it is void for vagueness, and that it is not amply supported by the factual evidence.

II. DISCUSSION

A. Standard of Review

We must uphold OSHA's factual determinations underlying its regulations if they are supported by substantial evidence in the record considered as a whole. Substantial evidence is "such relevant evidence as a reasonable mind might accept as adequate to support a conclusion." "All that need be shown is that OSHA's determination is supported by substantial evidence presented to or produced by it and does not rest on faulty assumptions or factual foundations." OSHA's policy decisions are entitled to the same deference.

B. The Industry's Challenge

1. Retention of the Hierarchy-of-Controls Policy
The Industry's first challenge to the Standard is addressed to the retention of the Hierarchy-of-Controls Policy from the prior standard. The Hierarchy-of-Controls Policy reflects a general preference for engineering controls, which eliminate or arrest pollution at the source, over respirators in reducing employee exposure to airborne contaminants. Although it comprehensively revised those aspects of the prior standard relating to the manner and conditions of respirator use, OSHA altogether excluded the Hierarchy-of-Controls Policy from the rulemaking proceeding. Consequently, the Hierarchy-of-Controls Policy was not open to comment or scrutiny. In the issuing release for the Standard, OSHA explained its position in the following way:

By leaving paragraphs (a)(1) and (a)(2) of the final rule unchanged from the corresponding paragraphs of the respiratory protection standard that has been in effect since 1971, OSHA.... continues the protection that employees have relied on, ... retains the language that employers are familiar with, ... [and] allows OSHA and the affected public to continue to rely on OSHA interpretations....

....

The unchanged language of paragraph (a)(1) was included in the language of the proposed rule only to enable interested parties to view the rule as it would ultimately appear in the Code of Federal Regulations in its entirety. Since OSHA neither proposed nor adopted modifications to proposed paragraph (a)(1), the Agency believes that it is not legally required to reconsider this issue at this time. OSHA has the authority to identify which regulatory requirements it is proposing to revise and which issues are to receive regulatory priority. Limiting this rulemaking to issues concerning respirator programs is appropriate because such programs are the exclusive focus of this rulemaking and to collect comments and data on additional issues would divert resources from the task at hand.

We do not find a requirement that OSHA include all possible substances in one rulemaking. OSHA has never claimed that the Air Contaminants Standard constituted the entire universe of substances needing regulation, and it seems reasonable that some limit needed to be set as to what substances could be considered in this rulemaking. The list of [the standard-setting organization's] recommendations is a rational choice as the source for that limitation. [Those] recommendations are well known to industry and the safety and health community. Therefore, we find that the agency's choice to so limit this rulemaking is a valid exercise of OSHA's authority to set priorities for rulemaking.

The Industry also implies that the Hierarchy-of-Controls Policy has outlived its validity under § 6(a) because it no longer represents a national consensus standard. This argument is without merit because the Industry has proffered no evidence that the Hierarchy-of-Controls Policy no longer represents the national consensus standard. To the contrary, the most recent national consensus standard, ANSI Standard Z88.2-1992, § 4.2, retains the Hierarchy-of-Controls Policy. Thus, the Industry has failed to demonstrate that OSHA's decision to limit the instant rulemaking

to issues relating to the manner and conditions of respirator use was unreasonable.

For the foregoing reasons, we reject the Industry's challenge to the retention of the Hierarchy-of-Controls Policy.

2. Change Schedule Requirement for Air-Purifying Respirators

Because the Industry's challenge to the Change Schedule Condition is exclusively factual in nature, our review is limited to whether OSHA's determinations are "supported by substantial evidence in the record considered as a whole." After reviewing the record, we conclude that OSHA's decision to replace the subjective adequate-warning-properties approach with the Change Schedule Condition is supported by substantial evidence. There was a consensus among commentors that inherent unreliability problems exist with odor and irritation thresholds. Change schedules based on "objective information or data" better promote worker safety by ensuring on a consistent basis that APRs are properly serviced and maintained. Moreover, the record belies the Industry's argument that OSHA entirely failed to consider the fact that ASRs tend to be bulky and cumbersome. The record reflects that OSHA did consider the uncomfortableness and mobility restrictions caused by APRs and weighed those factors in the balance. Thus, the factual determinations and policy choices underlying the Change Schedule Condition are consistent with the OSH Act and supported by substantial evidence.

3. Annual Fit-Test and Retraining Requirements

We turn next to the Industry's challenge to the provisions in the Standard requiring annual fit-testing and retraining of respirator-using employees. With respect to the annual fit-testing requirement, a respirator cannot function properly unless it is properly fitted to the wearer's face. Accordingly, the Standard requires that an employee be fit tested with a respirator of the same make, model, style, and size as is proposed to be used, before he actually begins to use one in the course of employment. The Industry does not object to this initial-test requirement, but does object to a requirement that wearers be tested at least annually following the initial test.

We find that the annual retraining requirement is also supported by substantial evidence. "OSHA's compliance experience had demonstrated that inadequate respirator training is a common problem, and is often associated with respirator program deficiencies that could lead to employee exposures to workplace contaminants." OSHA stated that annual retraining is necessary so that "employees know about the respiratory protection program and . . . cooperate and actively participate in the program," "so that employees will be confident when using respirators," and to "eliminate complacency on the part of both the employer and employees." OSHA noted that commenters requesting less frequent or no retraining submitted no data indicating that less frequent training "would be sufficient for respirator users to retain information critical to the successful use of respirators on an individual basis." Additionally, OSHA explained that annual retraining is the norm with respect to a number of other, substance-specific OSHA standards that involve respirators.

While retraining at some other periodic interval might also be defensible, OSHA was entitled to require annual retraining as a precautionary measure to assure "that no employee will suffer material impairment of health or functional capacity even if such employee has regular exposure to the hazard." Moreover, OSHA could conclude based on the record that annual retraining is reasonably necessary to ensure that employee knowledge about respirators does not fall into obsolescence. Given that conscientiousness among employees is such a critical element in the formula for success of a respirator program, OSHA could reasonably find that the Industry's suggested alternative of screening employees to determine who needed retesting would not serve its goal of preventing misuse and "ensuring a reasonable amount of recall and performance on the part of the respirator user." We see no basis for disturbing OSHA's factual conclusions and policy decisions in this regard.

C. The Doctors' Challenge

In their petition for review, the Doctors challenge the Non-Physician Involvement Provision in paragraph (e) of the Standard, which for the first time allows non-physician licensed health care professionals, as opposed to only physicians, to perform the required medical evaluations to the extent permitted under state law. The Doctors contend that OSHA gave insufficient notice to interested parties of its intent to adopt this new policy, that the Non-

Physician Involvement Provision is void for vagueness, and that the Non-Physician Involvement Provision is not supported by substantial evidence.

The Standard does not distinguish between physicians and other licensed health care professionals. Rather, it allows all of the tasks associated with medical evaluations to be performed by any licensed health care professional to the same extent as they may be performed by a physician, to the extent permitted under state law. The Standard uses the term "physician or other licensed health care provider," which is defined as "an individual whose legally permitted scope of practice (i.e., license, registration, or certification) allows him or her to independently provide, or be delegated the responsibility to provide, some or all of the health care services required by paragraph (e) of this section." Because licensure, registration, and certification of health care professionals is basically a matter of state law, the Standard essentially defers to state law on the question of who may provide the medical evaluation services. In contrast, the prior standard provided that "persons should not be assigned to tasks requiring use of respirators unless it has been determined that they are physically able to perform the work and use the equipment. The local physician shall determine what health and physical conditions are pertinent."

We have reviewed the record and find OSHA's decision to be supported by substantial evidence. While the comments were extremely varied, a common thread running through many of the comments was that registered nurses, physician's assistants, and other such health care providers are well-equipped to perform basic medical functions, such as assessing responses to medical questionnaires, provided that appropriate measures are in place for referring non-routine cases to a physician. There also was evidence from several commenters to the effect that they had safely and efficaciously used non-physician licensed health care professionals in the past for medical evaluations involving respirators. Moreover, the Non-Physician Involvement Provision does not automatically allow non-physician individuals to perform medical evaluation services; rather, it merely defers to state law on the extent of permissible involvement. State licensure laws can be trusted, as they are relied upon in similar contexts, to ensure that individuals performing medical evaluations under the Standard have the requisite competence, and such laws in fact typically provide for physician oversight over other health care professionals.

III. CONCLUSION

For the foregoing reasons, the petitions for review are
DENIED.

Judgment for OSHA.

Case Commentary

The Eleventh Circuit determined that the standards adhered to by OSHA in enacting a new regulation regarding respiratory protection in the workplace were lawful.

Case Questions

1. Are you in accord with the Court's decision?
2. Why does the industry not want to accept the new OSHA standard?
3. Why do the physicians refuse to support the OSHA respiratory standard?

INSPECTIONS

Inspections of business premises and records may be made during working hours and at other times deemed reasonable by OSHA compliance officers. The employees and the employer may be questioned privately. Record-keeping relating to occupational accidents and illnesses is required and must be produced upon demand. Exposure of employees to toxic chemicals must be documented. Employees have the right of free access to the documents relating to their exposure. If the level exceeds the occupational safety and health standard, the employer must immediately notify the employee and take corrective action. If the employees believe a standard is being violated, they may notify the Secretary of Labor in writing. If the Secretary determines that there is a viable issue, he or she will authorize an investigation.

CITATIONS AND PENALTIES

If an employer has committed a violation, an OSHA director will issue a citation, which will describe the particulars as well as reference to the occupational safety and health standard that the Secretary believes has been violated. The employer, upon receipt, has 15 business days to contest the citation, or it will become a final order not subject to judicial review.

If the employer fails to correct the violation of a safety and health standard, a penalty will be assessed against the employer. The employer has 15 days to object to the penalty. Otherwise, it will become a final order not subject to judicial review.

Penalties may be assessed between $5,000 and $70,000 for each violation of an occupational safety and health standard. These penalties may be made in increments of up to $7,000 per day per violation. Payment for these penalties shall be made to the Secretary of Labor and deposited in the U.S. Treasury.

With regard to any issues of occupational safety and health not addressed by the Secretary of Labor, the individual states are free to develop their own standards.

If an employer timely contests the citation or penalty, the matter is referred to the Occupational Safety and Health Review Commission, which is an administrative agency composed of three commissioners, each of whom has been appointed by the

President. The Secretary of Labor has the burden of proving that the employer violated held an OSHA standard, in a hearing held before an administrative law judge. The judge's decision is then given to the Commission, which has the option of reviewing it.

The commission may render its own decision or else allow the administrative law judge's decision to be final. An appeal may be made in either case within 60 days from the Commission's decision to the Federal Circuit Court of Appeals.

There are no specific standards set forth in the Occupational Safety and Health Act itself. OSHA was empowered to adopt existing standards and to develop new ones as conditions warrant.

EMPLOYMENT PERSPECTIVE

Stan Meyers was installing aluminum siding on a house, working on a platform 22 feet high. The platform was flat and had no guardrails. An OSHA standard requires guardrails to be installed on all platforms that are 10 feet or higher above the ground. Stan has asked his employer to install guardrails, without success. Finally, Stan notifies OSHA, which sends a compliance officer to the work site. The compliance officer investigates and makes a determination that there is a violation of the OSHA standard regarding guardrails. The OSHA director then issues a citation. Must the employer install the guardrails? Yes! ▪

EMERGENCY STANDARDS

The Secretary of Labor has the power to institute health and safety standards for OSHA. These standards may be emergency or permanent.

Emergency standards are imposed where an immediate concern for the health and safety of workers has just arisen and needs to be addressed in an expeditious manner. Emergency standards are effective for only six months. The Secretary of Labor must explain what the emergency is and then follow regular procedures to have the standard become permanent, if it is believed that the problem will continue to exist.

EMPLOYMENT PERSPECTIVE

Pesto, Inc., created a new cleanser for industrial ovens. When workers began to use the cleanser, they felt a burning sensation on the hands and face. It was discovered that the product contained a caustic acid that would burn exposed areas of the skin that were exposed to its fumes. What recourse is available? Through the Secretary of Labor, an emergency standard can be imposed, requiring breathing ventilators and appropriate gloves, uniforms, and masks to guard against the caustic effects of the acid in the oven cleanser. ▪

The next case deals with a conflict between the Secretary of Labor and the Occupational Safety and Health Review Commission over the power to interpret the OSHA.

LYNN MARTIN, SECRETARY OF LABOR v. OCCUPATIONAL SAFETY AND HEALTH REVIEW COMMISSION

499 U.S. 144 (1991)

JUSTICE MARSHALL delivered the opinion of the Court Per Curiam.

In this case, we consider the question to whom should a reviewing court defer when the Secretary of Labor and the Occupational Safety and Health Review Commission furnish reasonable but conflicting interpretations of an ambiguous regulation promulgated by the Secretary under the Occupational Safety and Health Act of 1970. The Court of Appeals concluded that it should defer to the Commission's interpretation under such circumstances. We reverse.

The Occupational Safety and Health Act of 1970 (OSH Act or Act) establishes a comprehensive regulatory scheme designed "to assure so far as possible . . . safe and healthful working conditions" for "every working man and woman in the Nation." To achieve this objective, the Act assigns distinct regulatory tasks to two independent administrative actors: the Secretary of Labor (Secretary); and the Occupational Safety and Health Review Commission (Commission), a three-member board appointed by the President with the advice and consent of the Senate.

The Act charges the Secretary with responsibility for setting and enforcing workplace health and safety standards. The Secretary establishes these standards through the exercise of rulemaking powers. If the Secretary (or the Secretary's designate) determines upon investigation that an employer is failing to comply with such a standard, the Secretary is authorized to issue a citation and to assess the employer a monetary penalty.

The Commission is assigned to "carry out adjudicatory functions" under the Act. If an employer wishes to contest a citation, the Commission must afford the employer an evidentiary hearing and "thereafter issue an order, based on findings of fact, affirming, modifying, or vacating the Secretary's citation or proposed penalty."

Initial decisions are made by an administrative law judge (ALJ), whose ruling becomes the order of the Commission unless the Commission grants discretionary review. Both the employer and the Secretary have the right to seek review of an adverse Commission order in the court of appeals, which must treat as "conclusive" Commission findings of fact that are "supported by substantial evidence."

This case arises from the Secretary's effort to enforce compliance with OSH Act standards relating to coke-oven emissions. Promulgated pursuant to the Secretary's rulemaking powers, these standards establish maximum permissible emissions levels and require the use of employee respirators in certain circumstances. An investigation by one of the Secretary's compliance officers revealed that respondent CF&I Steel Corporation (CF&I) had equipped 28 of its employees with respirators that failed an "atmospheric test" designed to determine whether a respirator provides a sufficiently tight fit to protect its wearer from carcinogenic emissions. As a result of being equipped with these loose-fitting respirators, some employees were exposed to coke-oven emissions exceeding the regulatory limit. Based on these findings, the compliance officer issued a citation to CF&I and assessed it a $10,000 penalty which requires an employer to "institute a respiratory protection program in accordance with OSHAct." CF&I contested the citation.

The ALJ sided with the Secretary, but the full Commission subsequently granted review and vacated the citation. In the Commission's view, the "respiratory protection program" expressly requires only that an employer train employees in the proper use of respirators. The obligation to assure proper fit of an individual employee's respirator, the Commission noted, was expressly stated in another regulation.

The Secretary petitioned for review in the Court of Appeals for the Tenth Circuit, which affirmed the Commission's order. The court concluded that the relevant regulations were ambiguous as to the employer's obligation to assure proper fit of an employee's respirator. The court thus framed the issue before it as whose reasonable interpretation of the regulations, the Secretary's or the Commission's, merited the court's deference. The court held that the Commission's interpretation was entitled to deference under such circumstances, reasoning that Congress had intended to delegate to the Commission "the normal complement of adjudicative powers possessed by traditional administrative agencies" and that "such an adjudicative function necessarily encompasses the power to 'declare' the law."

The Secretary thereafter petitioned this Court for a writ of certiorari. We granted the petition in order to resolve a conflict among the Circuits on the question whether a reviewing court should defer to the Secretary or to the Commission when these actors furnish reasonable but conflicting interpretations of an ambiguous regulation under the OSH Act.

It is well established "that an agency's construction of its own regulations is entitled to substantial deference." In situations in which "the meaning of regulatory language is not free from doubt," the reviewing court should give effect to the agency's interpretation so long as it is "reasonable," that is, so long as the interpretation "sensibly conforms to the purpose and wording of the regulations." Because applying an agency's regulation to complex or changing circumstances calls upon the agency's unique expertise and policymaking prerogatives, we presume that the power authoritatively to interpret its own regulations is a component of the agency's delegated lawmaking powers. The question before us in this case is to which administrative actor—the Secretary or the Commission—did Congress delegate this "interpretive" lawmaking power under the OSH Act.

To put this question in perspective, it is necessary to take account of the unusual regulatory structure established by the Act. Under most regulatory schemes, rulemaking, enforcement, and adjudicative powers are combined in a single administrative authority. Under the OSH Act, however, Congress separated enforcement and rulemaking powers from adjudicative powers, assigning these respective functions to two independent administrative authorities. The purpose of this "split enforcement" structure was to achieve a greater separation of functions than exists within the traditional "unitary" agency, which under the Administrative Procedure Act (APA) generally must divide enforcement and adjudication between separate personnel.

Although the Act does not expressly address the issue, we now infer from the structure and history of the statute, that the power to render authoritative interpretations of OSH Act regulations is a "necessary adjunct" of the Secretary's powers to promulgate and to enforce national health and safety standards. The Secretary enjoys readily identifiable structural advantages over the Commission in rendering authoritative interpretations of OSH Act regulations. Because the Secretary promulgates these standards, the Secretary is in a better position than is the Commission to reconstruct the purpose of the regulations in question. Moreover, by virtue of the Secretary's statutory role as enforcer, the Secretary comes into contact with a much greater number of regulatory problems than does the Commission, which encounters only those regulatory episodes resulting in contested citations.

Consequently, we think the more plausible inference is that Congress intended to delegate to the Commission the type of nonpolicymaking adjudicatory powers typically exercised by a court in the agency-review context. Under this conception of adjudication, the Commission is authorized to review the Secretary's interpretations only for consistency with the regulatory language and for reasonableness. In addition, of course, Congress expressly charged the Commission with making authoritative findings of fact and with applying the Secretary's standards to those facts in making a decision.

We emphasize the narrowness of our holding. We deal in this case only with the division of powers between the Secretary and the Commission under the OSH Act. We conclude from the available indicia of legislative intent that

Congress did not intend to sever the power authoritatively to interpret OSH Act regulations from the Secretary's power to promulgate and enforce them.

In addition, although we hold that a reviewing court may not prefer the reasonable interpretations of the Commission to the reasonable interpretations of the Secretary, we emphasize that the reviewing court should defer to the Secretary only if the Secretary's interpretation is reasonable. The Secretary's interpretation of an ambiguous regulation is subject to the same standard of substantive review as any other exercise of delegated lawmaking power.

The judgment of the Court of Appeals is reversed, and the case is remanded for further proceedings consistent with this opinion.

It is so ordered.
Judgment for Lynn Martin,
Secretary of Labor.

Case Commentary

The United States Supreme Court ruled that the power to promulgate and enforce OSHA regulations rests with the Secretary of Labor.

Case Questions

1. Are you in accord with the Court's decision?
2. Why do you think this conflict arose?

3. What is the purpose of the Occupational Safety and Health Review Commission?

PARTIAL AND PERMANENT DISABILITY

Over 10,000 workers die on the job each year. In the vicinity of 100,000 workers are permanently disabled. Permanent disability means that the worker is unable to work again and has suffered a serious physical impairment. Over two million workers are partially disabled, meaning that they have missed one or more days from work as a result of the work-related injury. All together, approximately two and one half million workers suffer some form of disabling injury each year. In addition, in excess of six million more suffer minor injuries for which no time is taken off from work.

In about half of the cases, manually handling an object or falling is the cause. Other major types of injuries include being struck by falling or moving objects; machinery-related injuries; motor-vehicle and other types of vehicle-induced injuries; stepping on or striking against objects; the use of hand tools, elevators, hoists, or conveyors; and being in the proximity of electric heat and explosives. Motor-vehicle accidents and falling account for a significant portion of fatalities.

ANCILLARY EXPENSES

There are numerous ancillary expenses which must be absorbed by an employer when a worker is injured on the job. At the time of the injury, other employees and their supervisors may have to stop working to assist their injured coworker or to view and discuss the event. This constitutes a loss of working time. If the injured worker suffered a temporary disability and remained out from work for a short duration, the injured employee would still be entitled to wages, and the employer would have to bear the corresponding loss of productivity. When the injury is permanent or death results, the costs for these losses are substantial. A replacement will have to be hired, and the cost of his or her training must be recognized. The time devoted to investigatory questioning about the accident is time lost for supervisors and coworkers. There is the cost to repair or replace the equipment and/or premises involved in the incident. Another consideration is the time taken for the repair or replacement that may have resulted in a partial work stoppage for those dependent on that equipment or access to the premises in question. The loss of productivity caused by the accident could result in overtime needed to facilitate a return to status quo. These ancillary costs may on occasion exceed the payments made on behalf of the insured worker.

There are two criteria which must be satisfied before an employer is held to be in violation of OSHAct. The first criterion is that the employer did not provide a workplace free from recognized hazards. A hazard is considered recognized when the employer either knew of it or should have known of it because the hazard is of the type that is understood throughout the industry. The second is that the hazard is likely to cause serious harm or death to the employees. When the Secretary of Labor brings an action against an employer, he or she must set forth the OSHA standard held to be violated. Standards vary among the four designated industries: general, maritime, construction, and agriculture. The Secretary must describe how, when, and where the violation took place and whether the employer knew or should have known of it, as well as the proximity of the employees to the hazard. The proximity requirement does not suggest that an employee must have been injured by the hazard, only that the potential for injury exists because the employee was in the vicinity of the hazard.

EMPLOYMENT PERSPECTIVE

The Boxer is a company that manufactures and recycles cardboard boxes. A mechanical forklift is used to carry and stack the flattened boxes. OSHA requires that all motorized vehicles emit a beeping sound when they are in reverse. Forklift 17's beeper is not functional, but the forklift is still being used until Friday when the repair is scheduled. On Wednesday morning, Ryan Madison has just turned a corner and is now walking in the aisle when forklift 17, operating in reverse, just misses hitting him. Is the Boxer in violation? Yes! The Boxer knew of the violation, because forklift 17 was scheduled for repair; an employee, Ryan Madison, was in proximity of the recognized hazard; and the potential for an injury to occur existed. ■

EMPLOYER DEFENSES

The greater hazard defense is applicable where the imposition of a safety standard while remedying one hazard actually has caused a greater hazard in its place. The employer should request a variance for noncompliance; otherwise, the employer's excuse for not adhering to the safety standard may be denied.

EMPLOYMENT PERSPECTIVE

Assume that during roadway construction, orange cones must be laid for a quarter mile before the construction work commences, and, furthermore, a flag-waver must stand by the first cone to wave off oncoming traffic. On days when there is fog, snow, or heavy rain, poor visibility makes it difficult for drivers to see the flag-waver. Does this situation pose a greater hazard? Yes! The imposition of this safety standard on clear days makes sense, but on days of poor visibility it exposes the flag-waver to a greater hazard than those workers one-quarter mile down the road. A variance should be requested for days when there is inclement weather. ∎

Another defense exists where compliance with the safety standard requires a device that is not available on the market. Finally, an employee's negligence or refusal to comply with an OSHA safety standard does not justify the employer's inaction. The employer will still be held in violation.

The following case addresses the question of whether a State Hazardous Waste Laborers Licensing Act must yield to the Occupational Safety and Health Act when they are in conflict.

CASE

MARY GADE, DIRECTOR, ILLINOIS ENVIRONMENTAL PROTECTION AGENCY v. NATIONAL SOLID WASTES MANAGEMENT ASSOCIATION

509 U.S. 88 (1992)

JUSTICE O'CONNOR delivered the opinion of the Court.

In 1988, the Illinois General Assembly enacted the Hazardous Waste Crane and Hoisting Equipment Operators Licensing Act, and the Hazardous Waste Laborers Licensing Act, (together, licensing acts). The stated purpose of the acts is both "to promote job safety" and "to protect life, limb and property." In this case, we consider whether these "dual impact" statutes, which protect both workers and the general public, are preempted by the federal Occupational Safety and Health Act of 1970, (OSH Act), and the standards promulgated thereunder by the Occupational Safety and Health Administration (OSHA).

The OSH Act authorizes the Secretary of Labor to promulgate federal occupational safety and health standards. In the Superfund Amendments and Reauthorization Act of 1986 (SARA), Congress directed the Secretary of Labor to "promulgate standards for the health and safety protection of employees engaged in hazardous waste operations" pursuant to her authority under the OSH Act. In relevant part, SARA requires the Secretary to establish standards for the initial and routine training of workers who handle hazardous wastes.

In response to this congressional directive, OSHA, to which the Secretary has delegated certain of her statutory responsibilities, promulgated regulations on "Hazardous Waste Operations and Emergency Response," including detailed regulations on worker training requirements. The OSHA regulations require, among other things, that workers engaged in an activity that may expose them to hazardous wastes receive a minimum of 40 hours of instruction off the site, and a minimum of three days actual field experience under the supervision of a trained supervisor. Workers who are on the site only occasionally or who are working in areas that have been determined to be under the permissible exposure limits must complete at least 24 hours of off-site instruction and one day of actual field experience. On-site managers and supervisors directly responsible for hazardous waste operations must receive the same initial training as general employees, plus at least eight additional hours of specialized training on various health and safety programs. Employees and supervisors are required to receive eight hours of refresher training annually. Those who have satisfied the training and field experience requirement receive a written certification; uncertified workers are prohibited from engaging in hazardous waste operations.

In 1988, while OSHA's interim hazardous waste regulations were in effect, the State of Illinois enacted the licensing acts at issue here. The laws are designated as acts "in relation to environmental protection," and their stated aim is to protect both employees and the general public by licensing hazardous waste equipment operators and laborers working at certain facilities. Both acts require a license applicant to provide a certified record of at least 40 hours of training under an approved program conducted within Illinois, to pass a written examination, and to complete an annual refresher course of at least eight hours of instruction. In addition, applicants for a hazardous waste crane operator's license must submit "a certified record showing operation of equipment used in hazardous waste handling for a minimum of 4,000 hours." Employees who work without the proper license, and employers who knowingly permit an unlicensed employee to work, are subject to escalating fines for each offense.

The respondent in this case, National Solid Waste Management Association (the Association), is a national trade association of businesses that remove, transport, dispose, and handle waste material, including hazardous waste. The Association's members are subject to the OSH Act and OSHA regulations, and are therefore required to train, qualify, and certify their hazardous waste remediation workers. For hazardous waste operations conducted in Illinois, certain of the workers employed by the Association's members are also required to obtain licenses pursuant to the Illinois licensing acts. Thus, for example, some of the Association's members must ensure that their employees receive not only the three days of field experience required for certification under the OSHA regulations, but also the 500 days of experience (4,000 hours) required for licensing under the state statutes.

The Association sought to enjoin Illinois Environmental Protection Agency (IEPA) from enforcing the Illinois licensing acts, claiming that the acts were pre-empted by the OSH Act and OSHA regulations and that they violated the Commerce Clause of the United States Constitution.

"The question whether a certain state action is pre-empted by federal law is one of congressional intent. The purpose of Congress is the ultimate touchstone."

In the OSH Act, Congress endeavored "to assure so far as possible every working man and woman in the Nation safe and healthful working conditions." To that end, Congress authorized the Secretary of Labor to set mandatory occupational safety and health standards applicable to all businesses affecting interstate commerce, and thereby brought the Federal Government into a field that traditionally had been occupied by the States. Federal regulation of the workplace was not intended to be all-encompassing, however. First, Congress expressly saved two areas from federal pre-emption. Section 4(b)(4) of the OSH Act states that the Act does not "supersede or in any manner affect any workmen's compensation law or . . . enlarge or diminish or affect in any other manner the common law or statutory rights, duties, or liabilities of employers and employees under any law with respect to injuries, diseases, or death of employees arising out of, or in the course of, employment." Section 18(a) provides that the Act does not "prevent any State agency or court from asserting jurisdiction under State law over any occupational safety or health issue with respect to which no federal standard is in effect."

Congress not only reserved certain areas to state regulation, but it also, in 18(b) of the Act, gave the States the option of pre-empting federal regulation entirely. That section provides:

"Submission of State plan for development and enforcement of State standards to pre-empt applicable Federal standards."

"Any State which, at any time, desires to assume responsibility for development and enforcement therein of occupational safety and health standards relating to any occupational safety or health issue with respect to which a Federal standard has been promulgated by the Secretary under the OSH Act shall submit a State plan for the development of such standards and their enforcement."

About half the States have received the Secretary's approval for their own state plans as described in this provision. Illinois is not among them.

Looking at the provisions of 18 as a whole, we conclude that the OSH Act precludes any state regulation of an occupational safety or health issue with respect to which a federal standard has been established, unless a state plan has been submitted and approved pursuant to 18(b). Our review of the Act persuades us that Congress sought to promote occupational safety and health while at the same time avoiding duplicative, and possibly counterproductive, regulation. It thus established a system of uniform federal occupational health and safety standards, but gave States the option of pre-empting federal regulations by developing their own occupational safety and health programs. In addition, Congress offered the States substantial federal grant monies to assist them in developing their own programs. To allow a State selectively to "supplement," certain federal regulations with ostensibly nonconflicting standards would be inconsistent with this federal scheme of establishing uniform federal standards, on the one hand, and encouraging States to assume full responsibility for development and enforcement of their own OSH programs, on the other.

The OSH Act defines an "occupational safety and health standard" as "a standard which requires conditions, or the adoption or use of one or more practices, means, methods, operations, or processes, reasonably necessary or appropriate to provide safe or healthful employ-ment and places of employment." Any state law requirement designed to promote health and safety in the workplace falls neatly within the Act's definition of an "occupational safety and health standard." Clearly, under this definition, a state law that expressly declares a legislative purpose of regulating occupational health and safety would, in the absence of an approved state plan, be pre-empted by an OSHA standard regulating the same subject matter.

We recognize that "the States have a compelling interest in the practice of professions within their boundaries, and that as part of their power to protect the public health, safety, and other valid interests they have broad power to establish standards for licensing practitioners and regulating the practice of professions." But under the Supremacy Clause, from which our pre-emption doctrine is derived, "any state law, however clearly within a State's acknowledged power, which interferes with or is contrary to federal law, must yield" ("even state regulation designed to protect vital state interests must give way to paramount federal legislation"). We therefore reject petitioner's argument that the State's interest in licensing various occupations can save from OSH Act pre-emption those provisions that directly and substantially affect workplace safety.

The judgment of the Court of Appeals is hereby Affirmed.

Judgment for National Solid Wastes
Management Association.

Case Commentary

The United States Supreme Court concluded that an Illinois state law regulating occupational safety and health must yield, since it is in conflict with the OSHAct.

Case Questions

1. Are you in agreement with the Court's decision?
2. Why cannot Illinois enact measures stricter than OSHA requirements in certifying individuals who deal with hazardous waste?

3. Is National Solid Waste Management Association's argument that requiring its members to comply with individual state standards more stringent than OSHA standards would be an undue burden?

An employer is required to provide its employees with a safe working environment. Inherent in this requirement is the employer's duty to inspect and maintain the working environment. An employer breaches its duty when it knew or should have known of a workplace hazard and failed either to correct the defect or notify its employees of it.

An employer is not an insurer of the employee's safety. Liability attaches when the employer had a better understanding of the hazards to be anticipated. However, the employer's liability ceases when the employee's knowledge of the hazard is at least the equivalent of the employer's.

❖ EMPLOYER LESSONS

- Understand that NIOSH makes recommendations regarding health and safety measures.
- Know that the Secretary of Labor takes into account those recommendations in promulgating safety standards.
- Appreciate that the Occupational Safety and Health Administration inspects the plants and offices of employers to assure compliance.
- Be aware that the OSHRC holds hearings and imposes fines and penalties on derelict employers.
- Maintain a clean, safe, and healthy work environment.
- Look for possible OSHA violations and correct them immediately.
- Differentiate between the various gradations of disabilities.
- Be apprised of the annual figure regarding work-related injuries.
- Be cognizant that on occasion a repair may lead to a greater hazard.
- Educate your employees regarding executing their work in a safe and responsible manner.

❖ EMPLOYEE LESSONS

- Be apprised of the significance of the OSHAct.
- Learn what safety measures are required in your place of employment.
- Determine whether your employer is adhering to the required standards.
- Consider whether to report your employer for OSHA violations.
- Know whom to contact for reporting unsafe conditions.
- Be aware of the numerous injuries that occur each year during the scope of employment.
- Guard against injuring yourself on the job by wearing safety equipment and following safety procedures.
- Appreciate the distinctions among the various types of disabilities.
- Make sure you have adequate disability insurance.

❖ REVIEW QUESTIONS

1. Explain the significance of the OSHAct.
2. Who is responsible for establishing OSHA standards?
3. If an employer is unable to comply with an OSHA standard, what alternative is available to it?
4. Absent OSHAct, what should provide employers with enough incentive to ensure a safe working environment?
5. Explain the purpose of the Occupational Safety and Health Administration.
6. May OSHA representatives inspect an employer's place of business?
7. Explain the purpose of the NIOSH.
8. What kind of record-keeping is mandated by OSHA?
9. Explain National Consensus Standards.
10. What is the procedure once a determination has been made that an employer is in violation of OSHA standards?
11. Is the burden and cost of compliance with OSHA standards justified by the injuries and lives saved?
12. How should a decision ethically be made when compliance with OSHA standards perpetrates discrimination against women?
13. Should OSHA take precedence in all conflicts with state law?

14. At issue is whether OSHA preempts all state laws regarding regulation of worker health and safety or only those state laws in direct conflict with it. What was the result? *National Solid Wastes Management Association v. Killian,* 918 F.2d 671 (1990)

15. OWCP, the Court of Appeals for the Fourth Circuit, struck down the DOL interim regulations. John Taylor, a respondent in No. 90-113, applied for black lung benefits in 1976, after having worked for almost 12 years as a coal loader and roof bolter in underground coal mines. The Administrative Law Judge found that Taylor properly had invoked the presumption of eligibility for benefits under MDRV 727.203 (a) (3), based on qualifying arterial blood gas studies demonstrating an impairment in the transfer of oxygen from his lungs to his blood. The ALJ then proceeded to weigh the rebuttal evidence, consisting of negative X-ray evidence, nonqualifying ventilatory study scores, and several medical reports submitted respectively by Taylor and by his employer, petitioner Clinchfield Coal Company. In light of this evidence, the ALJ concluded that Taylor neither suffered from pneumoconiosis nor was totally disabled. Rather, the evidence demonstrated that Taylor suffered from chronic bronchitis caused by 30 years of cigarette smoking and obesity. The Benefits Review Board affirmed, concluding that the ALJ's decision was supported by substantial evidence. Section 410.416 (a) provides: "If a miner was employed for 10 years or more in the Nation's coal mines, and is suffering or suffered from pneumoconiosis, it will be presumed, in the absence of persuasive evidence to the contrary, that the pneumoconiosis arose out of such employment." What was the result? *Clinchfield Coal Co. v. Director, Office of Workers' Compensation Programs, U.S. Dept. of Labor,* 501 U.S. 680 (1991)

16. Albert Dayton, a respondent in No. 90-114, applied for black lung benefits in 1979, after having worked as a coal miner for 17 years. The ALJ found that Dayton invoked the presumption of eligibility based on ventilatory test scores showing a chronic pulmonary condition. The judge then determined that petitioner Consolidated Coal Company had successfully rebutted the presumption under 15 727.203 (b) (2) and (4) by demonstrating that Dayton did not have pneumoconiosis and, in any event, that Dayton's pulmonary impairment was not totally disabling. The Benefits Review Board affirmed, concluding that the medical evidence demonstrated that Dayton's pulmonary condition was unrelated to coal and dust exposure, but was instead secondary to his smoking and "other ailments," and that the ALJ had correctly concluded that Consolidation had rebutted the presumption. *Consolidation Coal Co. v. Director, Office of Workers' Compensation Programs,* U.S. Dept. of Labor, 501 U.S. 680 (1991)

17. In 1986, while walking in a dark train tunnel, Sinclair fell over a depression in a bent trap door covering a manhole. Sinclair immediately experienced "sharp low back pains" and could not stand straight or walk normally. He was out of work for almost three weeks, during which time he was treated and examined twice by a private physician and three times by LIRR physicians.

   Sinclair commenced this FELA (Fair Employment Labor Authority) action in September 1989, alleging a single theory of liability: the LIRR breached its duty to exercise reasonable care in providing a safe workplace. The claim was limited to the September 1986 incident with the manhole cover. What was the result? *Sinclair v. Long Island R.R.,* 985 F.2d 74 (2nd Cir. 1993)

❖ **WEB SITES**

www.osh.net/
www.findlaw.com
www.westbuslaw.com
www.nycash.org/
www.worksafe.org
www.eng.auburn.edu/ie/ose/
http://laborsafety.about.com/?once=true&

WORKERS' COMPENSATION

INTRODUCTION

Workers' compensation originated under the Master/Servant Doctrine where a master was liable for the death or injury of his servant. Master/Servant evolved into Employer/Employee. Originally the liability of the employer was not absolute. If the employee was contributorily negligent, assumed the risk, or was injured by another employee, he or she would be barred from recovery. As employee issues gained importance, those roadblocks to recovery were removed and the employer's negligence became absolute.

CHAPTER CHECKLIST

❖ Appreciate the purpose of workers' compensation.

❖ Know the function of the Workers' Compensation Board.

❖ Learn that eligibility hinges upon the injury occurring within the scope of employment.

❖ Be aware that an employee must notify the employer of the injury sustained.

❖ Be apprised that employees may not sue their employer in court.

❖ Be cognizant that employers will pay for medical expenses, lost wages, retraining, and death benefits.

❖ Realize that workers' compensation is governed by each state.

❖ Recognize that some employees submit fraudulent claims hoping to collect benefits.

❖ Understand that workers' compensation is absolute regardless of fault.

❖ Appreciate that workers' compensation is a form of no-fault insurance.

EMPLOYMENT SCENARIO

Mary Fields, an inventory control analyst for the Long and the Short of It, was injured when a shelf containing heavy boxes collapsed, knocking her to the floor. The injury occurred in the stockroom while Mary was taking inventory. She suffered a severe concussion, broken collarbone, and injuries to her ribs. Tom Long and Mark Short were very sympathetic to Mary until they learned she intended to file a workers' compensation claim.

They attempted to dissuade Mary, informing her that they would cover all of her medical expenses. Mary replied that she wanted compensation for her pain and suffering. Tom empathized with Mary, saying that he felt Mary's pain, but then rebuked her, telling Mary that she would feel his wrath if she filed with the Workers' Compensation Board. Tom admonished Mary that she could take her time convalescing, because her days at L&S were over.

Tom and Mark were afraid of an increase in L&S's workers' compensation insurance premiums. Susan North, L&S's attorney, was notified by Mary's attorney of Tom Long's outburst and threats. She scolded Tom, and then informed Mark and Tom that acts of retaliation were public policy exceptions to the at-will employment doctrine. Susan addressed Tom and Mark's concern with the potential rise in insurance costs, but indicated this should be viewed as a cost of doing business. Susan convinced Tom and Mark to permit her to apologize on their behalf and to support Mary's entitlement to workers' compensation benefits.

PURPOSE

In return for absolute liability for injury or death, employers are immune from lawsuits for unintentional torts. When an injury occurs on the job the employer is liable without regard to fault. It makes no difference whether the negligent act was committed on the part of the employee, employer, or coworker. The term *injury* also includes diseases that occur in the workplace, such as lung-related diseases from asbestos.

Workers' compensation affords employers and employees the following benefits. Employers save the time and expense of defending a lawsuit. Employees, in turn, receive immediate medical benefits, continued wage earnings, retraining, and death or disfigurement benefits, if applicable.

EMPLOYMENT PERSPECTIVE
P's and Q's Grammar School has discovered that its building is laced with asbestos. An asbestos removal firm has estimated the cost of removal at $175,000. School administrators decide to have Oscar Clark, their maintenance man, do the work over the summer. Oscar is not particularly knowledgeable about what asbestos is and how to remove it properly. Oscar works all summer on the job, without proper clothing or equipment. Seventeen years later, he is diagnosed with lung cancer. He sues P's and Q's Grammar School in court, claiming that the school administrators intentionally exposed him to asbestos, knowing its harmful effects. Will Oscar win? Yes! ■

The question presented in the case that follows is whether the employee's disability was completely caused by asbestosis.

IN THE MATTER OF BLAIR v. BENDIX CORPORATION

85 N.Y.2d 834 (1995)

MEMORANDUM:

The order of the Appellate Division should be affirmed, with costs.

Until July 1, 1974, an employee disabled by a dust disease, such as asbestosis, was entitled to workers' compensation only in the event of total disability. Workers' Compensation Law § 39 was amended, effective July 1, 1974, to afford a remedy to any employee disabled, whether partially or completely, as a result of exposure to noxious dust in the course of employment, provided such exposure occurred on or after July 1, 1974.

Claimant-appellant was exposed to asbestos from August 1956 through September 1970 in the course of her employment as a stenciler and packer of brake linings for Respondent.

Claimant became totally disabled and stopped working in 1978 as a result of asthma and emphysema, diseases that were unrelated to her employment. She was awarded Social Security disability benefits accordingly. On March 15, 1988, claimant was diagnosed with asbestosis and, subsequently, instituted this workers' compensation proceeding against respondent alleging injurious exposure to asbestos as a result of her employment.

The Workers' Compensation Board found that claimant's asbestosis was causally related to her employment at respondent's plant. However, it also found that claimant was previously partially disabled, as a result of a "pre-existing lung disability from unrelated pulmonary emphysema and asthma" and that the combination of the two unrelated conditions—asbestosis and pulmonary disease—caused her total disablement.

This Court agrees with that part of the Appellate Division's reasoning that concluded claimant's pre-existing lung disability and her asbestosis were not inseparable causative agents of her total disability. The Workers' Compensation Board, therefore, erroneously found that claimant sustained a compensable injury and was entitled to benefits. Since claimant's period of exposure to asbestos predated the 1974 amendment to section 39, the recovery of workers' compensation was contingent on her complete disablement as a result of asbestosis, a fact not evidenced by this record. The fact that claimant's asbestosis contributed to her pre-existing lung disability could not create an entitlement to compensation, prior to the 1974 amendment to section 39, absent proof that the disabling causative agents were inseparable or that the asbestosis completely disabled her.

Judgment for Bendix Corp.

Case Commentary

The New York Court of Appeals concluded that Blair's lung deficiency was not completely due to asbestosis. Therefore, she was not entitled to benefits under workers' compensation.

Case Questions

1. Are you in accord with the Court's decision?
2. Do you think it was unfair that Blair received no compensation?

3. Do you believe the 1974 amendment, which granted benefits where asbestosis was only partially responsible, should have been retroactive?

An employee must report an injury to his or her employer and then file a claim with the Workers' Compensation Board.

The issue in the case that follows is whether the awarding of attorney's fees should be based solely on past workers' compensation benefits or should also include the amount of future benefits that would have been paid had the worker not recovered from a third party tortfeasor.

CASE

STONE v. FLUID AIR COMPONENTS OF ALASKA

990 P.2d 621 (Alaska 1999)

MATTHEWS, Chief Justice.

INTRODUCTION

This workers' compensation case presents the question of whether an employer's pro rata share of attorney's fees and costs due on a recovery from a third party should be based on the amount of the compensation benefits already paid, or on such benefits plus those that would have been paid in the future if there had been no recovery from a third party.

FACTS AND PROCEEDINGS

Duncan Stone was injured at work. He received workers' compensation payments from Fluid Air Components, his employer, through Liberty Northwest, the employer's insurance carrier, (collectively, "the employer") in the amount of approximately $74,408. He subsequently recovered a $600,000 judgment in a suit against a third-party tortfeasor. The employer filed a petition for reimbursement of the payments already made to Stone. Stone filed an answer to the petition, contending that he owed the employer no money, as the amount of its right to reimbursement was exceeded by the employer's prorated share of the at-

torney's fees and costs based on the total of past and future benefits. The employer conceded that its reimbursement should be reduced by a prorated share of fees and costs, but contended that the apportionment should be based on past compensation payments alone. The Workers' Compensation Board held that "the proration of attorney fees should be calculated on the employer's total potential liability," rather than past benefits actually paid. The Board retained jurisdiction to determine the appropriate amount of future liability.

In a later hearing, the Board determined, based on the testimony of Stone, his doctor, and an economist, that Stone's injury was permanent and would require lifelong medical treatment costing an estimated $158,371 when reduced to present value. This sum represented the employer's "future compensation liability, for the purpose of prorating litigation costs and expenses." As attorney's fees and costs apportionable to the past and future liability exceeded the employer's request for reimbursement Stone owed nothing. In addition, Stone was awarded attorney's fees for defending the employer's reimbursement petition.

The employer appealed to the superior court. After briefing and argument, the court reversed the Board, holding that pro rata fees can only be based on past benefits paid rather than past benefits and future liability. The court therefore ordered reimbursement to the employer of $46,892. The court further ordered that the attorney's fees paid by the employer for services before the Board be repaid.

Is the Employer's Pro Rata Share of Attorney's Fees and Costs in a Third-Party Tort Case Based Solely on Compensation Benefits Paid, or on Total Benefits?

Employees injured on the job are entitled to benefits from their employers under the Workers' Compensation Act. These benefits are the exclusive remedy that employees have against their employers. But employees may sue third parties who may be legally responsible for on-the-job injuries. If damages are recovered by an employee in a third-party suit after compensation benefits have been paid by the employer, the employer is entitled to reimbursement from the recovery for the benefits paid, less the employer's prorated share of litigation costs and attorney's fees.

In Cooper v. Argonaut, we interpreted AS 23.30.015(g) to require this result. This subsection provides in part:

If the employee or the employee's representative recovers damages from the third person, the employee or representative shall promptly pay to the employer the total amounts paid by the employer under (e)(1)(A)-(C) of this section insofar as the recovery is sufficient after deducting all litigation costs and expenses. Any excess recovery by the employee or representative shall be credited against any amount payable by the employer thereafter.

We read the language "after deducting all litigation costs and expenses" to require a pro rata sharing of costs and expenses between employee and employer.

In Cooper the question was not presented as to whether the employer's prorated "share of the recovery" against which its fees would be calculated should include future as well as past compensation payments. The accident in Cooper was fatal, so there were no future unpaid benefits. But the reasons underlying the Cooper holding support the conclusion that the employer's prorated share includes all benefits, both past and future.

The first reason given by the Cooper court was that prorating fees and expenses to the employer made subsection (g) of AS 23.30.015 "harmonious with provisions of the Act which permit

such a deduction by the employer when he brings suit."

Under subsection (e) of AS 23.30.015, an employer who recovers from a third party can deduct reasonable fees, the cost of benefits actually paid, and the present value of benefits "to be furnished later" before remitting any excess to the employee. The reasonableness of the fee depends in part on the "results obtained." As past and future benefits are treated similarly under subsection (e)(1)(B) and (D), the "results obtained" guideline for subsection (e) fees must refer to total benefits rather than just to past compensation. Construing pro rata fees under subsection (g) to also refer to future benefits thus makes it harmonious with subsection (e).

An additional reason relied on by the Cooper court was the prevention of unjust enrichment: "If an employer or compensation carrier is not required to pay its pro rata share to recover this unanticipated return, the entire burden of the litigation would be borne by the employee. The carrier would take the benefit of both the employer's premium and the employee's litigation effort." Unjust enrichment occurs whether the benefits have already been paid or would have been paid in the future. The unjust enrichment rationale of Cooper therefore also applies to future benefits.

Finally, among the other jurisdictions that prorate fees between employees and employers in third-party tort recoveries, the vast majority hold that the employer's pro rata share is calculated on the total benefits to the employer. Most courts in these jurisdictions have concluded that since the employer's right of reimbursement extends to future liability, the employer's equitable share of the fees and costs involved in the employee's third-party recovery should likewise be calculated on the employer's total potential liability.

The employer argues that Alaska's statutory scheme, in contrast to the majority of jurisdictions, does not include the right to future reimbursement on the part of the employer. However, AS 23.30.015(g) includes future benefits in the employer's right to reimbursement in the form of a credit. It provides that the employee's recovery "shall be credited against any amount payable by the employer thereafter." In other words, if the employee recovers an amount in excess of the compensation paid, the employee can keep it, subject to the employer's credit for future benefits that would otherwise be paid. It is as if the employer were to pay a doctor's bill and be instantaneously reimbursed for it. If the "excess" is not sufficient to cover future benefits, the employer will again be liable.

Thus, based on the rationale of Cooper, and because the law of most other states is in accord, we conclude that the employer's pro rata share of fees and costs should be based on both past and future benefits to the employee. In this case the employee seeks only an offset against the employer's reimbursement request. The offset remedy readily fits the language of AS 23.30.015(g) which speaks of "deducting" litigation costs before reimbursing the employer.

CONCLUSION

For the reasons discussed above, we REVERSE the superior court's decision and direct reinstatement of the decision of the Workers' Compensation Board, including the Board's award of attorney's fees.

Judgment for Stone.

Case Commentary

The Alaska Supreme Court ruled that the employer's share of Stone's attorney fees in his suit against a third party tortfeasor should be proportionately based on the future workers' compensation benefits Stone would have received absent this suit as a percentage of the total tort case recovery.

Case Questions

1. Are you in agreement with the Court's decision?
2. Why should the employer be liable for attorney fees in a lawsuit to which it is not a party?
3. Why should the tortfeasor be responsible for the employee's attorney fees, rather than the employer?

EMPLOYMENT PERSPECTIVE

Peter Hallmark worked at Freedom Printing Press. One day, Sam Houseman, a coworker, caught his hand in a press. When Peter attempted to extricate Sam from his peril, Peter banged his head on the press and suffered a bad head injury that resulted in his death. Peter's widow filed a claim with the Workers' Compensation Board for Peter's wrongful death. Sam filed a claim for the injury to his hand. Will they be successful? Yes! Fault is not at issue here. Peter may have been contributorily negligent. Sam may have been contributorily negligent in jamming his hand. Freedom may have been negligent if the machine was not functioning properly. All that matters is that the injuries occurred on the job. Freedom is liable for the medical expenses, loss of wages, death benefits, and a possible benefit for disfigurement depending on the severity of the injury to Sam's hand. ▪

EMPLOYMENT PERSPECTIVE

Tom Woodstock was working on the third floor of a new office building. While walking along a beam, his attention was distracted when two waitresses came out of the Masters Restaurant across the street. Tom slipped off the beam and fell 30 feet. As a result, he became quadraplegic. Tom filed a claim with the Workers' Compensation Board for permanent disability. His employer, Build-Rite, claimed that Tom should have watched where he was walking. Will Tom recover? Yes! Although Tom was clearly negligent, he will recover because his injury occurred on the job. ▪

EMPLOYMENT PERSPECTIVE

Sidney Wood was cleaning debris off the railroad tracks that are owned and operated by Northwest Railway System. Billy Thomas, a teenager, threw a rock that hit Sidney on the head. Sidney suffered a concussion and blurred vision and was out of work for one month. He filed a workers' compensation claim. Northwest Railway claimed that only the perpetrator of this intentional tort can be held liable. Is Northwest correct? No! Sidney was injured on the job. Northwest Railway is liable for medical expenses and lost wages. This situation does not preclude Sidney from suing Billy for pain and suffering for the intentional tort of battery or from pressing criminal charges against him for assault. ■

EMPLOYMENT PERSPECTIVE

Herman Munsun worked for the West Virginia Coal Mining Company for 30 years. At 51 years of age, while still employed, Herman was diagnosed with black lung disease. He filed a claim under workers' compensation for a work-related disease. West Virginia Coal disputed the claim, asserting it was not conclusive that Herman contracted the disease while on the job. Will Herman be successful? Yes! Expert opinion is on the side of Herman because of the multitude of case histories. West Virginia Coal Mining Company will probably be liable. ■

The question presented in the following case is whether it is within the power of the Director of the Office of Workers' Compensation to seek compensation for an employee, who has been denied by the Benefits Review Board.

CASE

DIRECTOR, OWCP v. NEWPORT NEWS SHIPBUILDING

514 U.S. 122 (1995)

JUSTICE SCALIA delivered the opinion of the Court.

The question before us in this case is whether the Director of the Office of Workers' Compensation Programs in the United States Department of Labor has standing under the Longshore and Harbor Workers' Compensation Act (LHWCA) to seek judicial review of decisions by the Benefits Review Board that in the Director's view deny claimants compensation to which they are entitled.

I

On October 24, 1984, Jackie Harcum, an employee of respondent Newport News Shipbuilding and Dry Dock Co., was working in the bilge of a steam barge when a piece of metal grating fell and struck him in the lower back. His injury required surgery to remove a herniated disc, and caused prolonged disability. Respondent paid Harcum benefits under the LHWCA until he returned to light-duty work in April 1987. In November 1987,

Harcum returned to his regular department under medical restrictions. He proved unable to perform essential tasks, however, and the company terminated his employment in May 1988. Harcum ultimately found work elsewhere, and started his new job in February 1989.

Harcum filed a claim for further benefits under the LHWCA. Respondent contested the claim, and the dispute was referred to an Administrative Law Judge (ALJ). One of the issues was whether Harcum was entitled to benefits for total disability, or instead only for partial disability, from the date he stopped work for respondent until he began his new job. "Disability" under the LHWCA means "incapacity because of injury to earn the wages which the employee was receiving at the time of injury in the same or any other employment."

After a hearing on October 20, 1989, the ALJ determined that Harcum was partially, rather than totally, disabled when he left respondent's employ, and that he was therefore owed only partial-disability benefits for the interval of his unemployment. On appeal, the Benefits Review Board affirmed the ALJ's judgment, and also ruled that the company was entitled to cease payments to Harcum after 104 weeks, after which time the LHWCA special fund would be liable for disbursements.

The Director petitioned the United States Court of Appeals for the Fourth Circuit for review of both aspects of the Board's ruling. Harcum did not seek review and, while not opposing the Director's pursuit of the action, expressly declined to intervene on his own behalf in response to an inquiry by the Court of Appeals. The Court of Appeals raised the question whether the Director had standing to appeal the Board's order. It concluded that she did not have standing with regard to that aspect of the order denying Harcum's claim for full-disability compensation, since she was not "adversely affected or aggrieved" by that decision. We granted certiorari.

II

The LHWCA provides for compensation of workers injured or killed while employed on the navigable waters or adjoining, shipping-related land areas of the United States. With the exception of those duties imposed by 919(d), 921(b), and 941, the Secretary of Labor has delegated all responsibilities of the Department with respect to administration of the LHWCA to the Director of the Office of Workers' Compensation Programs (OWCP). For ease of exposition, the Director will hereinafter be referred to as the statutory recipient of those responsibilities.

A worker seeking compensation under the Act must file a claim with an OWCP district director. If the district director cannot resolve the claim informally, it is referred to an ALJ authorized to issue a compensation order. The ALJ's decision is reviewable by the Benefits Review Board, whose members are appointed by the Secretary. The Board's decision is in turn appealable to a United States court of appeals, at the instance of "any person adversely affected or aggrieved by" the Board's order.

With regard to claims that proceed to ALJ hearings, the Act does not by its terms make the Director a party to the proceedings, or grant her authority to prosecute appeals to the Board, or thence to the federal court of appeals. The Director argues that she nonetheless had standing to petition the Fourth Circuit for review of the Board's order, because she is "a person adversely affected or aggrieved." Specifically, she contends the Board's decision injures her because it impairs her ability to achieve the Act's purposes and to perform the administrative duties the Act prescribes.

The LHWCA assigns four broad areas of responsibility to the Director: (1) supervising, administering, and making rules and regulations for calculation of benefits and processing of claims, (2) supervising, administering, and making rules and regulations for provision of medical care to covered workers, (3) assisting claimants with processing claims and receiving medical and vocational rehabilitation, and (4) enforcing compensation orders and administering payments to and disbursements from the special fund established by the Act for the payment of certain benefits. The Director does not assert that the Board's decision hampers her performance of these express statutory responsibilities. She claims only two categories of interest that are affected, neither of which remotely suggests that she has authority to appeal Board determinations.

For these reasons, the judgment of the United States Court of Appeals for the Fourth Circuit is affirmed.

Judgment for Newport News Shipbuilding.

Case Commentary

The United States Supreme Court resolved that it was not within the authority granted to the Director of the Office of Workers' Compensation to seek compensation for an employee who was refused by the Benefits Review Board.

Case Questions

1. Are you in accord with the decision of the Court?
2. Why do you think the Director wanted to intervene?
3. What made the Director believe it was within her authority to intervene?

WORKERS' COMPENSATION BOARD

The social purposes of workers' compensation are to provide injured workers with support and medical treatment expeditiously and to provide an incentive to employers to create and maintain a safe working environment for their employees.

The Workers' Compensation Board is administered by the state. Each employer must carry its own workers' compensation insurance unless it is a self-insurer.

Insurance companies assess premiums on the basis of the number of claims that are made. There has been an abuse of the system by some lawyers and physicians. Certain lawyers steer individuals with skeptical claims to physicians who will always diagnose a work-related injury. In deciding whether to pay, insurance companies have to weigh the investigation and litigation expenses against the cost of the settlement. Employers should consult with their insurers before a settlement to assess whether the claim is bogus and what the potential pubic relations ramifications are. Employers are concerned with keeping premiums low. Litigating bogus claims may result in fewer doubtful claims in the future.

Employers often do not want to hire people who have a condition that could be aggravated on the job, for they fear an almost certain workers' compensation claim in the future. If an individual is not hired because of his or her physical condition and he or she could perform the job at the present time, the person may file a claim with the EEOC for violation of the Americans with Disabilities Act (ADA).

EMPLOYMENT PERSPECTIVE

Susan Hampton is a registered nurse. She applies for a position with the Midway Hospital. While Susan is undergoing a physical exam, it is discovered that she suffered a lower back strain. Midway refuses to hire Susan, although she can do the job required. Susan files a claim with the EEOC, alleging a violation of the ADA. Midway claims that eventually Susan will reinjure her back and file a workers' compensation claim. Will Susan win? Yes! Midway is discriminating against Susan for a past disability. Although the odds may favor a reinjury, this is discrimination. There is no way for Midway to guard against a future workers' compensation claim by Susan if she reinjures her back. ∎

EMPLOYMENT PERSPECTIVE

Ken Warren delivers groceries for Foodway. His main hobby is playing racquetball. One night, Ken is late for a match and forgoes his usual preplay routine. During the intensive match, Ken injures his groin muscle. Ken will be out of work for at least six weeks. The next day he files a workers' compensation claim, alleging that the injury resulted from carrying two heavy packages up the flights of stairs to Thelma Johnson's apartment, one of the previous day's deliveries. Foodway does not believe Ken. North Star Insurance wants to settle the claim. What should Foodway do? It should insist that North Star investigate by speaking to his racquetball partners and by questioning how he could play at night if he suffered such a painful injury earlier during the day. This investigation will keep costs down and discourage other employees from submitting fraudulent claims. ■

FALSE REPRESENTATIONS

A worker who makes a false representation with regard to his or her physical or mental state of health will be prevented from recouping compensation if the following are true: the representation was made intentionally; reliance was justifiably placed on the representation; the representation influenced the employer in the hiring of the employee; and the resulting injury is of the same condition as the one falsely represented. The burden of proving this is on the employer.

EMPLOYER DEFENSES

During the Industrial Age many workers labored under the most deplorable conditions, such as lack of heat, lighting, ventilation, and having to use unsafe equipment and machinery. Workers for the most part assumed the risk of injury. Recovering damages for loss of earnings, medical expenses, and pain and suffering was rare. The employee suffered not only an injury but possibly the loss of his or her job as well for nonperformance. Coworkers were afraid to testify for fear of employer retaliation. Even worse than that was the courts' allowance of the legal defenses of fellow servant negligence and assumption of risk. The fellow servant rule prohibited an employee from suing the employer when the injury occurred because of the negligence of a coworker. The employer's deep pocket was immune from liability. The injured employee's only recourse was to sue the coworker.

When a worker is injured, the employer sustains an economic loss due to the non-productivity of the worker. The employer must absorb this loss. The employee's entitlement to compensation depends on whether the injury was in the scope of employment. If the employer provides health and disability benefits, this will compensate the employee for medical expenses and loss of earnings while temporarily or partially disabled because of an injury or illness that occurred outside the scope of employment. The employee must make up the difference.

When the injury occurs on the job and is within the scope of employment, the employee may seek retribution from the employer's workers' compensation plan.

The issue in the case that follows is whether the employee's involvement in a customer sponsored bowling league was in some way work related.

IN THE MATTER OF DOROSZ v. GREEN & SEIFTER AND WORKERS COMPENSATION BOARD

92 N.Y.2d 672 (1999).

ROSENBLATT, Judge.

Decedent, an accountant who worked for a private accounting firm, suffered a fatal heart attack while bowling for a team sponsored by one of the firm's clients. We must decide whether the Workers' Compensation Board properly denied his widow's claim for Workers' Compensation benefits. Reversing the Workers' Compensation Law Judge, the Board ruled that decedent's death did not arise out of an injury sustained in the course of his employment. In disallowing the claim, the Board concluded that decedent's participation in bowling was an after-hours, voluntary athletic activity for which benefits are barred by section 10 of the Workers' Compensation Law. The Appellate Division, by a divided court, upheld the Board's decision. We affirm.

The Workers' Compensation Law requires every employer to carry workers' compensation insurance, so that employees, or those claiming through them, may recover for "accidental injuries arising out of and in the course of employmen." Pursuant to Workers' Compensation Law § 10, this entitlement exists without regard to fault as a cause of the injury, but the section contains a number of restrictions, including the one at issue in this case. The pertinent restriction reads:

"There shall be no liability for compensation under this chapter where the injury was sustained in or caused by voluntary participation in an off-duty athletic activity not constituting part of the employee's work related duties unless the employer (a) requires the employee to participate in such activity, (b) compensates the employee for participating in such activity or (c) otherwise sponsors the activity."

The Board found that decedent bowled in a Monday night league, on a team sponsored by

Tom Cardinal, a client of decedent's firm. The two were friends, and, as was their custom, would discuss business before and after bowling on these Monday nights. No other employees of Cardinal's or decedent's firm were involved in the activity. On the night in question, Cardinal picked decedent up and the two went to the bowling alley, where they discussed business and then bowled three games. Minutes later, decedent had a cardiovascular collapse and died. The Board noted that there was conflicting evidence as to whether the act of bowling caused the decedent's heart attack, or whether, owing to his pre-existing severe obstructive coronary artery disease, it would have happened at that time, no matter what he was doing. The Board, however, made no determination as to that issue, and it is not before us.

By enacting section 10, the Legislature narrowed the standards for what constitutes a compensable work-related sports injury, so that an award would not be based upon insufficient employer involvement. In the record before us it is obvious that the decedent, who was an accountant, was not engaging in work-related duties when he was bowling. To conclude otherwise would be inconsistent with the Board's findings, which are supported by substantial evidence.

Under section 10, an award is thus foreclosed here unless one of three conditions permitting compensation for off-duty athletic-related injuries exists: that the employer (1) required the employee to participate in the activity, (2) paid the worker to do so, or (3) sponsored the activity. In the case before us, none of these conditions is met. The employer did not require the decedent to bowl in the Monday league, nor did it pay him to do so.

As to the third condition, that the employer "otherwise sponsors the activity," we note that the legislative memorandum to the 1983 amendment of section 10 states that the amendment "will not change the liability of the employer when participation in an activity is overtly encouraged by the employer." In the case before us, there is no evidence of overt encouragement by the employer. That the employer may have known of the activity, and even acquiesced in it, does not constitute overt encouragement, let alone formal sponsorship of the activity. An employee's activity may be beneficial to his or her health or morale or may confer a benefit on the employer, but that alone is not enough to justify an award, given the restrictions set forth in section 10.

Based on the testimony adduced, we conclude that the Board's determination was supported by substantial evidence.

Accordingly, the order of the Appellate Division should be affirmed, with costs.

Judgment for Green Seifter.

Case Commentary

The New York Court of Appeals decided that Dorosz's death did not occur within the scope of employment. The bowling league where Dorosz

Case Questions

1. Are you in agreement with the Court's decision?
2. Was it not enough that Dorosz and Cardinal were discussing business at the bowling alley?

died of a heart attack was not company sponsored and Dorosz was not otherwise obligated to be at the bowling alley.

3. Why should the employer be responsible if it sponsored the bowling league?

The next case deals with an injury to a teacher arising out of a faculty/student basketball game. Being present on the court or in the stands was required of each teacher. The teacher claimed that the game was work-related and filed for workers' compensation for the injury sustained during that game.

CASE

HIGHLANDS CTY. SCHOOL v. SAVAGE

609 So.2d 133 (Fla. App. 1 Dist. 1992)

WOLF, Judge.

Highlands County School Board and McCreary Corporation (E/C), appeal from a final order of the judge of compensation claims (JCC) determining that the injury sustained by claimant, Rosalie Savage, was compensable. The E/C asserted that the JCC erred in finding that claimant's injury while participating in a basketball game was a result of an incident of her employment, and therefore, com-

pensable. We find that the basketball game during which claimant was injured constituted part of her employment rather than social or recreational activity and is, therefore, compensable.

The facts are undisputed. The claimant, a teacher at Sebring Middle School, was injured in December 1990 during a basketball game between the teachers and students. The game was an annual charity event. The game occurred during regular school hours, and the teachers received their regular salary. The teachers were required to participate in the game, either as a spectator or a player. No benefit or detriment resulted from a teacher's decision to play or to act as a spectator.

The claimant's claim for benefits to cover the injury sustained in the faculty basketball game was denied by the E/C, on the grounds that the recreational or social activity was not an expressly required incident of employment nor did it produce a benefit to the employer beyond improvement in employee health and morale. The JCC found, following a June 7, 1991, hearing, that the claimant's participation was an incident of her employment and, therefore, compensable.

The E/C's main argument on appeal is that the JCC erred in finding the accident to be compensable in light of section 440.092(1), Florida Statutes (1991), where there was no proof that playing in the basketball games was expressly required as an incident of employment. Section 440.092(1) was created in 1990 and was in effect on December 21, 1990, the date of the claimant's injury. The statute provides as follows:

Recreational or social activities are not compensable unless such recreational or social activities are an expressly required incident of employment and produce a substantial direct benefit to the employer beyond improvement in employee health and morale that is common to all kinds of recreation and social life.

Prior to the adoption of the statute, the law concerning compensability of recreational and social activities was as follows:

Social activities . . . are deemed to be in the course and scope of employment when *any one* of the following criteria are met: (1) They occur on the premises during a lunch or recreation period as a regular incident of the employment; or (2) the employer,

by expressly or impliedly requiring participation, or by making the activity part of the services of an employee, brings the activity within the orbit of the employment; or (3) the employer derives substantial direct benefits from the activity beyond the intangible value of improvement in employee health and morale that is common to all kinds of recreation and social life.

It appears that the statutory change was enacted to avoid compensability in situations where the activity in question was neither part of the job duties of an individual or expressly required by the employer. There is nothing in the statute as adopted which would indicate a desire to preclude compensation where a person was injured in conducting actual job duties. Thus, the JCC did not ignore the requirement for a finding of an "express incident of employment" as argued by the E/C. As a matter of fact, the JCC specifically found that the activity in which the claimant was injured was *not* social and recreational but was a regular incident of her employment. This finding is supported by competent substantial evidence; therefore, the E/C's reliance on the statute to deny benefits was inappropriate.

Even if the JCC had found that the facts of this case are controlled by section 440.092 (1), there would be record support for finding of both "an expressly required incident of employment" *and* "a substantial direct benefit to the employer beyond improvement in employee health and morale" as required by the statute. It was uncontradicted that the basketball game was a school activity which required attendance of both students and faculty. Teachers were expressly required to participate in the basketball game in some manner. The event was a part of developing community awareness by requiring students to participate in a community service project. The order of the JCC is affirmed.

Judgment for Savage.

Case Commentary

The Florida Appellate District Court decided that the teacher's participation in the playing of a faculty/student basketball game, which resulted in an injury to her, occurred within the scope of employment.

Case Questions

1. Are you in agreement with the Court's decision?
2. Why should the school be liable when Savage could have watched the game, instead of playing?

3. Did Savage not assume the risk of injury when she stepped out onto the court?

Temporarily debilitating injuries are paid according to a schedule of benefits that determines the amount of compensation given during each pay period and its duration. Once the time limit has been reached, payments cease. The benefit to both the employer and the employee is the time and expense saved by not engaging in litigation. Also, employees do not have to lay out money for medical expenses and to wonder how they will support themselves until the case is tried or a settlement is reached.

Workers' compensation is a form of no-fault insurance. Under most workers' compensation plans, medical expenses for on-the-job injuries resulting in permanent disability or death will be fully covered, and disability payments for loss of earnings will be payable for life at a fixed rate, *i.e.,* two-thirds of the wage earned at the time the employee was disabled. In cases of death, benefits will be paid to the surviving spouse until remarriage or death and to any children until they reach the age of majority.

Injured workers may also seek compensation for pain and suffering. An employee must file an accident report at the time of the injury, and if the injury results in a disability, then a workers' compensation claim must also be filed with the insurance company administering the plan. Some states administer the plan themselves. In other jurisdictions, the employer may choose a private carrier or may self-insure. After an award is made, the employee will be notified. If the employee is not satisfied with the amount given, he or she may appeal to the state workers' compensation board. If the board affirms the award, the employee may appeal the decision in court. This will result in legal fees, court costs, and the loss of time. However, it may be a necessary evil when an award is unjustifiably deficient.

❖ EMPLOYER LESSONS

- Understand that workers' compensation applies only to work-related injuries.
- Learn that employees must give notice that a work-related injury was sustained.
- Know that employers are immune from lawsuits for employee work-related injuries.
- Be aware that, as an employer, you are absolutely liable for all injuries to employees occurring within the scope of employment.
- Be cognizant that workers' compensation is governed by a state board.
- Realize that employees may fraudulently claim that their injuries occurred on the job.
- Appreciate that you can contest an employee's claim if it is fraudulent.
- Be apprised that employees may collect workers' compensation even if they were negligent.
- Recognize that employers pay into the state funded workers' compensation program.
- Attempt to minimize work-related injuries to avoid having to pay workers' compensation.

❖ EMPLOYEE LESSONS

- Learn the history of the Master/Servant relationship.
- Know that employers were not liable for work-related injuries if employees were partially negligent.
- Understand the purpose of workers' compensation was to hold the employer absolutely liable for work-related injuries.
- Appreciate that employees gave up their right to sue in return for workers' compensation coverage.
- Be aware that you must report an injury to your employer.
- Be cognizant that you must then file a claim with the workers' compensation board.
- Recognize that workers' compensation is governed by each state.
- Realize that the injury must occur on the job.
- Do not submit a claim for an injury that is not work related and/or not fake an injury.
- Understand that discharge in retaliation for filing a workers' compensation claim is an exception to at-will termination.

❖ REVIEW QUESTIONS

1. Define workers' compensation.
2. Before workers' compensation, what procedure was followed when an employee was injured?
3. What defenses were available before workers' compensation that are no longer applicable?
4. Are there any instances in which an employer is not liable for an injured employee?
5. Explain the advantages of workers' compensation.
6. Define the fellow servant rule.
7. Who administers workers' compensation claims?
8. Prior to workers' compensation, why were employees afraid to testify?
9. Explain the benefits that an employee who suffers a temporary disability is entitled to receive.
10. What factor will determine an employer's liability?
11. Kunze was criminally assaulted on the way home from work. Kunze claimed that this situation was within the scope of employment and filed a claim for workers' compensation. The employer argued that it was no longer responsible once the employees had left for home. What was the result? *Kunze v. Columbus Police Dept.,* 600 N.E.2d. 697 (1991)
12. Robatin made a left turn from a busy intersection into the employer's plant. Robatin claimed this "turn" qualified him for workers' compensation under the special hazard rule. The employer argued that this risk was similar to risks encountered by the public in general. What was the result? *MTD Products, Inc. v. Robatin,* 572 N.E.2d 661 (1991)
13. Cory Grote, 16 years old, was a high school rodeo champion. After receiving permission from Bruce Bushnell, foreman, he was allowed to visit his brother Brad, at Joy Ranch, a division of Meyers. During his visit, Cory helped Brad release 12 colts into a corral. One of the colts, known to the ranchers to be uncontrollable, kicked Cory, causing him to have a skull fracture. Cory sued the ranch, claiming that the ranch was negligent in not informing him of the colt's dangerous propensities. Does Cory qualify for workers' compensation? *Grote v. Meyers Land and Cattle Co.,* 485 N.W.2d 748 (Neb. 1992)
14. Does a psychological condition qualify as a permanent disability? The employer claimed that only physical injuries meet the test. What was the result? *Bingham Memorial Hosp. v. Special Indemnity Fund,* 842 P.2d 273 (Idaho 1992)
15. Is an employee's voluntary exposure of himself to danger that results in an injury a bar to receiving workers' compensation? The employee argued that the employer is absolutely liable. What was the result? *Farmer v. Heard,* Ky. App. 844 S.W.2d 425 (1993)

16. Here, an injured worker has been found capable of part-time work in an occupation, but her earnings would be approximately one-third of her pre-injury wages. She claims that her earnings are so greatly reduced as to entitle her to a permanent total disability (PTD) award. What was the result? *Tee v. Albertsons,* Inc., 842 P.2d 3774 (Or. 1992)

17. The issue concerns whether the employee's disability is permanent. The employee argued that he is unable to do light work without interruption and that he could not find suitable employment elsewhere. The company claimed that the employee's contentions are unfounded. What was the result? *Asplundh Tree Expert Co. v. Challis,* 609 So.2d 135 (Fla. App. 1 Dist. 1992)

18. Can an employer question a prospective employee about whether he or she ever received workers' compensation and for what type of injury it was given? On an employment application, the employee was not forthcoming about his prior employment-related back injury. After he was hired, he sustained further back injuries. Must the new employer pay him although he lied on the job application? *Huisenga v. Opus Corp.,* 494 N.W.2d 469 (Minn. 1992)

19. Is an employer absolutely liable for an employee's injuries when the employee has voluntarily exposed himself to danger?

20. How is a decision regarding permanent disability arrived at?

❖ **WEB SITES**

www.findlaw.com

www.westbuslaw.com

www.benefitsnext.com/content/cats.cfm?cats_id-10&source=MiQ&effort=50

www.workcompsite.com/

www.business.com/directory/human_resources/compensation_and_benefits/
  workers_compensation/

www.encyclopedia.com/articles/13999.html

www.wcboard.com

21

EMPLOYEE RETIREMENT INCOME SECURITY ACT

INTRODUCTION

The Employee Retirement Income Security Act of 1974 (ERISA) divides employee benefit plans into pension plans and welfare plans. Pension plans provide income for retirement. Welfare plans include, but are not limited to, medical and insurance benefits.

CHAPTER CHECKLIST

❖ Define ERISA.

❖ Understand why ERISA was enacted.

❖ Learn what motivates employers to underfund their companies' pensions.

❖ Know what a defined benefit plan is.

❖ Be aware that a defined benefit pension is fixed.

❖ Be cognizant of what a defined contribution plan is.

❖ Appreciate the concept of vesting.

❖ Recognize the concept of graduated vesting.

❖ Realize the significance of pension income to retirees.

❖ Be apprised of the age for eligibility to participate in pension plans.

EMPLOYMENT SCENARIO

The Long and the Short of It, which is now in its tenth year of operation, set up a pension plan during its second year of operation. L&S's pension plan provides for a generous 12 percent contribution based on present salary for employees who contribute 5 percent to the plan. L&S's motivation for creating this plan was to entice superior salespeople to work for L&S. To date, their plan is severely underfunded due to L&S's failure to make any contributions to the pension plan after its third year of existence. Fourteen of L&S's employees have reached retirement age. L&S began funding payouts to the retirees from current operations, but now with layoffs and the closing of four stores, operating losses are mounting. Paying retirees is no longer possible. Susan North is notified of the ERISA violations. The retirees seek supplementation from the Pension Benefit Guarantee Corporation. L&S is sued for underfunding. Susan learns that Tom Long and Mark Short have been milking the company by paying themselves astronomical salaries. Susan pleads with Tom and Mark to personally make up the shortfall, but they will not relent. They state they would rather see L&S go into bankruptcy than to admit guilt.

DEFINED BENEFIT PLAN

Originally, pension plans provided a defined benefit based on the employee's salary and the number of years of service. The determination of the "employee's salary" may be based on an average over more than one year. The amount determined to be paid will be fixed for the remainder of the retiree's life. This amount, which may be generous on the date of retirement, may become seriously eroded after many years. While providing a larger percentage of a retiree's income initially, this will gradually decrease in comparison with social security and investment income, which will move to some extent with inflation.

DEFINED CONTRIBUTION PLAN

A more popular type of pension is the defined contribution plan. The income generated at retirement is not guaranteed as in the defined benefit plan. Rather, it depends on the contributions made by the employee. The employer may also contribute to this plan. The amount of the employer's contribution may be conditioned on the employee's contribution, or it may be independent. A positive element of this plan is that the payment upon retirement may either be fixed or vary with the investments in the employee's retirement plan.

Profit-sharing plans provide for employer contributions based on a formula or at the discretion of the employer.

ELIGIBILITY

An employee must be 21 years of age and have worked one year with the employer before becoming eligible to participate in that employer's pension plan.

The issue in the following case is whether the requirement for an amendment procedure to an employee benefit plan is satisfied by the language that the company reserves the right to amend the plan at any time.

CURTISS-WRIGHT CORP. v. SCHOONEJONGEN

514 U.S. 73 (1995)

JUSTICE O'CONNOR delivered the opinion of the Court.

Section 402(b)(3) of the Employee Retirement Income Security Act of 1974 (ERISA) requires that every employee benefit plan provide "a procedure for amending such plan, and for identifying the persons who have authority to amend the plan." This case presents the question whether the standard provision in many employer-provided benefit plans stating that "The Company reserves the right at any time to amend the plan" sets forth an amendment procedure that satisfies 402(b)(3). We hold that it does.

For many years, petitioner Curtiss-Wright voluntarily maintained a postretirement health plan for employees who had worked at certain Curtiss-Wright facilities; respondents are retirees who had worked at one such facility in Wood-Ridge, New Jersey. The specific terms of the plan, the District Court determined, could be principally found in two plan documents: the plan constitution and the Summary Plan Description (SPD), both of which primarily covered active employee health benefits.

In early 1983, presumably due to the rising cost of health care, a revised SPD was issued with the following new provision: "TERMINATION OF HEALTH CARE BENEFITS .... Coverage under this Plan will cease for retirees and their dependents upon the termination of business operations of the facility from which they retired." The two main authors of the new SPD provision, Curtiss-Wright's director of benefits and its labor counsel, testified that they did not think the provision effected a "change" in the plan, but rather merely clarified it. Probably for this reason, the record is less than clear as to which Curtiss-Wright officers or committees had authority to make plan amendments on behalf of the company and whether such officers or committees approved or ratified the new SPD provision. In any

event, later that year, Curtiss-Wright announced that the Wood-Ridge facility would close. Shortly thereafter, an executive vice president wrote respondents a series of letters informing them that their postretirement health benefits were being terminated.

Respondents brought suit in federal court over the termination of their benefits, and many years of litigation ensued. The District Court ultimately rejected most of respondents' claims, including their contention that Curtiss-Wright had bound itself contractually to provide health benefits to them for life. The District Court agreed, however, that the new SPD provision effected a significant change in the plan's terms and thus constituted an "amendment" to the plan; that the plan documents nowhere contained a valid amendment procedure, as required by 402(b)(3); and that the proper remedy for the 402(b)(3) violation was to declare the new SPD provision void. The court eventually ordered Curtiss-Wright to pay respondents $2,681,086 in back benefits.

On appeal, Curtiss-Wright primarily argued that the plan documents did contain an amendment procedure, namely, the standard reservation clause contained in the plan constitution and in a few secondary plan documents. The clause states: "The Company reserves the right at any time and from time to time to modify or amend, in whole or in part, any or all of the provisions of the Plan." In Curtiss-Wright's view, this clause sets forth an amendment procedure as required by the statute. It says, in effect, that the plan is to be amended by "the Company."

The Court of Appeals for the Third Circuit rejected this argument, as well as all other arguments before it, and affirmed the District Court's remedy.

In interpreting 402(b)(3), we are mindful that ERISA does not create any substantive entitlement to employer-provided health benefits or any other kind of welfare benefits. Employers or other plan sponsors are generally free under ERISA, for any reason at any time, to adopt, modify, or terminate welfare plans. "A company does not act in a fiduciary capacity when deciding to amend or terminate a welfare benefits plan." Nor does ERISA establish any minimum participation, vesting, or funding requirements for welfare plans as it does for pension Plans. Accordingly, that Curtiss-Wright amended its plan to deprive respondents of health benefits is not a cognizable complaint under ERISA; the only cognizable claim is that the company did not do so in a permissible manner.

The text of 402(b)(3) actually requires two things: a "procedure for amending the plan" and "a procedure for identifying the persons who have authority to amend the plan." With respect to the second requirement, the general "Definitions" section of ERISA makes quite clear that the term "person," wherever it appears in the statute, includes companies. ("The term 'person' means an individual, partnership, joint venture, corporation, mutual company, joint-stock company, trust, estate, unincorporated organization, association, or employee organization"). The Curtiss-Wright reservation clause thus appears to satisfy the statute's identification requirement by naming "the Company" as "the person" with amendment authority.

The more difficult question in this case is whether the Curtiss-Wright reservation clause contains a "procedure for amending the plan." To recall, the reservation clause says in effect that the plan may be amended "by the Company." Curtiss-Wright is correct, we think, that this states an amendment procedure and one that, like the identification procedure, is more substantial than might first appear. It says the plan may be amended by a unilateral company decision to amend, and only by such a decision - and not, for example, by the unilateral decision of a third-party trustee or upon the approval of the union. Moreover, to the extent that this procedure is the barest of procedures, that is because the Curtiss-Wright plan is the simplest of plans: a voluntarily maintained single-employer health plan that is administered by the employer and funded by the employer. More complicated plans, such as multiemployer plans, may have more complicated amendment procedures, and 402(b)(3) was designed to cover them as well.

In any event, the literal terms of 402(b)(3) are ultimately indifferent to the level of detail in an amendment procedure, or in an identification procedure for that matter. The provision requires only that there be an amendment procedure, which here there is.

Having determined that the Curtiss-Wright plan satisfies 402(b)(3), we do not reach the question of the proper remedy for a 402(b)(3) violation. On remand, the Court of Appeals will have to decide the question that has always been at the heart of this case: whether Curtiss-Wright's valid amendment procedure—amendment "by the Company"—was complied with in this case. The answer will depend on a fact-intensive inquiry, under applicable corporate law principles, into what persons or committees within Curtiss-Wright possessed plan amendment authority, either by express delegation or impliedly, and whether those persons or committees actually approved the new plan provision contained in the revised SPD. If the new plan provision is found not to have been properly authorized when issued, the question would then arise whether any subsequent actions, such as the executive vice president's letters informing respondents of the termination, served to ratify the provision. The judgment of the Court of Appeals is reversed, and the case is remanded for further proceedings consistent with this opinion.

Judgment for Curtiss-Wright Corp.

Case Commentary

The United States Supreme Court determined that the ERISA requirements for an amendment procedure and who will be responsible for administering it are satisfied by the language that the company reserves the right to amend the employee benefit plan at any time.

Case Questions

1. Are you in agreement with the Court's decision?
2. How could such general language be construed to identify an amendment procedure?
3. How can you determine from the term "company" who within the company is responsible for administering the amendment procedure?

VESTING

Vesting occurs when the employee acquires the right to the contribution made on his or her behalf by the employer. An employee may be partially or fully vested. An employee becomes partially vested if, beginning in the third year, the plan provides for 20 percent vesting for each of the next five years. In that way, by the end of the seventh year, the employee will be completely vested. This means that all contributions made by the employer belong to the employee. Vesting applies only to the employer's contribution. When the employee contributes his or her own money in a defined contribution plan, it always belongs to the employee.

The question presented in the following case is whether the employer's demand for a release of employment-related claims by an employee before payments are made according to an early retirement program is in violation of ERISA.

CASE

LOCKHEED CORP. v. SPINK

517 U.S. 882 (1996)

JUSTICE THOMAS delivered the opinion of the Court.
In this case, we decide whether the payment of benefits pursuant to an early retirement program conditioned on the participants' release of employment-related claims constitutes a prohibited transaction under the Employee Retirement Income Security Act of 1974 (ERISA). We also determine whether the 1986 amendments to ERISA and the Age Discrimination in Employment Act of 1967 (ADEA), forbidding age-based discrimination in pension plans apply retroactively.

I.

Respondent Paul Spink was employed by petitioner Lockheed Corporation from 1939 until 1950, when he left to work for one of Lockheed's competitors. In 1979, Lockheed persuaded Spink to return. Spink was 61 years old when he resumed employment with Lockheed. At that time, the terms of the Lockheed Retirement Plan for Certain Salaried Individuals (Plan), a defined benefit plan, excluded from participation employees who were over the age of 60 when hired. This was expressly permitted by ERISA.

Congress subsequently passed the Omnibus Budget Reconciliation Act of 1986 (OBRA), Section 9203(a)(1) of OBRA repealed the age-based exclusion provision of ERISA, and the statute now flatly mandates that "no pension plan may exclude from participation (on the basis of age) employees who have attained a specified age." In an effort to comply with these new laws, Lockheed ceased its prior practice of age-based exclusion from the Plan, effective December 25, 1988.

As of that date, all employees, including Spink, who had previously been ineligible to participate in the Plan due to their age at the time of hiring became members of the Plan. Lockheed made clear, however, that it would not credit those employees for years of service rendered before they became members.

Spink brought this suit, in his individual capacity and on behalf of others similarly situated, against Lockheed and several of its directors and officers. Among other things, the complaint alleged that Lockheed and the members of the board of directors violated ERISA's duty of care and prohibited transaction provisions by amending the Plan to create the retirement programs. The complaint also asserted that the OBRA amendments to ERISA and the ADEA required Lockheed to count Spink's pre-1988 service years toward his accrued pension benefits. Lockheed moved to dismiss the complaint for failure to state a claim, and the District Court granted the motion.

The Court of Appeals for the Ninth Circuit reversed in relevant part. The Plan was unlawful under ERISA, which prohibits a fiduciary from causing a plan to engage in a transaction that transfers plan assets to a party in interest or involves the use of plan assets for the benefit of a party in interest. The court reasoned that because the amendments offered increased benefits in exchange for a release of employment claims, they constituted a use of Plan assets to "purchase" a significant benefit for Lockheed. In addition, the Court of Appeals agreed with Spink that Lockheed had violated the OBRA amendments by refusing to include Spink's service years prior to 1988 in determining his benefits. In so holding, the court found that the OBRA amendments apply retroactively. We issued a writ of certiorari and now reverse.

II.

Nothing in ERISA requires employers to establish employee benefits plans. Nor does ERISA mandate what kind of benefits employers must provide if they choose to have such a plan. ERISA does, however, seek to ensure that employees will not be left empty-handed once employers have guaranteed them certain benefits. Accordingly, ERISA tries to "make as certain as possible that pension fund assets will be adequate" to meet expected benefits payments.

To increase the chances that employers will be able to honor their benefits commitments—that is, to guard against the possibility of bankrupt pension funds—Congress incorporated several key measures into the Act. Section 302 of ERISA sets minimum annual funding levels for all covered plans and creates tax liens in favor of such plans when those funding levels are not met. Sections 404 and 409 of ERISA impose respectively a duty of care with respect to the management of existing trust funds, along with liability for breach of that duty, upon plan fiduciaries. Finally, Section 406 of ERISA prohibits fiduciaries from involving the plan and its assets in certain kinds of business deals. It is this last feature of ERISA that is at issue today.

Congress enacted Section 406 "to bar categorically a transaction that is likely to injure the pension plan." That section mandates, in relevant part, that "a fiduciary with respect to a plan shall not cause the plan to engage in a transaction, if he knows or should know that such transaction constitutes a direct or indirect . . . transfer to, or use by or for the benefit of a party in interest, of any assets of the plan." The question here is whether this provision of ERISA prevents an employer from conditioning the receipt of early retirement benefits upon the participants' waiver of employment claims. For the following reasons, we hold that it does not.

III.

Section 406(a)(1) regulates the conduct of plan fiduciaries, placing certain transactions outside the scope of their lawful authority. When a fiduciary violates the rules set forth in Section 406(a)(1), Section 409 of ERISA renders him personally liable for any losses incurred by the plan, any ill-gotten profits, and other equitable and remedial relief deemed appropriate by the court. But in order to sustain an alleged transgression of Section(s) 406(a), a plaintiff must show that a fiduciary caused the plan to engage in the allegedly unlawful transaction. Unless a plaintiff can make that showing, there can be no violation of Section(s) 406(a)(1) to warrant relief under the enforcement provisions.

A.

We first address the allegation in Spink's complaint that Lockheed and the board of directors breached their fiduciary duties when they adopted

to work as a brokerage manager for the Greater New York Brokerage Agency. In 1978, Lehman was relocated and promoted to agency manager of the brokerage agency in Boston, Massachusetts. In 1986, Prudential expanded the territory of the agency run by Lehman, making him director of its New England Brokerage Agency which included all of New England except Fairfield County in Connecticut. Even after the expansion, the New England agency was relatively small; nevertheless, it performed very well under Lehman's direction. In 1988, Prudential created Pru Select, a separate sales division of Prudential's life insurance business, to supervise the twelve regional brokerage agencies. Ira Kleinman was appointed President of Pru Select, and he hired Roger Dunker as Pru Select's Senior Vice President. Dunker, along with Lehman's prior supervisors, gave Lehman glowing performance reviews.

Effective January 1, 1990, Pru Select revised its pension plan by changing the commencement year for calculating average eligible earnings from 1979 to 1983, benefitting more senior employees, and by providing a 50% annuity to widows without charge to the employee, benefitting Lehman whose wife is fifteen years younger than he. Lehman projected the additional cost to Prudential of his pension, in light of the above modifications, to be $500,000.

Also at that time, Pru Select overhauled and streamlined its brokerage agencies. It consolidated its twelve regions and directors into five regions and seven directors. In December of 1990, Dunker told Lehman that as of April 1, 1991, his New England office was going to be consolidated with the entire New York territory and part of the New Jersey territory. Lehman was to assume the duties and compensation scheme of a brokerage manager and report to the co-managing directors in the newly created Northeast region: Robert Kiley, the pre-consolidation director of the New York office, and the newly hired David Dietz. According to Lehman, his income potential as brokerage manager could be less than 25% of what it had been as a director. Lehman was instructed to formulate his own unit of brokers in New England from whom he could solicit business. However, he did not feel that this was possible, and after several meetings in which he attempted to define his new unit, he wrote to Dunker stating

that the reassignment of his responsibilities constituted involuntary termination motivated by age discrimination. Lehman then accepted an early retirement package.

Before the merger, Lehman, aged 61, directed the New England office, and Kiley, aged 57, directed the New York office. After consolidation of the two offices into the new Northeast region, the latter was headed jointly by Kiley and the 42-year-old Dietz.

II. THIS COURT REVIEWS THE DISTRICT COURT'S GRANT OF SUMMARY JUDGMENT

Pension Discrimination Claim (ERISA) Lehman's second claim against Prudential was for unlawful pension discrimination in violation of section 510 of ERISA: any person to discharge, fine, suspend, expel, discipline, or discriminate against a participant or beneficiary for exercising any right to which he is entitled under the provisions of an employee benefit plan . . . for the purpose of interfering with the attainment of any right to which such participant may become entitled under the plan.

Lehman alleged that Prudential hired a younger person for the co-managing director position to avoid the high cost of funding his pension. This circuit, along with most others, analyzes ERISA discrimination claims under the same three stage burden-shifting paradigm described above. In the first stage, Lehman must set forth a prima facie case by demonstrating that: (1) he had the opportunity to attain rights under an ERISA benefit plan; (2) he was qualified for the position at issue; and (3) he was subjected to adverse action under circumstances that give rise to an inference of discrimination. We again assume *arguendo*, without deciding, that Lehman set forth a prima facie case.

To dispel the inference of discrimination arising from a prima facie case, Prudential must only articulate, it need not prove, a non-discriminatory reason for its hiring decision. Lehman conceded that Prudential "articulated a legitimate, non-discriminatory reason for its action . . . namely that it selected Dietz instead of Lehman for the position of co-Managing Director because of Dietz' supposedly superior qualifications for the position."

At the third stage, Lehman must show that Prudential was motivated by "the specific intent of interfering with the employee's ERISA benefits." ERISA provides no relief if the loss of an employee's benefits was incidental to, and not the reason for, the adverse employment action. Were this not so, every discharged employee who had been a member of a benefit plan would have a potential cause of action against his or her former employer under ERISA. To demonstrate that Prudential acted with the specific intention of interfering with Lehman's ERISA benefits, Lehman must show "(1) that Prudential's articulated reason for its employment actions was a pretext; *and* (2) that the true reason was to interfere with Lehman's receipt of benefits." On this record, we find no genuine issue of fact either that Prudential was motivated by a discriminatory purpose or that Prudential's reason for not hiring Lehman co-managing director was not credible.

Effective January 1, 1990, Prudential made adjustments to its company-wide pension plan which Lehman estimates increased Prudential's cost of funding his pension by about $500,000 over time. Lehman contends that Prudential was aware of the high cost of his benefits and refused to offer him the co-managing director position in an effort to reduce this cost (pension benefit obligations being lesser for younger people). Lehman again points to Kleinman's statement

that benefits actually cost more than they had been estimating because of "the age of some of the Directors."

Viewing the evidence in the light most favorable to Lehman, we find nothing that would cause a reasonable fact-finder to doubt Prudential's explanation for its hiring decision. Prudential's mere awareness of the high cost of pension obligations combined with the single isolated ambiguous remark by Kleinman were insufficient, by themselves, to establish Prudential's discriminatory intent. Lehman did not contradict deposition testimony that Prudential's benefit costs were calculated on a company-wide basis, and that Pru Select's top management, who made the hiring decision, received no individual employee calculation of pension costs. Nor did Lehman contradict deposition testimony that Prudential did not have knowledge of his wife's age, knowledge that would be necessary to compute his pension obligation. No material connection appears between the cost of funding Lehman's pension and Prudential's decision to hire Dietz rather than Lehman. We are satisfied that the record would not support a finding that Prudential did not hire Lehman as co-managing director because of the cost of funding his pension.

Affirmed.

Judgment for Prudential Ins. Co.

Case Commentary

The First Circuit Court of Appeals resolved that Prudential was not guilty of pension discrimination when it terminated Lehman and

replaced him with a younger worker who was more experienced.

Case Questions

1. Are you in agreement with the Court's decision?
2. Do you believe the cost of funding Lehman's pension had nothing to do with his termination?

3. Is there any protection afforded to Lehman in this situation?

PURPOSE

ERISA was introduced in response to unfair practices by employers. Numerous pension funds were underfunded. Therefore, when an employee retired, there was no guarantee that the money would be there for his or her pension. This situation occurred often in companies that went out of business. ERISA imposed minimum funding standards in response to this problem. Companies also had peculiar rules regarding age and years of service as the following examples will illustrate.

EMPLOYMENT PERSPECTIVE

Joan Thompson worked for 41 years for Bullseye Distillery in Memphis, Tennessee. When the plant closed down, Joan was offered a position in the Lexington, Kentucky, plant. She refused because she was 63½. When she reached age 65, she applied to Bullseye for pension benefits but was turned down because she had left the company before retirement. How would ERISA have addressed this problem? Joan would have been completely vested after either five years or seven years if the graduated method had been used. The retirement benefits lost by leaving the job one and one-half years before her retirement would have been negligible. ■

EMPLOYMENT PERSPECTIVE

Dennis Lynch had worked as a blackjack dealer for Shore Road Casino for 17 years. He left for a job in Crazy Horse Casino when he was 55. At 65, he applied to Shore Road for pension benefits. Dennis was denied because he had worked for Shore Road only 10 out of the last 20 years, whereas 15 years out of 20 years immediately prior to retirement is required. How would this situation work out under ERISA? Dennis would have been completely vested for the contributions made by Shore Road Casino for his 17 years of service and would have been entitled to collect these upon his retirement. ■

EMPLOYMENT PERSPECTIVE

Marjorie Quinn worked as a legal stenographer for Westfield, Morgan, and Kane (WMK) for 15 years before resigning at age 35 after the birth of her son. At age 50, after her sons had entered high school, she resumed stenographic work with WMK until retirement. When she applied for pension benefits, the law firm denied her because she had not served 20 years consecutively. Under ERISA, what would happen today? Marjorie would have become fully vested during her first service with the firm. Her 15-year absence would have had no effect on the situation. On her return, she would have continued to be fully vested in all the contributions made both before and after her absence. Marjorie would have been entitled to all these benefits upon retirement. ■

EMPLOYMENT PERSPECTIVE

Matthew Price had worked as a foreman for the Stingray Automobile Company for 35 years when he was forced to resign because of kidney failure. He was 53 years old at the time. When he reached 65, he applied for pension benefits. Matthew was turned down because only those who worked with the company until age 55 were entitled to a pension. How would he be treated under ERISA? Matthew would have been fully vested and entitled to all the employer contributions made during his 35 years of service. Under ERISA, mistreatment of an individual who had contributed lengthy service to one employer would have been prevented. ■

The issue in the case that follows is whether an officer of the corporation was a fiduciary under ERISA, and thus personally liable for fraudulent transfers of corporate assets that were going to be used to fund an ERISA judgment against the corporation.

PEACOCK v. THOMAS

516 U.S. 349 (1996)

JUSTICE THOMAS delivered the opinion of the Court.

This case presents the issue whether federal courts possess ancillary jurisdiction over new actions in which a federal judgment creditor seeks to impose liability for a money judgment on a person not otherwise liable for the judgment. We hold that they do not.

I

Respondent Jack L. Thomas is a former employee of Tru-Tech, Inc. In 1987, Thomas filed an ERISA class action in federal court against Tru-Tech and petitioner D. Grant Peacock, an officer and shareholder of Tru-Tech, for benefits due under the corporation's pension benefits plan. Thomas alleged primarily that Tru-Tech and Peacock breached their fiduciary duties to the class in administering the plan. The District Court found that Tru-Tech had breached its fiduciary duties, but ruled that Peacock was not a fiduciary. On November 28, 1988, the District Court entered judgment in the amount of $187,628.93 against Tru-Tech only. On April 3, 1990, the Court of Appeals for the Fourth Circuit affirmed. Thomas did not execute the judgment while the case was on appeal and, during that time, Peacock settled many of Tru-Tech's accounts with favored creditors, including himself.

After the Court of Appeals affirmed the judgment, Thomas unsuccessfully attempted to collect the judgment from Tru-Tech. Thomas then sued Peacock in federal court, claiming that Peacock had entered into a civil conspiracy to siphon assets from Tru-Tech to prevent satisfaction of the ERISA judgment. Thomas also claimed that Peacock fraudulently conveyed Tru-Tech's assets in violation of South Carolina and Pennsylvania law. Thomas later amended his complaint to assert a claim for "Piercing the Corporate Veil Under ERISA and Applicable Federal Law." The District Court ultimately agreed to pierce the corporate veil and entered judgment against Peacock in the amount of $187,628.93—the precise amount of the judgment against Tru-Tech—plus interest and fees, notwithstanding the fact that Peacock's alleged fraudulent transfers totalled no more than $80,000. The Court of Appeals affirmed, holding that the District Court properly exercised ancillary jurisdiction over Thomas' suit. We granted certiorari to determine whether the District Court had subject-matter jurisdiction and to resolve a conflict among the Courts of Appeals. We now reverse.

II

Thomas relies on the Employee Retirement Income Security Act of 1974 (ERISA) as the source of federal jurisdiction for this suit. The District Court did not expressly rule on subject matter jurisdiction, but found that Thomas had properly stated a claim under ERISA for piercing the corporate veil. We disagree. We are not aware of, and Thomas does not point to, any provision of ERISA that provides for imposing liability for an extant ERISA judgment against a third party.

("ERISA does not provide an enforcement mechanism for collecting judgments ....")

Moreover, Thomas' veil-piercing claim does not state a cause of action under ERISA and cannot independently support federal jurisdiction. Even if ERISA permits a plaintiff to pierce the corporate veil to reach a defendant not otherwise subject to suit under ERISA, Thomas could invoke the jurisdiction of the federal courts only by independently alleging a violation of an ERISA provision or term of the plan. Piercing the corporate veil is not itself an independent ERISA cause of action, "but rather is a means of imposing liability on an underlying cause of action." Because Thomas alleged no "underlying" violation of any provision of ERISA or an ERISA plan, neither ERISA's jurisdictional provision, supplied the District Court with subject matter jurisdiction over this suit.

In this suit, Thomas alleged civil conspiracy and fraudulent transfer of Tru-Tech's assets, but, as we have noted, no substantive ERISA violation. The alleged wrongdoing in this case occurred after the ERISA judgment was entered, and Thomas' claims—civil conspiracy, fraudulent conveyance, and "veil-piercing"—all involved new theories of liability not asserted in the ERISA suit. Other than the existence of the ERISA judgment itself, this suit has little connection to the ERISA case. This is a new action based on theories of relief that did not exist, and could not have existed, at the time the court entered judgment in the ERISA case.

For these reasons, we hold that the District Court lacked jurisdiction over Thomas' subsequent suit. Accordingly, the judgment of the Court of Appeals is

Reversed.
Judgment for Peacock.

Case Commentary

The United States Supreme Court determined that ERISA does not provide for the collection of judgments against third parties.

Case Questions

1. Are you in accord with the Court's decision?
2. Is it unfair that Peacock should be able to fraudulently transfer corporate assets to obviate the payment of corporate pension benefits?
3. Is there any other way for Thomas to enforce the judgment against Peacock?

MINIMUM FUNDING REQUIREMENTS

ERISA requires minimum funding requirements. The fiduciaries who administer the plan are required to act prudently when making investments. In addition, ERISA established the Pension Benefit Guarantee Corporation (PBGC), a not-for-profit enterprise administered by the Secretary of Labor to guard against loss of benefits when pension plans are terminated by companies. Employers are required to purchase pension termination insurance. There are maximum limits; retirees are insured up to the full value of their pensions, as long as the value does not exceed the maximum limit. Employees currently working who are vested are insured up to the value of the pension upon termination.

EMPLOYMENT PERSPECTIVE

Nancy Woodward worked for Z Mart Department Stores for 40 years. Two years after her retirement at age 65, Nancy began to collect her pension. When Z Mart went out of business, her benefits were reduced by 70 percent because the pension plan was underfunded. How would she be treated under ERISA? The likelihood is that Z Mart's pension would be better funded and more prudently invested under ERISA to guard against loss of benefits. But if the plan was still inadequate, PBGC would step in and provide proceeds from its termination insurance fund. The amount that Z Mart was underfunded would be covered up to a maximum amount. ■

FIDUCIARY DUTIES

A fiduciary's duty is one of trust and confidence. A pension plan trustee is required to exercise prudence in the management of a pension's investments. In a defined contribution plan, the employee usually has discretion to allocate risk by selecting among a number of mutual funds. The range of funds will usually be from conservative to aggressive.

In a defined benefit plan, the employee has no say over the risk level of the pension plan's investments. Because of thus, the duty of care owed by the fiduciary is greater in that the total responsibility falls upon him or her to act in a prudent manner. The defined benefit is paid according to a formula such as an average of the three final years of salary times the number of years of service times 2 percent.

EMPLOYMENT PERSPECTIVE

Ronald Fishburn was employed by Marvelous Muffins, a gourmet bakery chain, where he worked for 30 years until retirement. Ronald's salaries for his final three years were $38,000, $40,000, and $42,000. How much will Ronald's pension be? His average salary was $40,000; $40,000 $\times$ 30 years of service = $1,200,000 $\times$ 2% = $24,000 per year pension. ■

The issue in the following case is whether a group of beneficiaries, who transferred out of the company's welfare benefit plan base because of false information provided by the company, can seek reinstatement into the company's plan.

CASE

VARITY CORP. v. HOWE

516 U.S. 489 (1996)

JUSTICE BREYER delivered the opinion of the Court.
A group of beneficiaries of a firm's employee welfare benefit plan, protected by the Employee Retirement Income Security Act of 1974 (ERISA) have sued their plan's administrator, who was also their employer. They claim that the administrator, through trickery, led them to withdraw from the plan and to forfeit their benefits. They seek, among other things, an order that, in essence, would reinstate each of them as a participant in the employer's ERISA plan. The lower courts entered judgment in the employees' favor, and we agreed to review that judgment.

In conducting our review, we do not question the lower courts' findings of serious deception by the employer, but instead consider three legal questions. First, in the factual circumstances (as determined by the lower courts), was the employer acting in its capacity as an ERISA "fiduciary" when it significantly and deliberately misled the beneficiaries? Second, in misleading the beneficiaries, did the employer violate the fiduciary obligations that ERISA 404 imposes upon plan administrators? Third, does ERISA 502(a)(3) authorize ERISA plan beneficiaries to bring a lawsuit, such as this one, that seeks relief for individual beneficiaries harmed by an administrator's breach of fiduciary obligations?

We answer each of these questions in the beneficiaries' favor, and we therefore affirm the judgment of the Court of Appeals.

The key facts, as found by the District Court after trial, include the following: Charles Howe, and the other respondents, used to work for Massey-Ferguson, Inc., a farm equipment manufacturer, and a wholly-owned subsidiary of the petitioner, Varity Corporation. (Since the lower courts found that Varity and Massey-Ferguson were "alter egos," we shall refer to them interchangeably.) These employees all were participants in, and beneficiaries of, Massey-Ferguson's self-funded employee welfare benefit plan—an ERISA-protected plan that Massey-Ferguson itself administered. In the mid-1980's, Varity became concerned that some of Massey-Ferguson's divisions were losing too much money and developed a business plan to deal with the problem.

The business plan—which Varity called "Project Sunshine"—amounted to placing many of Varity's money-losing eggs in one financially rickety basket. It called for a transfer of Massey-Ferguson's money-losing divisions, along with various other debts, to a newly created, separately incorporated subsidiary called Massey Combines. The plan foresaw the possibility that Massey Combines would fail. But it viewed such a failure, from Varity's business perspective, as closer to a victory than to a defeat. That is because Massey Combine's failure would not only eliminate several of Varity's poorly performing divisions, but it would also eradicate various debts that Varity would transfer to Massey Combines, and which, in the absence of the reorganization, Varity's more profitable subsidiaries or divisions might have to pay.

Among the obligations that Varity hoped the reorganization would eliminate were those arising from the Massey-Ferguson benefit plan's promises to pay medical and other nonpension benefits to employees of Massey-Ferguson's money-losing divisions. Rather than terminate those benefits directly (as it had retained the right to do), Varity attempted to avoid the undesirable fallout that could have accompanied cancellation by inducing the failing divisions' employees to switch employers and thereby voluntarily release Massey-Ferguson from its obligation to provide them benefits (effectively substituting the new, self-funded Massey Combines benefit plan for the former Massey-Ferguson plan). Insofar as Massey-Ferguson's employees did so, a subsequent Massey Combines failure would eliminate—simply and automatically, without distressing the remaining Massey-

Ferguson employees—what would otherwise have been Massey-Ferguson's obligation to pay those employees their benefits.

To persuade the employees of the failing divisions to accept the change of employer and benefit plan, Varity called them together at a special meeting and talked to them about Massey Combines' future business outlook, its likely financial viability, and the security of their employee benefits. The thrust of Varity's remarks was that the employees' benefits would remain secure if they voluntarily transferred to Massey Combines. As Varity knew, however, the reality was very different. Indeed, the District Court found that Massey Combines was insolvent from the day of its creation and that it hid a $46 million negative net worth by overvaluing its assets and underestimating its liabilities.

After the presentation, about 1,500 Massey-Ferguson employees accepted Varity's assurances and voluntarily agreed to the transfer. (Varity also unilaterally assigned to Massey Combines the benefit obligations it owed to some 4,000 workers who had retired from Massey-Ferguson prior to this reorganization, without requesting permission or informing them of the assignment.) Unfortunately for these employees, Massey Combines ended its first year with a loss of $88 million, and ended its second year in a receivership, under which its employees lost their nonpension benefits. Many of those employees (along with several retirees whose benefit obligations Varity had assigned to Massey Combines and others whose claims we do not now consider) brought this lawsuit, seeking the benefits they would have been owed under their old, Massey-Ferguson plan, had they not transferred to Massey Combines.

After trial, the District Court found, among other things, that Varity and Massey-Ferguson, acting as ERISA fiduciaries, had harmed the plan's beneficiaries through deliberate deception. The court held that Varity and Massey-Ferguson thereby violated an ERISA-imposed fiduciary obligation to administer Massey-Ferguson's benefit plan "solely in the interest of the participants and beneficiaries" of the plan. ERISA 404(a). The Court added that ERISA 502(a)(3) gave the former Massey-Ferguson employees a right to "appropriate equitable relief . . . to redress" the harm that this deception had caused them individually. Among other remedies the Court considered "appropriate equitable relief," was an order that

Massey-Ferguson reinstate its former employees into its own plan (which had continued to provide benefits to employees of Massey-Ferguson's profitable divisions). The court also ordered certain monetary relief which is not at issue here. The Court of Appeals later affirmed the District Court's determinations, in relevant part.

We granted certiorari in this case primarily because the Courts of Appeals have disagreed about the proper interpretation of ERISA 502(a)(3), the provision the District Court held authorized the lawsuit and relief in this case. ERISA protects employee pensions and other benefits by providing insurance for vested pension rights, specifying certain plan characteristics in detail (such as when and how pensions vest), and by setting forth certain general fiduciary duties applicable to the management of both pension and nonpension benefit plans.

We begin with the question of Varity's fiduciary status. In relevant part, the statute says that a "person is a fiduciary with respect to a plan," and therefore subject to ERISA fiduciary duties, "to the extent" that he or she "exercises any discretionary authority or discretionary control respecting management" of the plan, or "has any discretionary authority or discretionary responsibility in the administration" of the ERISA plan.

Varity was both an employer and the benefit plan's administrator, as ERISA permits. But, obviously, not all of Varity's business activities involved plan management or administration. Varity argues that when it communicated with its Massey-Ferguson workers about transferring to Massey Combines, it was not administering or managing the plan; rather, it was acting only in its capacity as an employer and not as a plan administrator.

The eight questions and answers on the question-and-answer sheet include three that relate to welfare benefits or to the ERISA pension plan Varity also administered:

"Q. 3. What happens to my benefits, pension, etc.?

"A. 3. When you transfer to MCC [Massey Combines], pay levels and benefit programmes will remain unchanged.

There will be no loss of seniority or pensionable service.

"Q. 4. Do you expect the terms and conditions of employment to change?

"A. 4. Employment conditions in the future will depend on our ability to make Massey Combines Corporation a success and if changes are considered necessary or appropriate, they will be made.

. . . . .

"Q. 8. Are the pensions protected under MCC?

"A. 8. Responsibility for pension benefits earned by employees transferring to Massey Combines Corporation is being assumed by the Massey Combines Corporation Pension Plan.

"The assets which are held in the Massey Ferguson Pension Plan to fund such benefits as determined by actuarial calculations, are being transferred to the Massey Combines Corporation Plan. Such benefits and assets will be protected by the same legislation that protect the Massey Ferguson Pension Plan.

"There will be no change in pension benefits as a result of your transfer to Massey Combines Corporation."

The transcript of the 90-second videotape message repeated much of the information in the question-and-answer sheet, adding assurances about Massey Combines' viability.

The cover letter, in five short paragraphs, repeated verbatim these benefit-related assurances.

Given this record material, the District Court determined, as a factual matter, that the key meeting, to a considerable extent, was about benefits, for the documents described them in detail, explained the similarity between past and future plans in principle, and assured the employees that they would continue to receive similar benefits in practice. The District Court concluded that the basic message conveyed to the employees was that transferring from Massey-Ferguson to Massey Combines would not significantly undermine the security of their benefits. And, given this view of the facts, we believe that the District Court reached the correct legal conclusion, namely, that Varity spoke, in significant part, in its capacity as plan administrator.

The second question—whether Varity's deception violated ERISA-imposed fiduciary obligations—calls for a brief, affirmative answer. ERISA requires a "fiduciary" to "discharge his duties with respect to a plan solely in the interest of the participants and beneficiaries." To participate knowingly and significantly in deceiving a plan's beneficiaries in order to save the employer money at the beneficiaries' expense, is not to act "solely in the interest of the participants and beneficiaries."

The remaining question before us is whether or not the remedial provision of ERISA that the beneficiaries invoked, ERISA 502(a)(3), authorizes this lawsuit for individual relief. That subsection is the third of six subsections contained within ERISA's "Civil Enforcement" provision (as it stood at the times relevant to this lawsuit):

"Sec. 502. (a) A civil action may be brought—

"(1) by a participant or beneficiary—

"(A) for the relief provided for in subsection (c) of this section [providing for liquidated damages for failure to provide certain information on request], or

"(B) to recover benefits due to him under the terms of his plan, to enforce his rights under the terms of the plan, or to clarify his rights to future benefits under the terms of the plan;

"(2) by the Secretary, or by a participant, beneficiary or fiduciary for appropriate relief;

"(3) by a participant, beneficiary, or fiduciary (A) to enjoin any act or practice which violates any provision of this title or the terms of the plan, or (B) to obtain other appropriate equitable relief (i) to redress such violations or (ii) to enforce any provisions of this title or the terms of the plan;

"(4) by the Secretary, or by a participant, or beneficiary for appropriate relief in the case of a violation of 105(c) [requiring disclosure of certain tax registration statements];

"(5) except as otherwise provided in subsection (b), by the Secretary (A) to enjoin any act or practice which violates any provision of this title, or (B) to obtain other appropriate equitable relief (i) to redress such violation or (ii) to enforce any provision of this title; or

"(6) by the Secretary to collect any civil penalty under subsection (i)

The District Court held that the third subsection, which we have italicized, authorized this suit and the relief awarded. Varity concedes that the plaintiffs satisfy most of this provision's requirements, namely that the plaintiffs are plan "participants" or "beneficiaries," and that they are suing for "equitable" relief to "redress" a violation of 404(a), which is a "provision of this title."

Section 409(a), in turn, reads:

"Liability for Breach of Fiduciary Duty

Sec. 409. (a) Any person who is a fiduciary with respect to a plan who breaches any of the responsibilities, obligations, or duties imposed upon fiduciaries by this title shall be personally liable to make good to such plan any losses to the plan resulting from each such breach, and to restore to such plan any profits of such fiduciary which have been made through use of assets of the plan by the fiduciary, and shall be subject to such other equitable or remedial relief as the court may deem appropriate, including removal of such fiduciary. . . ."

ERISA makes clear that a fiduciary has obligations other than, and in addition to, managing plan assets. The plaintiffs in this case could not proceed under the first subsection because they were no longer members of the Massey-Ferguson plan and, therefore, had no "benefits due them under the terms of the plan."

They could not proceed under the second subsection because that provision, tied to 409, does not provide a remedy for individual beneficiaries. They must rely on the third subsection or they have no remedy at all. We are not aware of any ERISA-related purpose that denial of a remedy would serve. Rather, we believe that granting a remedy is consistent with the literal language of the statute, the Act's purposes, and pre-existing trust law.

For these reasons, the judgment of the Court of Appeals is Affirmed.

Judgment for Howe.

Case Commentary

The United States Supreme Court ruled that the company must reinstate those beneficiaries who opted out of welfare benefit program because of false information provided by the company. The company was a fiduciary, and was guilty of deception. The beneficiaries have the right to maintain an action for reinstatement under ERISA.

Case Questions

1. Are you in accord with the Court's resolution?
2. What motivated the company to provide false information to the beneficiaries?
3. How did the company think it was going to get away with this deception?
4. Do you believe whatever officers devised this scheme should be held personally liable?

INFLATION

In a defined benefit pension, the amount per year is fixed. What may seem to be a generous amount initially will erode over time because of inflation. Defined contribution plans usually offer a choice of graduated payments that will increase as time goes by. If a fixed amount is taken, the retiree must be disciplined enough to save a portion to offset the loss of purchasing power down the road.

EMPLOYMENT PERSPECTIVE

John Jacobs retired from Bull and Bear Investment Company after 40 years of service at age 65. The defined benefit pension plan paid him $7,000, which was a generous amount at the time. He is now 92 years old. The pension, which by itself provided for him and his wife at retirement, today provides about one-quarter of their needs. ■

A multifunded pension plan is one into which several companies contribute. It is usually formed in response to provisions in collective bargaining agreements, which stipulate that employees be given credit for length of service toward a pension when they work for more than one member of the plan.

TAX INCENTIVES

Although employers are not obligated to offer any benefits, a tax incentive exists for an employer that makes contributions to a qualified plan. A qualified plan is one that meets the requirements of the Internal Revenue Code. The tax incentive is a deduction for all employer contributions to the pension trust fund from which benefits will ultimately be paid to the employees. The monies paid into the trust fund do not have to be reported by the employees until they receive the benefits. This deferral helps the income grow faster because it is tax free. Thus, pension benefits can be paid out with smaller initial investments by the employer. This tax-free deferral plan can be withdrawn if the plan no longer qualifies under the Internal Revenue code because of violations surrounding vesting or other fiduciary responsibilities. Enforcement of ERISA is spread out among various federal departments. The Department of Labor receives ERISA plan reports and initiates civil suits for violations of reporting and disclosure. The employee plans and exempt organizations component of the Internal Revenue Service deals with tax law violations of the Internal Revenue Code and can authorize removal of qualified plan status for tax deferral of pension contributions. The Pension Benefit Guaranty corporation actively pursues employers that have underfunded plans, particularly those employers that are in bankruptcy. Finally, the Department of Justice pursues criminal violations of ERISA, such as embezzlement of funds.

❖ EMPLOYER LESSONS

- Understand the ramifications of ERISA.
- Keep your pension plan fully funded.
- Learn what constitutes a defined benefit plan.
- Know how to construct a defined contribution plan.
- Realize that a defined contribution plan invites employees to allocate income to the plan.
- Recognize that a defined contribution plan may guard against inflation.
- Be cognizant that defined benefit plans are fully funded by employers.
- Be aware that an employer can determine the amount, if any, that it wants to allocate to a defined contribution plan.
- Determine when an employee becomes vested.
- Be apprised that the age for pension eligibility is 21.

❖ EMPLOYEE LESSONS

- Know the impact ERISA has on your pension.
- Determine whether your employer is fully funding your pension plan.
- Be aware whether your employer offers a defined benefit plan or a defined contribution plan.
- Understand what each plan is about.
- Learn whether your employer will match your pension contribution up to a predetermined amount.
- Realize the importance pension income has on your retirement income.
- Appreciate the concept of vesting.
- Be apprised of the amount of time required before you become vested.
- Be cognizant of the fact that pension eligibility begins at 21 years of age.
- Recognize that the PBGC aids retirees who are victimized by underfunded pension plans.

❖ REVIEW QUESTIONS

1. Define ERISA.
2. Explain the difference between a defined benefit plan and a defined contribution plan.
3. Define profit-sharing plans.
4. When does an employee become eligible to participate in a company's pension plan?
5. Define vesting.
6. Explain the graduated method of vesting.
7. If an employee is discharged prior to vesting, what happens to his or her contributions?
8. When can employees access their contributions?
9. Are many pension plans underfunded?
10. Who administers pension plans?
11. Can a company's contributions to its employees' pension fund be something other than cash?
12. Why would a company want to be part of a multifunded pension plan?
13. McGann sued H&H Music Co., claiming violation of ERISA when H&H severely reduced health benefits for employees with AIDS. What was the result? *McGann v. H&H Music Co.,* 946 F.2d 401 (5th Cir. 1991)
14. Seaman was discharged by Arvida Realty Sales when it learned of Seaman's life-threatening illness. Seaman contended that Arvida violated ERISA by discharging him

to avoid paying benefits. What was the result? *Seaman v. Arvida Realty Co.,* 985 F.2d 543 (11th Cir. 1993)

15. This case addresses the issue of whether an insurance agent is an employee and, if so, must forfeit his retirement benefits if he violates a restrictive covenant. The restrictive covenant was designed to prohibit the employee from working for competitors in the same vicinity for a period of one year. What was the result? *Nationwide Mutual Insurance Company v. Robert T. Darden,* 112 S. Ct. 1344 (1992)

16. Petitioner Ingersoll-Rand employed respondent Perry McClendon as a salesman and distributor of construction equipment. In 1981, after McClendon had worked for the company for nine years and eight months, the company fired him citing a companywide reduction in force. McClendon sued the company in Texas state court, alleging that his pension would have vested in another four months and that a principal reason for his termination was the company's desire to avoid making contributions to his pension fund. What was the result? *Ingersoll-Rand Company v. Perry McClendon,* 494 U.S. 133 (1990)

17. The Hazens hired respondent Walter F. Biggins as their technical director in 1977. They fired him in 1986, when he was 62 years old.

    The Hazen Paper pension plan had a 10-year vesting period and respondent would have reached the 10-year mark had he worked "a few more weeks" after being fired. There was also testimony that petitioners had offered to retain respondent as a consultant to Hazen Paper, in which capacity he would not have been entitled to receive pension benefits. What was the result? *Hazen Paper Company v. Walter F. Biggins,* 113 S. Ct. 1701 (1993)

18. Can a company contribute real property to the pension fund and, if so, what are the tax consequences of such a contribution? What was the result? *Commissioner of Internal Revenue v. Keystone Consolidated Industries, Inc.,* 113 S. Ct. 2006 (1993)

19. The question presented is whether a non-fiduciary who knowingly participates in the breach of a fiduciary duty imposed by the Employee Retirement Income Security Act of 1974 (ERISA) is liable for losses that an employee benefit plan suffers as a result of the breach. What was the result? *Mertens v. Hewitt Associates,* 113 S. Ct. 2063 (1993)

20. Construction Laborers Pension Trust for Southern California (the Plan) is a multiemployer pension trust fund established under a Trust Agreement executed in 1962. Concrete Pipe is an employer and former contributor to the Plan that withdrew from it and was assessed "withdrawal liability" under provisions of the Employee Retirement Income Security Act of 1974 (ERISA), added by the Multiemployer Pension Plan Amendments Act of 1980 (MPPAA). Concrete Pipe contends that the MPPAA's assessment and arbitration provisions worked to deny it procedural due process. What was the result? *Concrete Pipe Inc. v. Construction Laborers Pension Trust,* 113 S. Ct. 2264 (1993)

21. Multiemployers withdrew from one fund and became affiliated with another. The second fund acquired some of the original fund's liabilities. The employers on behalf of the second fund sought the transfer of contributions from the original fund to offset the liabilities assumed. The original fund refused. What was the result? *Local 144 Nursing Home Pension Fund v. Nicholas Demisay,* 113 S. Ct. 2252 (1993)

❖ **WEB SITES**

www.law.cornell.edu/topics/pensions.html
www.hmopage.org/erisa.html
www.findlaw.com
www.westbuslaw.com
www.eric.org/
www.freeerisa.com
www.mednets.com/erisa.htm

CASE INDEX

A

A.L. Blades & Sons v. Yerusalim, 63
Alaska Housing Finance Corp. v. Salvucci, 131
Albertsons, Inc v. Kirkingburg, 432
Allen v. Dept. of Employment Training, 314
Aloia v. Eastman Kodak Co., 227
American Friends Service Committee v. Thornburgh, 406
American Hospital Assoc. v. N.L.R.B., 470
American Iron v. OSHA, 488
Amirmokri v. Baltimore Gas and Electric Co., 396
Amoroso v. Samuel Friedland Family Ent., 30
Anderson v. SUNY New Paltz, 528
Andrews v. Town of Skiatook, OK, 477
Armour & Co. v. Wantock, 483
Armstrong , et al v. Martin Marietta Corp., 166
Asplundh Tree Expert Co. v. Challis, 518
Auciello Iron Works v. National Labor Relations Board, 467
Aucutt v. Six Flags Over Mid America, 455
August v. Offices Unlimited, Inc., 455

B

Badih v. Myers, 337
Baehr v. Mike, Dir. of Dept.of Health, Hawaii, 354
Bahadirli v. Domino's Pizza, 402
Baker v. State of Vermont, 355
Beall v. Abbott Labs, 144
Becerra v. Dalton, Secretary of the Navy, 245
Belhomme v. Windhall, Secretary of Air Force, 219
Benton v. State of Delaware, 108
Bernstein v. Board of Ed of School District 200, 369
Bickerstaff v. Vassar College, 214
Biggs v. Wilson, 484
Bingham Memorial Hosp. v. Special Indemnity Fund, 517
Blackburn v. UPS, 45
Blackwell v. Shelter Mutual Insurance Co., 139
Blair v. Bendix Corp., 505
Blare v. Husky Injection Systems, Inc., 176
Bobcat Enterprises, Inc. v. Duwell, 31

Boyd v. Harding Academy of Memphis, Inc., 327
Bragdon v. Abbot, 446
Brown v. Coach Store Inc., 225
Brown v. Board of Education of Topeka, 154
Bruhn v. Foley, 57
Buhrmaster v. Overnite Transport Co., 238
Bullington v. United Airlines, Inc., 240
Bunce v. Parkside Lodge of Columbus, 33, 313
Burkhart v. WMATA, 24
Burlington Industries, Inc. v. Ellerth, 293
Burns v. McGregor Electronic Industries, Inc., 313

C

Canada v. Boyd Group, Inc., 313
Car Parts Distribution Ctr. v. Auto Wholesaler's Assoc., 456
Carl v. Angelone, 255
Carpenter v. City of Denver, CO, 480
Carr v. F.W. Woolworth Co., 234
Carreno v. Local Union, 366
Carter v. Caring for the Homeless of Peekskill, 314
Carter v. South Central Bell, 56
Casserly v. State, 484
Chambers v. Omaha Girls Club, Inc., 329
Chance v. Rice University, 266
Chandler v. Miller, 77
Chaudmuri v. State of Tennessee, 233, 383
Clay v. City of Chicago Department of Health, 324
Cleghorn v. Hess, 65
Clinchfield Coal Co. v. U.S. Dept. of Labor, 502
Clowes v. Allegheny Valley Hosp., 152
Coalition v. Pete Wilson, 201
Collum v. Argo, 32
Comm. of IRS v. Keystone Industries, 540
Concrete Pipe, Inc. v. Construction Laborers, 540
Conroy v. Anchor Savings Bank, 424
Consolidation Coal Co. v. U.S. Dept. of Labor, 502
Cruz v. Ecolab, 405
Cumpiano v. Banco Santander Puerto Rico, 314
Curtiss-Wright Corp v. Schoonejongen, 521

All entries that appear in italic appear in the Review Questions within the chapters.